P9-ECY-982

The Quotable Shakespeare

The Quotable Shakespeare

A Topical Dictionary

compiled by
Charles DeLoach

McFarland & Company, Inc., Publishers
Jefferson, North Carolina, and London

REF.

PR
2892
.D37
1988

DeLoach, Charles,
1927–

The quotable
Shakespeare

60,594

Library of Congress Cataloguing-in-Publication Data

DeLoach, Charles, 1927–
  The quotable Shakespeare.

  Includes indexes.
  1. Shakespeare, William, 1564–1616—Dictionaries,
indexes, etc.   2. Shakespeare, William, 1564–1616—
Quotations.   I. Title.
PR2892.D37   1988   822.3'3   87-35362

ISBN 0-89950-303-9 (50# acid-free natural paper) ∞

© 1988 Charles DeLoach. All rights reserved.

Manufactured in the United States of America.

McFarland & Company, Inc., Publishers
  Box 611, Jefferson, North Carolina 28640

Table of Contents

CAMROSE LUTHERAN COLLEGE
LIBRARY

Table of Contents

Table of Contents

Table of Contents

Table of Contents

Table of Contents

Table of Contents

Table of Contents

Foreword

We don't know the exact year that William Shakespeare, with a few belongings, took his farewell of the picturesque little market town of Stratford-on-Avon and set out for London. But the day he rode his horse over Clopton Bridge to seek his fame and fortune in that big city marked the beginning of a literary career unequaled in mankind's history. We do know that he was young, in his early twenties, and that he already had a wife and three children to support. He seems to have enjoyed a measure of success at every stage — first as an actor and poet, then as play director, theater manager and playwright. Obviously, he was a prolific writer. In the span of less than twenty-five years, he penned the thirty-eight plays, one hundred and fifty-four sonnets and several other poems that would make his name immortal.

It was a multifaceted genius that launched Shakespeare on the path to greatness. You cannot read the Bard of Avon's works without being struck by his tremendous powers of observation. He seems to have taken a consummate interest in everything around him — in the customs and fashions of the court, the workings of the law, the practice of medicine and religion, things pertaining to the sea, all horticulture, indeed, practically every facet of nature, even down to the tiny dewdrop that the early morning hung on a cowslip's ear. "His frame of reference is so far-ranging, and he is so concretely versed in the tricks of so many trades," states Harry Levin, "that lawyers have written to prove he was trained in the law, sailors about his expert seamanship, naturalists upon his botanizing, and so on through the professions."

He took the same keen interest in people. He was, according to the accounts of those who knew him, a friendly, self-effacing, unpretentious man, with an empathy for people in all walks of life. It was this empathy, perhaps, that enabled his mind to penetrate the facades of those around him and see to their bare soul. Coleridge, taking note of this ability, once referred to the poet as "our myriad-minded Shakespeare." He also listened, as no writer before or since has listened. Thus, even though he created more than a thousand characters, the voice of every one is so individualized, according to Pope, "that, even if the speech-prefixes were removed, we should have little difficulty in identifying the speaker."

He also had an extraordinary *inner ear* that enabled him, when he sat down to write his poems and plays, to put words to work like no one else ever has. His writing vocabulary totaled over 21,000 words, of which he had such great command that he could give just the right nuance to any thought he was trying to express. Such was the force of his words that some who attended his plays prior to their being published in the First Folio in 1623, would, after leaving the theater, write down what they could remember from his most memorable passages. He said so many things so well, in fact, that a half-dozen books now carry a collection of his thoughts. So why another book? First, because these other collections are far from complete, and, second, because they are not bona fide books of quotes at all, but contain a very heavy volume of selections that have to do with plot, scene description or characterization. For this book I have followed a different formula. Each quote I selected had to contain not only a philosophical axiom, a general truth or a fundamental principle, but also had to be immediately clear in meaning and capable of inspiring or delighting the reader. Thus *The Quotable Shakespeare* is a rich collection of the gems that resulted from Shakespeare's flashes of philosophical brilliance.

This volume, a work of love that took several years to construct, is based in its entirety on *The Riverside Shakespeare*, a highly regarded edition published in 1974 by Houghton Mifflin Company, with G. Blakemore Evans as textual editor.

— Charles DeLoach

How To Use This Book

The 6,516 quotes that make up this book are arranged under some one thousand topics that cover almost the entire range of man's thoughts and emotions. Because these topics appear in alphabetical order, the reader will be able to locate quickly any general topic he chooses for study. For the convenience of those who want to make a more extensive search, a Topical Index has been provided; it should prove of much value to readers who want to illustrate or develop an idea. It can also be used to find quotes when the reader remembers only a key word or an idea. In addition to the entries under each heading, this index lists the other topical headings that might yield additional Shakespearean thoughts related to that particular subject.

A Character Index has also been included, providing a list of what each character said, according to topic. This should prove helpful to those who want to study such favorite characters as Othello, Macbeth, Hamlet or the unforgettable Sir John Falstaff. This index will also help to locate a quote when only the character can be remembered.

A Title Index will enable the fans of certain plays and the long poems to easily find all the quotes gleaned from them.

Anyone who has ever used the index of a book of quotes that gives only page numbers for entries knows the frustration and inconvenience of that method. To remedy this, each quote in *The Quotable Shakespeare* has been assigned a number, and index entries refer to that number. Using this numbering system, the reader can quickly find a quote without having to search it out from a page full of quotes.

The Quotable Shakespeare

Ability

1 HAMLET [soliloquy]: He that made
   us with such large discourse,
Looking before and after, gave us not
That capability and godlike reason
To fust in us unus'd.
                              Hamlet 4.4.36
[*fust*: grow mouldy]

2 NORFOLK [on Wolsey]: There's in
   him stuff that puts him to these
   ends;
For being not propp'd by ancestry,
   whose grace
Chalks successors their way, nor call'd
   upon
For high feats done to th' crown,
   neither allied
To eminent assistants, but spider-like
Out of his self-drawing web, 'a gives us
   note,
The force of his own merit makes his
   way—
A gift that heaven gives for him, which
   buys
A place next to the King.
                              Henry VIII 1.1.58
['*a*: he]

Absence

3 O absence, what a torment wouldst
   thou prove,
Were it not thy sour leisure gave sweet
   leave
To entertain the time with thoughts of
   love.
                              Sonnet 39

4 FIRST GENTLEMAN: Our absence
makes us unthrifty to our knowledge.
                              Winter's Tale 5.2.111

5 K. HENRY: 'Tis ever common
That men are merriest when they are
   from home.
                              Henry V 1.2.271

6 All days are nights to see till I see
   thee,

All nights bright days when dreams do
   show thee me.
                              Sonnet 43

7 How like a winter hath my absence
   been
From thee, the pleasure of the fleeting
   year!
What freezings have I felt, what dark
   days seen!
What old December's bareness every
   where!
                              Sonnet 97

8 CASSIO [to Bianca]: I have this
   while with leaden thoughts been
   press'd,
But I shall in a more continuate time
Strike off this score of absence.
                              Othello 3.4.176

9 BIANCA [to Cassio]: What? keep a
   week away? seven days and nights?
Eightscore eight hours? and lovers' absent hours,
More tedious than the dial eightscore
   times?
O weary reck'ning!
                              Othello 3.4.173

10 VALENTINE [about Silvia]: Banish'd
   from her
Is self from self, a deadly banishment.
       Two Gentlemen of Verona 3.1.172

11 VALENTINE [soliloquy]: O thou that
   dost inhabit in my breast,
Leave not the mansion so long
   tenantless,
Lest growing ruinous, the building fall
And leave no memory of what it was!
Repair me with thy presence, Silvia.
       Two Gentlemen of Verona 5.4.7

12 O, never say that I was false in
   heart,
Though absence seem'd my flame to
   qualify;
As easy might I from myself depart
As from my soul which in thy breast
   doth lie:
That is my home of love; if I have
   rang'd,

Like him that travels I return again.
Sonnet 109

13 Were I with her, the night would
post too soon,
But now are minutes added to the
hours;
To spite me now, each minute seems a
moon.
The Passionate Pilgrim xiv.25

Abstinence

14 BEROWNE: Abstinence engenders
maladies.
Love's Labor's Lost 4.3.291

15 PROSPERO [to Ferdinand]: Do not
give dalliance
Too much the rein. The strongest oaths
are straw
To th' fire i' th' blood. Be more
abstenious,
Or else good night your vow!
The Tempest 4.1.52

16 HAMLET [to the Queen]: Refrain
to-night,
And that shall lend a kind of easiness
To the next abstinence, the next more
easy;
For use almost can change the stamp of
nature.
Hamlet 3.4.165

Abundance

17 The sea, all water, yet receives rain
still,
And in abundance addeth to his store.
Sonnet 135

Abuse

18 They that level
At my abuses reckon up their own.
Sonnet 121

Access

19 FORD: They say, if money goes
before, all ways do lie open.
Merry Wives of Windsor 2.2.169

Accident

20 FLORIZEL: As th' unthought-on ac-
cident is guilty
To what we wildly do, so we profess
Ourselves to be the slaves of chance,
and flies
Of every wind that blows.
Winter's Tale 4.4.538

Accommodation

21 ANTONY: The hated, grown to
strength,
Are newly grown to love.
Antony and Cleopatra 1.3.48

Accusation

22 HERMIONE: Innocence shall make
False accusation blush.
Winter's Tale 3.2.30

23 HAMLET: I could accuse me of such
things that it were better my mother
had not borne me.
Hamlet 3.1.122

Achievement

24 CRESSIDA: Joy's soul lies in the
doing.
Troilus and Cressida 1.2.287

25 HELENA: Oft expectation fails, and
most oft there
Where most it promises; and oft it hits
Where hope is coldest, and despair
most fits.
All's Well That Ends Well 2.1.142

26 ANTONY: To business that we love
we rise betime,

And go to't with delight.
Antony and Cleopatra 4.4.20

27 AARON: So must you resolve,
That what you cannot as you would achieve,
You must perforce accomplish as you may.
Titus Andronicus 2.1.105

28 ULYSSES: To have done is to hang
Quite out of fashion, like a rusty mail
In monumental mock'ry. Take the instant away,
For honor travels in a strait so narrow,
Where one but goes abreast. Keep then the path,
For emulation hath a thousand sons
That one by one pursue. If you give way,
Or hedge aside from the direct forthright,
Like to an ent'red tide, they all rush by
And leave you hindmost.
Troilus and Cressida 3.3.151
[*mail:* suit of armor; *direct forthright:* straight path]

Acquisition

29 K. RICHARD: They well deserve to have
That know the strong'st and surest way to get.
Richard II 3.3.200

Act

30 FIRST CLOWN: An act has three branches—it is to act, to do, to perform.
Hamlet 5.1.11

31 BRUTUS [soliloquy]: Between the acting of a dreadful thing
And the first motion, all the interim is
Like a phantasma or a hideous dream.
The Genius and the mortal instruments

Are then in council; and the state of man,
Like to a little kingdom, suffers then
The nature of an insurrection.
Julius Caesar 2.1.63
[*the Genius:* the soul; *mortal instruments:* man's reason and his will; *in council:* at war]

32 BASTARD [to King John]: Be great in act, as you have been in thought...
Be stirring as the time, be fire with fire,
Threaten the threat'ner, and outface the brow
Of bragging horror.
King John 5.1.45

Acting

33 CLEOPATRA: When good will is show'd, though 't come too short,
The actor may plead pardon.
Antony and Cleopatra 2.5.8

34 HAMLET: The players ... are the abstract and brief chronicles of the time. After your death you were better have a bad epitaph than their ill report while you live.
Hamlet 2.2.522

35 JAQUES: All the world's a stage,
And all the men and women merely players;
They have their exits and their entrances,
And one man in his time plays many parts.
As You Like It 2.7.139

36 HAMLET: The purpose of playing, whose end, both at the first and now, was and is, to hold as 'twere the mirror up to nature: to show virtue her feature, scorn her own image, and the very age and body of the time his form and pressure.
Hamlet 3.2.20

37 HAMLET: O, there be players that I have seen play—and heard others

praise, and that highly—not to speak it profanely, that, neither having th' accent of Christians nor the gait of Christian, pagan, nor man, have so strutted and bellow'd that I have thought some of Nature's journeymen had made men, and not made them well, they imitated humanity so abominably.
Hamlet 3.2.28

38 HAMLET [soliloquy]: Is it not monstrous that this player here,
But in a fiction, in a dream of passion,
Could force his soul so to his own conceit
That from her working all the visage wann'd,
Tears in his eyes, distraction in his aspect,
A broken voice, an' his whole function suiting
With forms of his conceit? And all for nothing,
For Hecuba!
What's Hecuba to him, or he to Hecuba,
That he should weep for her? What would he do
Had he the motive and the cue for passion
That I have? He would drown the stage with tears,
And cleave the general ear with horrid speech,
Make mad the guilty, and appall the free,
Confound the ignorant, and amaze indeed
The very faculties of eyes and ears.
Hamlet 2.2.551

39 HAMLET: O, it offends me to the soul to hear a robustious periwig-pated fellow tear a passion to totters, to very rags, to spleet the ears of the groundlings, who for the most part are capable of nothing but inexplicable dumb shows and noise. I would have such a fellow whipt.
Hamlet 3.2.8
[*totters:* tatters; *spleet:* split; *groundlings:* those who paid the lowest admission price and stood on the ground to watch a play]

40 YORK: In a theatre the eyes of men,
After a well-graced actor leaves the stage,
Are idly bent on him that enters next,
Thinking his prattle to be tedious.
Richard II 5.2.23

41 PHILOSTRATE [to Theseus]: A play there is, my lord, some ten words long,
Which is as brief as I have known a play;
But by ten words, my lord, it is too long,
Which makes it tedious.
Midsummer Night's Dream 5.1.61

42 QUINCE: Come, sit down, every mother's son, and rehearse your parts.
Midsummer Night's Dream 3.1.72

43 ULYSSES [about Patroclus]: He pageants us . . .
Like a strutting player, whose conceit
Lies in his hamstring, and doth think it rich
To hear the wooden dialogue and sound
'Twixt his stretch'd footing and the scaffolage.
Troilus and Cressida 1.3.151

Action

44 VOLUMNIA: Action is eloquence.
Coriolanus 3.2.76

45 REIGNIER: Defer no time, delays have dangerous ends.
1 Henry VI 3.2.33

46 LEWIS: Strong reasons make strange actions.
King John 3.4.182

47 MACBETH: The flighty purpose never is o'ertook
Unless the deed go with it.
Macbeth 4.1.145

48 AGAMEMNON: A stirring dwarf we do allowance give
Before a sleeping giant.
Troilus and Cressida 2.3.137

49 CLEOPATRA: Celerity is never more admir'd
Than by the negligent.
Antony and Cleopatra 3.7.24

50 HOTSPUR: The blood more stirs
To rouse a lion than to start a hare!
1 Henry IV 1.3.197

51 HAMLET [to some actors]: Suit the action to the word, the word to the action, with this special observance, that you o'erstep not the modesty of nature.
Hamlet 3.2.17

52 HOTSPUR [to his men prior to battle]: I profess not talking; only this —
Let each man do his best.
1 Henry IV 5.2.91

53 WOLSEY: We must not stint
Our necessary actions in the fear
To cope malicious censurers.
Henry VIII 1.2.76

54 FIRST MURDERER [to Gloucester]:
Tut, tut, my lord, we will not stand to prate;
Talkers are no good doers. Be assur'd;
We go to use our hands, and not our tongues.
Richard III 1.3.350

55 POLONIUS: 'Tis too much prov'd —
that with devotion's visage
And pious action we do sugar o'er
The devil himself.
Hamlet 3.1.46

56 ULYSSES: Things in motion sooner catch the eye
Than what stirs not.
Troilus and Cressida 3.3.183

57 PROSPERO: The rarer action is
In virtue than in vengeance.
The Tempest 5.1.27

58 ARVIRAGUS [to Belarius]: What pleasure, sir, find we in life, to lock it
From action and adventure.
Cymbeline 4.4.2

59 CANTERBURY: As many arrows loosed several ways
Come to one mark; as many ways meet in one town;
As many fresh streams meet in one salt sea;
As many lines close in the dial's centre;
So may a thousand actions, once afoot,
End in one purpose.
Henry V 1.2.207

Activity

60 FALSTAFF: Better to be eaten to death with a rust than to be scour'd to nothing with perpetual motion.
2 Henry IV 1.2.218

Adaptation

61 PORTIA: How many things by season season'd are
To their right praise and true perfection!
Merchant of Venice 5.1.107

62 ENOBARBUS: Every time
Serves for the matter that is then born in't.
Antony and Cleopatra 2.2.10

63 Q. MARGARET: What cannot be avoided,
'Twere childish weakness to lament or fear.
3 Henry VI 5.4.37

64 GAUNT: All places that the eye of heaven visits
Are to a wise man ports and happy havens.
Richard II 1.3.275

Admiration

65 ENOBARBUS [on Cleopatra]: For her own person,
It beggar'd all description.
Antony and Cleopatra 2.2.197

66 CAMILLO [to Perdita]: I should
leave grazing, were I of your flock,
And only live by gazing.
Winter's Tale 4.4.109

67 HORATIO [to Hamlet about the
ghost]: Season your admiration for a
while.
Hamlet 1.2.193

Adolescence

68 CLOWN: Youth's a stuff will not
endure.
Twelfth Night 2.3.52

69 FALSTAFF: Youth, the more it is
wasted, the sooner it wears.
1 Henry IV 2.4.400

70 CLEOPATRA: My salad days,
When I was green in judgment.
Antony and Cleopatra 1.5.73

Adulation

71 K. HENRY [soliloquy]: Thinks thou
the fiery fever will go out
With titles blown from adulation?
Henry V 4.1.253

Adultery

72 HAMLET [to Queen, on her quick
marriage to Claudius]: O, such a
deed
As from the body of contraction plucks
The very soul, and sweet religion
makes
A rhapsody of words. Heaven's face
doth glow
O'er this solidity and compound mass
With heated visage, as against the
doom;
Is thought-sick at the act.
Hamlet 3.4.45

73 HAMLET [to Queen, on her mar-
riage]: To live
In the rank sweat of an enseamed bed,

Stew'd in corruption, honeying and
making love o'er the nasty sty!
Hamlet 3.4.92

74 DEMETRIUS: Easy it is
Of a cut loaf to steal a shive.
Titus Andronicus 2.1.86
[*shive:* slice]

Advantage

75 MONTJOY: Advantage is a better
soldier than rashness.
Henry V 3.6.120

76 Make use of the time, let not advantage slip.
Venus and Adonis 129

Adventure

77 ARVIRAGUS [to Belarius]: What
pleasure, sir, find we in life, to lock
it
From action and adventure?
Cymbeline 4.4.2

Adversary

78 TRANIO: Do as adversaries do in
law,
Strive mightily, but eat and drink as
friends.
Taming of the Shrew 1.2.276

Adversity

79 K. HENRY: Let me embrace thee,
sour adversities,
For wise men say it is the wisest course.
3 Henry VI 3.1.24

80 DUKE: Sweet are the uses of
adversity,
Which, like the toad, ugly and
venomous,
Wears yet a precious jewel in his head.
As You Like It 2.1.12

[The idea that the toad was venomous comes from Pliny's *Natural History*. The *jewel*, or toadstone, was believed to have curative powers.]

81 K. HENRY: 'Tis good for men to love their present pains
Upon example; so the spirit is eased.
Henry V 4.1.18

82 TRINCULO: Misery acquaints a man with strange bedfellows.
The Tempest 2.2.39

83 EDGAR: The worst is not
So long as we can say, "This is the worst."
King Lear 4.1.27

84 BELARIUS: Many times
Doth ill deserve by doing well.
Cymbeline 3.3.53

85 ADRIANA: A wretched soul, bruis'd with adversity,
We bid be quiet when we hear it cry;
But were we burd'ned with like weight of pain,
As much, or more, we should ourselves complain.
Comedy of Errors 2.1.34

86 GRIFFITH [to Katherine about Cardinal Wolsey]: His overthrow heap'd happiness upon him;
For then, and not till then, he felt himself,
And found the blessedness of being little.
Henry VIII 4.2.64

87 VALENTINE [to three outlaws]:
Know that I have little wealth to lose.
A man I am cross'd with adversity;
My riches are these poor habiliments,
Of which if you should here disfurnish me,
You take the sum and substance that I have.
Two Gentlemen of Verona 4.1.11

88 FRIAR LAWRENCE: Adversity's sweet milk, philosophy.
Romeo and Juliet 3.3.55

Advice

89 KING: Friendly counsel cuts off many foes.
1 Henry VI 3.1.184

90 Will is deaf and hears no heedful friends.
Rape of Lucrece 495

91 Advice is sporting while infection breeds.
Rape of Lucrece 907

92 YORK: Direct not him whose way himself will choose,
'Tis breath thou lack'st, and that breath wilt thou lose.
Richard II 2.1.29

93 POLONIUS [to Laertes]: Give thy thoughts no tongue,
Nor any unproportion'd thought his act.
Be thou familiar, but by no means vulgar:
Those friends thou hast, and their adoption tried,
Grapple them unto thy soul with hoops of steel,
But do not dull thy palm with entertainment
Of each new-hatch'd, unfledg'd courage. Beware
Of entrance to a quarrel, but being in,
Bear't that th' opposed may beware of thee.
Give every man thy ear, but few thy voice,
Take each man's censure, but reserve thy judgment.
Costly thy habit as thy purse can buy,
But not express'd in fancy, rich, not gaudy,
For the apparel oft proclaims the man . . .
Neither a borrower nor a lender be,
For loan oft loses both itself and friend,

And borrowing dulleth th' edge of husbandry.
This above all: to thine own self be true,
And it must follow, as the night the day,
Thou canst not then be false to any man.
Hamlet 1.3.59
[*courage:* spirited, young blood]

94 COUNTESS [to Bertram]: Love all, trust a few,
Do wrong to none. Be able for thine enemy
Rather in power than use, and keep thy friend
Under thy own life's key. Be check'd for silence,
But never tax'd for speech.
All's Well That Ends Well 1.1.64

95 PORTIA: If to do were as easy as to know what were good to do, chapels had been churches, and poor men's cottages princes' palaces. It is a good divine that follows his own instructions; I can easier teach twenty what were good to be done, than to be one of the twenty to follow mine own teaching.
Merchant of Venice 1.2.12

96 FOOL: Have more than thou showest,
Speak less than thou knowest,
Lend less than thou owest.
King Lear 1.4.118

97 FOOL: When a wise man gives thee better counsel, give me mine again.
King Lear 2.4.74

98 MARIANA [about Duke Vincentio]:
Here comes a man of comfort, whose advice
Hath often still'd my brawling discontent.
Measure for Measure 4.1.8

99 When we rage, advice is often seen
By blunting us to make our wits more keen.
A Lover's Complaint 160

Affairs

100 GARDINER: Affairs that walk
(As they say spirits do) at midnight, have
In them a wilder nature than the business
That seeks dispatch by day.
Henry VIII 5.1.13

Affectation

101 POLONIUS: 'Tis too much prov'd —
that with devotion's visage
And pious action we do sugar o'er
The devil himself.
Hamlet 3.1.46

Affection

102 Affection faints not like a pale-fac'd coward,
But then woos best when most his choice is froward.
Venus and Adonis 569

103 Nothing can affection's course control,
Or stop the headlong fury of his speed.
Rape of Lucrece 500

104 LEONTES: Affection! thy intention stabs the centre.
Thou dost make possible things not so held,
Communicat'st with dreams.
Winter's Tale 1.2.138
[*not so held:* not supposed possible]

105 Affection is my captain, and he leadeth;
And when his gaudy banner is display'd,
The coward fights, and will not be dismay'd.
Rape of Lucrece 271

106 HORTENSIO: Kindness in women, not their beauteous looks,
Shall win my love.
Taming of the Shrew 4.2.41

107 LAERTES: Keep you in the rear of your affection,
Out of the shot and danger of desire.
Hamlet 1.3.34

108 SHYLOCK: Affection,
Mistress of passion, sways it to the mood
Of what it likes or loathes.
Merchant of Venice 4.1.51

109 Affection is a coal that must be cool'd,
Else suffer'd it will set the heart on fire.
Venus and Adonis 387

110 Where Love reigns, disturbing Jealousy
Doth call himself Affection's sentinel.
Venus and Adonis 649

111 IAGO: 'Tis the curse of service;
Preferment goes by letter and affection,
And not by old gradation, where each second
Stood heir to th' first.
Othello 1.1.35
[*old gradation:* seniority]

112 LADY MACBETH: I have given suck, and know
How tender 'tis to love the babe that milks me.
Macbeth 1.7.54

113 MARTIUS [to some citizens]: Your affections are
A sick man's appetite, who desires most that
Which would increase his evil.
Coriolanus 1.1.177

114 ULYSSES: One touch of nature makes the whole world kin.
Troilus and Cressida 3.3.175

115 LADY MACDUFF: The poor wren,
The most diminutive of birds, will fight,
Her young ones in her nest, against the owl.
Macbeth 4.2.9

Affliction

116 ISABELLA: 'Tis a physic
That's bitter to sweet end.
Measure for Measure 4.6.7

117 KING: When sorrows come, they come not single spies,
But in battalions.
Hamlet 4.5.78

118 GLOUCESTER: Henceforth I'll bear
Affliction till it do cry out itself
"Enough, enough," and die.
King Lear 4.6.75

119 OTHELLO: Had it pleas'd heaven
To try me with affliction, had they rain'd
All kinds of sores and shames on my bare head,
Steep'd me in poverty to the very lips,
Given to captivity me and my utmost hopes,
I should have found in some place of my soul
A drop of patience.
Othello 4.2.47

120 LEAR [to Cordelia]: Thou art a soul in bliss, but I am bound
Upon a wheel of fire, that mine own tears
Do scald like molten lead.
King Lear 4.7.45

121 FRIAR LAWRENCE [about Romeo]:
Affliction is enamor'd of thy parts,
And thou art wedded to calamity.
Romeo and Juliet 3.3.2

122 COSTARD: Affliction may one day smile again, and till then, sit thee down, sorrow!
Love's Labor's Lost 1.1.314

Age

123 FRIAR LAWRENCE: Care keeps his watch in every old man's eye,
And where care lodges, sleep will never lie;

But where unbruised youth with unstuff'd brain
Doth couch his limbs, there golden sleep doth reign.
Romeo and Juliet 2.3.35

124 GONERIL [to Lear]: As you are old and reverend, [you] should be wise.
King Lear 1.4.240

125 ALCIBIADES: Reverend ages love Security.
Timon of Athens 3.5.79

126 DOGBERRY: When the age is in, the wit is out.
Much Ado About Nothing 3.5.34

127 FALSTAFF: Lord, Lord, how subject we old men are to this vice of lying!
2 Henry IV 3.2.303

128 NERISSA: Superfluity comes sooner by white hairs, but competency lives longer.
Merchant of Venice 1.2.8

129 ROSENCRANTZ: They say an old man is twice a child.
Hamlet 2.2.385

130 ADAM: Though I look old, yet I am strong and lusty;
For in my youth I never did apply
Hot and rebellious liquors in my blood,
Nor did not with unbashful forehead woo
The means of weakness and debility;
Therefore my age is as a lusty winter,
Frosty, but kindly.
As You Like It 2.3.47

131 KING [to Falstaff]: How ill white hairs become a fool and jester!
2 Henry IV 5.5.48

132 DUKE: [It is] as dangerous to be ag'd in any kind of course, as it is virtuous to to be constant in any undertaking.
Measure for Measure 3.2.224

133 Time doth transfix the flourish set on youth,
And delves the parallels in beauty's brow.
Sonnet 60

134 K. HENRY: A good leg will fall, a straight back will stoop, a black beard will turn white, a curl'd pate will grow bald, a fair face will wither, a full eye will wax hollow; but a good heart, Kate, is the sun ... for it shines bright and never changes, but keeps his course truly.
Henry V 5.2.159

135 FALSTAFF: You that are old consider not the capacities of us that are young, you do measure the heat of our livers with the bitterness of your galls ...
CHIEF JUSTICE: Do you set down your name in the scroll of youth, that are written down old with all the characters of age? Have you not a moist eye, a dry hand, a yellow cheek, a white beard, a decreasing leg, an increasing belly? Is not your voice broken, your wind short, your chin double, your wit single, and every part about you blasted with antiquity? and will you yet call yourself young? Fie, fie, fie, Sir John!
2 Henry IV 1.2.173

136 That time of year thou mayst in me behold
When yellow leaves, or none, or few, do hang
Upon those boughs which shake against the cold,
Bare ruin'd choirs, where late the sweet birds sang.
Sonnet 73

137 EGEON: Though now this grained face of mine be hid
In sap-consuming winter's drizzled snow,
And all the conduits of my blood froze up,
Yet hath my night of life some memory.
Comedy of Errors 5.1.312

138 MACBETH: My way of life
Is fall'n into the sear, the yellow leaf,
And that which should accompany old age,
As honor, love, obedience, troops of friends,
I must not look to have; but in their stead,
Curses, not loud but deep, mouth-honor, breath,
Which the poor heart would fain deny, and dare not.
Macbeth 5.3.22

139 JAQUES: And so from hour to hour, we ripe and ripe,
And then from hour to hour, we rot and rot;
And thereby hangs a tale.
As You Like It 2.7.26

140 TIMON: These old fellows
Have their ingratitude in them hereditary:
Their blood is cak'd, 'tis cold, it seldom flows;
'Tis lack of kindly warmth they are not kind;
And nature, as it grows again toward earth,
Is fashion'd for the journey, dull and heavy.
Timon of Athens 2.2.214

141 Crabbed age and youth cannot live together:
Youth is full of pleasance, age is full of care,
Youth like summer morn, age like winter weather,
Youth like summer brave, age like winter bare.
Youth is full of sport, age's breath is short,
Youth is nimble, age is lame,
Youth is hot and bold, age is weak and cold,
Youth is wild, and age is tame.
Age, I do abhor thee, youth, I do adore thee.
The Passionate Pilgrim xii.1

142 Age in love loves not t' have years told.
Sonnet 138

143 BEROWNE: Beauty doth varnish age.
Love's Labor's Lost 4.3.240

144 CAPULET [to a cousin]: You and I are past our dancing days.
Romeo and Juliet 1.5.33

145 To me, fair friend, you never can be old,
For as you were when first your eye I ey'd,
Such seems your beauty still.
Sonnet 104

146 FOOL [to Lear]: Thou shouldst not have been old till thou hadst been wise.
King Lear 1.5.44

147 GLOUCESTER [reading a letter from Edgar]: "This policy and reverence of age makes the world bitter to the best of times; keeps our fortunes from us till our oldness cannot relish them..."
King Lear 1.2.46

148 CLEOPATRA: Though age from folly could not give me freedom,
It does from childishness.
Antony and Cleopatra 1.3.57

149 OTHELLO [to Brabantio]: You shall more command with years
Than with your weapons.
Othello 1.2.60

150 HAMLET [to the Queen]: At your age
The heyday in the blood is tame, it's humble,
And waits upon the judgment.
Hamlet 3.4.68

151 REGAN [to Lear]: O sir, you are old,
Nature in you stands on the very verge
Of her confine. You should be rul'd and led

By some discretion that discerns your state
Better than you yourself.
King Lear 2.4.146

152 ADAM: At seventeen years many their fortunes seek,
But at fourscore it is too late a week.
As You Like It 2.3.73

153 K. RICHARD [soliloquy]: I wasted time, and now doth time waste me.
Richard II 5.5.49

154 KING: We are old, and on our quick'st decrees
Th' inaudible and noiseless foot of time
Steals ere we can effect them.
All's Well That Ends Well 5.3.40

155 DROMIO SYRACUSE: What he [Time] hath scanted men in hair he hath given them in wit.
Comedy of Errors 2.2.80

156 JAQUES: One man in his time plays many parts,
His acts being seven ages. At first the infant,
Mewling and puking in the nurse's arms.
Then the whining schoolboy, with his satchel
And shining morning face, creeping like snail
Unwillingly to school. And then the lover,
Sighing like furnace, with a woeful ballad
Made to his mistress' eyebrow. Then a soldier,
Full of strange oaths, and bearded like the pard,
Jealous in honor, sudden, and quick in quarrel,
Seeking the bubble reputation
Even in the cannon's mouth. And then the justice,
In fair round belly with good capon lin'd,
With eyes severe and beard of formal cut,
Full of wise saws and modern instances;
And so he plays his part. The sixt age shifts
Into the lean and slipper'd pantaloon,
With spectacles on nose, and pouch on side,
His youthful hose, well sav'd, a world too wide
For his shrunk shank, and his big manly voice,
Turning again toward childish treble, pipes
And whistles in his sound. Last scene of all,
That ends this strange eventful history,
Is second childishness, and mere oblivion,
Sans teeth, sans eyes, sans taste, sans every thing.
As You Like It 2.7.142

[*sixt:* sixth]

157 YOUNG CLIFFORD: The silver livery of advised age.
2 Henry VI 5.2.47

158 MORTIMER [dying]: Grey locks, the pursuivants of death,
Nestor-like aged, in an age of care,
Argue the end of Edmund Mortimer.
1 Henry VI 2.5.5

159 APEMANTUS: Men shut their doors against a setting sun.
Timon of Athens 1.2.145

160 ENOBARBUS [about Cleopatra]:
Age cannot wither her, nor custom stale
Her infinite variety. Other women cloy
The appetites they feed, but she makes hungry
Where most she satisfies.
Antony and Cleopatra 2.2.234

161 CHARMIAN: I love long life better than figs.
Antony and Cleopatra 1.2.32

162 MISTRESS QUICKLY: Old folks, you know, have discretion, as they say, and know the world.
Merry Wives of Windsor 2.2.129

163 Respect and reason wait on wrinkled age!
Rape of Lucrece 275

Agony

164 BEROWNE: Mirth cannot move a soul in agony.
Love's Labor's Lost 5.2.857

165 LEAR [to Cordelia]: Thou art a soul in bliss, but I am bound
Upon a wheel of fire, that mine own tears
Do scald like molten lead.
King Lear 4.7.45

Aim

166 ANTIOCHUS: An arrow shot
From a well-experienc'd archer hits the mark
His eye doth level at.
Pericles 1.1.161

Aloneness

167 DUKE: I myself am best
When least in company.
Twelfth Night 1.4.37

168 Now counting best to be with you alone,
Then better'd that the world may see my pleasure;
Sometime all full with feasting on your sight,
And by and by clean starved for a look.
Sonnet 75

169 EDGAR [soliloquy]: Who alone suffers, suffers most i' th' mind,
Leaving free things and happy shows behind,
But then the mind much sufferance doth o'erskip,
When grief hath mates, and bearing fellowship.
King Lear 3.6.104

170 K. HENRY: I and my bosom must debate a while,
And then I would no other company.
Henry V 4.1.31

Aloofness

171 JULIA: They do not love that do not show their love.
Two Gentlemen of Verona 1.2.31

Amazement

172 BASTARD: Wild amazement hurries up and down.
King John 5.1.35

Ambition

173 WOLSEY [to Cromwell]: I charge thee, fling away ambition!
By that sin fell the angels.
Henry VIII 3.2.440

174 SALISBURY: Pride went before, ambition follows him.
2 Henry VI 1.1.180

175 K. RICHARD [soliloquy]: Thoughts tending to ambition, they do plot
Unlikely wonders.
Richard II 5.5.18

176 MACBETH [soliloquy]: I have no spur
To prick the sides of my intent, but only
Vaulting ambition, which o'erleaps itself.
Macbeth 1.7.25

177 GLOUCESTER: Virtue is chok'd with foul ambition.
2 Henry VI 3.1.143

178 Q. MARGARET: They that stand high have many blasts to shake them,
And if they fall, they dash themselves to pieces.
Richard III 1.3.258

179 DIONYZA: Who digs hills because they do aspire
Throws down one mountain to cast up a higher.
Pericles 1.4.5

180 MOROCCO: Men that hazard all
Do it in hope of fair advantage;
A golden mind stoops not to shows of dross.
Merchant of Venice 2.7.18

181 GLOUCESTER: Banish the canker of ambitious thoughts!
2 Henry VI 1.2.18

182 ANTONY [at The Forum]: The noble Brutus
Hath told you Caesar was ambitious;
If it were so, it was a grievous fault,
And grievously hath Caesar answer'd it.
Julius Caesar 3.2.77

183 WOLSEY [soliloquy]: Farewell? a long farewell to all my greatness!
This is the state of man: to-day he puts forth
The tender leaves of hopes, to-morrow blossoms,
And bears his blushing honors thick upon him;
The third day comes a frost, a killing frost,
And when he thinks, good easy man, full surely
His greatness is a-ripening, nips his root,
And then he falls as I do.
Henry VIII 3.2.351

184 PUCELLE: Glory's like a circle in the water,
Which never ceases to enlarge itself,
Till by broad spreading it disperse to nought.
1 Henry VI 1.2.133

185 PRINCE [about Percy]: Ill-weav'd ambition, how much art thou shrunk!
When that this body did contain a spirit,
A kingdom for it was too small a bound,
But now two paces of the vilest earth
Is room enough.
1 Henry IV 5.4.88

186 BRUTUS [soliloquy]: 'Tis a common proof
That lowliness is young ambition's ladder,
Whereto the climber-upward turns his face;
But when he once attains the upmost round,
He then unto the ladder turns his back,
Looks in the clouds, scorning the base degrees
By which he did ascend.
Julius Caesar 2.1.21

187 GUILDENSTERN: Dreams indeed are ambition, for the very substance of the ambitious is merely the shadow of a dream.
HAMLET: A dream itself is but a shadow.
ROSENCRANTZ: Truly, and I hold ambition of so airy and light a quality that it is but a shadow's shadow.
Hamlet 2.2.257

Amity

188 ULYSSES: The amity that wisdom knits not, folly may easily untie.
Troilus and Cressida 2.3.101

189 CONSTABLE: There is flattery in friendship.
Henry V 3.7.114

Amusement

190 THESEUS [about Philostrate]:
Where is our usual manager of mirth?
What revels are in hand? Is there no play
To ease the anguish of a torturing hour?
Midsummer Night's Dream 5.1.35

191 PRINCESS: There's no such sport as sport by sport o'erthrown.
Love's Labor's Lost 5.2.153

Anarchy

192 DUKE: Now, as fond fathers,
Having bound up the threat'ning twigs of birch,
Only to stick it in their children's sight
For terror, not to use, in time the rod
Becomes more mock'd than fear'd; so our decrees,
Dead to infliction, to themselves are dead,
And liberty plucks justice by the nose;
The baby beats the nurse, and quite athwart
Goes all decorum.
Measure for Measure 1.3.23

193 ULYSSES: O, when degree is shak'd,
Which is the ladder of all high designs,
The enterprise is sick. How could communities,
Degrees in schools, and brotherhoods in cities,
Peaceful commerce from dividable shores,
The primogenity and due of birth,
Prerogative of age, crowns, sceptres, laurels,
But by degree stand in authentic place?
Take but degree away, untune that string,
And hark what discord follows. Each thing meets
In mere oppugnancy: the bounded waters
Should lift their bosoms higher than the shores,
And make a sop of all this solid globe;
Strength should be lord of imbecility,
And the rude son should strike his father dead;
Force should be right, or rather, right and wrong
(Between whose endless jar justice resides)
Should lose their names, and so should justice too!
Then every thing includes itself in power,
Power into will, will into appetite,
And appetite, an universal wolf
(So doubly seconded with will and power),
Must make perforce an universal prey,
And last eat up himself . . .
This chaos, when degree is suffocate,
Follows the choking.
And this neglection of degree it is
That by a pace goes backward with a purpose
It hath to climb. The general's disdain'd
By him one step below, he by the next,
That next by him beneath; so every step,
Exampled by the first pace that is sick
Of his superior, grows to an envious fever
Of pale and bloodless emulation.
Troilus and Cressida 1.3.101
[*primogenity . . . of birth:* rights of the eldest-born]

194 CONSTANCE: When law can do no right,
Let it be lawful that law bar no wrong.
King John 3.1.185

Angel

195 MALCOLM: Angels are bright still, though the brightest fell.
Macbeth 4.3.22

196 K. RICHARD: If angels fight,
Weak men must fall, for heaven still guards the right.
Richard II 3.2.61

197 Two loves I have, of comfort and despair,
That like two spirits do suggest me still:
My better angel is a man (right fair),
My worser spirit a woman (color'd ill).
To win me soon to hell, my female evil

Tempteth my better angel from my
  side;
And would corrupt my saint to be a
  devil,
Wooing his purity with her fair pride.
And whether that my angel be turn'd
  fiend,
Suspect I may (yet not directly tell):
For being both to me, both to each
  friend,
I guess one angel in another's hell:
The truth I shall not know, but live in
  doubt,
Till my bad angel fire my good one
  out.
                The Passionate Pilgrim ii.1

198 DUKE [soliloquy]: O, what may
  man within him hide,
Though angel on the outward side!
                Measure for Measure 3.2.271

199 CRESSIDA: Women are angels,
  wooing.
                Troilus and Cressida 1.2.286

200 CHANCELLOR: We all are men,
In our own natures frail, and capable
Of our flesh; few are angels.
                Henry VIII 5.2.45

201 BOYET: Fair ladies mask'd are
  roses in their bud;
Dismask'd, their damask sweet commixture shown,
Are angels vailing clouds, or roses
  blown.
                Love's Labor's Lost 5.2.295
[*damask:* red and white; *vailing:* letting
fall, shedding]

Anger

202 NORFOLK: Heat not a furnace for
  your foe so hot
That it do singe yourself.
                Henry VIII 1.1.140

203 MAECENAS: Never anger
Made good guard for itself.
                Antony and Cleopatra 4.1.8

204 NORFOLK: Anger is like
A full hot horse, who being allow'd his
  way,
Self-mettle tires him.
                Henry VIII 1.1.132

205 VOLUMNIA: Anger's my meat; I
  sup upon myself,
And so shall starve with feeding.
                Coriolanus 4.2.50

206 PORTIA: The brain may devise
laws for the blood, but a hot temper
leaps o'er a cold decree.
                Merchant of Venice 1.2.18

207 KENT: Anger hath a privilege.
                King Lear 2.2.70

208 IAGO: Men in rage strike those
  that wish them best.
                Othello 2.3.243

209 KATHERINA: A woman mov'd is
  like a fountain troubled,
Muddy, ill-seeming, thick, bereft of
  beauty.
                Taming of the Shrew 5.2.142

210 KATHERINA: My tongue will tell
  the anger of my heart,
Or else my heart concealing it will
  break.
                Taming of the Shrew 4.3.77

211 ALCIBIADES: To be in anger is
  impiety;
But who is man that is not angry?
                Timon of Athens 3.5.56

212 CONSTANCE: O that my tongue
  were in the thunder's mouth!
Then with a passion would I shake the
  world.
                King John 3.4.38

Answer

213 CASSIO [fearing Othello's discipline following a drunken brawl]: I
will ask him for my place again, he
shall tell me I am a drunkard! Had I as

many mouths as Hydra, such an answer
would stop them all.

Othello 2.3.304

Anticipation

214 GRATIANO: All things that are,
Are with more spirit chased than
enjoy'd.

Merchant of Venice 2.6.13

215 TROILUS: I am giddy; expectation
whirls me round;
Th' imaginary relish is so sweet
That it enchants my sense.

Troilus and Cressida 3.2.18

216 NORTHUMBERLAND: Hope to joy is
little less in joy
Than hope enjoyed.

Richard II 2.3.15

Anxiety

217 GRATIANO [to Antonio]: You
have too much respect upon the
world.
They lose it that do buy it with much
care.

Merchant of Venice 1.1.74

Apparel

218 LEAR: Through tatter'd clothes
small vices do appear;
Robes and furr'd gowns hide all. Plate
sin with gold,
And the strong lance of justice hurtless
breaks;
Arm it in rags, a pigmy's straw does
pierce it.

King Lear 4.6.164

219 POLONIUS: Costly thy habit as thy
purse can buy,
But not express'd in fancy, rich, not
gaudy,
For the apparel oft proclaims the man.

Hamlet 1.3.70

Apparition

220 MACBETH [soliloquy, on Duncan's
murder]: Is this a dagger which I see
before me,
The handle toward my hand? Come,
let me clutch thee:
I have thee not, and yet I see thee still.
Art thou not, fatal vision, sensible
To feeling as to sight? or art thou but
A dagger of the mind, a false creation,
Proceeding from the heat-oppressed
brain?

Macbeth 2.1.33

Appearance

221 ANGELO [soliloquy]: O place, O
form,
How often dost thou with thy case, thy
habit,
Wrench awe from fools, and tie the
wiser souls
To thy false seeming!

Measure for Measure 2.4.12

222 BASSANIO: So may the outward
shows be least themselves —
The world is still deceiv'd with
ornament.

Merchant of Venice 3.2.73

223 BASSANIO: There is no vice so simple but assumes
Some mark of virtue on his outward
parts.

Merchant of Venice 3.2.81

224 VIOLA: Nature with a beauteous
wall
Doth oft close in pollution.

Twelfth Night 1.2.48

225 ANTONIO: O, what a goodly outside falsehood hath!

Merchant of Venice 1.3.102

226 DUKE [soliloquy]: O, what may
man within him hide,
Though angel on the outward side!

Measure for Measure 3.2.271

227 HAMLET: One may smile, and smile, and be a villain!
Hamlet 1.5.108

228 WORCESTER: Look how we can, or sad or merrily,
Interpretation will misquote our looks.
1 Henry IV 5.2.12

229 KENT: I am much more
Than my out-wall.
King Lear 3.1.44

[*out-wall:* exterior]

230 O, what a mansion have those vices got
Which for their habitation chose out thee,
Where beauty's veil doth cover every blot,
And all things turn to fair that eyes can see!
Sonnet 95

231 SECOND LORD [about Parolles]: I will never trust a man again for keeping his sword clean, nor believe he can have every thing in him by wearing his apparel neatly.
All's Well That Ends Well 4.3.144

232 HENRY [incognito, to some soldiers]: The King is but a man, as I am. The violet smells to him as it doth to me; the element shows to him as it doth to me; all his senses have but human conditions. His ceremonies laid by, in his nakedness he appears but a man; and though his affections are higher mounted than ours, yet when they stoop, they stoop with like wing.
Henry V 4.1.101

Appetite

233 O appetite, from judgment stand aloof!
A Lover's Complaint 166

234 FALSTAFF: The latter end of a fray and the beginning of a feast
Fits a dull fighter and a keen guest.
1 Henry IV 4.2.79

235 BENEDICK [soliloquy]: Doth not the appetite alter? A man loves the meat in his youth that he cannot endure in his age.
Much Ado About Nothing 2.3.238

236 To make our appetites more keen,
With eager compounds we our palate urge.
Sonnet 118

237 MACBETH: Now good digestion wait on appetite,
And health on both!
Macbeth 3.4.37

238 GRATIANO: Who riseth from a feast
With that keen appetite that he sits down?
Merchant of Venice 2.6.8

239 FRIAR LAWRENCE: The sweetest honey
Is loathsome in his own deliciousness,
And in the taste confounds the appetite.
Romeo and Juliet 2.6.11

240 ABBESS: Unquiet meals make ill digestions.
Comedy of Errors 5.1.74

241 MARTIUS [to some citizens]: Your affections are
A sick man's appetite, who desires most that
Which would increase his evil.
Coriolanus 1.1.177

242 ULYSSES: Appetite, an universal wolf
(So doubly seconded with will and power),
Must make perforce an universal prey,
And last eat up himself.
Troilus and Cressida 1.3.121

243 KING [to Falstaff]: Make less thy body hence and more thy grace,
Leave gormandizing.
2 Henry IV 5.5.52

Applause

244 MACBETH [to doctor, on healing
Lady Macbeth]: I would applaud
thee to the very echo,
That should applaud again.
Macbeth 5.3.53

Appreciation

245 CRESSIDA: Men prize the thing
ungain'd more than it is.
Troilus and Cressida 1.2.289

Apprehension

246 BULLINGBROOK: Apprehension of
the good
Gives but the greater feeling to the
worst.
Richard II 1.3.300

247 ISABELLA: The sense of death is
most in apprehension.
Measure for Measure 3.1.77

248 IAGO: Who has that breast so pure
But some uncleanly apprehensions
Keep leets and law-days and in sessions
sit
With meditations lawful?
Othello 3.3.138
[*keep leets:* hold courts]

April

249 CAPULET: Well-apparell'd April
on the heels
Of limping winter treads.
Romeo and Juliet 1.2.27

250 ROSALIND: Men are April when
they woo, December when they wed.
As You Like It 4.1.147

251 PROTEUS [soliloquy]: O, how this
spring of love resembleth
The uncertain glory of an April day,
Which now shows all the beauty of the
sun,

And by and by a cloud takes all away.
Two Gentlemen of Verona 1.3.84

252 Proud-pied April (dress'd in all his
trim)
Hath put a spirit of youth in every
thing.
Sonnet 98

Argument

253 DROMIO SYRACUSE: Every why
hath a wherefore.
Comedy of Errors 2.2.44

254 FLUELLEN: There is occasions and
causes why and wherefore in all things.
Henry V 5.1.3

255 ANTONIO: The devil can cite
Scripture for his purpose.
Merchant of Venice 1.3.98

256 TOUCHSTONE [to Jaques]: O sir,
we quarrel in print, by the book—as
you have books for good manners. I
will name you the degrees. The first,
the Retort Courteous; the second, the
Quip Modest; the third, the Reply
Churlish; the fourth, the Reproof
Valiant; the fift, the Countercheck
Quarrelsome; the sixt, the Lie with Circumstance; the seventh, the Lie Direct.
As You Like It 5.4.90
[*fift:* fifth; *sixt:* sixth]

257 The argument all bare is of more
worth
Than when it hath my added praise
beside.
Sonnet 103
[*argument all bare:* subject unadorned]

258 HOLOFERNES [about Armado]: He
draweth out the thread of his verbosity
finer than the staple of his argument.
Love's Labor's Lost 5.1.16

259 GUILDENSTERN: O, there has been
much throwing about of brains.
Hamlet 2.2.358

260 CLAUDIO [about Isabella]: She
hath prosperous art
When she will play with reason and
discourse,
And well she can persuade.
Measure for Measure 1.2.184

261 MOWBRAY: The bitter clamor of
two eager tongues.
Richard II 1.1.48

262 How can my Muse want subject to
invent
While thou dost breathe, that pour'st
into my verse
Thine own sweet argument, too
excellent
For every vulgar paper to rehearse?
Sonnet 38
[*argument:* subject, theme]

263 O, know, sweet love, I always
write of you,
And you and love are still my
argument.
Sonnet 76
[*argument:* theme]

Aristocracy

264 KING: Strange is it that our
bloods,
Of color, weight, and heat, pour'd all
together,
Would quite confound distinction, yet
stands off
In differences so mighty.
All's Well That Ends Well 2.3.118

265 ULYSSES: O, when degree is
shak'd,
Which is the ladder of all high
designs,
The enterprise is sick. How could
communities,
Degrees in schools, and brotherhoods
in cities,
Peaceful commerce from dividable
shores,
The primogenity and due of birth,
Prerogative of age, crowns, sceptres,
laurels,

But by degree stand in authentic
place?
Troilus and Cressida 1.3.101
[*primogenity ... of birth:* the rights of the
eldest-born]

Arms

266 KING: Thrice is he arm'd that
hath his quarrel just;
And he but naked, though lock'd up
in steel,
Whose conscience with injustice is
corrupted.
2 Henry VI 3.2.233

267 KING: What stronger breastplate
than a heart untainted!
2 Henry VI 3.2.232

268 HOTSPUR: The arms are fair
When the intent of bearing them is
just.
1 Henry IV 5.2.87

269 SECOND SENATOR: What thou
wilt,
Thou rather shall enforce it with thy
smile
Than hew to't with thy sword.
Timon of Athens 5.4.44

Arrogance

270 ULYSSES: Supple knees
Feed arrogance and are the proud
man's fees.
Troilus and Cressida 3.3.48

271 MENENIUS [about Martius]: The
tartness of his face sours ripe grapes.
When he walks, he moves like an
engine, and the ground shrinks before
his treading. He is able to pierce a
corslet with his eye, talks like a knell,
and his hum is a battery. He sits in his
state, as a thing made for Alexander.
What he bids be done is finish'd with
his bidding. He wants nothing of a
god but eternity and a heaven to
throne in.
Coriolanus 5.4.17

Arrow

272 ANTIOCHUS: An arrow shot
From a well-experienc'd archer hits the
mark
His eye doth level at.
Pericles 1.1.161

Art

273 Perspective it is best painter's art.
Sonnet 24

274 Through the painter must you see
his skill.
Sonnet 24

275 POLIXENES [to Perdita]: Nature is
made better by no mean
But Nature makes that mean; so over
that art
Which you say adds to Nature, is an
art
That Nature makes. You see, sweet
maid, we marry
A gentler scion to the wildest stock,
And make conceive a bark of baser
kind
By bud of nobler race. This is an art
Which does mend Nature—change it
rather; but
The art itself is Nature.
Winter's Tale 4.4.89

276 LEAR: Nature's above art.
King Lear 4.6.86

277 TIMON: The painting is almost the
natural man;
For since dishonor traffics with man's
nature,
He is but outside; these pencill'd
figures are
Even such as they give out.
Timon of Athens 1.1.157

Aspiration

278 CHORUS: O for a Muse of fire,
that would ascend
The brightest heaven of invention!
Henry V, Prologue 1

279 GLOUCESTER: 'Tis but a base ignoble mind
That mounts no higher than a bird can
soar.
2 Henry VI 2.1.13

280 CLEOPATRA: I have
Immortal longings in me.
Antony and Cleopatra 5.2.280

Ass

281 FIRST CLOWN: Your dull ass will
not mend his pace with beating.
Hamlet 5.1.57

282 FOOL: May not the ass know when
the cart draws the horse?
King Lear 1.4.223

Assassination

283 K. JOHN: There is no sure foundation set on blood,
No certain life achiev'd by others'
death.
King John 4.2.104

284 MACBETH [soliloquy, on Duncan]:
If th' assassination
Could trammel up the consequence,
and catch
With his surcease, success; that but this
blow
Might be the be-all and the end-all—
here,
But here, upon this bank and shoal of
time,
We'ld jump the life to come.
Macbeth 1.7.2

Association

285 FALSTAFF [soliloquy]: It is certain
that either wise bearing or ignorant
carriage is caught, as men take
diseases, one of another; therefore let
men take heed of their company.
2 Henry IV 5.1.75

286 CASSIUS [soliloquy]: It is meet
That noble minds keep ever with their
    likes;
For who so firm that cannot be
    seduc'd?
                    Julius Caesar 1.2.310

287 BRUTUS: For mine own part,
I shall be glad to learn of noble men.
                    Julius Caesar 4.3.54

Astrology

288 EDMUND [soliloquy]: This is the
excellent foppery of the world, that
when we are sick in fortune — often the
surfeits of our own behavior — we make
guilty of our disasters the sun, the
moon, and stars, as if we were villains
on necessity, fools by heavenly compulsion, knaves, thieves, and treachers by
spherical predominance; drunkards,
liars, and adulterers by an enforc'd
obedience of planetary influence; and
all that we are evil in, by a divine
thrusting on. An admirable evasion of
whoremaster man, to lay his goatish
disposition on the charge of a star!
                    King Lear 1.2.118
[*goatish:* lecherous]

289 CASSIUS: Men at some time are
    masters of their fates;
The fault, dear Brutus, is not in our
    stars,
But in ourselves, that we are under-
    lings.
                    Julius Caesar 1.2.139

290 PROSPERO: I find my zenith doth
    depend upon
A most auspicious star, whose influence
If now I court not, but omit, my for-
    tunes
Will ever after droop.
                    The Tempest 1.2.181

291 HERMIONE: There's some ill planet
    reigns;
I must be patient, till the heavens look
With an aspect more favorable.
                    Winter's Tale 2.1.105

292 KENT: It is the stars,
The stars above us, govern our conditions.
                    King Lear 4.3.32

Astronomy

293 BEROWNE: These earthly god-
fathers of heaven's lights,
That give a name to every fixed star,
Have no more profit of their shining
    nights
Than those that walk and wot not what
    they are.
                    Love's Labor's Lost 1.1.88
[*wot:* know]

Attractiveness

294 JACHIMO: That hook of wiving,
Fairness which strikes the eye.
                    Cymbeline 5.5.167

Authority

295 PAROLLES: There is no fettering of
    authority.
        All's Well That Ends Well 2.3.237

296 CLOWN: Though authority be a
stubborn bear, yet he is oft led by the
nose with gold.
                    Winter's Tale 4.4.801

297 LEAR: Thou hast seen a farmer's
dog bark at a beggar?
GLOUCESTER: Ay, sir.
LEAR: And the creature run from the
cur? There thou mightst behold the
great image of authority: a dog's
obey'd in office.
                    King Lear 4.6.154

298 ISABELLA: Man, proud man,
Dress'd in a little brief authority,
Most ignorant of what he's most assur'd
(His glassy essence), like an angry ape

Plays such fantastic tricks before high
  heaven
As make the angels weep.
            Measure for Measure 2.2.117
[*glassy:* fragile, highly susceptible of
damage]

299 ANGELO [soliloquy]: Authority
  bears of a credent bulk
That no particular scandal once can
  touch
But it confounds the breather.
            Measure for Measure 4.4.26
[*credent bulk:* massive credibility]

300 DUKE: Hence hath offense his
  quick celerity,
When it is borne in high authority.
            Measure for Measure 4.2.110

301 ISABELLA: Authority, though it err
  like others,
Hath yet a kind of medicine in itself,
That skins the vice o' th' top.
            Measure for Measure 2.2.134
[*skins the vice:* grows new skin over the
sore]

302 CLAUDIO: O, what authority and
  show of truth
Can cunning sin cover itself withal!
            Much Ado About Nothing 4.1.35

303 CORIOLANUS: When two authori-
  ties are up,
Neither supreme, how soon confusion
May enter 'twixt the gap of both, and
  take
The one by th' other.
            Coriolanus 3.1.109

304 CLAUDIO: Thus can the demigod,
  Authority,
Make us pay down for our offense by
  weight
The words of heaven.
            Measure for Measure 1.2.120

Authorship

305 ARMADO: Devise, wit, write, pen,
for I am for whole volumes in folio.
            Love's Labor's Lost 1.2.184

Autumn

306 The teeming autumn, big with
  rich increase,
Bearing the wanton burthen of the
  prime.
                            Sonnet 97
[*burthen:* burden]

307 TITANIA: The spring, the summer,
The chiding autumn, angry winter,
  change
Their wonted liveries.
            Midsummer Night's Dream 2.1.111

Avarice

308 KING: How quickly nature falls
  into revolt
When gold becomes her object!
                        2 Henry IV 4.5.65

309 FALSTAFF: A man can no more
separate age and covetousness than 'a
can part young limbs and lechery.
                        2 Henry IV 1.2.228
[*'a:* he]

310 MACDUFF: This avarice
Sticks deeper, grows with more per-
  nicious root
Than summer-seeming lust.
                            Macbeth 4.3.84

311 Poorly rich, so wanteth in his
  store,
That cloy'd with much, he pineth still
  for more.
                        Rape of Lucrece 97

312 MALCOLM: There grows
In my most ill-compos'd affection such
A stanchless avarice that, were I king,
I should cut off the nobles for their
  lands.
                            Macbeth 4.3.76

313 BASTARD: Bell, book, and candle
shall not drive me back,

When gold and silver becks me to
come on.
King John 3.3.12
[*bell, book, and candle:* symbols of Church
excommunication]

Aversion

314 JULIA: Love will not be spurr'd to
what it loathes.
Two Gentlemen of Verona 5.2.7

315 SHYLOCK: Some men there are
love not a gaping pig;
Some that are mad if they behold a
cat;
And others, when the bagpipe sings i'
th' nose,
Cannot contain their urine.
Merchant of Venice 4.1.47

Awe

316 CASSIUS [to Brutus, alluding to
Caesar]: I cannot tell what you and
other men
Think of this life; but, for my single
self,
I had as lief not be as live to be
In awe of such a thing as I myself.
Julius Caesar 1.2.93

Babes

317 Q. ELIZABETH: My poor princes!
ah, my tender babes!
My unblown flow'rs, new-appearing
sweets!
Richard III 4.4.9

Bachelor

318 TOUCHSTONE: As a wall'd town is
more worthier than a village, so is the
forehead of a married man more
honorable than the bare brow of a
bachelor.
As You Like It 3.3.59

319 CINNA: Wisely, I say, I am a
bachelor.
PLEBEIAN: That's as much as to say,
they are fools that marry.
Julius Caesar 3.3.16

320 DROMIO SYRACUSE: As from a
bear a man would run for life,
So fly I from her that would be my
wife.
Comedy of Errors 3.2.154

321 BENEDICK: All women shall pardon me. Because I will not do them
the wrong to mistrust any, I will do
myself the right to trust none . . . I
will live a bachelor.
Much Ado About Nothing 1.1.242

322 DON PEDRO: "In time the savage
bull doth bear the yoke."
BENEDICK: The savage bull may, but if
ever the sensible Benedick bear it,
pluck off the bull's horns, and set
them in my forehead, and let me be
vildly painted, and in such great letters
as they write "Here is good horse to
hire," let them signify under my sign,
"Here you may see Benedick the married man."
Much Ado About Nothing 1.1.261
[*vildly:* vilely]

323 BENEDICK [soliloquy]: When I
said I would die a bachelor, I did not
think I should live till I were married.
Much Ado About Nothing 2.3.242

Back

324 Q. KATHERINE: The back is sacrifice to th' load.
Henry VIII 1.2.50

325 BUCKINGHAM: Many
Have broke their backs with laying
manors on 'em.
Henry VIII 1.1.84

Badness

326 HAMLET: Bad begins and worse remains behind.

Hamlet 3.4.179

327 All men are bad and in their badness reign.

Sonnet 121

Balance

328 IAGO: If the beam of our lives had not one scale of reason to poise another of sensuality, the blood and baseness of our natures would conduct us to most prepost'rous conclusions. But we have reason to cool our raging motions, our carnal stings, our unbitted lusts.

Othello 1.3.326

[*beam:* balance; *raging motions:* desires, appetites]

Baldness

329 DROMIO SYRACUSE: There's no time for a man to recover his hair that grows bald by nature.

Comedy of Errors 2.2.72

330 DROMIO SYRACUSE: Time himself is bald, and therefore, to the world's end, will have bald followers.

Comedy of Errors 2.2.108

331 DROMIO SYRACUSE: What he [Time] hath scanted men in hair he hath given them in wit.

Comedy of Errors 2.2.81

332 LONGAVILLE: Fat paunches have lean pates.

Love's Labor's Lost 1.1.26

Ballad

333 CLOWN: I love a ballad but even too well, if it be doleful matter merrily set down, or a very pleasant

thing indeed and sung lamentably.

Winter's Tale 4.4.188

334 HOTSPUR: I had rather be a kitten and cry mew
Than one of these same metre ballet-mongers.
I had rather hear a brazen canstick turn'd,
Or a dry wheel grate on the axle-tree,
And that would set my teeth nothing on edge,
Nothing so much as mincing poetry.
'Tis like the forc'd gait of a shuffling nag.

1 Henry IV 3.1.127

[*ballet:* ballad]

Banishment

335 ROMEO [on his exile]: "Banished"?
O friar, the damned use that word in hell;
Howling attends it.

Romeo and Juliet 3.3.46

336 ROMEO: There is no world without Verona walls,
But purgatory, torture, hell itself.
Hence "banished" is banish'd from the world,
And world's exile is death; then "banished"
Is death misterm'd.

Romeo and Juliet 3.3.17

337 ROMEO: Exile hath more terror in his look,
Much more than death.

Romeo and Juliet 3.3.13

338 VALENTINE [soliloquy]: To die is to be banish'd from myself,
And Silvia is myself: banish'd from her
Is self from self, a deadly banishment.

Two Gentlemen of Verona 3.1.171

339 BULLINGBROOK [on his years in exile]: How long a time lies in one little word!
Four lagging winters and four wanton springs

End in a word: such is the breath of kings.
Richard II 1.3.213

340 MOWBRAY: To dwell in solemn shades of endless night.
Richard II 1.3.177

341 Q. MARGARET [to Gloucester, the usurper]: I do find more pain in banishment
Than death can yield me here by my abode.
Richard III 1.3.167

Bargain

342 COSTARD: To sell a bargain well is as cunning as fast and loose.
Love's Labor's Lost 3.1.103

343 BEROWNE: To things of sale a seller's praise belongs.
Love's Labor's Lost 4.3.236

344 HOTSPUR: I'll give thrice so much land
To any well-deserving friend;
But in the way of a bargain, mark ye me,
I'll cavil on the ninth part of a hair.
1 Henry IV 3.1.135

345 PARIS: Fair Diomed, you do as chapmen do,
Dispraise the thing that they desire to buy.
Troilus and Cressida 4.1.76

Baseness

346 HELENA [soliloquy]: Things base and vile, holding no quantity,
Love can transpose to form and dignity.
Midsummer Night's Dream 1.1.232
[*holding no quantity:* lacking proportion, unshapely]

347 GLOUCESTER: 'Tis but a base ignoble mind

That mounts no higher than a bird can soar.
2 Henry VI 2.1.13

348 SUFFOLK: Small things make base men proud.
2 Henry VI 4.1.106

349 FERDINAND: Some kinds of baseness
Are nobly undergone.
The Tempest 3.1.2.

350 PISTOL: Base is the slave that pays.
Henry V 2.1.96

351 BELARIUS: Cowards father cowards and base things sire base.
Cymbeline 4.2.26

Bashfulness

352 FRANCE: Is it but this—a tardiness in nature
Which often leaves the history unspoke
That it intends to do?
King Lear 1.1.235

Bastard

353 EDMUND [soliloquy]: Why bastard? Wherefore base?
When my dimensions are as well compact,
My mind as generous, and my shape as true,
As honest madam's issue? Why brand they us
With base? with baseness? bastardy? base, base?
Who, in the lusty stealth of nature, take
More composition, and fierce quality,
Than doth within a dull, stale, tired bed
Go to th' creating of a whole tribe of fops,
Got 'tween asleep and wake?
King Lear 1.2.6

354 POSTHUMUS [soliloquy]: We are all bastards,

And that most venerable man which I
Did call my father, was I know not
   where
When I was stamp'd.
                              Cymbeline 2.5.2

355 THERSITES [to Margarelon, bastard
son of Priam]: I am a bastard too, I
love bastards. I am a bastard begot,
bastard instructed, bastard in mind,
bastard in valor, in every thing ille-
gitimate. One bear will not bite
another, and wherefore should one
bastard?
             Troilus and Cressida 5.7.16

Battle

356 WILLIAMS: There are few die well
that die in a battle; for how can they
charitably dispose of any thing, when
blood is their argument?
                              Henry V 4.1.141

357 MACDUFF [attacking Macbeth]:
Make all our trumpets speak, give
   them all breath,
Those clamorous harbingers of blood
and death.
                              Macbeth 5.6.9

358 K. HENRY [at the battle of
   Harfleur]: Once more into the
   breach, dear friends, once more;
Or close the wall up with our English
dead.
                              Henry V 3.1.1

359 SECOND WITCH: When the hurly-
   burly's done,
When the battle's lost and won.
                              Macbeth 1.1.3

Bawd

360 POMPEY: I do find your hangman
is a more penitent trade than your
bawd: he doth oft'ner ask forgiveness.
             Measure for Measure 4.2.49

Bear

361 THESEUS: In the night, imagining
   some fear,
How easy is a bush suppos'd a bear!
             Midsummer Night's Dream 5.1.21

362 K. LEAR: Thou'dst shun a bear,
But if thy flight lay toward the roaring
   sea,
Thou'dst meet the bear i' th' mouth.
                              King Lear 3.4.9

363 BRUTUS [about Martius]: He's a
lamb indeed, that baes like a bear.
                              Coriolanus 2.1.11

Beard

364 BEATRICE: He that hath a beard is
more than a youth, and he that hath
no beard is less than a man.
             Much Ado About Nothing 2.1.36

365 BASSANIO: How many cowards,
   whose hearts are all as false
As stairs of sand, wear yet upon their
   chins
The beards of Hercules and frowning
   Mars,
Who inward search'd, have livers white
as milk.
             Merchant of Venice 3.2.83

366 GOWER: What a beard of the
general's cut and a horrid suit of the
camp will do among foaming bottles
and ale-wash'd wits, is wonderful to be
thought on.
                              Henry V 3.6.77

367 KING [to Laertes]: You must not
   think
That we are made of stuff so flat and
dull
That we can let our beard be shook
   with danger
And think it pastime.
                              Hamlet 4.7.30

Beast

368 ANNE [to Gloucester]: No beast so
fierce but knows some touch of pity.
Richard III 1.2.71

369 SICINIUS: Nature teaches beasts to
know their friends.
Coriolanus 2.1.6

370 FALSTAFF [soliloquy]: O powerful
love, that in some respects makes a
beast a man; in some other, a man a
beast.
Merry Wives of Windsor 5.5.4

371 HAMLET [soliloquy]: What is a
man,
If his chief good and market of his
time
Be but to sleep and feed? a beast, no
more.
Hamlet 4.4.33

372 HAMLET: Let a beast be lord of
beasts, and his crib shall stand at the
King's mess.
Hamlet 5.2.85

373 TIMON [to Apemantus]: If thou
wert the lion, the fox would beguile
thee; if thou wert the lamb, the fox
would eat thee; if thou wert the fox,
the lion would suspect thee, when
peradventure thou wert accus'd by the
ass; if thou wert the ass, thy dullness
would torment thee, and still thou
liv'dst but as a breakfast to the wolf; if
thou wert the wolf, thy greediness
would afflict thee, and oft thou
shouldst hazard thy life for thy dinner:
wert thou the unicorn, pride and wrath
would confound thee and make thine
own self the conquest of thy fury; wert
thou a bear, thou wouldst be kill'd by
the horse; wert thou a horse, thou
wouldst be seiz'd by the leopard; wert
thou a leopard, thou wert germane to
the lion, and the spots of thy kindred
were jurors on thy life; all thy safety
were remotion and thy defense
absence. What beast couldst thou be,
that were not subject to a beast? And

what a beast art thou already, that
seest not thy loss in transformation!
Timon of Athens 4.3.327

Beauty

374 All orators are dumb when beauty
pleadeth.
Rape of Lucrece 268

375 BASSANIO: Look on beauty,
And you shall see 'tis purchas'd by the
weight,
Which therein works a miracle of
nature,
Making them lightest that wear most
of it.
Merchant of Venice 3.2.88
[*lightest*: most wanton]

376 ROMEO [about Juliet, on first seeing her]: O, she doth teach the
torches to burn bright!
It seems she hangs upon the cheek of
night
As a rich jewel in an Ethiop's ear—
Beauty too rich for use, for earth too
dear!
So shows a snowy dove trooping with
crows,
As yonder lady o'er her fellows
shows . . .
Did my heart love till now? Foreswear
it, sight!
For I ne'er saw true beauty till this
night.
Romeo and Juliet 1.5.44

377 Beauty within itself should not be
wasted.
Venus and Adonis 130

378 CLOWN: Beauty's a flower.
Twelfth Night 1.5.52

379 SONG: Beauty lives with kindness.
Love doth to her eyes repair,
To help him of his blindness;
And, being help'd, inhabits there.
Two Gentlemen of Verona 4.2.45

380 BEROWNE: Beauty doth varnish age.
Love's Labor's Lost 4.3.240

381 BEROWNE: 'Tis the sun that maketh all things shine!
Love's Labor's Lost 4.3.243

382 ROSALIND: Beauty provoketh thieves sooner than gold.
As You Like It 1.3.112

383 Beauty is but a vain and doubtful good,
A shining gloss, that vadeth suddenly,
A flower that dies when first it gins to bud,
A brittle glass that's broken presently:
A doubtful good, a gloss, a glass, a flower,
Lost, vaded, broken, dead within an hour.
And as goods lost are seld or never found,
As vaded gloss no rubbing will refresh,
As flowers dead lie withered on the ground,
As broken glass no cement can redress:
So beauty blemish'd once, for ever lost,
In spite of physic, painting, pain, and cost.
The Passionate Pilgrim xiii.1
[*vaded*: to depart, to disappear; *seld*: seldom]

384 O how much more doth beauty beauteous seem
By that sweet ornament which truth doth give!
Sonnet 54

385 CLAUDIO [soliloquy]: Beauty is a witch
Against whose charms faith melteth into blood.
Much Ado About Nothing 2.1.179

386 Beauty itself doth of itself persuade
The eyes of men without an orator.
Rape of Lucrece 29

387 PRINCESS: Beauty is bought by judgment of the eye.
Love's Labor's Lost 2.1.15

388 ANTONIO: Virtue is beauty.
Twelfth Night 3.4.369

389 TOUCHSTONE: For honesty coupled to beauty is to have honey a sauce to sugar.
As You Like It 3.3.30

390 Were beauty under twenty locks kept fast,
Yet love breaks through, and picks them all at last.
Venus and Adonis 575

391 The rose looks fair, but fairer we it deem
For that sweet odor which doth in it live.
Sonnet 54

392 SUFFOLK: Beauty's princely majesty is such,
'Confounds the tongue and makes the senses rough.
1 Henry VI 5.3.70
[*'Confounds*: That it confounds]

393 HAMLET: If you be honest and fair, your honesty should admit no discourse to your beauty.
OPHELIA: Could beauty, my lord, have better commerce than with honesty?
HAMLET: Ay, truly, for the power of beauty will sooner transform honesty from what it is to a bawd than the force of honesty can translate beauty into his likeness.
Hamlet 3.1.106

394 YORK: 'Tis beauty that doth oft make women proud.
3 Henry VI 1.4.128

395 CONSTANCE [to her son, Arthur]:
Of Nature's gifts thou mayst with lilies boast,
And with the half-blown rose.
King John 3.1.53

396 IAGO: She never yet was foolish that was fair.

Othello 2.1.136

397 BEROWNE: Where is any author in the world
Teaches such beauty as a woman's eye?

Love's Labor's Lost 4.3.308

398 Truth needs no color with his color fix'd,
Beauty no pencil, beauty's truth to lay;
But best is best, if never intermix'd.

Sonnet 101

399 To me, fair friend, you never can be old,
For as you were when first your eye I ey'd,
Such seems your beauty still.

Sonnet 104

400 From fairest creatures we desire increase,
That thereby beauty's rose might never die.

Sonnet 1

401 All that beauty that doth cover thee
Is but the seemly raiment of my heart.

Sonnet 22

402 SERVANT [about Perdita]: The most peerless piece of earth, I think,
That e'er the sun shone bright on.

Winter's Tale 5.1.94

403 BEROWNE [about the beautiful Rosaline]: A wither'd hermit, five-score winters worn,
Might shake off fifty, looking in her eye.

Love's Labor's Lost 4.3.238

404 ULYSSES [about Cressida]: Fie, fie upon her!
There's language in her eye, her cheek, her lip,
Nay, her foot speaks; her wanton spirits look out
At every joint and motive of her body.

Troilus and Cressida 4.5.54

405 When in the chronicle of wasted time
I see descriptions of the fairest wights,
And beauty making beautiful old rhyme
In praise of ladies dead and lovely knights,
Then in the blazon of sweet beauty's best,
Of hand, of foot, of lip, of eye, of brow,
I see their antique pen would have express'd
Even such a beauty as you master now.
So all their praises are but prophecies
Of this our time, all you prefiguring.

Sonnet 106

[*wights:* persons]

406 Thy outward thus with outward praise is crown'd,
But those same tongues that give thee so thine own,
In other accents do this praise confound
By seeing farther than the eye hath shown.
They look into the beauty of thy mind,
And that in guess they measure by thy deeds.

Sonnet 69

407 Beauty breedeth beauty.

Venus and Adonis 167

Bed

408 Weary with toil, I haste me to my bed,
The dear repose for limbs with travel tired.

Sonnet 27

409 TOBY: Not to be a-bed after midnight is to be up betimes ... To be up after midnight and to go to bed then, is early; so that to go to bed after midnight is to go to bed betimes.

Twelfth Night 2.3.1

410 GARDINER: These should be hours for necessities,

Not for delights; times to repair our
nature
With comforting repose, and not for
us
To waste these times.
Henry VIII 5.1.2

Bee

411 CANTERBURY: So works the
honey-bees,
Creatures that by a rule in nature
teach
The act of order to a peopled king-
dom.
They have a king, and officers of sorts,
Where some, like magistrates, correct
at home;
Others, like merchants, venter trade
abroad;
Others, like soldiers, armed in their
stings,
Make boot upon the summer's velvet
buds,
Which pillage they with merry march
bring home
To the tent-royal of their emperor;
Who busied in his majesty surveys
The singing masons building roofs of
gold,
The civil citizens kneading up the
honey,
The poor mechanic porters crowding in
Their heavy burthens at his narrow
gate,
The sad-ey'd justice, with his surly
hum,
Delivering o'er to executioners pale
The lazy yawning drone.
Henry V 1.2.187
[*venter:* venture; *boot:* booty; *burthens:*
burdens]

412 PANDARUS: Full merrily the
humble-bee doth sing,
Till he hath lost his honey and his
sting;
And being once subdu'd in armed tail,
Sweet honey and sweet notes together
fail.
Troilus and Cressida 5.10.41

Beetle

413 ISABELLA: The poor beetle that we
tread upon
In corporal sufferance finds a pang as
great
As when a giant dies.
Measure for Measure 3.1.78

414 BELARIUS: Often, to our comfort,
shall we find
The sharded beetle in a safer hold
Than is the full-wing'd eagle.
Cymbeline 3.3.19

Beggar

415 JULIET: They are but beggars that
can count their worth.
Romeo and Juliet 2.6.32

416 YORK: The adage must be
verified,
That beggars mounted run their horse
to death.
3 Henry VI 1.4.126

417 CALPHURNIA: When beggars die
there are no comets seen;
The heavens themselves blaze forth the
death of princes.
Julius Caesar 2.2.30

418 BASTARD [soliloquy]: Well, whiles
I am a beggar, I will rail,
And say there is no sin but to be rich;
And being rich, my virtue then shall
be
To say there is no vice but beggary.
King John 2.1.593

419 ANTONY: There's beggary in the
love that can be reckon'd.
Antony and Cleopatra 1.1.15

420 FALSTAFF [to a servant of the
Chief Justice]: What? a young knave,
and begging? is there not wars? is
there not employment? doth not the
King lack subjects? do not the rebels
need soldiers? Though it be a shame to
be on any side but one, it is worse

shame to beg than to be on the worst side.
2 Henry IV 1.2.72

Beginnings

421 MACBETH: Things bad begun make strong themselves by ill.
Macbeth 3.2.55

422 CASSIUS: Those that with haste will make a mighty fire
Begin it with weak straws.
Julius Caesar 1.3.107

423 The colt that's back'd and burthen'd being young,
Loseth his pride, and never waxeth strong.
Venus and Adonis 419
[*burthen'd:* burdened]

Behavior

424 FOOL: Have more than thou showest,
Speak less than thou knowest,
Lend less than thou owest,
Ride more than thou goest,
Learn more than thou trowest,
Set less than thou throwest;
Leave thy drink and thy whore,
And keep in a' door,
And thou shall have more
Than two tens to a score.
King Lear 1.4.118
[*a' door:* indoors]

425 COUNTESS: Love all, trust a few,
Do wrong to none.
All's Well That Ends Well 1.1.64

Belief

426 When my love swears that she is made of truth,
I do believe her, though I know she lies.
Sonnet 138

427 ORLANDO [on Ganymede's promise to win Rosalind for him]: I sometimes do believe, and sometimes do not;
As those that fear they hope, and know they fear.
As You Like It 5.4.3

428 CLOWN: He that will believe all that they say, shall never be sav'd by half that they do.
Antony and Cleopatra 5.2.255

Bell

429 K. JOHN: The midnight bell
Did with his iron tongue and brazen mouth
Sound on into the drowsy race of night.
King John 3.3.37

430 BASTARD: Bell, book, and candle shall not drive me back,
When gold and silver becks me to come on.
King John 3.3.12
[*bell, book, and candle:* symbols of Church excommunication]

Belly

431 MENENIUS: There was a time when all the body's members
Rebell'd against the belly; thus accus'd it:
That only like a gulf it did remain
I' th' midst 'a th' body, idle and unactive,
Still cupboarding the viand, never bearing
Like labor with the rest, where th' other instruments
Did see and hear, devise, instruct, walk, feel,
And, mutually participate, did minister
Unto the appetite and affection common
To the whole body . . .
Note me this, good friend:

Your most grave belly was deliberate,
Not rash like his accusers, and thus
    answered:
"True is it, my incorporate friends,"
    quoth he,
"That I receive the general food first
Which you do live upon; and fit it is,
Because I am the store-house and the
    shop
Of the whole body. But, if you do
    remember,
I send it through rivers of your blood,
Even to the court, the heart, to th' seat
    o' th' brain,
And, through the cranks and offices of
    man,
The strongest nerves and small inferior
    veins
From me receive that natural compe-
    tency
Whereby they live. And though that
    all at once . . . cannot
See what I do deliver out to each,
Yet I can make my audit up, that all
From me do back receive the flour of
    all,
And leave me but the bran."
                          Coriolanus 1.1.96
['a: of]

Benefits

432 AMIENS [singing]:
Freeze, freeze, thou bitter sky,
Thou dost not bite so nigh
As benefits forgot;
Though thou the waters warp,
Thy sting is not so sharp
As a friend rememb'red not.
                       As You Like It 2.7.184

Bereavement

433 MACDUFF [on the slaughter of his
    family]: I cannot but remember such
    things were,
That were most precious to me.
                          Macbeth 4.3.222

Betrayal

434 Q. ELIZABETH: Trust not him that
    hath once broken faith.
                          3 Henry VI 4.4.30

435 IMOGEN: Though those that are
    betray'd
Do feel the treason sharply, yet the
    traitor
Stands in worse case of woe.
                          Cymbeline 3.4.85

436 BEROWNE [to King Ferdinand,
    Longaville and Dumaine]: I am
    betrayed by keeping company
With men like you, men of incon-
    stancy.
                    Love's Labor's Lost 4.3.177

437 AARON [to Chiron]: Fie,
    treacherous hue, that will betray
    with blushing
The close enacts and counsels of thy
    heart!
                    Titus Andronicus 4.2.117

438 BANQUO: Oftentimes, to win us
    to our harm,
The instruments of darkness tell us
    truths,
Win us with honest trifles, to betray 's
In deepest consequence.
                          Macbeth 1.3.123

Betrothal

439 THESEUS: The sealing-day betwixt
    my love and me.
                Midsummer Night's Dream 1.1.84

440 PRIEST: A contract of eternal bond
    of love,
Confirm'd by mutual joinder.
                          Twelfth Night 5.1.156

Birds

441 K. HENRY: The bird that hath
    been limed in a bush,

With trembling wings misdoubteth
every bush.
                    3 Henry VI 5.6.13
[Birdlime, a sticky substance, was used to
catch birds.]

442 K. HENRY [to Westmerland]:
Thou art a summer bird,
Which ever in the haunch of winter
sings
The lifting up of day.
                    2 Henry IV 4.4.91

443 PETRUCHIO: What, is the jay more
precious than the lark,
Because his feathers are more beautiful?
                    Taming of the Shrew 4.3.175

Birth

444 K. LEAR: When we are born, we
cry that we are come
To this great stage of fools.
                    King Lear 4.6.182

445 ANNE: I swear, 'tis better to be
lowly born,
And range with humble livers in
content,
Than to be perk'd up in a glist'ring
grief
And wear a golden sorrow.
                    Henry VIII 2.3.19

446 K. HENRY [to Gloucester, later
King Richard III]: The owl shriek'd
at thy birth, an evil sign;
The night-crow cried, aboding luckless
time;
Dogs howl'd, and hideous tempest
shook down trees;
The raven rook'd her on the chimney's
top,
And chatt'ring pies in dismal discords
sung;
Thy mother felt more than a mother's
pain,
And yet brought forth less than a
mother's hope,
To wit, an indigested and deformed
lump,

Not like the fruit of such a goodly
tree.
Teeth hadst thou in thy head when
thou wast born,
To signify thou cam'st to bite the
world.
                    3 Henry VI 5.6.44

447 BEATRICE: There was a star danc'd,
and under that I was born.
                    Much Ado About Nothing 2.1.335

Black

448 KING: Black is the badge of hell,
The hue of dungeons, and the school
of night.
                    Love's Labor's Lost 4.3.250

449 In the old age black was not
counted fair,
Or if it were it bore not beauty's name;
But now is black beauty's successive
heir,
And beauty slander'd with a bastard
shame.
                    Sonnet 127

450 AARON: Coal-black is better than
another hue,
In that it scorns to bear another hue;
For all the water in the ocean
Can never turn the swan's black legs to
white,
Although she lave them hourly in the
flood.
                    Titus Andronicus 4.2.99

Blame

451 No man inveigh against the
withered flow'r,
But chide rough winter that the flow'r
hath kill'd.
                    Rape of Lucrece 1254

452 POSTHUMUS [soliloquy]: There's no
motion
That tends to vice in man, but I affirm
It is the woman's part: be it lying, note
it,

The woman's; flattering, hers; deceiving, hers;
Lust and rank thoughts, hers, hers; revenges, hers;
Ambitions, covetings, change of prides, disdain,
Nice longing, slanders, mutability,
All faults that may be named, nay that hell knows,
Why hers.
                         Cymbeline 2.5.20
[*change of prides:* varying vanities and extravagances; *nice longing:* wanton appetites]

Blasphemy

453 ISABELLA: That in the captain's but a choleric word,
Which in the soldier is flat blasphemy.
                    Measure for Measure 2.2.130

Blemish

454 ANTONIO: In nature there's no blemish but the mind.
                         Twelfth Night 3.4.367

Blessing

455 LAERTES: A double blessing is a double grace.
                         Hamlet 1.3.53

456 SON: Ill blows the wind that profits nobody.
                         3 Henry VI 2.5.55

457 GAUNT: The world's ransom, blessed Mary's Son.
                         Richard II 2.1.56

Blindness

458 JESSICA: Love is blind, and lovers cannot see
The pretty follies that themselves commit.
                    Merchant of Venice 2.6.36

459 ROMEO: He that is strooken blind cannot forget
The precious treasure of his eyesight lost.
                    Romeo and Juliet 1.1.232
[*strooken:* stricken]

Blood

460 POLONIUS: I do know,
When the blood burns, how prodigal the soul
Lends the tongue vows.
                         Hamlet 1.3.115

461 K. JOHN: There is no sure foundation set on blood;
No certain life achiev'd by others' death.
                         King John 4.2.104

462 MACBETH: Blood will have blood.
                         Macbeth 3.4.121

463 K. HENRY [on the prospect of war with France]: Never two such kingdoms did contend
Without much fall of blood, whose guiltless drops
Are every one a woe.
                         Henry V 1.2.24

464 HUBERT [on the war between England and France]: Blood hath bought blood, and blows have answer'd blows;
Strength match'd with strength, and power confronted power.
                         King John 2.1.329

465 FIRST SENATOR: Friend, or brother,
He forfeits his own blood that spills another.
                    Timon of Athens 3.5.86

466 PUCELLE [to Burgundy]: One drop of blood drawn from thy country's bosom
Should grieve thee more than streams of foreign gore.
                         1 Henry VI 3.3.54

467 PANDULPH: Your mind is all as youthful as your blood.
King John 3.4.125

468 BEROWNE: Young blood doth not obey an old decree.
Love's Labor's Lost 4.3.213

469 PARIS: Hot blood begets hot thoughts, and hot thoughts beget hot deeds.
Troilus and Cressida 3.1.129

470 IAGO: The blood is made dull with the act of sport.
Othello 2.1.227

471 KING: Strange is it that our bloods,
Of color, weight, and heat, pour'd all together,
Would quite confound distinction, yet stands off
In differences so mighty.
All's Well That Ends Well 2.3.118

472 COUNTESS: Our blood to us, this to our blood is born.
It is the show and seal of nature's truth,
Where love's strong passion is impress'd in youth.
All's Well That Ends Well 1.3.131

473 MACBETH [after murdering Duncan]: What hands are here?
Hah! they pluck out mine eyes.
Will all great Neptune's ocean wash this blood
Clean from my hand? No; this my hand will rather
The multitudinous seas incarnadine,
Making the green one red.
Macbeth 2.2.56

474 LADY MACBETH [haunted by Duncan's murder]: Here's the smell of the blood still. All the perfumes of Arabia will not sweeten this little hand. O, O, O!
Macbeth 5.1.50

Blows

475 Alas, how many bear such shameful blows,
Which not themselves but he that gives them knows!
Rape of Lucrece 832

476 HUBERT: Blows have answer'd blows.
King John 2.1.329

Bluntness

477 ANTONY: I have neither wit, nor words, nor worth,
Action, nor utterance, nor the power of speech
To stir men's blood; I only speak right on.
Julius Caesar 3.2.221

478 CORNWALL [about Kent]: This is some fellow
Who, having been prais'd for bluntness, doth affect
A saucy roughness, and constrains the garb
Quite from his nature. He cannot flatter, he,
An honest mind and plain, he must speak truth!
And they will take't, so; if not, he's plain.
These kind of knaves I know, which in this plainness
Harbor more craft and far corrupter ends
Than twenty silly-ducking observants
That stretch their duty nicely.
King Lear 2.2.95

Blushing

479 HERMIONE: Innocence shall make False accusation blush.
Winter's Tale 3.2.30

480 CLAUDIO [about Hero]: Comes not that blood as modest evidence
To witness simple virtue?
Much Ado About Nothing 4.1.37

481 AARON [to Chiron]: Fie, treacherous hue, that will betray with blushing
The close enacts and counsels of thy heart!
Titus Andronicus 4.2.117

482 MOTH: If she be made of white and red,
Her faults will ne'er be known,
For blush in cheeks by faults are bred,
And fears by pale white shown:
Then if she fear, or be to blame,
By this you shall not know,
For still her cheeks possess the same
Which native she doth owe.
Love's Labor's Lost 1.2.99

483 AENEAS [to Agamemnon]: Bid the cheek be ready with a blush
Modest as morning when she coldly eyes
The youthful Phoebus.
Troilus and Cressida 1.3.228

484 HAMLET [to his mother, on her remarriage]: O shame, where is thy blush?
Hamlet 3.4.81

485 PETRUCHIO [about Kate]: Such war of white and red within her cheeks!
Taming of the Shrew 4.5.30

486 ADRIANA [to Luciana about Antipholus Ephesus]: Look'd he red or pale, or sad or merrily?
What observation mad'st thou in this case
Of his heart's meteors tilting in his face?
Comedy of Errors 4.2.4

Blustering

487 FIRST CONSPIRATOR: Splitting the air with noise.
Coriolanus 5.6.51

488 BOY: The empty vessel makes the greatest sound.
Henry V 4.4.69

489 GUIDERIUS [to Cloten]: What art thou? Have not I
An arm as big as thine? a heart as big?
Thy words I grant are bigger; for I wear not
My dagger in my mouth.
Cymbeline 4.2.76

490 BOY [about Pistol]: He hath a killing tongue and a quiet sword.
Henry V 3.2.34

Boasting

491 ROMEO: A gentleman ... that loves to hear himself talk ... will speak more in a minute that he will stand to in a month.
Romeo and Juliet 2.4.147

492 CRESSIDA: They that have the voice of lions and the act of hares, are they not monsters?
Troilus and Cressida 3.2.88

493 STEWARD: We wound our modesty, and make foul the clearness of our deservings, when of ourselves we publish them.
All's Well That Ends Well 1.3.5

494 JULIET: Conceit, more rich in matter than in words,
Brags of his substance, not of ornament;
They are but beggars that can count their worth.
Romeo and Juliet 2.6.30

495 OTHELLO: (O vain boast!)
Who can control his fate?
Othello 5.2.264

496 ANTONIO [about Don Pedro and Claudio]: I know them, yea,
And what they weigh, even to the utmost scruple —
Scrambling, outfacing, fashion-monging boys,
That lie and cog and flout, deprave and slander,
Go anticly, and show outward hideousness,

And speak off half a dozen dang'rous
words,
How they might hurt their enemies — if
they durst —
And that is all.
Much Ado About Nothing 5.1.93

497 PAROLLES: Who knows himself a
braggart,
Let him fear this; for it will come to
pass
That every braggart shall be found an
ass.
All's Well That Ends Well 4.3.334

Boat

498 AGAMEMNON: Light boats sail
swift, though greater hulks draw deep.
Troilus and Cressida 2.3.266

Body

499 PETRUCHIO: 'Tis the mind that
makes the body rich.
Taming of the Shrew 4.3.172

500 IAGO: Our bodies are our gardens,
to the which our wills are gardeners . . .
either to have it sterile with idleness or
manur'd with industry.
Othello 1.3.320

501 My body or my soul, which was
the dearer,
When the one pure, the other made
divine?
Rape of Lucrece 1163

502 LEAR: We are not ourselves
When nature, being oppress'd, com-
mands the mind
To suffer with the body.
King Lear 2.4.107

503 K. EDWARD [to Warwick]: What
is the body when the head is off?
3 Henry VI 5.1.41

504 WARWICK [soliloquy]: My sick
heart shows,

That I must yield my body to the
earth,
And by my fall, the conquest to my
foe.
Thus yields the cedar to the axe's edge,
Whose arms gave shelter to the
princely eagle,
Under whose shade the ramping lion
slept,
Whose top-branch overpeer'd Jove's
spreading tree,
And kept low shrubs from winter's
pow'rful wind.
3 Henry VI 5.2.7

505 CHARMIAN: The soul and body
rive not more in parting
Than greatness going off.
Antony and Cleopatra 4.13.5
[*rive:* cleave]

Boldness

506 DUKE: Virtue is bold, and
goodness never fearful.
Measure for Measure 3.1.208

507 Things out of hope are compass'd
oft with vent'ring.
Venus and Adonis 567
[*vent'ring:* venturing]

508 K. LEWIS [to Margaret]: Yield not
thy neck
To fortune's yoke, but let thy dauntless
mind
Still ride in triumph over all mischance.
3 Henry VI 3.3.16

509 BASTARD [to King John]: Be stir-
ring as the time, be fire with fire,
Threaten the threat'ner, and outface
the brow
Of bragging horror.
King John 5.1.48

510 Youth is hot and bold.
The Passionate Pilgrim xii.7

511 Who is so faint that dares not be
so bold

To touch the fire, the weather being cold?

Venus and Adonis 401

Bondage

512 GLOUCESTER [reading a letter from Edgar]: "This policy and reverence of age makes the world bitter to the best of our times; keeps our fortunes from us till our oldness cannot relish them. I begin to find an idle and fond bondage in the oppression of aged tyranny, who sways, not as it hath power, but as it is suffer'd..."

King Lear 1.2.46

513 JULIET: Bondage is hoarse, and may not speak aloud.

Romeo and Juliet 2.2.160

514 PISTOL: Base is the slave that pays.

Henry V 2.1.96

515 CASCA: Every bondsman in his own hand bears
The power to cancel his captivity.

Julius Caesar 1.3.101

516 JACHIMO: To think that man, who knows
By history, report, or his own proof,
What woman is, yea, what she cannot choose
But must be, will 's free hours languish for
Assured bondage.

Cymbeline 1.6.69

[*'s:* his]

Bones

517 ARMADO: Beat not the bones of the buried.

Love's Labor's Lost 5.2.661

Books

518 LADY CAPULET: That book in many's eyes doth share the glory,

That in gold clasps locks in the golden story.

Romeo and Juliet 1.3.91

519 POSTHUMUS: A book? O rare one!
Be not, as is our fangled world, a garment
Nobler than that its covers!

Cymbeline 5.4.133

520 BEROWNE: Study is like the heaven's glorious sun,
That will not be deep search'd with saucy looks;
Small have continual plodders ever won,
Save base authority from others' books.

Love's Labor's Lost 1.1.84

521 PROSPERO: My library
Was dukedom large enough.

The Tempest 1.2.109

522 TITUS [to Lavinia]: Come and take choice of all my library,
And so beguile thy sorrow.

Titus Andronicus 4.1.34

Bores

523 BEATRICE [concerning Benedick and his latest companion, Claudio]: O Lord, he will hang upon him like a disease; he is sooner caught than the pestilence, and the taker runs presently mad.

Much Ado About Nothing 1.1.86

524 AUSTRIA [about the Bastard]: What cracker is this same that deafs our ears with this abundance of superfluous breath?

King John 2.1.147

525 HOTSPUR [about Glendower]: O, he is as tedious
As a tired horse, a railing wife,
Worse than a smoky house. I had rather live
With cheese and garlic in a windmill, far,

Than feed on cates and have him talk
   to me
In any summer house in Christendom.
                 1 Henry IV 3.1.157
[*cates:* delicacies]

Borrowing

526 FALSTAFF: I can get no remedy
against this consumption of the purse;
borrowing only lingers and lingers it
out, but the disease is incurable.
               2 Henry IV 1.2.236

527 POLONIUS: Neither a borrower nor
a lender be,
For loan oft loses both itself and
   friend,
And borrowing dulleth th' edge of
   husbandry.
               Hamlet 1.3.75

528 EDGAR: Keep . . . thy pen from
lenders' books.
               King Lear 3.4.97

Bounty

529 JULIET [to Romeo]: My bounty is
as boundless as the sea,
My love as deep; the more I give to
   thee,
The more I have, for both are infinite.
         Romeo and Juliet 2.2.133

530 HAMLET: Use every man after his
desert, and who shall scape whipping?
Use them after your own honor and
dignity—the less they deserve, the
more merit is in your bounty.
              Hamlet 2.2.528

531 CLOWN [to Duke]: Sir, let your
bounty take a nap, I will awake it
anon.
           Twelfth Night 5.1.48

Bow

532 He is no woodman that doth bend
his bow
To strike a poor unseasonble doe.
          Rape of Lucrece 580

Boy

533 POLIXENES [to Hermione]: We
were, fair queen,
Two lads that thought there was no
   more behind
But such a day to-morrow as to-day,
And to be boy eternal.
           Winter's Tale 1.2.63

Braggart

534 PAROLLES: Who knows himself a
braggart,
Let him fear this; for it will come to
pass
That every braggart shall be found an
ass.
    All's Well That Ends Well 4.3.334

535 K. HENRY: The man that once
did sell the lion's skin
While the beast liv'd, was kill'd with
   hunting him.
             Henry V 4.3.93

Brain

536 THESEUS: Lovers and madmen
   have such seething brains,
Such shaping fantasies, that apprehend
More than cool reason ever compre-
   hends.
The lunatic, the lover, and the poet
Are of imagination all compact.
    Midsummer Night's Dream 5.1.4

537 CAESAR [drinking wine]: It's
   monstrous labor when I wash my
   brain
And it grows fouler.
      Antony and Cleopatra 2.7.98

538 What's in the brain that ink may character...?

Sonnet 108

539 GUIDERIUS [about Cloten]: Not Hercules
Could have knock'd out his brains, for he had none.

Cymbeline 4.2.114

Bravery

540 CELIA: All's brave that youth mounts and folly guides.

As You Like It 3.4.45

541 BEVIS: There's no better sign of a brave mind than a hard hand.

2 Henry VI 4.2.19

542 MARTIUS: Brave death outweighs bad life.

Coriolanus 1.6.71

543 FIRST SENATOR: He's truly valiant that can wisely suffer
The worst that man can breathe, and make his wrongs
His outsides, to wear them like his raiment, carelessly,
And ne'er prefer his injuries to his heart,
To bring it into danger.

Timon of Athens 3.5.31

544 NORTHUMBERLAND: What valor were it, when a cur doth grin,
For one to thrust his hand between his teeth,
When he might spurn him with his foot away?

3 Henry VI 1.4.56

545 PETRUCHIO [to Gremio, about Kate]: Think you a little din can daunt mine ears?
Have I not in my time heard lions roar?
Have I not heard the sea, puff'd up with winds,
Rage like an angry boar chafed with sweat?
Have I not heard great ordnance in the field,

And heaven's artillery thunder in the skies?
Have I not in a pitched battle heard
Loud 'larums, neighing steeds, and trumpets' clang?
And do you tell me of a woman's tongue,
That gives not half so great a blow to hear
As will a chestnut in a farmer's fire?
Tush, tush, fear boys with bugs.

Taming of the Shrew 1.2.199

[*'larums:* alarums, calls to arms]

546 ORLEANCE: That's a valiant flea that dare eat his breakfast on the lip of a lion.

Henry V 3.7.145

Breach

547 K. HENRY [at the battle of Harfleur]: Once more into the breach, dear friends, once more;
Or close the wall up with our English dead.

Henry V 3.1.1

Breast

548 IAGO: Who has that breast so pure
But some uncleanly apprehensions
Keep leets and law-days and in sessions sit
With meditations lawful?

Othello 3.3.138

[*keep leets:* hold courts]

Breath

549 LONGAVILLE: Vows are but breath, and breath a vapor is.

Love's Labor's Lost 4.3.66

550 PROSPERO: Words
Are natural breath.

The Tempest 5.1.156

551 DUKE [to the condemned Claudio]: A breath thou art.

Measure for Measure 3.1.8

552 FIRST CITIZEN: They say poor suitors have strong breaths.
Coriolanus 1.1.59

553 BEATRICE: Foul words is but foul wind, and foul wind is but foul breath, and foul breath is noisome.
Much Ado About Nothing 5.2.52

554 PERICLES: Life's but breath.
Pericles 1.1.46

555 Age's breath is short.
The Passionate Pilgrim xii.5

556 YORK: Direct not him whose way himself will choose,
'Tis breath thou lack'st, and that breath wilt thou lose.
Richard II 2.1.29

Breeding

557 KING: Strange it is that our bloods,
Of color, weight, and heat, pour'd all together,
Would quite confound distinction, yet stands off
In differences so mighty.
All's Well That Ends Well 2.3.118

558 From fairest creatures we desire increase,
That thereby beauty's rose might never die.
Sonnet 1

559 BELARIUS: Cowards father cowards and base things sire base.
Cymbeline 4.2.26

560 DUKE [to Isabella]: The hand that hath made you fair hath made you good.
Measure for Measure 3.1.180

561 IMOGEN: Clay and clay differs in dignity
Whose dust is both alike.
Cymbeline 4.2.4

Brevity

562 POLONIUS: Brevity is the soul of wit.
Hamlet 2.2.90

563 BOY: Men of few words are the best men.
Henry V 3.2.36

564 FIRST MURDERER: I would speak with Clarence, and I came hither on my legs.
BRAKENBURY: What, so brief?
SECOND MURDERER: 'Tis better, sir, than to be tedious.
Richard III 1.4.88

565 HAMLET: Is this a prologue, or the posy of a ring?
OPHELIA: 'Tis brief, my lord.
HAMLET: As woman's love.
Hamlet 3.2.152
[*posy of a ring:* short verse motto inscribed in a ring]

566 K. RICHARD: We must be brief when traitors brave the field.
Richard III 4.3.57

Bribery

567 CLOTEN [soliloquy]: 'Tis gold
Which buys admittance (oft it doth), yea, and makes
Diana's rangers false themselves, yield up
Their deer to th' stand o' th' stealer; and 'tis gold
Which makes the true man kill'd and saves the thief;
Nay, sometimes hangs both thief and true man. What
Can it not do, and undo?
Cymbeline 2.3.67

568 CLOWN: Though authority be a subborn bear, yet he is oft led by the nose with gold.
Winter's Tale 4.4.801

Brightness

569 KING: To the brightest beams
Distracted clouds give way.
All's Well That Ends Well 5.3.34

Britain

570 CLOTEN: Britain's a world
By itself.
Cymbeline 3.1.12

Broker

571 HUME: A crafty knave does need
no broker.
2 Henry VI 1.2.100

Building

572 LORD BARDOLPH: When we mean
to build,
We first survey the plot, then draw the
model,
And when we see the figure of the
house,
Then must we rate the cost of the
erection,
Which if we find outweighs ability,
What do we do then but draw anew
the model
In fewer offices, or at least desist
To build at all?
2 Henry IV 1.3.41

573 SECOND LORD: Goodly buildings
left without a roof
Soon fall to ruin.
Pericles 2.4.36

574 VOLUMNIA: I have lived
To see inherited my very wishes
And the buildings of my fancy.
Coriolanus 2.1.199

Bull

575 DON PEDRO: In time the savage
bull doth bear the yoke.
Much Ado About Nothing 1.1.261

Burden

576 Q. KATHERINE: The back is
sacrifice to th' load.
Henry VIII 1.2.50

577 BUCKINGHAM: Many
Have broke their backs with laying
manors on 'em.
Henry VIII 1.1.84

Burlesque

578 PORTIA: It is a sin to be a mocker.
Merchant of Venice 1.2.57

Bush

579 GLOUCESTER: Suspicion always
haunts the guilty mind;
The thief doth fear each bush an
officer.
3 Henry VI 5.6.11

580 THESEUS: In the night, imagining
some fear,
How easy is a bush suppos'd a bear!
Midsummer Night's Dream 5.1.21

Business

581 ANTONY: To business that we
love we rise betime,
And go to't with delight.
Antony and Cleopatra 4.4.20

582 HAMLET: Every man hath business
and desire,
Such as it is.
Hamlet 1.5.130

583 GARDINER: Affairs that walk
(As they say spirits do) at midnight,
have
In them a wilder nature than the
business
That seeks dispatch by day.
Henry VIII 5.1.13

584 KING [soliloquy]: Like a man to double business bound,
I stand in pause where I shall first begin.

Hamlet 3.3.41

Butterfly

585 MENENIUS: There is differency between a grub and a butterfly, yet your butterfly was a grub.

Coriolanus 5.4.11

Buying

586 PARIS: Fair Diomed, you do as chapmen do,
Dispraise the thing that they desire to buy,
But we in silence hold this virtue well,
We'll not commend what we intend to sell.

Troilus and Cressida 4.1.76

587 AUTOLYCUS [singing]: Gloves as sweet as damask roses,
Masks for faces and for noses;
Bugle-bracelet, necklace amber,
Perfume for a lady's chamber;
Golden quoifs and stomachers
For my lads to give their dears;
Pins and poking-sticks of steel;
What maids lack from head to heel:
Come buy of me, come; come buy, come buy,
Buy, lads, or else your lasses cry:
Come buy.

Winter's Tale 4.4.220

Caesar

588 CAESAR [to Antony]: I rather tell thee what is to be fear'd
Than what I fear; for always I am Caesar.

Julius Caesar 1.2.211

589 CAESAR: The cause is in my will.

Julius Caesar 2.2.71

590 ANTONY: When Caesar says, "Do this," it is perform'd.

Julius Caesar 1.2.10

591 CLOTEN: There be many Caesars, ere such another Julius . . . Other of them may have crook'd noses, but to owe such straight arms, none.

Cymbeline 3.1.11, 37

[*owe:* own]

592 CASSIUS [about Caesar]: Why, man, he doth bestride the narrow world
Like a Colossus, and we petty men
Walk under his huge legs, and peep about
To find ourselves dishonorable graves.

Julius Caesar 1.2.135

593 CAESAR: Et tu, Brute!

Julius Caesar 3.1.77

[And thou, Brutus!]

594 BRUTUS [at The Forum]: As Caesar lov'd me, I weep for him; as he was fortunate, I rejoice at it; as he was valiant, I honor him; but, as he was ambitious, I slew him. There is tears for his love; joy for his fortune; honor for his valor; and death for his ambition.

Julius Caesar 3.2.24

595 ANTONY [at The Forum]: Friends, Romans, countrymen, lend me your ears!
I come to bury Caesar, not to praise him.
The evil that men do lives after them,
The good is oft interred with their bones;
So let it be with Caesar. The noble Brutus
Hath told you Caesar was ambitious;
If it were so, it was a grievous fault,
And grievously hath Caesar answer'd it.
Here, under leave of Brutus and the rest
(For Brutus is an honorable man,
So are they all, all honorable men),
Come I to speak in Caesar's funeral.

He was my friend, faithful and just to me;
But Brutus says he was ambitious,
And Brutus is an honorable man.
He hath brought many captives home to Rome,
Whose ransoms did the general coffers fill;
Did this in Caesar seem ambitious?
When that the poor have cried, Caesar hath wept;
Ambition should be made of sterner stuff:
Yet Brutus says he was ambitious,
And Brutus is an honorable man.
You all did see that on the Lupercal
I thrice presented him a kingly crown,
Which he did thrice refuse. Was this ambition?
Yet Brutus says he was ambitious,
And sure he is an honorable man.
I speak not to disprove what Brutus spoke,
But here I am to speak what I do know.
You all did love him once, not without cause;
What cause withholds you then to mourn for him?
O judgment! thou art fled to brutish beasts,
And men have lost their reason. Bear with me,
My heart is in the coffin there with Caesar,
And I must pause till it come back to me.
Julius Caesar 3.2.73

596 ANTONY [at The Forum]: But yesterday the word of Caesar might
Have stood against the world; now lies he there,
And none so poor to do him reverence.
Julius Caesar 3.2.118

597 HAMLET: Imperious Caesar, dead and turn'd to clay,
Might stop a hole to keep the wind away.
O that that earth which kept the world in awe

Should patch a wall t' expel the winter's flaw!
Hamlet 5.1.213

598 PRINCE: That Julius Caesar was a famous man;
With what his valor did enrich his wit,
His wit set down to make his valure live.
Richard III 3.1.84
[*valure:* valor]

Cake

599 PANDARUS: He that will have a cake out of the wheat must tarry the grinding.
Troilus and Cressida 1.1.14

Calamity

600 CLOWN: There is no true cuckold but calamity.
Twelfth Night 1.5.51

601 FRIAR LAWRENCE [about Romeo]:
Affliction is enamor'd of thy parts,
And thou art wedded to calamity.
Romeo and Juliet 3.3.2

Calumny

602 LAERTES: Virtue itself scapes not calumnious strokes.
Hamlet 1.3.38

603 HAMLET: Be thou as chaste as ice, as pure as snow, thou shalt not escape calumny.
Hamlet 3.1.135

604 DUKE [soliloquy]: No might nor greatness in mortality
Can censure scape; back-wounding calumny
The whitest virtue strikes. What king so strong
Can tie the gall up in the slanderous tongue?
Measure for Measure 3.2.185
[*scape:* escape]

605 LEONTES: Calumny will sear
Virtue itself, these shrugs, these hums
and ha's.
Winter's Tale 2.1.73

Camel

606 K. RICHARD: It is as hard to come
as for a camel
To thread the postern of a small
needle's eye.
Richard II 5.5.16

Candle

607 PORTIA: How far that little candle
throws his beams!
So shines a good deed in a naughty
world.
Merchant of Venice 5.1.90

Candor

608 IAGO: Men should be what they
seem,
Or those that be not, would they
might seem none!
Othello 3.3.126

609 OLIVIA: To be generous, guiltless,
and of free disposition, is to take those
things for bird-bolts that you deem
cannon-bullets.
Twelfth Night 1.5.91
[*bird-bolts:* blunt-headed arrows for
shooting birds]

610 IAGO: Take note, take note, O
world,
To be direct and honest is not safe.
Othello 3.3.377

611 MENENIUS: We call a nettle but a
nettle, and
The faults of fools but folly.
Coriolanus 2.1.190

612 DON PEDRO [about Benedick]: He
hath a heart as sound as a bell, and his
tongue is the clapper, for what his
heart thinks, his tongue speaks.
Much Ado About Nothing 3.2.12

Canker

613 PROTEUS: In the sweetest bud
The eating canker dwells.
Two Gentlemen of Verona 1.1.42

614 GLOUCESTER: Banish the canker of
ambitious thoughts!
2 Henry VI 1.2.18

615 LAERTES: The canker galls the infants of the spring
Too oft before their buttons be
disclos'd.
Hamlet 1.3.39
[*buttons:* buds]

Cannon

616 K. JOHN [warning Angiers of the
French]: The cannons have their
bowels full of wrath,
And ready mounted are they to spit
forth
Their iron indignation 'gainst your
walls.
King John 2.1.210

Cant

617 POLONIUS: 'Tis too much
prov'd—that with devotion's visage
And pious action we do sugar o'er
The devil himself.
Hamlet 3.1.46

Caprice

618 CLOTEN: A woman's fitness comes
by fits.
Cymbeline 4.1.5

619 JULIA [soliloquy]: How wayward is
this foolish love,

That (like a testy babe) will scratch the
nurse
And presently, all humbled, kiss the
rod!
Two Gentlemen of Verona 1.2.57

Captain

620 VENTIDIUS: Who does i' th' wars
more than his captain can
Becomes his captain's captain.
Antony and Cleopatra 3.1.21

621 ISABELLA: That in the captain's
but a choleric word,
Which in the soldier is flat blasphemy.
Measure for Measure 2.2.130

Captivity

622 CASCA: Every bondsman in his
own hand bears
The power to cancel his captivity.
Julius Caesar 1.3.101

Care

623 MACBETH: The innocent sleep,
Sleep that knits up the ravell'd sleave
of care.
Macbeth 2.2.33

624 K. RICHARD [to the victorious
Bullingbrook]: My care is loss of
care, by old care done,
Your care is gain of care, by new care
won.
Richard II 4.1.196

625 SIR TOBY: I am sure care's an
enemy to life.
Twelfth Night 1.3.2

626 FRIAR LAWRENCE: Care keeps his
watch in every old man's eye,
And where care lodges, sleep will never
lie.
Romeo and Juliet 2.3.35

627 PUCELLE: Care is no cure, but
rather corrosive,
For things that are not to be remedied.
1 Henry VI 3.3.3

628 YORK: Things past redress are now
with me past care.
Richard II 2.3.171

629 GRATIANO [to Antonio]: You
have too much respect upon the
world.
They lose it that do buy it with much
care.
Merchant of Venice 1.1.74

630 YORK: Comfort's in heaven, and
we are on the earth,
Where nothing lives but crosses, cares,
and grief.
Richard II 2.2.79

631 ROSALINE: Past care is still past
cure.
Love's Labor's Lost 5.2.28

632 PERICLES [soliloquy]: The passions
of the mind,
That have their first conception by
misdread,
Have after-nourishment and life by
care.
Pericles 1.2.11

633 DON PEDRO: In faith, lady, you
have a merry heart.
BEATRICE: Yea, my lord, I thank it—
poor fool, it keeps on the windy side
of care.
Much Ado About Nothing 2.1.312

634 Age is full of care.
The Passionate Pilgrim xii.2

635 K. RICHARD: Say, is my kingdom
lost? Why, 'twas my care,
And what loss is it to be rid of care?
Richard II 3.2.95

636 PRINCE [soliloquy]: O, polish'd
perturbation! golden care!

That keep'st the ports of slumber open
  wide
To many a watchful night.
       2 Henry IV 4.5.23

637 LEAR [to his daughters]: Know
  that we have divided
In three our kingdom; and 'tis our fast
  intent
To shake all cares and business from
  our age,
Conferring them on younger strengths,
  while we
Unburthen'd crawl toward death.
       King Lear 1.1.38
[*unburthen'd:* unburdened]

638 GLOUCESTER: Thus sometimes
  hath the brightest day a cloud,
And after summer evermore succeeds
Barren winter, with his wrathful nip-
  ping cold;
So cares and joys abound, as seasons
  fleet.
       2 Henry VI 2.4.1

639 ARIEL [singing]: If of life you keep
  a care,
Shake off slumber, and beware.
Awake, awake!
       The Tempest 2.1.303

Carnality

640 COSTARD: Such is the simplicity of
man to harken after the flesh.
       Love's Labor's Lost 1.1.217

641 The flesh being proud, Desire
  doth fight with Grace.
       Rape of Lucrece 712

Cat

642 HAMLET: Let Hercules himself do
  what he may,
The cat will mew, and dog will have
  his day.
       Hamlet 5.1.291
[That is, nothing under the sun can prevent
justice being done for his father's murder.]

Cause

643 DROMIO SYRACUSE: Every why
hath a wherefore.
       Comedy of Errors 2.2.44

644 FLUELLEN: There is occasions and
causes why and wherefore in all things.
       Henry V 5.1.3

645 BRUTUS [to his fellow con-
  spirators]: What need we any spur
but our own cause
To prick us to redress?
       Julius Caesar 2.1.123

646 WESTMERLAND: A rotten case
abides no handling.
       2 Henry IV 4.1.159

647 POLONIUS [to Queen, about
  Hamlet]: Mad let us grant him then,
  and now remains
That we find out the cause of this
  effect,
Or rather say, the cause of this defect,
For this effect defective comes by
  cause.
       Hamlet 2.2.100

648 BATES: We know enough, if we
know we are the King's subjects. If his
cause be wrong, our obedience to the
King wipes the crime of it out of us.
       Henry V 4.1.131

Caution

649 BAPTISTA: Pitchers have ears.
       Taming of the Shrew 4.4.52

650 THIRD CITIZEN: When clouds are
seen, wise men put on their cloaks.
       Richard III 2.3.32

651 HECTOR: The wound of peace is
  surety,
Surety secure, but modest doubt is
  call'd

The beacon of the wise, the tent that searches
To th' bottom of the worst.
Troilus and Cressida 2.2.14
[*wound of peace:* i.e. the danger to peace lies in a false sense of security; *tent:* probe]

652 AUTOLYCUS: It behooves men to be wary.
Winter's Tale 4.4.254

653 Q. ELIZABETH: Trust not him that hath once broken faith.
3 Henry VI 4.4.30

654 PANDULPH: He that stands upon a slipp'ry place
Makes nice of no vild hold to stay him up.
King John 3.4.137
[*vild:* vile]

655 PISTOL: Trust none;
For oaths are straws, men's faiths are wafer-cakes,
And Hold-fast is the only dog.
Henry V 2.3.50
[*wafer-cakes:* i.e. fragile; *Hold-fast:* an allusion to the proverb: "Brag is a good dog, but Holdfast is a better."]

Cedar

656 The cedar stoops not to the base shrub's foot,
But low shrubs wither at the cedar's root.
Rape of Lucrece 664

Celerity

657 CLEOPATRA: Celerity is never more admir'd
Than by the negligent.
Antony and Cleopatra 3.7.24

658 DUKE: Hence hath offense his quick celerity,
When it is borne in high authority.
Measure for Measure 4.2.110

Censure

659 WOLSEY: We must not stint
Our necessary actions in the fear
To cope malicious censurers.
Henry VIII 1.2.76

660 POLONIUS: Take each man's censure, but reserve thy judgment.
Hamlet 1.3.69

Ceremony

661 TIMON: Ceremony was but devis'd at first
To set a gloss on faint deeds, hollow welcomes,
Recanting goodness, sorry ere 'tis shown;
But where there is true friendship, there needs none.
Timon of Athens 1.2.15

662 K. HENRY [soliloquy]: What infinite heart's ease
Must kings neglect, that private men enjoy!
And what have kings, that privates have not too,
Save ceremony, save general ceremony?
And what art thou, thou idol Ceremony?
What kind of god art thou, that suffer'st more
Of mortal griefs than do thy worshippers?
What are thy rents? what are thy comings-in?
O Ceremony, show me but thy worth!
What is thy soul of adoration?
Art thou aught else but place, degree, and form,
Creating awe and fear in other men?
Wherein thou art less happy, being fear'd,
Than they in fearing.
What drink'st thou oft, in stead of homage sweet,
But poison'd flattery? O, be sick, great greatness,
And bid thy ceremony give thee cure!
Henry V 4.1.236
[*rents:* revenues]

663 K. HENRY: The King is but a man ... His ceremonies laid by, in his nakedness he appears but a man.
Henry V 4.1.101

664 BRUTUS: When love begins to sicken and decay
It useth an enforced ceremony.
There are no tricks in plain and simple faith.
Julius Caesar 4.2.20

665 LADY MACBETH: To feed were best at home;
From thence, the sauce to meat is ceremony,
Meeting were bare without it.
Macbeth 3.4.34

666 HAMLET: Th' appurtenance of welcome is fashion and ceremony.
Hamlet 2.2.371

667 PAROLLES [to Bertram concerning the nobles going off to war]: Use a more spacious ceremony to the noble lords ... for they wear themselves in the cap of the time, there do muster true gait; eat, speak, and move under the influence of the most receiv'd star, and though the devil lead the measure, such are to be follow'd. After them, and take a more dilated farewell.
All's Well That Ends Well 2.1.50
[*dilated:* expansive]

Certainty

668 Q. MARGARET: What cannot be avoided,
'Twere childish weakness to lament or fear.
3 Henry VI 5.4.37

669 IMOGEN: Certainties
Either are past remedies, or, timely knowing,
The remedy then born.
Cymbeline 1.6.96

670 K. HENRY: When the mind is quick'ned, out of doubt,

The organs, though defunct and dead before,
Break up their drowsy grave, and newly move
With casted slough and fresh legerity.
Henry V 4.1.20
[*legerity:* nimbleness]

671 MACBETH: Make assurance double sure.
Macbeth 4.1.83

Challenge

672 VIOLA: I have heard of some kind of men that put quarrels purposely on others, to taste their valor.
Twelfth Night 3.4.242

Chance

673 ARCHBISHOP: Against ill chances men are ever merry,
But heaviness foreruns the good event.
2 Henry IV 4.2.81

674 NESTOR: In the reproof of chance Lies the true proof of men.
Troilus and Cressida 1.3.33

675 FLORIZEL: But as th' unthought on accident is guilty
To what we wildly do, so we profess Ourselves to be the slaves of chance, and flies
Of every wind that blows.
Winter's Tale 4.4.538

676 CLEOPATRA: I shall show the cinders of my spirits
Through th' ashes of my chance.
Antony and Cleopatra 5.2.173
[*chance:* her misfortune]

677 K. RICHARD: I have set my life upon a cast,
And I will stand the hazard of the die.
Richard III 5.4.9
[*cast:* throw of the dice; *die:* singular of dice]

Change

678 HAMLET: Use almost can change the stamp of nature.
Hamlet 3.4.168

679 CAPULET [supposing Juliet to be dead]: All things that we ordained festival,
Turn from their office to black funeral:
Our instruments to melancholy bells,
Our wedding cheer to a sad burial feast;
Our solemn hymns to sullen dirges change;
Our bridal flowers serve for a buried corse;
And all things change them to the contrary.
Romeo and Juliet 4.5.84

680 KING: That we would do,
We should do when we would; for this "would" changes,
And hath abatements and delays as many
As there are tongues, are hands, are accidents,
And then this "should" is like a spend-thrift's sigh,
That hurts by easing.
Hamlet 4.7.118
[*spendthrift's sigh:* a sigh, which, it was supposed, drew blood from the heart]

681 WOLSEY [soliloquy]: This is the state of man: to-day he puts forth
The tender leaves of hopes, to-morrow blossoms,
And bears his blushing honors thick upon him;
The third day comes a frost, a killing frost,
And when he thinks, good easy man, full surely
His greatness is a-ripening, nips his root,
And then he falls as I do.
Henry VIII 3.2.352

682 K. RICHARD: The love of wicked men converts to fear,

That fear to hate, and hate turns one or both
To worthy danger and deserved death.
Richard II 5.1.66

683 BENEDICK [soliloquy]: Happy are they that hear their detractions, and can put them to mending.
Much Ado About Nothing 2.3.229

684 BENEDICK [soliloquy]: A man loves the meat in his youth that he cannot endure in his age.
Much Ado About Nothing 2.3.238

685 PLAYER KING: This world is not for aye, nor 'tis not strange
That even our loves should with our fortunes change.
Hamlet 3.2.200

686 MENENIUS: There is difference between a grub and a butterfly, yet your butterfly was a grub.
Coriolanus 5.4.11

687 ANTONY: The hated, grown to strength,
Are newly grown to love.
Antony and Cleopatra 1.3.48

688 TITANIA [to Oberon and his train of fairies]: The seasons alter: hoary-headed frosts
Fall in the fresh lap of the crimson rose,
And on old Hiems' thin and icy crown
An odorous chaplet of sweet summer buds
Is, as in mockery, set; the spring, the summer,
The chiding autumn, angry winter, change
Their wonted liveries; and the mazed world,
By their increase, now knows not which is which.
And this same progeny of evils comes
From our debate, from our dissension.
Midsummer Night's Dream 2.1.107

689 PROTEUS [soliloquy]: Even as one heat another heat expels,

Or as one nail by strength drives out another,
So the remembrance of my former love
Is by a newer object quite forgotten.
Two Gentlemen of Verona 2.4.192

Character

690 DUNCAN: There's no art
To find the mind's construction in the face.
Macbeth 1.4.12

691 IAGO: 'Tis in ourselves that we are thus or thus. Our bodies are our gardens, to the which our wills are gardeners; so that if we will plant nettles or sow lettuce, set hyssop and weed up tine, supply it with one gender of herbs or distract it with many, either to have it sterile with idleness or manur'd with industry—why, the power and corrigible authority of this lies in our wills.
Othello 1.3.319
[*tine:* tares, wild grasses]

692 CRESSIDA: Mighty states characterless are grated
To dusty nothing.
Troilus and Cressida 3.2.188

693 FIRST SENATOR: He's truly valiant that can wisely suffer
The worst that man can breathe, and make his wrongs
His outsides, to wear them like his raiment, carelessly,
And ne'er prefer his injuries to his heart,
To bring it into danger.
Timon of Athens 3.5.31

694 PROTEUS: He wants wit that wants resolved will.
Two Gentlemen of Verona 2.6.12

695 AMIENS [to Duke Senior, in exile]:
Happy is your Grace,
That can translate the stubbornness of fortune
Into so quiet and so sweet a style.
As You Like It 2.1.18

696 HAMLET [to Horatio]: Thou hast been
As one in suff'ring all that suffers nothing,
A man that Fortune's buffets and rewards
Has ta'en with equal thanks.
Hamlet 3.2.65

Charity

697 HAMLET: Use every man after his desert, and who shall scape whipping? Use them after your own honor and dignity—the less they deserve, the more merit is in your bounty.
Hamlet 2.2.529

698 BEROWNE: Charity itself fulfills the law,
And who can sever love from charity?
Love's Labor's Lost 4.3.361

699 GLOUCESTER [to Anne]: Lady, you know no rules of charity,
Which renders good for bad, blessings for curses.
Richard III 1.2.68

700 ORLANDO: I will chide no breather in the world but myself,
against whom I know most faults.
As You Like It 3.2.280

701 PRINCESS: A giving hand, though foul, shall have fair praise.
Love's Labor's Lost 4.1.23

702 OPHELIA: To the noble mind
Rich gifts wax poor when givers prove unkind.
Hamlet 3.1.99

703 TIMON: 'Tis not enough to help the feeble up,
But to support him after.
Timon of Athens 1.1.107

704 DUKE: The robb'd that smiles steals something from the thief.
Othello 1.3.208

Chastity

705 EMILIA: If she be not honest,
chaste, and true,
There's no man happy.
Othello 4.2.17

706 MISTRESS PAGE: I will find you
twenty lascivious turtles ere one chaste
man.
Merry Wives of Windsor 2.1.80

707 LAERTES: The chariest maid is
prodigal enough
If she unmask her beauty to the moon.
Hamlet 1.3.36

708 TOUCHSTONE: To cast away honesty upon a foul slut were to put good
meat into an unclean dish.
As You Like It 3.3.35

709 DIANA: My chastity's the jewel of
our house.
All's Well That Ends Well 4.2.46

710 Fruitless chastity,
Love-lacking vestals, and self-loving
nuns,
That on the earth would breed a
scarcity
And barren dearth of daughters and of
sons.
Venus and Adonis 751

711 Pure Chastity is rifled of her store,
And Lust, the thief, far poorer than
before.
Rape of Lucrece 692

712 She hath lost a dearer thing than
life,
And he hath won what he would lose
again.
Rape of Lucrece 687

713 BENVOLIO [about Juliet]: Then she
hath sworn that she will still live
chaste?
ROMEO: She hath, and in that sparing
makes huge waste;
For beauty starv'd with her severity
Cuts beauty off from all posterity.
Romeo and Juliet 1.1.217

714 ORLANDO [soliloquy, about Rosa-
lind]: Run, run, Orlando, carve on
every tree
The fair, the chaste, and unexpressive
she.
As You Like It 3.2.9
[*unexpressive:* inexpressive]

715 CLAUDIO [to Hero]: You seem to
me as Dian in her orb,
As chaste as is the bud ere it be blown.
Much Ado About Nothing 4.1.57
[*Dian:* Diana, emblematic of virginity]

716 POSTHUMUS [about Imogen]: I
thought her
As chaste as unsunn'd snow.
Cymbeline 2.5.12

717 MARIANA: The honor of a maid is
her name, and no legacy is so rich as
honesty.
All's Well That Ends Well 3.5.12

718 FORD [to Falstaff, concerning his
wife]: She dwells so securely on the excellency of her honor, that the folly of
my soul dares not present itself.
Merry Wives of Windsor 2.2.242

719 Touches so soft still conquer
chastity.
The Passionate Pilgrim iv.8

720 EMILIA: Of all flow'rs
Methinks a rose is best.
WOMAN: Why, gentle madam?
EMILIA: It is the very emblem of a
maid;
For when the west wind courts her
gently,
How modestly she blows, and paints
the sun
With her chaste blushes! When the
north comes near her,
Rude and impatient, then, like
chastity,
She locks her beauties in her bud
again,
And leaves him to base briers.
Two Noble Kinsmen 2.2.135

Cheerfulness

721 AUTOLYCUS [singing]: A merry heart goes all the day,
Your sad tires in a mile-a.
Winter's Tale 4.3.126

722 BUSHY: Lay aside life-harming heaviness
And entertain a cheerful disposition.
Richard II 2.2.3

723 KATHERINE: A light heart lives long.
Love's Labor's Lost 5.2.18

724 ORLANDO: Live a little, comfort a little, cheer thyself a little.
As You Like It 2.6.5

725 CAESAR [to Octavia]: Cheer your heart,
Be you not troubled with the time, which drives
O'er your content these strong necessities,
But let determin'd things to destiny
Hold unbewail'd their way.
Antony and Cleopatra 3.6.81

726 GRATIANO: Let me play the fool,
With mirth and laughter let old wrinkles come,
And let my liver rather heat with wine
Than my heart cool with mortifying groans.
Why should a man, whose blood is warm within,
Sit like his grandsire cut in alabaster?
Sleep when he wakes? and creep into the jaundies
By being peevish?
Merchant of Venice 1.1.79
[*jaundies:* jaundice]

727 Youth is full of pleasance.
The Passionate Pilgrim xii.2

Chiding

728 MRS. PAGE: Better a little chiding than a great deal of heart-break.
Merry Wives of Windsor 5.3.9

Children

729 Q. ELIZABETH: Ah, my young princes! ah, my tender babes!
My unblown flow'rs, new-appearing sweets!
Richard III 4.4.10

730 MALCOLM: Wife and child,
Those precious motives, those strong knots of love.
Macbeth 4.3.26

731 VINCENTIO: 'Tis a good hearing when children are toward.
Taming of the Shrew 5.2.182

732 MISTRESS QUICKLY: 'Tis not good that children should know any wickedness.
Merry Wives of Windsor 2.2.128

733 K. EDWARD: 'Tis a happy thing
To be the father unto many sons.
3 Henry VI 3.2.104

734 LAUNCELOT: It is a wise father that knows his own child.
Merchant of Venice 2.2.76

735 CONSTANCE: O Lord, my boy, my Arthur, my fair son!
My life, my joy, my food, my all the world!
My widow-comfort, and my sorrow's cure!
King John 3.4.103

736 FOOL: Fathers that wear rags
Do make their children blind,
But fathers that bear bags
Shall see their children kind.
King Lear 2.4.48
[*bags:* i.e. money bags]

737 GARDENER: Unruly children make their sire stoop.
Richard II 3.4.30

738 K. LEAR: How sharper than a serpent's tooth it is
To have a thankless child!
King Lear 1.4.288

739 LADY MACBETH: 'Tis the eye of childhood
That fears a painted devil.
Macbeth 2.2.51

740 THIRD CITIZEN: Woe to that land that's govern'd by a child!
Richard III 2.3.11

741 JULIET [soliloquy]: So tedious is this day
As is the night before some festival
To an impatient child that hath new robes
And may not wear them.
Romeo and Juliet 3.2.28

742 Thou art thy mother's glass, and she in thee
Calls back the lovely April of her prime,
So thou through windows of thine age shalt see,
Despite of wrinkles, this thy golden time.
Sonnet 3

743 That's for thyself to breed another thee,
Or ten times happier be it ten for one;
Ten times thyself were happier than thou art,
If ten of thine ten times refigur'd thee,
Then what could death do if thou shouldst depart,
Leaving thee living in posterity?
Sonnet 6

Choice

744 HORTENSIO: There's small choice in rotten apples.
Taming of the Shrew 1.1.134

745 IAGO: 'Tis the curse of service;
Preferment goes by letter and affection,
And not by old gradation, where each second
Stood heir to th' first.
Othello 1.1.35

[*old gradation:* seniority]

746 HAMLET: Madness would not err,
Nor sense to ecstasy was ne'er so thrall'd
But it reserv'd some quantity of choice.
Hamlet 3.4.73

[*thrall'd:* enslaved; *quantity of choice:* some power to choose]

747 ARRAGON: I will not choose what many men desire,
Because I will not jump with common spirits,
And rank me with the barbarous multitudes.
Merchant of Venice 2.9.31

748 TROILUS: My election
Is led on in the conduct of my will,
My will enkindled by mine eyes and ears,
Two traded pilots 'twixt the dangerous shores
Of will and judgment.
Troilus and Cressida 2.2.61

[*election:* choice; *traded pilots:* intermediaries constantly going back and forth]

749 LEAR: Thou'dst shun a bear,
But if thy flight lay toward the roaring sea,
Thou'dst meet the bear i' th' mouth.
King Lear 3.4.9

Choler

750 TYBALT: Patience perforce with willful choler meeting
Makes my flesh tremble in their different greeting.
Romeo and Juliet 1.5.89

[*different greeting:* i.e. the confrontation of these opposed states of mind]

Christ

751 KING [announcing a crusade to Jerusalem]: We are impressed and engag'd to fight . . .
To chase these pagans in those holy fields,

Over whose acres walk'd those blessed
feet
Which fourteen hundred years ago
were nail'd
For our advantage on the bitter cross.
1 Henry IV 1.1.21

752 KING: Let never day nor night
unhallowed pass,
But still remember what the Lord hath
done.
2 Henry VI 2.1.83

753 WARWICK: My soul intends to live
With that dread King that took our
state upon him,
To free us from his Father's wrathful
curse.
2 Henry VI 3.2.153

754 GAUNT: The world's ransom,
blessed Mary's Son.
Richard II 2.1.56

Christian

755 CRANMER [to Gardiner]: Love and
meekness, lord,
Become a churchman better than
ambition;
Win straying souls with modesty again,
Cast none away.
Henry VIII 5.2.97

756 RIVERS: A virtuous and Christian-
like conclusion—
To pray for them that have done scathe
to us.
Richard III 1.3.315

Circumstance

757 PETRUCHIO: Leave frivolous
circumstances.
Taming of the Shrew 5.1.26

758 The summer's flow'r is to the summer sweet,
Though to itself it only live and die,
But if that flow'r with base infection
meet,

The basest weed outbraves his dignity.
Sonnet 94
[*outbraves:* surpasses in splendor]

Citizen

759 K. HENRY: Every subject's duty is
the King's, but every subject's soul is
his own.
Henry V 4.1.176

City

760 SICINIUS: What is the city but the
people?
Coriolanus 3.1.198

Civility

761 STEPHANO: While thou liv'st,
keep a good tongue in thy head.
The Tempest 3.2.112

762 ORLANDO: The thorny point
Of bare distress hath ta'en from me the
show
Of smooth civility.
As You Like It 2.7.94

Clergy

763 CARDINAL: Clergy's bags
Are lank and lean.
2 Henry VI 1.3.128

764 CRANMER [to Gardiner]: Love and
meekness, lord,
Become a churchman better than
ambition;
Win straying souls with modesty again,
Cast none away.
Henry VIII 5.2.97

765 OPHELIA: Do not, as some
ungracious pastors do,
Show me the steep and thorny way to
heaven,
Whiles, like a puff'd and reckless
libertine,

Himself the primrose path of dalliance
treads,
And reaks not his own rede.
                    Hamlet 1.3.47
[*reaks:* recks, heeds; *rede:* advice]

Cleverness

766 ANTONIO: The devil can cite
Scripture for his purpose.
                    Merchant of Venice 1.3.98

Cloak

767 FALSTAFF: An old cloak makes a
new jerkin.
                    Merry Wives of Windsor 1.3.17

Clothing

768 SLY: Ne'er ask me what raiment
I'll wear, for I have no more doublets
than backs, no more stockings than
legs, nor no more shoes than feet; nay,
sometimes more feet than shoes.
                    Taming of the Shrew, Induction 2.9

769 PETRUCHIO: Our purses shall be
proud, our garments poor,
For 'tis the mind that makes the body
rich;
And as the sun breaks through the
darkest clouds,
So honor peereth in the meanest habit.
What, is the jay more precious than
the lark,
Because his feathers are more beauti-
ful?
Or is the adder better than the eel,
Because his painted skin contents the
eye?
O no, good Kate; neither art thou the
worse
For this poor furniture and mean array.
                    Taming of the Shrew 4.3.171

770 LAFEW [about Parolles]: The soul
of this man is his clothes.
                    All's Well That Ends Well 2.5.43

Clouds

771 KING: To the brightest beams
Distracted clouds give way.
                    All's Well That Ends Well 5.3.34

772 THIRD CITIZEN: When clouds are
seen, wise men put on their cloaks.
                    Richard III 2.3.32

773 CLARENCE: Every cloud engenders
not a storm.
                    3 Henry VI 5.3.13

774 ANTONY: Sometime we see a
cloud that's dragonish,
A vapor sometime like a bear or lion,
A tower'd citadel, a pendant rock,
A forked mountain, or blue promon-
tory
With trees upon't, that nod unto the
world,
And mock our eyes with air.
                    Antony and Cleopatra 4.14.2

Clown

775 TOUCHSTONE: It is meat and
drink to me to see a clown.
                    As You Like It 5.1.10

776 HAMLET: The clown shall make
those laugh whose lungs are tickled a'
th' sere.
                    Hamlet 2.2.323
[*tickled a' th' sere:* those quick to laugh, as
a gun with a hair-trigger is quick to fire]

Cock

777 HORATIO: The cock, that is the
trumpet to the morn,
Doth with his lofty and shrill-sounding
throat
Awake the god of day.
                    Hamlet 1.1.150

Cockle

778 BEROWNE: Sow'd cockle reap'd no
corn.
Love's Labor's Lost 4.3.380

Coldness

779 How like a winter hath my
absence been
From thee, the pleasure of the fleeting
year!
What freezings have I felt, what dark
days seen!
Sonnet 97

Colt

780 The colt that's back'd and
burthen'd being young,
Loseth his pride, and never waxeth
strong.
Venus and Adonis 419
[*burthen'd:* burdened]

Comeback

781 LUCIUS: Some falls are means the
happier to arise.
Cymbeline 4.2.403

Comet

782 CALPHURNIA: When beggars die
there are no comets seen;
The heavens themselves blaze forth the
death of princes.
Julius Caesar 2.2.30

783 BEDFORD [mourning the death of
Henry V]: Comets, importing
change of times and states,
Brandish your crystal tresses in the
sky,
And with them scourge the bad
revolting stars.
1 Henry VI 1.1.2

Comfort

784 Love comforteth like sunshine
after rain.
Venus and Adonis 799

785 YORK: Comfort's in heaven, and
we are on the earth,
Where nothing lives but crosses, cares,
and grief.
Richard II 2.2.78

786 ADAM: He that doth the ravens
feed,
Yea, providently caters for the sparrow,
Be comfort to my age!
As You Like It 2.3.43

787 FIRST LORD: How mightily
sometimes we make us comforts of our
losses!
All's Well That Ends Well 4.3.65

788 CAPUCHIUS: The King's request
that I would visit you,
Who grieves much for your weakness,
and by me
Sends you his princely commendations,
And heartily entreats you take good
comfort.
KATHERINE: O my good lord, that
comfort comes too late,
'Tis like a pardon after execution.
That gentle physic given in time had
cur'd me;
But now I am past all comforts here
but prayers.
Henry VIII 4.2.116

789 MARIANA [about Duke Vincentio]:
Here comes a man of comfort, whose
advice
Hath often still'd my brawling discon-
tent.
Measure for Measure 4.1.8

790 Two loves I have, of comfort and
despair,
That like two spirits do suggest me
still:
My better angel is a man (right fair),
My worser spirit a woman (color'd ill).
To win me soon to hell, my female evil

CAMROSE LUTHERAN COLLEGE
LIBRARY

Tempteth my better angel from my side;
And would corrupt my saint to be a devil,
Wooing his purity with her fair pride.
And whether that my angel be turn'd fiend,
Suspect I may (yet not directly tell):
For being both to me, both to each friend,
I guess one angel in another's hell:
The truth I shall not know, but live in doubt,
Till my bad angel fire my good one out.

The Passionate Pilgrim ii.1

Command

791 ARRAGON: O that estates, degrees, and offices
Were not deriv'd corruptly, and that clear honor
Were purchas'd by the merit of the wearer!
How many then should cover that stand bare?
How many be commanded that command?

Merchant of Venice 2.9.41

Commiseration

792 Grief best is pleas'd with grief's society.

Rape of Lucrece 1111

793 JULIET: Sour woe delights in fellowship.

Romeo and Juliet 3.2.116

794 K. RICHARD: Two together weeping make one woe.

Richard II 5.1.86

795 EDGAR [soliloquy]: The mind much sufferance doth o'erskip,
When grief hath mates, and bearing fellowship.

King Lear 3.6.106

796 EDGAR [soliloquy]: When we our betters see bearing our woes,
We scarcely think our miseries our foes.

King Lear 3.6.102

797 Fellowship in woe doth woe assuage.

Rape of Lucrece 790

Commonality

798 K. HENRY [soliloquy]: What infinite heart's ease
Must kings neglect, that private men enjoy!
And what have kings, that privates have not too,
Save ceremony, save general ceremony?

Henry V 4.1.236

799 GRIFFITH [about Wolsey]: His overthrow heap'd happiness upon him;
For then, and not till then, he felt himself,
And found the blessedness of being little.

Henry VIII 4.2.64

800 FALSTAFF: It was always yet the trick of our English nation, if they have a good thing, to make it too common.

2 Henry IV 1.2.214

801 Sweets grown common lose their dear delight.

Sonnet 102

Company

802 Sad souls are slain in merry company.

Rape of Lucrece 1110

803 FALSTAFF [soliloquy]: It is certain that either wise bearing or ignorant carriage is caught, as men take diseases, one of another; therefore let men take the heed of their company.

2 Henry IV 5.1.75

804 CASSIUS [soliloquy]: Therefore it is meet
That noble minds keep ever with their likes;
For who so firm that cannot be seduc'd?
Julius Caesar 1.2.310

805 FALSTAFF: Company, villainous company, hath been the spoil of me.
1 Henry IV 3.3.11

806 PORTIA: In companions
That do converse and waste the time together,
Whose souls do bear an egall yoke of love,
There must be needs a like proportion
Of lineaments, of manners, and of spirit.
Merchant of Venice 3.4.11
[*egall:* equal; *like proportion:* agreement]

807 BEROWNE [to King Ferdinand, Longaville and Dumaine]: I am betrayed by keeping company
With men like you, men of inconstancy.
Love's Labor's Lost 4.3.177

808 BEROWNE: One drunkard loves another of the name.
Love's Labor's Lost 4.3.48

Comparisons

809 CORIN: Those that are good manners at the court are as ridiculous in the country as the behavior of the country is most mockable at the court.
As You Like It 3.2.45

810 K. LEAR: Where the greater malady is fix'd,
The lesser is scarce felt.
King Lear 3.4.8

811 PETRUCHIO: What, is the jay more precious than the lark,
Because his feathers are more beautiful?
Or is the adder better than the eel,
Because his painted skin contents the eye?
Taming of the Shrew 4.3.175

812 NERISSA: When the moon shone, we did not see the candle.
PORTIA: So doth the greater glory dim the less:
A substitute shines brightly as a king
Until a king be by, and then his state
Empties itself, as doth an inland brook
Into the main of waters.
Merchant of Venice 5.1.92

813 BELARIUS: Nature hath meal and bran, contempt and grace.
Cymbeline 4.2.27

814 DOGBERRY: Comparisons are odorous.
Much Ado About Nothing 3.5.17

Compassion

815 ALCIBIADES: Pity is the virtue of the law,
And none but tyrants use it cruelly.
Timon of Athens 3.5.8

816 PROSPERO: As you from crimes would pardon'd be,
Let your indulgence set me free.
The Tempest, Epilogue 19

817 LEAR: Poor naked wretches, wheresoe'er you are,
That bide the pelting of this pitiless storm,
How shall your houseless heads and unfed sides,
Your loop'd and window'd raggedness, defend you
From seasons such as these? O, I have ta'en
Too little care of this! Take physic, pomp,
Expose thyself to feel what wretches feel,
That thou mayst shake the superflux to them,
And show the heavens more just.
King Lear 3.4.28

Competency

818 NERISSA: Superfluity comes sooner by white hairs, but competency lives longer.
Merchant of Venice 1.2.9

Competition

819 OTHELLO: They laugh that win.
Othello 4.1.122

820 K. EDWARD: The harder match'd, the greater victory.
3 Henry VI 5.1.70

821 TRANIO: Do as adversaries do in law,
Strive mightily, but eat and drink as friends.
Taming of the Shrew 1.2.276

Complacency

822 The path is smooth that leadeth on to danger.
Venus and Adonis 788

823 QUEEN: Now 'tis the spring, and weeds are shallow-rooted;
Suffer them now, and they'll o'ergrow the garden,
And choke the herbs for want of husbandry.
2 Henry VI 3.1.31

Compliment

824 OLIVIA: 'Twas never merry world Since lowly feigning was call'd compliment.
Twelfth Night 3.1.98
[*lowly feigning:* pretending humility]

825 JAQUES: That they call compliment is like th' encounter of two dog-apes.
As You Like It 2.5.26
[*dog-apes:* baboons]

Compulsion

826 FALSTAFF [to Poins]: Give you a reason on compulsion! if reasons were as plentiful as blackberries, I would give no man a reason upon compulsion.
1 Henry IV 2.4.238

Concealment

827 IAGO [soliloquy]: Knavery's plain face is never seen till us'd.
Othello 2.1.312

828 MARCUS: Sorrow concealed, like an oven stopp'd,
Doth burn the heart to cinders.
Titus Andronicus 2.4.36

829 K. EDWARD: 'Tis wisdom to conceal our meaning.
3 Henry VI 4.7.60

Conceit

830 GHOST: Conceit in weakest bodies strongest works.
Hamlet 3.4.114

831 IAGO [soliloquy]: Dangerous conceits are in their natures poisons.
Othello 3.3.326

832 BOYET: Conceits have wings Fleeter than arrows, bullets, wind, thought, swifter things.
Love's Labor's Lost 5.2.260

833 JULIET: Conceit, more rich in matter than in words,
Brags of his substance, not of ornament;
They are but beggars that can count their worth.
Romeo and Juliet 2.6.30

834 STEWARD: We wound our modesty, and make foul the clearness of our deservings, when of ourselves we publish them.
All's Well That Ends Well 1.3.5

835 AJAX: I do hate a proud man, as I hate the engend'ring of toads.
Troilus and Cressida 2.3.158

836 EDGAR: I know not how conceit may rob
The treasury of life, when life itself
Yields to the theft.
King Lear 4.6.42

[*yields:* consents]

837 QUEEN: Conceit is still deriv'd
From some forefather grief.
Richard II 2.2.34

838 KING [to Berowne, about Armado]: Our court you know is haunted
With a refined traveller of Spain ...
One who the music of his own vain tongue
Doth ravish like enchanting harmony.
Love's Labor's Lost 1.1.162

839 ADRIANA: I am press'd down with conceit—
Conceit, my comfort and my injury.
Comedy of Errors 4.2.65

Conception

840 HAMLET: Conception is a blessing.
Hamlet 2.2.184

Conciliation

841 TOUCHSTONE: Your If is the only peacemaker; much virtue in If.
As You Like It 5.4.102

Condemnation

842 ANGELO: Condemn the fault, and not the actor of it?
Why, every fault's condemn'd ere it be done.
Measure for Measure 2.2.37

843 HERMIONE [to Leontes]: If I shall be condemn'd
Upon surmises (all proofs sleeping else
But what your jealousies awake), I tell you
'Tis rigor and not law.
Winter's Tale 3.2.111

Condolences

844 LEONATO: Men
Can counsel and speak comfort to that grief
Which they themselves not feel.
Much Ado About Nothing 5.1.20

845 LEONATO: 'Tis all men's office to speak patience
To those that wring under the load of sorrow,
But no man's virtue nor sufficiency
To be so moral when he shall endure
The like himself.
Much Ado About Nothing 5.1.27

846 LEONATO: Charm ache with air, and agony with words.
Much Ado About Nothing 5.1.26

847 LEONATO: Patch grief with proverbs.
Much Ado About Nothing 5.1.17

848 PAULINA: What's gone and what's past help
Should be past grief.
Winter's Tale 3.2.222

Conduct

849 EDGAR: Obey thy parents, keep thy word's justice, swear not, commit not with man's sworn spouse, set not thy sweet heart on proud array ...
Keep thy foot out of brothels, thy hand out of plackets, thy pen from lenders' books.
King Lear 3.4.80

[*plackets:* openings in petticoats]

850 FOOL: Have more than thou showest,
Speak less than thou knowest,

Lend less than thou owest,
Ride more than thou goest,
Learn more than thou trowest,
Set less than thou throwest.
King Lear 1.4.118

Confession

851 KING: Teach us, sweet madam,
for our rude transgression
Some fair excuse.
PRINCESS: The fairest is confession.
Love's Labor's Lost 5.2.431

852 HAMLET [to Queen]: Confess
yourself to heaven,
Repent what's past, avoid what is to
come.
Hamlet 3.4.149

Confidence

853 Q. ELIZABETH: Trust not him that
hath once broken faith.
3 Henry VI 4.4.30

854 CALPHURNIA [to Caesar]: Alas, my
lord,
Your wisdom is consum'd in
confidence.
Julius Caesar 2.2.49

855 HECAT: Security
Is mortals' chiefest enemy.
Macbeth 3.5.32

Confusion

856 MALCOLM: Nay, had I pow'r, I
should
Pour the sweet milk of concord into
hell,
Uproar the universal peace, confound
All unity on earth.
Macbeth 4.3.97

Conquest

857 LEONATO: A victory is twice itself
when the achiever brings home full
numbers.
Much Ado About Nothing 1.1.8

858 PANDULPH [to King Philip]: Bet-
ter conquest never canst thou make
Than arm thy constant and thy nobler
parts
Against these giddy loose suggestions.
King John 3.1.290

859 ENOBARBUS: He that can endure
To follow with allegiance a fall'n lord
Does conquer him that did his master
conquer,
And earns a place i' th' story.
Antony and Cleopatra 3.13.43

860 KING [to his three ascetic lords]:
Brave conquerors—for so you are,
That war against your own affections
And the huge army of the world's
desires.
Love's Labor's Lost 1.1.8

Conscience

861 HAMLET [soliloquy]: Conscience
does make cowards of us all.
Hamlet 3.1.82

862 KING: Conscience, conscience!
O, 'tis a tender place.
Henry VIII 2.2.142

863 K. RICHARD [soliloquy]: My conscience hath a thousand several
tongues,
And every tongue brings in a several
tale,
And every tale condemns me for a
villain.
Richard III 5.3.193

864 K. RICHARD: Conscience is but a
word that cowards use,
Devis'd at first to keep the strong in
awe.
Richard III 5.3.309

865 SECOND MURDERER: I'll not meddle with it, it makes a man a coward. A man cannot steal, but it accuseth him; a man cannot swear, but it checks him; a man cannot lie with his neighbor's wife, but it detects him. 'Tis a blushing, shame-fac'd spirit that mutinies in a man's bosom. It fills a man full of obstacles. It made me once restore a purse of gold that (by chance) I found. It beggars any man that keeps it. It is turn'd out of towns and cities for a dangerous thing, and every man that means to live well endeavors to trust to himself and live without it.
Richard III 1.4.134

866 They whose guilt within their
bosoms lie
Imagine every eye beholds their blame.
Rape of Lucrece 1342

867 IAGO: Guiltiness will speak,
Though tongues were out of use.
Othello 5.1.109

868 OXFORD: Every man's conscience
is a thousand men.
Richard III 5.2.17
[Most other editions have: Every man's conscience is a thousand swords.]

869 HAMLET [soliloquy]: Murther,
though it hath no tongue, will speak
With most miraculous organ.
Hamlet 2.2.593
[*murther:* murder]

870 FIRST MURDERER: How dost thou feel thyself now?
SECOND MURDERER: 'Faith, some dregs of conscience are yet within me.
FIRST MURDERER: Remember our reward when the deed's done.
SECOND MURDERER: 'Zounds, he dies! I had forgot the reward.
FIRST MURDERER: Where's thy conscience now?
SECOND MURDERER: O, in the Duke of Gloucester's purse.
FIRST MURDERER: When he opens his purse to give us our reward, thy conscience flies out.

SECOND MURDERER: 'Tis no matter, let it go. There's few or none will entertain it.
FIRST MURDERER: What if it come to thee again?
SECOND MURDERER: I'll not meddle with it, it makes a man a coward.
Richard III 1.4.120

871 GLOUCESTER: Suspicion always haunts the guilty mind;
The thief doth fear each bush an officer.
3 Henry VI 5.6.11

872 KING: Thrice is he arm'd that
hath his quarrel just;
And he but naked, though lock'd up
in steel,
Whose conscience with injustice is corrupted.
2 Henry VI 3.2.233

873 MACBETH: Better be with the
dead,
Whom we, to gain our peace, have
sent to peace,
Than on the torture of the mind to lie
In restless ecstasy.
Macbeth 3.2.19

874 DOCTOR [on Lady Macbeth's sleepwalking confession]: Foul whisp'rings are abroad. Unnatural deeds
Do breed unnatural troubles; infected minds
To their deaf pillows will discharge their secrets.
Macbeth 5.1.71

875 IAGO: Who has that breast so pure
But some uncleanly apprehensions
Keep leets and law-days and in sessions sit
With meditations lawful?
Othello 3.3.138
[*keep leets:* hold courts]

876 CLARENCE: O, I have pass'd a
miserable night,
So full of fearful dreams, of ugly
sights,

That, as I am a Christian faithful man,
I would not spend another such a
  night
Though 'twere to buy a world of happy
days.
                          Richard III 1.4.2

877 K. RICHARD [soliloquy]: Give me
another horse! Bind up my wounds!
Have mercy, Jesu! Soft, I did but
dream.
O coward conscience, how dost thou
  afflict me!
The lights burn blue. It is now dead
  midnight.
Cold fearful drops stand on my trembling flesh.
What do I fear? Myself?
                        Richard III 5.3.178

878 SALISBURY [about King John]:
The color of the king doth come and
  go
Between his purpose and his conscience,
Like heralds 'twixt two dreadful battles
set:
His passion is so ripe, it needs must
  break.
                         King John 4.2.76

879 FIRST STRANGER: Policy sits above
conscience.
                    Timon of Athens 3.2.87

880 POLONIUS: 'Tis too much
prov'd—that with devotion's visage
And pious action we do sugar o'er
The devil himself.
                          Hamlet 3.1.46

881 Q. MARGARET [to Gloucester]:
The worm of conscience still begnaw
thy soul!
                      Richard III 1.3.221

882 KING: What a sign it is of evil
life,
Where death's approach is seen so
  terrible!
                       2 Henry VI 3.3.5

883 K. HENRY: Every subject's duty is
the King's, but every subject's soul is
his own.
                          Henry V 4.1.176

884 OTHELLO [on unfaithful wives]:
They do let God see the pranks
They dare not show their husbands;
  their best conscience
Is not to leave't undone, but keep't
unknown.
                          Othello 3.3.202

885 MACBETH: To know my deed,
'twere best not know myself.
                          Macbeth 2.2.70

886 K. HENRY: Our bad neighbor
  makes us early stirrers,
Which is both healthful and good
  husbandry.
Besides, they are our outward consciences
And preachers to us all, admonishing
That we should dress us fairly for our
  end.
                            Henry V 4.1.8

887 WOLSEY: I feel within me
A peace above all earthly dignities,
A still and quiet conscience.
                        Henry VIII 3.2.378

888 DIONYZA [to Leonine]: Let not
conscience,
Which is but cold in flaming, thy lone
bosom
Inflame too nicely.
                          Pericles 4.1.4

889 Love is too young to know what
  conscience is,
Yet who knows not conscience is born
  of love?
                            Sonnet 151

890 ISABELLA [to Angelo]: Go to your
bosom,
Knock there, and ask your heart what
  it doth know
That's like my brother's fault. If it
confess
A natural guiltiness such as is his,

Let it not sound a thought upon your
tongue
Against my brother's life.
Measure for Measure 2.2.136

891 MACBETH [after Duncan's
assassination]: What hands are here?
Hah! they pluck out mine eyes.
Will all great Neptune's ocean wash
this blood
Clean from my hand? No; this my
hand will rather
The multitudinous seas incarnadine,
Making the green one red.
Macbeth 2.2.56

892 LADY MACBETH: Out, damn'd
spot! out, I say!
Macbeth 5.1.35

893 LADY MACBETH [haunted by Duncan's murder]: Here's the smell of the
blood still. All the perfumes of Arabia
will not sweeten this little hand. O,
O, O!
Macbeth 5.1.50

894 GHOST [to Hamlet, on the
Queen]: Leave her to heaven,
And to those thorns that in her bosom
lodge
To prick and sting her.
Hamlet 1.5.86

Consideration

895 TIMON [soliloquy]: Ingrateful
man, with liquorish draughts
And morsels unctuous, greases his pure
mind,
That from it all consideration slips.
Timon of Athens 4.3.194

Consolation

896 ENOBARBUS: Grief is crown'd with
consolation.
Antony and Cleopatra 1.2.167

Conspiracy

897 BRUTUS [soliloquy]: Between the
acting of a dreadful thing
And the first motion, all the interim is
Like a phantasma or a hideous dream.
The Genius and the mortal instru-
ments
Are then in council; and the state of
man,
Like to a little kingdom, suffers then
The nature of an insurrection.
Julius Caesar 2.1.63
[*The Genius:* the soul; *mortal instruments:*
man's reason and his will; *in council:* at
war]

898 BRUTUS [soliloquy]: O Conspiracy,
Sham'st thou to show thy dang'rous
brow by night,
When evils are most free? O then, by
day
Where wilt thou find a cavern dark
enough
To mask thy monstrous visage? Seek
none, Conspiracy!
Hide it in smiles and affability;
For if thou path, thy native semblance
on,
Not Erebus itself were dim enough
To hide thee from prevention.
Julius Caesar 2.1.77
[*path:* i.e. go about; *native semblance:*
natural expression; *Erebus:* underworld, a
region of darkness]

Constancy

899 PROTEUS: O heaven, were man
But constant, he were perfect; that one
error
Fills him with faults; makes him run
through all th' sins:
Inconstancy falls off ere it begins.
Two Gentlemen of Verona 5.4.110

900 BALTHAZAR [singing]: Sigh no
more, ladies, sigh no more,
Men were deceivers ever,
One foot in sea, and one on shore,
To one thing constant never.
Much Ado About Nothing 2.3.62

901 HOTSPUR: Constant you are,
But yet a woman, and for secrecy,
No lady closer, for I well believe
Thou wilt not utter what thou dost not know,
And so far will I trust thee, gentle Kate.
1 Henry IV 2.3.108

902 DUKE: Novelty is only in request, and, as it is, as dangerous to be ag'd in any kind of course, as it is virtuous to be constant in any undertaking.
Measure for Measure 3.2.224

903 CRESSIDA: Who shall be true to us,
When we are so unsecret to ourselves?
Troilus and Cressida 3.2.124

904 FIRST BANDITTI: There is no time so miserable but a man may be true.
Timon of Athens 4.3.456

905 DUKE: If ever thou shalt love,
In the sweet pangs of it remember me;
For such as I am, all true lovers are,
Unstaid and skittish in all motions else,
Save in the constant image of the creature
That is belov'd.
Twelfth Night 2.4.15

906 PORTIA: O constancy, be strong upon my side,
Set a huge mountain 'tween my heart and tongue!
Julius Caesar 2.4.6

907 CAESAR: I am constant as the northern star,
Of whose true-fix'd and resting quality
There is no fellow in the firmament.
Julius Caesar 3.1.60

Constituency

908 ARCHBISHOP: An habitation giddy and unsure

Hath he that buildeth on the vulgar heart.
2 Henry IV 1.3.89

[*vulgar:* plebeian]

Contamination

909 DOGBERRY: They that touch pitch will be defil'd.
Much Ado About Nothing 3.3.57

Contemplation

910 BUCKINGHAM: So sweet is zealous contemplation.
Richard III 3.7.94

Contempt

911 ANTONY: What our contempts doth often hurl from us,
We wish it ours again.
Antony and Cleopatra 1.2.123

912 BOYET: Contempt will kill the speaker's heart,
And quite divorce his memory from his part.
Love's Labor's Lost 5.2.149

913 Hot desire converts to cold disdain.
Rape of Lucrece 691

914 SLENDER [to Shallow about the maid Anne Page]: If there be no great love in the beginning, yet heaven may decrease it upon better acquaintance, when we are married and have more occasion to know one another. I hope, upon familiarity will grow more content.
Merry Wives of Windsor 1.1.246

Contention

915 BENEDICK: In a false quarrel there is no true valor.
Much Ado About Nothing 5.1.120

916 Time's glory is to calm contending kings.
Rape of Lucrece 939

917 NORTHUMBERLAND [on the rebellion]: Contention, like a horse Full of high feeding, madly hath broke loose,
And bears down all before him.
2 Henry IV 1.1.9

Contentment

918 PORTIA: He is well paid that is well satisfied.
Merchant of Venice 4.1.415

919 OLD LADY: Our content Is our best having.
Henry VIII 2.3.23

920 LADY MACBETH [soliloquy]: Nought's had, all's spent,
Where our desire is got without content.
Macbeth 3.2.5

921 IAGO: Poor and content is rich, and rich enough,
But riches fineless is as poor as winter To him that ever fears he shall be poor.
Othello 3.3.172
[*fineless:* boundless]

922 CORIN: He that wants money, means, and content is without three good friends.
As You Like It 3.2.24

923 ANTIPHOLUS EPHESUS [soliloquy]: He that commends me to mine own content,
Commends me to the thing I cannot get.
Comedy of Errors 1.2.33

924 PETRUCHIO: 'Tis the mind that makes the body rich.
Taming of the Shrew 4.3.173

925 CORIN: I earn that I eat, get that I wear, owe no man hate, envy no man's happiness, glad of other men's good, content with my harm.
As You Like It 3.2.73

926 K. HENRY: My crown is in my heart, not on my head;
Not deck'd with diamonds and Indian stones,
Nor to be seen. My crown is call'd content,
A crown it is that seldom kings enjoy.
3 Henry VI 3.1.62

927 WORCESTER: For mine own part, I could be well content
To entertain the lag end of my life With quiet hours.
1 Henry IV 5.1.23

928 ORLANDO: Live a little, comfort a little, cheer thyself a little.
As You Like It 2.6.5

929 APEMANTUS: Best state, content-less,
Hath a distracted and most wretched being,
Worse than the worst, content.
Timon of Athens 4.3.246

930 MALCOLM: My more-having would be as a sauce
To make me hunger more.
Macbeth 4.3.81

931 ANNE: I swear, 'tis better to be lowly born,
And range with humble livers in content,
Than to be perk'd up in a glist'ring grief
And wear a golden sorrow.
Henry VIII 2.3.19

932 PRINCESS: Zeal strives to content, and the contents
Die in the zeal of that which it presents.
Love's Labor's Lost 5.2.517

933 K. RICHARD [soliloquy]: No thought is contented.
Richard II 5.5.11

934 GLENDOWER [interpreting to Mortimer what his wife, who speaks only Welsh, is saying to him]: She bids you on the wanton rushes lay you down,
And rest your gentle head upon her lap,
And she will sing the song that pleaseth you,
And on your eyelids crown the god of sleep,
Charming your blood with pleasing heaviness,
Making such difference 'twixt wake and sleep
As is the difference betwixt day and night
The hour before the heavenly-harness'd team
Begins his golden progress in the east.
1 Henry IV 3.1.211

935 DUKE SENIOR [to Amiens and others, in exile]: Hath not old custom made this life more sweet
Than that of painted pomp? Are not these woods
More free from peril than the envious court?
Here feel we not the penalty of Adam,
The season's difference, as the icy fang
And churlish chiding of the winter's wind,
Which when it bites and blows upon my body,
Even till I shrink with cold, I smile and say,
"This is no flattery: these are counsellors
That feelingly persuade me what I am."
Sweet are the uses of adversity,
Which like the toad, ugly and venomous,
Wears yet a precious jewel in his head;
And this our life, exempt from public haunt,
Finds tongues in trees, books in the running brooks,
Sermons in stones, and good in every thing.
As You Like It 2.1.2
[The idea that the toad was venomous

comes from Pliny's *Natural History*. The *jewel,* or toadstone, was believed to have curative powers.]

936 FOOL [singing]: He that has a little tine wit—
With heigh-ho, the wind and the rain—
Must make content with his fortunes fit,
Though the rain it raineth every day.
King Lear 3.2.74
[*tine:* tiny]

Conversation

937 ADRIANA: If voluble and sharp discourse be marr'd,
Unkindness blunts it more than marble hard.
Comedy of Errors 2.1.92

938 NATHANIEL [to Holofernes]: Your reasons . . . have been sharp and sententious: pleasant without scurrility, witty without affection, audacious without impudency, learned without opinion, and strange without heresy.
Love's Labor's Lost 5.1.2

Cooperation

939 CASCA [to Cassius]: I will set this foot of mine as far
As who goes farthest.
Julius Caesar 1.3.118

Coquetry

940 CRESSIDA: Women are angels, wooing:
Things won are done, joy's soul lies in the doing.
That she belov'd knows nought that knows not this:
Men prize the thing ungain'd more than it is.
Troilus and Cressida 1.2.286

941 VALENTINE [to Duke, on court-
ship]: If she do frown, 'tis not in
hate of you,
But rather to beget more love in you.
If she do chide, 'tis not to have you
  gone,
For why, the fools are mad, if left
  alone.
Take no repulse, what ever she doth
  say;
For "get you gone," she doth not mean
  "away!"
Two Gentlemen of Verona 3.1.96

942 CHARMIAN [on Antony]: In each
thing give him way, cross him in
nothing.
CLEOPATRA: Thou teachest like a fool:
the way to lose him.
Antony and Cleopatra 1.3.8

943 BERTRAM [about Helena]: She
knew her distance, and did angle for
me,
Maddening my eagerness with her
  restraint,
As all impediments in fancy's course
Are motives of more fancy, and in
  fine,
Her inf'nite cunning, with her modern
  grace,
Subdu'd me to her rate. She got the
  ring.
All's Well That Ends Well 5.3.212

944 FALSTAFF [on Ford's wife]: I spy
entertainment in her. She discourses,
she carves, she gives the leer of invitation.
Merry Wives of Windsor 1.3.44

Corn

945 BEROWNE: Sow'd cockle reap'd no
corn.
Love's Labor's Lost 4.3.379

Correction

946 MRS. PAGE: Better a little chiding
than a great deal of heart-break.
Merry Wives of Windsor 5.3.9

947 DUKE [on Pompey's imprison-
ment]: Correction and instruction
must both work
Ere this rude beast will profit.
Measure for Measure 3.2.32

Corruption

948 KING [soliloquy]: In the corrupted
currents of this world
Offense's gilded hand may shove by
justice,
And oft 'tis seen the wicked prize itself
Buys out the law, but 'tis not so above.
Hamlet 3.3.57
[*gilded hand:* offer of a bribe; *wicked prize:*
i.e. ill-gotten gains]

949 MARCELLUS: Something is rotten
in the state of Denmark.
Hamlet 1.4.90

950 ARRAGON: O that estates, degrees,
and offices
Were not deriv'd corruptly, and that
clear honor
Were purchas'd by the merit of the
wearer!
Merchant of Venice 2.9.41

951 WOLSEY: Corruption wins not
more than honesty.
Henry VIII 3.2.444

952 HAMLET: Rank corruption, mining
all within,
Infects unseen.
Hamlet 3.4.148

953 Loathsome canker lives in sweetest
bud.
Sonnet 35

954 Lilies that fester smell far worse
than weeds.
Sonnet 94

955 K. JOHN [to King Philip, about
the Pope]: You and all the kings of
Christendom
Are led so grossly by this meddling
priest,

Dreading the curse that money may
buy out,
And by the merit of vild gold, dross,
dust,
Purchase corrupted pardon of a man
Who in that sale sells pardon from
himself.

King John 3.1.162

[*vild:* vile]

Cosmetics

956 HAMLET [to Ophelia, about
women]: God hath given you one face,
and you make yourselves another.

Hamlet 3.1.143

Counsel

957 APEMANTUS [soliloquy]: O that
men's ears should be
To counsel deaf, but not to flattery!

Timon of Athens 1.2.249

958 They that thrive well take counsel
of their friends.

Venus and Adonis 640

959 K. HENRY: Friendly counsel cuts
off many foes.

1 Henry VI 3.1.184

960 Counsel may stop a while what
will not stay.

A Lover's Complaint 159

961 MONTAGUE: He, his own affections' counsellor,
Is to himself I will not say how true.

Romeo and Juliet 1.1.147

962 YORK: All too late comes counsel
to be heard,
Where will doth mutiny with wit's
regard.

Richard II 2.1.27

963 NURSE: Two may keep counsel,
putting one away.

Romeo and Juliet 2.4.197

964 AARON: Two may keep counsel
when the third's away.

Titus Andronicus 4.2.144

965 When as thine eye hath chose the
dame,
And stall'd the deer that thou shouldst
strike,
Let reason rule things worthy blame,
As well as fancy, partial might.
Take counsel of some wiser head,
Neither too young not yet unwed.

The Passionate Pilgrim xviii.1

966 FOOL [to Kent]: When a wise man
gives thee better counsel, give me mine
again.

King Lear 2.4.74

Counsellor

967 POMPEY: Good counsellors lack no
clients.

Measure for Measure 1.2.106

968 PERICLES [to Helicanus]: Fit
counsellor and servant for a
prince . . .
By thy wisdom makes a prince thy
servant.

Pericles 1.2.63

Countenance

969 NORTHUMBERLAND [to Morton,
with news of war]: Thou tremblest,
and the whiteness in thy cheek
Is apter than thy tongue to tell thy
errand.

2 Henry IV 1.1.69

970 LADY MACBETH [to Macbeth]:
Your face, my thane, is as a book,
where men
May read strange matters.

Macbeth 1.5.62

Counterfeit

971 HAMLET: [soliloquy]: The dev'l hath power
T' assume a pleasing shape.
Hamlet 2.2.599

972 FALSTAFF: He is but the counterfeit of a man who hath not the life of a man.
1 Henry IV 5.4.116

973 POSTHUMUS [soliloquy]: We are all bastards,
And that most venerable man which I
Did call my father, was I know not where
When I was stamp'd. Some coiner with his tools
Made me a counterfeit.
Cymbeline 2.5.5

Country

974 COMINIUS: I do love
My country's good with a respect more tender,
More holy and profound, than mine own life.
Coriolanus 3.3.111

975 CORIN: Those that are good manners at the court are as ridiculous in the country as the behavior of the country is most mockable at the court.
As You Like It 3.2.45

Courage

976 GLOUCESTER: A heart unspotted is not easily daunted.
2 Henry VI 3.1.100

977 NESTOR: The thing of courage,
As rous'd with rage, with rage doth sympathize,
And with an accent tun'd in self-same key
Retires to chiding fortune.
Troilus and Cressida 1.3.51

978 GLOUCESTER: Fearless minds climb soonest unto crowns.
3 Henry VI 4.7.62

979 EDMUND: To be tender-minded
Does not become a sword.
King Lear 5.3.31

980 ENOBARBUS [soliloquy]: When valor preys on reason,
It eats the sword it fights with.
Antony and Cleopatra 3.13.198

981 K. LEWIS [to Margaret]: Yield not thy neck
To fortune's yoke, but let thy dauntless mind
Still ride in triumph over all mischance.
3 Henry VI 3.3.16

982 Q. MARGARET: Wise men ne'er sit and wail their loss,
But cheerly seek how to redress their harms.
3 Henry VI 5.4.1

983 AUSTRIA: Courage mounteth with occasion.
King John 2.1.82

984 HOTSPUR: O, the blood more stirs
To rouse a lion than start a hare!
1 Henry IV 1.3.197

985 CLIFFORD: Patience is for poltroons.
3 Henry VI 1.1.62
[*poltroons:* arrant cowards]

986 CLOTEN: Winning will put any man into courage.
Cymbeline 2.3.7

987 FIRST SENATOR: He's truly valiant that can wisely suffer
The worst that man can breathe, and make his wrongs
His outsides, to wear them like his raiment, carelessly,
And ne'er prefer his injuries to his heart,
To bring it into danger.
Timon of Athens 3.5.31

988 MACBETH: I dare do all that may become a man;
Who dares do more is none.
Macbeth 1.7.45

989 CAESAR [to Antony]: I rather tell thee what is to be fear'd
Than what I fear; for always I am Caesar.
Julius Caesar 1.2.211

990 K. HENRY [to Gloucester at Agincourt]: 'Tis true that we are in great danger,
The greater therefore should our courage be.
Henry V 4.1.1

991 LADY MACBETH [to Macbeth, on Duncan's murder plot]: Screw your courage to the sticking place,
And we'll not fail.
Macbeth 1.7.60

992 VOLUMNIA: Had I a dozen sons, each in my love alike . . . I had rather had eleven die nobly for their country than one voluptuously surfeit out of action.
Coriolanus 1.3.24

993 CLIFFORD: The smallest worm will turn, being trodden on,
And doves will peck in safeguard of their brood.
3 Henry VI 2.2.17

994 HOTSPUR: Doomsday is near, die all, die merrily.
1 Henry IV 4.1.134

Court

995 CORIN: Those that are good manners at the court are as ridiculous in the country as the behavior of the country is most mockable at the court.
As You Like It 3.2.45

996 FIRST GENTLEMAN: Not a courtier, Although they wear their faces to the bent

Of the King's looks, hath a heart that is not
Glad at the thing they scowl at.
Cymbeline 1.1.12

997 BELARIUS: Did you but know . . . The art o' th' court . . .
Whose top to climb
Is certain falling, or so slipp'ry that The fear's as bad as falling.
Cymbeline 3.3.46

998 POSTHUMUS: Poor wretches that depend
On greatness' favor dream as I have done,
Wake, and find nothing.
Cymbeline 5.4.127

999 SHALLOW: A friend i' th' court is better than a penny in purse.
2 Henry IV 5.1.30

Courtesy

1000 IMOGEN: O
Dissembling courtesy! How fine this tyrant
Can tickle where she wounds!
Cymbeline 1.1.84

1001 PERICLES: How courtesy would seem to cover sin.
Pericles 1.1.121

1002 ULYSSES: The elephant hath joints, but none for courtesy; his legs are legs for necessity, not for flexure.
Troilus and Cressida 2.3.105

1003 ORLANDO: The thorny point Of bare distress hath ta'en from me the show
Of smooth civility.
As You Like It 2.7.94

1004 STEPHANO: While thou liv'st, keep a good tongue in thy head.
The Tempest 3.2.112

1005 LEPIDUS: Touch you the sourest
points with sweetest terms.
Antony and Cleopatra 2.2.24

Courtier

1006 FIRST GENTLEMAN: Not a
courtier,
Although they wear their faces to the
bent
Of the King's looks, hath a heart that
is not
Glad at the thing they scowl at.
Cymbeline 1.1.12

Courtship

1007 SALERIO [quoting Antonio's advice to Bassanio]: "Be merry, and
employ your chiefest thoughts
To courtship, and such fair ostents of
love
As shall conveniently become you
there."
Merchant of Venice 2.8.43

1008 VALENTINE [to Duke, on court-
ship]: Win her with gifts, if she
respect not words:
Dumb jewels often in their silent kind
More than quick words do move a
woman's mind.
Two Gentlemen of Verona 3.1.89

1009 PETRUCHIO [soliloquy, on Kate]:
Say that she rail, why then I'll tell her
plain
She sings as sweetly as a nightingale;
Say that she frown, I'll say she looks as
clear
As morning roses newly wash'd with
dew;
Say she be mute, and will not speak a
word,
Then I'll commend her volubility,
And say she uttereth piercing
eloquence.
Taming of the Shrew 2.1.170

1010 JULIET [to Romeo]: My bounty is
as boundless as the sea,
My love as deep; the more I give to
thee,
The more I have, for both are infinite.
Romeo and Juliet 2.2.33

1011 JULIET: O Romeo, Romeo,
wherefore art thou Romeo?
Romeo and Juliet 2.2.33

1012 PROSPERO [to Ferdinand]: Look
thou be true; do not give dalliance
Too much the rein. The strongest oaths
are straw
To th' fire i' th' blood. Be more ab-
stenious,
Or else good night your vow!
The Tempest 4.1.51

1013 OPHELIA [giving out flowers after
Polonius' death]: There's rosemary,
that's for remembrance; pray you, love,
remember. And there is pansies, that's
for thoughts.
Hamlet 4.5.176
[*rosemary:* used as a symbol of remembrance at both weddings and funerals; *pansies:* emblems of love and courtship]

Covetousness

1014 FALSTAFF: A man can no more
separate age and covetousness than 'a
can part young limbs and lechery.
2 Henry IV 1.2.228
[*'a:* he]

1015 MACDUFF [to Malcolm]: Avarice
Sticks deeper, grows with more per-
nicious root
Than summer-seeming lust; and it
hath been
The sword of our slain kings.
Macbeth 4.3.84

1016 Those that much covet are with
gain so fond,
That what they have not, that which
they possess,
They scatter and unloose it from their
bond,
And so by hoping more they have but
less.
Rape of Lucrece 134

1017 The aged man that coffers up his gold
Is plagu'd with cramps and gouts and painful fits,
And scarce hath eyes his treasure to behold,
But like still-pining Tantalus he sits,
And useless barns the harvest of his wits;
Having no other pleasure of his gain
But torment that it cannot cure his pain.
Rape of Lucrece 855

1018 K. HENRY: I am not covetous for gold,
Nor care I who doth feed upon my cost;
It yearns me not if men my garments wear;
Such outward things dwell not in my desires.
But if it be a sin to covet honor,
I am the most offending soul alive.
Henry V 4.3.24

1019 PEMBROKE: When workmen strive to do better than well,
They do confound their skill in covetousness.
King John 4.2.28

1020 CLOWN [to Duke]: I would not have you think that my desire of having is the sin of covetousness; but as you say, sir, let your bounty take a nap, I will awake it anon.
Twelfth Night 5.1.46

Cow

1021 BEATRICE: It is said, "God sends a curst cow short horns"—but to a cow too curst he sends none.
Much Ado About Nothing 2.1.22

Cowardice

1022 HAMLET [soliloquy]: Conscience does make cowards of us all.
Hamlet 3.1.82

1023 IMOGEN: Plenty and peace breed cowards; hardness ever
Of hardiness is mother.
Cymbeline 3.6.21

1024 CAESAR: Cowards die many times before their deaths,
The valiant never taste of death but once.
Of all the wonders that I yet have heard,
It seems to me most strange that men should fear,
Seeing that death, a necessary end,
Will come when it will come.
Julius Caesar 2.2.32

1025 BRUTUS: I do find it cowardly and vile,
For fear of what might fall, so to prevent
The time of life.
Julius Caesar 5.1.103

1026 BASSANIO: How many cowards, whose hearts are all as false
As stairs of sand, wear yet upon their chins
The beards of Hercules and frowning Mars,
Who inward search'd, have livers white as milk.
Merchant of Venice 3.2.83

1027 BRUTUS: Hollow men, like horses hot at hand,
Make gallant show and promise of their mettle;
But when they should endure the bloody spur,
They fall their crests, and like deceitful jades
Sink in the trial.
Julius Caesar 4.2.23
[*jades:* inferior horses, nags]

1028 LADY MACBETH [to Macbeth]: Wouldst thou have that
Which thou esteem'st the ornament of life,
And live a coward in thine own esteem,

Letting "I dare not" wait upon "I
would,"
Like the poor cat i' th' adage?
Macbeth 1.7.41

[*th' adage:* i.e. "The cat would eat fish, and
would not wet her feet."]

1029 ROSENCRANTZ: Many wearing
rapiers are afraid of goose-quills.
Hamlet 2.2.343

[*goose-quills:* pens of satirical writers]

1030 BELARIUS: Cowards father
cowards and base things sire base.
Cymbeline 4.2.26

1031 FALSTAFF: A coward is worse
than a cup of sack with lime in it.
1 Henry IV 2.4.126

1032 DOLPHIN: Coward dogs
Most spend their mouths when what
they seem to threaten
Runs far before them.
Henry V 2.4.69

1033 CLIFFORD: Cowards fight when
they can fly no further,
So doves do peck the falcon's piercing
talons,
So desperate thieves, all hopeless of
their lives,
Breathe out invectives 'gainst the
officers.
3 Henry VI 1.4.40

1034 DUCHESS: That which in mean
men we entitle patience
Is pale cold cowardice in noble breasts.
Richard II 1.2.33

1035 CLIFFORD: Patience is for
poltroons.
3 Henry VI 1.1.62

[*poltroons:* arrant cowards]

1036 FALSTAFF: Instinct is a great matter; I was now a coward on instinct.
1 Henry IV 2.4.272

1037 PRINCE: I may speak it to my
shame,
I have a truant been to chivalry.
1 Henry IV 5.1.93

1038 BOY: I would give all my fame
for a pot of ale and safety.
Henry V 3.2.13

1039 CONSTANCE [to Austria]: Thou
slave, thou wretch, thou coward!
Thou little valiant, great in villainy!
Thou ever strong upon the stronger
side!
Thou Fortune's champion that dost
never fight
But when her humorous ladyship is by
To teach thee safety!
King John 3.1.115

1040 POSTHUMUS [reporting a Roman
rout of the British]: To-day how
many would have given their honors
To have sav'd their carcasses! took heel
to do't,
And yet died too!
Cymbeline 5.3.66

1041 WARWICK [to Clarence]: I hold
it cowardice
To rest mistrustful where a noble heart
Hath pawn'd an open hand in sign of
love.
3 Henry VI 4.2.7

1042 PAROLLES [soliloquy]: Who
knows himself a braggart,
Let him fear this; for it will come to
pass
That every braggart shall be found an
ass.
All's Well That Ends Well 4.3.334

1043 BASTARD [to Austria]: You are
the hare of whom the proverb goes,
Whose valor plucks dead lions by the
beard.
King John 2.1.137

1044 HAMLET [soliloquy]: The native
hue of resolution
Is sicklied o'er with the pale cast of
thought.
Hamlet 3.1.83

Cozener

1045 LEAR: The usurer hangs the
Cozener.
King Lear 4.6.163
[That is, the judge—guilty himself of
usury—condemns the petty cheat.]

Craftiness

1046 HUME: A crafty knave does need
no broker.
2 Henry VI 1.2.100

Crime

1047 FIRST LORD: Our crimes would
despair, if they were not cherish'd by
our virtues.
All's Well That Ends Well 4.3.73

1048 K. JOHN: How oft the sight of
means to do ill deeds
Makes deeds ill done!
King John 4.2.219

1049 HAMLET [soliloquy]: Foul deeds
will rise,
Though all the earth o'erwhelm them,
to men's eyes.
Hamlet 1.2.256

1050 K. HENRY: If little faults, pro-
ceeding on distemper,
Shall not be wink'd at, how shall we
stretch our eye
When capital crimes, chew'd, swal-
low'd, and digested,
Appear before us?
Henry V 2.2.54

1051 BRUTUS [soliloquy]: Between the
acting of a dreadful thing
And the first motion, all the interim is
Like a phantasma or a hideous dream.
The Genius and the mortal instru-
ments
Are then in council; and the state of a
man,
Like to a little kingdom, suffers then
The nature of an insurrection.
Julius Caesar 2.1.63

[*The Genius:* the soul; *mortal instruments:*
man's reason and his will; *in council:* at
war]

1052 BATES: We know enough, if we
know we are the King's subjects. If his
cause be wrong, our obedience to the
King wipes the crime of it out of us.
Henry V 4.1.131

Crisis

1053 ROSSE: Things at the worst will
cease, or else climb upward
To what they were before.
Macbeth 4.2.24

Criticism

1054 ISABELLA: 'Tis a physic
That's bitter to sweet end.
Measure for Measure 4.6.7

1055 ORLANDO: I will chide no
breather in the world but myself,
against whom I know most faults.
As You Like It 3.2.280

1056 MRS. PAGE: Better a little
chiding than a great deal of heart-
break.
Merry Wives of Windsor 5.3.9

1057 BENEDICK [soliloquy]: Happy are
they that hear their detractions, and
can put them to mending.
Much Ado About Nothing 2.3.229

1058 POLONIUS: Take each man's censure, but reserve thy judgment.
Hamlet 1.3.69

1059 IAGO: I am nothing if not
critical.
Othello 2.1.119

1060 OLIVIA: To be generous,
guiltless, and of free disposition, is to

take those things for bird-bolts that
you deem cannon-bullets.
Twelfth Night 1.5.91
[*bird-bolts:* blunt-headed arrows for
shooting birds]

1061 WOLSEY: We must not stint
Our necessary actions in the fear
To cope malicious censurers, which
ever,
As rav'nous fishes, do a vessel follow.
Henry VIII 1.2.76

1062 BENEDICK: These paper bullets
of the brain.
Much Ado About Nothing 2.3.240

Crow

1063 PORTIA: The crow doth sing as
sweetly as the lark
When neither is attended.
Merchant of Venice 5.1.102

1064 The crow may bathe his coal-
black wings in mire,
And unperceiv'd fly with the filth
away,
But if the like the snow-white swan
desire,
The stain upon his silver down will
stay.
Rape of Lucrece 1009

Crown

1065 K. HENRY: My crown is in my
heart, not on my head;
Not deck'd with diamonds and Indian
stones,
Nor to be seen. My crown is call'd
content,
A crown it is that seldom kings enjoy.
3 Henry VI 3.1.62

1066 KING [soliloquy]: Uneasy lies the
head that wears a crown.
2 Henry IV 3.1.31

1067 GAUNT [to King Richard]: A
thousand flatterers sit within thy
crown,

Whose compass is no bigger than thy
head.
Richard II 2.1.100

1068 K. RICHARD: Within the hollow
crown
That rounds the mortal temples of a
king
Keeps Death his court, and there the
antic sits,
Scoffing his state and grinning at his
pomp.
Richard II 3.2.160

1069 ANNE: I swear, 'tis better to be
lowly born,
And range with humble livers in
content,
Than to be perk'd up in a glist'ring
grief
And wear a golden sorrow.
Henry VIII 2.3.19

1070 PRINCE [soliloquy]: O polish'd
perturbation! golden care!
That keep'th the ports of slumber open
wide
To many a watchful night, sleep with
it now!
Yet not so sound, and half so deeply
sweet,
As he whose brow with homely biggen
bound
Snores out the watch of night.
2 Henry IV 4.5.23
[*biggen:* nightcap]

1071 GLOUCESTER: Fearless minds
climb soonest unto crowns.
3 Henry VI 4.7.62

1072 K. RICHARD: Our holy lives must
win a new world's crown.
Richard II 5.1.24

Cruelty

1073 CROMWELL: 'Tis a cruelty
To load a falling man.
Henry VIII 5.2.111

1074 HAMLET [to Queen]: I must be cruel only to be kind.
                        Hamlet 3.4.178

1075 LADY MACBETH [soliloquy, on Duncan's assassination]: Come, you spirits
That tend on mortal thoughts, unsex me here,
And fill me from the crown to the toe topful
Of direst cruelty! Make thick my blood,
Stop up th' access and passage to remorse,
That no compunctious visitings of nature
Shake my fell purpose.
                        Macbeth 1.5.40
[*mortal:* deadly, murderous]

Cuckold

1076 LEONTES: Should all despair
That have revolted wives, the tenth of mankind
Would hang themselves.
                        Winter's Tale 1.2.198
[*revolted:* unfaithful]

1077 CLOWN: There is no true cuckold but calamity.
                        Twelfth Night 1.5.51

1078 FIRST SERVANT: Let me have war, say I: it exceeds peace as far as day does night; it's spritely, waking, audible, and full of vent. Peace is a very apoplexy, lethargy; mulled, deaf, sleepy, insensible; a getter of more bastard children than war's the destroyer of men.
SECOND SERVANT: 'Tis so . . . but peace is a great maker of cuckolds.
                        Coriolanus 4.5.228
[*cuckold:* a nickname for husbands of unfaithful wives]

Cunning

1079 GLOUCESTER [aside]: When the fox hath once got in his nose,

He'll soon find means to make the body follow.
                        3 Henry VI 4.7.25

1080 CORDELIA: Time shall unfold what plighted cunning hides.
                        King Lear 1.1.280
[*plighted:* pleated, i.e. what is concealed under the folds]

1081 HUME: A crafty knave does need no broker.
                        2 Henry VI 1.2.100

1082 POLONIUS: Thus do we of wisdom and of reach,
With windlasses and with assays of bias,
By indirections find directions out.
                        Hamlet 2.1.61

1083 OTHELLO [on Desdemona's supposed adultery]: Sir, she can turn, and turn; and yet go on
And turn again.
                        Othello 4.1.253

1084 HAMLET: O, 'tis most sweet
When in one line two crafts directly meet.
                        Hamlet 3.4.209
[*two crafts:* two acts of guile]

Cupid

1085 ROSALIND: That blind rascally boy . . . abuses every one's eyes because his own are out.
                        As You Like It 4.1.213

1086 BEROWNE [soliloquy]: This wimpled, whining, purblind, wayward boy,
This senior-junior, giant-dwarf, Dan Cupid,
Regent of love-rhymes, lord of folded arms,
Th' anointed sovereign of sighs and groans,
Liege of all loiterers and malcontents,
Dread prince of plackets, king of codpieces,

Sole imperator and great general
Of trotting paritors (O my little
heart!),
And I to be a corporal of his field,
And wear his colors like a tumbler's
hoop!
Love's Labor's Lost 3.1.179
[*plackets*: slits in petticoats; *codpieces*:
baggy appendages at the front of breeches]

1087 HELENA [soliloquy]: Love looks
not with the eyes but with the
mind;
And therefore is wing'd Cupid painted
blind.
Midsummer Night's Dream 1.1.234

1088 HERO: Loving goes by haps:
Some Cupid kills with arrows, some
with traps.
Much Ado About Nothing 3.1.105

1089 PUCK: Cupid is a knavish lad.
Midsummer Night's Dream 3.2.440

1090 BEROWNE: Rhymes are guards on
wanton Cupid's hose.
Love's Labor's Lost 4.3.56

Cure

1091 MACBETH: The labor we delight
in physics pain.
Macbeth 2.3.50

1092 BENVOLIO: One fire burns out
another's burning,
One pain is less'ned by another's
anguish.
Romeo and Juliet 1.2.45

1093 PUCELLE: Care is no cure, but
rather corrosive,
For things that are not to be remedied.
1 Henry VI 3.3.3

1094 Past cure am I, now reason is
past care.
Sonnet 147

1095 ROSALINE: Past care is still past
cure.
Love's Labor's Lost 5.2.28

Cursing

1096 CALIBAN [to Miranda]: You
taught me language, and my profit
on't
Is, I know how to curse. The red-
plague rid you
For learning me your language!
The Tempest 1.2.363

Custom

1097 VALENTINE [soliloquy]: How use
doth breed a habit in a man!
This shadowy desert, unfrequented
woods,
I better brook than flourishing peopled
towns.
Two Gentlemen of Verona 5.4.1

1098 HAMLET: Use almost can change
the stamp of nature.
Hamlet 3.4.168

1099 IMOGEN: The breach of custom
Is breach of all.
Cymbeline 4.2.10

1100 SANDS: New customs,
Though they be never so ridiculous
(Nay, let 'em be unmanly), yet are
follow'd.
Henry VIII 1.3.3

1101 K. HENRY: Nice customs cur'sy
to great kings.
Henry V 5.2.268

1102 HAMLET: That monster custom,
who all sense doth eat,
Of habits devil, is angel yet in this,
That to the use of actions fair and
good
He likewise gives a frock or livery
That aptly is put on.
Hamlet 3.4.161

1103 DUKE SENIOR [on his exile]:
Hath not custom made this life more
sweet
Than that of painted pomp?
As You Like It 2.1.2

1104 ANGELO: We must not make a scarecrow of the law,
Setting it up to fear the birds of prey,
And let it keep one shape, till custom make it
Their perch and not their terror.
Measure for Measure 2.1.1

1105 GLOWER: But custom what they did begin
Was with long use account'd no sin.
Pericles, Prologue 1.29

1106 My nature is subdu'd
To what it works in, like the dyer's hands.
Sonnet 111

1107 OTHELLO: The tyrant custom, most grave senators,
Hath made the flinty and steel couch of war
My thrice-driven bed of down.
Othello 1.3.229

1108 CORIOLANUS: What custom wills, in all things should we do't.
Coriolanus 2.3.118

Daffodils

1109 PERDITA: Daffodils,
That come before the swallow dares . . . take
The winds of March with beauty.
Winter's Tale 4.4.118

Dagger

1110 DONALBAIN: There's daggers in men's smiles.
Macbeth 2.3.140

Dalliance

1111 PROSPERO [to Ferdinand]: Do not give dalliance
Too much the rein. The strongest oaths are straw
To th' fire i' th' blood.
The Tempest 4.1.51

1112 OPHELIA: Do not, as some ungracious pastors do,
Show me the steep and thorny way to heaven,
Whiles, like a puff'd and reckless libertine,
Himself the primrose path of dalliance treads,
And reaks not his own rede.
Hamlet 1.3.47
[*reaks:* recks, heeds; *rede:* advice]

Dancing

1113 ROMEO: Let wantons light of heart
Tickle the senseless rushes with their heels.
Romeo and Juliet 1.4.35
[*rushes:* floor coverings]

1114 CAPULET [to a cousin]: You and I are past our dancing days.
Romeo and Juliet 1.5.33

Danger

1115 Danger deviseth shifts, wit waits on fear.
Venus and Adonis 690

1116 PATROCLUS: Omission to do what is necessary
Seals a commission to a blank of danger,
And danger like an ague subtly taints
Even then when they sit idly in the sun.
Troilus and Cressida 3.3.230

1117 Q. MARGARET: They that stand high have many blasts to shake them,
And if they fall, they dash themselves to pieces.
Richard III 1.3.258

1118 GLOUCESTER: Many men that stumble at the threshold
Are well foretold that danger lurks within.
3 Henry VI 4.7.11

1119 REIGNIER: Defer no time, delays have dangerous ends.
1 Henry VI 3.2.33

1120 HOTSPUR: Out of this nettle, danger, we pluck this flower, safety.
1 Henry IV 2.3.9

1121 The path is smooth that leadeth on to danger.
Venus and Adonis 788

1122 PANDULPH: He that stands upon a slipp'ry place
Makes nice of no vild hold to stay him up.
King John 3.4.137
[*vild:* vile]

1123 K. HENRY [to Gloucester at Agincourt]: 'Tis true that we are in great danger,
The greater therefore should our courage be.
Henry V 4.1.1

1124 CAESAR: Let me have men about me that are fat,
Sleek-headed men and such as sleep a-nights.
Yond Cassius hath a lean and hungry look,
He thinks too much; such men are dangerous.
Julius Caesar 1.2.192

1125 HOTSPUR: O, the blood more stirs
To rouse a lion than to start a hare!
1 Henry IV 1.3.197

Daring

1126 MACBETH: I dare do all that may become a man;
Who dares do more is none.
Macbeth 1.7.46

Darkness

1127 CLOWN: There is no darkness but ignorance.
Twelfth Night 4.2.42

1128 PROSPERO: The morning steals upon the night,
Melting the darkness.
The Tempest 5.1.65

1129 IRAS [to Cleopatra]: The bright day is done,
And we are for the dark.
Antony and Cleopatra 5.2.193

Dating

1130 EGLAMOUR: Lovers break not hours,
Unless it be to come before their time.
Two Gentlemen of Verona 5.1.4

Dawn

1131 CINNA: Yon grey lines
That fret the clouds are messengers of day.
Julius Caesar 2.1.103

1132 PUCK: Night's swift dragons cut the clouds full fast,
And yonder shines Aurora's harbinger,
At whose approach, ghosts, wand'ring here and there,
Troop home to churchyards.
Midsummer Night's Dream 3.2.379

1133 FRIAR LAWRENCE: The grey-ey'd morn smiles on the frowning night,
Check'ring the eastern clouds with streaks of light.
Romeo and Juliet 2.3.1

1134 BEDFORD: The day begins to break, and night is fled,
Whose pitchy mantle over-veil'd the earth.
1 Henry VI 2.2.1

1135 OBERON: The eastern gate, all
fiery red,
Opening on Neptune with fair blessed
beams,
Turns into yellow gold his salt green
streams.
                 Midsummer Night's Dream 3.2.392

1136 SONG: Hark, hark, the lark at
heaven's gate sings,
And Phoebus gins arise,
His steeds to water at those springs
On chalic'd flow'rs that lies;
And winking Mary-buds begin to ope
their golden eyes;
With every thing that pretty is, my
lady sweet, arise:
Arise, arise!
                              Cymbeline 2.3.20
[*gins:* begins to]

Day

1137 ROMEO: Night's candles are burnt
out, and jocund day
Stands tiptoe on the misty mountain
tops.
                       Romeo and Juliet 3.5.9

1138 SCROOP: Men judge by the complexion of the sky
The state and inclination of the day.
                          Richard II 3.2.194

1139 CONSTANCE: What hath this day
deserv'd? what hath it done,
That it in golden letters should be set
Among the high tides in the calendar?
                            King John 3.1.84

1140 TROILUS [to Cressida]: The busy
day,
Wak'd by the lark, hath rous'd the
ribald crows,
And dreaming night will hide our joys
no longer.
                    Troilus and Cressida 4.2.8

1141 CAPTAIN: The gaudy, blabbing,
and remorseful day
Is crept into the bosom of the sea.
                           2 Henry VI 4.1.1

1142 IRAS [to Cleopatra]: The bright
day is done,
And we are for the dark.
                    Antony and Cleopatra 5.2.193

1143 BEDFORD: The day begins to
break, and night is fled,
Whose pitchy mantle over-veil'd the
earth.
                            1 Henry VI 2.2.1

1144 BRUTUS: That we shall die, we
know, 'tis but the time,
And drawing days out, that men stand
upon.
                       Julius Caesar 3.1.99

Daydream

1145 KING HENRY [soliloquy, near the
battlefield]: O God! Methinks it
were a happy life
To be no better than a homely swain,
To sit upon a hill, as I do now,
To carve out dials quaintly, point by
point,
Thereby to see the minutes how they
run:
How many makes the hour full com-
plete,
How many hours brings about the day,
How many days will finish up the year,
How many years a mortal man may
live.
When this is known, then to divide
the times:
So many hours must I tend my flock,
So many hours must I take my rest,
So many hours must I contemplate,
So many hours must I sport myself,
So many days my ewes have been with
young,
So many weeks ere the poor fools will
ean,
So many years ere I shall shear the
fleece:
So minutes, hours, days, months, and
years,
Pass'd over to the end they were
created,
Would bring white hairs unto a quiet
grave.

Ah! what a life were this! how sweet!
how lovely!

3 Henry VI 2.5.21

[*homely swain:* simple shepherd; *ean:* yean,
bring forth]

Dearness

1146 HECTOR: Life every man holds
dear, but the dear man
Holds honor far more precious-dear
than life.

Troilus and Cressida 5.3.27

1147 PROTEUS [soliloquy]: I to myself
am dearer than a friend.

Two Gentlemen of Verona 2.6.23

1148 KING: Praising what is lost
Makes the remembrance dear.

All's Well That Ends Well 5.3.19

1149 Pain pays the income of each
precious thing.

Rape of Lucrece 334

1150 O, that is gone for which I
sought to live,
And therefore now I need not fear to
die.

Rape of Lucrece 1051

Death

1151 THIRD QUEEN: This world's a city
full of straying streets,
And death's the market-place, where
each one meets.

Two Noble Kinsmen 1.5.16

1152 BASTARD [at Angiers]: O now
doth Death line his dead chaps with
steel,
The swords of soldiers are his teeth, his
fangs,
And now he feasts, mousing the flesh
of men,
In undetermin'd differences of kings.

King John 2.1.352

1153 MACBETH: To-morrow, and to-
morrow, and to-morrow,

Creeps in this petty pace from day to
day,
To the last syllable of recorded time;
And all our yesterdays have lighted
fools
The way to dusty death. Out, out,
brief candle!
Life's but a walking shadow, a poor
player,
That struts and frets his hour upon the
stage,
And then is heard no more. It is a tale
Told by an idiot, full of sound and
fury,
Signifying nothing.

Macbeth 5.5.19

1154 STEPHANO: He that dies pays all
debts.

The Tempest 3.2.131

1155 FEEBLE: He that dies this year is
quit for the next.

2 Henry IV 3.2.238

1156 ROMEO [soliloquy]: How oft
when men are at the point of death
Have they been merry, which their
keepers call
A lightning before death!

Romeo and Juliet 5.3.88

1157 YORK: Though death be poor, it
ends a mortal woe.

Richard II 2.1.152

1158 CYMBELINE: By med'cine life
may be prolong'd, yet death
Will seize the doctor too.

Cymbeline 5.5.29

1159 K. HENRY: Ah, what a sign it is
of evil life,
Where death's approach is seen so
terrible!

2 Henry VI 3.3.5

1160 BRUTUS: That we shall die, we
know, 'tis but the time,
And drawing days out, that men stand
upon.

Julius Caesar 3.1.99

1161 HAMLET: Imperious Caesar, dead
and turn'd to clay,
Might stop a hole to keep the wind
away.
O that that earth which kept the world
in awe
Should patch a wall t' expel the
winter's flaw!
Hamlet 5.1.213

1162 CLAUDIO: Ay, but to die, and go
we know not where;
To lie in cold obstruction, and to rot;
This sensible warm motion to become
A kneaded clod; and the delighted
spirit
To bathe in fiery floods, or to reside
In thrilling region of thick-ribbed ice;
To be imprison'd in the viewless winds
And blown with restless violence round
about
The pendent world; or to be worse
than worst
Of those that lawless and incertain
thought
Imagine howling—'tis too horrible!
The weariest and most loathed worldly
life
That age, ache, penury, and imprison-
ment
Can lay on nature is a paradise
To what we fear of death.
Measure for Measure 3.1.117

1163 HAMLET [soliloquy]: To be, or
not to be, that is the question:
Whether 'tis nobler in the mind to
suffer
The slings and arrows of outrageous
fortune,
Or to take arms against a sea of
troubles,
And by opposing, end them. To die,
to sleep—
No more, and by a sleep to say we end
The heart-ache and the thousand
natural shocks
That flesh is heir to; 'tis a consummation
Devoutly to be wish'd. To die, to
sleep—
To sleep, perchance to dream—ay,
there's the rub,

For in that sleep of death what dreams
may come,
When we have shuffled off this mortal
coil,
Must give us pause; there's the respect
That makes calamity of so long life.
Hamlet 3.1.55

1164 PRINCE: The end of life cancels
all bands.
1 Henry IV 3.2.157
[*bands:* bonds, debts]

1165 Death once dead, there's no
more dying then.
Sonnet 146

1166 CASCA: Why, he that cuts off
twenty years of life
Cuts off so many years of fearing
death.
BRUTUS: Grant that, and then is death
a benefit.
Julius Caesar 3.1.101

1167 POSTHUMUS: Th' sure physician,
death . . . is the key
T' unbar these locks.
Cymbeline 5.4.7

1168 MORTIMER [dying]: Now, the arbitrator of despairs,
Just Death, kind umpire of men's
miseries,
With sweet enlargement doth dismiss
me hence.
1 Henry VI 2.5.28

1169 TALBOT [dying with his son on
the battlefield]: Thou antic Death,
which laugh'st us here to scorn,
Anon, from thy insulting tyranny,
Coupled in bonds of perpetuity,
Two Talbots, winged through the
lither sky,
In thy spite shall scape mortality.
1 Henry VI 4.7.18
[*lither:* yielding]

1170 CLAUDIO: If I must die,
I will encounter darkness as a bride,
And hug it in mine arms.
Measure for Measure 3.1.83

1171 MENENIUS: He that hath a will to die by himself fears it not from another.

Coriolanus 5.2.104

1172 CONSTANCE: Death, death. O amiable lovely death!
Thou odoriferous stench! sound rottenness!
Arise forth from the couch of lasting night,
Thou hate and terror to prosperity,
And I will kiss thy detestable bones,
And put my eyeballs in thy vaulty brows,
And ring these fingers with thy household worms,
And stop this gap of breath with fulsome dust,
And be a carrion monster like thyself.
Come, grin on me, and I will think thou smil'st,
And buss thee as a wife. Misery's love,
O, come to me!

King John 3.4.25

1173 MALCOLM [reporting to Duncan, on Cawdor's execution]: Nothing in his life
Became him like the leaving it. He died
As one that had been studied in his death,
To throw away the dearest thing he ow'd,
As 'twere a careless trifle.

Macbeth 1.4.7

1174 WARWICK [soliloquy]: Why, what is pomp, rule, reign, but earth and dust?
And live we how we can, yet die we must.

3 Henry VI 5.2.27

1175 EDGAR: O, our lives' sweetness!
That we the pain of death would hourly die
Rather than die at once!

King Lear 5.3.185

1176 CAESAR: Cowards die many times before their deaths,

The valiant never taste of death but once.
Of all the wonders that I yet have heard,
It seems to me most strange that men should fear,
Seeing that death, a necessary end,
Will come when it will come.

Julius Caesar 2.2.32

1177 DUKE: That life is better life, past fearing death,
Than that which lives to fear.

Measure for Measure 5.1.397

1178 DUKE [to the condemned Claudio]: Thou art death's fool,
For him thou labor'st by thy flight to shun,
And yet run'st toward him still.

Measure for Measure 3.1.11

1179 HAMLET: This fell sergeant, Death,
Is strict in his arrest.

Hamlet 5.2.336

1180 CARLISLE: Fear, and be slain—no worse can come to fight,
And fight and die is death destroying death,
Where fearing dying pays death servile breath.

Richard II 3.2.183

1181 WILLIAMS: There are few die well that die in a battle.

Henry V 4.1.141

1182 HAMLET [soliloquy]: The dread of something after death,
The undiscover'd country, from whose bourn
No traveller returns, puzzles the will,
And makes us rather bear those ills we have,
Than fly to others that we know not of.

Hamlet 3.1.77

[*bourn:* boundary, i.e. region]

1183 K. RICHARD: Nothing can we call our own but death,

And that small model of the barren
earth
Which serves as paste and cover to our
bones.
                              Richard II 3.2.152

1184 ANTONY [on viewing the slain
Roman general]: O mighty Caesar!
dost thou lie so low?
Are all thy conquests, glories, tri-
umphs, spoils,
Shrunk to this little measure?
                              Julius Caesar 3.1.148

1185 PRINCE [about Percy]: Ill-weav'd
ambition, how much art thou
shrunk!
When that this body did contain a
spirit,
A kingdom for it was too small a
bound,
But now two paces of the vilest earth
Is room enough.
                              1 Henry IV 5.4.88

1186 CAPTAIN: We go to gain a little
patch of ground
That hath in it no profit but the name.
                              Hamlet 4.4.18

1187 PERICLES: Death remembered
should be like a mirror,
Who tells us life's but breath, to trust
it error.
                              Pericles 1.1.45

1188 EDGAR: Men must endure
Their going hence even as their coming
hither.
                              King Lear 5.2.9

1189 CALPHURNIA: When beggars die
there are no comets seen;
The heavens themselves blaze forth the
death of princes.
                              Julius Caesar 2.2.30

1190 GAUNT: More are men's ends
mark'd than their lives before.
                              Richard II 2.1.11

1191 MARTIUS: Brave death outweighs
bad life.
                              Coriolanus 1.6.71

1192 RODERIGO: It is silliness to live,
when to live is torment; and then have
we a prescription to die, when death is
our physician.
                              Othello 1.3.308

1193 Do I delight to die, or life
desire?
But now I liv'd, and life was death's
annoy,
But now I died, and death was lively
joy.
                              Venus and Adonis 496
[*death's annoy:* i.e. painful as death]

1194 OTHELLO: 'Tis happiness to die.
                              Othello 5.2.290

1195 Q. MARGARET [to Oxford and
Somerset]: So part we sadly in this
troublous world,
To meet with joy in sweet Jerusalem.
                              3 Henry VI 5.5.7

1196 To live or die which of the twain
were better,
When life is sham'd and death
reproach's debtor.
                              Rape of Lucrece 1154

1197 DUKE [to the condemned
Claudio]: Be absolute for death:
either death or life
Shall thereby be the sweeter.
                              Measure for Measure 3.1.5

1198 DUKE [to the condemned
Claudio]: What's yet in this
That bears the name of life? Yet in
this life
Lie hid moe thousand deaths; yet
death we fear
That makes these odds all even.
                              Measure for Measure 3.1.38
[*moe:* more]

1199 CATESBY: 'Tis a vile thing to
die . . .
When men are unprepar'd and look
not for it.
                              Richard III 3.2.62

1200 K. RICHARD: Cry woe, destruction, ruin, and decay:

The worst is death, and death will have his day.
Richard II 3.2.103

1201 TALBOT: Kings and mightiest potentates must die,
For that's the end of human misery.
1 Henry VI 3.2.136

1202 ROMEO [soliloquy]: Eyes, look your last!
Arms, take your last embrace! and, lips, O you
The doors of breath, seal with a righteous kiss
A dateless bargain to engrossing death!
Romeo and Juliet 5.3.112

1203 OTHELLO: Here is my journey's end, here is my butt
And very sea-mark of my utmost sail.
Othello 5.2.267

1204 NORTHUMBERLAND: Even through the hollow eyes of death
I spy life peering.
Richard II 2.1.270

1205 CLARENCE: My dream was lengthen'd after life.
O then began the tempest to my soul!
I pass'd (methought) the melancholy flood,
With that sour ferryman which poets write of,
Unto the kingdom of perpetual night.
Richard III 1.4.43

1206 YORK [after being stabbed]:
Open thy gate of mercy, gracious God!
My soul flies through these wounds to seek out thee.
3 Henry VI 1.4.177

1207 QUEEN [to Hamlet]: Do not for ever with thy vailed lids
Seek for thy noble father in the dust.
Thou know'st 'tis common, all that lives must die,
Passing through nature to eternity.
Hamlet 1.2.70

1208 K. RICHARD [falling, wounded by Exton]: Mount, mount, my soul!
thy seat is up on high,
Whilst my gross flesh sinks downward, here to die.
Richard II 5.5.111

1209 GAUNT: They say the tongues of dying men
Enforce attention like deep harmony.
Where words are scarce, they are seldom spent in vain,
For they breathe truth that breathe their words in pain.
Richard II 2.1.5

1210 FEEBLE: A man can die but once, we owe God a death.
2 Henry IV 3.2.234

1211 GRIFFITH [on Wolsey's death]:
He gave his honors to the world again,
His blessed part to heaven, and slept in peace.
Henry VIII 4.2.29

1212 K. HENRY: Every subject's duty is the King's, but every subject's soul is his own. Therefore should every soldier in the wars do as every sick man in his bed, wash every mote out of his conscience; and dying so, death is to him advantage; or not dying, the time was blessedly lost wherein such preparation was gain'd; and in him that escapes, it were not sin to think that making God so free an offer, He let him outlive that day to see His greatness and to teach others how they should prepare.
Henry V 4.1.178

1213 WARWICK [soliloquy]: My sick heart shows,
That I must yield my body to the earth.
3 Henry VI 5.2.8

1214 HOTSPUR [dying]: Thoughts, the slaves of life, and life, time's fool,
And time, that takes survey of all the world,
Must have a stop.
1 Henry IV 5.4.81

1215 SHALLOW: Death, as the Psalmist saith, is certain to all, all shall die.
2 Henry IV 3.2.37

1216 PRINCE: Thou owest God a death.
1 Henry IV 5.1.126

1217 LADY MACBETH: The sleeping and the dead
Are but as pictures.
Macbeth 2.2.50

1218 ISABELLA: The sense of death is most in apprehension,
And the poor beetle that we tread upon
In corporal sufferance finds a pang as great
As when a giant dies.
Measure for Measure 3.1.77

1219 LORD: Grim death, how foul and loathsome is thine image!
Taming of the Shrew, Induction 1.35

1220 IRAS [to Cleopatra, after Caesar's victory]: Finish, good lady, the bright day is done
And we are for the dark.
Antony and Cleopatra 5.2.193
[*finish:* end, die]

Debts

1221 PANDARUS: Words pay no debts.
Troilus and Cressida 3.2.55

1222 PLAYER KING: Most necessary 'tis that we forget
To pay ourselves what to ourselves is debt.
Hamlet 3.2.192

1223 FALSTAFF: I can get no remedy against this consumption of the purse; borrowing only lingers and lingers it out, but the disease is incurable.
2 Henry IV 1.2.236

1224 STEPHANO: He that dies pays all debts.
The Tempest 3.2.131

Decay

1225 MACBETH: I have liv'd long enough: my way of life
Is fall'n into the sear, the yellow leaf.
Macbeth 5.3.23

1226 PROTEUS: In the sweetest bud
The eating canker dwells.
Two Gentlemen of Verona 1.1.42

Deceit

1227 CLAUDIO: O, what authority and show of truth
Can cunning sin cover itself withal!
Much Ado About Nothing 4.1.35

1228 When my love swears that she is made of truth,
I do believe her, though I know she lies.
Sonnet 138

1229 BANQUO: 'Tis strange;
And oftentimes, to win us to our harm,
The instruments of darkness tell us truths,
Win us with honest trifles, to betray 's
In deepest consequence.
Macbeth 1.3.122

1230 CLEON: Who makes the fairest show means most deceit.
Pericles 1.4.75

1231 MACBETH: False face must hide what the false heart doth know.
Macbeth 1.7.82

1232 HAMLET: One may smile, and smile, and be a villain!
Hamlet 1.5.108

1233 BASSANIO: I like not fair terms and a villain's mind.
Merchant of Venice 1.3.179

1234 BASSANIO: The world is still deceiv'd with ornament.

In law, what plea so tainted and corrupt
But, being season'd with a gracious voice,
Obscures the show of evil? In religion,
What damned error but some sober brow
Will bless it, and approve it with a text,
Hiding the grossness with fair ornament?
There is no vice so simple but assumes
Some mark of virtue on his outward parts.
Merchant of Venice 3.2.74

1235 MOROCCO: All that glitters is not gold.
Merchant of Venice 2.7.65

1236 DUCHESS [on Gloucester's feigned love to young Edward]: Ah! that deceit should steal such gentle shape,
And with a virtuous vizor hide deep vice!
Richard III 2.2.27

1237 JULIET [about Romeo, after Tybalt's death]: O that deceit should dwell
In such a gorgeous palace!
Romeo and Juliet 3.2.84

1238 SUFFOLK: The fox barks not when he would steal the lamb.
2 Henry VI 3.1.55

1239 POLONIUS: Thus do we of wisdom and of reach,
With windlasses and with assays of bias,
By indirections find directions out.
Hamlet 2.1.61

1240 SUFFOLK: That is good deceit
Which mates him first that first intends deceit.
2 Henry VI 3.1.264

1241 Time's glory is . . .
To mock the subtle in themselves beguil'd.
Rape of Lucrece 939

1242 HERMIA [to Lysander]: You speak not as you think.
Midsummer Night's Dream 3.2.191

1243 TIMON [soliloquy, on gold and its power]: Much of this will make
Black white, foul fair, wrong right,
Base noble, old young, coward valiant.
Timon of Athens 4.3.28

1244 BALTHAZAR [singing]: Sigh no more, ladies, sigh no more,
Men were deceivers ever,
One foot in sea, and one on shore,
To one thing constant never.
Much Ado About Nothing 2.3.62

1245 K. HENRY: The tongues of men are full of deceits.
Henry V 5.2.117

1246 CORDELIA: That glib and oily art
To speak and purpose not.
King Lear 1.1.224

1247 ISABELLA: It oft falls out,
To have what we would have, we speak not what we mean.
Measure for Measure 2.4.117

1248 HAMLET: We must speak by the card, or equivocation will undo us.
Hamlet 5.1.137

1249 My true eyes have never practic'd how
To cloak offenses with a cunning brow.
Rape of Lucrece 748

1250 OPHELIA [giving flowers to Claudius and Gertrude]: There's a daisy. I would give you some violets, but they wither'd all when my father died.
Hamlet 4.5.184
[*daisy:* emblem of dissembling, faithlessness]

December

1251 How like a winter hath my absence been

From thee, the pleasure of the fleeting
    year!
What freezings have I felt, what dark
    days seen!
What old December's bareness every
    where!
                    Sonnet 97

1252 ROSALIND: Men are April when
they woo, December when they wed.
          As You Like It 4.1.147

Deception

1253 K. HENRY: When the lion fawns
  upon the lamb,
The lamb will never cease to follow
  him.
              3 Henry VI 4.8.49

1254 CICERO: Men may construe
  things after their fashion,
Clean from the purpose of the things
  themselves.
          Julius Caesar 1.3.34

1255 SUFFOLK: The fox barks not
  when he would steal the lamb.
            2 Henry VI 3.1.55

1256 BASSANIO: So may the outward
  shows be least themselves—
The world is still deceiv'd with
  ornament.
In law, what plea so tainted and cor-
  rupt
But, being season'd with a gracious
  voice,
Obscures the show of evil? In religion,
What damned error but some sober
  brow
Will bless it, and approve it with a
  text,
Hiding the grossness with fair orna-
  ment?
There is no vice so simple but assumes
Some mark of virtue on his outward
  parts.
How many cowards, whose hearts are
  all as false
As stairs of sand, wear yet upon their
  chins

The beards of Hercules and frowning
  Mars,
Who inward search'd, have livers white
  as milk,
And these assume but valor's excre-
  ment
To render them redoubted! Look on
  beauty,
And you shall see 'tis purchas'd by the
  weight,
Which therein works a miracle in
  nature,
Making them lightest that wear most
  of it.
So are those crisped snaky golden
  locks,
Which make such wanton gambols
  with the wind
Upon supposed fairness, often known
To be the dowry of a second head,
The skull that bred them in the
  sepulchre.
Thus ornament is but the guiled shore
To a most dangerous sea; the beau-
  teous scarf
Veiling an Indian beauty; in a word,
The seeming truth which cunning
  times put on
To entrap the wisest.
        Merchant of Venice 3.2.73
[*valor's excrement:* beard of a brave man;
render them redoubted: make themselves
feared; *lightest:* most wanton]

1257 GLOUCESTER [soliloquy]: Why, I
  can smile, and murther whiles I
  smile,
And cry "Content" to that which
  grieves my heart,
And wet my cheeks with artificial tears,
And frame my face to all occasions.
I'll drown more sailors than the mer-
  maid shall,
I'll slay more gazers than the basilisk,
I'll play the orator as well as Nestor,
Deceive more slily than Ulysses could,
And like a Sinon, take another Troy.
I can add colors to the chameleon,
Change shapes with Proteus for advan-
  tages,
And set the murtherous Machevil to
  school.
Can I do this, and cannot get a crown?

Tut, were it farther off, I'll pluck it
down.
3 Henry VI 3.2.182
[*murther:* murder; *basilisk:* fabulous, fabled
serpent whose look could cause death;
Sinon: the Greek warrior whose wooden-
horse ruse led to the fall of Troy; *Proteus:*
the sea god, who could assume many
different shapes; *Machevil:* for Machiavelli,
a Florentine philosopher and statesman who
expounded excessive political immorality as
a means to an end]

1258 Testy sick men, when their
    deaths be near,
No news but health from their physi-
cians know.
Sonnet 140

1259 CLAUDIO: O, what authority and
    show of truth
Can cunning sin cover itself withal!
Much Ado About Nothing 4.1.35

Decision

1260 BRUTUS: There is a tide in the
affairs of men,
Which taken at the flood, leads on to
fortune;
Omitted, all the voyage of their life
Is bound in shallows and in mis-
eries . . .
We must take the current when it
serves,
Or lose our ventures.
Julius Caesar 4.3.218

1261 HECTOR: Pleasure and revenge
Have ears more deaf than adders to the
voice
Of any true decision.
Troilus and Cressida 2.2.171

1262 ANTONIO: What I will, I will,
    and there an end.
Two Gentlemen of Verona 1.3.65

Decline

1263 APEMANTUS: Men shut their
doors against a setting sun.
Timon of Athens 1.2.145

Decree

1264 PORTIA: The brain may devise
laws for the blood, but a hot temper
leaps o'er a cold decree.
Merchant of Venice 1.2.18

1265 DUKE: Our decrees,
Dead to infliction, to themselves are
dead.
Measure for Measure 1.3.27

Deeds

1266 KING: 'Tis a kind of good deed
    to say well,
And yet words are no deeds.
Henry VIII 3.2.153

1267 AGAMEMNON: Whatever praises
itself but in the deed, devours the
deed in the praise.
Troilus and Cressida 2.3.156

1268 BAPTISTA: 'Tis deeds must win
    the prize.
Taming of the Shrew 2.1.342

1269 MACBETH: The flighty purpose
    never is o'ertook
Unless the deed go with it.
Macbeth 4.1.145

1270 KING: From lowest place when
    virtuous things proceed,
The place is dignified by th' doer's
    deed.
Where great additions swell 's, and vir-
tue none,
It is a dropsied honor. Good alone
Is good, without a name.
All's Well That Ends Well 2.3.125
[*additions:* honorific titles and other marks
of distinction; *'s:* us]

1271 LUCIANA: Ill deeds is doubled
with an ill word.
Comedy of Errors 3.2.20

1272 DOCTOR: Unnatural deeds
Do breed unnatural troubles.
Macbeth 5.1.71

1273 PROTEUS [soliloquy]: Truth hath
better deeds than words to grace it.
Two Gentlemen of Verona 2.2.18

1274 KING: Things done well
And with care exempt themselves from
fear;
Things done without example, in their
issue
Are to be fear'd.
Henry VIII 1.2.88

1275 KING: That we would do,
We should do when we would.
Hamlet 4.7.118

1276 K. JOHN: How oft the sight of
means to do ill deeds
Make deeds ill done!
King John 4.2.219

1277 AGRIPPA: Strange it is
That nature must compel us to lament
Our most persisted deeds.
Antony and Cleopatra 5.1.28

1278 ULYSSES [to Achilles]: Time
hath, my lord, a wallet at his back,
Wherein he puts alms for oblivion,
A great-siz'd monster of ingratitudes.
Those scraps are good deeds past,
which are devour'd
As fast as they are made, forgot as
soon
As done.
Troilus and Cressida 3.3.145

1279 HAMLET [soliloquy]: Foul deeds
will rise,
Though all the earth o'erwhelm them,
to men's eyes.
Hamlet 1.2.256

1280 LADY MACBETH: Things without
all remedy

Should be without regard: what's
done, is done.
Macbeth 3.2.11

1281 K. RICHARD: What is done cannot be now amended.
Richard III 4.4.291

1282 CRESSIDA: Things won are done,
joy's soul lies in the doing.
Troilus and Cressida 1.2.287

1283 VENTIDIUS: Better to leave undone, than by our deed
Acquire too high a fame when him we
serve's away.
Antony and Cleopatra 3.1.14

1284 CLAUDIO: O, what men dare do!
What men may do! What men daily
do, not knowing what they do!
Much Ado About Nothing 4.1.19

1285 MACBETH [soliloquy, on murder-
ing Duncan]: If it were done, when
'tis done, then 'twere well
It were done quickly. If th' assassina-
tion
Could trammel up the consequence,
and catch
With his surcease, success; that but this
blow
Might be the be-all and end-all—here,
But here, upon this bank and shoal of
time,
We'ld jump the life to come.
Macbeth 1.7.1

1286 MACBETH: Come, seeling night,
Scarf up the tender eye of pitiful day,
And with thy bloody and invisible
hand
Cancel and tear to pieces that great
bond
Which keeps me pale! Light thickens,
and the crow
Makes wing to th' rooky wood;
Good things of the day begin to droop
and drowse,
Whiles night's black agents to their
preys do rouse.
Thou marvel'st at my words, but hold
thee still:

Things bad begun make strong
themselves by ill.
                    Macbeth 3.2.46

1287 CLEOPATRA [to a 'rural fellow'
giving her some figs]: What poor an
instrument
May do a noble deed!
        Antony and Cleopatra 5.2.236

1288 FLORIZEL: What you do
Still betters what is done.
            Winter's Tale 4.4.135

1289 HERMIONE: One good deed dying tongueless
Slaughters a thousand waiting upon
that.
Our praises are our wages.
            Winter's Tale 1.2.92

1290 AARON: Let my deeds be witness
of my worth.
        Titus Andronicus 5.1.103

1291 PORTIA: How far that little candle throws his beams!
So shines a good deed in a naughty
world.
        Merchant of Venice 5.1.90

Deer

1292 He is no woodman that doth
bend his bow
To strike a poor unseasonable doe.
            Rape of Lucrece 580

Defeat

1293 IRAS [to Cleopatra, after Caesar's
victory]: Finish, good lady, the
bright day is done,
And we are for the dark.
        Antony and Cleopatra 5.2.193
[*finish:* end, die]

Defect

1294 HAMLET: So, oft it chances in
particular men,

That for some vicious mole of nature
in them,
As in their birth, wherein they are not
guilty
(Since nature cannot choose his origin),
By their o'ergrowth of some com-
plexion
Oft breaking down the pales and forts
of reason,
Or by some habit, that too much o'er-
leavens
The form of plausive manners—that
these men,
Carrying, I say, the stamp of one
defect,
Being nature's livery, or fortune's star,
His virtues else, be they as pure as
grace,
As infinite as man may undergo,
Shall in the general censure take cor-
ruption
From that particular fault.
                    Hamlet 1.4.23

1295 FERDINAND: For several virtues
Have I lik'd several women, never any
With so full soul but some defect in
her
Did quarrel with the noblest grace she
ow'd,
And put it to the foil.
            The Tempest 3.1.42

1296 GLOUCESTER: Full oft 'tis seen,
Our means secure us, and our mere
defects
Prove our commodities.
                King Lear 4.1.19
[*means:* prosperity, which makes us careless;
defects: disadvantages, which sometimes
prove beneficial]

1297 K. HENRY: Defect of manners,
want of government,
Pride, haughtiness, opinion, and
disdain,
The least of which haunting a noble-
man
Loseth men's hearts and leaves behind
a stain

Upon the beauty of all parts besides,
Beguiling them of commendation.
                           1 Henry IV 3.1.182
[*want of government:* self-control; *opinion:*
conceit]

Defense

1298 DOLPHIN: In cases of defense 'tis
    best to weigh
The enemy more mighty than he
    seems,
So the proportions of defense are fill'd;
Which, of a weak and niggardly pro-
    jection,
Doth like a miser spoil his coat with
    scanting
A little cloth.
                           Henry V 2.4.43

1299 ALCIBIADES: To kill, I grant, is
    sin's extremest gust,
But in defense, by mercy, 'tis most
    just.
                           Timon of Athens 3.5.54

1300 CLIFFORD: Doves will peck in
    safeguard of their brood.
                           3 Henry VI 2.2.18

Defiance

1301 WARWICK [to Gloucester]: I had
    rather chop this hand off at a blow,
And with the other fling it at thy face,
Than bear so low a sail to strike to
    thee.
                           3 Henry VI 5.1.50

Defilement

1302 DOGBERRY: They that touch
pitch will be defil'd.
                    Much Ado About Nothing 3.3.57

Deformity

1303 ANTONIO: In nature there's no
    blemish but the mind;

None can be call'd deform'd but the
    unkind.
                           Twelfth Night 3.4.367

1304 ALBANY: Proper deformity shows
    not in the fiend
So horrid as in woman.
                           King Lear 4.2.60

Degrees

1305 ULYSSES: O, when degree is
    shak'd,
Which is the ladder of all high de-
    signs,
The enterprise is sick. How could
    communities,
Degrees in schools, and brotherhoods
    in cities,
Peaceful commerce from dividable
    shores,
The primogenity and due of birth,
Prerogative of age, crowns, sceptres,
    laurels,
But by degree stand in authentic
    place?
Take but degree away, untune that
    string,
And hark what discord follows.
                           Troilus and Cressida 1.3.101
[*primogenity ... of birth:* the rights of the
eldest-born]

1306 ISABELLA: That in the captain's
    but a choleric word,
Which in the soldier is flat blasphemy.
                           Measure for Measure 2.2.130

1307 TOUCHSTONE [to Jaques]: O sir,
we quarrel in print, by the book—as
you have books for good manners. I
will name you the degrees. The first,
the Retort Courteous; the second, the
Quip Modest; the third, the Reply
Churlish; the fourth, the Reproof
Valiant; the fift, the Countercheck
Quarrelsome; the sixt, the Lie with Cir-
cumstance; the seventh, the Lie Direct.
All these you may avoid but the Lie
Direct; and you may avoid that too,

with an If . . . Your If is the only
peacemaker; much virtue in If.
As You Like It 5.4.90

[*fift:* fifth; *sixt:* sixth]

1308 ARRAGON: O that estates,
degrees, and offices
Were not deriv'd corruptly, and that
clear honor
Were purchas'd by the merit of the
wearer!
Merchant of Venice 2.9.41

Delay

1309 REIGNIER: Defer no time, delays
have dangerous ends.
1 Henry VI 3.2.33

1310 MERCUTIO: In delay
We waste our lights in vain, like lights
by day!
Romeo and Juliet 1.4.44

1311 K. RICHARD: I have learn'd that
fearful commenting
Is leaden servitor to dull delay;
Delay leads impotent and snail-pac'd
beggary.
Richard III 4.3.51

1312 IAGO: Dull not device by coldness and delay.
Othello 2.3.388

1313 HAMLET: "By and by" is easily
said.
Hamlet 3.2.387

Delicacy

1314 HAMLET: The hand of little
employment hath the daintier sense.
Hamlet 5.1.69

Delight

1315 PHILOSTRATE: How shall we beguile

The lazy time, if not with some delight?
Midsummer Night's Dream 5.1.40

1316 BEROWNE: All delights are vain,
but that most vain,
Which, with pain purchas'd, doth inherit pain.
Love's Labor's Lost 1.1.72

1317 FRIAR LAWRENCE: Violent
delights have violent ends,
And in their triumph die, like fire and
powder,
Which as they kiss consume.
Romeo and Juliet 2.6.9

1318 CELIA: O wonderful, wonderful,
and most wonderful wonderful! and
yet again wonderful, and after that,
out of all hooping!
As You Like It 3.2.191

[*hooping:* whooping]

Dependence

1319 WOLSEY [soliloquy]: O how
wretched
Is that poor man that hangs on princes'
favors!
Henry VIII 3.2.366

1320 POSTHUMUS: Poor wretches that
depend
On greatness' favor dream as I have
done,
Wake, and find nothing.
Cymbeline 5.4.127

1321 HELICANUS: Plants look up to
heaven, from whence
They have their nourishment.
Pericles 1.2.55

Depravity

1322 APEMANTUS: Who lives that's not
depraved or depraves?
Timon of Athens 1.2.140

Deserts

1323 K. RICHARD: They well deserve to have
That know the strong'st and surest way to get.
Richard II 3.3.200

1324 HAMLET: Use every man after his desert, and who shall scape whipping?
Hamlet 2.2.529

1325 STEWARD: We wound our modesty, and make foul the clearness of our deservings, when of ourselves we publish them.
All's Well That Ends Well 1.3.5

1326 BELARIUS: Many times
Doth ill deserve by doing well.
Cymbeline 3.3.53

Desire

1327 LADY MACBETH [soliloquy]:
Nought's had, all's spent,
Where our desire is got without content.
Macbeth 3.2.5

1328 LAERTES: Keep you in the rear of your affection,
Out of the shot and danger of desire.
Hamlet 1.3.34

1329 POINS: Is it not strange that desire should so many years outlive performance?
2 Henry IV 2.4.260

1330 Now quick desire hath caught the yielding prey,
And glutton-like she feeds, yet never filleth.
Venus and Adonis 547

1331 The sea hath bounds, but deep desire hath none.
Venus and Adonis 389

1332 Hot desire converts to cold disdain.
Rape of Lucrece 691

1333 Had doting Priam check'd his son's desire,
Troy had been bright with fame, and not with fire.
Rape of Lucrece 1490

1334 BEROWNE: Where nothing wants that want itself doth seek.
Love's Labor's Lost 4.3.233

1335 HERMIA: My legs can keep no pace with my desires.
Midsummer Night's Dream 3.2.445

1336 ARMADO: If drawing my sword against the humor of affection would deliver me from the reprobate thought of it, I would take Desire prisoner.
Love's Labor's Lost 1.2.59

1337 BERTRAM: All impediments in fancy's course
Are motives of more fancy.
All's Well That Ends Well 5.3.214
[*fancy's:* i.e. love's]

1338 True respect will prison false desire.
Rape of Lucrece 642

1339 IMOGEN: Most miserable
Is the desire that's glorious.
Cymbeline 1.6.6

1340 THESEUS [to Hermia]: Question your desires,
Know of your youth, examine well your blood.
Midsummer Night's Dream 1.1.67

1341 HAMLET: Every man has business and desire,
Such as it is.
Hamlet 1.5.130

1342 FALSTAFF: A man can no more separate age and coveteousness than 'a can part young limbs and lechery.
2 Henry IV 1.2.228
[*'a:* he]

1343 CRESSIDA: Men prize the thing ungain'd more than it is.
Troilus and Cressida 1.2.289

1344 DUKE [on falling in love with Olivia]: My desires, like fell and cruel hounds,
E'er since pursue me.
Twelfth Night 1.1.21

1345 Then can no horse with my desire keep pace.
Sonnet 51

1346 Drunken Desire must vomit his receipt
Ere he can see his own abomination.
Rape of Lucrece 703

1347 Feeble Desire, all recreant, poor, and meek,
Like to a bankrout beggar wails his case:
The flesh being proud, Desire doth fight with Grace,
For there it revels.
Rape of Lucrece 710
[*bankrout:* bankrupt]

1348 ROSALIND: Can one desire too much of a good thing?
As You Like It 4.1.123

1349 PRINCE: I never thought to hear you speak again.
KING: Thy wish was father, Harry, to that thought.
2 Henry IV 4.5.91

1350 CLEOPATRA: I have
Immortal longings in me.
Antony and Cleopatra 5.2.280

1351 CLAUDIO: Come thronging soft and delicate desires.
Much Ado About Nothing 1.1.303

1352 In night . . . desire sees best of all.
Venus and Adonis 720

Desolation

1353 CLEOPATRA: My desolation does begin to make
A better life.
Antony and Cleopatra 5.2.1

Despair

1354 PROTEUS: Hope is a lover's staff; walk hence with that
And manage it against despairing thoughts.
Two Gentlemen of Verona 3.1.248

1355 HAMLET [soliloquy]: O that this too too sallied flesh would melt,
Thaw, and resolve itself into a dew!
Or that the Everlasting had not fix'd
His canon 'gainst self-slaughter! O God, God,
How weary, stale, flat, and unprofitable
Seem to me all the uses of this world!
Hamlet 1.2.129
[*sallied:* sullied; many editors prefer *solid*]

1356 K. RICHARD: Of comfort no man speak:
Let's talk of graves, of worms, and epitaphs.
Richard II 3.2.144

1357 SALISBURY: Discomfort guides my tongue
And bids me speak of nothing but despair.
Richard II 3.2.65

1358 KING: I am wrapp'd in dismal thinkings.
All's Well That Ends Well 5.3.128

1359 SECOND MURDERER [accepting Macbeth's hire to kill Banquo]: I am one, my liege,
Whom the vile blows and buffets of the world
Have so incens'd that I am reckless what
I do to spite the world.
FIRST MURDERER: And I another,

So weary with disasters, tugg'd with
    fortune,
That I would set my life on any
    chance,
To mend it, or be rid of it.
                              Macbeth 3.1.108

1360 OTHELLO [to Iago, on Desdemona's 'adultery']: Nothing canst
thou to damnation add
Greater than that.
                              Othello 3.3.372

1361 Despair and hope makes thee
    ridiculous:
The one doth flatter thee in thoughts
    unlikely,
In likely thoughts the other kills thee
    quickly.
                        Venus and Adonis 988

1362 MACBETH: All is but toys:
    renown and grace is dead,
The wine of life is drawn, and the
    mere lees
Is left this vault to brag of.
                              Macbeth 2.3.94

1363 PETER: When griping griefs the
    heart doth wound,
And doleful dumps the mind oppress,
Then music with her silver sound . . .
With speedy help doth lend redress.
                        Romeo and Juliet 4.5.126

1364 JULIET [on learning of her
    betrothal to Paris]: Come weep with
    me, past hope, past cure, past help!
                        Romeo and Juliet 4.1.45

1365 O, that is gone for which I
    sought to live,
And therefore now I need not fear to
    die.
                        Rape of Lucrece 1051

1366 K. RICHARD [soliloquy]: I shall
    despair; there is no creature loves
    me,
And if I die no soul shall pity me.
And wherefore should they, since that
    I myself
Find in myself no pity to myself?
                              Richard III 5.3.200

1367 Two loves I have, of comfort and
    despair,
That like two spirits do suggest me
    still:
My better angel is a man (right fair),
My worser spirit a woman (color'd ill).
To win me soon to hell, my female evil
Tempteth my better angel from my
    side;
And would corrupt my saint to be a
    devil,
Wooing his purity with her fair pride.
And whether that my angel be turn'd
    fiend,
Suspect I may (yet not directly tell):
For being both to me, both to each
    friend,
I guess one angel in another's hell:
The truth I shall not know, but live in
    doubt,
Till my bad angel fire my good one
    out.
                        The Passionate Pilgrim ii.1

Desperation

1368 ROMEO [soliloquy]: O mischief,
    thou art swift
To enter in the thoughts of desperate
    men!
                        Romeo and Juliet 5.1.35

1369 PANDULPH: He that stands upon
    a slipp'ry place
Makes nice of no vild hold to stay him
    up.
                              King John 3.4.137
[*vild:* vile]

1370 ROMEO: Tempt not a desp'rate
    man.
                        Romeo and Juliet 5.3.59

1371 CLIFFORD: Doves will peck in
    safeguard of their brood.
                              3 Henry VI 2.2.18

Destiny

1372 K. RICHARD: All unavoided is
    the doom of destiny.
                              Richard III 4.4.218

1373 CORIOLANUS: 'Tis fond to wail inevitable strokes,
As 'tis to laugh at 'em.
Coriolanus 4.1.26

1374 Q. MARGARET: What cannot be avoided,
'Twere childish weakness to lament or fear.
3 Henry VI 5.4.37

1375 NERISSA: The ancient saying is no heresy,
Hanging and wiving goes by destiny.
Merchant of Venice 2.9.82

1376 CAESAR: Let determin'd things to destiny
Hold unbewail'd their way.
Antony and Cleopatra 3.6.84

1377 HAMLET: There's a divinity that shapes our ends,
Rough-hew them how we will.
Hamlet 5.2.10

1378 K. EDWARD: What fates impose, that men must needs abide;
It boots not to resist both wind and tide.
3 Henry VI 4.3.58
[*boots;* helps]

1379 WOLSEY [soliloquy]: Farewell? a long farewell to all my greatness!
This is the state of man: to-day he puts forth
The tender leaves of hopes, to-morrow blossoms,
And bears his blushing honors thick upon him;
The third day comes a frost, a killing frost,
And when he thinks, good easy man, full surely
His greatness is a-ripening, nips his root,
And then he falls as I do.
Henry VIII 3.2.351

1380 HAMLET: A man may fish with the worm that hath eat of a king, and eat of the fish that hath fed of that worm.
Hamlet 4.3.27

1381 HAMLET: There is special providence in the fall of a sparrow. If it be now, 'tis not to come; if it be not to come, it will be now; if it be not now, yet it will come — the readiness is all.
Hamlet 5.2.219

1382 HAMLET: Some must watch while some must sleep,
Thus runs the world away.
Hamlet 3.2.273

Destruction

1383 LADY MACBETH: 'Tis safer to be that which we destroy
Than by destruction dwell in doubtful joy.
Macbeth 3.2.6

Determination

1384 MALVOLIO: Thou art made if thou desir'st to be so.
Twelfth Night 2.5.155

1385 LADY MACBETH [to Macbeth]: Screw your courage to the sticking place,
And we'll not fail.
Macbeth 1.7.60

Detraction

1386 BENEDICK [soliloquy]: Happy are they that hear their detractions, and can put them to mending.
Much Ado About Nothing 2.3.229

1387 FABIAN [to Malvolio]: Ay, and you had an eye behind you, you might see more detraction at your heels than fortunes before you.
Twelfth Night 2.5.136

Device

1388 IAGO: Dull not device by coldness and delay.
Othello 2.3.388

Devil

1389 SERVANT: The devil knew not
what he did when he made man politic; he cross'd himself by't.
Timon of Athens 3.3.28

1390 HAMLET [soliloquy]: The dev'l
hath power
T' assume a pleasing shape.
Hamlet 2.2.599

1391 ANTONIO: The devil can cite
Scripture for his purpose.
Merchant of Venice 1.3.98

1392 CLOWN: He is prince of this
world.
All's Well That Ends Well 4.5.49

1393 EDGAR: The prince of darkness is
a gentleman.
King Lear 3.4.143

1394 PRINCE: The devil shall have his
bargain, for he was never yet a breaker
of proverbs. He will give the devil his
due.
1 Henry IV 1.2.117
[*his due:* i.e. Falstaff's soul]

1395 K. HENRY: Other devils that
suggest by treasons
Do botch and bungle up damnation
With patches, colors, and with forms
being fetch'd
From glist'ring semblances of piety.
Henry V 2.2.114

1396 IAGO [soliloquy]: When devils
will the blackest sins put on,
They do suggest at first with heavenly
shows.
Othello 2.3.351

1397 HOTSPUR: O, while you live, tell
the truth and shame the devil!
1 Henry IV 3.1.61

1398 DROMIO SYRACUSE: He must
have a long spoon that must eat with
the devil.
Comedy of Errors 4.3.63

1399 CLOWN: I am driven on by the
flesh, and he must needs go that the
devil drives.
All's Well That Ends Well 1.3.28

1400 ARIEL: Hell is empty,
And all the devils are here.
The Tempest 1.2.214

1401 BEROWNE: Devils soonest tempt,
resembling spirits of light.
Love's Labor's Lost 4.3.253

1402 BANQUO: Oftentimes, to win us
to our harm,
The instruments of darkness tell us
truths,
Win us with honest trifles, to betray 's
In deepest consequence.
Macbeth 1.3.123

1403 TROILUS: Sometimes we are
devils to ourselves,
When we will tempt the frailty of our
powers,
Presuming on their changeful potency.
Troilus and Cressida 4.4.95

1404 POLONIUS: 'Tis too much
prov'd—that with devotion's visage
And pious action we do sugar o'er
The devil himself.
Hamlet 3.1.46

1405 LADY MACBETH: 'Tis the eye of
childhood
That fears a painted devil.
Macbeth 2.2.51

1406 SIR TOBY [to Malvolio]: Defy the
devil!
Consider, he's an enemy to mankind.
Twelfth Night 3.4.97

1407 SOLANIO: Let me say amen betimes, lest the devil cross my prayer.
Merchant of Venice 3.1.20

1408 FALSTAFF [soliloquy]: I think the devil will not have me damn'd, lest the oil that's in me should set hell on fire.
Merry Wives of Windsor 5.5.34

Devotion

1409 POLONIUS: 'Tis too much prov'd—that with devotion's visage And pious action we do sugar o'er The devil himself.
Hamlet 3.1.46

1410 BARDOLPH [mourning Falstaff]: Would I were with him, wheresome'er he is, either in heaven or in hell!
Henry V 2.3.7

Dew

1411 FAIRY: I must go seek some dewdrops here, And hang a pearl in every cowslip's ear.
Midsummer Night's Dream 2.1.14

1412 LYSANDER: Decking with liquid pearl the bladed grass.
Midsummer Night's Dream 1.1.211

1413 QUINTUS: As fresh as morning dew distill'd on flowers.
Titus Andronicus 2.3.201

Differences

1414 KING: Strange is it that our bloods,
Of color, weight, and heat, pour'd all together,
Would quite confound distinction, yet stands off
In differences so mighty.
All's Well That Ends Well 2.3.118

1415 IMOGEN: Clay and clay differs in dignity,
Whose dust is both alike.
Cymbeline 4.2.4

Difficulty

1416 DUKE: All difficulties are but easy when they are known.
Measure for Measure 4.2.205

Diffidence

1417 FRANCE: Is it but this—a tardiness in nature
Which often leaves the history unspoke That it intends to do?
King Lear 1.1.235

Digestion

1418 ABBESS: Unquiet meals make ill digestions.
Comedy of Errors 5.1.74

1419 GAUNT: Things sweet to taste prove in digestion sour.
Richard II 1.3.236

1420 MACBETH: Now good digestion wait on appetite,
And health on both!
Macbeth 3.4.37

Dignity

1421 HELENA [soliloquy]: Things base and vile, holding no quantity,
Love can transpose to form and dignity.
Midsummer Night's Dream 1.1.232
[*holding no quantity:* lacking proportion, unshapely]

1422 ARRAGON: Let none presume To wear an undeserved dignity.
Merchant of Venice 2.9.39

1423 IMOGEN: Clay and clay differs in dignity,
Whose dust is both alike.
Cymbeline 4.2.4

Dilemma

1424 LAUNCELOT: When I shun Scylla, your father, I fall into Charybdis, your mother.
Merchant of Venice 3.5.18
[In Homer's fable, Scylla was a rock and Charybdis was a whirlpool in the straits of Messina, Sicily. Each was the habitat of a sea-monster who lured sailors to their death.]

Diligence

1425 KENT: That which ordinary men are fit for, I am qualified in, and the best of me is diligence.
King Lear 1.4.34

Dining

1426 MENENIUS: The veins unfill'd, our blood is cold, and then
We pout upon the morning, are unapt
To give or to forgive; but when we have stuff'd
These pipes and these conveyances of our blood
With wine and feeding, we have suppler souls
Than in our priest-like fasts.
Coriolanus 5.1.51

Diplomacy

1427 PHEBE [about Ganymede]: Faster than his tongue
Did make offense, his eye did heal it up.
As You Like It 3.5.116

Disappointment

1428 GRATIANO: All things that are,
Are with more spirit chased than enjoy'd.
Merchant of Venice 2.6.12

1429 The sweets we wish for turn to loathed sours,
Even in the moment that we call them ours.
Rape of Lucrece 867

1430 GAUNT: Things sweet to taste prove in digestion sour.
Richard II 1.3.236

1431 THESEUS: Earthlier happy is the rose distill'd,
Than that which withering on the virgin thorn
Grows, lives, and dies in single blessedness.
Midsummer Night's Dream 1.1.76

Disapprobation

1432 PARIS: Fair Diomed, you do as chapmen do,
Dispraise the thing that they desire to buy.
Troilus and Cressida 4.1.76

Discipline

1433 GARDENER: Unruly children make their sire stoop.
Richard II 3.4.30

1434 DUKE: Now, as fond fathers,
Having bound up the threat'ning twigs of birch,
Only to stick it in their children's sight
For terror, not to use, in time the rod
Becomes more mock'd than fear'd; so our decrees,
Dead to infliction, to themselves are dead,
And liberty plucks justice by the nose;

The baby beats the nurse, and quite athwart
Goes all decorum.
Measure for Measure 1.3.23

1435 GARDINER: Those that tame wild horses
Pace 'em not in their hands to make 'em gentle,
But stop their mouths with stubborn bits and spur 'em
Till they obey the manage.
Henry VIII 5.2.56

Discomfort

1436 SERGEANT: As whence the sun gins his reflection
Shipwracking storms and direful thunders break,
So from that spring whence comfort seem'd to come
Discomfort swells.
Macbeth 1.2.25
[*gins his reflection:* begins its turning back at the vernal equinox]

1437 SALISBURY: Discomfort guides my tongue
And bids me speak of nothing but despair.
Richard II 3.2.65

Discontent

1438 PANDULPH [predicting a rebellion of the English people against King John]: 'Tis wonderful
What may be wrought out of their discontent.
King John 3.4.178

1439 APEMANTUS: Best state, contentless,
Hath a distracted and most wretched being,
Worse than the worst, content.
Timon of Athens 4.3.245

1440 ARCHBISHOP: Past and to come seems best; things present worst.
2 Henry IV 1.3.108

1441 ANTONY: The present pleasure,
By revolution low'ring, does become
The opposite of itself.
Antony and Cleopatra 1.2.124

1442 KING: What's more miserable than discontent?
2 Henry VI 3.1.201

1443 LADY MACBETH [soliloquy]:
Nought's had, all's spent,
Where our desire is got without content.
Macbeth 3.2.5

1444 K. RICHARD [soliloquy]: Nor I, nor any man that but man is,
With nothing shall be pleas'd, till he be eas'd
With being nothing.
Richard II 5.5.39

1445 ANTIPHOLUS SYRACUSE [soliloquy]: He that commends me to mine own content,
Commends me to a thing I cannot get.
Comedy of Errors 1.2.33

1446 DUKE [to the condemned Claudio]: Happy thou art not,
For what thou hast not, still thou striv'st to get,
And what thou hast, forget'st.
Measure for Measure 3.1.21

1447 GLOUCESTER [soliloquy, on King Edward]: Now is the winter of our discontent
Made glorious summer by this son of York.
Richard III 1.1.1

1448 CONRADE [to Don John]: Can you make no use of your discontent?
Much Ado About Nothing 1.3.38

Discord

1449 KING: Civil dissension is a viperous worm
That gnaws the bowels of the commonwealth.
1 Henry VI 3.1.72

1450 K. RICHARD [soliloquy]: How sour sweet music is
When time is broke, and no proportion kept!
So is it in the music of men's lives.
Richard II 5.5.42

Discourse

1451 ADRIANA: If voluble and sharp discourse be marr'd,
Unkindness blunts it more than marble hard.
Comedy of Errors 2.1.92

1452 BELARIUS: Discourse is heavy, fasting.
Cymbeline 3.6.90

1453 Bid me discourse, I will enchant thine ear.
Venus and Adonis 145

Discretion

1454 ARMADO: I have seen the day of wrong through the little hole of discretion.
Love's Labor's Lost 5.2.724

1455 POLONIUS: Give thy thoughts no tongue,
Nor any unproportion'd thought his act.
Hamlet 1.3.59

1456 FALSTAFF: The better part of valor is discretion.
1 Henry IV 5.4.119

1457 MACBETH [about Banquo]: 'Tis much he dares,
And to that dauntless temper of his mind,
He hath a wisdom that doth guide his valor
To act in safety.
Macbeth 3.1.49

1458 K. HENRY: Where they fear'd the death, they have borne life away;
and where they would be safe, they perish.
Henry V 4.1.171

1459 OTHELLO: Let's teach ourselves that honorable stop,
Not to outsport discretion.
Othello 2.3.2

1460 HAMLET: Let your own discretion be your tutor.
Hamlet 3.2.16

1461 POLONIUS: It is common for the younger sort
To lack discretion.
Hamlet 2.1.113

1462 MORTIMER [to Plantagenet]: With silence, nephew, be thou politic.
1 Henry VI 2.5.101

1463 PISTOL: Trust none;
For oaths are straws, men's faiths are wafer-cakes,
And Hold-fast is the only dog.
Henry V 2.3.50
[*wafer-cakes:* i.e. fragile; *Hold-fast:* an allusion to the proverb: Brag is a good dog, but Holdfast is a better.]

1464 REGAN [to Lear]: O sir, you are old,
Nature in you stands on the very verge
Of his confine. You should be rul'd and led
By some discretion that discerns your state
Better than you yourself.
King Lear 2.4.146

1465 KING [to Thomas, on dealing with Prince Henry]: Chide him for faults, and do it reverently,
When you perceive his blood inclin'd to mirth.
But, being moody, give him time and scope,
Till that his passions, like a whale on ground,
Confound themselves with working.
2 Henry IV 4.4.37

1466 MISTRESS QUICKLY: Old folks, you know, have discretion, as they say, and know the world.
Merry Wives of Windsor 2.2.129

Discrimination

1467 LEAR: Plate sin with gold,
And the strong lance of justice hurtless breaks;
Arm it in rags, a pigmy's straw does pierce it.
King Lear 4.6.165

1468 SHYLOCK [to Bassanio]: I will buy with you, sell with you, talk with you, walk with you, and so following; but I will not eat with you, drink with you, nor pray with you.
Merchant of Venice 1.3.35

Disdain

1469 Hot desire converts to cold disdain.
Rape of Lucrece 691

Disease

1470 PANDULPH: Before the curing of a strong disease,
Even in the instant of repair and health,
The fit is strongest.
King John 3.4.112

1471 LEAR: Where the greater malady is fix'd,
The lesser is scarce felt.
King Lear 3.4.8

1472 KING: Diseases desperate grown
By desperate appliance are reliev'd,
Or not at all.
Hamlet 4.3.9

1473 BEROWNE: Abstinence engenders maladies.
Love's Labor's Lost 4.3.291

1474 PROTEUS: In the sweetest bud
The eating canker dwells.
Two Gentlemen of Verona 1.1.42

1475 ARCHBISHOP: We are all diseas'd,
And with our surfeiting and wanton hours
Have brought ourselves into a burning fever,
And we must bleed for it.
2 Henry IV 4.1.54
[*bleed:* to be bled, as a medical treatment]

1476 LEAR [to Cordelia]: Thou art a soul in bliss, but I am bound
Upon a wheel of fire, that mine own tears
Do scald like molten lead.
King Lear 4.7.45

Disguise

1477 VIOLA [soliloquy]: Disguise, I see thou art a wickedness
Wherein the pregnant enemy does much.
How easy is it for the proper-false
In women's waxen hearts to set their forms!
Alas, our frailty is the cause, not we,
For such as we are made of, such we be.
Twelfth Night 2.2.27
[*pregnant enemy:* devil]

1478 LADY MACBETH [to Macbeth]: To beguile the time,
Look like the time; bear welcome in your eye,
Your hand, your tongue; look like th' innocent flower,
But be the serpent under't.
Macbeth 1.5.63

1479 IAGO [soliloquy]: When devils will the blackest sins put on,
They do suggest at first with heavenly shows.
Othello 2.3.351

Dishonesty

1480 CLOWN: Bid the dishonest man mend himself: if he mend, he is no longer dishonest; if he cannot, let the botcher mend him.

Twelfth Night 1.5.45

[*botcher:* a mender of old clothes and shoes]

Dishonor

1481 YORK: I rather would have lost my life betimes
Than bring a burthen of dishonor home.

2 Henry VI 3.1.297

[*burthen:* burden]

Dislike

1482 HORATIO: If your mind dislike any thing, obey it.

Hamlet 5.2.217

Disobedience

1483 GARDENER: Unruly children make their sire stoop.

Richard II 3.4.30

Disparity

1484 Crabbed age and youth cannot live together:
Youth is full of pleasance, age is full of care,
Youth like summer morn, age like winter weather,
Youth like summer brave, age like winter bare.
Youth is full of sport, age's breath is short,
Youth is nimble, age is lame,
Youth is hot and bold, age is weak and cold,
Youth is wild, and age is tame.
Age, I do abhor thee, youth, I adore thee.

The Passionate Pilgrim xii.1

Displeasure

1485 KING: Oft our displeasures, to ourselves unjust,
Destroy our friends, and after weep their dust;
Our own love waking cries to see what's done,
While shameful hate sleeps out the afternoon.

All's Well That Ends Well 5.3.63

1486 BASTARD [to King John, urging courage]: Run
To meet displeasure farther from the doors,
And grapple with him ere he comes so nigh.

King John 5.1.59

Dissension

1487 KING: Civil dissension is a viperous worm
That gnaws the bowels of the commonwealth.

1 Henry VI 3.1.72

1488 KING [on his state marriage to Margaret]: I feel such sharp dissension in my breast,
Such fierce alarums both of hope and fear,
As I am sick with working of my thoughts.

1 Henry VI 5.5.84

Dissimulation

1489 When my love swears that she is made of truth,
I do believe her, though I know she lies.

Sonnet 138

1490 FIRST GENTLEMAN: Not a courtier,
Although they wear their faces to the bent

Of the King's looks, hath a heart that
is not
Glad at the thing they scowl at.
Cymbeline 1.1.12

1491 MACBETH: Away, and mock the
time with fairest show:
False face must hide what false heart
doth know.
Macbeth 1.7.81

Distinction

1492 DUCHESS: That which in mean
men we entitle patience
Is pale cold cowardice in noble breasts.
Richard II 1.2.33

1493 TIMON: Faults that are rich are
fair.
Timon of Athens 1.2.13

1494 AGAMEMNON: Distinction, with a
broad and powerful fan,
Puffing at all, winnows the light away.
Troilus and Cressida 1.3.27

Distress

1495 Distress likes dumps when time
is kept with tears.
Rape of Lucrece 1127

1496 ORLANDO: The thorny point
Of bare distress hath ta'en from me the
show
Of smooth civility.
As You Like It 2.7.94

1497 QUEEN [to Hamlet]: Upon the
heat and flame of thy distemper
Sprinkle cool patience.
Hamlet 3.4.123

1498 How want of love tormenteth.
Venus and Adonis 202

Distrust

1499 CHARLES: One sudden foil shall
never breed distrust.
1 Henry VI 3.3.11
[*foil:* repulse]

1500 BASTARD [to King John]: Let not
the world see fear and sad distrust
Govern the motion of a kingly eye.
King John 5.1.46

1501 WARWICK [to Somerset]: I hold
it cowardice
To rest mistrustful where a noble heart
Hath pawn'd an open hand in sign of
love.
3 Henry VI 4.2.7

1502 K. HENRY: The bird that hath
been limed in a bush,
With trembling wings misdoubteth
every bush.
3 Henry VI 5.6.13
[Birdlime, a sticky substance, was used to
catch birds.]

Divinity

1503 HAMLET: There's a divinity that
shapes our ends,
Rough-hew them how we will.
Hamlet 5.2.10

1504 KING: There's such divinity doth
hedge a king
That treason can but peep to what it
would.
Hamlet 4.5.124

Division

1505 CORIOLANUS: When two
authorities are up,
Neither supreme, how soon confusion
May enter 'twixt the gap of both, and
take
The one by th' other.
Coriolanus 3.1.109

1506 DESDEMONA: My noble father,
I do perceive here a divided duty:
To you I am bound for life and educa-
tion;
My life and education both do learn
me
How to respect you; you are the lord of
duty;

I am hitherto your daughter. But here's
my husband.

Othello 1.3.180

Doctor

1507 CYMBELINE: By med'cine life
may be prolong'd, yet death
Will seize the doctor too.

Cymbeline 5.5.29

1508 TIMON: Trust not the physician,
His antidotes are poison, and he slays
Moe than you rob.

Timon of Athens 4.3.431

[*moe:* more]

1509 The patient dies while the physician sleeps.

Rape of Lucrece 904

1510 KENT [to Lear]: Kill thy physician, and the fee bestow
Upon thy foul disease.

King Lear 1.1.163

1511 RODERIGO: Have we a prescription to die, when death is our
physician.

Othello 1.3.309

1512 POSTHUMUS: Cur'd
By the sure physician, death.

Cymbeline 5.4.7

Dog

1513 LEAR: Thou hast seen a farmer's
dog bark at a beggar?
GLOUCESTER: Ay, sir.
LEAR: And the creature run from the
cur? There thou mightst behold the
great image of authority: a dog's
obey'd in office.

King Lear 4.6.154

1514 DOLPHIN: Coward dogs
Most spend their mouths when what
they seem to threaten
Runs far before them.

Henry V 2.4.68

1515 HAMLET: Let Hercules himself do
what he may,
The cat will mew, and dog will have
his day.

Hamlet 5.1.291

[That is, nothing under the sun can prevent
justice being done for his father's murder.]

1516 MACBETH [to his two hired
murderers]: Ay, in the catalogue ye
go for men,
As hounds and greyhounds, mongrels,
spaniels, curs,
Shoughs, water-rugs, and demi-wolves
are clipt
All by the name of dogs; the valued
file
Distinguishes the swift, the slow, the
subtle,
The house-keeper, the hunter, every
one,
According to the gift which bounteous
nature
Hath in him clos'd.

Macbeth 3.1.91

[*clipt:* called]

1517 KING [to Gardiner]: You play
the spaniel,
And think with wagging of your
tongue to win me.

Henry VIII 5.2.161

Dogmatism

1518 GRATIANO: There are a sort of
men whose visages
Do cream and mantle like a standing
pond,
And do a wilful stillness entertain,
With purpose to be dress'd in an
opinion
Of wisdom, gravity, profound conceit,
As who should say, "I am Sir Oracle,
And when I ope my lips let no dog
bark!"

Merchant of Venice 1.1.88

Domesticity

1519 DON PEDRO: In time the savage
bull doth bear the yoke.

Much Ado About Nothing 1.1.261

Doomsday

1520 HAMLET: What news?
ROSENCRANTZ: None, my lord, but
the world's grown honest.
HAMLET: Then is doomsday near.
Hamlet 2.2.236

1521 SECOND CLOWN: Who builds
stronger than a mason, a shipwright, or
a carpenter?
FIRST CLOWN: . . . When you are asked
this question next, say "a grave-
maker": The houses he makes lasts till
doomsday.
Hamlet 5.1.50

1522 HOTSPUR: Doomsday is near, die
all, die merrily.
1 Henry IV 4.1.134

Doubt

1523 LUCIO: Our doubts are traitors,
And make us lose the good we oft
might win,
By fearing to attempt.
Measure for Measure 1.4.77

1524 HECTOR: Modest doubt is call'd
The beacon of the wise, the tent that
searches
To th' bottom of the worst.
Troilus and Cressida 2.2.15
[*tent:* probe]

1525 OTHELLO: To be once in doubt
Is once to be resolv'd.
Othello 3.3.179

1526 PERICLES: Truth can never be
confirm'd enough,
Though doubts did ever sleep.
Pericles 5.1.201

1527 IMOGEN: Doubting things go ill
often hurts
More than to be sure they do.
Cymbeline 1.6.95

1528 ARCHBISHOP: To end one doubt
by death

Revives two greater in the heirs of
life.
2 Henry IV 4.1.197

1529 MACBETH [on the witches'
predictions]: I pull in resolution,
and begin
To doubt th' equivocation of the fiend
That lies like truth.
Macbeth 5.5.41

1530 YORK [soliloquy]: Steel thy fearful thoughts,
And change misdoubt to resolution;
Be that thou hop'st to be, or what
thou art
Resign to death.
2 Henry VI 3.1.331

1531 MESSENGER: But yet, madam—
CLEOPATRA: I do not like "but yet," it
does allay
The good precedence; fie upon "but
yet"!
"But yet" is as a jailer to bring forth
Some monstrous malefactor.
Antony and Cleopatra 2.5.49
[*good precedence:* i.e. the good news that
preceded the *but yet*]

Dove

1532 CLIFFORD: Cowards fight when
they can fly no further,
So doves do peck the falcon's piercing
talons.
3 Henry VI 1.4.40

1533 ENOBARBUS [soliloquy]: To be
furious
Is to be frighted out of fear, and in
that mood
The dove will peck the estridge.
Antony and Cleopatra 3.13.194

1534 CLIFFORD: Doves will peck in
safeguard of their brood.
3 Henry VI 2.2.18

Drama

1535 JAQUES: All the world's a stage,
And all the men and women merely
   players;
They have their exits and their
   entrances,
And one man in his time plays many
   parts.
                     As You Like It 2.7.139

Dreams

1536 PROSPERO: We are such stuff
As dreams are made on; and our little
   life
Is rounded with a sleep.
                     The Tempest 4.1.156

1537 HAMLET: O God, I could be
bounded in a nutshell, and count
myself a king of infinite space—were it
not that I have bad dreams.
GUILDENSTERN: Which dreams indeed
are ambition, for the very substance of
the ambitious is merely the shadow of
a dream.
HAMLET: A dream itself is but a
shadow.
                     Hamlet 2.2.254

1538 MERCUTIO: I talk of dreams,
Which are the children of an idle
   brain,
Begot of nothing but vain fantasy,
Which is as thin of substance as the
   air,
And more inconstant than the wind.
                     Romeo and Juliet 1.4.96

1539 MACBETH [soliloquy]: Wicked
   dreams abuse
The curtain'd sleep.
                     Macbeth 2.1.50

1540 CLARENCE: O, I have pass'd a
   miserable night,
So full of fearful dreams, of ugly
   sights,
That, as I am a Christian faithful man,
I would not spend another such a
   night

Though 'twere to buy a world of happy
days.
                     Richard III 1.4.2

1541 K. RICHARD: Let not our babbling dreams affright our souls.
                     Richard III 5.3.308

1542 IAGO: There are a kind of men,
   so loose of soul,
That in their sleep will mutter their
   affairs.
                     Othello 3.3.416

1543 SEBASTIAN: I am mad, or else
   this is a dream.
Let fancy still my sense in Lethe steep;
If it be thus to dream, still let me
   sleep!
                     Twelfth Night 4.1.61

1544 K. RICHARD [soliloquy]: Give me
   another horse! Bind up my wounds!
Have mercy, Jesu! Soft, I did but
   dream.
O coward conscience, how dost thou
   afflict me!
The lights burn blue. It is now dead
   midnight.
Cold fearful drops stand on my trembling flesh.
What do I fear? Myself? There's none
   else by.
                     Richard III 5.3.177

1545 What win I if I gain the thing I
   seek?
A dream, a breath, a froth of fleeting
   joy.
                     Rape of Lucrece 211

Dress

1546 BEVIS: The clothier means to
dress the commonwealth, and turn it,
and set a new nap upon it.
                     2 Henry VI 4.2.4

1547 SIMONIDES: Opinion's but a fool,
   that makes us scan
The outward habit by the inward man.
                     Pericles 2.2.56

1548 POLONIUS: Costly thy habit as thy purse can buy,
But not express'd in fancy, rich, not gaudy,
For the apparel oft proclaims the man.
Hamlet 1.3.70

1549 LAFEW [about Parolles]: The soul of this man is his clothes.
All's Well That Ends Well 2.5.43

1550 KING: Youth no less becomes
The light and careless livery that it wears
Than settled age his sables and his weeds,
Importing health and graveness.
Hamlet 4.7.78

1551 LEAR: Through tatter'd clothes small vices do appear;
Robes and furr'd gowns hide all. Plate sin with gold,
And the strong lance of justice hurtless breaks;
Arm it in rags, a pygmy's straw does pierce it.
King Lear 4.6.164

1552 PETRUCHIO [to Kate]: Our purses shall be proud, our garments poor,
For 'tis the mind that makes the body rich;
And as the sun breaks through the darkest clouds,
So honor peereth in the meanest habit.
Taming of the Shrew 4.3.173

1553 PETRUCHIO: What, is the jay more precious than the lark,
Because his feathers are more beautiful?
Or is the adder better than the eel,
Because his painted skin contents the eye?
Taming of the Shrew 4.3.175

Drowning

1554 'Tis double death to drown in ken of shore.
Rape of Lucrece 1114
[*ken:* sight]

Drunkenness

1555 CASSIO: O God, that men should put an enemy in their mouths to steal away their brains! that we should, with joy, pleasance, revel, and applause, transform ourselves into beasts!
Othello 2.3.289

1556 BEROWNE: One drunkard loves another of the name.
Love's Labor's Lost 4.3.48

1557 CASSIO: O thou invisible spirit of wine, if thou hast no name to be known by, let us call thee devil!
Othello 2.3.281

1558 CASSIO: I have very poor and unhappy brains for drinking. I could well wish courtesy would invent some other custom of entertainment.
Othello 2.3.33

1559 IAGO: Good wine is a good familiar creature, if it be well us'd.
Othello 2.3.309

1560 CASSIO: To be now a sensible man, by and by a fool, and presently a beast! O strange! Every inordinate cup is unbless'd, and the ingredient is a devil.
Othello 2.3.305

1561 APEMANTUS: Great men should drink with harness on their throats.
Timon of Athens 1.2.52

1562 OLIVIA: What is a drunken man like, fool?
CLOWN: Like a drown'd man, a fool, and a madman. One draught above heat makes him a fool, the second mads him, and a third drowns him.
Twelfth Night 1.5.130
[*above heat:* above the point at which the body grows warm with drinking]

1563 PORTER: It provokes the desire, but it takes away the performance.
Macbeth 2.3.29

1564 SONG: Come, thou monarch of
the vine,
Plumpy Bacchus with pink eyne!
In thy fats our cares be drown'd,
With thy grapes our hairs be crown'd!
Cup us, till the world go round,
Cup us, till the world go round!
Antony and Cleopatra 2.7.113
[*pink eyne:* half-shut eyes]

Duplicity

1565 FALSTAFF: I, I, I myself
sometimes, leaving the fear of God on
the left hand, and hiding mine honor
in my necessity, am fain to shuffle, to
hedge, and to lurch.
Merry Wives of Windsor 2.2.22

1566 BANQUO: Oftentimes, to win us
to our harm,
The instruments of darkness tell us
truths,
Win us with honest trifles, to betray 's
In deepest consequence.
Macbeth 1.3.123

1567 ANTONIO: The devil can cite
Scripture for his purpose.
Merchant of Venice 1.3.98

1568 IAGO [soliloquy]: When devils
will the blackest sins put on,
They do suggest at first with heavenly
shows.
Othello 2.3.351

1569 DUKE [soliloquy]: O, what may
man within him hide,
Though angel on the outward side!
Measure for Measure 3.2.271

Duty

1570 THESEUS: Never any thing can be
amiss,
When simpleness and duty tender it.
Midsummer Night's Dream 5.1.83

1571 SILVIA: Duty never yet did want
his meed.
Two Gentlemen of Verona 2.4.112
[*want his meed:* lack his reward]

1572 WOLSEY: We must not stint
Our necessary actions in the fear
To cope malicious censures.
Henry VIII 1.2.76

1573 CLOTEN: Be but duteous, and
true preferment shall tender itself to
thee.
Cymbeline 3.5.153

1574 K. HENRY: Every subject's duty
is the King's, but every subject's soul is
his own.
Henry V 4.1.176

1575 KATHERINA: Such a duty as the
subject owes the prince,
Even such a woman oweth to her
husband.
Taming of the Shrew 5.2.155

1576 DESDEMONA: My noble father,
I do perceive here a divided duty:
To you I am bound for life and educa-
tion;
My life and education both do learn
me
How to respect you; you are the lord of
duty;
I am hitherto your daughter. But here's
my husband.
Othello 1.3.181

1577 KENT [to Lear]: Think'st thou
that duty shall have dread to speak
When power to flattery bows?
King Lear 1.1.147

1578 ARMADO: The words of Mercury
are harsh after the songs of Apollo.
Love's Labor's Lost 5.2.930
[The reference is to Mercury as the god of
eloquence and, in antithesis, to Apollo as
the god of music.]

1579 Fleet-wing'd duty with thought's
feathers flies.
Rape of Lucrece 1216

Dwarf

1580 AGAMEMNON: A stirring dwarf we do allowance give
Before a sleeping giant.
Troilus and Cressida 2.3.137

Eagles

1581 TAMORA: The eagle suffers little birds to sing,
And is not careful what they mean thereby,
Knowing that with the shadow of his wings
He can at pleasure stint their melody.
Titus Andronicus 4.4.83

1582 Gnats are unnoted wheresoe'er they fly,
But eagles gaz'd upon with every eye.
Rape of Lucrece 1014

Ear

1583 APEMANTUS [soliloquy]: O that men's ears should be
To counsel deaf, but not to flattery!
Timon of Athens 1.2.249

1584 Will is deaf and hears no heedful friends.
Rape of Lucrece 495

1585 HAMLET: A knavish speech sleeps in a foolish ear.
Hamlet 4.2.22

1586 By our ears our hearts oft tainted be.
Rape of Lucrece 38

1587 To see sad sights moves more than hear them told.
Rape of Lucrece 1324

1588 BEROWNE: Honest plain words best pierce the ear of grief.
Love's Labor's Lost 5.2.753

1589 ROSALINE: A jest's prosperity lies in the ear
Of him that hears it, never in the tongue
Of him that makes it.
Love's Labor's Lost 5.2.861

1590 BRABANTIO: I never yet did hear That the bruis'd heart was pierced through the ear.
Othello 1.3.218

1591 HERMIA: Dark night, that from the eye his function takes,
The ear more quick of apprehension makes;
Wherein it doth impair the seeing sense,
It pays the hearing double recompense.
Midsummer Night's Dream 3.2.177

1592 To hear with eyes belongs to love's fine wit.
Sonnet 23

1593 BEROWNE: A lover's ears will hear the lowest sound.
Love's Labor's Lost 4.3.332

1594 Mine ears, that to your wanton talk attended,
Do burn themselves for having so offended.
Venus and Adonis 809

1595 POLONIUS: Give every man thine ear, but few thy voice,
Take each man's censure, but reserve thy judgment.
Hamlet 1.3.68

1596 TROILUS: My election Is led on in the conduct of my will,
My will kindled by mine eyes and ears,
Two traded pilots 'twixt the dangerous shores
Of will and judgment.
Troilus and Cressida 2.2.61
[*election:* choice; *traded pilots:* intermediaries constantly going back and forth]

Earth

1597 HAMLET: This goodly frame, the earth, seems to me a sterile promontory; this most excellent canopy, the air, look you, this brave o'erhanging firmament, this majestical roof fretted with golden fire, why, it appeareth nothing to me but a foul and pestilent congregation of vapors.
Hamlet 2.2.298

1598 The earth can have but earth, which is his due,
My spirit is thine, the better part of me.
Sonnet 74

Earthquake

1599 HOTSPUR: Diseased nature oftentimes breaks forth
In strange eruptions; oft the teeming earth
Is with a kind of colic pinch'd and vex'd
By the imprisoning of unruly wind
Within her womb, which, for enlargement striving,
Shakes the old beldam earth, and topples down
Steeples and moss-grown towers.
1 Henry IV 3.1.26

Eating

1600 ABBESS: Unquiet meals make ill digestions.
Comedy of Errors 5.1.74

1601 ARCITE: Hunger needs no sauce.
Two Noble Kinsmen 3.3.24

1602 NERISSA: They are as sick that surfeit with too much as they that starve with nothing.
Merchant of Venice 1.2.5

1603 LADY MACBETH: To feed were best at home;

From thence, the sauce to meat is ceremony,
Meeting were bare without it.
Macbeth 3.4.34

1604 FOOL: He that keeps nor crust nor crumb,
Weary of all, shall want some.
King Lear 1.4.198

1605 LONGAVILLE: Fat paunches have lean pates; and dainty bits
Make rich the ribs, but bankrout quite the wits.
Love's Labor's Lost 1.1.26
[*bankrout:* bankrupt]

1606 GAUNT: With eager feeding food doth choke the feeder.
Richard II 2.1.37

1607 MACBETH: Now good digestion wait on appetite,
And health on both!
Macbeth 3.4.37

1608 LYSANDER: A surfeit of the sweetest things
The deepest loathing to the stomach brings.
Midsummer Night's Dream 2.2.137

1609 TRANIO: Do as adversaries do in law,
Strive mightily, but eat and drink as friends.
Taming of the Shrew 1.2.276

1610 CONSTABLE [about English soldiers]: Give them great meals of beef and iron and steel, they will eat like wolves and fight like devils.
Henry V 3.7.149

1611 HOSTESS [to Chief Justice about Falstaff]: He hath eaten me out of house and home, he hath put all my substance into that fat belly of his.
2 Henry IV 2.1.74

Echo

1612 VIOLA [to Olivia]: Hallow your name to the reverberate hills,
And make the babbling gossip of the air
Cry out "Olivia!"
Twelfth Night 1.5.272
[*hallow:* halloo, shout]

1613 MURELLUS: The replication of your sounds.
Julius Caesar 1.1.46

Economy

1614 K. HENRY: I may conquer fortune's spite
By living low, where fortune cannot hurt me.
3 Henry VI 4.6.19

1615 FALSTAFF: I can get no remedy against this consumption of the purse; borrowing only lingers and lingers it out, but the disease is incurable.
2 Henry IV 1.2.236

Ecstasy

1616 HAMLET: Madness would not err, Nor sense to ecstasy was ne'er so thrall'd
But it reserv'd some quantity of choice
To serve in such a difference.
Hamlet 3.4.73
[*thrall'd:* enslaved; *quantity of choice:* some power to choose]

1617 QUEEN [to Hamlet, on his father's ghost]: This is the very coinage of your brain,
This bodiless creation ecstasy
Is very cunning in.
Hamlet 3.4.137

1618 PERICLES: O Helicanus, strike me, honored sir,
Give me a gash, put me to present pain,

Lest this great sea of joys rushing upon me
O'erbear the shores of my mortality,
And drown me with their sweetness.
Pericles 5.1.190

Education

1619 BEROWNE: Study is like the heaven's glorious sun,
That will not be deep search'd with saucy looks;
Small have continual plodders ever won,
Save base authority from others' books.
Love's Labor's Lost 1.1.84

1620 REGAN: To willful men,
The injuries that they themselves procure
Must be their schoolmasters.
King Lear 2.4.302

1621 DOGBERRY: To be a well-favor'd man is the gift of fortune, but to write and read comes by nature.
Much Ado About Nothing 3.3.14
[*well-favor'd:* good-looking]

1622 DON PEDRO: In time the savage bull doth bear the yoke.
Much Ado About Nothing 1.1.261

Eel

1623 PETRUCHIO: Is the adder better than the eel,
Because his painted skin contents the eye?
Taming of the Shrew 4.3.177

Effect

1624 BELARIUS: Defect of judgment Is oft the cause of fear.
Cymbeline 4.2.111

1625 KENT: Good effects may spring from words of love.
King Lear 1.1.185

Effeminacy

1626 PATROCLUS: A woman impudent
and manish grown
Is not more loathed than an effeminate
man.
Troilus and Cressida 3.3.217

Efficiency

1627 GARDENER: Superfluous branches
We lop away, that bearing boughs may
live.
Richard II 3.4.63

Effort

1628 LEAR: Nothing will come of
nothing.
King Lear 1.1.90

Egotist

1629 FALSTAFF: I have a whole school
of tongues in this belly of mine, and
not a tongue of them all speaks any
other word but my name.
2 Henry IV 4.3.18

1630 MENENIUS [about Martius]: He
wants nothing of a god but eternity
and a heaven to throne in.
Coriolanus 5.4.23

Elephant

1631 ULYSSES: The elephant hath
joints, but none for courtesy; his legs
are legs for necessity, not for flexure.
Troilus and Cressida 2.3.111

Eloquence

1632 VOLUMNIA: Action is eloquence.
Coriolanus 3.2.76

1633 ARMADO: The words of Mercury
are harsh after the songs of Apollo.
Love's Labor's Lost 5.2.930
[The reference is to Mercury as the god of
eloquence and, in antithesis, to Apollo as
the god of music.]

1634 CASSIUS [to Antony]: But for
your words, they rob the Hybla bees,
And leave them honeyless.
Julius Caesar 5.1.35

1635 BEROWNE: Taffata phrases, silken
terms precise,
Three-pil'd hyperboles, spruce affec-
tion,
Figures pedantical.
Love's Labor's Lost 5.2.406

1636 CANTERBURY [about King
Henry]: When he speaks,
The air, a charter'd libertine, is still,
And the mute wonder lurketh in men's
ears
To steal his sweet and honeyed
sentences.
Henry V 1.1.47

1637 SUFFOLK: Words sweetly plac'd
and modestly directed.
1 Henry VI 5.3.179

1638 FIRST GENTLEMAN [concerning
Leontes' and Camillo's reaction when
Perdita is revealed as the King's lost
daughter]: There was speech in their
dumbness, language in their very gesture.
Winter's Tale 5.2.13

Empathy

1639 ANTONY [to servant, weeping at
Caesar's death]: Passion, I see, is
catching; for mine eyes,
Seeing those beads of sorrow stand in
thine,
Begin to water.
Julius Caesar 3.1.282

Employment

1640 HAMLET: The hand of little
employment hath the daintier sense.
Hamlet 5.1.69

Emulation

1641 ULYSSES: Emulation hath a thou-
sand sons
That one by one pursue. If you give
way,
Or hedge aside from the direct forth-
right,
Like to an ent'red tide, they all rush by
And leave you hindmost.
Troilus and Cressida 3.3.156
[*forthright:* straight path]

1642 ARTEMIDORUS: My heart laments
that virtue cannot live
Out of the teeth of emulation.
Julius Caesar 2.3.14

1643 ULYSSES: The general's disdain'd
By him one step below, he by the
next,
That next by him beneath; so every
step,
Exampled by the first pace that is sick
Of his superior, grows to an envious
fever
Of pale and bloodless emulation.
Troilus and Cressida 1.3.129

End

1644 PRINCE: The end of life cancels
all bands.
1 Henry IV 3.2.157
[*bands:* bonds, debts]

1645 HELENA: All's well that ends
well!
All's Well That Ends Well 4.4.35

1646 HELENA: What e'er the course,
the end is the renown.
All's Well That Ends Well 4.4.36

1647 HECTOR: The end crowns all.
Troilus and Cressida 4.5.224

1648 PRINCE: Let the end try the man.
2 Henry IV 2.2.47

1649 GAUNT: More are men's ends
mark'd than their lives before.
Richard II 2.1.11

1650 REIGNIER: Delays have dangerous
ends.
1 Henry VI 3.2.33

1651 BULLINGBROOK: I regreet
The daintiest last, to make the end
most sweet.
Richard II 1.3.68
[*regreet:* greet, salute]

1652 BRUTUS [to Cassius, on the eve
of battle]: O that a man might know
The end of this day's business ere it
come!
But it sufficeth that the day will end,
And then the end is known.
Julius Caesar 5.1.122

1653 WOLSEY [to Cromwell]: Let all
the ends thou aim'st at be thy
country's,
Thy God's, and truth's.
Henry VIII 3.2.447

1654 HAMLET [soliloquy]: To die, to
sleep—
No more, and by a sleep to say we end
The heart-ache and the thousand
natural shocks
That flesh is heir to; 'tis a consum-
mation
Devoutly to be wish'd.
Hamlet 3.1.62

Endurance

1655 PAGE: What cannot be eschew'd
must be embrac'd.
Merry Wives of Windsor 5.5.237

1656 Q. MARGARET: What cannot be
avoided,
'Twere childish weakness to lament or
fear.
3 Henry VI 5.4.37

1657 K. HENRY: Let me embrace thee, sour adversities,
For wise men say it is the wisest course.
3 Henry VI 3.1.24

1658 LEONATO: There was never yet philosopher
That could endure the toothache patiently,
However they have writ the style of gods,
And make a push at chance and sufferance.
Much Ado About Nothing 5.1.35

1659 CLOWN: Things may serve long, but not serve ever.
All's Well That Ends Well 2.2.59

1660 NATHANIEL: Many can brook the weather that love not the wind.
Love's Labor's Lost 4.2.33

Enemy

1661 DOLPHIN: 'Tis best to weigh The enemy more mighty than he seems.
Henry V 2.4.43

1662 COUNTESS: Be able for thine enemy
Rather in power than use.
All's Well That Ends Well 1.1.65

1663 KING [to Wolsey]: You have many enemies, that know not
Why they are so, but, like to village curs,
Bark when their fellows do.
Henry VIII 2.4.159

1664 K. HENRY: They are our outward consciences.
Henry V 4.1.8

1665 PLAYER KING: Who in want a hollow friend doth try,
Directly seasons him his enemy.
Hamlet 3.2.208

1666 VALENTINE [to Proteus]: O time most accurst!

'Mongst all foes that a friend should be the worst!
Two Gentlemen of Verona 5.4.71

1667 GLOUCESTER: 'Tis death to me to be at enmity;
I hate it, and desire all good men's love.
Richard III 2.1.61

England

1668 HASTINGS: England is safe, if true within itself.
3 Henry VI 4.1.40

1669 RAMBURES: That island of England breeds very valiant creatures; their mastiffs are of unmatchable courage.
Henry V 3.7.140

1670 GAUNT: This royal throne of kings, this sceptred isle,
This earth of majesty, this seat of Mars,
This other Eden, demi-paradise,
This fortress built by Nature for herself
Against infection and the hand of war,
This happy breed of men, this little world,
This precious stone set in the silver sea,
Which serves it in the office of a wall,
Or as a moat defensive to a house,
Against the envy of less happier lands;
This blessed plot, this earth, this realm, this England.
Richard II 2.1.40

1671 GAUNT: England, bound in with the triumphant sea,
Whose rocky shore beats back the envious siege
Of wat'ry Neptune.
Richard II 2.1.61

1672 BASTARD: This England never did, nor never shall,
Lie at the proud foot of a conqueror.
King John 5.7.112

1673 FALSTAFF: It was always yet the trick of our English nation, if they

have a good thing, to make it too
common.
                    2 Henry IV 1.2.214

1674 CHORUS: O England! model to
thy inward greatness,
Like little body with a mighty heart.
                    Henry V Prologue 2.16

1675 BASTARD: Come the three corners
of the world in arms,
And we shall shock them. Nought
shall make us rue,
If England to itself do rest but true.
                    King John 5.7.116

1676 GAUNT: This land of such dear
souls, this dear dear land,
Dear for her reputation through the
world.
                    Richard II 2.1.57

Enjoyment

1677 FRIAR: What we have we prize
not to the worth
Whiles we enjoy it, but being lack'd
and lost,
Why then we rack the value; then we
find
The virtue that possession would not
show us
Whiles it was ours.
                    Much Ado About Nothing 4.1.218

Ennui

1678 KING: I am wrapp'd in dismal
thinkings.
                    All's Well That Ends Well 5.3.128

Entertainment

1679 POLONIUS: Do not dull thy palm
with entertainment.
                    Hamlet 1.3.64

Enthusiasm

1680 GAUNT [on King Richard]: His
rash fierce blaze of riot cannot last,
For violent fires soon burn out themselves;
Small show'rs last long, but sudden
storms are short.
                    Richard II 2.1.33

Enticement

1681 BANQUO: Oftentimes, to win us
to our harm,
The instruments of darkness tell us
truths,
Win us with honest trifles, to betray 's
In deepest consequence.
                    Macbeth 1.3.123

Envy

1682 ORLANDO [on the marriage of
Oliver to Celia]: O, how bitter a thing
it is to look into happiness through
another man's eyes!
                    As You Like It 5.2.43

1683 CRANMER: Men that make
Envy and crooked malice nourishment
Dare bite the best.
                    Henry VIII 5.2.78

1684 TROILUS: What envy can say
worst shall be a mock for his truth.
                    Troilus and Cressida 3.2.96

1685 EXETER [soliloquy]: When envy
breeds unkind division:
There comes the ruin, there begins
confusion.
                    1 Henry VI 4.1.193

1686 CAESAR [about Cassius]: Such
men as he be never at heart's ease
Whiles they behold a greater than
themselves,
And therefore are they very dangerous.
                    Julius Caesar 1.2.208

1687 ULYSSES: The general's disdain'd
By him one step below, he by the
    next,
The next by him beneath; so every
    step,
Exampled by the first pace that is sick
Of his superior, grows to an envious
    fever.
                Troilus and Cressida 1.3.129

Epilogue

1688 ROSALIND: If it be true that good
wine needs no bush, 'tis true that a
good play needs no epilogue. Yet to
good wine they do use good bushes;
and good plays prove the better by the
help of good epilogues.
            As You Like It, Epilogue 1.3

Equality

1689 HAMLET: Your worm is your only
emperor for diet: we fat all creatures
else to fat us, and we fat ourselves for
maggots; your fat king and your lean
beggar is but variable service, two
dishes, but to one table — that's the
end.
KING: Alas, alas!
HAMLET: A man may fish with the
worm that hath eat of a king, and eat
of the fish that hath fed of that worm.
KING: What dost thou mean by this?
HAMLET: Nothing but to show you
how a king may go a progress through
the guts of a beggar.
                            Hamlet 4.3.21

1690 BELARIUS: Mean and mighty,
    rotting
Together, have one dust.
                Cymbeline 4.2.246

1691 ANTONY: Equality of two
    domestic powers
Breeds scrupulous faction.
            Antony and Cleopatra 1.3.47

1692 K. HENRY [incognito, to some
soldiers]: The King is but a man, as I

am. The violet smells to him as it doth
to me; the element shows to him as it
doth to me; all his senses have but
human conditions. His ceremonies laid
by, in his nakedness he appears but a
man; and though his affections are
higher mounted than ours, yet when
they stoop, they stoop with the like
wing.
                            Henry V 4.1.101

1693 GUIDERIUS: Thersites' body is as
    good as Ajax',
When neither are alive.
                Cymbeline 4.2.252

1694 GUIDERIUS [song]: Golden lads
    and girls all must,
As chimney-sweepers, come to dust.
                Cymbeline 4.2.263

1695 FIRST KNIGHT [to Pericles]: Con-
tend not, sir, for we are gentlemen
Have neither in our hearts nor outward
    eyes
Envied the great, nor shall the low
    despise.
                            Pericles 2.3.24

1696 CELIA [to Rosalind]: Let us sit
and mock the good huswife Fortune
from her wheel, that her gifts may
henceforth be bestow'd equally.
                As You Like It 1.2.31
[*huswife:* housewife]

Equanimity

1697 OLIVIA: To be generous,
guiltless, and of free disposition, is to
take those things for bird-bolts that
you deem cannon-bullets.
                Twelfth Night 1.5.91
[*bird-bolts:* blunt-headed arrows for
shooting birds]

1698 HAMLET [to Horatio]: Thou hast
    been
As one in suff'ring all that suffers
    nothing,

A man that Fortune's buffets and
rewards
Hast ta'en with equal thanks.

Hamlet 3.2.65

Equivocation

1699 MACBETH [on the witches'
predictions]: I pull in resolution,
and begin
To doubt th' equivocation of the fiend
That lies like truth.

Macbeth 5.5.41

1700 MACBETH [on the witches'
predictions]: Be these juggling fiends
no more believ'd,
That palter with us in a double sense,
That keep the word of promise to our
ear,
And break it to our hope.

Macbeth 5.8.19

1701 HAMLET: We must speak by the
card, or equivocation will undo us.

Hamlet 5.1.137

Error

1702 CRESSIDA: The error of our eye
directs our mind.
What error leads must err.

Troilus and Cressida 5.2.110

1703 MESSALA: O hateful error, melancholy's child,
Why dost thou show to the apt
thoughts of men
The things that are not? O error, soon
conceiv'd,
Thou never com'st unto a happy birth,
But kill'st the mother that engend'red
thee!

Julius Caesar 5.3.67

1704 PATROCLUS: Omission to do what
is necessary
Seals a commission to a blank of
danger.

Troilus and Cressida 3.3.230

1705 ALBANY: Striving to better, oft
we mar what's well.

King Lear 1.4.346

1706 PERICLES: Death remembered
should be like a mirror,
Who tells us life's but breath, to trust
it error.

Pericles 1.1.45

Escape

1707 DROMIO SYRACUSE: As from a
bear a man would run for life,
So fly I from her that would be my
wife.

Comedy of Errors 3.2.154

1708 DON PEDRO [about Beatrice]:
Look! here she comes.
BENEDICK [as she approaches]: Will
your Grace command me any service to
the world's end? I will go on the
slightest arrand now to the Antipodes
that you can devise to send me on; I
will fetch you a toothpicker now from
the furthest inch of Asia, bring you the
length of Prester John's foot, fetch you
a hair of the Great Cham's beard, do
you any embassage to the Pigmies,
rather than hold three words' conference with this harpy.

Much Ado About Nothing 2.1.263
[*arrand:* errand]

Eternity

1709 QUEEN: All that lives must die,
Passing through nature to eternity.

Hamlet 1.2.72

1710 What win I if I gain the thing I
seek?
A dream, a breath, a froth of fleeting
joy.
Who buys a minute's mirth to wail a
week?
Or sells eternity to get a toy?

Rape of Lucrece 211

1711 ORLANDO: For ever and a day.
As You Like It 4.1.145

Etiquette

1712 ANGELO [soliloquy]: O place, O form,
How oft dost thou with thy case, thy habit,
Wrench awe from fools, and tie the wiser souls
To thy false seeming!
Measure for Measure 2.4.12

Eunuch

1713 CLOTEN: The voice of unpav'd eunuch . . . can never amend.
Cymbeline 2.3.30

Evening

1714 CLIFFORD: Now Phaeton hath tumbled from his car,
And made an evening at the noontide prick.
3 Henry VI 1.4.33

Evidence

1715 WARWICK: Who finds the heifer dead and bleeding fresh,
And sees fast by a butcher with an axe,
But will suspect 'twas he that made the slaughter?
2 Henry VI 3.2.188

Evil

1716 ANTONY: The evil that men do lives after them,
The good is oft interred with their bones.
Julius Caesar 3.2.75

1717 GRIFFITH: Men's evil manners live in brass, their virtues
We write in water.
Henry VIII 4.2.45

1718 FRIAR LAWRENCE [soliloquy]:
Nought so vile that on the earth doth live
But to the earth some special good doth give.
Romeo and Juliet 2.3.17

1719 K. HENRY: There is some soul of goodness in things evil,
Would men observingly distil it out;
For our bad neighbor makes us early stirrers,
Which is both healthful and good husbandry.
Besides, they are our outward consciences
And preachers to us all, admonishing
That we should dress us fairly for our end.
Thus may we gather honey from the weed,
And make a moral of the devil himself.
Henry V 4.1.4

1720 LUCIANA: Ill deeds is doubled with an evil word.
Comedy of Errors 3.2.20

1721 LADY MACDUFF: I am in this earthly world—where to do harm
Is often laudable, to do good sometime
Accounted dangerous folly.
Macbeth 4.2.75

1722 APEMANTUS: Who lives that's not depraved or depraves?
Timon of Athens 1.2.140

1723 CASSIUS [to Brutus]: Of your philosophy you make no use,
If you give place to accidental evils.
Julius Caesar 4.3.145

1724 BASSANIO: In law, what plea so tainted and corrupt
But, being season'd with a gracious voice,
Obscures the show of evil?
Merchant of Venice 3.2.75

1725 KING: Ah, what a sign it is of evil life,

Where death's approach is seen so terrible!

2 Henry VI 3.3.5

1726 CLAUDIO: Our natures do pursue,
Like rats that ravin down their proper bane,
A thirsty evil, and when we drink we die.

Measure for Measure 1.2.128

[*ravin down:* devour greedily; *proper bane:* rat poison]

1727 LUCIANA: No evil lost is wail'd when it is gone.

Comedy of Errors 4.2.24

1728 QUEEN: Now 'tis spring, and weeds are shallow-rooted;
Suffer them now, and they'll o'ergrow the garden,
And choke the herbs for want of husbandry.

2 Henry VI 3.1.31

1729 K. HENRY: Didst thou never hear
That things ill got had ever bad success?

3 Henry VI 2.2.45

1730 In men, as in a rough-grown grove, remain
Cave-keeping evils that obscurely sleep.

Rape of Lucrece 1249

1731 Unruly blasts wait on the tender spring,
Unwholesome weeds take root with precious flow'rs,
The adder hisses where the sweet birds sing,
What virtue breeds iniquity devours.

Rape of Lucrece 869

1732 Unstain'd thoughts do seldom dream on evil.

Rape of Lucrece 87

1733 PANDULPH: Evils that take leave,
On their departure most of all show evil.

King John 3.4.114

1734 ENOBARBUS [soliloquy]: I have done ill,
Of which I do accuse myself so sorely
That I will joy no more.

Antony and Cleopatra 4.6.17

1735 HAMLET [soliloquy]: Foul deeds will rise,
Though all the earth o'erwhelm them, to men's eyes.

Hamlet 1.2.256

1736 GLOUCESTER: The world is grown so bad
That wrens make prey where eagles dare not perch.

Richard III 1.3.69

1737 HAMLET: There is nothing either good or bad, but thinking makes it so.

Hamlet 2.2.249

1738 ROMEO [soliloquy]: O mischief, thou art swift
To enter in the thoughts of desperate men!

Romeo and Juliet 5.1.35

1739 Two loves I have, of comfort and despair,
That like two spirits do suggest me still:
My better angel is a man (right fair),
My worser spirit a woman (color'd ill).
To win me soon to hell, my female evil
Tempteth my better angel from my side;
And would corrupt my saint to be a devil,
Wooing his purity with her fair pride.
And whether that my angel be turn'd fiend,
Suspect I may (yet not directly tell):
For being both to me, both to each friend,
I guess one angel in another's hell:
The truth I shall not know, but live in doubt,
Till my bad angel fire my good one out.

The Passionate Pilgrim ii.1

Example

1740 ANGELO [soliloquy]: Thieves for their robbery have authority
When judges steal themselves.
Measure for Measure 2.2.175

1741 FALSTAFF [soliloquy]: It is certain that either wise bearing or ignorant carriage is caught, as men take diseases, one of another; therefore let men take heed of their company.
2 Henry IV 5.1.75

1742 PORTIA: It is a good divine that follows his own instructions; I can easier teach twenty what were good to be done, than to be one of the twenty to follow mine own teaching.
Merchant of Venice 1.2.14

1743 Princes are the glass, the school, the book,
Where subjects' eyes do learn, do read, do look.
Rape of Lucrece 615
[*glass:* mirror]

1744 LADY PERCY [on Percy]: He was indeed the glass
Wherein the noble youth did dress themselves.
2 Henry IV 2.3.21

1745 KING: Things done well
And with a care exempt themselves from fear;
Things done without example, in their issue
Are to be fear'd.
Henry VIII 1.2.88

1746 BASTARD [to King John]: Be stirring as the time, be fire with fire,
Threaten the threat'ner, and outface the brow
Of bragging horror; so shall inferior eyes,
That borrow their behaviors from the great,
Grow great by your example and put on
The dauntless spirit of resolution.
King John 5.1.48

1747 CANTERBURY: So work the honey-bees,
Creatures that by a rule in nature teach
The art of order to a peopled kingdom.
Henry V 1.2.187

1748 PORTIA: How far that little candle throws his beams!
So shines a good deed in a naughty world.
Merchant of Venice 5.1.90

Excellence

1749 DON PEDRO: It is the witness still of excellency
To put a strange face on his own perfection.
Much Ado About Nothing 2.3.46

1750 AGRIPPA: Graces speak
That which none else can utter.
Antony and Cleopatra 2.2.129

Excelsior

1751 GLOUCESTER: 'Tis but a base ignoble mind
That mounts no higher than a bird can soar.
2 Henry VI 2.1.13

1752 GLOUCESTER: Fearless minds climb soonest unto crowns.
3 Henry VI 4.7.62

Exception

1753 MESSENGER: But yet, madam—
CLEOPATRA: I do not like "but yet," it does allay
The good precedence; fie upon "but yet"!
"But yet" is as a jailer to bring forth
Some monstrous malefactor.
Antony and Cleopatra 2.5.49
[*good precedence:* i.e. the good news that preceded the *but yet*]

Excess

1754 COUNTESS: If the living be enemy to grief, the excess makes it soon mortal.
All's Well That Ends Well 1.1.57

1755 SALISBURY: To gild refined gold, to paint the lily,
To throw a perfume on the violet,
To smooth the ice, or add another hue
Unto the rainbow, or with taper-light
To seek the beauteous eye of heaven to garnish,
Is wasteful and ridiculous excess.
King John 4.2.11

1756 LEAR: Allow not nature more than nature needs.
King Lear 2.4.266

1757 NERISSA: They are sick that surfeit with too much as they that starve with nothing.
Merchant of Venice 1.2.5

1758 CLAUDIO: As surfeit is the father of much fast,
So every scope by the immoderate use
Turns to restraint.
Measure for Measure 1.2.126
[*scope:* freedom]

1759 LYSANDER: A surfeit of the sweetest things
The deepest loathing to the stomach brings.
Midsummer Night's Dream 2.2.137

1760 CASSIO [on wine]: Every inordinate cup is unbless'd, and the ingredient is a devil.
Othello 2.3.307

1761 OTHELLO: Let's teach ourselves that honorable stop,
Not to outsport discretion.
Othello 2.3.2

1762 NERISSA: Superfluity comes sooner by white hairs, but competency lives longer.
Merchant of Venice 1.2.9

1763 GLOUCESTER: Distribution should undo excess,
And each man have enough.
King Lear 4.1.70

1764 DUKE: If music be the food of love, play on,
Give me excess of it; that surfeiting,
The appetite may sicken, and so die.
Twelfth Night 1.1.2

1765 FRIAR LAWRENCE: Violent delights have violent ends,
And in their triumph die, like fire and powder,
Which as they kiss consume.
Romeo and Juliet 2.6.9

1766 ROSALIND: Can one desire too much of a good thing?
As You Like It 4.1.123

Excuse

1767 GLOUCESTER: A staff is quickly found to beat a dog.
2 Henry VI 3.1.171

1768 FIRST OUTLAW: We cite our faults
That they may hold excus'd our lawless lives.
Two Gentlemen of Verona 4.1.51

1769 PEMBROKE: Oftentimes excusing of a fault
Doth make the fault the worse by th' excuse:
As patches set upon a little breach
Discredit more in hiding of the fault
Than did the fault before it was so patch'd.
King John 4.2.30

1770 EDMUND [soliloquy]: This is the excellent foppery of the world, that when we are sick in fortune—often the surfeits of our own behavior—we make guilty of our disasters the sun, the moon, and stars, as if we were villains on necessity, fools by heavenly compulsion, knaves, thieves, and treachers

by spherical predominance; drunkards, liars, and adulterers, by an enforc'd obedience of planetary influence; and all that we are evil in, by a divine thrusting on. An admirable evasion of whoremaster man, to lay his goatish disposition on the change of a star!
King Lear 1.2.118

[*goatish:* lecherous]

1771 AUFIDIUS: I must excuse
What cannot be amended.
Coriolanus 4.7.11

1772 IMOGEN: Why should excuse be born or ere begot?
Cymbeline 3.2.65

Execution

1773 SILVIUS: The common executioner,
Whose heart th' accustom'd sight of death makes hard,
Falls not the axe upon the humbled neck
But first begs pardon.
As You Like It 3.5.3

1774 PROVOST: I have seen
When, after execution, judgment hath Repented o'er his doom.
Measure for Measure 2.2.10

Exercise

1775 BELARIUS: Weariness
Can snore upon the flint, when resty sloth
Finds the down pillow hard.
Cymbeline 3.6.33

Exile

1776 ROMEO: Exile hath more terror in his look,
Much more than death.
Romeo and Juliet 3.3.13

1777 ROMEO: Exile is death.
Romeo and Juliet 3.3.20

1778 ROMEO: "Banished"
Is death misterm'd.
Romeo and Juliet 3.3.20

1779 BULLINGBROOK [on his years in exile]: How long a time lies in one little word!
Four lagging winters and four wanton springs
End in a word: such is the breath of kings.
Richard II 1.3.213

Expectation

1780 HELENA: Oft expectation fails, and most oft there
Where it most promises; and oft it hits
Where hope is coldest, and despair most fits.
All's Well That Ends Well 2.1.142

1781 PAINTER: Promising is the very air o' th' time;
It opens the eyes of expectation.
Performance is ever duller for his act.
Timon of Athens 5.1.22

1782 TROILUS: I am giddy; expectation whirls me round;
Th' imaginary relish is so sweet
That it enchants my sense.
Troilus and Cressida 3.2.18

1783 JULIET [soliloquy]: So tedious is this day
As is the night before some festival
To an impatient child that hath new robes
And may not wear them.
Romeo and Juliet 3.2.28

1784 CAESAR: Expectation fainted, Longing for what it had not.
Antony and Cleopatra 3.6.47

1785 THIRD CITIZEN: Untimely storms make men expect a dearth.
Richard III 2.3.35

1786 CHORUS: Now sits Expectation in the air.
Henry V, Prologue 2.8

Expediency

1787 FIRST STRANGER: Policy sits above conscience.
Timon of Athens 3.2.87

1788 MACBETH: Th' expedition of my violent love
Outrun the pauser, reason.
Macbeth 2.3.110

Experience

1789 ROMEO: He jests at scars that never felt a wound.
Romeo and Juliet 2.2.1

1790 REGAN: To wilful men,
The injuries that they themselves procure
Must be their schoolmasters.
King Lear 2.4.302

1791 ARMADO: How hast thou purchased this experience?
MOTH: By my penny of observation.
Love's Labor's Lost 3.1.26

1792 FORD: Experience be a jewel—
that I have purchas'd at an infinite rate.
Merry Wives of Windsor 2.2.204

1793 LEONATO: Men
Can counsel and speak comfort to that grief
Which they themselves not feel, but tasting it,
Their counsel turns to passion, which before
Would give preceptial med'cine to rage,
Fetter strong madness in a silken thread,
Charm ache with air, and agony with words.
Much Ado About Nothing 5.1.20

1794 ANTONIO: Experience is by industry achiev'd,
And perfected by the swift course of time.
Two Gentlemen of Verona 1.3.22

1795 ROSALIND: I had rather have a fool to make me merry than experience to make me sad.
As You Like It 4.1.27

1796 KING: The bitter past, more welcome is the sweet.
All's Well That Ends Well 5.3.334

Expression

1797 ULYSSES [about Cressida]: Fie, fie upon her!
There's language in her eye, her cheek, her lip,
Nay, her foot speaks; her wanton spirits look out
At every joint and motive of her body.
Troilus and Cressida 4.5.55

Extravagance

1798 SALISBURY: To be possess'd with double pomp,
To guard a title that was rich before,
To gild refined gold, to paint the lily,
To throw a perfume on the violet,
To smooth the ice, to add another hue
Unto the rainbow, or with taper-light
To seek the beauteous eye of heaven to garnish,
Is wasteful and ridiculous excess.
King John 4.2.10

Extremes

1799 PRINCE HENRY: Fierce extremes
In their continuance will not feed themselves.
King John 5.7.13

1800 CORIOLANUS [to Volumnia]:
Where is your ancient courage? You were us'd
To say extremities was the trier of spirits.
Coriolanus 4.1.3

Eye

1801 ULYSSES: Things in motion sooner catch the eye
Than what not stirs.
Troilus and Cressida 3.3.183

1802 PRINCESS: Beauty is bought by judgment of the eye,
Not utter'd by base sale of chapmen's tongues.
Love's Labor's Lost 2.1.15

1803 MACBETH [soliloquy]: Mine eyes are made the fools o' th' other senses.
Macbeth 2.1.44

1804 CRESSIDA: The error of our eye directs our mind.
What error leads must err.
Troilus and Cressida 5.2.110

1805 ULYSSES: The present eye praises the present object.
Troilus and Cressida 3.3.180

1806 LEAR: A man may see how this world goes with no eyes.
Look with thine ears.
King Lear 4.6.150

1807 To hear with eyes belongs to love's fine wit.
Sonnet 23

1808 HELENA [soliloquy]: Love looks not with the eyes but with the mind.
Midsummer Night's Dream 1.1.234

1809 FRIAR LAWRENCE: Young men's love then lies
Not truly in their hearts, but in their eyes.
Romeo and Juliet 2.3.67

1810 BEROWNE: But love, first learned in a lady's eyes,
Lives not alone immured in the brain,
But with the motion of all elements,
Courses as swift as thought in every power,
And gives to every power a double power,
Above their functions and their offices.
It adds a precious seeing to the eye.
Love's Labor's Lost 4.3.324

1811 BEROWNE: Where is any author in the world
Teaches such beauty as a woman's eye?
Love's Labor's Lost 4.3.308

1812 BEROWNE: A lover's eyes will gaze an eagle blind.
Love's Labor's Lost 4.3.331

1813 IAGO [concerning Desdemona]: What an eye she has! Methinks it sounds a parley to provocation.
Othello 2.3.22

1814 BASSANIO [about Portia]: Sometimes from her eyes I did receive fair speechless messages.
Merchant of Venice 1.1.163

1815 LEWIS [about Blanch]: In her eye I find
A wonder, or a wondrous miracle.
King John 2.1.496

1816 ROMEO: He that is strooken blind cannot forget
The precious treasure of his eyesight lost.
Romeo and Juliet 1.1.232
[*strooken:* stricken]

1817 If I could write the beauty of your eyes,
And in fresh numbers number all your graces,
The age to come would say, "This poet lies,
Such heavenly touches ne'er touch'd earthly faces."
Sonnet 17

1818 There lives more life in one of your fair eyes
Than both your poets can in praise devise.
Sonnet 83

1819 DUMAINE: By heaven, the wonder in a mortal eye!
Love's Labor's Lost 4.3.83

1820 BEROWNE: From women's eyes this doctrine I derive:
They sparkle still the right Promethean fire.
Love's Labor's Lost 4.3.347

1821 FRIAR LAWRENCE: Care keeps his watch in every old man's eye.
Romeo and Juliet 2.3.35

1822 BELARIUS: To apprehend thus Draws us a profit from all things we see.
Cymbeline 3.3.17

1823 ROSALIND: To have seen much, and to have nothing, is to have rich eyes and poor hands.
As You Like It 4.1.23

1824 Beauty itself doth of itself persuade
The eyes of men without an orator.
Rape of Lucrece 29

1825 MERCUTIO: Men's eyes were made to look, and let them gaze.
Romeo and Juliet 3.1.54

1826 ABBESS [to Adriana about Antipholus Ephesus]: Hath not else his eye
Stray'd his affection in unlawful love—
A sin prevailing much in youthful men,
Who give their eyes the liberty of gazing?
Comedy of Errors 5.1.50

1827 Oft the eye mistakes, the brain being troubled.
Venus and Adonis 1068

1828 SPEED [to the love-sick Valentine]: Not an eye that sees you but is a physician to comment on your malady.
Two Gentlemen of Verona 2.1.40

1829 Thou blind fool, Love, what dost thou to mine eyes,
That they behold and see not what they see?
Sonnet 137

1830 IMOGEN: Our very eyes Are sometimes like our judgments, blind.
Cymbeline 4.2.301

1831 LADY MACBETH: 'Tis the eye of childhood
That fears a painted devil.
Macbeth 2.2.51

1832 HERMIA: Dark night, that from the eye his function takes,
The ear more quick of apprehension makes;
Wherein it doth impair the seeing sense,
It pays the hearing double recompense.
Midsummer Night's Dream 3.2.177

1833 BASTARD [to King John]: Let not the world see fear and sad distrust
Govern the motion of a kingly eye.
King John 5.1.46

1834 BRUTUS: The eye sees not itself But by reflection, by some other things.
Julius Caesar 1.2.52

1835 TROILUS: My election Is led on in the conduct of my will,
My will enkindled by mine eyes and ears,
Two traded pilots 'twixt the dangerous shores
Of will and judgment.
Troilus and Cressida 2.2.61
[*election:* choice; *traded pilots:* intermediaries constantly going back and forth]

1836 CLAUDIO [soliloquy]: Let every eye negotiate for itself,
And trust no agent; for beauty is a witch
Against whose charms faith melteth into blood.
Much Ado About Nothing 2.1.178

1837 ROMEO [to Juliet]: Alack, there
lies more peril in thine eye
Than twenty of their swords!
Romeo and Juliet 2.2.71

1838 PHEBE [about Ganymede]: Faster
than his tongue
Did make offense, his eye did heal it
up.
As You Like It 3.5.116

1839 HAMLET: An eye like Mars, to
threaten and command.
Hamlet 3.4.57

1840 JACHIMO: Windows, white and
azure lac'd
With blue of heaven's own tinct.
Cymbeline 2.2.22

1841 SONG: Tell me where is fancy
bred,
Or in the heart or in the head?
How begot, how nourished?
Reply, reply.
It is engender'd in the eyes,
With gazing fed, and fancy dies
In the cradle where it lies.
Merchant of Venice 3.2.63

Eyewitness

1842 To see sad sights moves more
than hear them told.
Rape of Lucrece 1324

Face

1843 IAGO [soliloquy]: Knavery's plain
face is never seen till us'd.
Othello 2.1.312

1844 DUNCAN: There's no art
To find the mind's construction in the
face.
Macbeth 1.4.11

1845 HAMLET: [to Ophelia, about
women]: God hath given you one face,
and you make yourselves another.
Hamlet 3.1.143

1846 Q. KATHERINE [to Cardinals
Wolsey and Campeius]: Ye have
angels' faces, but heaven knows your
hearts.
Henry VIII 3.1.145

1847 ENOBARBUS: Never a fair woman
has a true face.
Antony and Cleopatra 2.6.100

1848 Though men can cover crimes
with bold stern looks,
Poor women's faces are their own
faults' books.
Rape of Lucrece 1252

1849 POMPEY: I know not
What counts harsh Fortune casts upon
my face,
But in my bosom shall she never come,
To make my heart her vassal.
Antony and Cleopatra 2.6.53

1850 MENAS: All men's faces are true,
whatsome'er their hands are.
Antony and Cleopatra 2.6.97

1851 WORCESTER: Look how we can,
or sad or merrily,
Interpretation will misquote our looks.
1 Henry IV 5.2.12

1852 LADY MACBETH [to Macbeth]:
Your face, my thane, is as a book,
where men
May read strange matters.
Macbeth 1.5.62

1853 MACBETH [to Lady Macbeth]: We
Must lave our honors in these flattering
streams,
And make our faces vizards to our
hearts,
Disguising what they are.
Macbeth 3.2.32

1854 Thus is his cheek the map of
days outworn,
When beauty liv'd and died as flowers
do now,
Before these bastard signs of fair were
born,
Or durst inhabit on a living brow.
Sonnet 68

1855 It cannot be, I find,
But such a face should bear a wicked mind.
                    Rape of Lucrece 1539

Faction

1856 ANTONY: Equality of two domestic powers
Breeds scrupulous faction.
                    Antony and Cleopatra 1.3.47

1857 FIRST SENATOR: Quarrelling . . .
Is valor misbegot, and came into the world
When sects and factions were newly born.
                    Timon of Athens 3.5.27

Failure

1858 MACBETH: We have scotch'd the snake, not kill'd it.
                    Macbeth 3.2.13
[*scotch'd:* slashed, i.e. merely wounded]

Faith

1859 PISTOL: Oaths are straws, men's faiths are wafer-cakes.
                    Henry V 2.3.51
[*wafer-cakes:* i.e. fragile]

1860 K. HENRY: O, where is faith? O, where is loyalty?
If it be banish'd from the frosty head,
Where shall it find a harbor in the earth?
                    2 Henry VI 5.1.166

1861 BRUTUS: There are no tricks in plain and simple faith.
                    Julius Caesar 4.2.22

1862 Q. ELIZABETH: Trust not him that hath once broken faith.
                    3 Henry VI 4.4.30

1863 SILVIA: Better have none
Than plural faith, which is too much by one.
                    Two Gentlemen of Verona 5.4.51

1864 HELENA: Most it is presumption in us when
The help of heaven we count the act of men.
                    All's Well That Ends Well 2.1.151

1865 FLORIZEL: My desires
Run not before mine honor, nor my lusts
Burn hotter than my faith.
                    Winter's Tale 4.4.33

1866 PERICLES [to Helicanus]: I'll take thy word for faith, not ask thine oath:
Who shuns not to break one will crack them both.
                    Pericles 1.2.120

1867 BEATRICE [about Benedick]: He wears his faith but as the fashion of his hat: it ever changes with the next block.
                    Much Ado About Nothing 1.1.75

1868 CAMILLO: You may as well
Forbid the sea for to obey the moon
As or by oath remove or counsel shake
The fabric of his folly, whose foundation
Is pil'd upon his faith.
                    Winter's Tale 1.2.427

1869 FRANCE [about Cordelia]: Which to believe of her
Must be a faith that reason without miracle
Should never plant in me.
                    King Lear 1.1.221
[*should:* could]

Faithfulness

1870 DIANA: My chastity's the jewel of our house.
                    All's Well That Ends Well 4.2.46

1871 OPHELIA [giving flowers to Claudius and Gertrude]: There's a daisy. I would give you some violets,

but they wither'd all when my father
died.
Hamlet 4.5.184
[*daisy, violets:* emblems respectively of
faithlessness and faithfulness]

Falling

1872 K. RICHARD: Pride must have a
fall, and break the neck
Of the proud man that did usurp his
back.
Richard II 5.5.88

1873 ESCALUS: Some rise by sin, and
some by virtue fall.
Measure for Measure 2.1.38

1874 CHAMBERLAIN: Press not a falling
man too far!
Henry VIII 3.2.333

1875 CROMWELL: 'Tis a cruelty
To load a falling man.
Henry VIII 5.2.111

1876 LUCIUS: Be cheerful; wipe thine
eyes:
Some falls are means the happier to
arise.
Cymbeline 4.2.402

1877 ANGELO: 'Tis one thing to be
tempted . . .
Another thing to fall.
Measure for Measure 2.1.17

1878 WOLSEY [soliloquy]: I have
touch'd the highest point of all my
greatness,
And, from that full meridian of my
glory,
I haste now to my setting. I shall fall
Like a bright exhalation in the eve-
ning,
And no man see me more.
Henry VIII 3.2.223

1879 DUKE: Frailty hath examples for
his falling.
Measure for Measure 3.1.186

Falsehood

1880 ANTONIO: O, what a goodly outside falsehood hath!
Merchant of Venice 1.3.103

1881 PANDULPH: Falsehood falsehood
cures, as fire cools fire.
King John 3.1.277

1882 BEROWNE: We to ourselves prove
false,
By being once false for ever to be true
To those that make us both—fair
ladies, you;
And even that falsehood, in itself a
sin,
Thus purifies itself and turns to grace.
Love's Labor's Lost 5.2.772

1883 IMOGEN: To lapse in fullness
Is sorer than to lie for need; and false-
hood
Is worse in kings than beggars.
Cymbeline 3.6.12

1884 FALSTAFF: Lord, Lord, how subject we old men are to this vice of
lying!
2 Henry IV 3.2.303

1885 AUTOLYCUS: Let me have no lying. It becomes none but tradesmen.
Winter's Tale 4.4.722

1886 LEONTES: Past all shame . . .
So past all truth.
Winter's Tale 3.2.84

Falsity

1887 MALCOLM: To show an unfelt
sorrow is an office
Which the false man does easy.
Macbeth 2.3.136

1888 OLIVIA: 'Twas never merry world
Since lowly feigning was call'd compliment.
Twelfth Night 3.1.98
[*lowly feigning:* pretending humility]

1889 MACBETH: False face must hide what the false heart doth know.
Macbeth 1.7.82

1890 HAMLET: As false as dicers' oaths.
Hamlet 3.4.45

Fame

1891 BRUTUS: Fame ... cannot
Better be held nor more attain'd than by
A place below the first; for what miscarries
Shall be the general's fault, though he perform
To th' utmost of a man.
Coriolanus 1.1.263

1892 BEROWNE: Too much to know is to know nought but fame.
Love's Labor's Lost 1.1.92

1893 PUCELLE: Glory is like a circle in the water,
Which never ceaseth to enlarge itself,
Till by broad spreading it disperse to nought.
1 Henry VI 1.2.133

1894 ANTONY: The evil that men do lives after them,
The good is oft interred with their bones.
Julius Caesar 3.2.75

1895 BENEDICK: If a man do not erect in this age his own tomb ere he dies, he shall live no longer in monument than the bell rings and the widow weeps.
Much Ado About Nothing 5.2.77

1896 HAMLET: There's hope a great man's memory may outlive his life half a year.
Hamlet 3.2.131

1897 GRIFFITH: Men's evil manners live in brass, their virtues
We write in water.
Henry VIII 4.2.45

1898 The painful warrior famoused for fight,
After a thousand victories once foil'd,
Is from the book of honor rased quite,
And all the rest forgot for which he toil'd.
Sonnet 25
[*rased:* erased, blotted out]

1899 ALL: He lives in fame, that died in virtue's cause.
Titus Andronicus 1.1.390

1900 VENTIDIUS: Better to leave undone, than by our deed
Acquire too high a fame when him we serve's away.
Antony and Cleopatra 3.1.14

1901 KING: Let fame, that all hunt after in their lives,
Live regist'red upon our brazen tombs.
Love's Labor's Lost 1.1.1

1902 PRINCE: That Julius Caesar was a famous man;
With what his valor did enrich his wit,
His wit set down to make his valure live.
Death makes no conquest of this conqueror,
For now he lives in fame though not in life.
Richard III 3.1.84
[*valure:* valor]

1903 DUKE: It deserves with characters of brass
A forted residence 'gainst the tooth of time
And razure of oblivion.
Measure for Measure 5.1.11

1904 LUCIANA: Shame hath a bastard fame, well managed.
Comedy of Errors 3.2.19

1905 BOY: I would give all my fame for a pot of ale and safety.
Henry V 3.2.13

Familiarity

1906 POLONIUS: Be thou familiar, but by no means vulgar.

Hamlet 1.3.61

1907 Sweets grown common lose their dear delight.

Sonnet 102

Fancy

1908 BERTRAM: All impediments in fancy's course
Are motives of more fancy.

All's Well That Ends Well 5.3.214

1909 SEBASTIAN: Let fancy still my sense in Lethe steep;
If it be thus to dream, still let me sleep!

Twelfth Night 4.1.61

1910 SILVIUS: If ever . . .
You meet in some fresh cheek the power of fancy,
Then shall you know the wounds invisible
That love's keen arrows make.

As You Like It 3.5.28

1911 VOLUMNIA: I have lived
To see . . . the buildings of my fancy.

Coriolanus 2.1.198

1912 DUKE: However we do praise ourselves,
Our fancies are more giddy and unfirm,
More longing, wavering, sooner lost and worn,
Than women's are.

Twelfth Night 2.4.32

1913 SONG: Tell me where is fancy bred,
Or in the heart or in the head?
How begot, how nourished?
Reply, reply.
It is engend'red in the eyes,
With gazing fed, and fancy dies
In the cradle where it lies.

Merchant of Venice 3.2.63

1914 BANQUO [to Macbeth, on the witches]: The earth hath bubbles, as the water has,
And these are of them.

Macbeth 1.3.79

Farewell

1915 ULYSSES: Welcome ever smiles,
And farewell goes out sighing.

Troilus and Cressida 3.3.168

1916 WOLSEY [soliloquy]: Farewell? a long farewell to all my greatness!
This is the state of man: to-day he puts forth
The tender leaves of hopes, to-morrow blossoms,
And bears his blushing honors thick upon him;
The third day comes a frost, a killing frost,
And when he thinks, good easy man, full surely
His greatness is a-ripening, nips his root,
And then he falls as I do.

Henry VIII 3.2.351

1917 OTHELLO: O now, for ever
Farewell the tranquil mind! farewell content!
Farewell the plumed troop and the big wars
That makes ambition virtue! O, farewell!
Farewell the neighing steed and the shrill trump,
The spirit-stirring drum, th' ear-piercing fife,
The royal banner, and all quality,
Pride, pomp, and circumstance of glorious war!
And O you mortal engines, whose rude throats
Th' immortal Jove's dread clamors counterfeit,
Farewell! Othello's occupation's gone.

Othello 3.3.347

[*mortal engines:* cannons]

1918 ROMEO [soliloquy]: Eyes, look your last!

Arms, take your last embrace! and,
  lips, O you
The doors of breath, seal with a
  righteous kiss
A dateless bargain to engrossing death!
  Romeo and Juliet 5.3.112

1919 MORTIMER [dying]: Just Death,
  kind umpire of men's miseries,
With sweet enlargement doth dismiss
me hence.
  1 Henry VI 2.5.29

1920 JULIET [to Romeo]: Good night,
  good night! Parting is such sweet
sorrow,
That I shall say good night till it be
morrow.
  Romeo and Juliet 2.2.184

Fascination

1921 My love is as a fever, longing still
For that which longer nurseth the
  disease,
Feeding on that which doth preserve
  the ill,
Th' uncertain sickly appetite to please.
My reason, the physician to my love,
Angry that his prescriptions are not
  kept,
Hath left me, and I desperate now
  approve
Desire is death, which physic did
  except.
Past cure I am, now reason is past care,
And frantic mad with evermore unrest;
My thoughts and my discourse as mad-
  men's are,
At random from the truth vainly ex-
  press'd;
For I have sworn thee fair, and thought
  thee bright,
Who art as black as hell, as dark as
night.
  Sonnet 147

1922 ENOBARBUS [about Cleopatra]:
  Other women cloy

The appetites they feed, but she makes
  hungry
Where most she satisfies.
  Antony and Cleopatra 2.2.235

Fashion

1923 POLONIUS: The apparel oft proclaims the man.
  Hamlet 1.3.72

1924 CONRADE: Fashion wears out
more apparel than the man.
  Much Ado About Nothing 3.3.139

1925 SANDS: New customs,
Though they be never so ridiculous
(Nay, let 'em be unmanly), yet are
  follow'd.
  Henry VIII 1.3.2

1926 SIMONIDES: Opinion's but a fool,
  that makes us scan
The outward habit by the inward man.
  Pericles 2.2.56

1927 BORACHIO: Seest thou not, I say,
what a deformed thief this fashion is,
how giddily 'a turns about all the hot-
bloods between fourteen and
five-and-thirty?
  Much Ado About Nothing 3.3.130
['a: he]

1928 BEVIS: The clothier means to
dress the commonwealth, and turn it,
and set a new nap on it.
  2 Henry VI 4.2.4

1929 GLOUCESTER [soliloquy]: I'll be
  at charges for a looking-glass,
And entertain a score or two of tailors
To study fashions to adorn my body:
Since I am crept in favor with myself,
I will maintain it with some little cost.
But first I'll turn yon fellow in his
  grave,
And then return lamenting to my love.
Shine out, fair sun, till I have bought
  a glass,
That I may see my shadow as I pass.
  Richard III 1.2.255
[yon fellow: the corpse of Henry VI]

1930 MERCUTIO: Strange flies, these fashion-mongers, these pardon-me's, who stand so much on the new form, that they cannot sit at ease on the old bench? O, their bones, their bones!
Romeo and Juliet 2.4.32
[*pardon-me's:* those with affected manners; *bones:* a pun on the French word *bons*]

1931 BIANCA: Old fashions please me best; I am not so nice
To change true rules for odd inventions.
Taming of the Shrew 3.1.80

1932 BORACHIO: Thou knowest that the fashion of a doublet, or a hat, or a cloak, is nothing to a man.
CONRADE: Yes, it is apparel.
BORACHIO: I mean the fashion.
CONRADE: Yes, the fashion is the fashion.
Much Ado About Nothing 3.3.117

1933 POSTHUMUS: To shame the guise o' th' world, I will begin
The fashion: less without and more within.
Cymbeline 5.1.32
[*guise:* custom]

1934 OPHELIA [about Prince Hamlet]: The glass of fashion and the mould of form,
Th' observ'd of all observers.
Hamlet 3.1.153

1935 HAMLET: Th' appurtenance of welcome is fashion and ceremony.
Hamlet 2.2.371

1936 LAFEW [about Parolles]: The soul of this man is his clothes.
All's Well That Ends Well 2.5.43

Fasting

1937 CLAUDIO: Surfeit is the father of much fast.
Measure for Measure 1.2.126

1938 KING [to Falstaff]: Make less thy body hence and more thy grace,
Leave gormandizing.
2 Henry IV 5.5.52

1939 LONGAVILLE: The mind shall banquet, though the body pine.
Love's Labor's Lost 1.1.25

1940 MENENIUS: The veins unfill'd, our bood is cold, and then
We pout upon the morning, are unapt
To give or to forgive; but when we have stuff'd
These pipes and these conveyances of our blood
With wine and feeding, we have suppler souls
Than in our priest-like fasts.
Coriolanus 5.1.51

Fate

1941 CLOWN: That that is is.
Twelfth Night 4.2.14

1942 HAMLET: There's a divinity that shapes our ends,
Rough-hew them how we will.
Hamlet 5.2.10

1943 HAMLET: We defy augury. There's special providence in the fall of a sparrow. If it be now, 'tis not to come; if it be not to come, it will be now; if it be not now, yet it will come—the readiness is all.
Hamlet 5.2.219

1944 K. RICHARD: All unavoided is the doom of destiny.
Richard III 4.4.218

1945 K. EDWARD: What fates impose, that men must needs abide;
It boots not to resist both wind and tide.
3 Henry VI 4.3.58
[*boots:* helps]

1946 CAESAR: Let determin'd things to destiny
Hold unbewail'd their way.
Antony and Cleopatra 3.6.84

1947 PLAYER QUEEN: Our wills and
fates do so contrary run
That our devices still are overthrown,
Our thoughts are ours, their ends none
of our own.
Hamlet 3.2.211

1948 OTHELLO: (O vain boast!)
Who can control his fate?
Othello 5.2.264

1949 CASSIUS: Men at some time are
masters of their fates;
The fault, dear Brutus, is not in our
stars,
But in ourselves, that we are underlings.
Julius Caesar 1.2.139

1950 FLORIZEL: But as th' unthought-
on accident is guilty
To what we wildly do, so we profess
Ourselves to be the slaves of chance,
and flies
Of every wind that blows.
Winter's Tale 4.4.538

1951 BRUTUS: That we shall die, we
know, 'tis but the time,
And drawing days out, that men stand
upon.
Julius Caesar 3.1.99

1952 K. HENRY: O God, that one
might read the book of fate,
And see the revolutions of the times
Make mountains level, and the conti-
nent,
Weary of solid firmness, melt itself
Into the sea, and other times to see
The beachy girdle of the ocean
Too wide for Neptune's hips; how
chance's mock
And changes fill the cup of alteration
With divers liquors! O, if this were
seen,
The happiest youth, viewing his prog-
ress through,
What perils past, what crosses to
ensue,
Would shut the book, and sit him
down and die.
2 Henry IV 3.1.45

1953 ANTONY: Do not please sharp
fate
To grace it with your sorrows. Bid that
welcome
Which comes to punish us, and we
punish it
Seeming to bear it lightly.
Antony and Cleopatra 4.14.135

1954 CAESAR: What can be avoided
Whose end is purpos'd by the mighty
gods?
Julius Caesar 2.2.26

1955 MALVOLIO: Some are born
great ...
Some achieve greatness ...
And some have greatness thrust upon
them.
Twelfth Night 3.4.41

Father

1956 LAUNCELOT: It is a wise father
that knows his own child.
Merchant of Venice 2.2.76

1957 K. EDWARD: 'Tis a happy thing
To be the father unto many sons.
3 Henry VI 3.2.104

1958 GARDENER: Unruly children
make their sire stoop.
Richard II 3.4.30

1959 POLIXENES: Methinks a father
Is at the nuptial of his son a guest
That best becomes the table.
Winter's Tale 4.4.394

1960 THESEUS [to Hermia]: To you
your father should be as a god;
One that compos'd your beauties; yea,
and one
To whom you are but as a form in
wax,
By him imprinted, and within his
power,
To leave the figure, or disfigure it.
Midsummer Night's Dream 1.1.47

1961 FOOL: Fathers that wear rags
Do make their children blind,
But fathers that bear bags
Shall see their children kind.
King Lear 2.4.48
[*bags:* i.e. money bags]

Fatness

1962 HAMLET [to King]: Your worm is
your only emperor for diet: we fat all
creatures else to fat us, and we fat ourselves for maggots; your fat king and
your lean beggar is but variable service,
two dishes, but to one table—that's
the end.
Hamlet 4.3.21

1963 LONGAVILLE: Fat paunches have
lean pates.
Love's Labor's Lost 1.1.26

1964 PRINCE: Falstaff sweats to death,
And lards the lean earth as he walks
along.
1 Henry IV 2.2.108

1965 FALSTAFF: I have more flesh than
another man, and therefore more
frailty.
1 Henry IV 3.3.166

1966 FALSTAFF [soliloquy]: I think the
devil will not have me damn'd, lest the
oil that's in me should set hell on fire.
Merry Wives of Windsor 5.5.34

1967 KING [to Falstaff]: Make less thy
body hence and more thy grace,
Leave gormandizing.
2 Henry IV 5.5.52

1968 CORIN: Good pasture makes fat
sheep.
As You Like It 3.2.27

1969 KING: Most subject is the fattest
soil to weeds.
2 Henry IV 4.4.54

Faults

1970 LUCULLUS: Every man has his
fault.
Timon of Athens 3.1.27

1971 MARIANA: They say best men are
moulded out of faults,
And for the most, become much more
better
For being a little bad.
Measure for Measure 5.1.439

1972 Men's faults do seldom to
themselves appear.
Rape of Lucrece 633

1973 TIMON: Faults that are rich are
fair.
Timon of Athens 1.2.13

1974 ANNE [about Slender]: O, what
a world of vild ill-favor'd faults
Looks handsome in three hundred
pounds a year!
Merry Wives of Windsor 3.4.32
[*vild:* vile]

1975 PEMBROKE: Oftentimes excusing
of a fault
Doth make the fault the worse by th'
excuse.
King John 4.2.30

1976 The fault unknown is as a
thought unacted.
Rape of Lucrece 527

1977 COUNTESS: It is the show and
seal of nature's truth,
Where love's strong passion is im-
press'd in youth.
By our remembrances of days foregone,
Such were our faults, or then we
thought them none.
All's Well That Ends Well 1.3.134

1978 KING: Our rash faults
Make trivial price of serious things we
have,
Not knowing them until we know their
grave.
All's Well That Ends Well 5.3.60

1979 PAULINA: All faults I make,
when I shall come to know them,
I do repent.
Winter's Tale 3.2.219

1980 TIMON: Wilt thou whip thine
own faults in other men?
Timon of Athens 5.1.39

1981 OLIVIA: There's something in me
that reproves my fault;
But such a headstrong potent fault it is
That it but mocks reproof.
Twelfth Night 3.4.203

1982 DUKE [soliloquy]: Shame to him
whose cruel striking
Kills for faults of his own liking!
Measure for Measure 3.2.267

1983 HAMLET: So, oft it chances in
particular men,
That for some vicious mole of nature
in them,
As in their birth, wherein they are not
guilty
(Since nature cannot choose his origin),
By their o'ergrowth of some com-
plexion
Oft breaking down the pales and forts
of reason,
Or by some habit, that too much o'er-
leavens
The form of plausive manners — that
these men,
Carrying, I say, the stamp of one
defect,
Being nature's livery, or fortune's star,
His virtues else, be they as pure as
grace,
As infinite as man may undergo,
Shall in the general censure take cor-
ruption
From that particular fault.
Hamlet 1.4.23

1984 IAGO: Oft my jealousy
Shapes faults that are not.
Othello 3.3.147

1985 ISABELLA [to Angelo]: Go to your
bosom,
Knock there, and ask your heart what
it doth know

That's like my brother's fault. If it
confess
A natural guiltiness such as is his,
Let it not sound a thought upon your
tongue
Against my brother's life.
Measure for Measure 2.2.136

1986 ORLANDO: I will chide no
breather in the world but myself,
against whom I know most faults.
As You Like It 3.2.280

1987 FIRST OUTLAW: We cite our
faults
That they may hold excus'd our lawless
lives.
Two Gentlemen of Verona 4.1.51

1988 BRUTUS: I do not like your
faults.
CASSIUS: A friendly eye could never see
such faults.
BRUTUS: A flatterer's would not,
though they do appear
As huge as high Olympus.
Julius Caesar 4.3.89

1989 CASSIUS: The fault, dear Brutus,
is not in our stars,
But in ourselves, that we are underlings.
Julius Caesar 1.2.140

1990 KING [to Thomas, on dealing
with Prince Henry]: Chide him for
faults, and do it reverently,
When you perceive his blood inclin'd
to mirth;
But, being moody, give him time and
scope,
Till that his passions, like a whale on
ground,
Confound themselves with working.
2 Henry IV 4.4.37

1991 ROSALIND [to Orlando, on
women and their faults]: They were all
like one another as halfpence are, every
one fault seeming monstrous till his
fellow-fault came to match it.
As You Like It 3.2.353

1992 ANGELO: Condemn the fault,
and not the actor of it?
Why, every fault's condemn'd ere it be
done.
Measure for Measure 2.2.37

1993 ANTONY: Read not my
blemishes in the world's report.
Antony and Cleopatra 2.3.5

1994 PEMBROKE: Patches set upon a
little breach
Discredit more in hiding the fault
Than did the fault before it was
patch'd.
King John 4.2.32

1995 MOTH: If she be made of white
and red,
Her faults will ne'er be known,
For blush in cheeks by faults are bred,
And fears by pale white shown.
Love's Labor's Lost 1.2.99

1996 Though men can cover crimes
with bold stern looks,
Poor women's faces are their own
faults' books.
Rape of Lucrece 1252

1997 FALSTAFF: If sack and sugar be a
fault, God help the wicked!
1 Henry IV 2.4.470

1998 ANGELO: We are made to be no
stronger
Than faults may shake our frames.
Measure for Measure 2.4.132

1999 DUKE: That we were all, as some
would seem to be,
From our faults, as faults from seeming, free!
Measure for Measure 3.2.38

2000 FERDINAND: For several virtues
Have I lik'd several women, never any
With so full soul but some defect in
her
Did quarrel with the noblest grace she
ow'd
And put it to the foil.
The Tempest 3.1.42

2001 CHAMBERLAIN: Press not a falling
man too far! 'tis virtue.
His faults lie open to the laws, let
them,
Not you, correct him.
Henry VIII 3.2.333

2002 No more be griev'd at that which
thou hast done:
Roses have thorns, and silver fountains
mud,
Clouds and eclipses stain both moon
and sun,
And loathsome canker lives in sweetest
bud.
All men make faults.
Sonnet 35

2003 AGRIPPA [on Antony]: A rarer
spirit never
Did steer humanity; but you gods will
give us
Some faults to make us men.
Antony and Cleopatra 5.1.31

Favor

2004 IAGO: 'Tis the curse of service;
Preferment goes by letter and affection,
And not by old gradation, where each
second
Stood heir to th' first.
Othello 1.1.35
[*old gradation:* seniority]

2005 POSTHUMUS [soliloquy]: Poor
wretches that depend
On greatness' favor dream as I have
done,
Wake, and find nothing. But, alas, I
swerve.
Many dream not to find, neither de-
serve,
And yet are steep'd in favors.
Cymbeline 5.4.127

2006 MARTIUS [to some citizens]: He
that depends
Upon your favors swims with fins of
lead,
And hews down oaks with rushes.
Coriolanus 1.1.179

Fear

2007 MACBETH: Present fears
Are less than horrible imaginings.
Macbeth 1.3.137

2008 PUCELLE: Of all base passions,
fear is most accurs'd.
1 Henry VI 5.2.18

2009 DUKE: That life is better life,
past fearing death,
Than that which lives to fear.
Measure for Measure 5.1.397

2010 K. RICHARD: Fearful commenting
Is leaden servitor to dull delay.
Richard III 4.3.51

2011 CRESSIDA: Blind fear that seeing
reason leads finds safer footing than
blind reason stumbling without fear.
To fear the worst oft cures the worst.
Troilus and Cressida 3.2.71

2012 ENOBARBUS [soliloquy]: To be
furious
Is to be frighted out of fear, and in
that mood
The dove will peck the estridge.
Antony and Cleopatra 3.13.194

2013 KING: Things done well
And with care exempt themselves from
fear;
Things done without example, in their
issue
Are to be fear'd.
Henry VIII 1.2.88

2014 LAERTES: Best safety lies in fear.
Hamlet 1.3.43

2015 BELARIUS: Nothing routs us but
the villainy of our fears.
Cymbeline 5.2.12

2016 LADY MACBETH: When our actions do not,
Our fears do make us traitors.
Macbeth 4.2.3

2017 CARLISLE [to King Richard]: To
fear the foe, since fear oppresseth
strength,
Gives in your weakness strength unto
your foe,
And so your follies fight against yourself.
Richard II 3.2.180

2018 PERICLES: 'Tis time to fear when
tyrants seem to kiss.
Pericles 1.2.79

2019 MACBETH: I have almost forgot
the taste of fears.
The time has been, my senses would
have cool'd
To hear a night-shriek, and my fell of
hair
Would at a dismal treatise rouse and
stir
As life were in't. I have supp'd full
with horrors;
Direness, familiar to my slaughterous
thoughts,
Cannot once start me.
Macbeth 5.5.9

2020 LAFEW: They say miracles are
past, and we have our philosophical
persons, to make modern and familiar,
things supernatural and causeless.
Hence is it that we make trifles of terrors, ensconcing ourselves into seeming
knowledge, when we should submit
ourselves to an unknown fear.
All's Well That Ends Well 2.3.1
[*terrors:* i.e. occurrences that should inspire
awe]

2021 ROSSE: Cruel are the times when
we are traitors,
And do not know ourselves; when we
hold rumor
From what we fear, yet know not what
we fear.
Macbeth 4.2.18

2022 MACBETH: Hang those that talk
of fear.
Macbeth 5.3.36

2023 MOTH: Blush in cheeks by faults are bred,
And fears by pale white shown.
Love's Labor's Lost 1.2.101

2024 MACBETH [to servant reporting Macduff's imminent attack]: Those linen cheeks of thine
Are counsellors to fear.
Macbeth 5.3.16

2025 POSTHUMUS: It is a basilisk unto mine eye,
Kills me to look on't.
Cymbeline 2.4.107
[*basilisk:* fabulous serpent which could kill with a glance]

2026 BELARIUS: Defect of judgment Is oft the cause of fear.
Cymbeline 4.2.111

2027 LADY MACBETH: 'Tis the eye of childhood
That fears a painted devil.
Macbeth 2.2.51

2028 THESEUS: In the night, imagining some fear,
How easy is a bush suppos'd a bear!
Midsummer Night's Dream 5.1.21

2029 GLOUCESTER: Suspicion always haunts the guilty mind;
The thief doth fear each bush an officer.
3 Henry VI 5.6.11

2030 Q. MARGARET: What cannot be avoided,
'Twere childish weakness to lament or fear.
3 Henry VI 5.4.37

2031 BRUTUS: I do find it cowardly and vile,
For fear of what might fall, so to prevent
The time of life.
Julius Caesar 5.1.103

2032 YORK [soliloquy]: Let pale-fac'd fear keep with the mean-born man,
And find no harbor in a royal heart.
2 Henry VI 3.1.335

2033 BASTARD [to King John]: Let not the world see fear and sad distrust
Govern the motion of a kingly eye.
King John 5.1.46

2034 SUFFOLK: True nobility is exempt from fear.
2 Henry VI 4.1.129

2035 Extreme fear can neither fight nor fly,
But coward-like with trembling terror die.
Rape of Lucrece 230

2036 KING: Ah, what a sign it is of evil life,
Where death's approach is seen so terrible!
2 Henry VI 3.3.5

2037 ISABELLA: The sense of death is most in apprehension.
Measure for Measure 3.1.77

2038 PLAYER QUEEN: Where love is great, the littlest doubts are fear;
When little fears grow great, great love grows there.
Hamlet 3.2.171

2039 Against love's fire fear's frost hath dissolution.
Rape of Lucrece 355

2040 SECOND CITIZEN: Truly, the hearts of men are full of fear.
You cannot reason (almost) with a man That looks not heavily and full of fear.
Richard III 2.3.38

2041 JULIET [soliloquy, after her mother's departure]: Farewell! God knows when we shall meet again.
I have a faint cold fear thrills through my veins,
That almost freezes up the heat of life.
Romeo and Juliet 4.3.15

2042 HAMLET [to Horatio, on the ghost]: What should be the fear?
I do not set my life at a pin's fee,
And for my soul, what can it do to that,
Being a thing immortal as itself?
Hamlet 1.4.64

2043 CHARMIAN: In time we hate that which we often fear.
Antony and Cleopatra 1.3.12

2044 NORTHUMBERLAND [on the death of his son]: He that but fears the thing he would not know
Hath by instinct knowledge from others' eyes
That what he fear'd is chanced.
2 Henry IV 1.1.85

2045 BASTARD [to King John]: As I travell'd hither through the land,
I find the people strangely fantasied,
Possess'd with rumors, full of idle dreams,
Not knowing what they fear, but full of fear.
King John 4.2.143

2046 GUIDERIUS [singing a funeral dirge for Cloten]: Fear no more the heat o' th' sun,
Nor the furious winter's rages,
Thou thy worldly task hast done,
Home art gone, and ta'en thy wages.
Golden lads and girls all must,
As chimney-sweepers, come to dust.
ARVIRAGUS [joining in]: Fear no more the frown o' th' great,
Thou art past the tyrant's stroke;
Care no more to clothe and eat,
To thee the reed is as the oak.
The sceptre, learning, physic, must
All follow this and come to dust.
GUIDERIUS: Fear no more the lightning-flash.
ARVIRAGUS: Nor th' all-dreaded thunder-stone.
GUIDERIUS: Fear not slander, censure rash.
ARVIRAGUS: Thou hast finish'd joy and moan:
BOTH: All lovers young, all lovers must

Consign to thee and come to dust.
GUIDERIUS: No exorciser harm thee.
ARVIRAGUS: Nor no witchcraft charm thee.
GUIDERIUS: Ghost unlaid forbear thee.
ARVIRAGUS: Nothing ill come near thee.
BOTH: Quiet consummation have,
And renowned be thy grave.
Cymbeline 4.2.258

2047 CONSTANCE [to Salisbury]: Thou shalt be punish'd for thus frighting me,
For I am sick and capable of fears,
Oppress'd with wrongs, and therefore full of fears,
A widow, husbandless, subject to fears,
A woman, naturally born to fears;
And though thou now confess thou didst but jest,
With my vex'd spirits I cannot take a truce,
But they will quake and tremble all this day.
King John 3.1.11

Feasting

2048 BALTHAZAR: Small cheer and great welcome makes a merry feast.
Comedy of Errors 3.1.26
[*cheer*: used here as a metaphor for food]

2049 ANTIPHOLUS EPHESUS: A table full of welcome makes scarce one dainty dish.
Comedy of Errors 3.1.23

2050 FALSTAFF: The latter end of a fray and the beginning of a feast
Fits a dull fighter and a keen guest.
1 Henry IV 4.2.79

2051 GRATIANO: Who riseth from a feast
With that keen appetite that he sits down?
Merchant of Venice 2.6.8

2052 SECOND LORD: Thou art going to Lord Timon's feast?

APEMANTUS: Ay, to see meat fill knaves, and wine heat fools.

Timon of Athens 1.1.260

Fellow

2053 SOLANIO: Nature hath fram'd strange fellows in her time:
Some that will evermore peep through their eyes,
And laugh like parrots at a bagpiper;
And other of such vinegar aspect
That they'll not show their teeth in way of smile
Though Nestor swear the jest be laughable.

Merchant of Venice 1.1.51

[*Nestor:* a character in the *Iliad,* noted for his excessive gravity]

2054 K. HENRY: These fellows of infinite tongue, that can rhyme themselves into ladies' favors, they do always reason themselves out again.

Henry V 5.2.155

Fellowship

2055 DUKE: There is scarce truth enough alive to make societies secure, but security enough to make fellowships accurs'd. Much upon this riddle runs the wisdom of the world.

Measure for Measure 3.2.226

2056 EDGAR [soliloquy]: Who alone suffers, suffers most i' th' mind,
Leaving free things and happy shows behind,
But then the mind much sufferance doth o'erskip,
When grief hath mates, and bearing fellowship.

King Lear 3.6.104

2057 JULIET: Sour woe delights in fellowship.

Romeo and Juliet 3.2.116

2058 Fellowship in woe doth woe assuage.

Rape of Lucrece 790

Fever

2059 ABBESS: What's fever but a fit of madness?

Comedy of Errors 5.1.76

2060 K. HENRY [soliloquy]: Thinks thou the fiery fever will go out
With titles blown from adulation?

Henry V 4.1.253

2061 DUMAINE [about Kate]: I would forget her, but a fever she
Reigns in my blood, and will rememb'red be.

Love's Labor's Lost 4.3.93

Fickleness

2062 Love is not love
Which alters when it alteration finds.

Sonnet 116

2063 HAMLET: Frailty, thy name is woman!

Hamlet 1.2.146

2064 BALTHAZAR [singing]:
Sigh no more, ladies, sigh no more,
Men were deceivers ever,
One foot in sea, and one on shore,
To one thing constant never.

Much Ado About Nothing 2.3.62

2065 IAGO: Dull not device by coldness and delay.

Othello 2.3.388

2066 OLD ATHENIAN: Our own precedent passions do instruct us
What levity's in youth.

Timon of Athens 1.1.133

2067 MARTIUS [to some citizens in Rome]: What's the matter, you dissentious rogues,

That rubbing the poor itch of your
opinion
Make yourself scabs?
Coriolanus 1.1.164

2068 BEATRICE [about Benedick]: He
wears his faith but as the fashion of his
hat: it ever changes with the next
block.
Much Ado About Nothing 1.1.75

Fiction

2069 THESEUS: More strange than true.
I never may believe
These antic fables, nor these fairy toys.
Midsummer Night's Dream 5.1.3

Fidelity

2070 POLONIUS: This above all: to
thine own self be true,
And it must follow, as the night the
day,
Thou canst not then be false to any
man.
Hamlet 1.3.78

2071 KING: O, where is faith? O,
where is loyalty?
If it be banish'd from the frosty head,
Where shall it find a harbor in the
earth?
2 Henry VI 5.1.166

2072 HELICANUS [to Pericles]: Day
serves not light more faithful than
I'll be.
Pericles 1.2.110

2073 HELENA: My heart
Is as true as steel.
Midsummer Night's Dream 2.1.196

Fiend

2074 ALBANY: Proper deformity shows
not in the fiend
So horrid as in woman.
King Lear 4.2.60

2075 MACBETH [on the witches'
predictions]: I pull in resolution,
and begin
To doubt th' equivocation of the fiend
That lies like truth.
Macbeth 5.5.41

2076 MACBETH [on the witches'
predictions]: Be these juggling fiends
no more believ'd,
That palter with us in a double sense,
That keep the word of promise to our
ear,
And break it to our hope.
Macbeth 5.8.19

Fighting

2077 MARTIUS [to his soldiers preparing for battle]: Put your shields
before your hearts, and fight
With hearts more proof than shields.
Coriolanus 1.4.24

2078 ANTONY: The next time I do
fight
I'll make death love me; for I will
contend
Even with his pestilent scythe.
Antony and Cleopatra 3.13.191

Filth

2079 ALBANY: Filths savor but themselves.
King Lear 4.2.39

Finality

2080 LADY MACBETH: What's done, is
done.
Macbeth 3.2.12

2081 LADY MACBETH: What's done
cannot be undone.
Macbeth 5.1.68

2082 CLOWN: That that is is.
Twelfth Night 4.2.14

Finger

2083 DESDEMONA: Men's natures
wrangle with inferior things,
Though great ones are their object. 'Tis
even so;
For let our finger ache, and it endues
Our other healthful members even to a
sense
Of pain.
Othello 3.4.144

Fire

2084 CLARENCE: A little fire is quickly
trodden out,
Which being suffer'd, rivers cannot
quench.
3 Henry VI 4.8.7

2085 CASSIUS: Those that with haste
will make a mighty fire
Begin it with weak straws.
Julius Caesar 1.3.107

2086 PETRUCHIO: Where two raging
fires meet together,
They do consume the thing that feeds
their fury.
Taming of the Shrew 2.1.132

2087 GAUNT: Violent fires soon burn
out themselves.
Richard II 2.1.34

2088 LUCETTA: Fire that's closest kept
burns most of all.
Two Gentlemen of Verona 1.2.30

2089 BENVOLIO: One fire burns out
another's burning.
Romeo and Juliet 1.2.45

2090 PETRUCHIO: Though little fire
grows great with little wind,
Yet extreme gusts will blow out fire
and all.
Taming of the Shrew 2.1.134

2091 BULLINGBROOK: Who can hold a
fire in his hand

By thinking on the frosty Caucasus?
Richard II 1.3.294

2092 POET: The fire i' th' flint
Shows not till it be strook.
Timon of Athens 1.1.22
[*strook:* struck]

2093 BRUTUS: As fire drives out fire,
so pity pity.
Julius Caesar 3.1.171

2094 Small lights are soon blown out,
huge fires abide,
And with the wind in greater fury fret.
Rape of Lucrece 647

2095 NORFOLK [to Buckingham]:
Know you not
The fire that mounts the liquor till't
runs o'er,
In seeming to augment it wastes it?
Henry VIII 1.1.143

2096 JULIA [to Lucetta]: Didst thou
but know the inly touch of love,
Thou wouldst as soon go kindle fire
with snow
As seek to quench the fire of love with
words.
Two Gentlemen of Verona 2.7.18

2097 PAULINA: It is an heretic that
makes the fire,
Not she which burns in't.
Winter's Tale 2.3.115

2098 DROMIO SYRACUSE: Light is an
effect of fire.
Comedy of Errors 4.3.56

2099 CORIN: The property of rain is to
wet and fire to burn.
As You Like It 3.2.26

Firmness

2100 SLY: I'll not budge an inch.
Taming of the Shrew, Intro. 1.14

Fish

2101 THIRD FISHERMAN: Master, I marvel how the fishes live in the sea.
FIRST FISHERMAN: Why, as men do a-land; the great ones eat up the little ones.
Pericles 2.1.26

Fishing

2102 CLAUDIO [aside, about Benedick]: Bait the hook well, this fish will bite.
Much Ado About Nothing 2.3.108

2103 SECOND FISHERMAN: A fish hangs in the net, like a poor man's right in the law.
Pericles 2.1.116

2104 HAMLET: A man may fish with the worm that hath eat of a king, and eat of the fish that hath fed of that worm.
Hamlet 4.3.27

2105 URSULA: The pleasant'st angling is to see the fish
Cut with her golden oars the silver stream,
And greedily devour the treacherous bait.
Much Ado About Nothing 3.1.26

Flattery

2106 APEMANTUS: He that loves to be flatter'd is worthy o' th' flatterer.
Timon of Athens 1.1.226

2107 K. RICHARD: He does me double wrong
That wounds me with the flatteries of his tongue.
Richard II 3.2.215

2108 HELICANUS: They do abuse the King that flatter him,
For flattery is the bellows blows up sin.
Pericles 1.2.38

2109 K. HENRY: 'Tis sin to flatter.
3 Henry VI 5.6.3

2110 APEMANTUS [soliloquy]: O that men's ears should be
To counsel deaf, but not to flattery!
Timon of Athens 1.2.249

2111 HAMLET: Why should the poor be flatter'd?
No, let the candied tongue lick absurd pomp,
And crook the pregnant hinges of the knee
Where thrift may follow fawning.
Hamlet 3.2.59

[*candied*: flattering]

2112 LUCIANA: 'Tis holy sport to be a little vain,
When the sweet breath of flattery conquers strife.
Comedy of Errors 3.2.27

2113 GLOUCESTER: Because I cannot flatter and look fair,
Smile in men's faces, smooth, deceive, and cog,
Duck with French nods and apish courtesy,
I must be held a rancorous enemy.
Cannot a plain man live and think no harm,
But thus his simple truth must be abus'd
With silken, sly, insinuating Jacks?
Richard III 1.3.51

[*cog*: cheat; *duck*: bow; *Jacks*: worthless fellows]

2114 KENT [about Oswald]: Such smiling rogues as these ...
Smooth every passion
That in the natures of their lords rebel,
Being oil to fire, snow to their colder moods;
Renege, affirm, and turn their halcyon beaks
With every gale and vary of their masters,

Knowing nought (like dogs) but following.
                                        King Lear 2.2.73
[*smooth:* humor, flatter; *renege:* deny; *gale
and vary:* changing wind]

2115 GONERIL: Old fools are babes
again, and must be us'd
With checks as flatteries.
                                        King Lear 1.3.19

2116 K. HENRY [soliloquy]: What
drink'st thou oft, in stead of homage
sweet,
But poison'd flattery?
                                        Henry V 4.1.250

2117 K. HENRY [to Gardiner]: You
play the spaniel,
And think with wagging of your
tongue to win me.
                                        Henry VIII 5.2.161

2118 DECIUS [about Caesar]: When I
tell him he hates flatterers
He says he does, being then most
flattered.
                                        Julius Caesar 2.1.207

2119 GOWER: No visor does become
black villainy
So well as soft and tender flattery.
                                        Pericles 4.4.44

2120 VALENTINE: O, flatter me; for
love delights in praises.
                        Two Gentlemen of Verona 2.4.149

2121 TIMON [soliloquy]: Who dares,
In purity of manhood stand upright
And say, "This man's a flatterer"? If
one be,
So are they all; for every grize of for-
tune
Is smooth'd by that below. The learned
pate
Ducks to the golden fool. All's
obliquy;
There's nothing level in our cursed
natures
But direct villainy. Therefore be
abhorr'd
All feasts, societies, and throngs of
men!

His semblable, yea, himself, Timon
disdains.
                                        Timon of Athens 4.3.13
[*grize:* step; *semblable:* his own kind;
ducks: bows]

2122 APEMANTUS: What things in the
world canst thou nearest compare to
thy flatterers?
TIMON: Women nearest, but men—
men are the things themselves.
                                        Timon of Athens 4.3.318

2123 POET: When we for recompense
have prais'd the vild,
It stains the glory in that happy verse
Which aptly sings the good.
                                        Timon of Athens 1.1.15
[*vild:* vile]

2124 BRUTUS: I do not like your
faults.
CASSIUS: A friendly eye could never see
such faults.
BRUTUS: A flatterer's would not,
though they do appear
As huge as high Olympus.
                                        Julius Caesar 4.3.89

2125 TIMON [to some lords]: Live
loath'd, and long,
Most smiling, smooth, detested para-
sites,
Courteous destroyers, affable wolves,
meek bears,
You fools of fortune, trencher-friends,
time's flies,
Cap-and-knee slaves, vapors, and
minute-jacks!
                                        Timon of Athens 3.6.93

2126 CONSTABLE: There is flattery in
friendship.
                                        Henry V 3.7.114

2127 Drink up the monarch's plague,
this flattery.
                                        Sonnet 114

2128 CLOWN [to Duke, concerning a
fault he found in his friends]: Sir, they
praise me, and make an ass of me.
Now my foes tell me plainly I am an

ass; so that by my foes, sir, I profit in the knowledge of myself, and by my friends I am abus'd.

Twelfth Night 5.1.17

2129 OPHELIA [giving flowers to King]: There's fennel for you, and columbines.

Hamlet 4.5.180

[*fennel, columbines:* symbols respectively of flattery and ingratitude]

Flea

2130 ORLEANCE: That's a valiant flea that dare eat his breakfast on the lip of a lion.

Henry V 3.7.145

Flesh

2131 HAMLET [soliloquy]: O that this too too sallied flesh would melt, Thaw, and resolve itself into a dew!

Hamlet 1.2.129

[*sallied:* sullied; many editors prefer *solid*]

2132 COSTARD: Such is the simplicity of man to harken after the flesh.

Love's Labor's Lost 1.1.217

2133 FALSTAFF: I have more flesh than another man, and therefore more frailty.

1 Henry IV 3.3.166

Flight

2134 HASTINGS: To fly the boar before the boar pursues, Were to incense the boar to follow us, And make pursuit where he did mean no chase.

Richard III 3.2.28

2135 LADY MACBETH: Little is the wisdom, where the flight So runs against all reason.

Macbeth 4.2.13

2136 MALCOLM [to Donalbain]: Let us not be dainty of leave-taking, But shift away.

Macbeth 2.3.144

Flirtation

2137 BASSANIO [about Portia]: Sometimes from her eyes I did receive fair speechless messages.

Merchant of Venice 1.1.163

2138 BERTRAM [about Helena]: She knew her distance, and did angle for me, Maddening my eagerness with her restraint, As all impediments in fancy's course Are motives of more fancy, and in fine, Her inf'nite cunning, with her modern grace, Subdu'd me to her rate. She got the ring.

All's Well That Ends Well 5.3.212

Flood

2139 HELENA: Great floods have flown From simple sources; and great seas have dried When miracles have by the great'st been denied.

All's Well That Ends Well 2.1.139

[*great floods:* perhaps a reference to Moses smiting the rock at Horeb; *great seas have dried:* probably the parting of the Red Sea, permitting the Israelites to escape Egypt]

Flowers

2140 IMOGEN: Flow'rs are like the pleasures of the world.

Cymbeline 4.2.296

2141 CLOWN: Beauty's a flower.

Twelfth Night 1.5.51

2142 OBERON: I know a bank where the wild thyme blows,

Where oxlips and the nodding violet
  grows,
Quite over-canopied with luscious
  woodbine,
With sweet musk-roses and with eglan-
  tine;
There sleeps Titania sometime of the
  night,
Lull'd in these flowers with dances and
  delight.
          Midsummer Night's Dream 2.1.249

2143 No man inveigh against the
  withered flow'r,
But chide rough winter that the flow'r
  hath kill'd.
                    Rape of Lucrece 1254

2144 Flowers distill'd, though they
  with winter meet,
Leese but their show, their substance
  still lives sweet.
                              Sonnet 5
[*leese:* lose]

2145 YORK: Sweet flow'rs are slow and
  weeds make haste.
                    Richard III 2.4.15

2146 Fair flowers that are not gath'red
  in their prime
Rot, and consume themselves in little
  time.
                    Venus and Adonis 131

2147 Unwholesome weeds take root
  with precious flow'rs.
                    Rape of Lucrece 870

2148 The summer's flow'r is to the
  summer sweet,
Though to itself it only live and die,
But if that flow'r with base infection
  meet,
The basest weed outbraves his dignity:
For sweetest things turn sourest by
  their deeds;
Lilies that fester smell far worse than
  weeds.
                              Sonnet 94
[*outbraves:* surpasses in splendor]

2149 SONG [of Spring]: When daisies
  pied, and violets blue,
And lady-smocks all silver-white,
And cuckoo-buds of yellow hue
Do paint the meadows with delight.
              Love's Labor's Lost 5.2.894

2150 AUTOLYCUS [singing]: When
  daffadils begin to peer,
With heigh, the doxy over the dale!
Why, then comes in the sweet o' the
  year,
For the red blood reigns in the winter's
  pale.
                    Winter's Tale 4.3.1
[*daffadils:* daffodils]

2151 PERDITA: The marigold . . . goes
  to bed wi' th' sun,
And with him rises weeping.
                    Winter's Tale 4.4.105

2152 CONSTANCE [to her son, Arthur]:
Of Nature's gifts thou mayst with lilies
  boast,
And with the half-blown rose.
                    King John 3.1.53

2153 SALISBURY: To gild refined gold,
  to paint the lily,
To throw perfume on the violet . . .
Is wasteful and ridiculous excess.
                    King John 4.2.11

2154 PERDITA: Daffadils,
That come before the swallow dares,
  and take
The winds of March with beauty;
  violets, dim,
But sweeter than the lids of Juno's
  eyes,
Or Cytherea's breath; pale primroses,
That die unmarried, ere they can
  behold
Bright Phoebus in his strength (a
  malady
Most incident to maids); bold oxlips,
  and
The crown imperial; lilies of all kinds

(The flower-de-luce being one). O,
these I lack,
To make you garlands of.
Winter's Tale 4.4.118
[*daffadils:* daffodils]

2155 FRIAR LAWRENCE: Within the infant rind of this weak flower
Poison hath residence and medicine
power;
For this, being smelt, with that part
cheers each part,
Being tasted, stays all senses with the
heart.
Romeo and Juliet 2.3.23
[*stays:* brings to a halt]

2156 HELICANUS: The plants look up
to heaven, from whence
They have their nourishment.
Pericles 1.2.54

2157 Though the rose have prickles,
yet 'tis pluck'd.
Venus and Adonis 574

2158 O how much more doth beauty
beauteous seem
By that sweet ornament which truth
doth give!
The rose looks fair, but fairer we it
deem
For that sweet odor which doth in it
live.
Sonnet 54

2159 JULIET: What's in a name? That
which we call a rose
By any other word would smell as
sweet.
Romeo and Juliet 2.2.43

2160 EMILIA: Of all flow'rs
Methinks a rose is best.
WOMAN: Why, gentle madam?
EMILIA: It is the very emblem of a
maid;
For when the west wind courts her
gently,
How modestly she blows, and paints
the sun
With her chaste blushes! When the
north comes near her,

Rude and impatient, then, like
chastity,
She locks her beauties in her bud
again,
And leaves him to base briers.
Two Noble Kinsmen 2.2.135

2161 OPHELIA [giving out flowers after
Polonius' death]: There's rosemary,
that's for remembrance; pray you, love,
remember. And there is pansies, that's
for thoughts ... [to Claudius] There's
fennel for you, and columbines. [to
Gertrude]: There's rue for you, and
here's some for me; we may call it herb
of grace a' Sundays. You may wear
your rue with a difference. There's a
daisy. I would give you some violets,
but they wither'd all when my father
died.
Hamlet 4.5.175
[*rosemary:* used as a symbol of remembrance at both weddings and funerals; *pansies:* emblems of love and courtship; *fennel:* emblem of flattery; *columbines:* emblems of ingratitude; *rue:* emblem of sorrow and repentance, which, when mingled with holy water, was called the *herb of grace; daisy:* emblem of dissembling, faithlessness; *violets:* emblems of faithfulness]

2162 BOY [singing]:
Roses, their sharp spines being gone,
Not royal in their smells alone,
But in their hue;
Maiden pinks, of odor faint,
Daisies smell-less, yet most quaint,
And sweet thyme true;
Primrose, first-born child of Ver,
Merry spring-time's harbinger,
With her bells dim;
Oxlips in their cradles growing,
Marigolds on death-beds blowing,
Larks'-heels trim;
All dear Nature's children sweet,
Lie 'fore bride and bridegroom's feet,
Blessing their sense;
Not an angel of the air,
Bird melodious, or bird fair
Is absent hence.
The crow, the sland'rous cuckoo, nor
The boding raven, nor chough hoar
Nor chatt'ring pie,

May on our bridehouse perch or sing,
Or with them any discord bring,
But from it fly.
Two Noble Kinsmen 1.1.1

Folly

2163 CELIA: All's brave that youth
mounts and folly guides.
As You Like It 3.4.45

2164 HELENA: Full oft we see
Cold wisdom waiting on superfluous
folly.
All's Well That Ends Well 1.1.104

2165 ULYSSES: The amity that wisdom
knits not, folly may easily untie.
Troilus and Cressida 2.3.101

2166 PRINCE: In every thing the purpose must weigh with the folly.
2 Henry IV 2.2.175

2167 MENENIUS: We call a nettle but
a nettle, and
The faults of fools but folly.
Coriolanus 2.1.190

2168 CLOWN [to Viola]: Foolery, sir,
does walk about the orb like the sun,
it shines every where.
Twelfth Night 3.1.38

2169 SILVIUS: If thou rememb'rest not
the slightest folly
That ever love did make thee run into,
Thou hast not lov'd.
As You Like It 2.4.34

2170 VALENTINE: By love the young
and tender wit
Is turn'd to folly.
Two Gentlemen of Verona 1.1.47

2171 JESSICA: Love is blind, and lovers
cannot see
The petty follies that themselves
commit.
Merchant of Venice 2.6.36

2172 TOUCHSTONE: As all is mortal in
nature, so is all nature in love mortal
in folly.
As You Like It 2.4.55

2173 CLEOPATRA: Though age from
folly could not give me freedom,
It does from childishness.
Antony and Cleopatra 1.3.57

2174 FIRST SENATOR: What folly 'tis to
hazard life for ill!
Timon of Athens 3.5.37

2175 LADY MACDUFF: I am in this
earthly world — where to do harm
Is often laudable, to do good sometime
Accounted dangerous folly.
Macbeth 4.2.75

2176 EDMUND [soliloquy]: This is the
excellent foppery of the world, that
when we are sick in fortune — often the
surfeits of our own behavior — we make
guilty of our disasters the sun, the
moon, and stars, as if we were villains
on necessity, fools by heavenly compulsion, knaves, thieves, and treachers by
spherical predominance; drunkards,
liars, and adulterers by an enforc'd
obedience of planetary influence; and
all that we are evil in, by a divine
thrusting on.
King Lear 1.2.118

2177 THERSITES [to Patroclus]: The
common curse of mankind, folly and
ignorance, be thine.
Troilus and Cressida 2.3.27

2178 FORD [to Falstaff]: As you have
one eye upon my follies . . . turn
another into the register of your own,
that I may pass with reproof the easier.
Merry Wives of Windsor 2.2.185

Food

2179 BALTHAZAR: Small cheer and
great welcome makes a merry feast.
Comedy of Errors 3.1.26
[*cheer:* used here as a metaphor for food]

2180 ANTIPHOLUS EPHESUS: A table full of welcome makes scarce one dainty dish.
Comedy of Errors 3.1.23

2181 JULIA [to Lucetta, on Proteus]: Know'st thou not his looks are my soul's food?
Two Gentlemen of Verona 2.7.15

2182 GAUNT: With eager feeding food doth choke the feeder.
Richard II 2.1.37

2183 CORIN: Good pasture makes fat sheep.
As You Like It 3.2.27

Fools

2184 PUCK: Lord, what fools these mortals be!
Midsummer Night's Dream 3.2.115

2185 IMOGEN: Fools are not mad folks.
Cymbeline 2.3.101

2186 LEAR: When we are born, we cry that we are come
To this great stage of fools.
King Lear 4.6.182

2187 BOTTOM: Man is but a patch'd fool.
Midsummer Night's Dream 4.1.209

2188 ORLEANCE: A fool's bolt is soon shot.
Henry V 3.7.122

2189 CLOWN: Better a witty fool than a foolish wit.
Twelfth Night 1.5.36

2190 TOUCHSTONE: The fool doth think he is wise, but the wise man knows himself to be a fool.
As You Like It 5.1.31

2191 CELIA: Always the dullness of the fool is the whetstone of the wits.
As You Like It 1.2.54

2192 CLEOPATRA: Wishers were ever fools.
Antony and Cleopatra 4.15.37

2193 OLIVIA: There is no slander in an allow'd fool, though he do nothing but rail.
Twelfth Night 1.5.94

2194 CLOWN [to Viola]: Foolery, sir, does walk about the orb like the sun, it shines every where.
Twelfth Night 3.1.38

2195 VIOLA: To play the fool,
And do that well craves a kind of wit.
Twelfth Night 3.1.60

2196 KING [to Falstaff]: How ill white hairs become a fool and jester!
2 Henry IV 5.5.48

2197 GONERIL: Old fools are babes again, and must be us'd
With checks as flatteries.
King Lear 1.3.19

2198 CLOWN: God give them wisdom that have it; and those that are fools, let them use their talents.
Twelfth Night 1.5.14

2199 CLOWN: These wise men that give fools money get themselves a good report—after fourteen years' purchase.
Twelfth Night 4.1.21

2200 MALVOLIO: I take these wise men that crow so at these set kind of fools no better than fools' zanies.
Twelfth Night 1.5.88
[*fools' zanies:* fools' fools]

2201 LUCIANA: How many fond fools serve mad jealousy?
Comedy of Errors 2.1.116

2202 THURIO: I hold him but a fool that will endanger
His body for a girl that loves him not.
Two Gentlemen of Verona 5.4.133

2203 MARIA: Folly in fools bears not so strong a note

As fool'ry in the wise, when wit doth
dote.
Love's Labor's Lost 5.2.75

2204 THERSITES: I will keep where
there is wit stirring, and leave the faction of fools.
Troilus and Cressida 2.1.118

2205 PRINCE: Thus we play the fools
with the time, and the spirits of the
wise sit in the clouds and mock us.
2 Henry IV 2.2.141

2206 FIRST LORD: To wisdom he's a
fool that will not yield.
Pericles 2.4.54

2207 GUIDERIUS [about Cloten]: Not
Hercules
Could have knock'd out his brains, for
he had none.
Cymbeline 4.2.114

Foot

2208 CASCA [to Cassius]: I will set this
foot of mine as far
As who goes farthest.
Julius Caesar 1.3.118

2209 K. JOHN: Make haste; the better
foot before.
King John 4.2.170

2210 FRIAR LAWRENCE [about Juliet]:
Here comes the lady. O, so light a
foot
Will ne'er wear out the everlasting
flint.
Romeo and Juliet 2.6.16

Foppery

2211 LUCIO: I had as lief have the foppery of freedom as the mortality of
imprisonment.
Measure for Measure 1.2.133
[Most editors prefer *morality*, in antithesis
to *foppery*.]

2212 SHYLOCK: Let not the sound of
shallow fopp'ry enter
My sober house.
Merchant of Venice 2.5.35

2213 EDMUND [soliloquy]: This is the
excellent foppery of the world, that
when we are sick in fortune—often the
surfeits of our own behavior—we make
guilty of our disasters the sun, the
moon, and stars, as if we were villains
on necessity, fools by heavenly compulsion, knaves, thieves, and treachers by
spherical predominance.
King Lear 1.2.118

2214 LAFEW [about Parolles]: The soul
of this man is his clothes.
All's Well That Ends Well 2.5.43

2215 BRABANTIO: The wealthy curled
darlings of our nation.
Othello 1.2.68

2216 HOTSPUR [about a certain lord]:
He made me mad
To see him shine so brisk, and smell so
sweet,
And talk so like a waiting-
gentlewoman.
1 Henry IV 1.3.53

Foreboding

2217 ARCHBISHOP: Against ill chances
men are ever merry,
But heaviness foreruns the good event.
2 Henry IV 4.2.81

Foresight

2218 PORTIA: If to do were as easy as
to know what were good to do, chapels
had been churches, and poor men's
cottages princes' palaces.
Merchant of Venice 1.2.12

2219 CRESSIDA: To fear the worst oft
cures the worst.
Troilus and Cressida 3.2.73

Forgetfulness

2220 AGAMEMNON: What's past and
what's to come is strew'd with husks
And formless ruin of oblivion.
Troilus and Cressida 4.5.166

2221 PERCY: That is not forgot
Which ne'er I did remember.
Richard II 2.3.37

2222 IAGO: Men are men: the best
sometimes forget.
Othello 2.3.241

2223 PLAYER KING: Most necessary 'tis
that we forget
To pay ourselves what to ourselves is
debt.
Hamlet 3.2.192

2224 MACBETH [to doctor, on Lady
Macbeth]: Canst thou not minister
to a mind diseas'd,
Pluck from the memory a rooted sor-
row,
Raze out the written troubles of the
brain,
And with some sweet oblivious anti-
dote
Cleanse the stuff'd bosom of that
perilous stuff
Which weighs upon the heart?
Macbeth 5.3.40

2225 K. RICHARD: That I could forget
what I have been!
Or not remember what I must be now!
Richard II 3.3.138

2226 CONSTANCE: I am not mad, I
would to heaven I were!
For then 'tis like I should forget
myself.
O, if I could, what grief should I
forget!
King John 3.4.48

2227 DUMAINE [about Kate]: I would
forget her, but a fever she
Reigns in my blood, and will rememb'red be.
Love's Labor's Lost 4.3.93

Forgiveness

2228 PROSPERO: The rarer action is
In virtue than in vengeance.
The Tempest 5.1.27

2229 PROSPERO: As you from crimes
would pardon'd be,
Let your indulgence set me free.
The Tempest, Epilogue 19

2230 HAMLET [begging pardon from
Laertes]: Let my disclaiming from a
purpos'd evil
Free me so far in your most generous
thoughts,
That I have shot mine arrow o'er the
house
And hurt my brother.
Hamlet 5.2.241

2231 CLEOMINES [to Leontes]: Do as
the heavens have done, forget your
evil,
With them, forgive yourself.
Winter's Tale 5.1.5

2232 K. RICHARD [to two quarreling
dukes]: Deep malice makes too deep
incision.
Forget, forgive, conclude and be
agreed.
Richard II 1.1.155

2233 KING [soliloquy]: May one be
pardon'd and retain th' offense?
Hamlet 3.3.56

2234 OTHELLO [to Desdemona, before
killing her]: If you bethink yourself
of any crime
Unreconcil'd as yet to heaven and
grace,
Solicit for it straight.
Othello 5.2.26

2235 No more be griev'd at that which
thou hast done:
Roses have thorns, and silver fountains
mud,
Clouds and eclipses stain both moon
and sun,

And loathsome canker lives in sweetest
  bud.
All men make faults.
                              Sonnet 35

Form

2236 ANGELO [soliloquy]: O place, O
  form,
How often doth thou with thy case,
  thy habit,
Wrench awe from fools, and tie the
  wiser souls
To thy false seeming!
              Measure for Measure 2.4.12

2237 HELENA [soliloquy]: Things base
  and vile, holding no quantity,
Love can transform to form and dignity.
      Midsummer Night's Dream 1.1.232
[*holding no quantity:* lacking proportion,
unshapely]

2238 FOOL: That sir which serves and
  seeks for gain,
And follows but for form,
Will pack when it begins to rain,
And leave thee in the storm.
                        King Lear 2.4.78

Fortitude

2239 ANTONY: Bid that welcome
Which comes to punish us, and we
  punish it
Seeming to bear it lightly.
          Antony and Cleopatra 4.14.136

2240 GAUNT: Gnarling sorrow hath
  less power to bite
The man that mocks at it and sets it
  light.
                      Richard II 1.3.292

2241 HAMLET [to Horatio]: Blest are
  those
Whose blood and judgment are so well
  co-meddled,

That they are not a pipe for Fortune's
  finger
To sound what stop she please.
                        Hamlet 3.2.68
[*co-meddled:* commingled]

Fortress

2242 TALBOT: God is our fortress.
                    1 Henry VI 2.1.26

Fortune

2243 PANDULPH: When Fortune
  means to men most good,
She looks upon them with a
  threat'ning eye.
                    King John 3.4.119

2244 ANTONY: Fortune is merry,
And in this mood will give us any
  thing.
                Julius Caesar 3.2.266

2245 DUKE: What cannot be preserv'd
  when Fortune takes,
Patience her injury a mock'ry makes.
                      Othello 1.3.206

2246 THIDIAS: Wisdom and fortune
  combating together,
If that the former dare but what it can,
No chance may shake it.
          Antony and Cleopatra 3.13.79

2247 LUCIUS: Some falls are means the
  happier to arise.
                    Cymbeline 4.2.403

2248 PISANIO: Fortune brings in some
  boats that are not steer'd.
                    Cymbeline 4.3.46

2249 POSTHUMUS: Many dream not to
  find, neither deserve,
And yet are steep'd in favors.
                    Cymbeline 5.4.130

2250 MARIA: Some are born great ...
Some achieve greatness ...

And some have greatness thrust upon
them.
Twelfth Night 3.4.41

2251 ANTONY: Fortune knows
We scorn her most when most she
offers blows.
Antony and Cleopatra 3.11.73

2252 TIMON: Every grize of fortune
Is smooth'd by that below.
Timon of Athens 4.3.16
[*grize:* step]

2253 ENOBARBUS: Men's judgments
are
A parcel of their fortunes.
Antony and Cleopatra 3.13.31

2254 K. HENRY: I may conquer fortune's spite
By living low, where fortune cannot
hurt me.
3 Henry VI 4.6.19

2255 NESTOR: The thing of courage,
As rous'd with rage, with rage doth
sympathize,
And with an accent tun'd in self-same
key
Retires to chiding fortune.
Troilus and Cressida 1.3.51

2256 K. HENRY: Will fortune never
come with both hands full,
But write her fair words still in foulest
terms?
She either gives a stomach and no
food—
Such are the poor, in health; or else a
feast
And takes away the stomach—such are
the rich,
That have abundance and enjoy it not.
2 Henry IV 4.4.103

2257 BRUTUS: There is a tide in the
affairs of men,
Which taken at the flood, leads on to
fortune;
Omitted, all the voyage of their life
Is bound in shallows and in
miseries . . .

We must take the current when it
serves,
Or lose our ventures.
Julius Caesar 4.3.218

2258 JULIET: O Fortune, Fortune, all
men call thee fickle.
Romeo and Juliet 3.5.60

2259 FOOL: Fortune, that arrant
whore,
Ne'er turns the key to th' poor.
King Lear 2.4.52

2260 KENT: A good man's fortune
may grow out at heels.
King Lear 2.2.157

2261 ANTONIO: It is still her use
To let the wretched man outlive his
wealth,
To view with hollow eye and wrinkled
brow
An age of poverty.
Merchant of Venice 4.1.268

2262 HAMLET [to Horatio]: Blest are
those
Whose blood and judgment are so well
co-meddled,
That they are not a pipe for Fortune's
finger
To sound what stop she please.
Hamlet 3.2.68
[*co-meddled:* commingled]

2263 ULYSSES: How some men creep
in skittish Fortune's hall,
While others play the idiots in her
eyes!
Troilus and Cressida 3.3.134

2264 GUILDENSTERN: On Fortune's cap
we are not the very button.
Hamlet 2.2.229

2265 GLOUCESTER [reading a letter
from Edgar]: "This policy and
reverence of age makes the world bitter
to the best of our times; keeps our fortunes from us till our oldness cannot
relish them. I begin to feel an idle and
fond bondage in the oppression of

aged tyranny, who sways, not as it hath
power, but as it is suffer'd . . ."
King Lear 1.2.46

2266 POMPEY: I know not
What counts harsh Fortune casts upon
my face,
But in my bosom shall she never come,
To make my heart her vassal.
Antony and Cleopatra 2.6.53

2267 K. LEWIS [to Margaret]: Yield
not thy neck
To fortune's yoke, but let thy dauntless
mind
Ride in triumph over all mischance.
3 Henry VI 3.3.16

2268 K. EDWARD: Though Fortune's
malice overthrow my state,
My mind exceeds the compass of her
wheel.
3 Henry VI 4.3.46

2269 FLUELLEN: Fortune is painted
blind, with a muffler afore her eyes, to
signify to you that Fortune is blind;
and she is painted also with a wheel,
to signify to you, which is the moral of
it, that she is turning, and inconstant,
and mutability, and variation; and her
foot, look you, is fixed upon a
spherical stone, which rolls, and rolls,
and rolls. In good truth, the poet
makes a most excellent description of
it. Fortune is an excellent moral.
Henry V 3.6.30

2270 ACHILLES: 'Tis certain, greatness,
once fall'n out with fortune,
Must fall out with men too.
Troilus and Cressida 3.3.75

2271 ROSALIND: Fortune reigns in gifts
of the world, not in the lineaments of
Nature.
As You Like It 1.2.41
[*gifts of the world:* e.g. wealth, power, as
contrasted with beauty and intelligence—
gifts of nature]

2272 MALVOLIO: All is fortune.
Twelfth Night 2.5.23

2273 FIRST PLAYER: Out, out, thou
strumpet, Fortune! All you gods,
In general synod take away her power!
Break all the spokes and fellies from
her wheel,
And bowl the round nave down the
hill of heaven.
Hamlet 2.2.493

2274 LEAR [to Cordelia]: Mend your
speech a little,
Lest you may mar your fortunes.
King Lear 1.1.93

2275 AMIENS [to Duke Senior, in ex-
ile]: Happy is your Grace,
That can translate the stubbornness of
fortune
Into so quiet and so sweet a style.
As You Like It 2.1.18

2276 HAMLET [soliloquy]: To be, or
not to be, that is the question:
Whether 'tis nobler in the mind to
suffer
The slings and arrows of outrageous
fortune,
Or to take arms against a sea of
troubles,
And by opposing, end them. To die,
to sleep—
No more, and by a sleep to say we end
The heart-ache and the thousand
natural shocks
That flesh is heir to; 'tis a consum-
mation
Devoutly to be wish'd.
Hamlet 3.1.55

2277 ADAM: At seventeen years many
their fortunes seek,
But at fourscore it is too late a week.
As You Like It 2.3.73

2278 FLORIZEL: As th' unthought-on
accident is guilty
To what we wildly do, so we profess
Ourselves to be the slaves of chance,
and flies
Of every wind that blows.
Winter's Tale 4.4.538

Fox

2279 SUFFOLK: The fox barks not
when he would steal the lamb.
2 Henry VI 3.1.55

2280 GLOUCESTER [aside]: When the
fox hath once got in his nose,
He'll soon find means to make the
body follow.
3 Henry VI 4.7.25

2281 WORCESTER: Treason is but
trusted like the fox,
Who never so tame, so cherish'd and
lock'd up,
Will have a wild trick of his ancestors.
1 Henry IV 5.2.9

Foundation

2282 K. JOHN: There is no sure foundation set on blood;
No certain life achiev'd by others'
death.
King John 4.2.104

Fountain

2283 Mud not the fountain that gave
drink to thee.
Rape of Lucrece 577

Frailty

2284 CHANCELLOR: We are all men,
In our own natures frail, and capable
Of our flesh; few are angels.
Henry VIII 5.2.45

2285 DUKE: Frailty hath examples for
his falling.
Measure for Measure 3.1.186

2286 TROILUS: Sometimes we are
devils to ourselves,
When we will tempt the frailty of our
powers,
Presuming on their changeful potency.
Troilus and Cressida 4.4.95

2287 HAMLET: Frailty, thy name is
woman!
Hamlet 1.2.146

2288 VIOLA [soliloquy]: How easy it is
for the proper-false
In women's waxen hearts to set their
forms!
Alas, our frailty is the cause, not we,
For such as we are made of, such we
be.
Twelfth Night 2.2.29

Freedom

2289 PROSPERO: As you from crimes
would pardon'd be,
Let your indulgence set me free.
The Tempest, Epilogue 19

2290 CLAUDIO: As surfeit is the father
of much fast,
So every scope by the immoderate use
Turns to restraint.
Measure for Measure 1.2.126
[*scope:* freedom]

2291 LUCIO: I had as lief have the foppery of freedom as the mortality of
imprisonment.
Measure for Measure 1.2.133
[Most editors prefer *morality*, in antithesis
to *foppery*.]

Frenzy

2292 MESSENGER: Melancholy is the
nurse of frenzy.
Taming of the Shrew, Intro. 2.133

Friend

2293 SHALLOW: A friend 'n th' court is
better than a penny in purse.
2 Henry IV 5.1.30

2294 K. EDWARD: We are advertis'd
by our loving friends.
3 Henry VI 5.3.18

2295 BULLINGBROOK: I count myself in nothing else so happy
As in a soul rememb'ring my good friends.
Richard II 2.3.46

2296 TIMON: I am wealthy in my friends.
Timon of Athens 2.2.184

2297 Faithful friends are hard to find:
Every man will be thy friend,
Whilst thou hast wherewith to spend.
The Passionate Pilgrim xx.32

2298 PLAYER KING: Hitherto doth love on fortune tend,
For who not needs shall never lack a friend,
And who in want a hollow friend doth try,
Directly seasons him his enemy.
Hamlet 3.2.206

2299 BUCKINGHAM: Where you are liberal of your loves and counsels,
Be sure you be not lose; for those you make friends
And give your hearts to, when they once perceive
The least rub in your fortunes, fall away
Like water from ye, never found again
But where they mean to sink ye.
Henry VIII 2.1.126

2300 CORIN: He that wants money, means, and content is without three good friends.
As You Like It 3.2.24

2301 POLONIUS: Neither a borrower nor a lender be,
For loan oft loses both itself and friend.
Hamlet 1.3.75

2302 CASSIUS: A friend should bear his friend's infirmities.
Julius Caesar 4.3.86

2303 KING: To wail friends lost
Is not by much so wholesome-profitable

As to rejoice at friends but newly found.
Love's Labor's Lost 5.2.749

2304 TIMON: What need we have any friends, if we should ne'er have need of 'em? They were the most needless creatures living, should we ne'er have use for 'em; and would most resemble sweet instruments hung up in cases, that keep their sounds to themselves.
Timon of Athens 1.2.95

2305 BEATRICE: I will never love that which my friend hates.
Much Ado About Nothing 5.2.70

2306 There is no hate in loving.
Rape of Lucrece 240

2307 COUNTESS: Keep thy friend
Under thy own life's key.
All's Well That Ends Well 1.1.66

2308 SICINIUS: Nature teaches beasts to know their friends.
Coriolanus 2.1.6

2309 OTHELLO: Thou dost conspire against thy friend, Iago,
If thou but think'st him wrong'd, and mak'st his ear
A stranger to thy thoughts.
Othello 3.3.142

2310 ROSENCRANTZ: You do surely bar the door upon your own liberty if you deny your griefs to your friends.
Hamlet 3.2.338

2311 They that thrive well take counsel of their friends.
Venus and Adonis 640

2312 KING: Friendly counsel cuts off many foes.
1 Henry VI 3.1.184

2313 POLONIUS: Those friends thou hast, and their adoption tried,
Grapple them unto thy soul with hoops of steel,
But do not dull thy palm with entertainment

Of each new-hatch'd, unfledg'd
courage.
Hamlet 1.3.62

[*courage:* spirited, young blood]

2314 PROTEUS: In love
Who repects friend?
Two Gentlemen of Verona 5.4.54

2315 PROTEUS [soliloquy]: I to myself
am dearer than a friend.
Two Gentlemen of Verona 2.6.23

2316 He that is thy friend indeed,
He will help thee in thy need:
If thou sorrow, he will weep;
If thou wake, he cannot sleep;
Thus of every grief in heart
He with thee doth bear a part.
These are certain signs to know
Faithful friend from flatt'ring foe.
The Passionate Pilgrim xx.49

2317 VALENTINE [to Proteus]: O time
most accurst!
'Mongst all foes that a friend should be
the worst!
Two Gentlemen of Verona 5.4.71

2318 FLAVIUS: What vilder thing upon
the earth than friends
Who can bring noblest minds to basest
ends!
Timon of Athens 4.3.463

[*vilder:* viler]

Friendship

2319 CONSTABLE: There is flattery in
friendship.
Henry V 3.7.114

2320 ULYSSES: The amity that wisdom
knits not, folly may easily untie.
Troilus and Cressida 2.3.101

2321 CLAUDIO [soliloquy]: Friendship
is constant in all other things
Save in the office and affairs of love.
Much Ado About Nothing 2.1.175

2322 ANTONIO [to Shylock]: If thou
wilt lend this money, lend it not

As to thy friends, for when did friend-
ship take
A breed for barren metal of his friend?
But lend it rather to thine enemy,
Who if he break, thou mayst with bet-
ter face
Exact the penalty.
Merchant of Venice 1.3.132

[*breed:* offspring or increase]

2323 TIMON: Ceremony was but
devis'd at first
To set a gloss on faint deeds, hollow
welcomes,
Recanting goodness, sorry ere 'tis
shown;
But where there is true friendship,
there needs none.
Timon of Athens 1.2.15

2324 AMIENS: Most friendship is
feigning.
As You Like It 2.7.181

2325 APEMANTUS: Friendship's full of
dregs.
Timon of Athens 1.2.233

2326 Let me not to the marriage of
true minds
Admit impediments; love is not love
Which alters when it alteration finds,
Or bends with the remover to remove.
O no, it is an ever-fixed mark
That looks on tempests and is never
shaken;
It is the star to every wand'ring bark,
Whose worth's unknown, although his
highth be taken.
Love's not Time's fool, though rosy lips
and cheeks
Within his bending sickle's compass
come,
Love alters not with his brief hours and
weeks,
But bears it out even to the edge of
doom.
Sonnet 116

[*highth:* height]

Frivolity

2327 PETRUCHIO: Leave frivolous
circumstances.
Taming of the Shrew 5.1.26

Frown

2328 Looks kill love, and love by looks
reviveth:
A smile recures the wounding of a
frown.
Venus and Adonis 464

Frugality

2329 K. HENRY: I may conquer fortune's spite
By living low, where fortune cannot
hurt me.
3 Henry VI 4.6.19

Fruit

2330 FALSTAFF: The tree may be
known by the fruit, as the fruit by the
tree.
1 Henry IV 2.4.428

2331 IAGO: Fruits that blossom first
will first be ripe.
Othello 2.3.377

2332 K. RICHARD: The ripest fruit first
falls.
Richard II 2.1.153

2333 The mellow plum doth fall, the
green sticks fast,
Or being early pluck'd, is sour to taste.
Venus and Adonis 527

Fruitfulness

2334 GARDENER: Superfluous branches
We lop away, that bearing boughs may
live.
Richard II 3.4.63

Function

2335 WINCHESTER: Each hath his place
and function to attend.
1 Henry VI 1.1.173

Fury

2336 ENOBARBUS [soliloquy]: To be
furious
Is to be frighted out of fear, and in
that mood
The dove will peck the estridge.
Antony and Cleopatra 3.13.194

2337 PETRUCHIO: Where two raging
fires meet together,
They do consume the thing that feeds
their fury.
Taming of the Shrew 2.1.132

Futility

2338 BEROWNE: Climb o'er the house
to unlock the little gate.
Love's Labor's Lost 1.1.109

2339 GREEN [on York's war with Bullingbrook]: Alas, poor duke, the task
he undertakes
Is numb'ring sands and drinking
oceans dry.
Richard II 2.2.145

2340 KING [to Laertes, on why Hamlet
was not charged for the murder of
Polonius]: My arrows,
Too slightly timber'd for so loud a
wind,
Would have reverted to my bow again,
And not where I have aim'd them.
Hamlet 4.7.21

2341 PANDARUS: I have had my labor
for my travail.
Troilus and Cressida 1.1.70

Future

2342 ARCHBISHOP: Past and to come
seems best; things present worst.
2 Henry IV 1.3.108

2343 AGAMEMNON: What's past and what's to come is strew'd with husks
And formless ruin of oblivion.
Troilus and Cressida 4.5.166

2344 KING: O God, that one might read the book of fate,
And see the revolution of the times
Make mountains level, and the continent,
Weary of solid firmness, melt itself
Into the sea, and other times to see
The beachy girdle of the ocean
Too wide for Neptune's hips; how chance's mocks
And changes fill the cup of alteration
With divers liquors! O, if this were seen,
The happiest youth, viewing his progress through,
What perils past, what crosses to ensue,
Would shut the book, and sit him down and die.
2 Henry IV 3.1.45

2345 BANQUO [to the three witches]:
If you can look into the seeds of time,
And say which grain will grow, and which will not,
Speak then to me, who neither beg nor fear
Your favors nor your hate.
Macbeth 1.3.58

2346 OPHELIA: We know what we are, but know not what we may be.
Hamlet 4.5.43

2347 BRUTUS [to Cassius, on the eve of battle]: O that a man might know
The end of this day's business ere it come!
But it sufficeth that the day will end,
And then the end is known.
Julius Caesar 5.1.122

2348 FLAVIUS: The future comes apace;
What shall defend the interim?
Timon of Athens 2.2.148

2349 My grief lies onward and my joy behind.
Sonnet 50

Gain

2350 Despair to gain doth traffic oft for gaining,
And when great treasure is the meed proposed,
Though death be adjunct, there's no death supposed.
Rape of Lucrece 131

2351 Those that much covet are with gain so fond,
That what they have not, that which they possess,
They scatter and unloose it from their bond,
And so by hoping more they have but less.
Rape of Lucrece 134

2352 TRANIO: No profit grows where is no pleasure ta'en.
Taming of the Shrew 1.1.39

2353 MOROCCO: Men that hazard all
Do it in hope of fair advantages;
A golden mind stoops not to shows of dross.
Merchant of Venice 2.7.18

2354 K. HENRY: Didst thou never hear
That things ill got had ever bad success?
3 Henry VI 2.2.45

2355 FIRST LORD: How mightily sometimes we make us comforts of our losses!
SECOND LORD: And how mightily some other times we drown our gain in tears!
All's Well That Ends Well 4.3.65

2356 FOOL: That sir which serves and seeks for gain,
And follows but for form,

Will pack when it begins to rain,
And leave thee in the storm.
King Lear 2.4.78

2357 What win I if I gain the thing I
seek?
A dream, a breath, a froth of fleeting
joy.
Who buys a minute's mirth to wail a
week?
Or sells eternity to get a toy?
Rape of Lucrece 211

Gall

2358 ULYSSES: O deadly gall, and
theme of all our scorns,
For which we lose our heads to gild his
horns!
Troilus and Cressida 4.5.30

2359 FALSTAFF [to Chief Justice]: You
that are old consider not the capacities
of us that are young, you do measure
the heat of our livers with the bitterness of your galls.
2 Henry IV 1.2.173

Gallows

2360 FIRST CLOWN: The gallows does
well; but how does it well? It does well
to those that do ill.
Hamlet 5.1.45

Gamble

2361 K. RICHARD: I have set my life
upon a cast,
And I will stand the hazard of the die.
Richard III 5.4.9
[*cast:* throw of the dice; *die:* singular of
dice]

Gardening

2362 QUEEN: Now 'tis spring, and
weeds are shallow rooted;
Suffer them now, and they'll o'ergrow
the garden,

And choke the herbs for want of husbandry.
2 Henry VI 3.1.31

Gate

2363 CLOWN: I am for the house with
the narrow gate, which I take to be too
little for pomp to enter.
All's Well That Ends Well 4.5.50

Generosity

2364 PRINCESS: A giving hand, though
foul, shall have fair praise.
Love's Labor's Lost 4.1.23

2365 TIMON: 'Tis not enough to help
the feeble up,
But to support him after.
Timon of Athens 1.1.107

2366 OLIVIA: To be generous,
guiltless, and of a free disposition, is to
take those things for bird-bolts that
you deem cannon-bullets.
Twelfth Night 1.5.91
[*bird-bolts:* blunt-headed arrows for
shooting birds]

2367 FLAVIUS: Being free itself, it
[bounty] thinks all others so.
Timon of Athens 2.2.233

2368 FALVIUS [to Timon]: O my good
lord, the world is but a word;
Were it all yours to give it in a breath,
How quickly were it gone!
Timon of Athens 2.2.152

Gentlemen

2369 MOTH: You are a gentleman and
a gamester, sir.
ARMADO: I confess both, they are both
the varnish of a complete man.
Love's Labor's Lost 1.2.42

2370 HOLLAND: It was never merry world in England since gentlemen came up.

2 Henry VI 4.2.8

[*came up:* i.e. into fashion]

2371 FIRST CLOWN: There is no ancient gentlemen but gard'ners, ditchers, and grave-makers; they hold up Adam's profession.

Hamlet 5.1.29

2372 GLOUCESTER: The world is grown so bad
That wrens make prey where eagles dare not perch.
Since every Jack became a gentleman,
There's many a gentle person made a Jack.

Richard III 1.3.69

2373 SHEPHERD [to Autolycus]: We must be gentle, now we are gentlemen.

Winter's Tale 5.2.152

2374 FIRST KNIGHT [to Pericles]: We are gentlemen
Have neither in our hearts nor outward eyes
Envied the great, nor shall the low despise.

Pericles 2.3.24

Gentleness

2375 DUKE SENIOR [to Orlando]: Your gentleness shall force,
More than your force move us to gentleness.

As You Like It 2.7.102

2376 SECOND SENATOR: What thou wilt,
Thou rather shalt enforce it with thy smile
Than hew to't with thy sword.

Timon of Athens 5.4.44

2377 DESDEMONA: Those that do teach young babes

Do it with gentle means and easy tasks.

Othello 4.2.111

2378 ORLANDO: Let gentleness my strong enforcement be.

As You Like It 2.7.118

Giant

2379 AGAMEMNON: A stirring dwarf we do allowance give
Before a sleeping giant.

Troilus and Cressida 2.3.137

2380 ISABELLA: The poor beetle that we tread upon
In corporal sufferance finds a pang as great
As when a giant dies.

Measure for Measure 3.1.78

2381 ISABELLA: It is excellent
To have a giant's strength; but it is tyrannous
To use it like a giant.

Measure for Measure 2.2.108

2382 BELARIUS: The gates of monarchs
Are arch'd so high that giants may jet through
And keep their impious turbands on.

Cymbeline 3.3.4

[*jet:* strut]

Gift

2383 OPHELIA: Rich gifts wax poor when givers prove unkind.

Hamlet 3.1.100

2384 KING: The gift doth stretch itself as 'tis receiv'd.

All's Well That Ends Well 2.1.4

2385 TIMON: There's none
Can truly say he gives if he receives.

Timon of Athens 1.2.10

2386 VALENTINE [to Duke, on courtship]: Win her with gifts, if she respect not words:

Dumb jewels often in their silent kind
More than quick words do move a
woman's mind.
Two Gentlemen of Verona 3.1.89

2387 CAMILLO: You pay a great deal
too dear for what's given freely.
Winter's Tale 1.1.17

Glibness

2388 K. HENRY: These fellows of infinite tongue, that can rhyme
themselves into ladies' favors, they do
always reason themselves out again.
Henry V 5.2.155

Glory

2389 PUCELLE: Glory is like a circle in
the water,
Which never ceaseth to enlarge itself,
Till by broad spreading it disperse to
nought.
1 Henry VI 1.2.133

2390 Some glory in their birth, some
in their skill,
Some in their wealth, some in their
body's force,
Some in their garments, though new-
fangled ill,
Some in their hawks and hounds, some
in their horse;
And every humor hath his adjunct
pleasure,
Wherein it finds a joy above the rest.
Sonnet 91

2391 APEMANTUS: Like madness is the
glory of this life.
Timon of Athens 1.2.134

2392 Time's glory is to calm contending kings.
Rape of Lucrece 939

2393 FLAVIUS: O, the fierce wretched-
ness that glory brings us!
Timon of Athens 4.2.30

2394 CAPTAIN: We go to gain a little
patch of ground

That hath in it no profit but the
name.
Hamlet 4.4.18

2395 WOLSEY [soliloquy]: Farewell? a
long farewell to all my greatness!
This is the state of man: today he puts
forth
The tender leaves of hopes, tomorrow
blossoms,
And bears his blushing honors thick
upon him;
The third day comes a frost, a killing
frost,
And when he thinks, good easy man,
full surely
His greatness is a-ripening, nips his
root,
And then he falls as I do. I have
ventur'd,
Like little wanton boys that swim on
bladders,
This many summers in the sea of glory,
But far beyond my depth. My high-
blown pride
At length broke under me, and now
has left me,
Weary and old with service, to the
mercy
Of a rude stream that must for ever
hide me.
Vain pomp and glory of this world, I
hate ye!
I feel my heart new open'd. O how
wretched
Is that poor man that hangs on princes'
favors!
There is, betwixt that smile we would
aspire to,
That sweet aspect of princes, and their
ruin,
More pangs and fears than wars or
women have;
And when he falls, he falls like Lucifer,
Never to hope again.
Henry VIII 3.2.351

2396 NERISSA: When the moon
shown, we did not see the candle.
PORTIA: So doth the greater glory dim
the less:
A substitute shines brightly as a king
Until a king be by, and then his state

Empties itself, as doth an inland brook
Into the main of waters.
Merchant of Venice 5.1.92

2397 PRINCESS: Glory grows guilty of
detested crimes.
Love's Labor's Lost 4.1.31

Gluttony

2398 LONGAVILLE: Fat paunches have
lean pates; and dainty bits
Makes rich the ribs, but bankrout quite
the wits.
Love's Labor's Lost 1.1.26
[*bankrout:* bankrupt]

2399 CAESAR: Let me have men about
me that are fat,
Sleek-headed men and such as sleep
a-nights.
Yond Cassius has a lean and hungry
look,
He thinks too much; such men are
dangerous.
Julius Caesar 1.2.192

2400 HOSTESS [to Chief Justice about
Falstaff]: He hath eaten me out of
house and home, he hath put all my
substance into that fat belly of his.
2 Henry IV 2.1.74

2401 KING [to Falstaff]: Make less thy
body hence and more thy grace,
Leave gormandizing.
2 Henry IV 5.5.52

Goals

2402 MACBETH: The flighty purpose
never is o'ertook
Unless the deed go with it.
Macbeth 4.1.145

2403 DESDEMONA: Men's natures
wrangle with inferior things,
Though great ones are their object.
Othello 3.4.144

2404 ALBANY: Striving to better, oft
we mar what's well.
King Lear 1.4.346

God

2405 K. HENRY: Let never day nor
night unhallowed pass,
But still remember what the Lord hath
done.
2 Henry VI 2.1.83

2406 TALBOT: God is our fortress.
1 Henry VI 2.1.26

2407 DOGBERRY: God is to be worshipp'd.
Much Ado About Nothing 3.5.39

2408 ADAM: He that doth the ravens
feed,
Yea, providently caters for the sparrow,
Be comfort to my age!
As You Like It 2.3.43

2409 K. HENRY: God shall be my
hope,
My stay, my guide, and lanthorn to my
feet.
2 Henry VI 2.3.24
[*lanthorn:* lantern]

2410 K. HENRY: Some, peradventure,
have on them the guilt of premeditated and contriv'd murther; some, of
beguiling virgins with the broken seals
of perjury; some, making the wars
their bulwark, that have before gor'd
the gentle bosom of peace with pillage
and robbery. Now, if these men have
defeated the law and outrun native
punishment, though they can outstrip
men, they have no wings to fly from
God.
Henry V 4.1.161
[*murther:* murder]

2411 Q. KATHERINE: Heaven is above
all yet; there sits a judge
That no king can corrupt.
Henry VIII 3.1.100

2412 KING [on fleeing St. Albans]:
Can we outrun the heavens?
2 Henry VI 5.2.73

2413 HELENA: It is not so with Him
that all things knows
As 'tis with us that square our guess by
shows;
But most it is presumption in us when
The help of heaven we count the act of
men.
All's Well That Ends Well 2.1.149

2414 HAMLET: There's a divinity that
shapes our ends,
Rough-hew them how we will.
Hamlet 5.2.10

2415 YORK [after being stabbed]:
Open thy gate of mercy, gracious God!
My soul flies through these wounds to
seek out thee.
3 Henry VI 1.4.177

2416 SUFFOLK: Rather let my head
Stoop to the block than these knees
bow to any
Save to the God of heaven and to my
king.
2 Henry VI 4.1.124

2417 WOLSEY: Had I but serv'd my
God with half the zeal
I serv'd my king, He would not in
mine age
Have left me naked to mine enemies.
Henry VIII 3.2.455

2418 CASSIO: God's above all; and
there be souls must be sav'd, and there
be souls must not be sav'd.
Othello 2.3.102

2419 PORTIA: Mercy is above this scep-
tred sway,
It is enthroned in the hearts of kings,
It is an attribute of God himself;
And earthly power doth then show
likest God's
When mercy seasons justice.
Merchant of Venice 4.1.193

2420 WARWICK: My soul intends to
live
With that dread King that took our
state upon him,
To free us from his Father's wrathful
curse.
2 Henry VI 3.2.153

2421 GRIFFITH [on Wolsey]: To add
greater honors to his age
Than man could give him, he died
fearing God.
Henry VIII 4.2.67

2422 HELENA: Great floods have flown
From simple sources; and great seas
have dried
When miracles have by the great'st
been denied.
All's Well That Ends Well 2.1.139
[*great floods:* Perhaps a reference to Moses
smiting the rock at Horeb; *great seas have
dried:* probably the parting of the Red Sea,
permitting the Israelites to escape Egypt]

Gods

2423 EDGAR: The gods are just, and of
our pleasant vices
Make instruments to plague us.
King Lear 5.3.171

2424 GLOUCESTER: As flies to wanton
boys are we to th' gods,
They kill us for their sport.
King Lear 4.1.36

Gold

2425 PAGE: Gold were as good as
twenty orators.
Richard III 4.2.38

2426 The strongest castle, tower, and
town,
The golden bullet beats it down.
The Passionate Pilgrim xviii.17

2427 K. HENRY: How quickly nature
falls into revolt
When gold becomes her object!

For this the foolish over-careful fathers
Have broke their sleep with thoughts,
their brains with care,
Their bones with industry;
For this they have engrossed and pil'd
up
The cank'red heaps of strange-achieved
gold;
For this they have been thoughtful to
invest
Their sons with arts and martial exercises.
2 Henry IV 4.5.65

2428 TIMON: What a god's gold,
That he is worshipp'd in a baser
temple
Than where swine feed!
Timon of Athens 5.1.47

2429 Foul cank'ring rust the hidden
treasure frets,
But gold that's put to use more gold
begets.
Venus and Adonis 767

2430 CLOWN: Though authority be a
stubborn bear, yet he is oft led by the
nose with gold.
Winter's Tale 4.4.801

2431 CLOTEN [soliloquy]: 'Tis gold
Which buys admittance (oft it doth),
yea, and makes
Diana's rangers false themselves, yield
up
Their deer to th' stand o' th' stealer;
and 'tis gold
Which makes the true man kill'd and
saves the thief;
Nay, sometimes hangs both thief and
true man. What
Can it not do, and undo?
Cymbeline 2.3.67

2432 HOSTESS: A good heart's worth
gold.
2 Henry IV 2.4.31

2433 TIMON: The learned pate
Ducks to the golden fool.
Timon of Athens 4.3.17
[*ducks:* bows]

2434 TIMON: O thou sweet king-killer,
and dear divorce
'Twixt natural son and sire! thou bright
defiler
Of Hymen's purest bed! thou valiant
Mars!
Thou ever young, fresh, lov'd, and
delicate wooer,
Whose blush doth thaw the conse-
crated snow
That lies on Dian's lap! thou visible
god,
That sold'rest close impossibilities,
And mak'st them kiss! that speak'st
with every tongue
To every purpose!
Timon of Athens 4.3.381

2435 LEAR: Plate sin with gold,
And the strong lance of justice hurtless
breaks;
Arm it in rags, a pigmy's straw does
pierce it.
King Lear 4.6.165

2436 ANNE [about Slender]: O, what
a world of vild ill-favor'd faults
Looks handsome in three hundred
pounds a-year!
Merry Wives of Windsor 3.4.32
[*vild:* vile]

2437 TIMON [soliloquy, on gold]: This
yellow slave
Will knit and break religions, bless th'
accurs'd,
Make the hoar leprosy ador'd, place
thieves,
And give them title, knee, and appro-
bation
With senators on the bench. This is it
That makes the wappen'd widow wed
again;
She, whom the spittle-house and
ulcerous sores
Would cast the gorge at, this embalms
and spices
To th' April day again.
Timon of Athens 4.3.34

2438 ROMEO [buying poison from the
Apothecary]: There is thy gold,
worse poison to men's souls,

Doing more murther in this loathsome world,
Than these poor compounds that thou mayest not sell.
I sell thee poison, thou hast sold me none.
Romeo and Juliet 5.1.80
[*murther:* murder]

2439 ROSALIND: Beauty provoketh thieves sooner than gold.
As You Like It 1.3.110

2440 BASTARD: Bell, book, and candle shall not drive me back,
When gold and silver becks me to come on.
King John 3.3.12
[*bell, book, and candle:* symbols of Church excommunication]

2441 ARVIRAGUS: All gold and silver rather turn to dirt,
As 'tis no better reckon'd, but of those Who worship dirty gods.
Cymbeline 3.6.53

Goodness

2442 LAUNCE: Good things should be prais'd.
Two Gentlemen of Verona 3.1.347

2443 HERMIONE: One good deed dying tongueless
Slaughters a thousand waiting upon that.
Our praises are our wages.
Winter's Tale 1.2.92

2444 KING: 'Tis a kind of good deed to say well,
And yet words are no deeds.
Henry VIII 3.2.153

2445 ANTONY: The evil that men do lives after them,
The good is oft interred with their bones.
Julius Caesar 3.2.75

2446 KING: Good alone
Is good, without a name.
All's Well That Ends Well 2.3.128

2447 HAMLET: There is nothing either good or bad, but thinking makes it so.
Hamlet 2.2.249

2448 FRIAR LAWRENCE [soliloquy]: Nought so vile that on earth doth live
But to the earth some special good doth give.
Romeo and Juliet 2.3.17

2449 ALBANY: Wisdom and goodness to the vild seem vild,
Filths savor but themselves.
King Lear 4.2.38
[*vild:* vile]

2450 POET: When we for recompense have prais'd the vild,
It stains the glory in that happy verse Which aptly sings the good.
Timon of Athens 1.1.15
[*vild:* vile]

2451 K. HENRY: There is some soul of goodness in things evil,
Would men observingly distil it out;
For our bad neighbor makes us early stirrers,
Which is both healthful and good husbandry.
Besides, they are our outward consciences
And preachers to us all, admonishing That we should dress us fairly for our end.
Thus may we gather honey from the weed,
And make a moral of the devil himself.
Henry V 4.1.4

2452 FALSTAFF: There lives not three good men unhang'd in England, and one of them is fat and grows old.
1 Henry IV 2.4.130

2453 PORTIA: If to do were as easy as to know what were good to do, chapels

had been churches, and poor men's cottages princes' palaces.
Merchant of Venice 1.2.12

2454 DUKE: Virtue is bold, and goodness never fearful.
Measure for Measure 3.1.208

2455 LADY MACDUFF: I am in this earthly world—where to do harm
Is often laudable, to do good sometime
Accounted dangerous folly.
Macbeth 4.2.75

2456 KING: There lives within the flame of love
A kind of week or snuff that will abate it,
And nothing is at a like goodness still,
For goodness, growing to a plurisy,
Dies in his own too much.
Hamlet 4.7.114
[*week:* wick; *plurisy:* excess, plethora]

2457 DUKE [to Isabella]: The goodness that is cheap in beauty makes beauty brief in goodness; but grace, being the soul of your complexion, shall keep the body of it ever fair.
Measure for Measure 3.1.181

2458 PORTIA: How far that little candle throws his beams!
So shines a good deed in a naughty world.
Merchant of Venice 5.1.90

Gossip

2459 HERO: How much an ill word may empoison liking!
Much Ado About Nothing 3.1.86

2460 HAMLET: A knavish speech sleeps in a foolish ear.
Hamlet 4.2.23

2461 CAPTAIN: What great ones do, the less will prattle of.
Twelfth Night 1.2.33

2462 WORCESTER: We in the world's wide mouth
Live scandaliz'd and foully spoken of.
1 Henry IV 1.3.153

2463 DOGBERRY: To babble and to talk, is most tolerable, and not to be endur'd.
Much Ado About Nothing 3.3.35
[*tolerable:* for intolerable]

2464 DOCTOR: Foul whisp'rings are abroad.
Macbeth 5.1.71

2465 CAMILLO: The injury of tongues.
Winter's Tale 1.2.338

2466 AARON: A long-tongu'd babbling gossip.
Titus Andronicus 4.2.150

Government

2467 EXETER: Government, though high, and low, and lower,
Put into parts, doth keep in one consent,
Congreeing in a full and natural close,
Like music.
Henry V 1.2.180
[*congreeing:* agreeing]

2468 YORK: Let them obey that know not how to rule.
2 Henry VI 5.1.6

2469 CRESSIDA: Mighty states characterless are grated
To dusty nothing.
Troilus and Cressida 3.2.188

2470 ANTONY: Equality of two domestic powers
Breeds scrupulous faction.
Antony and Cleopatra 1.3.47

2471 REGAN [answering Lear's request to visit her]: How in one house
Should many people under two commands

Hold amity? 'Tis hard, almost impossible.
King Lear 2.4.240

2472 MENENIUS [to some factious citizens]: You slander
The helms o' th' state, who care for you like fathers,
When you curse them as enemies.
Coriolanus 1.1.76

2473 GLOUCESTER [to Clarence, on his imprisonment]: Why, this it is, when men are rul'd by women.
Richard III 1.1.62

2474 YORK: 'Tis government that makes them [women] seem divine.
3 Henry VI 1.4.132
[*government:* discipline, self-control]

2475 CANTERBURY: So work the honey-bees,
Creatures that by a rule in nature teach
The act of order to a peopled kingdom.
They have a king, and officers of sorts,
Where some, like magistrates, correct at home;
Others, like merchants, venter trade abroad;
Others, like soldiers, armed in their stings,
Make boot upon the summer's velvet buds,
Which pillage they with merry march bring home
To the tent-royal of their emperor;
Who busied in his majesty surveys
The singing masons building roofs of gold,
The civil citizens kneading up the honey,
The poor mechanic porters crowding in
Their heavy burthens at his narrow gate,
The sad-ey'd justice, with his surly hum,
Delivering o'er to executioners pale
The lazy yawning drone.
Henry V 1.2.187
[*venter:* venture; *boot:* booty; *burthens:* burdens]

Grace

2476 MALCOLM: The king-becoming graces,
As justice, verity, temp'rance, stableness,
Bounty, perseverance, mercy, lowliness,
Devotion, patience, courage, fortitude,
I have no relish of them.
Macbeth 4.3.91

2477 ANGELO [soliloquy]: When once our grace we have forgot,
Nothing goes right.
Measure for Measure 4.4.33

2478 HASTINGS: O momentary grace of mortal men,
Which we more hunt for than the grace of God!
Who builds his hope in air of your good looks
Lives like a drunken sailor on a mast,
Ready with every nod to tumble down
Into the fatal bowels of the deep.
Richard III 3.4.96

2479 ORLANDO: To some kind of men
Their graces serve them but as enemies.
As You Like It 2.3.10

2480 FERDINAND: For several virtues
Have I lik'd several women, never any
With so full soul but some defect in her
Did quarrel with the noblest grace she ow'd,
And put it to the foil.
The Tempest 3.1.42

2481 BENEDICK [soliloquy]: Till all graces be in one woman, one woman shall not come in my grace. Rich she shall be, that's certain; wise, or I'll none; virtuous, or I'll never cheapen her; fair, or I'll never look on her; mild, or come not near me; noble, or not I for an angel; of good discourse, an excellent musician, and her hair shall be of what color it please God.
Much Ado About Nothing 2.3.28

2482 The flesh being proud, Desire
doth fight with Grace,
For there it revels.
Rape of Lucrece 712

2483 YORK: That word "grace"
In an ungracious mouth is but profane.
Richard II 2.3.88

2484 SIR ANDREW [concerning Sir
Toby's foolery]: He does it with a bet-
ter grace, but I do it more natural.
Twelfth Night 2.3.82

Grandmother

2485 K. RICHARD: A grandam's name
is little less in love
Than is the doting title of mother;
They are as children but one step
below.
Richard III 4.4.299

Gratitude

2486 KING: The gift doth stretch itself
as 'tis receiv'd.
All's Well That Ends Well 2.1.4

2487 KING: God's goodness hath been
great to thee.
Let never day nor night unhallowed
pass,
But still remember what the Lord hath
done.
2 Henry VI 2.1.82

2488 BULLINGBROOK: Evermore thanks
[is] the exchequer of the poor.
Richard II 2.3.65
[Gratitude being the only payment the poor
can make for favors.]

Grave

2489 CAPTAIN: We go to gain a little
patch of ground
That hath in it no profit but the name.
Hamlet 4.4.18

2490 K. RICHARD: Nothing can we call
our own but death,
And that small model of the barren
earth
Which serves as paste and cover to our
bones.
Richard II 3.2.152

2491 K. RICHARD: Let's talk of graves,
of worms, and epitaphs,
Make dust our paper, and with rainy
eyes
Write sorrow on the bosom of the
earth.
Let's choose executors and talk of wills;
And yet not so, for what can we be-
queath
Save our deposed bodies to the
ground?
Richard II 3.2.148

2492 KING: Our rash faults
Make trivial price of serious things we
have,
Not knowing them until we know their
grave.
All's Well That Ends Well 5.3.60

2493 HAMLET: To what base uses we
may return, Horatio! Why may not imagination trace the noble dust of Alexander, till 'a find it stopping a bunghole?
Hamlet 5.1.202

['a: he]

2494 HAMLET: Alexander died, Alexander was buried, Alexander returneth
to dust, the dust is earth, of earth we
make loam, and why of that loam
whereunto he was converted might
they not stop a beer-barrel?
Hamlet 5.1.208

2495 HAMLET: Imperious Caesar, dead
and turn'd to clay,
Might stop a hole to keep the wind
away.
O that that earth which kept the world
in awe
Should patch a wall t' expel the winter's flaw!
Hamlet 5.1.213

2496 ANTONY [on viewing the slain Roman general]: O mighty Caesar! dost thou lie so low?
Are all thy conquests, glories, triumphs, spoils,
Shrunk to this little measure?
Julius Caesar 3.1.148

2497 PRINCE [about Percy]: Ill-weav'd ambition, how much art thou shrunk!
When that this body did contain a spirit,
A kingdom for it was too small a bound,
But now two paces of the vilest earth
Is room enough.
1 Henry IV 5.4.88

2498 SECOND CLOWN: Who builds stronger than a mason, a shipwright, or a carpenter?
FIRST CLOWN: . . . When you are asked this question next, say "a grave-maker": the houses that he makes lasts till doomsday.
Hamlet 5.1.50

2499 MOROCCO: Gilded tombs do worms infold.
Merchant of Venice 2.7.69

2500 LEAR: So be my grave my peace.
King Lear 1.1.125

2501 GRIFFITH [on Wolsey, at his death]: He gave his honors to the world again,
His blessed part to heaven, and slept in peace.
Henry VIII 4.2.29

2502 VIOLA [to Olivia]: Lady, you are the cruell'st she alive
If you will lead these graces to the grave,
And leave the world no copy.
Twelfth Night 1.5.241

Gravity

2503 FALSTAFF: What doth gravity out of his bed at midnight?
1 Henry IV 2.4.294

Greatness

2504 HOTSPUR: Greatness knows itself.
1 Henry IV 4.3.74

2505 SUFFOLK: Great men oft die by vild besonians.
2 Henry VI 4.1.134
[*vild:* vile; *besonians:* scoundrels]

2506 APEMANTUS: Great men should drink with harness on their throats.
Timon of Athens 1.2.52

2507 DUKE [soliloquy]: O place and greatness! millions of false eyes
Are stuck upon thee. Volumes of report
Run with these false, and most contrarious quests
Upon thy doings; thousand escapes of wit
Make thee the father of their idle dream,
And rack thee in their fancies.
Measure for Measure 4.1.59

2508 ACHILLES: 'Tis certain, greatness, once fall'n out with fortune,
Must fall out with men too.
Troilus and Cressida 3.3.75

2509 MALVOLIO: Some are born great . . .
Some achieve greatness . . .
And some have greatness thrust upon them.
Twelfth Night 3.4.41

2510 PERICLES [on Antiochus]: He's so great can make his will his act.
Pericles 1.2.18

2511 Q. MARGARET: They that stand high have many blasts to shake them,
And if they fall, they dash themselves to pieces.
Richard III 1.3.258

2512 BRUTUS [soliloquy]: Th' abuse of greatness is when it disjoins
Remorse from power.
Julius Caesar 2.1.18

2513 HAMLET: 'Tis dangerous when
the baser nature comes
Between the pass and fell incensed
points
Of mighty opposites.
Hamlet 5.2.60
[*pass:* thrust; *fell incensed:* fiercely angered]

2514 K. HENRY [soliloquy]: O, be
sick, great greatness,
And bid thy ceremony give thee cure!
Thinks thou the fiery fever will go out
With titles blown from adulation?
Henry V 4.1.251

2515 The mightier man, the mightier
is the thing
That makes him honor'd, or begets
him hate;
For greatest scandal waits on greatest
state.
Rape of Lucrece 1004

2516 OTHELLO [soliloquy]: 'Tis the
plague of great ones,
Prerogativ'd are they less than the base.
Othello 3.3.273
[*prerogativ'd:* privileged]

2517 SAY: Great men have reaching
hands.
2 Henry VI 4.7.81

2518 MARTIUS [to some factious
citizens]: Who deserves greatness
Deserves your hate.
Coriolanus 1.1.176

2519 CHARMIAN: The soul and body
rive not more in parting
Than greatness going off.
Antony and Cleopatra 4.13.5
[*rive:* cleave]

2520 BASTARD [to King John]: Be stirring as the time, be fire with fire,
Threaten the threat'ner, and outface
the brow
Of bragging horror; so shall inferior
eyes,
That borrow their behaviors from the
great,

Grow great by your example and put
on
The dauntless spirit of resolution.
King John 5.1.48

2521 ISABELLA: Great men may jest
with saints; 'tis wit in them,
But in the less foul profanation.
Measure for Measure 2.2.128

2522 ISABELLA: That in the captain's
but a choleric word,
Which in the soldier is flat blasphemy.
Measure for Measure 2.2.130

2523 WOLSEY [soliloquy]: Farewell? a
long farewell, to all my greatness!
This is the state of man: to-day he puts
forth
The tender leaves of hopes, tomorrow
blossoms,
And bears his blushing honors thick
upon him;
The third day comes a frost, a killing
frost,
And when he thinks, good easy man,
full surely
His greatness is a-ripening, nips his
root,
And then he falls as I do.
Henry VIII 3.2.351

2524 HAMLET [soliloquy]: Rightly to
be great
Is not to stir without great argument,
But greatly to find quarrel in a straw
When honor's at the stake.
Hamlet 4.4.53

2525 FOOL: Let go thy hold when a
great wheel runs down a hill, lest it
break thy neck with following; but the
great one that goes upward, let him
draw thee after.
King Lear 2.4.71

2526 CLEOPATRA: Be it known that
we, the greatest, are misthought
For things that others do; and, when
we fall,
We answer others' merits in our name.
Antony and Cleopatra 5.2.176

2527 WOLSEY [soliloquy]: Nay then, farewell!
I have touch'd the highest point of all my greatness,
And, from that full meridian of my glory,
I haste now to my setting. I shall fall
Like a bright exhalation in the evening,
And no man see me more.
Henry VIII 3.2.222

2528 KING: Madness in great ones must not unwatch'd go.
Hamlet 3.1.189

2529 POSTHUMUS: Many dream not to find, neither deserve,
And yet are steep'd in favors.
Cymbeline 5.4.130

2530 TIMON: The greater scorns the lesser.
Timon of Athens 4.3.6

2531 The crow may bathe his coal-black wings in mire,
And unperceiv'd fly with the filth away,
But if the like the snow-white swan desire,
The stain upon his silver down will stay.
Poor grooms are sightless night, kings glorious day;
Gnats are unnoted wheresoe'er they fly,
But eagles gaz'd upon with every eye.
Rape of Lucrece 1009

Greed

2532 DUKE [to the condemned Claudio]: Happy thou art not,
For what thou hast not, still thou striv'st to get,
And what thou hast, forget'st.
Measure for Measure 3.1.21

2533 KING: How quickly nature falls into revolt
When gold becomes her object!
2 Henry IV 4.5.65

2534 MALCOLM: My more-having would be as a sauce
To make me hunger more.
Macbeth 4.3.81

2535 Poorly rich, so wanteth in his store,
That cloy'd with much, he pineth still for more.
Rape of Lucrece 97

Greek

2536 CASSIUS: Did Cicero say anything?
CASCA: Ay, he spoke Greek.
CASSIUS: To what effect?
CASCA: Nay, and I tell you that, I'll ne'er look you i' th' face again. But those that understood him smil'd at one another, and shook their heads; but, for mine own part, it was Greek to me.
Julius Caesar 1.2.278

Green

2537 ARMADO: Green indeed is the color of lovers.
Love's Labor's Lost 1.2.86

Grief

2538 BULLINGBROOK: Grief makes one hour ten.
Richard II 1.3.261

2539 CONSTANCE: Grief is proud and makes his owner stoop.
King John 3.1.69

2540 LEONATO: Men
Can counsel and speak comfort to the grief
Which they themselves not feel, but tasting it,
Their counsel turns to passion, which before
Would give preceptial med'cine to rage,

Fetter strong madness in a silken thread,
Charm ache with air, and agony with words.
Much Ado About Nothing 5.1.20

2541 BEROWNE: Honest plain words best pierce the ear of grief.
Love's Labor's Lost 5.2.753

2542 COUNTESS [to a French lord]: If thou engrossest all the griefs are thine,
Thou robb'st me of a moi'ty.
All's Well That Ends Well 3.2.65
[*engrossest:* monopolize]

2543 MALCOLM [to Macduff]: The grief that does not speak
Whispers the o'erfraught heart, and bids it break.
Macbeth 4.3.209

2544 MALCOLM [to Rosse and Macduff]: Let's make us med'cines of our great revenge
To cure this deadly grief.
Macbeth 4.3.214

2545 FALSTAFF: A plague of sighing and grief, it blows a man up like a bladder.
1 Henry IV 2.4.331

2546 BUSHY: Each substance of a grief hath twenty shadows,
Which show like grief itself, but is not so;
For sorrow's eye, glazed with blinding tears,
Divides one thing entire to many objects.
Richard II 2.2.14

2547 PAULINA: What's gone and what's past help
Should be past grief.
Winter's Tale 3.2.222

2548 DUKE: When remedies are past, the griefs are ended.
Othello 1.3.202

2549 PROTEUS: Cease to lament for that thou canst not help,
And study help for that which thou lament'st.
Two Gentlemen of Verona 3.1.244

2550 Sorrow, like a heavy hanging bell,
Once set on ringing, with his own weight goes;
Then little strength rings out the doleful knell.
Rape of Lucrece 1493

2551 BENEDICK: Every one can master a grief but he that has it.
Much Ado About Nothing 3.2.28

2552 Sad souls are slain in merry company,
Grief best is pleas'd with grief's society.
Rape of Lucrece 1110

2553 DUKE: To mourn a mischief that is past and gone
Is the next way to draw new mischief on.
Othello 1.3.204

2554 CONSTANCE: My grief's so great
That no supporter but the huge firm earth
Can hold it up.
King John 3.1.71

2555 ROSENCRANTZ [to Hamlet]: You do surely bar the door upon your own liberty, if you deny your griefs to your friend.
Hamlet 3.2.338

2556 DUKE: The robb'd that smiles steals something from the thief;
He robs himself that spends a bootless grief.
Othello 1.3.208

2557 GLOUCESTER: None can help our harms by wailing them.
Richard III 2.2.103

2558 It is a greater grief
To bear love's wrong than hate's known
injury.
Sonnet 40

2559 LADY CAPULET: Some grief
shows much of love,
But much of grief shows still some
want of wit.
Romeo and Juliet 3.5.73

2560 IMOGEN: Some griefs are
med'cinable.
Cymbeline 3.2.33

2561 Grief hath two tongues, and
never woman yet
Could rule them both without ten
women's wit.
Venus and Adonis 1007

2562 LAFEW: Moderate lamentation is
the right of the dead, excessive grief
the enemy of the living.
All's Well That Ends Well 1.1.55

2563 HELICANUS: Bear with patience
Such griefs as you yourself do lay upon
yourself.
Pericles 1.2.65

2564 LEONATO: Patch grief with
proverbs.
Much Ado About Nothing 5.1.17

2565 RICHARD: To weep is to make
less the depth of grief.
3 Henry VI 2.1.85

2566 PLAYER KING: The violence of
either grief or joy
Their own enactures with themselves
destroy.
Hamlet 3.2.196

2567 PLAYER KING: Where joy most
revels, griefs doth most lament;
Grief joys, joy grieves, on slender accident.
Hamlet 3.2.198

2568 COUNTESS: If the living be
enemy to the grief, the excess makes it
soon mortal.
All's Well That Ends Well 1.1.57

2569 YORK: Comfort's in heaven, and
we are on the earth,
Where nothing lives but crosses, cares,
and grief.
Richard II 2.2.78

2570 ANNE: 'Tis better to be lowly
born,
And range with humble livers in con-
tent,
Than to be perk'd up in a glist'ring
grief
And wear a golden sorrow.
Henry VIII 2.3.19

2571 QUEEN: Conceit is still deriv'd
From some forefather grief.
Richard II 2.2.33

2572 MRS. PAGE: Better a little
chiding than a great deal of
heart-break.
Merry Wives of Windsor 5.3.9

2573 ENOBARBUS: Grief is crown'd
with consolation.
Antony and Cleopatra 1.2.167

2574 EDGAR [soliloquy]: The mind
much sufferance doth o'erskip,
When grief hath mates, and bearing
fellowship.
King Lear 3.6.106

2575 QUEEN: Oft have I heard that
grief softens the mind,
And makes it fearful and degenerate.
2 Henry VI 4.4.1

2576 CONSTANCE: I am not mad, I
would to heaven I were!
For then 'tis like I should forget myself.
O, if I could, what grief should I
forget!
King John 3.4.48

2577 BELARIUS: Great griefs, I see,
med'cine the less.
Cymbeline 4.2.243

2578 MALCOLM: What's the newest
grief?
ROSSE: That of an hour's age doth hiss
the speaker;
Each minute teems a new one.
Macbeth 4.3.174
[*hiss the speaker:* for telling stale news]

2579 To see the salve doth make the
wound ache more.
Rape of Lucrece 1116

2580 K. RICHARD [to Bullingbrook]:
You may my glories and my state de-
pose,
But not my griefs; still am I king of
those.
Richard II 4.1.192

2581 BRABANTIO [to Duke]: Take hold
on me; for my particular grief
Is of so flood-gate and o'erbearing
nature
That it engluts and swallows other
sorrows.
Othello 1.3.55

2582 HAMLET: Why, let the strooken
deer go weep,
The hart ungalled play,
For some must watch while some must
sleep,
Thus runs the world away.
Hamlet 3.2.271
[*strooken:* stricken, wounded; *ungalled:*
unwounded]

2583 PETER: When griping griefs the
heart doth wound,
And doleful dumps the mind oppress,
Then music with her silver sound . . .
With speedy help doth lend redress.
Romeo and Juliet 4.5.126

2584 K. RICHARD: 'Tis very true, my
grief lies all within,
And these external manners of laments
Are merely shadows to the unseen grief

That swells with silence in the tortur'd
soul.
Richard II 4.1.295

2585 My grief lies onward and my joy
behind.
Sonnet 50

Growth

2586 Things growing to themselves are
growth's abuse.
Seeds spring from seeds, and beauty
breedeth beauty;
Thou wast begot, to get it is thy duty.
Venus and Adonis 166

2587 YORK: Idle weeds are fast in
growth.
Richard III 3.1.103

2588 YORK: Small herbs have grace,
great weeds do grow apace.
Richard III 2.4.13

Grub

2589 MENENIUS: There is differency
between a grub and a butterfly, yet
your butterfly was a grub.
Coriolanus 5.4.11

Guest

2590 BEDFORD: Unbidden guests
Are often welcomest when they are
gone.
1 Henry VI 2.2.55

Guilt

2591 GLOUCESTER: Suspicion always
haunts the guilty mind;
The thief doth fear each bush an
officer.
3 Henry VI 5.6.11

2592 IAGO: Guiltiness will speak,
Though tongues were out of use.
Othello 5.1.109

2593 They whose guilt within their
bosoms lie
Imagine every eye beholds their blame.
Rape of Lucrece 1342

2594 HAMLET [soliloquy]: Conscience
does make cowards of us all.
Hamlet 3.1.82

2595 QUEEN: So full of artless jealousy
is guilt,
It spills itself in fearing to be spilt.
Hamlet 4.5.19

2596 The guilt being great, the fear
doth still exceed.
Rape of Lucrece 229

2597 GHOST [to Hamlet, on the
Queen]: Leave her to heaven,
And to those thorns that in her bosom
lodge
To prick and sting her.
Hamlet 1.5.86

2598 HAMLET: Use every man after his
desert, and who shall scape whipping?
Hamlet 2.2.529

2599 MACBETH: Full of scorpions is my
mind.
Macbeth 3.2.36

2600 HAMLET: Let the gall'd jade
winch, our withers are unwrung.
Hamlet 3.2.242
[*gall'd jade:* chafed horse; *winch:* wince;
withers: ridge between a horse's shoulders;
unwrung: not rubbed sore]

Gullibility

2601 CLAUDIO [aside, about
Benedick]: Bait the hook well, this fish
will bite.
Much Ado About Nothing 2.3.108

Habit

2602 VALENTINE: How use doth breed
a habit in a man!
Two Gentlemen of Verona 5.4.1

2603 HAMLET: Use almost can change
the stamp of nature.
Hamlet 3.4.168

Hair

2604 DROMIO SYRACUSE: What [Time]
hath scanted men in hair he hath given
them in wit.
Comedy of Errors 2.2.80

2605 MORTIMER: These grey locks, the
pursuivants of death,
Nestor-like aged, in an age of care,
Argue the end of Edmund Mortimer.
1 Henry VI 2.5.5

Hallucination

2606 MACBETH [soliloquy, before slay-
ing Duncan]: Is this a dagger which
I see before me,
The handle toward my hand? Come,
let me clutch thee:
I have thee not, and yet I see thee still.
Art thou not, fatal vision, sensible
To feeling as to sight? or art thou but
A dagger of the mind, a false creation,
Proceeding from the heat-oppressed
brain?
Macbeth 2.1.38

2607 QUEEN [to Hamlet, on his
father's ghost]: This is the very
coinage of your brain,
This bodiless creation ecstasy
Is very cunning in.
Hamlet 3.4.137

Hand

2608 BEVIS: There's no better sign of a
brave mind that a hard hand.
2 Henry VI 4.2.19

2609 HAMLET: The hand of little
employment hath the daintier sense.
Hamlet 5.1.69

2610 MENAS: All men's faces are true, whatsome'er their hands are.
Antony and Cleopatra 2.6.97

2611 PRINCESS: A giving hand, though foul, shall have fair praise.
Love's Labor's Lost 4.1.23

2612 GLOUCESTER: O, let me kiss that hand!
LEAR: Let me wipe it first, it smells of mortality.
King Lear 4.6.132

2613 MACBETH [soliloquy, on Duncan's murder]: What hands are here? Hah! they pluck out mine eyes.
Will all great Neptune's ocean wash this blood
Clean from my hand? No; this my hand will rather
The multitudinous seas incarnadine,
Making the green one red.
Macbeth 2.2.56

2614 LADY MACBETH [haunted by Duncan's murder]: Here's the smell of the blood still. All the perfumes of Arabia will not sweeten this little hand. O, O, O!
Macbeth 5.1.50

2615 Sweating palm,
The president of pith and livelihood.
Venus and Adonis 25
[*president:* precedent]

Hanging

2616 POMPEY: He that drinks all night, and is hang'd betimes in the morning, may sleep the sounder all the next day.
Measure for Measure 4.3.46

2617 CLOWN: He that is well hang'd in this world needs to fear no colors.
Twelfth Night 1.5.5
[*fear no colors:* proverbial for "fear nothing"]

2618 LAUNCE: A man is never undone till he be hang'd.
Two Gentlemen of Verona 2.5.3

2619 NERISSA: The ancient saying is no heresy,
Hanging and wiving goes by destiny.
Merchant of Venice 2.9.83

2620 CLOWN: Many a good hanging prevents a bad marriage.
Twelfth Night 1.5.19

2621 POMPEY: I do find your hangman is a more penitent trade than your bawd: he doth oft'ner ask forgiveness.
Measure for Measure 4.2.49

Happiness

2622 AUTOLYCUS [singing]:
A merry heart goes all the day,
Your sad tires in a mile-a.
Winter's Tale 4.3.125

2623 DUKE [to the condemned Claudio]: Happy thou art not,
For what thou hast not, still thou striv'st to get,
And what thou hast, forget'st.
Measure for Measure 3.1.21

2624 BULLINGBROOK: I count myself in nothing else so happy
As in a soul remem'bring my good friends.
Richard II 2.3.46

2625 CLAUDIO: I were but little happy, if I could say how much!
Much Ado About Nothing 2.1.306

2626 O happiness enjoy'd but of a few,
And if possess'd, as soon decay'd and done
As is the morning's silver melting dew
Against the golden splendor of the sun!
Rape of Lucrece 22

2627 NATHANIEL: Society, saith the text, is the happiness of life.
Love's Labor's Lost 4.2.161

2628 EMILIA: If she be not honest, chaste, and true,
There's no man happy.
Othello 4.2.17

2629 ORLANDO [on the marriage of Oliver to Celia]: O, how bitter a thing it is to look into happiness through another man's eyes!
As You Like It 5.2.43

2630 OTHELLO: 'Tis happiness to die.
Othello 5.2.290

Hare

2631 CRESSIDA: They that have the voice of lions and the act of hares, are they not monsters?
Troilus and Cressida 3.2.88

2632 BASTARD [to Austria]: You are the hare of whom the proverb goes, Whose valor plucks dead lions by the beard.
King John 2.1.137

Harlotry

2633 EDGAR [in the guise of a madman, to Lear]: Keep thy foot out of brothels, thy hand out of plackets, thy pen from lenders' books.
King Lear 3.4.100
[*plackets:* openings in petticoats]

Harm

2634 MESSENGER: Frame your mind to mirth and merriment,
Which bars a thousand harms and lengthens life.
Taming of the Shrew, Intro. 2.135

2635 Q. MARGARET: Wise men ne'er sit and wail their loss,

But cheerly seek how to redress their harms.
3 Henry VI 5.4.1

2636 ANTONY: Ten thousand harms, more than the ills I know,
My idleness doth hatch.
Antony and Cleopatra 1.2.129

2637 EMILIA [to Othello]: Thou hast not half the pow'r to do me harm As I have to be hurt.
Othello 5.2.162
[*be hurt:* i.e. endure hurt]

2638 MENECRATES: We, ignorant of ourselves,
Beg often our own harms, which the wise pow'rs
Deny us for our good; so find we profit By losing of our prayers.
Antony and Cleopatra 2.1.5

2639 LADY MACDUFF: I am in this earthly world—where to do harm Is often laudable, to do good sometime Accounted dangerous folly.
Macbeth 4.2.75

2640 CORIN: I earn that I eat, get that I wear, owe no man hate, envy no man's happiness, glad of other men's good, content with my harm.
As You Like It 3.2.73

2641 GLOUCESTER: None can help our harms by wailing them.
Richard III 2.2.103

Harmony

2642 LORENZO: Soft stillness and the night
Become the touches of sweet harmony.
Merchant of Venice 5.1.56

2643 LORENZO: Such harmony is in immortal souls,
But whilst this muddy vesture of decay Doth grossly close it in, we cannot hear it.
Merchant of Venice 5.1.63

Harvest

2644 CONRADE [to Don John]: It is needful that you frame the season for your own harvest.
Much Ado About Nothing 1.3.25

2645 TOUCHSTONE: They that reap must sheaf and bind.
As You Like It 3.2.107

2646 ANTONY: The seedsman
Upon the slime and ooze scatters his grain,
And shortly comes to harvest.
Antony and Cleopatra 2.7.21

Haste

2647 FRIAR LAWRENCE: Wisely and slow, they stumble that run fast.
Romeo and Juliet 2.3.94

2648 FRIAR LAWRENCE: Too swift arrives as tardy as too slow.
Romeo and Juliet 2.6.15

2649 DUKE: Haste still pays haste, and leisure answers leisure.
Measure for Measure 5.1.410

2650 GAUNT: He tires betimes that spurs too fast betimes;
With eager feeding food doth choke the feeder.
Richard II 2.1.36

2651 CLEOPATRA: Celerity is never more admir'd
Than by the negligent.
Antony and Cleopatra 3.7.23

2652 K. JOHN: Make haste; the better foot before.
King John 4.2.170

2653 MALCOLM: Modest wisdom plucks me
From over-credulous haste.
Macbeth 4.3.119

2654 MACBETH [soliloquy, on slaying Duncan]: If it were done, when 'tis done, then 'twere well
It were done quickly.
Macbeth 1.7.1

2655 MALCOLM [to Donalbain]: Let us not be dainty of leave-taking,
But shift away.
Macbeth 2.3.144

Hate

2656 EXETER [soliloquy]: When envy breeds unkind division:
There comes the ruin, there begins confusion.
1 Henry VI 4.1.193

2657 JULIA: Love will not be spurr'd to what it loathes.
Two Gentlemen of Verona 5.2.7

2658 CHARMIAN: In time we hate that which we often fear.
Antony and Cleopatra 1.3.12

2659 It is a greater grief
To bear love's wrong than hate's known injury.
Sonnet 40

2660 SCROOP: Sweet love, I see, changing his property,
Turns to the sourest and most deadly hate.
Richard II 3.2.135

2661 K. RICHARD: The love of wicked men converts to fear,
That fear to hate, and hate turns one or both
To worthy danger and deserved death.
Richard II 5.1.66

2662 VALENTINE: Scorn at first makes after-love the more.
Two Gentlemen of Verona 3.1.95

Havens

2663 GAUNT: All places that the eye
of heaven visits
Are to the wise man ports and happy
havens.
Richard II 1.3.275

Hazard

2664 MOROCCO: Men that hazard all
Do it in hope of fair advantages.
Merchant of Venice 2.7.18

2665 FIRST SENATOR: What folly 'tis to
hazard life for ill!
Timon of Athens 3.5.37

2666 Things out of hope are compass'd
oft with vent'ring.
Venus and Adonis 567
[*vent'ring:* venturing]

2667 THURIO: I hold him but a fool
that will endanger
His body for a girl that loves him not.
Two Gentlemen of Verona 5.4.133

2668 K. RICHARD: I have set my life
upon a cast,
And I will stand the hazard of the die.
Richard III 5.4.9
[*cast:* throw of the dice; *die:* singular for
dice]

Healing

2669 PANDULPH: Before the curing of
a strong disease,
Even in the instant of repair and
health,
The fit is strongest.
King John 3.4.112

2670 IAGO: What wound did ever heal
but by degrees?
Othello 2.3.371

2671 KING: Diseases desperate grown
By desperate appliance are reliev'd,
Or not at all.
Hamlet 4.3.9

Health

2672 POINS: The immortal part needs
a physician, but that moves not him;
though that be sick, it dies not.
2 Henry IV 2.2.104

2673 Testy sick men, when their
deaths be near,
No news but health from their physicians know.
Sonnet 140

2674 LEAR: Infirmity doth still neglect
all office
Whereto our health is bound.
King Lear 2.4.106

Heart

2675 AUTOLYCUS [singing]:
A merry heart goes all the day,
Your sad tires in a mile-a.
Winter's Tale 4.3.125

2676 HOSTESS: A good heart's worth
gold.
2 Henry IV 2.4.31

2677 KATHERINE: A light heart lives
long.
Love's Labor's Lost 5.2.18

2678 PRINCESS: A heavy heart bears
not a humble tongue.
Love's Labor's Lost 5.2.737

2679 WOLSEY: Love thyself last,
cherish those hearts that hate thee;
Corruption wins not more than
honesty.
Henry VIII 3.2.444

2680 DON PEDRO: In faith, lady, you
have a merry heart.
BEATRICE: Yea, my lord, I thank it—
poor fool, it keeps on the windy side
of care.
Much Ado About Nothing 2.1.312

2681 GLOUCESTER: A heart unspotted
is not easily daunted.
2 Henry VI 3.1.100

2682 K. HENRY: A good heart . . . is the sun and moon, or rather the sun and not the moon; for it shines bright and never changes, but keeps his course truly.

Henry V 5.2.162

2683 Q. KATHERINE [to Cardinals Wolsey and Campeius]: Ye have angels' faces, but heaven knows your hearts.

Henry VIII 3.1.145

2684 BRABANTIO: I never yet did hear That the bruis'd heart was pierced through the ear.

Othello 1.3.218

2685 By our ears our hearts oft tainted be.

Rape of Lucrece 38

2686 For lovers say, the heart hath treble wrong When it is barr'd the aidance of the tongue.

Venus and Adonis 329

2687 Affection is a coal that must be cool'd, Else suffer'd it will set the heart on fire.

Venus and Adonis 387

2688 HELENA: My heart Is true as steel.

Midsummer Night's Dream 2.1.196

2689 MARGARET [on her betrothal to Henry]: A pure unspotted heart, Never yet taint with love, I send the King.

1 Henry VI 5.3.182

Heartbreak

2690 MRS. PAGE: Better a little chiding than a great deal of heart-break.

Merry Wives of Windsor 5.3.9

Heaven

2691 Q. KATHERINE: Heaven is above all yet; there sits a judge That no king can corrupt.

Henry VIII 3.1.100

2692 KING [soliloquy]: In the corrupted currents of this world Offense's gilded hand may shove by justice, And oft 'tis seen the wicked prize itself Buys out the law, but 'tis not so above: There is no shuffling, there the action lies In his true nature, and we ourselves compell'd, Even to the teeth and forehead of our faults, To give in evidence.

Hamlet 3.3.57

[*gilded hand*: offer of a bribe; *wicked prize*: ill-gotten gains]

2693 CASSIO: God's above all; and there be souls must be sav'd, and there be souls must not be sav'd.

Othello 2.3.102

2694 CARLISLE: The means that heavens yield must be embrac'd, And not neglected; else heaven would, And we will not. Heaven's offer we refuse, The proffered means of succors and redress.

Richard II 3.2.29

2695 HELENA: Most it is presumption in us when The help of heaven we count the act of men.

All's Well That Ends Well 2.1.151

2696 MARGARET: Though usurpers sway the rule a while, Yet heav'ns are just, and time suppresseth wrongs.

3 Henry VI 3.3.76

2697 DUKE: Heaven doth with us as we with torches do,
Not light them for themselves; for if our virtues
Did not go forth of us, 'twere all alike
As if we had them not.
Measure for Measure 1.1.32

2698 HELICANUS: Plants look up to heaven, from whence
They have their nourishment.
Pericles 1.2.55

2699 SAY: Ignorance is the curse of God,
Knowledge the wing wherewith we fly to heaven.
2 Henry VI 4.7.73

2700 K. RICHARD: Our holy lives must win a new world's crown.
Richard II 5.1.24

2701 BUCKINGHAM: Heaven has an end in all.
Henry VIII 2.1.124

2702 GLOUCESTER: I'll make my heaven in a lady's lap.
3 Henry VI 3.2.148

Hell

2703 ARIEL: Hell is empty,
And all the devils are here.
The Tempest 1.2.214

2704 FALSTAFF [about Gadshill]: If men were to be sav'd by merit, what hole in hell were hot enough for him?
1 Henry IV 1.2.107

2705 GREEN: My comfort is, that heaven will take our souls,
And plague injustice with the pains of hell.
Richard II 3.1.33

2706 KING: Black is the badge of hell,
The hue of dungeons, and the school of night.
Love's Labor's Lost 4.3.250

2707 SUFFOLK: What is wedlock forced, but a hell,
An age of discord and continual strife?
1 Henry VI 5.5.62

2708 FALSTAFF [soliloquy]: I think the devil will not have me damn'd, lest the oil that's in me should set hell on fire.
Merry Wives of Windsor 5.5.34

2709 OPHELIA: The primrose path of dalliance.
Hamlet 1.3.50

2710 ISABELLA: 'Tis the cunning livery of hell.
Measure for Measure 3.1.94

2711 Two loves I have, of comfort and despair,
That like two spirits do suggest me still:
My better angel is a man (right fair),
My worser spirit a woman (color'd ill).
To win me soon to hell, my female evil
Tempteth my better angel from my side;
And would corrupt my saint to be a devil,
Wooing his purity with her fair pride.
And whether that my angel be turn'd fiend,
Suspect I may (yet not directly tell):
For being both to me, both to each friend,
I guess one angel in another's hell:
The truth I shall not know, but live in doubt,
Till my bad angel fire my good one out.
The Passionate Pilgrim ii.1

Help

2712 PAULINA: What's past help
Should be past grief.
Winter's Tale 3.2.222

2713 PANDULPH: He that stands upon a slipp'ry place

Makes nice of no vild hold to stay him
up.
King John 3.4.137

[*vild:* vile]

2714 TIMON: 'Tis not enough to help
the feeble up,
But to support him after.
Timon of Athens 1.1.107

2715 PROTEUS: Cease to lament for
that thou canst not help,
And study help for that which thou
lament'st.
Two Gentlemen of Verona 3.1.243

Heresy

2716 LYSANDER: The heresies that
men do leave
Are hated most of those they did
deceive.
Midsummer Night's Dream 2.2.139

Heretic

2717 PAULINA: It is an heretic that
makes the fire,
Not she which burns in't.
Winter's Tale 2.3.115

Historian

2718 ULYSSES: Here's Nestor,
Instructed by the antiquary times;
He must, he is, he cannot but be wise.
Troilus and Cressida 2.3.250

History

2719 WARWICK: There is a history in
all men's lives,
Figuring the natures of the times
deceas'd,
The which observ'd, a man may
prophesy,
With a near aim, of the main chance
of things
As yet not come to life, who in their
seeds

And weak beginning lie intreasured.
Such things become the hatch and
brood of time.
2 Henry IV 3.1.80

Hoarding

2720 K. HENRY: Didst thou never
hear
That things ill got had ever bad
success?
And happy always for it was that son
Whose father for his hoarding went to
hell?
3 Henry VI 2.2.45

Holidays

2721 PRINCE: If all the year were playing holidays,
To sport would be as tedious as to
work.
1 Henry IV 1.2.204

2722 CONSTANCE: What hath this day
deserv'd? what hath it done,
That it in golden letters should be set
Among the high tides in the calendar?
King John 3.1.84

Holiness

2723 DUKE [soliloquy]: He who the
sword of heaven will bear
Should be as holy as severe;
Pattern in himself to know,
Grace to stand, and virtue go;
More nor less to others paying
Than by self-offenses weighing.
Shame to him whose cruel striking
Kills for faults of his own liking!
Measure for Measure 3.2.261

Home

2724 TOUCHSTONE: When I was at
home, I was in a better place, but
travellers must be content.
As You Like It 2.4.17

2725 K. HENRY: 'Tis ever common
That men are merriest when they are
from home.
Henry V 1.2.271

2726 VALENTINE: Home-keeping
youth have ever homely wits.
Two Gentlemen of Verona 1.1.2

Honesty

2727 MARIANA: No legacy is so rich as
honesty.
All's Well That Ends Well 3.5.12

2728 HAMLET: To be honest, as this
world goes, is to be one man pick'd
out of ten thousand.
Hamlet 2.2.178

2729 TOUCHSTONE [to Duke Senior]:
Rich honesty dwells like a miser, sir, in
a poor house, as your pearl in your
foul oyster.
As You Like It 5.4.59

2930 AUTOLYCUS: Though I am not
naturally honest, I am so sometimes by
chance.
Winter's Tale 4.4.712

2731 HAMLET: I am myself indifferent
honest, but yet I could accuse me of
such things that it were better my
mother had not borne me.
Hamlet 3.1.121

2732 IAGO: Take note, take note, O
world,
To be direct and honest is not safe.
Othello 3.3.377

2733 WOLSEY: Corruption wins not
more than honesty.
Henry VIII 3.2.444

2734 HAMLET: The power of beauty
will sooner transform honesty from
what it is to a bawd than the force of
honesty can translate beauty into his
likeness.
Hamlet 3.1.110

2735 TOUCHSTONE: Honesty coupled
to beauty is to have honey a sauce to
sugar.
As You Like It 3.3.29

2736 HAMLET: What news?
ROSENCRANTZ: None, my lord, but
the world's grown honest.
HAMLET: Then is doomsday near.
Hamlet 2.2.236

2737 Q. ELIZABETH: An honest tale
speeds best being plainly told.
Richard III 4.4.358

2738 BRUTUS: There is no terror,
Cassius, in your threats,
For I am arm'd so strong in honesty
That they pass by me as the idle wind,
Which I respect not.
Julius Caesar 4.3.66

2739 LUCULLUS [about Timon]: Every
man has his fault, and honesty is his.
Timon of Athens 3.1.27

Honey

2740 FRIAR LAWRENCE: The sweetest
honey
Is loathsome in his own deliciousness,
And in the taste confounds the
appetite.
Romeo and Juliet 2.6.11

Honeybee

2741 CANTERBURY: So works the
honeybees,
Creatures that by a rule in nature teach
The act of order to a peopled
kingdom.
They have a king, and officers of sorts,
Where some, like magistrates, correct
at home;
Others, like merchants, venter trade
abroad;
Others, like soldiers, armed in their
stings,
Make boot upon the summer's velvet
buds,

Which pillage they with merry march
   bring home
To the tent-royal of their emperor;
Who busied in his majesty surveys
The singing masons building roofs of
   gold,
The civil citizens kneading up the
   honey,
The poor mechanic porters crowding in
Their heavy burthens at his narrow
   gate,
The sad-ey'd justice, with his surly
   hum,
Delivering o'er to executioners pale
The lazy yawning drone.
                Henry V 1.2.187
[*venter:* venture; *boot:* booty; *burthens:*
burdens]

Honor

2742 ULYSSES: Honor travels in a
   straight so narrow,
Where one but goes abreast.
       Troilus and Cressida 3.3.154

2743 PETRUCHIO: As the sun breaks
   through the darkest clouds,
So honor peereth in the meanest habit.
       Taming of the Shrew 4.3.173

2744 ANTONY: If I lose mine honor,
I lose myself.
       Antony and Cleopatra 3.4.22

2745 KING: What stronger breastplate
   than a heart untainted!
       2 Henry VI 3.2.232

2746 K. HENRY: If it be a sin to covet
   honor,
I am the most offending soul alive.
       Henry V 4.3.28

2747 MOWBRAY: Mine honor is my
   life, both grown in one,
Take honor from me, and my life is
   done.
       Richard II 1.1.182

2748 MOWBRAY: The purest treasure
   mortal times afford

Is spotless reputation; that away,
Men are but gilded loam or painted
   clay.
       Richard II 1.1.177

2749 BRUTUS: Set honor in one eye
   and death i' th' other,
And I will look on both indifferently;
For let the gods so speed me as I love
The name of honor more than I fear
   death.
       Julius Caesar 1.2.86

2750 CYMBELINE: The due of honor in
   no point omit.
       Cymbeline 3.5.11

2751 ACHILLES: Not a man, for being
   simply man,
Hath any honor, but honor for those
   honors
That are without him, as place, riches,
   and favor—
Prizes of accident as oft as merit.
       Troilus and Cressida 3.3.80

2752 ARRAGON: O that estates,
   degrees, and offices
Were not deriv'd corruptly, and that
   clear honor
Were purchas'd by the merit of the
   wearer!
       Merchant of Venice 2.9.41

2753 ARRAGON: Let none presume
To wear an undeserved dignity.
       Merchant of Venice 2.9.39

2754 FALSTAFF [soliloquy]: Well, 'tis
no matter, honor pricks me on. Yea,
but how if honor prick me off when I
come on? how then? Can honor set to
a leg? No. Or an arm? No. Or take
away the grief of a wound? No. Honor
hath no skill in surgery then? No.
What is honor? A word. What is in
that word honor? What is that honor?
Air. A trim reckoning! Who hath it?
He that died a' Wednesday. Doth he
feel it? No. Doth he hear it? No. 'Tis
insensible then? Yea, to the dead. But
will't not live with the living? No.
Why? Detraction will not suffer it.

Therefore I'll none of it, honor is a
mere scutcheon. And so ends my
catechism.

1 Henry IV 5.1.129

[*scutcheon:* an emblem carried in funerals]

2755 HAMLET [soliloquy]: Rightly to
be great
Is not to stir without great argument,
But greatly to find quarrel in a straw
When honor's at the stake.

Hamlet 4.4.53

2756 LAFEW: A scar nobly got, or a
nobles car, is a good liv'ry of honor.

All's Well That Ends Well 4.5.99

2757 KING: Honors thrive,
When rather from our acts we them
derive
Than our foregoers.

All's Well That Ends Well 2.3.135

2758 KING [to some lords leaving for
war]: See that you come
Not to woo honor, but to wed it.

All's Well That Ends Well 2.1.14

2759 OLD LADY: Honor's train
Is longer than his foreskirt.

Henry VIII 2.3.97

2760 KENT: To plainness honor's
bound,
When majesty falls to folly.

King Lear 1.1.148

2761 SEMPRONIUS: Who bates mine
honor shall not know my coin.

Timon of Athens 3.3.26

[*bates:* abates, diminishes]

2762 IAGO: Honor is an essence that's
not seen;
They have it very oft that have it not.

Othello 4.1.16

2763 MARIANA: The honor of a maid
is her name.

All's Well That Ends Well 3.5.12

2764 HELENA: Aged honor cites a virtuous youth.

All's Well That Ends Well 1.3.210

[*cites:* testifies to]

2765 VOLUMNIA: Honor and policy,
like unsever'd friends,
I' th' war do grow together.

Coriolanus 3.2.42

2766 POMPEY: 'Tis not my profit that
does lead mine honor;
Mine honor, it.

Antony and Cleopatra 2.7.76

2767 POSTHUMUS: Let there be no
honor
Where there is beauty; truth, where
semblance; love,
Where there's another man.

Cymbeline 2.4.108

2768 Honor and beauty, in the
owner's arms,
Are weakly fortess'd from a world of
harms.

Rape of Lucrece 27

2769 HECTOR: Life every man holds
dear, but the dear man
Holds honor far more precious-dear
than life.

Troilus and Cressida 5.3.27

2770 WOLSEY: Too much honor.
O, 'tis a burden, Cromwell, 'tis a
burden
Too heavy for a man that hopes for
heaven!

Henry VIII 3.2.383

2771 ULYSSES [to Achilles]:
Perseverance, dear my lord,
Keeps honor bright.

Troilus and Cressida 3.3.150

2772 Q. KATHERINE [to King]: Love
yourself, and in that love
Not unconsidered leave your honor.

Henry VIII 1.2.14

2773 GAUNT: Love they to live that
love and honor have.

Richard II 2.1.138

2774 The painful warrior famoused for
fight,

After a thousand victories once foil'd,
Is from the book of honor rased quite,
And all the rest forgot for which he
toil'd.

Sonnet 25

[*rased:* erased, blotted out]

Hope

2775 NORTHUMBERLAND: Hope to joy
is little less in joy
Than hope enjoyed.

Richard II 2.3.15

2776 CLAUDIO: The miserable have no
medicine
But only hope.

Measure for Measure 3.1.2

2777 HASTINGS: It never yet did hurt
To lay down likelihoods and forms of
hope.

2 Henry IV 1.3.34

2778 PROTEUS: Hope is a lover's staff;
walk hence with that
And manage it against despairing
thoughts.

Two Gentlemen of Verona 3.1.248

2779 PISTOL: Hope is a curtal dog in
some affairs.

Merry Wives of Windsor 2.1.110

[*curtal:* tail docked]

2780 LORD BARDOLPH: Indeed the in-
stant action, a cause on foot—
Lives so in hope, as in an early spring
We see th' appearing buds, which to
prove fruit
Hope gives not so much warrant, as
despair
That frosts will bite them.

2 Henry IV 1.3.37

2781 Things out of hope are compass'd
oft with vent'ring.

Venus and Adonis 567

[*vent'ring:* venturing]

2782 MACDUFF: I have lost my hopes.
MALCOLM: Perchance even there where
I did find my doubts.

Macbeth 4.3.24

[*hopes:* i.e. of Malcolm's cooperation;
doubts: i.e. of Macduff's loyalty]

2783 ROSSE: Things at the worst will
cease, or else climb upward
To what they were before.

Macbeth 4.2.24

2784 RICHMOND: True hope is swift
and flies with swallow's wings,
Kings it makes gods, and meaner
creatures kings.

Richard III 5.2.23

2785 QUEEN: I will despair, and be at
enmity
With cozening hope. He is a flatterer,
A parasite, a keeper-back of death,
Who gently would dissolve the bands
of life,
Which false hope lingers in extremity.

Richard II 2.2.68

2786 Despair and hope make thee
ridiculous:
The one doth flatter thee in thoughts
unlikely,
In likely thoughts the other kills thee
quickly.

Venus and Adonis 988

Horror

2787 OTHELLO: On horror's head horrors accumulate.

Othello 3.3.370

2788 MACDUFF [on Duncan's murder]:
O horror, horror, horror! Tongue nor
heart
Cannot conceive nor name thee!

Macbeth 2.3.64

Horse

2789 DOLPHIN: I will not change my
horse with any that treads but on four

pasterns ... When I bestride him, I
soar, I am a hawk; he trots the air; the
earth sings when he touches it.
                            Henry V 3.7.11
[*pasterns:* hoofs]

2790 K. RICHARD [after his horse was
slain in battle]: A horse! a horse! my
kingdom for a horse!
                            Richard III 5.4.7

2791 GRATIANO: Where is the horse
that doth untread again
His tedious measures with the unbated
fire
That he did pace them first? All things
that are,
Are with more spirit chased than
enjoy'd.
                    Merchant of Venice 2.6.10

2792 GARDINER: Those that tame wild
horses
Pace 'em not in their hands to make
'em gentle,
But stop their mouths with stubborn
bits and spur 'em
Till they obey the manage.
                            Henry VIII 5.2.56

Horticulture

2793 POLIXENES [to Perdita]: Nature is
made better by no mean
But Nature makes that mean; so over
that art
Which you say adds to Nature, is an
art
That nature makes. You see, sweet
maid, we marry
A gentler scion to the wildest stock,
And make conceive a bark of baser
kind
By bud of nobler race. This is an art
Which does mend Nature — change it
rather; but
The art itself is Nature.
                        Winter's Tale 4.4.89

2794 GARDENER: Superfluous branches
We lop away, that bearing boughs may
live.
                            Richard II 3.4.63

Hostess

2795 A woeful hostess brooks not
merry guests.
                    Rape of Lucrece 1125

Hours

2796 KING [soliloquy, on being a
shepherd]: So many hours must I
tend my flock,
So many hours must I take my rest,
So many hours must I contemplate,
So many hours must I sport myself.
                        3 Henry VI 2.5.31

2797 GARDINER: These should be
hours for necessities,
Not for delights; times to repair our
nature
With comforting repose, and not for us
To waste these times.
                            Henry VIII 5.1.2

2798 ROMEO: Sad hours seem long.
                    Romeo and Juliet 1.1.161

House

2799 FOOL: He that has a house to put
's head in has a good head-piece.
                            King Lear 3.2.25
[*'s:* his]

2800 CLOWN: I am for the house with
the narrow gate, which I take to be too
little for pomp to enter.
                All's Well That Ends Well 4.5.50

2801 SECOND VARRO SERVANT: Who
can speak broader than he that has no
house to put his head in? Such may
rail against great buildings.
                    Timon of Athens 3.4.63

2802 Who lets so fair a house fall to
decay,
Which husbandry in honor might
uphold
Against the stormy gusts of winter's
day

And barren rage of death's eternal
cold?
O, none but unthrifts.
Sonnet 13

2803 CLEON: Houses are defil'd for
want of use.
Pericles 1.4.37

2804 LORD BARDOLPH: When we
mean to build,
We first survey the plot, then draw the
model,
And when we see the figure of the
house,
Then we must rate the cost of the
erection,
Which if we find outweighs ability,
What do we then but draw anew the
model
In fewer offices, or at least desist
To build at all?
2 Henry IV 1.3.41

Humanity

2805 ALBANY: Humanity must per-
force prey on itself,
Like monsters of the deep.
King Lear 4.2.48

Humility

2806 PRINCESS: A heavy heart bears
not a humble tongue.
Love's Labor's Lost 5.2.737

2807 CLOWN: Though honesty be no
puritan, yet it will do no hurt; it will
wear the surplice of humility over the
black gown of a big heart.
All's Well That Ends Well 1.3.93

2808 K. HENRY: In peace there's
nothing so becomes a man
As modest stillness and humility;
But when the blast of war blows in our
ears,
Then imitate the action of the tiger.
Henry V 3.1.3

2809 ORLANDO: In the world I fill up
a place, which may be better supplied
when I have made it empty.
As You Like It 1.2.191

2810 CRANMER [to Gardiner]: Love
and meekness . . .
Become a churchman better than
ambition.
Henry VIII 5.2.97

2811 DON PEDRO: It is the witness still
of excellency
To put a strange face on his own
perfection.
Much Ado About Nothing 2.3.46

2812 CASSIUS [alluding to Caesar]: I
cannot tell what you and other men
Think of this life; but, for my single
self,
I had as lief not be as live to be
In awe of such a thing as I myself.
Julius Caesar 1.2.93

2813 PRINCE: I have sounded the very
base-string of humility.
1 Henry IV 2.4.5

Humor

2814 ROSALINE: A jest's prosperity lies
in the ear
Of him that hears it, never in the
tongue
Of him that makes it.
Love's Labor's Lost 5.2.861

2815 Every humor hath his adjunct
pleasure,
Wherein it finds a joy above the rest.
Sonnet 91

2816 K. JOHN: It is the curse of kings
to be attended
By slaves that take their humors for a
warrant
To break within the bloody house of
life,
And on the winking of authority
To understand a law; to know the
meaning

Of dangerous majesty, when perchance
  it frowns
More upon humor than advis'd respect.
                        King John 4.2.208

Humorless

2817 SOLANIO: Nature hath fram'd
strange fellows in her time:
Some that will evermore peep through
  their eyes,
And laugh like parrots at a bagpiper;
And other of such vinegar aspect
That they'll not show their teeth in the
  way of a smile
Though Nestor swear the jest be
  laughable.
                Merchant of Venice 1.1.51
[*Nestor:* a character in the *Iliad*, noted for
his excessive gravity]

Hunger

2818 He ten times pines that pines
beholding food.
                        Rape of Lucrece 1115

2819 NERISSA: They are as sick that
surfeit with too much as they that
starve with nothing.
                Merchant of Venice 1.2.5

Husband

2820 KATHERINA: Thy husband is thy
lord, thy life, thy keeper,
Thy head, thy sovereign; one that cares
  for thee,
And for thy maintenance; commits his
  body
To painful labor, both by sea and
  land;
To watch the night in storms, the day
  in cold,
Whilst thou li'st warm at home, secure
  and safe;
And craves no other tribute at thy
  hands
But love, fair looks, and true
  obedience —

Too little payment for so great a debt.
Such duty as the subject owes the
  prince,
Even such a woman oweth to her
  husband;
And when she is froward, peevish,
  sullen, sour,
And not obedient to his honest will,
What is she but a foul contending
  rebel,
And graceless traitor to her loving
  lord?
I am asham'd that women are so
  simple
To offer war where they should kneel
  for peace,
Or seek for rule, supremacy, and sway,
When they are bound to serve, love,
  and obey.
                Taming of the Shrew 5.2.146

2821 PLAYER QUEEN: The instances
that second marriage move
Are base respects of thrift, but none of
  love.
                        Hamlet 3.2.182

2822 ROMAN: The fittest time to corrupt a man's wife is when she's fall'n
out with her husband.
                        Coriolanus 4.3.32

2823 LEONATO: Well, niece, I hope to
see you one day fitted with a husband.
BEATRICE: Not till God make men of
some other mettle than earth. Would
it not grieve a woman to be over-
master'd with a piece of valiant dust?
to make an account of her life to a
clod of wayward marl?
                Much Ado About Nothing 2.1.57
[*mettle:* substance; *marl:* clay]

2824 PORTIA: A light wife doth make
a heavy husband.
                Merchant of Venice 5.1.130

2825 ADRIANA [to Antipholus
Syracuse]: Thou art an elm, my husband, I a vine,
Whose weakness, married to thy
  stronger state,
Makes me with thy strength to
  communicate.
                Comedy of Errors 2.2.174

2826 PERICLES [reading a riddle]: I
sought a husband, in which labor
I found that kindness in a father.
He's father, son, and husband mild;
I mother, wife—and yet his child.
Pericles 1.1.66

2827 LUCIANA: Man, more divine, the
masters of all these,
Lord of the wide world and wild wat'ry
seas,
Indu'd with intellectual sense and
souls,
Of more pre-eminence than fish and
fowls,
Are masters to their females, and their
lords.
Comedy of Errors 2.1.20

2828 ADRIANA: I will attend my hus-
band, be his nurse,
Diet his sickness, for it is my office.
Comedy of Errors 5.1.98

Husbandry

2829 CORIN: Good pasture makes fat
sheep.
As You Like It 3.2.27

2830 POLONIUS: Borrowing dulleth th'
edge of husbandry.
Hamlet 1.3.77

2831 QUEEN: Now 'tis spring, and
weeds are shallow-rooted;
Suffer them now, and they'll o'ergrow
the garden,
And choke the herbs for want of
husbandry.
2 Henry VI 3.1.31

2832 Where is she so fair whose
unear'd womb
Disdains the tillage of thy husbandry?
Sonnet 3

2833 K. HENRY: Our bad neighbor
makes us early stirrers,
Which is both healthful and good
husbandry.
Henry V 4.1.6

2834 BANQUO: There's husbandry in
heaven,
Their candles are all out.
Macbeth 2.1.4

Hypocrisy

2835 ANGELO [soliloquy]: Thieves for
their robbery have authority
When judges steal themselves.
Measure for Measure 2.2.175

2836 LEAR [to Gloucester]: See how
yond justice rails upon yond simple
thief. Hark in thine ear: change places,
and handy-dandy, which is the justice,
which is the thief?
King Lear 4.6.151

2837 IAGO [soliloquy]: When devils
will the blackest sins put on,
They do suggest at first with heavenly
shows.
Othello 2.3.351

2838 HAMLET: One may smile, and
smile, and be a villain!
Hamlet 1.5.108

2839 ISABELLA: It oft falls out,
To have what we would have, we speak
not what we mean.
Measure for Measure 2.4.117

2840 MACBETH: Away, and mock the
time with fairest show:
False face must hide what the false
heart doth know.
Macbeth 1.7.82

2841 DUKE [soliloquy]: Shame to him
whose cruel striking,
Kills for faults of his own liking!
Measure for Measure 3.2.267

2842 BASSANIO: There is no vice so
simple but assumes
Some mark of virtue on his outward
parts.
Merchant of Venice 3.2.81

2843 DUKE [soliloquy]: O, what may man within him hide,
Though angel on the outward side!
Measure for Measure 3.2.271

2844 CLAUDIO: O, what authority and show of truth
Can cunning sin cover itself withal!
Much Ado About Nothing 4.1.35

2845 DUCHESS [on Gloucester's feigned love to young Edward]: Ah! that deceit should steal such gentle shape,
And with a virtuous vizard hide deep vice!
Richard III 2.2.27

2846 ANTONIO: The devil can cite Scripture for his purpose.
Merchant of Venice 1.3.98

2847 POLONIUS: 'Tis too much prov'd—that with devotion's visage
And pious action we do sugar o'er
The devil himself.
Hamlet 3.1.46

2848 PORTIA: It is a good divine that follows his own instructions; I can easier teach twenty what were good to be done, than to be one of the twenty to follow mine own teaching.
Merchant of Venice 1.2.14

2849 GLOUCESTER [soliloquy]: Thus I clothe my naked villainy
With odd old ends stol'n forth of holy writ,
And seem a saint, when most I play the devil.
Richard III 1.3.335

2850 OPHELIA: Do not, as some ungracious pastors do,
Show me the steep and thorny way to heaven,
Whiles, like a puff'd and reckless libertine,
Himself the primrose path of dalliance treads,
And reaks not his own rede.
Hamlet 1.3.47
[*reaks:* recks, heeds; *rede:* advice]

2851 O, what a mansion have those vices got
Which for their habitation chose out thee,
Where beauty's veil doth cover every blot,
And all things turn to fair that eyes can see!
Sonnet 95

2852 HAMLET [to Ophelia, on women]: God has given you one face, and you make yourselves another.
Hamlet 3.1.143

2853 MALCOLM: To show an unfelt sorrow is an office
Which the false man does easy.
Macbeth 2.3.136

2854 FIRST GENTLEMAN: Not a courtier,
Although they wear their faces to the bent
Of the King's looks, hath a heart that is not
Glad at the thing they scowl at.
Cymbeline 1.1.12

2855 LADY MACBETH [to Macbeth]: To beguile the time,
Look like the time; bear welcome in your eye,
Your hand, your tongue; look like th' innocent flower,
But be the serpent under't.
Macbeth 1.5.63

2856 LUCIANA [to Antipholus Syracuse]: Be not thy tongue thy own shame's orator:
Look sweet, speak fair, become disloyalty;
Apparel vice like virtue's harbinger;
Bear a fair presence, though your heart be tainted;
Teach sin the carriage of a holy saint.
Comedy of Errors 3.2.10

Idleness

2857 HAMLET [soliloquy]: What is man,

If his chief good and market of his
time
Be but to sleep and feed? a beast, no
more.
Sure He that made us with such large
discourse,
Looking before and after, gave us not
That capability and godlike reason
To fust in us unus'd.
Hamlet 4.4.33
[*fust:* grow mouldy]

2858 ANTONY: Ten thousand harms,
more than the ills I know,
My idleness doth hatch.
Antony and Cleopatra 1.2.129

2859 IAGO: Our bodies are our
gardens, to the which our wills are
gardeners . . . either to have it sterile
with idleness or manur'd with industry.
Othello 1.3.320

2860 HAMLET: The hand of little
employment hath the daintier sense.
Hamlet 5.1.69

2861 ANTONY: We bring forth weeds
When our quick winds lie still.
Antony and Cleopatra 1.2.109
[*quick winds:* fresh breezes thought to be
good for the soil]

2862 YORK: Idle weeds are fast in
growth.
Richard III 3.1.103

2863 VALENTINE [to Proteus]: I rather
would entreat thy company,
To see the wonders of the world
abroad,
Than (living dully sluggardiz'd at
home)
Wear out thy youth with shapeless
idleness.
Two Gentlemen of Verona 1.1.5

Idolatry

2864 HECTOR: 'Tis mad idolatry
To make the service greater than the
god.
Troilus and Cressida 2.2.56

2865 K. HENRY [soliloquy]: What art
thou, thou idol Ceremony?
What kind of god art thou . . . ?
Henry V 4.1.240

If

2866 TOUCHSTONE [to Jaques]: O sir,
we quarrel in print, by the book — as
you have books for good manners. I
will name you the degrees. The first,
the Retort Courteous; the second, the
Quip Modest; the third, the Reply
Churlish; the fourth, the Reproof
Valiant; the fift, the Countercheck
Quarrelsome; the sixt, the Lie with Circumstance; the seventh, the Lie Direct.
All these you may avoid but the Lie
Direct; and you may avoid that too,
with an If. I knew when seven justices
could not take up a quarrel, but when
the parties were met themselves, one of
them thought but of an If, as, "If you
said so, then I said so"; and they shook
hands and swore brothers. Your If is
the only peacemaker; much virtue in
If.
As You Like It 5.4.90

Ignorance

2867 LORD SAY: Ignorance is the curse
of God,
Knowledge the wing wherewith we fly
to heaven.
2 Henry VI 4.7.73

2868 CLOWN: There is no darkness
but ignorance.
Twelfth Night 4.2.42

2869 ISABELLA: Man, proud man,
Dress'd in a little brief authority,
Most ignorant of what he's most assur'd
(His glassy essence), like an angry ape
Plays such fantastic tricks before high
heaven
As make the angels weep.
Measure for Measure 2.2.117
[*glassy:* fragile, highly susceptible of
damage]

2870 MENECRATES: We, ignorant of ourselves,
Beg often our own harms, which the wise pow'rs
Deny us for our good; so find we profit
By losing of our prayers.
Antony and Cleopatra 2.1.5

2871 DESDEMONA: O heavy ignorance! thou praisest the worst best.
Othello 2.1.143

2872 HOLOFERNES: O thou monster Ignorance, how deformed dost thou look!
Love's Labor's Lost 4.2.23

2873 MOWBRAY: Dull unfeeling barren ignorance
Is made my jailer to attend on me.
Richard II 1.3.168

2874 THERSITES [about Achilles]: I had rather be a tick in a sheep than such a valiant ignorance.
Troilus and Cressida 3.3.311

Ill

2875 BELARIUS: Many times
Doth ill deserve by doing well.
Cymbeline 3.3.53

2876 O benefit of ill, now I find true
That better is by evil still made better.
Sonnet 119

Illusion

2877 O me! what eyes hath Love put in my head,
Which have no correspondence with true sight,
Or if they have, where is my judgment fled,
That censures falsely what they see aright?
If that be fair whereon my false eyes dote,
What means the world to say it is not so?

If it be not, then love doth well denote
Love's eye is not so true as all men's: no,
How can it? O, how can Love's eye be true,
That is so vex'd with watching and with tears?
No marvel then though I mistake my view,
The sun itself sees not till heaven clears.
O cunning Love, with tears thou keep'st me blind,
Lest eyes well seeing thy foul faults should find.
Sonnet 148

Imagination

2878 HAMLET: My mind's eye.
Hamlet 1.2.186

2879 THESEUS: Lovers and madmen have such seething brains,
Such shaping fantasies, that apprehend
More than cool reason ever comprehends.
The lunatic, the lover, and the poet
Are of imagination all compact.
Midsummer Night's Dream 5.1.4

2880 THESEUS: As imagination bodies forth
The forms of things unknown, the poet's pen
Turns them to shapes, and gives to aery nothing
A local habitation and a name.
Midsummer Night's Dream 5.1.14

2881 MACBETH: Present fears
Are less than horrible imaginings.
Macbeth 1.3.137

2882 TROILUS: Expectation whirls me round;
Th' imaginary relish is so sweet
That it enchants my sense.
Troilus and Cressida 3.2.18

2883 BULLINGBROOK: O, who can hold a fire in his hand
By thinking on the frosty Caucasus?

Or cloy the hungry edge of appetite
By bare imagination of a feast?
Or wallow naked in December snow
By thinking on fantastic summer's
heat?
O no, the apprehension of the good
Gives but the greater feeling to the
worse.
Richard II 1.3.294

2884 HOLOFERNES: This is a gift that I
have, simple, simple; a foolish extravagant spirit, full of forms, figures,
shapes, objects, ideas, apprehensions,
motions, revolutions. These are begot
in the ventricle of memory, nourish'd
in the womb of pia mater, and
delivered upon the mellowing of
occasion.
Love's Labor's Lost 4.2.65

2885 QUEEN [to Hamlet, on his
father's ghost]: This is the very
coinage of your brain,
This bodiless creation ecstasy.
Hamlet 3.4.137

2886 LONGAVILLE: The mind shall
banquet, though the body pine.
Love's Labor's Lost 1.1.25

2887 Weary with toil, I haste me to
my bed,
The dear repose for limbs with travel
tired,
But then begins a journey in my head
To work my mind, when body's work's
expired;
For then my thoughts (from far where
I abide)
Intend a zealous pilgrimage to thee,
And keep my drooping eyelids open
wide,
Looking on darkness which the blind
do see;
Save that my soul's imaginary sight
Presents thy shadow to my sightless
view,
Which like a jewel hung in ghastly
night,
Makes black night beauteous, and her
old face new.
Sonnet 27

Imitation

2888 FALSTAFF [soliloquy]: It is certain
that either wise bearing or ignorant
carriage is caught, as men take
diseases, one of another; therefore, let
men take heed of their company.
2 Henry IV 5.1.75

Immaturity

2889 CLEOPATRA: Though age from
folly could not give me freedom,
It does from childishness.
Antony and Cleopatra 1.3.57

2890 MALVOLIO [about Viola, dis-
guised as a page]: One would think his
mother's milk were scarce out of him.
Twelfth Night 1.5.161

Immodesty

2891 STEWARD: We wound our
modesty, and make foul the clearness
of our deservings, when of ourselves we
publish them.
All's Well That Ends Well 1.3.5

2892 LAERTES: The chariest maid is
prodigal enough
If she unmask her beauty to the moon.
Hamlet 1.3.36

Immortality

2893 HAMLET [soliloquy]: Who would
fardels bear,
To grunt and sweat under a weary life,
But that the dread of something after
death,
The undiscover'd country, from whose
bourn
No traveler returns, puzzles the will,
And makes us rather bear those ills we
have,
Than fly to others that we know not
of?
Hamlet 3.1.75
[*fardels:* burdens; *bourn:* boundary, i.e.
region]

2894 CERIMON: I hold it ever
Virtue and cunning were endowments
　greater
Than nobleness and riches. Careless
　heirs
May the two latter darken and expend;
But immortality attends the former,
Making a man a god.
　　　　　　　　　　　Pericles 3.2.27

2895 PROVOST: Look, here's the war-
　rant, Claudio, for thy death.
'Tis now dead midnight, and by eight
　to-morrow
Thou must be made immortal.
　　　　Measure for Measure 4.2.63

2896 NORTHUMBERLAND: Even
　through the hollow eyes of death
I spy life peering.
　　　　　　　　Richard II 2.1.270

2897 LORENZO: Soft stillness and the
　night
Become the touches of sweet har-
　mony...
Such harmony is in immortal souls,
But whilst this muddy vesture of decay
Doth grossly close it in, we cannot hear
　it.
　　　　　Merchant of Venice 5.1.56

2898 YORK [after being stabbed]:
　Open thy gate of mercy, gracious
　God!
My soul flies through these wounds to
　seek out thee.
　　　　　　　　3 Henry VI 1.4.177

2899 K. RICHARD [falling, wounded
　by Exton]: Mount, mount, my soul!
　thy seat is up on high,
Whilst my gross flesh sinks downward,
　here to die.
　　　　　　　　Richard II 5.5.111

2900 HAMLET [to Horatio, on the
　ghost before them]: I do not set my
　life at a pin's fee,
And for my soul, what can it do to
　that,
Being a thing immortal as itself?
　　　　　　　　　Hamlet 1.4.65

2901 CLEOPATRA: I have
Immortal longings in me.
　　　　Antony and Cleopatra 5.2.280

2902 ISABELLA: All the souls that were
　were forfeit once,
And He that might the vantage best
　have took
Found out the remedy.
　　　　Measure for Measure 2.2.73

Impatience

2903 CLEOPATRA: Patience is sottish,
　and impatience doth
Become a dog that's mad.
　　　　Antony and Cleopatra 4.15.79
[*sottish:* stupid, very foolish]

2904 PEMBROKE: Impatience hath his
　privilege.
　　　　　　　　King John 4.3.32

Impediment

2905 BERTRAM: All impediments in
　fancy's course
Are motives of more fancy.
　　　　All's Well That Ends Well 5.3.214
[*fancy's:* i.e. love's]

Imperfection

2906 Loathsome canker lives in
　sweetest bud.
　　　　　　　　　Sonnet 35

2907 LUCULLUS: Every man has his
　fault.
　　　　　Timon of Athens 3.1.27

Impermanence

2908 CLOWN: Things may serve long,
but not serve ever.
　　　　All's Well That Ends Well 2.2.58

Impiety

2909 ALCIBIADES: To be in anger is impiety;
But who is man that is not angry?
Timon of Athens 3.5.56

Impossibility

2910 ISABELLA: Make not impossible
That which but seems unlike.
Measure for Measure 5.1.51

2911 LAUNCE: Nothing is impossible.
Two Gentlemen of Verona 3.1.370

2912 KING: What impossibility would slay
In common sense, sense saves another way.
All's Well That Ends Well 2.1.177
[*sense saves:* i.e. reason saves]

2913 K. RICHARD: It is as hard to come as for a camel
To thread the postern of a small needle's eye.
Richard II 5.5.16

Imprisonment

2915 CASSIUS: Stoney tower, nor walls of beaten brass,
Nor airless dungeon, nor strong links of iron,
Can be retentive to the strength of spirit.
Julius Caesar 1.3.93

2915 LUCIO: I had as lief have the foppery of freedom as the mortality of imprisonment.
Measure for Measure 1.2.133
[Most editors prefer *morality*, in antithesis to *foppery*.]

2916 LUCIO: Why, how now, Claudio? whence comes this restraint?
CLAUDIO: From too much liberty, my Lucio.
Measure for Measure 1.2.128
[*restraint:* Claudio, in custody of the Provost, is being taken to prison]

Improvement

2917 ALBANY: Striving to better, oft we mar what's well.
King Lear 1.4.346

Impurity

2918 No perfection is so absolute,
That some impurity doth not pollute.
Rape of Lucrece 853

Inactivity

2919 LEAR: When the mind's free,
The body's delicate.
King Lear 3.4.11

2920 ANTONY: Quietness, grown sick of rest, would purge
By any desperate change.
Antony and Cleopatra 1.3.53

Inappropriateness

2921 LADY GRAY: 'Tis better said than done.
3 Henry VI 3.2.90

Inconstancy

2922 Fair is my love, but not so fair as fickle,
Mild as a dove, but neither true nor trusty,
Brighter than glass, and yet as glass is brittle,
Softer than wax, and yet as iron rusty:
A lily pale, with damask dye to grace her,
None fairer, nor none falser to deface her.
The Passionate Pilgrim vii.1

2923 BEROWNE [to King Ferdinand, Longaville and Dumaine]: I am betrayed by keeping company
With men like you, men of inconstancy.
Love's Labor's Lost 4.3.177

2924 PROTEUS: O heaven, were man
But constant, he were perfect; that one
   error
Fills him with faults; makes him run
   through all th' sins:
Inconstancy falls off ere it begins.
   Two Gentlemen of Verona 5.4.110

2925 LEONTES: I am a feather for each
   wind that blows.
   Winter's Tale 2.3.154

2926 BALTHAZAR [singing]:
Sigh no more, ladies, sigh no more,
Men were deceivers ever,
One foot in sea, and one on shore,
To one thing constant never.
   Much Ado About Nothing 2.3.62

2927 HAMLET: Frailty, thy name is
   woman!
   Hamlet 1.2.146

2928 PROTEUS [soliloquy]: As one nail
   by strength drives out another,
So the remembrance of my former love
Is by a newer object quite forgotten.
   Two Gentlemen of Verona 2.4.193

Indebtedness

2929 BUCKINGHAM: Many
Have broke their backs with laying
   manors on 'em.
   Henry VIII 1.1.84

2930 FALSTAFF: I can get no remedy
against this consumption of the purse;
borrowing only lingers and lingers it
out, but the disease is incurable.
   2 Henry IV 1.2.236

2931 POLONIUS: Neither a borrower
   nor a lender be.
   Hamlet 1.3.75

2932 EDGAR: Keep ... thy pen from
   lenders' books.
   King Lear 3.4.97

Indecision

2933 KING [soliloquy]: Like a man to
   double business bound,
I stand in pause where I shall first
   begin.
   Hamlet 3.3.41

2934 ISABELLA: I am
At war 'twixt will and will not.
   Measure for Measure 2.2.32

2935 LEONTES: I am a feather for each
   wind that blows.
   Winter's Tale 2.3.154

2936 HAMLET [soliloquy]: To be, or
   not to be, that is the question.
   Hamlet 3.1.55

2937 HAMLET [soliloquy]: Thus the
   native hue of resolution
Is sicklied o'er with the pale cast of
   thought,
And enterprises of great pitch and
   movement
With this regard their currents turn
   awry,
And lose the name of action.
   Hamlet 3.1.83

Indiscretion

2938 GONERIL: All's not offense that
   indiscretion finds.
   King Lear 2.4.196

2939 HAMLET: Our indiscretion
sometimes serves us well.
   Hamlet 5.2.8

Individuality

2940 Who is it that says most, which
   can say more
Than this rich praise, that you alone
   are you...?
   Sonnet 84

2941 GLOUCESTER: I am myself alone.
   3 Henry VI 5.6.83

Indulgence

2942 Had doting Priam check'd his
son's desire,
Troy had been bright with fame, and
not with fire.
Rape of Lucrece 1490

2943 DUKE: Now, as fond fathers,
Having bound up the threat'ning twigs
of birch,
Only to stick it in their children's sight
For terror, not to use, in time the rod
Becomes more mock'd than fear'd.
Measure for Measure 1.3.23

Industry

2944 BELARIUS: The sweat of industry
would dry and die,
But for the end it works to.
Cymbeline 3.6.31

2945 ANTONIO: Experience is by industry achiev'd,
And perfected by the swift course of
time.
Two Gentlemen of Verona 1.3.22

2946 IAGO: Our bodies are our
gardens, to which our wills are
gardeners . . . either to have it sterile
with idleness or manur'd with industry.
Othello 1.3.320

2947 HELENA: Our remedies oft in
ourselves do lie,
Which we ascribe to heaven. The fated
sky
Gives us free scope, only doth
backward pull
Our slow designs when we ourselves are
dull.
All's Well That Ends Well 1.1.216

Inequality

2948 SECOND FISHERMAN: A fish
hangs in the net, like a poor man's
right in the law; 'twill hardly come
out.
Pericles 2.1.116

2949 LEAR: Plate sin with gold,
And the strong lance of justice hurtless
breaks;
Arm it in rags, a pigmy's straw does
pierce it.
King Lear 4.6.165

Infirmity

2950 MALVOLIO: Infirmity, that decays
the wise,
Doth ever make the better fool.
Twelfth Night 1.5.76

2951 LEAR: Infirmity doth still neglect
all office
Whereto our health is bound; we are
not ourselves
When nature, being oppress'd, com-
mands the mind
To suffer with the body.
King Lear 2.4.106

Influence

2952 SHALLOW: A friend i' th' court is
better than a penny in purse.
2 Henry IV 5.1.30

2953 ENOBARBUS: Things outward
Do draw the inward quality after
them,
To suffer all alike.
Antony and Cleopatra 3.13.32

2954 LADY PERCY [on Percy]: He was
indeed the glass
Wherein the noble youth did dress
themselves.
2 Henry IV 2.3.21

2955 Princes are the glass, the school,
the book,
Where subjects' eyes do learn, do read,
do look.
Rape of Lucrece 615

[*glass:* mirror]

2956 FALSTAFF [soliloquy]: It is certain
that either wise bearing or ignorant
carriage is caught, as men take

diseases, one of another; therefore let men take heed of their company.
2 Henry IV 5.1.75

Ingratitude

2957 K. LEAR: How sharper than a serpent's tooth it is
To have a thankless child!
King Lear 1.4.288

2958 K. LEAR: Filial ingratitude!
Is it not as this mouth should tear this hand
For lifting food to't?
King Lear 3.4.14

2959 TIMON [soliloquy]: Ingrateful man, with liquorish draughts
And morsels unctuous, greases his pure mind,
That from it all consideration slips.
Timon of Athens 4.3.194

2960 VIOLA: I hate ingratitude more in a man
Than lying, vainness, babbling, drunkenness,
Or any taint of vice whose strong corruption
Inhabits our frail blood.
Twelfth Night 3.4.354

2961 THIRD CITIZEN: Ingratitude is monstrous, and for the multitude to be ingrateful were to make a monster of the multitude.
Coriolanus 2.3.9

2962 LEAR: Blow, winds, and crack your cheeks! rage, blow!
You cataracts and hurricanoes, spout
Till you have drench'd our steeples, drown'd the cocks!
You sulph'rous and thought-executing fires,
Vaunt-couriers of oak-cleaving thunderbolts,
Singe my white head! And thou, all-shaking thunder,
Strike flat the thick rotundity o' th' world!

Crack nature's moulds, all germains spill at once
That makes ingrateful man!
King Lear 3.2.1

[*germains:* seeds of all living things]

2963 AMIENS [singing]:
Blow, blow, thou winter wind,
Thou art not so unkind
As man's ingratitude;
Thy tooth is not so keen,
Because thou art not seen,
Although thy breath be rude ...
Freeze, freeze, thou bitter sky,
That dost not bite so nigh
As benefits forgot;
Though thou the waters warp,
Thy sting is not so sharp
As friend rememb'red not.
As You Like It 2.7.174

2964 K. LEAR: Ingratitude! thou marble-hearted fiend,
More hideous when thou show'st thee in a child
Than the sea-monster.
King Lear 1.4.259

2965 ULYSSES [to Achilles]: Time hath, my lord, a wallet at his back,
Wherein he puts alms for oblivion,
A great-siz'd monster of ingratitudes.
Those scraps are good deeds past, which are devour'd
As fast as they are made, forgot as soon as done.
Troilus and Cressida 3.3.145

2966 MENENIUS [to some factious citizens]: You slander
The helms o' th' state, who care for you like fathers,
When you curse them as enemies.
Coriolanus 1.1.76

2967 OPHELIA [giving flowers to King]: There's fennel for you, and columbines.
Hamlet 4.5.180

[*columbines:* symbol of ingratitude]

Injury

2968 REGAN: To willful men,
The injuries that they themselves
　procure
Must be their schoolmasters.
　　　　　　　King Lear 2.4.302

Injustice

2969 ANGELO: What knows the laws
That thieves do pass on thieves?
　　　　　Measure for Measure 2.1.22

2970 KING: Thrice is he arm'd that
　hath his quarrel just;
And he but naked, though lock'd in
　steel,
Whose conscience with injustice is
　corrupted.
　　　　　　2 Henry VI 3.2.233

2971 HERMIONE [to Leontes]: If I shall
　be condemn'd
Upon surmises (all proofs sleeping else
But what your jealousies awake), I tell
　you
'Tis rigor and not law.
　　　　　　Winter's Tale 3.2.111

2972 LEAR: Plate sin with gold,
And the strong lance of justice hurtless
　breaks;
Arm it in rags, a pigmy's straw does
　pierce it.
　　　　　　King Lear 4.6.165

Innocence

2973 PAULINA: The silence often of
　pure innocence
Persuades when speaking fails.
　　　　　　Winter's Tale 2.3.38

2974 HERMIONE: Innocence shall make
False accusation blush.
　　　　　　Winter's Tale 3.2.30

2975 POLIXENES [to Hermione]: We
　were as twinn'd lambs that did frisk
　i' th' sun,

And bleat the one at th' other. What
　we chang'd
Was innocence for innocence; we knew
　not
The doctrine of ill-doing, nor dream'd
That any did.
　　　　　　Winter's Tale 1.2.67

2976 Unstain'd thoughts do seldom
　dream on evil.
　　　　　　Rape of Lucrece 87

2977 KING: What stronger breastplate
　than a heart untainted!
　　　　　　2 Henry VI 2.3.232

2978 HAMLET: Let the gall'd jade
winch, our withers are unwrung.
　　　　　　Hamlet 3.2.242
[*gall'd jade:* chafed horse; *winch:* wince;
withers: ridge between a horse's shoulders;
unwrung: not rubbed sore]

2979 GLOUCESTER: A heart unspotted
　is not easily daunted.
　　　　　　2 Henry VI 3.1.100

2980 MACBETH [to Lady Macbeth,
　after Duncan's murder]:
Methought I heard a voice cry, "Sleep
　no more!
Macbeth does murther sleep"　the in-
　nocent sleep,
Sleep that knits up the ravell'd sleave
　of care,
The death of each day's life, sore
　labor's bath,
Balm of hurt minds, great nature's sec-
　ond course,
Chief nourisher in life's feast.
　　　　　　Macbeth 2.2.32
[*murther:* murder]

Insanity

2981 LEAR: We are not ourselves
When nature, being oppress'd, com-
　mands the mind
To suffer with the body.
　　　　　　King Lear 2.4.107

2982 KING: Madness in great ones
must not unwatch'd go.
Hamlet 3.1.189

2983 HAMLET: I am but mad north-
north-west. When the wind is southerly I know a hawk from a hand-saw.
Hamlet 2.2.378

2984 POLONIUS: To define true
madness,
What is't but to be nothing else but
mad?
Hamlet 2.2.93

2985 HAMLET: Madness would not err,
Nor sense to ecstasy was ne'er so
thrall'd
But it reserv'd some quantity of choice.
Hamlet 3.4.73
[*thrall'd:* enslaved; *quantity of choice:* some
power to choose]

2986 CONSTANCE: I am not mad, I
would to heaven I were!
For then 'tis like I should forget
myself.
O, if I could, what grief should I
forget!
King John 3.4.48

2987 THESEUS: Lovers and madmen
have such seething brains,
Such shaping fantasies, that apprehend
More than cool reason ever compre-
hends.
Midsummer Night's Dream 5.1.4

2988 ROSALIND: Love is merely a
madness, and I tell you, deserves as
well a dark house and a whip as
madmen do; and the reason why they
are not so punish'd and cur'd is, that
the lunacy is so ordinary that the whippers are in love too.
As You Like It 3.2.400

2989 DOCTOR: Infected minds
To their deaf pillows will discharge
their secrets.
Macbeth 5.1.73

Insensitivity

2990 CLAUDIO: O, what men dare do!
What men may do! What men daily
do, not knowing what they do!
Much Ado About Nothing 4.1.19

2991 QUEEN [on Eleanor]: She bears a
duke's revenues on her back,
And in her heart she scorns our poverty.
2 Henry VI 1.3.80

Insolence

2992 HAMLET [soliloquy]: Who would
bear the whips and scorns of time,
Th' oppressor's wrong, the proud man's
contumely,
The pangs of despis'd love, the law's
delay,
The insolence of office...?
Hamlet 3.1.69

Inspiration

2993 POET: Our poesy is as a gum,
which oozes
From whence 'tis nourish'd. The fire i'
th' flint
Shows not till it be strook; our gentle
flame
Provokes itself and like the current flies
Each bound it chases.
Timon of Athens 1.1.21
[*strook:* struck]

Instinct

2994 FALSTAFF: Beware instinct . . .
Instinct is a great matter; I was now a
coward on instinct.
1 Henry IV 2.4.271

2995 THIRD CITIZEN: By divine in-
stinct men's minds mistrust
Ensuing dangers, as by proof we see
The water swell before a boist'rous
storm.
Richard III 2.3.42

2996 CORIOLANUS: I'll never
Be such a gosling to obey instinct, but
  stand
As if a man were author of himself,
And knew no other kin.
Coriolanus 5.3.34

2997 LUCETTA [on Proteus as Julia's
  best prospect]: I have no other but a
  woman's reason:
I think him so, because I think him so.
Two Gentlemen of Verona 1.2.23

Instruction

2998 DUKE [on Pompey's imprison-
  ment]: Correction and instruction
  must both work
Ere this rude beast will profit.
Measure for Measure 3.2.32

2999 DESDEMONA: Those that do teach
  young babes
Do it with gentle means and easy
  tasks.
Othello 4.2.111

3000 PORTIA: It is a good divine that
follows his own instructions; I can
easier teach twenty what were good to
be done, than to be one of the twenty
to follow mine own teaching. The
brain may devise laws for the blood,
but a hot temper leaps o'er a cold
decree.
Merchant of Venice 1.2.12

3001 REGAN: To willful men,
The injuries that they themselves
  procure
Must be their schoolmasters.
King Lear 2.4.302

Integrity

3002 POLONIUS: This above all: to
  thine own self be true,
And it must follow, as the night the
  day,
Thou canst not then be false to any
  man.
Hamlet 1.3.78

3003 ULYSSES: Honor travels in a strait
  so narrow,
Where one but goes abreast.
Troilus and Cressida 3.3.154

Intellect

3004 BEROWNE: Light, seeking light,
  doth light of light beguile.
Love's Labor's Lost 1.1.77

Intemperance

3005 CASSIO: O God, that men should
put an enemy in their mouths to steal
away their brains! that we should, with
joy, pleasance, revel, and applause,
transform ourselves into beasts!
Othello 2.3.289

3006 CASSIO: Every inordinate cup is
unbless'd, and the ingredient is a
devil.
Othello 2.3.307

3007 CASSIO: I have very poor and
unhappy brains for drinking. I could
well wish courtesy would invent some
other custom of entertainment.
Othello 2.3.33

3008 CASSIO: To be now a sensible
man, by and by a fool, and presently a
beast!
Othello 2.3.305

3009 MACDUFF: Boundless intem-
  perance
In nature is a tyranny; it hath been
Th' untimely emptying of the happy
  throne,
And fall of many kings.
Macbeth 4.3.67

3010 BEROWNE: One drunkard loves
  another of the name.
Love's Labor's Lost 4.3.48

Intensity

3011 LEAR: Where the greater malady
is fix'd,
The lesser is scarce felt.
King Lear 3.4.8

Intent

3012 ISABELLA: Thoughts are no
subjects,
Intents but merely thoughts.
Measure for Measure 5.1.453

Interest

3013 Foul cank'ring rust the hidden
treasure frets,
But gold that's put to use more gold
begets.
Venus and Adonis 767

3014 ANTONIO: When did friendship
take
A breed for barren metal of his friend?
Merchant of Venice 1.3.133
[*breed:* offspring or increase]

Interference

3015 JULIA [to Lucetta]: The current
that with gentle murmur glides,
Thou know'st, being stopp'd, impatiently doth rage.
Two Gentlemen of Verona 2.7.25

Interpretation

3016 AUFIDIUS: Our virtues
Lie in th' interpretation of the time.
Coriolanus 4.7.49

3017 WORCESTER: Look how we can,
or sad or merrily,
Interpretation will misquote our looks.
1 Henry IV 5.2.12

Investigation

3018 POLONIUS: Thus do we of
wisdom and of reach,
With windlasses and with assays of
bias,
By indirections find directions out.
Hamlet 2.1.61

Invitation

3019 IAGO [concerning Desdemona]:
What an eye she has! Methinks it
sounds a parley to provocation.
Othello 2.3.22

Invocation

3020 GLENDOWER: I can call spirits
from the vasty deep.
HOTSPUR: Why, so can I, or so can any
man,
But will they come when you do call
for them?
1 Henry IV 3.1.52

Irrevocableness

3021 LADY MACBETH: Things without
all remedy
Should be without regard: what's
done, is done.
Macbeth 3.2.11

Itch

3022 MARTIUS [to some dissentious
citizens]: Rubbing the poor itch of
your opinion
Make yourselves scabs.
Coriolanus 1.1.164

Jay

3023 PETRUCHIO: What, is the jay
more precious than the lark,
Because his feathers are more
beautiful?
Taming of the Shrew 4.3.175

Jealousy

3024 IAGO: Oft my jealousy
Shapes faults that are not.
Othello 3.3.147

3025 IAGO: O, what damned minutes
tells he o'er
Who dotes, yet doubts; suspects, yet
strongly loves!
Othello 3.3.169

3026 EMILIA: It is a monster
Begot upon itself, born on itself.
Othello 3.4.161

3027 OTHELLO [on Desdemona's supposed adultery]: I'll see before I
doubt; when I doubt, prove;
And on the proof, there is no more
but this—
Away at once with love or jealousy!
Othello 3.3.190

3028 IAGO [soliloquy]: Trifles light as
air
Are to the jealous confirmations strong
As proofs of holy writ.
Othello 3.3.322

3029 DESDEMONA [on Othello's
jealousy]: Alas the day, I never gave
him cause.
EMILIA: Jealous souls will not be
answer'd so;
They are not ever jealous for the cause,
But jealous for they're jealous.
Othello 3.4.158

3030 OTHELLO [soliloquy, on
Desdemona]: I had rather be a toad
And live upon the vapor of a dungeon
Than keep a corner in the thing I love
For others' uses.
Othello 3.3.270

3031 IAGO [to Othello]: O, beware,
my lord, of jealousy!
It is a green-ey'd monster which doth
mock
The meat it feeds on.
Othello 3.3.165

3032 Where Love reigns, disturbing
Jealousy
Doth call himself Affection's sentinel.
Venus and Adonis 649

3033 QUEEN: So full of artless jealousy
is guilt,
It spills itself in fearing to be spilt.
Hamlet 4.5.19

3034 Q. ISABEL: Fell jealousy . . .
Troubles oft the bed of blessed
marriage.
Henry V 5.2.363

3035 ABBESS: The venom clamors of a
jealous woman
Poison more deadly than a mad dog's
tooth.
Comedy of Errors 5.1.69

3036 This sour informer, this bate-
breeding spy,
This canker that eats up Love's tender
spring,
This carry-tale, dissentious Jealousy,
That sometimes true news, sometimes
false doth bring,
Knocks at my heart, and whispers in
mine ear.
Venus and Adonis 655

3037 LUCIANA: How many fond fools
serve mad jealousy?
Comedy of Errors 2.1.116

Jesting

3038 ROSALINE: A jest's prosperity lies
in the ear
Of him that hears it, never in the
tongue
Of him that makes it.
Love's Labor's Lost 5.2.861

3039 ISABELLA: Great men may jest
with saints; 'tis wit in them,
But in the less foul profanation.
Measure for Measure 2.2.127

3040 REGAN: Jesters do oft prove
prophets.
King Lear 5.3.71

3041 ROMEO: He jests at scars that never felt a wound.
Romeo and Juliet 2.2.1

3042 KING: How ill white hairs become a fool and jester!
2 Henry IV 5.5.48

3043 DIOMEDES: I do not like this fooling.
Troilus and Cressida 5.2.101

Jewel

3044 ANGELO: The jewel that we find, we stoop and take't,
Because we see it; but what we do not see
We tread upon, and never think of it.
Measure for Measure 2.1.24

3045 VALENTINE [to Duke, on courtship]: Win her with gifts, if she respect not words:
Dumb jewels often in their silent kind
More than quick words do move a woman's mind.
Two Gentlemen of Verona 3.1.89

Jews

3046 SHYLOCK: Suff'rance is the badge of all our tribe.
Merchant of Venice 1.3.110

3047 SHYLOCK: I am a Jew. Hath not a Jew eyes? Hath not a Jew hands, organs, dimensions, senses, affections, passions; fed with the same food, hurt with the same weapons, subject to the same diseases, heal'd by the same means, warm'd and cool'd by the same winter and summer, as a Christian is?
Merchant of Venice 3.1.58

3048 SHYLOCK [to Bassanio]: I will buy with you, sell with you, talk with you, walk with you, and so following; but I will not eat with you, drink with you, nor pray with you.
Merchant of Venice 1.3.37

Journeyman

3049 GAUNT: All the places that the eye of heaven visits
Are to the wise man ports and happy havens.
Richard II 1.3.275

Joy

3050 CLAUDIO: Silence is the perfectest herald of joy; I were but little happy, if I could say how much!
Much Ado About Nothing 2.1.306
[*herald:* herald]

3051 NORTHUMBERLAND: Hope to joy is little less in joy
Than hope enjoyed.
Richard II 2.3.15

3052 LEONATO: How much better is it to weep at joy than to joy at weeping!
Much Ado About Nothing 1.1.27

3053 PANDARUS: Things won are done, joy's soul lies in the doing.
Troilus and Cressida 1.2.287

3054 GRATIANO: All things that are,
Are with more spirit chased than enjoy'd.
Merchant of Venice 2.6.12

3055 Some glory in their birth, some in their skill,
Some in their wealth, some in their body's force,
Some in their garments, though new-fangled ill,
Some in their hawks and hounds, some in their horse;
And every humor hath his adjunct pleasure,
Wherein it finds a joy above the rest.
Sonnet 91

3056 PLAYER KING: The violence of either grief or joy
Their own enactures with themselves destroy.
Where joy most revels, grief doth most lament;

Grief joys, joy grieves, on slender
accident.

Hamlet 3.2.196

3057 Joy delights in joy.

Sonnet 8

3058 OTHELLO: They laugh that win.

Othello 4.1.122

3059 QUEEN: Joy, being altogether
wanting,
It doth remember me the more of
sorrow.

Richard II 3.4.13

3060 DUNCAN: My plenteous joys,
Wanton in fullness, seek to hide
themselves
In drops of sorrow.

Macbeth 1.4.33

3061 My grief lies onward and my joy
behind.

Sonnet 50

Judge

3062 When the judge is robb'd, the
prisoner dies.

Rape of Lucrece 1652

3063 ANGELO [soliloquy]: Thieves for
their robbery have authority
When judges steal themselves.

Measure for Measure 2.2.175

3064 DUKE [soliloquy]: He who the
sword of heaven will bear
Should be as holy as severe;
Pattern in himself to know,
Grace to stand, and virtue go;
More nor less to others paying
Than by self-offenses weighing.
Shame to him whose cruel striking
Kills for faults of his own liking!

Measure for Measure 3.2.261

3065 Q. KATHERINE: Heaven is above
all yet; there sits a judge
That no king can corrupt.

Henry VIII 3.1.100

3066 PORTIA: To offend and judge are
distinct offices,
And of opposed natures.

Merchant of Venice 2.9.61

3067 JAQUES: Then the justice,
In fair round belly with good capon
lin'd,
With eyes severe and beard of formal
cut,
Full of wise saws and modern
instances;
And so he plays his part.

As You Like It 2.7.153

Judgment

3068 ORLANDO: I will chide no
breather in the world but myself,
against whom I know most faults.

As You Like It 3.2.280

3069 BELARIUS: Defect of judgment
Is oft the cause of fear.

Cymbeline 4.2.111

3070 K. HENRY: Forbear to judge, for
we are sinners all.

2 Henry VI 3.3.31

3071 ANGELO: The jury, passing on
the prisoner's life,
May in the sworn twelve have a thief or
two
Guiltier than him they try.

Measure for Measure 2.1.19

3072 PROVOST: I have seen
When, after execution, judgment hath
Repented o'er his doom.

Measure for Measure 2.2.10

3073 ENOBARBUS: Men's judgments
are
A parcel of their fortunes, and things
outward
Do draw the inward quality after
them,
To suffer all alike.

Antony and Cleopatra 3.13.31

3074 HAMLET [to Horatio]: Blest are
those

Who blood and judgment are so well
  co-meddled,
That they are not a pipe for Fortune's
  finger
To sound what stop she please.
                          Hamlet 3.2.68
[*co-meddled:* commingled]

3075 ISABELLA [to Angelo]: How
would you be
If He, which is the top of judgment,
  should
But judge you as you are? O, think on
  that,
And mercy then will breathe on your
  lips,
Like a man new made.
              Measure for Measure 2.2.75

3076 HAMLET [about the King, kneeling in prayer]: How his audit stands
who knows save heaven?
                          Hamlet 3.3.82

3077 WARWICK: Between two blades,
  which bears the better temper,
Between two horses, which doth bear
  him best,
Between two girls, which hath the merriest eye —
I have perhaps some shallow spirit of
  judgment;
But in these nice sharp quillets of the
  law,
Good faith, I am no wiser than a daw.
                        1 Henry VI 2.4.13
[*quillets:* subtleties]

3078 SIR TOBY: [Judgment and
reason] have been grand-jurymen since
before Noah was a sailor.
                    Twelfth Night 3.2.16

3079 IMOGEN: Our very eyes
Are sometimes like our judgments,
blind.
                      Cymbeline 4.2.301

3080 JAQUES: Weed your better
  judgments
Of all opinion that grows rank in
  them.
                    As You Like It 2.7.45

3081 POLONIUS: Give every man thy
  ear, but few thy voice,
Take each man's censure, but reserve
  thy judgment.
                          Hamlet 1.3.68

3082 TROILUS: My election
Is led on in the conduct of my will,
My will enkindled by mine eyes and
  ears,
Two traded pilots 'twixt the dangerous
  shores
Of will and judgment.
              Troilus and Cressida 2.2.61
[*election:* choice; *traded pilots:* intermediaries constantly going back and
forth]

3083 CRESSIDA: To be wise and love
Exceeds man's might.
              Troilus and Cressida 3.2.156

3084 ANGELO: Condemn the fault,
  and not the actor of it?
              Measure for Measure 2.2.37

3085 FIRST SENATOR: He forfeits his
  own blood that spills another.
                    Timon of Athens 3.5.87

3086 SECOND MURDERER: The urging
of that word "judgment" hath bred a
kind of remorse in me.
                      Richard III 1.4.107

Jury

3087 ANGELO: The jury, passing on
  the prisoner's life,
May in the sworn twelve have a thief or
  two
Guiltier than him they try.
              Measure for Measure 2.1.19

Justice

3088 K. HENRY: Thrice is he arm'd
  that hath his quarrel just;
And he but naked, though lock'd up
  in steel,
Whose conscience with injustice is
  corrupted.
                        2 Henry VI 3.2.233

3089 K. HENRY: If little faults, pro-
ceeding on distemper,
Shall not be wink'd at, how shall we
stretch our eye
When capital crimes, chew'd,
swallow'd, and digested,
Appear before us?
Henry V 2.2.54

3090 K. HENRY: Some, peradventure,
have on them the guilt of
premeditated and contriv'd murther;
some, of beguiling virgins with the
broken seals of perjury; some, making
the wars their bulwark, that have
before gor'd the gentle bosom of peace
with pillage and robbery. Now, if these
men have defeated the law and outrun
native punishment, though they can
outstrip men, they have no wings to fly
from God.
Henry V 4.1.161
[*murther:* murder]

3091 HAMLET: Use every man after his
desert, and who shall scape whipping?
Hamlet 2.2.529

3092 ANGELO: I not deny
The jury, passing on the prisoner's life,
May in the sworn twelve have a thief or
two
Guiltier than him they try. What's
open made to justice,
That justice seizes. What know the
laws
That thieves do pass on thieves?
Measure for Measure 2.1.17

3093 BASSANIO: In law, what plea so
tainted and corrupt
But, being season'd with a gracious
voice,
Obscures the show of evil?
Merchant of Venice 3.2.75

3094 LEAR: Through tatter'd clothes
small vices do appear;
Robes and furr'd gowns hide all.
King Lear 4.6.164

3095 LEAR: Plate sin with gold,
And the strong lance of justice hurtless
breaks;

Arm it in rags, a pigmy's straw does
pierce it.
King Lear 4.6.165

3096 LEAR: The usurer hangs the
cozener.
King Lear 4.6.163
[That is, the judge—guilty himself of
usury—condemns the petty cheat.]

3097 Justice is feasting while the
widow weeps.
Rape of Lucrece 906

3098 BEROWNE: Justice always whirls
in equal measure.
Love's Labor's Lost 4.3.381

3099 KING: Where th' offense is, let
the great axe fall.
Hamlet 4.5.219

3100 PORTIA [to Shylock]: Though
justice be thy plea, consider this,
That in the course of justice, none of
us
Should see salvation. We do pray for
mercy,
And that same prayer doth teach us all
to render
The deeds of mercy.
Merchant of Venice 4.1.198

3101 PORTIA: Mercy is above this scep-
tred sway...
It is an attribute of God himself;
And earthly power doth then show
likest God's
When mercy seasons justice.
Merchant of Venice 4.1.193

3102 WOLSEY: Be just, and fear not:
Let all the ends thou aimest at be thy
country's,
Thy God's, and truth's.
Henry VIII 3.2.446

3103 EDGAR: The gods are just, and of
our pleasant vices
Make instruments to plague us.
King Lear 5.3.172

3014 K. RICHARD [to Mowbray, about Bullingbrook]: Were he my brother, nay, my kingdom's heir . . .
Such neighbor nearness to our sacred blood
Should nothing privilege him nor partialize
The unstooping firmness of my upright soul.
Richard II 1.1.116

3105 CANTERBURY: The sad-ey'd justice, with his surly hum,
Delivering o'er to executors pale
The lazy yawning drone.
Henry V 1.2.202

3106 ANTONY: The wise gods seel our eyes,
In our own filth drop our clear judgments, make us
Adore our errors, laugh at 's while we strut
To our confusion.
Antony and Cleopatra 3.13.112
[*seel:* sew up; *'s:* us]

Killing

3107 KING [soliloquy]: O, my offense is rank, it smells to heaven,
It hath the primal eldest curse upon't,
A brother's murther!
Hamlet 3.3.36
[*murther:* murder]

3108 K. JOHN: There is no sure foundation set on blood;
No certain life achiev'd by others' death.
King John 4.2.104

3109 BASSANIO: Do all men kill the things they do not love?
SHYLOCK: Hates any man the thing he would not kill?
Merchant of Venice 4.1.66

3110 ALCIBIADES: To kill, I grant, is sin's extremest gust,
But in defense, by mercy, 'tis most just.
Timon of Athens 3.5.54

3111 FIRST SENATOR: He forfeits his own blood that spills another.
Timon of Athens 3.5.87

Kin

3112 ULYSSES: One touch of nature makes the whole world kin.
Troilus and Cressida 3.3.175

3113 HAMLET [on Claudius, his uncle and step-father]:
A little more than kin, and less than kind.
Hamlet 1.2.65
[*less than kind:* indicating the enmity between them]

Kindness

3114 SONG: Beauty lives with kindness.
Two Gentlemen of Verona 4.2.45

3115 HERMIONE: You may ride 's
With one soft kiss a thousand furlongs ere
With spur we heat an acre.
Winter's Tale 1.2.94
[*'s:* us; *heat:* gallop]

3116 SECOND SENATOR: What thou wilt,
Thou rather shalt enforce it with thy smile
Than hew to't with thy sword.
Timon of Athens 5.4.44

3117 HORTENSIO: Kindness in women, not their beauteous looks,
Shall win my love.
Taming of the Shrew 4.2.41

3118 OLIVER: Kindness, nobler ever than revenge.
As You Like It 4.3.128

King

3119 PORTIA: A substitute shines brightly as a king
Until a king be by, and then his state

Empties itself, as doth an inland brook
Into the main of waters.
Merchant of Venice 5.1.94

3120 PERICLES: Kings are earth's gods.
Pericles 1.1.103

3121 K. RICHARD: The King's name is
a tower of strength.
Richard III 5.3.12

3122 KING: There's such divinity doth
hedge a king
That treason can but peep to what it
would.
Hamlet 4.5.124

3123 K. RICHARD: We were not born
to sue, but to command.
Richard II 1.1.196

3124 K. RICHARD: Not all the water in
the rough rude sea
Can wash the balm off from an
anointed king;
The breath of worldly men cannot
depose
The deputy elected by the Lord.
Richard II 3.2.54

3125 CONSTANCE: He that holds his
kingdom holds the law.
King John 3.1.188

3126 LAERTES [to Ophelia, about
Hamlet]: Perhaps he loves you now,
And now no soil nor cautel doth
besmirch
The virtue of his will, but you must
fear,
His greatness weigh'd, his will is not
his own,
For he himself is subject to his birth:
He may not, as unvalued persons do,
Carve for himself, for on his choice
depends
The safety and health of this whole
state.
Hamlet 1.3.14

[*soil:* stain; *cautel:* deceit]

3127 GLOUCESTER: The presence of a
king engenders love

Amongst his subjects and his loyal
friends,
As it disanimates his enemies.
1 Henry VI 3.1.180

3128 BATES: We know enough, if we
know we are the King's subjects. If his
cause be wrong, our obedience to the
King wipes the crime of it out of us.
Henry V 4.1.131

3129 K. HENRY: Every subject's duty
is the King's, but every subject's soul is
his own.
Henry V 4.1.176

3130 GLOUCESTER: Fearless minds
climb soonest unto crowns.
3 Henry VI 4.7.62

3131 KING [soliloquy]: How many
thousand of my poorest subjects
Are at this hour asleep! O sleep! O
gentle sleep!
Nature's soft nurse, how have I
frighted thee,
That thou no more wilt weigh my
eyelids down,
And steep my senses in forgetfulness?
Why rather, sleep, liest thou in smoky
cribs,
Upon uneasy pallets stretching thee,
And hush'd with buzzing night-flies to
thy slumber,
Than in the perfum'd chambers of the
great,
Under the canopies of costly state,
And lull'd with sound of sweetest
melody?
O thou dull god, why li'st thou with
the vile
In loathsome beds, and leavest the
kingly couch
A watch-case or a common 'larum-bell?
Wilt thou upon the high and giddy
mast
Seal up the ship-boy's eyes, and rock
his brains
In cradle of the rude imperious surge,
And in the visitation of the winds,
Who take the ruffian billows by the
top,
Curling their monstrous heads and
hanging them

With deafing clamor in the slippery
clouds,
That with the hurly death itself awakes?
Canst thou, O partial sleep, give then
repose
To a wet sea-boy in an hour so rude,
And in the calmest and most stillest
night,
With all appliances and means to boot,
Deny it to a king? Then happy low, lie
down!
Uneasy lies the head that wears a
crown.

2 Henry IV 3.1.4

[*hurly:* tumult; *low:* lowly ones]

3132 K. RICHARD: Within the hollow
crown
That rounds the mortal temples of a
king
Keeps Death his court, and there the
antic sits,
Scoffing his state and grinning at his
pomp.

Richard II 3.2.160

3133 K. RICHARD: Let us sit upon the
ground
And tell sad stories of the death of
kings:
How some have been depos'd, some
slain in war,
Some haunted by the ghosts they have
deposed,
Some poisoned by their wives, some
sleeping kill'd,
All murthered.

Richard II 3.2.155

[*murthered:* murdered]

3134 K. HENRY [soliloquy]: What infinite heart's-ease
Must kings neglect, that private men
enjoy!

Henry V 4.1.236

3135 K. HENRY [soliloquy]: What
have kings, that privates have not
too,
Save ceremony, save general ceremony?

Henry V 4.1.238

3136 BASTARD [to King John]: Let not
the world see fear and sad distrust
Govern the motion of a kingly eye.

King John 5.1.46

3137 MALCOLM: The king-becoming
graces,
As justice, verity, temp'rance,
stableness,
Bounty, perseverance, mercy, lowliness,
Devotion, patience, courage, fortitude,
I have no relish of them.

Macbeth 4.3.91

3138 K. HENRY [soliloquy]: The slave,
a member of the country's peace,
Enjoys it; but in gross brain little wots
What watch the King keeps to maintain the peace,
Whose hours the peasant best
advantages.

Henry V 4.1.281

[*wots:* knows]

3139 K. HENRY [soliloquy]: What
kind of god art thou, that suffer'st
more
Of mortal griefs than do thy worshippers?

Henry V 4.1.241

3140 K. HENRY [incognito, to some
soldiers]: The King is but a man, as I
am. The violet smells to him as it doth
to me; the element shows to him as it
doth to me; all his senses have but
human conditions. His ceremonies laid
by, in his nakedness he appears but a
man; and though his affections are
higher mounted than ours, yet when
they stoop, they stoop with the like
wing.

Henry V 4.1.101

3141 HELICANUS: They do abuse the
King that flatter him,
For flattery is the bellows blows up sin.

Pericles 1.2.38

3142 K. JOHN: It is the curse of kings
to be attended
By slaves that take their humors for a
warrant

To break within the bloody house of
life,
And on the winking of authority
To understand a law; to know the
meaning
Of dangerous majesty, when perchance
it frowns
More upon humor than advis'd respect.
King John 4.2.208

3143 PERICLES [about Simonides]: He
is a happy king, since he gains from
his subjects the name of good by his
government.
Pericles 2.1.106

3144 ROSENCRANTZ: The cess of
majesty
Dies not alone, but like a gulf doth
draw
What's near it with it. Or it is a massy
wheel
Fix'd on the summit of the highest
mount,
To whose huge spokes ten thousand
lesser things
Are mortis'd and adjoin'd, which when
it falls,
Each small annexment, petty
consequence,
Attends the boist'rous ruin. Never
alone
Did the King sigh, but with a general
groan.
Hamlet 3.3.15

[*cess:* cessation]

3145 HAMLET: A man may fish with
the worm that hath eat of a king, and
eat of the fish that hath fed of that
worm.
Hamlet 4.3.27

3146 WARWICK [soliloquy]: Who liv'd
king, but I could dig his grave?
3 Henry VI 5.2.21

3147 K. RICHARD: I had forgot myself,
am I not king?
Awake, thou coward majesty! thou
sleepest.
Is not the king's name twenty thousand
names?
Richard II 3.2.83

3148 K. HENRY [soliloquy, near the
battlefield]: O God! methinks it
were a happy life
To be no better than a homely swain,
To sit upon a hill, as I do now,
To carve out dials quaintly, point by
point,
Thereby to see the minutes how they
run:
How many make the hour full com-
plete,
How many hours bring about the day,
How many days will finish up the year,
How many years a mortal man may
live.
When this is known, then to divide
the times:
So many hours must I tend my flock,
So many hours must I take my rest,
So many hours must I contemplate,
So many hours must I sport myself,
So many days my ewes have been with
young,
So many weeks ere the poor fools will
ean,
So many years ere I shall shear the
fleece:
So minutes, hours, days, months, and
years,
Pass'd over to the end they were
created,
Would bring white hairs unto a quiet
grave.
Ah! what a life were this! how sweet!
how lovely!
Gives not the hawthorn bush a sweeter
shade
To shepherds looking on their silly
sheep
Than doth a rich embroider'd canopy
To kings that fear their subjects'
treachery?
O yes, it doth; a thousandfold it doth.
And to conclude, the shepherd's
homely curds,
His cold thin drink out of his leather
bottle,
His wonted sleep under a fresh tree's
shade,
All which secure and sweetly he enjoys,
Is far beyond a prince's delicates—
His viands sparkling in a golden cup,
His body couched in a curious bed,

When care, mistrust, and treason waits
on him.
                    3 Henry VI 2.5.21
[*homely swain:* simple shepherd; *ean:* yean,
bring forth]

Kiss

3149 HERMIONE: You may ride 's
With one soft kiss a thousand furlongs
ere
With spur we heat an acre.
                    Winter's Tale 1.2.95
[*'s:* us; *heat:* gallop]

3150 Were kisses all the joys in bed,
One woman would another wed.
                    The Passionate Pilgrim xviii.47

3151 ARRAGON: Some there be that
shadows kiss,
Such have but a shadow's bliss.
                    Merchant of Venice 2.9.66

3152 CRESSIDA: The kiss you take is
better than you give.
                    Troilus and Cressida 4.5.38

3153 WOLSEY: The hearts of princes
kiss obedience,
So much they love it.
                    Henry VIII 3.1.162

3154 PERICLES: 'Tis time to fear when
tyrants seem to kiss.
                    Pericles 1.2.79

3155 HELENA: Strangers and foes do
sunder, and not kiss.
                    All's Well That Ends Well 2.5.86

3156 GLOUCESTER [to Anne]: Teach
not thy lip such scorn; for it was
made
For kissing, lady, not for such
contempt.
                    Richard III 1.2.172

3157 Her lips to mine how often hath
she joined,
Between each kiss her oaths of true
love swearing!

How many tales to please me hath she
coined,
Dreading my love, the loss whereof
still fearing!
Yet in the midst of all her pure
protestings,
Her faith, her oaths, her tears, and all
were jestings.
                    The Passionate Pilgrim vii.7

3158 A thousand kisses buys my heart
from me.
                    Venus and Adonis 517

Knavery

3159 IAGO [soliloquy]: Knavery's plain
face is never seen till us'd.
                    Othello 2.1.312

3160 HAMLET [to Ophelia]: I am
myself indifferent honest, but yet I
could accuse me of such things that it
were better my mother had not borne
me: I am very proud, revengeful, ambitious, with more offenses at my beck
than I have thoughts to put them in,
imagination to give them shape, or
time to act them in. What should such
fellows as I do crawling between earth
and heaven? We are arrant knaves,
believe none of us.
                    Hamlet 3.1.121

3161 HUME: A crafty knave does need
no broker.
                    2 Henry VI 1.2.100

3162 HAMLET: A knavish speech
sleeps in a foolish ear.
                    Hamlet 4.2.23

Knee

3163 ULYSSES: Supple knees
Feed arrogance and are the proud
man's fees.
                    Troilus and Cressida 3.3.48

Knife

3164 The hardest knife ill us'd doth lose his edge.

Sonnet 95

Knot

3165 ULYSSES: Blunt wedges rive hard knots.

Troilus and Cressida 1.3.316

Knowledge

3166 BEROWNE: Learning is but an adjunct to ourself,
And where we are, our learning likewise is.

Love's Labor's Lost 4.3.310

3167 BEROWNE: What is the end of study, let me know.
KING: Why, that to know which else we should not know.
BEROWNE: Things hid and barr'd (you mean) from common sense.
KING: Ay, that is study's godlike recompense.

Love's Labor's Lost 1.1.55

3168 SAY: Ignorance is the curse of God,
Knowledge the wing wherewith we fly to heaven.

2 Henry VI 4.7.73

3169 OPHELIA: We know what we are, but know not what we may be.

Hamlet 4.5.43

3170 BEROWNE: Too much to know is to know nought but fame.

Love's Labor's Lost 1.1.92

Labor

3171 MACBETH: The labor we delight in physics pain.

Macbeth 2.3.50

3172 ANTONY: All labor
Mars what it does.

Antony and Cleopatra 4.14.47

3173 FIRST QUEEN: Bootless toil must recompense itself
With its own sweat.

Two Noble Kinsmen 1.1.153

3174 Old woes, not infant sorrows, bear them mild;
Continuance tames the one, the other wild,
Like an unpractic'd swimmer plunging still,
With too much labor drowns for want of skill.

Rape of Lucrece 1096

3175 FOOL: We'll set thee to school to an ant, to teach thee there's no laboring i' th' winter.

King Lear 2.4.67

3176 ORLANDO [to Adam]: O good old man, how well in thee appears
The constant service of the antique world,
When service sweats for duty, not for meed!
Thou art not for the fashion of these times,
Where none will sweat but for promotion.

As You Like It 2.3.56
[*meed:* reward]

3177 FERDINAND: Sweet thoughts do even refresh my labors.

The Tempest 3.1.14

Lady

3178 BOYET: Fair ladies mask'd are roses in their bud;
Dismask'd, their damask sweet commixture shown,
Are angels vailing clouds, or roses blown.

Love's Labor's Lost 5.2.295
[*damask:* red and white; *vailing:* letting fall, shedding]

3179 JAQUES: If ladies be but young
and fair,
They have the gift to know it.
As You Like It 2.7.37

3180 FRIAR LAWRENCE [about Juliet]:
Here comes the lady. O, so light a
foot
Will ne'er wear out the everlasting
flint.
Romeo and Juliet 2.6.16

Lameness

3181 Age is lame.
The Passionate Pilgrim xii.6

Lamentation

3182 LAFEW: Moderate lamentation is
the right of the dead, excessive grief
the enemy to the living.
All's Well That Ends Well 1.1.55

Language

3183 DON JOHN: There is not chastity
enough in language
Without offense to utter them.
Much Ado About Nothing 4.1.97

3184 FIRST GENTLEMAN [concerning
Leontes' and Camillo's reaction when
Perdita is revealed as the King's lost
daughter]: There was speech in their
dumbness, language in their very
gesture.
Winter's Tale 5.2.13

3185 ULYSSES [about Cressida]: Fie, fie
upon her!
There's language in her eye, her cheek,
her lip,
Nay, her foot speaks; her wanton
spirits look out
At every joint and motive of her body.
Troilus and Cressida 4.5.54

3186 CALIBAN [to Miranda]: You
taught me language, and my profit
on't

Is, I know how to curse. The red-
plague rid you
For learning me your language!
The Tempest 1.2.363

Lark

3187 CLOTEN: The lark at heaven's
gate sings.
Cymbeline 2.3.20

3188 SONG: Merry larks are plough-
men's clocks.
Love's Labor's Lost 5.2.904

3189 ROMEO: It was the lark, the
herald of the morn.
Romeo and Juliet 3.5.6

3190 Lo here the gentle lark, weary of
rest,
From his moist cabinet mounts up on
high,
And wakes the morning, from whose
silver breast
The sun ariseth in his majesty.
Venus and Adonis 853

3191 PETRUCHIO: What, is the jay
more precious than the lark,
Because his feathers are more beautiful?
Taming of the Shrew 4.3.175

Lateness

3192 FORD: Better three hours too
soon than a minute too late.
Merry Wives of Windsor 2.2.312

3193 PETRUCHIO: Better once than
never, for never too late.
Taming of the Shrew 5.1.150

3194 CLOTEN: I am glad I was up so
late, for that's the reason I was up so
early.
Cymbeline 2.3.33

Laughter

3195 OTHELLO: They laugh that win.
Othello 4.1.122

3196 BEROWNE: Mirth cannot move a
soul in agony.
Love's Labor's Lost 5.2.857

3197 K. JOHN: That idiot, laughter,
keep men's eyes
And strain their cheeks to idle merriment.
King John 3.3.45

3198 GRATIANO: With mirth and
laughter let old wrinkles come.
Merchant of Venice 1.1.80

Law

3199 ALCIBIADES: The law ... is past
depth
To those that (without heed) do
plunge into't.
Timon of Athens 3.5.12

3200 BEROWNE: Charity itself fulfills
the law,
And who can sever love from charity?
Love's Labor's Lost 4.3.361

3201 ALCIBIADES: Pity is the virtue of
the law,
And none but tyrants use it cruelly.
Timon of Athens 3.5.8

3202 CONSTANCE: He that holds his
kingdom holds the law.
King John 3.1.188

3203 CONSTANCE: When law can do
no right,
Let it be lawful that law bar no wrong.
King John 3.1.185

3204 ANGELO: We must not make a
scarecrow of the law,
Setting it up to fear the birds of prey,
And let it keep one shape, till custom
make it
Their perch and not their terror.
Measure for Measure 2.1.1

3205 DUKE: Now, as fond fathers,
Having bound up the threat'ning twigs
of birth,
Only to stick it in their children's sight
For terror, not to use, in time the rod
Becomes more mock'd than fear'd; so
our decrees,
Dead to infliction, to themselves are
dead,
And liberty plucks justice by the nose;
The baby beats the nurse, and quite
athwart
Goes all decorum.
Measure for Measure 1.3.23

3206 K. HENRY: Some, peradventure,
have on them the guilt of
premeditated and contriv'd murther;
some, of beguiling virgins with the
broken seals of perjury; some, making
the wars their bulwark, that have
before gor'd the gentle bosom of peace
with pillage and robbery. Now, if these
men have defeated the law and outrun
native punishment, though they can
outstrip men, they have no wings to fly
from God.
Henry V 4.1.161

[*murther:* murder]

3207 ISABELLA [soliloquy]: O perilous
mouths,
That bear in them one and the self-
same tongue,
Either of condemnation or approof,
Bidding the law make curtsy to their
will,
Hooking both right and wrong to th'
appetite,
To follow as it draws!
Measure for Measure 2.4.172

3208 BASSANIO: In law, what plea so
tainted and corrupt
But, being season'd with a gracious
voice,
Obscures the show of evil?
Merchant of Venice 3.2.75

3209 DUKE: Laws for all faults,
But faults so countenanc'd, that the
strong statutes

Stand like the forfeits in a barber's
  shop,
As much in mock as mark.
                    Measure for Measure 5.1.319

3210 ANGELO: The law hath not been
  dead, though it hath slept.
                    Measure for Measure 2.2.90

3211 ANGELO: What knows the laws
That thieves do pass on thieves?
                    Measure for Measure 2.1.22

3212 LUCIO: Give fear to use and
  liberty,
Which have for long run by the
  hideous law,
As mice by lions.
                    Measure for Measure 1.4.62

3213 SECOND FISHERMAN: A fish
hangs in the net, like a poor man's
right in the law; 'twill hardly come
out.
                    Pericles 2.1.116

3214 CHAMBERLAIN: Press not a falling
man too far! 'tis virtue.
His faults lie open to the laws, let
  them,
Not you, correct him.
                    Henry VIII 3.2.333

3215 KING [soliloquy, on his act of
  murder]: May one be pardon'd and
  retain th' offense?
In the corrupted currents of this world
Offense's gilded hand may shove by
  justice,
And oft 'tis seen the wicked prize itself
Buys out the law, but 'tis not so above:
There is no shuffling, but the action
  lies
In his true nature, and we ourselves
  compell'd,
Even to the teeth and forehead of our
  faults,
To give in evidence.
                    Hamlet 3.3.56
[*gilded hand:* offer of a bribe; *wicked prize:*
ill-gotten gains]

3216 HERMIONE [to Leontes]: If I shall
  be condemn'd
Upon surmises (all proofs sleeping else
But what your jealousies awake), I tell
  you
'Tis rigor and not law.
                    Winter's Tale 3.2.111

3217 WARWICK: Between two blades,
  which bears the better temper,
Between two horses, which doth bear
  him best,
Between two girls, which hath the merriest eye—
I have perhaps some shallow spirit of
  judgment;
But in these nice sharp quillets of the
  law,
Good faith, I am no wiser than a daw.
                    1 Henry VI 2.4.13
[*quillets:* subtleties]

3218 PORTIA: The brain may devise
laws for the blood, but a hot temper
leaps o'er a cold decree.
                    Merchant of Venice 1.2.18

3219 SUFFOLK: Faith, I have been a
  truant in the law,
And never yet could frame my will to
  it,
And therefore frame the law unto my
  will.
                    1 Henry VI 2.4.7

3220 FALSTAFF: The rusty curb of old
father antic the law.
                    1 Henry IV 1.2.61

3221 FIRST SENATOR [denying a man
  clemency]: We are for law, he dies.
                    Timon of Athens 3.5.85

Lawlessness

3222 CLIFFORD: What makes robbers
bold but too much lenity?
                    3 Henry VI 2.6.22

3223 FIRST OUTLAW: We cite our
  faults
That they may hold excus'd our lawless
lives.
                    Two Gentlemen of Verona 4.1.51

3224 ALCIBIADES: The law ... is past depth
To those that (without heed) do plunge into't.
Timon of Athens 3.5.12

Lawyer

3225 TIMON: Crack the lawyer's voice,
That he may never more false title plead,
Nor sound his quillets shrilly.
Timon of Athens 4.3.153
[*quillets:* sly tricks in argument]

3226 POMPEY: Good counsellors lack no clients.
Measure for Measure 1.2.106

3227 TRANIO: Do as adversaries do in law,
Strive mightily, but eat and drink as friends.
Taming of the Shrew 1.2.276

3228 DICK: The first thing we do, let's kill all the lawyers.
2 Henry VI 4.2.76
[A statement made after Cade's announcement that he wanted to take over the government through revolution and set up a new order.]

Laziness

3229 FALSTAFF: I were better to be eaten to death with a rust than to be scour'd to nothing with perpetual motion.
2 Henry IV 1.2.218

Learning

3230 GREMIO: O this learning, what a thing it is!
Taming of the Shrew 1.2.159

3231 BEROWNE: Study is like the heaven's glorious sun,
That will not be deep search'd with saucy looks;
Small have continual plodders ever won,

Save base authority from others' books.
Love's Labor's Lost 1.1.84

3232 BEROWNE: Learning is but an adjunct to ourself,
And where we are, our learning likewise is.
Love's Labor's Lost 4.3.310

3233 REGAN: To willful men,
The injuries that they themselves procure
Must be their schoolmasters.
King Lear 2.4.302

3234 APEMANTUS: Canst not read?
PAGE: No.
APEMANTUS: There will little learning die then that day thou art hang'd.
Timon of Athens 2.2.80

3235 BEROWNE: Love, first learned in a lady's eyes,
Lives not alone immured in the brain,
But with the motion of all elements,
Courses as swift as thought in every power,
And gives to every power a double power,
Above their functions and their offices.
It adds a precious seeing to the eye.
Love's Labor's Lost 4.3.324

3236 FALSTAFF [soliloquy]: Learning [is] a mere hoard of gold kept by a devil, till sack commences it and sets it in act and use.
2 Henry IV 4.3.115

3237 TIMON: The learned pate
Ducks to the golden fool.
Timon of Athens 4.3.17
[*ducks:* bows]

3238 LONGAVILLE: The mind shall banquet, though the body pine.
Love's Labor's Lost 1.1.25

Lechery

3239 FALSTAFF: A man can no more separate age and covetousness than 'a can part young limbs and lechery.
2 Henry IV 1.2.228
['*a:* he]

Legacy

3240 MARIANA: No legacy is so rich as honesty.
All's Well That Ends Well 3.5.12

Legs

3241 HERMIA: My legs can keep no pace with my desires.
Midsummer Night's Dream 3.2.445

3242 HELENA [to Hermia]: Your hands than mine are quicker for a fray;
My legs are longer though, to run away.
Midsummer Night's Dream 3.2.342

Leisure

3243 DUKE: Haste still pays haste, and leisure answers leisure.
Measure for Measure 5.1.410

3244 THESEUS: How shall we beguile
The lazy time, if not with some delight?
Midsummer Night's Dream 5.1.40

3245 A summer's day will seem an hour but short,
Being wasted in such time-beguiling sport.
Venus and Adonis 23

3246 PRINCE: If all the year were playing holidays,
To sport would be as tedious as to work.
1 Henry IV 1.2.204

Lending

3247 POLONIUS: Neither a borrower nor a lender be,
For loan oft loses both itself and friend.
Hamlet 1.3.75

3248 ANTONIO [to Shylock]: If thou wilt lend this money, lend it not

As to thy friends, for when did friendship take
A breed for barren metal of his friend?
But lend it rather to thine enemy,
Who if he break, thou mayst with better face
Exact the penalty.
Merchant of Venice 1.3.132
[*breed:* offspring or increase]

3249 LEAR: The usurer hangs the cozener.
King Lear 4.6.163
[That is, the judge—guilty himself of usury—condemns the petty cheat.]

Lenity

3250 CLIFFORD: What makes robbers bold but too much lenity?
3 Henry VI 2.6.22

3251 K. HENRY: When lenity and cruelty play for a kingdom, the gentler gamester is the soonest winner.
Henry V 3.6.112

3252 ESCALUS: Mercy is not itself, that oft looks so;
Pardon is still the nurse of second woe.
Measure for Measure 2.1.283

3253 GARDENER: Unruly children make their sire stoop.
Richard II 3.4.30

3254 DUKE: Now, as fond fathers,
Having bound up the threat'ning twigs of birch,
Only to stick it in their children's sight
For terror, nor to use, in time the rod
Becomes more mock'd than fear'd; so our decrees,
Dead to infliction, to themselves are dead,
And liberty plucks justice by the nose;
The baby beats the nurse, and quite athwart
Goes all decorum.
Measure for Measure 1.3.23

Leopard

3255 K. RICHARD: Lions make
leopards tame.
Richard II 1.1.174

Lewdness

3256 GHOST [to Hamlet]: But virtue,
as it never will be moved,
Though lewdness court it in a shape of
heaven,
So lust, though to a radiant angel
link'd,
Will sate itself in a celestial bed
And prey on garbage.
Hamlet 1.5.53

Liability

3257 BATES: We know enough, if we
know we are the King's subjects. If his
cause be wrong, our obedience to the
King wipes the crime of it out of us.
Henry V 4.1.131

3258 K. HENRY: Every subject's duty
is the King's, but every subject's soul is
his own.
Henry V 4.1.176

Liberality

3259 Gold that's put to use more gold
begets.
Venus and Adonis 768

3260 PRINCESS: A giving hand, though
foul, shall have fair praise.
Love's Labor's Lost 4.1.23

Liberty

3261 LUCIANA: Headstrong liberty is
lash'd with woe.
Comedy of Errors 2.1.15

3262 MACDUFF: Boundless intemperance

In nature is a tyranny; it hath been
Th' untimely emptying of the happy
throne,
And fall of many kings.
Macbeth 4.3.67

3263 DUKE: So our decrees,
Dead to infliction, to themselves are
dead,
And liberty plucks justice by the nose.
Measure for Measure 1.3.27

3264 LUCIO: Use and liberty . . .
Have for long run by the hideous law,
As mice by lions.
Measure for Measure 1.4.62

3265 LUCIO: Why, how now, Claudio!
whence comes this restraint?
CLAUDIO: From too much liberty, my
Lucio.
Measure for Measure 1.2.123
[*restraint:* Claudio, in custody of the Provost, is being led to prison]

3266 CASCA: Every bondman in his
own hand bears
The power to cancel his captivity.
Julius Caesar 1.3.101

3267 JAQUES: I must have liberty
Withal, as large a charter as the wind,
To blow on whom I please.
As You Like It 2.7.47

Library

3268 TITUS [to Lavinia]: Come and
take choice of all my library,
And so beguile thy sorrow.
Titus Andronicus 4.1.34

3269 PROSPERO: My library
Was dukedom large enough.
The Tempest 1.2.109

Licentiousness

3270 K. HENRY: What rein can hold
licentious wickedness
When down the hill he holds his fierce
career?
Henry V 3.3.22

Lies, Lying

3271 FALSTAFF: Lord, Lord, how this world is given to lying!
1 Henry IV 5.4.145

3272 JAQUES: How did you find the quarrel on the seventh cause?
TOUCHSTONE: Upon a lie seven times remov'd . . . as thus, sir. I did dislike the cut of a certain courtier's beard. He sent me word, if I said his beard was not cut well, he was in the mind it was: this is call'd the Retort Courteous. If I sent him word again, it was not well cut, he would send me word he cut it to please himself: this is call'd the Quip Modest. If again, it was not well cut, he disabled my judgment: this is call'd the Reply Churlish. If again, it was not well cut, he would answer I spake not true: this is call'd the Reproof Valiant. If again, it was not well cut he would say I lie: this is call'd the Countercheck Quarrelsome; and so to the Lie Circumstantial and the Lie Direct.
JAQUES: And how oft did you say his beard was not well cut?
TOUCHSTONE: I durst go no further than the Lie Circumstantial, nor he durst not give me the Lie Direct.
As You Like It 5.4.66

3273 TOUCHSTONE [to Jaques]: O sir, we quarrel in print, by the book — as you have books for good manners. I will name you the degrees. The first, the Retort Courteous; the second, the Quip Modest; the third, the Reply Churlish; the fourth, the Reproof Valiant; the fift, the Countercheck Quarrelsome; the sixt, the Lie with Circumstance; the seventh, the Lie Direct. All these you may avoid but the Lie Direct; and you may avoid that too, with an If.
As You Like It 5.4.90
[*fift:* fifth; *sixt:* sixth]

3274 ANTONIO: An evil soul producing holy witness
Is like a villain with a smiling cheek,
A goodly apple rotten at the heart.
O, what a goodly outside falsehood hath!
Merchant of Venice 1.3.99

3275 IMOGEN: To lapse in fullness
Is sorer than to lie for need; and falsehood
Is worse in kings than beggars.
Cymbeline 3.6.12

3276 AUTOLYCUS: Let me have no lying. It becomes none but tradesmen.
Winter's Tale 4.4.722

3277 PRINCE [to Falstaff]: These lies are like their father that begets them, gross as a mountain, open, palpable.
1 Henry IV 2.4.225

3278 HUBERT: Whose tongue soe'er speaks false,
Not truly speaks; who speaks not truly, lies.
King John 4.3.91

3279 PANDULPH: Falsehood falsehood cures, as fire cools fire.
King John 3.1.277

3280 When my love swears that she is made of truth,
I do believe her, though I know she lies.
Sonnet 138

3281 FALSTAFF: Lord, Lord, how subject we old men are to this vice of lying!
2 Henry IV 3.2.303

3282 PRINCE [to Falstaff, on Percy's slaying]: For my part, if a lie may do thee grace,
I'll gild it with the happiest terms I have.
1 Henry IV 5.4.157
[*grace:* credit]

3283 PAROLLES [to his captors about Dumaine]: He will lie, sir, with such volubility, that you would think truth were a fool.
All's Well That Ends Well 4.3.253

3284 LEONTES: I ne'er heard yet
That any of these bolder vices wanted
Less impudence to gainsay what they
did
Than to perform it first.
Winter's Tale 3.2.54

3285 LEONTES: Past all shame . . .
So past all truth.
Winter's Tale 3.2.84

3286 HAMLET: It is as easy as lying.
Hamlet 3.2.357

3287 ANTONIO: Travellers ne'er did
lie,
Though fools at home condemn 'em.
The Tempest 3.3.26

Life

3288 LEWIS: Life is as tedious as a
twice-told tale
Vexing the dull ear of a drowsy man.
King John 3.4.108

3289 IMOGEN: I see a man's life is a
tedious one.
Cymbeline 3.6.1

3290 EDGAR: O, our lives' sweetness!
That we the pain of death would
hourly die
Rather than die at once!
King Lear 5.3.185

3291 FIRST LORD: The web of our life
is of a mingled yarn, good and ill
together: our virtues would be proud,
if our faults whipt them not, and our
crimes would despair, if they were not
cherish'd by our virtues.
All's Well That Ends Well 4.3.71

3292 PROSPERO: We are such stuff
As dreams are made on; and our little
life
Is rounded with a sleep.
The Tempest 4.1.156

3293 HOTSPUR: The time of life is
short!

To spend that shortness basely were too
long.
1 Henry IV 5.2.81

3294 HECTOR: Life every man holds
dear, but the dear man
Holds honor far more precious-dear
than life.
Troilus and Cressida 5.3.27

3295 APEMANTUS: Like madness is the
glory of this life.
Timon of Athens 1.2.134

3296 CASSIUS [alluding to Caesar]: I
cannot tell what you and other men
Think of this life; but, for my single
self,
I had as lief not be as live to be
In awe of such a thing as I myself.
Julius Caesar 1.2.93

3297 SECOND MURDERER [accepting
Macbeth's hire to kill Banquo]: I am
one, my liege,
Whom the vile blows and buffets of
the world
Have so incens'd that I am reckless
what
I do to spite the world.
FIRST MURDERER: And I another,
So weary with disasters, tugg'd with
fortune,
That I would set my life on any
chance,
To mend it, or be rid of it.
Macbeth 3.1.108

3298 HAMLET [soliloquy]: Who would
fardels bear,
To grunt and sweat under a weary
life . . . ?
Hamlet 3.1.75

[*fardels:* burdens]

3299 O, that is gone for which I
sought to live,
And therefore now I need not fear to
die.
Rape of Lucrece 1051

3300 CLAUDIO: I am so out of love
with life that I will sue to be rid of it.
Measure for Measure 3.1.171

3301 RODERIGO: It is silliness to live, when to live is torment; and then we have a prescription to die, when death is our physician.

Othello 1.3.308

3302 MACBETH: Out, out, brief candle!
Life's but a walking shadow, a poor player,
That struts and frets his hour upon the stage,
And then is heard no more. It is a tale
Told by an idiot, full of sound and fury,
Signifying nothing.

Macbeth 5.5.23

3303 LEAR: When we are born, we cry that we are come
To this great stage of fools.

King Lear 4.6.182

3304 This huge stage presenteth nought but shows.

Sonnet 15

3305 MACBETH: All is but toys; renown and grace is dead,
The wine of life is drawn, and the mere lees
Is left this vault to brag of.

Macbeth 2.3.94

3306 Do I delight to die, or life desire?
But now I liv'd, and life was death's annoy,
But now I died, and death was lively joy.

Venus and Adonis 496
[*death's annoy:* i.e. painful as death]

3307 HOTSPUR [dying]: Thoughts, the slaves of life, and life, time's fool,
And time, that takes survey of all the world,
Must have a stop.

1 Henry IV 5.4.81

3308 KENT [to Lear]: My life I never held but as a pawn
To wage against thine enemies.

King Lear 1.1.157

3309 PRINCE: The end of life cancels all bands.

1 Henry IV 3.2.157
[*bands:* bonds, debts]

3310 DUKE [to the condemned Claudio]: Be absolute for death: either death or life
Shall thereby be the sweeter. Reason thus with life:
If I do lose thee, I do lose a thing
That none but fools would keep. A breath thou art,
Servile to all the skyey influences,
That dost this habitation where thou keep'st
Hourly afflict. Merely, thou art death's fool,
For him thou labor'st by thy flight to shun,
And yet run'st toward him still. Thou art not noble,
For all th' accommodations that thou bear'st
Are nurs'd by baseness. Thou'rt by no means valiant,
For thou dost fear the soft and tender fork
Of a poor worm. Thy best of rest is sleep,
And that thou oft provok'st, yet grossly fear'st
Thy death, which is no more. Thou art not thyself,
For thou exists on many a thousand grains
That issue out of dust. Happy thou art not,
For what thou hast not, still thou striv'st to get,
And what thou hast, forget'st. Thou art not certain,
For thy complexion shifts to strange effects,
After the moon. If thou art rich, thou'rt poor.
For like an ass, whose back with ingots bows,
Thou bear'st thy heavy riches but a journey,
And death unloads thee. Friend hast thou none,

For thy own bowels, which do call thee
sire,
The mere effusion of thy proper loins,
Do curse the gout, sapego, and the
rheum,
For ending thee no sooner. Thou hast
nor youth nor age,
But as it were an after-dinner's sleep,
Dreaming on both, for all thy blessed
youth
Becomes as aged, and doth beg the
alms
Of palsied eld; and when thou art old
and rich,
Thou hast neither heat, affection,
limb, nor beauty,
To make thy riches pleasant. What's
yet in this
That bears the name of life? Yet in
this life
Lie hid moe thousand deaths; yet
death we fear,
That makes these odds all even.
Measure for Measure 3.1.5
[*skyey influences:* influence of the stars; *eld:*
old age; *moe:* more]

3311 EDGAR: Life's a miracle.
King Lear 4.6.55

3312 PERICLES: Life's but breath.
Pericles 1.1.46

3313 ROSENCRANTZ: The single and
peculiar life is bound
With all the strength and armor of the
mind
To keep itself from noyance.
Hamlet 3.3.11
[*noyance:* injury]

3314 SIR TOBY: Does not our life con-
sist of the four elements?
SIR ANDREW: Faith, so they say, but I
think it rather consists of eating and
drinking.
Twelfth Night 2.3.9

3315 Like as the waves make towards
the pibbled shore,
So do our minutes hasten to their end.
Sonnet 60
[*pibbled:* pebbled]

3316 KATHERINE: A light heart lives
long.
Love's Labor's Lost 5.2.18

3317 YORK [soliloquy]: The sands are
numb'red that make up my life.
3 Henry VI 1.4.25

3318 FALSTAFF: I fear not Goliath with
a weaver's beam, because I know also
life is a shuttle.
Merry Wives of Windsor 5.1.22

3319 ORLANDO: Live a little, comfort
a little, cheer thyself a little.
As You Like It 2.6.5

3320 MESSENGER: Frame your mind to
mirth and merriment,
Which bars a thousand harms and
lengthens life.
Taming of the Shrew, Intro. 2.135

3321 ARIEL [singing]:
If of life you keep a care,
Shake off slumber, and beware.
Awake, awake!
The Tempest 2.1.303

3322 DUKE: That life is better life,
past fearing death,
Than that which lives to fear.
Measure for Measure 5.1.397

3323 QUEEN [to Hamlet]: Thou
know'st 'tis common, all that lives
must die,
Passing through nature to eternity.
Hamlet 1.2.72

3324 GAUNT: Love they to live that
love and honor have.
Richard II 2.1.138

3325 KING: Ah, what a sign it is of
evil life,
Where death's approach is seen so terrible!
2 Henry VI 3.3.5

3326 MARTIUS: Brave death outweighs
bad life.
Coriolanus 1.6.71

3327 HAMLET: A man's life's no more than to say "one."
Hamlet 5.2.74

3328 ARVIRAGUS [to Belarius]: What pleasure, sir, find we in life, to lock it
From action and adventure?
Cymbeline 4.4.2

3329 K. RICHARD [soliloquy]: How sour sweet music is
When time is broke, and no proportion kept!
So is it in the music of men's lives.
Richard II 5.5.43

3330 LORENZO: Harmony is in immortal souls,
But whilst this muddy vesture of decay
Doth grossly close it in, we cannot hear it.
Merchant of Venice 5.1.63

3331 NORTHUMBERLAND: Even through the hollow eyes of death
I spy life peering.
Richard II 2.1.270

3332 To live or die which of the twain were better,
When life is sham'd and death reproach's debtor.
Rape of Lucrece 1154

3333 JAQUES: So from hour to hour, we ripe and ripe,
And then from hour to hour, we rot and rot;
And thereby hangs a tale.
As You Like It 2.7.26

3334 FIRST CLOWN: He that is not guilty of his own death shortens not his own life.
Hamlet 5.1.19

3335 BELARIUS: O, this life
Is nobler than attending for a check;
Richer than doing nothing for a bable;
Prouder than rustling in unpaid-for silk.
Cymbeline 3.3.21

[*bable:* bribe]

3336 K. RICHARD: Our holy lives must win a new world's crown.
Richard II 5.1.24

3337 But thy eternal summer shall not fade,
Nor lose possession of that fair thou ow'st,
Nor shall Death brag thou wand'rest in his shade,
When in eternal lines to time thou grow'st.
So long as men can breathe or eyes can see,
So long lives this, and this gives life to thee.
Sonnet 18

[*ow'st:* ownest]

Light

3338 DROMIO SYRACUSE: Light is an effect of fire.
Comedy of Errors 4.3.56

3339 Light and lust are deadly enemies.
Rape of Lucrece 674

3340 BEROWNE: Light, seeking light, doth light of light beguile;
So ere you find where light in darkness lies,
Your light grows dark by losing of your eyes.
Love's Labor's Lost 1.1.77

3341 Small lights are soon blown out, huge fires abide.
Rape of Lucrece 647

Likeness

3342 BELARIUS: Cowards father cowards and base things sire base.
Cymbeline 4.2.26

Lion

3343 K. RICHARD: Lions make leopards tame.
Richard II 1.1.174

3344 QUEEN: Small curs are not regarded when they grin,
But great men tremble when the lion roars.
2 Henry VI 3.1.18

3345 CLIFFORD: To whom do lions cast their gentle looks?
Not to the beast that would usurp their den.
3 Henry VI 2.2.11

3346 ENOBARBUS: 'Tis better playing with a lion's whelp
Than with an old one dying.
Antony and Cleopatra 3.13.94

3347 HOTSPUR: O, the blood more stirs
To rouse a lion than to start a hare!
1 Henry IV 1.3.197

3348 K. HENRY: The man that once did sell the lion's skin
While the beast liv'd, was kill'd with hunting him.
Henry V 4.3.93

3349 OLIVER [to Celia and Rosalind on his rescue by Orlando]: A lioness, with udders all drawn dry,
Lay couching, head on ground, with cat-like watch
When that the sleeping man should stir; for 'tis
The royal disposition of that beast
To prey on nothing that doth seem as dead.
As You Like It 4.3.114
[*udders all drawn dry:* very hungry]

3350 BOTTOM: A lion among ladies, is a most dreadful thing.
Midsummer Night's Dream 3.1.30

3351 HELENA: The hind that would be mated by the lion
Must die for love.
All's Well That Ends Well 1.1.91

3352 ORLEANCE: That's a valiant flea that dare eat his breakfast on the lip of a lion.
Henry V 3.7.145

3353 BASTARD [to Lady Faulconbridge]: He that perforce robs lions of their hearts
May easily win a woman's.
King John 1.1.268

3354 CRESSIDA: They that have the voice of lions and the act of hares, are they not monsters?
Troilus and Cressida 3.2.88

Lips

3355 GLOUCESTER [to Anne]: Teach not thy lip such scorn; for it was made
For kissing, lady, not for such contempt.
Richard III 1.2.171

Liver

3356 ANNE: I swear, 'tis better to be lowly born,
And range with humble livers in content,
Than to be perk'd up in a glist'ring grief
And wear a golden sorrow.
Henry VIII 2.3.19

3357 FALSTAFF [to Chief Justice]: You that are old consider not the capacities of us that are young, you do measure the heat of our livers with the bitterness of your galls.
2 Henry IV 1.2.173

3358 BASSANIO: How many cowards, whose hearts are all as false
As stairs of sand, wear yet upon their chins
The beards of Hercules and frowning Mars,
Who inward search'd, have livers white as milk.
Merchant of Venice 3.2.83

3359 GRATIANO: Let my liver rather heat with wine
Than my heart cool with mortifying groans.
Merchant of Venice 1.1.81

3360 FALSTAFF [soliloquy]: The liver white and pale . . . is the badge of pusillanimity and cowardice.
2 Henry IV 4.3.104

Load

3361 Q. KATHERINE: The back is sacrifice to th' load.
Henry VIII 1.2.50

3362 BUCKINGHAM: Many
Have broke their backs with laying manors on 'em.
Henry VIII 1.1.84

3363 CROMWELL: 'Tis a cruelty
To load a falling man.
Henry VIII 5.2.111

Loathing

3364 JULIA: Love will not be spurr'd to what it loathes.
Two Gentlemen of Verona 5.2.7

3365 SHYLOCK: Affection,
Mistress of passion, sways it to the mood
Of what it likes or loathes.
Merchant of Venice 4.1.50

Logic

3366 CICERO: Men may construe things after their fashion,
Clean from the purpose of the things themselves.
Julius Caesar 1.3.34

3367 TRANIO: Balk logic with acquaintances that you have,
And practice rhetoric in your common talk.
Taming of the Shrew 1.1.34
[*balk logic:* chop logic, bandy words]

Looks

3368 Thy looks should nothing thence but sweetness tell.
Sonnet 93

3369 Looks kill love, and love by looks reviveth:
A smile recures the wounding of a frown.
Venus and Adonis 464

3370 JULIA [to Lucetta, on Proteus]:
O, know'st thou not his looks are my soul's food?
Two Gentlemen of Verona 2.7.15

3371 Ah, my love well knows
Her pretty looks have been mine enemies,
And therefore from my face she turns my foes,
That they elsewhere might dart their injuries:
Yet do not so, but since I am near slain,
Kill me outright with looks, and rid my pain.
Sonnet 139

3372 CAESAR: Let me have men about me that are fat,
Sleek-headed men and such as sleep a-nights.
Yond Cassius hath a lean and hungry look,
He thinks too much; such men are dangerous.
Julius Caesar 1.2.192

Loquacity

3373 CLOWN: Many a man's tongue shakes out his master's undoing.
All's Well That Ends Well 2.4.23

3374 ALONSO [to Gonzalo]: You cram these words into mine ears against the stomach of my sense.
The Tempest 2.1.107

3375 BASSANIO: Gratiano speaks an infinite deal of nothing, more than any
man in all Venice. His reasons are as
two grains of wheat hid in two bushels
of chaff; you seek all day ere you find
them, and when you have them, they
are not worth the search.
Merchant of Venice 1.1.114

3376 HOLOFERNES [about Armado]:
He draweth out the thread of his verbosity finer than the staple of his argument.
Love's Labor's Lost 5.1.16

Lord

3377 ULYSSES: No man is the lord of
any thing,
Though in and of him there be much
consisting,
Till he communicate his parts to
others;
Nor doth he of himself know them for
aught,
Till he behold them formed in th'
applause
Where th' are extended.
Troilus and Cressida 3.3.115
[*where th'*: where they]

3378 IAGO: We cannot all be masters,
nor all masters
Cannot be truly follow'd.
Othello 1.1.43

Loss

3379 Q. MARGARET: Wise men ne'er
sit and wail their loss,
But cheerly seek how to redress their
harms.
3 Henry VI 5.4.1

3380 OTHELLO: He that is robb'd, not
wanting what is stol'n,
Let him not know't, and he's not
robb'd at all.
Othello 3.3.342

3381 ROMEO: He that is strooken blind
cannot forget

The precious treasure of his eyesight
lost.
Romeo and Juliet 1.1.232
[*strooken*: stricken]

3382 FRIAR: It so falls out
That what we have we prize not to the
worth
Whiles we enjoy it, but being lack'd
and lost,
Why then we rack the value; then we
find
The virtue that possession would not
show us
Whiles it was ours.
Much Ado About Nothing 4.1.217

3383 KING: Praising what is lost
Makes the remembrance dear.
All's Well That Ends Well 5.3.19

3384 FIRST LORD: How mightily sometimes we make us comforts of our
losses!
All's Well That Ends Well 4.3.65

3385 K. RICHARD: What loss is it to
be rid of care?
Richard II 3.2.96

3386 KING [watching a tempest approach the Shrewsbury battlefield]:
With the losers let it sympathize,
For nothing can seem foul to those
that win.
1 Henry IV 5.1.7

3387 DUCHESS: It were lost sorrow to
wail one that's lost.
Richard III 2.2.11

3388 They that lose half with greater
patience bear it
Than they whose whole is swallowed in
confusion.
Rape of Lucrece 1158

3389 Q. MARGARET: Bett'ring thy loss
makes the bad causer worse.
Richard III 4.4.122

3390 K. RICHARD [to the victorious
Bullingbrook]:

Your cares set up do not pluck my
cares down:
My care is loss of care, by old care
done,
Your care is gain of care, by new care
won.
Richard II 4.1.195

3391 TITUS: Losers will have leave
To ease their stomachs with their bitter
tongues.
Titus Andronicus 3.1.232
[*stomachs:* resentments]

3392 QUEEN: I can give the loser leave
to chide.
2 Henry VI 3.1.182

Love

3393 BOTTOM: To say the truth,
reason and love keep little company
together now-a-days.
Midsummer Night's Dream 3.1.143

3394 HERMIA: O hell, to choose love
by another's eyes!
Midsummer Night's Dream 1.1.140

3395 CLAUDIO: Time goes on crutches
till love have all his rites.
Much Ado About Nothing 2.1.357

3396 PROTEUS: Hope is a lover's staff;
walk hence with that
And manage it against despairing
thoughts.
Two Gentlemen of Verona 3.1.248

3397 ROMEO: Love is a smoke raised
with the fume of sighs,
Being purg'd, a fire sparkling in lovers'
eyes,
Being vex'd, a sea nourish'd with lov-
ing tears.
What is it else? a madness most
discreet,
A choking gall, and a preserving sweet.
Romeo and Juliet 1.1.190

3398 Love keeps his revels where there
are but twain.
Venus and Adonis 123

3399 ANTONY: The hated, grown to
strength,
Are newly grown to love.
Antony and Cleopatra 1.3.48

3400 JULIA: They do not love that do
not show their love.
Two Gentlemen of Verona 1.2.31

3401 Age in love loves not t' have
years told.
Sonnet 138

3402 CAMILLO: Prosperity's the very
bond of love.
Winter's Tale 4.4.573

3403 JULIA: Love will not be spurr'd to
what it loathes.
Two Gentlemen of Verona 5.2.7

3404 VALENTINE: Scorn at first makes
after-love the more.
Two Gentlemen of Verona 3.1.95

3405 PROTEUS [soliloquy]: O, how this
spring of love resembleth
The uncertain glory of an April day,
Which now shows all the beauty of the
sun,
And by and by a cloud takes all away.
Two Gentlemen of Verona 1.3.84

3406 ROMEO: How silver-sweet sound
lovers' tongues by night,
Like softest music to attending ears!
Romeo and Juliet 2.2.165

3407 DUKE: If music be the food of
love, play on,
Give me excess of it.
Twelfth Night 1.1.1

3408 JULIET [to Romeo]: My bounty is
as boundless as the sea,
My love as deep; the more I give to
thee,
The more I have, for both are infinite.
Romeo and Juliet 2.2.133

3409 BEROWNE: Love is full of
unbefitting strains,
All wanton as a child, skipping and
vain,

Form'd by the eye and therefore like
the eye,
Full of straying shapes, of habits, and
of forms.
Love's Labor's Lost 5.2.760

3410 HELENA [soliloquy]: Love looks
not with the eyes but with the
mind.
Midsummer Night's Dream 1.1.234

3411 ROSALIND: Love is merely a
madness, and I tell you, deserves as
well a dark house and a whip as
madmen do; and the reason why they
are not so punish'd and cur'd is, that
the lunacy is so ordinary that the whippers are in love too.
As You Like It 3.2.400

3412 JESSICA: Love is blind, and lovers
cannot see
The pretty follies that themselves
commit.
Merchant of Venice 2.6.36

3413 FORD: Love like a shadow flies
when substance love pursues,
Pursuing that that flies, and flying
what pursues.
Merry Wives of Windsor 2.2.207

3414 ROSALIND [about Oliver and
Celia]: No sooner met but they look'd;
no sooner look'd but they lov'd; no
sooner lov'd but they sigh'd; no sooner
sigh'd but they ask'd one another the
reason; no sooner knew the reason but
they sought the remedy.
As You Like It 5.2.33

3415 DON PEDRO: Speak low if you
speak love.
Much Ado About Nothing 2.1.99

3416 ROMEO: Love goes toward love as
schoolboys from their books,
But love from love, toward school with
heavy looks.
Romeo and Juliet 2.2.156

3417 Love comforteth like sunshine
after rain.
Venus and Adonis 799

3418 POLONIUS [reading Hamlet's let-
ter to his daughter, Ophelia]:
"Doubt thou the stars are fire,
Doubt that the sun doth move,
Doubt truth to be a liar,
But never doubt I love..."
Hamlet 2.2.116

3419 PHEBE: Whoever lov'd that lov'd
not at first sight?
As You Like It 3.5.82

3420 FRIAR LAWRENCE: Love
moderately: long love doth so;
Too swift arrives as tardy as too slow.
Romeo and Juliet 2.6.14

3421 CLAUDIO [soliloquy]: Friendship
is constant in all other things
Save in the office and affairs of love.
Much Ado About Nothing 2.1.175

3422 VALENTINE [soliloquy]: Except I
be by Sylvia in the night,
There is no music in the nightingale.
Two Gentlemen of Verona 3.1.178

3423 Love is not love
Which alters when it alteration finds,
Or bends with the remover to remove.
O no, it is an ever-fixed mark
That looks on tempests and is never
shaken;
It is the star to every wand'ring bark,
Whose worth's unknown, although his
highth be taken.
Love's not Time's fool, though rosy lips
and cheeks
Within his bending sickle's compass
come,
Love alters not with his brief hours and
weeks,
But bears it out even to the edge of
doom.
If this be error and upon me proved,
I never writ, nor no man ever loved.
Sonnet 116
[*highth:* height]

3424 KING: There lives within the very
flame of love
A kind of week or snuff that will abate
it.
Hamlet 4.7.114
[*week:* wick]

3425 BRUTUS: When love begins to sicken and decay
It useth an enforced ceremony.
There are no tricks in plain and simple faith.
Julius Caesar 4.2.20

3426 LYSANDER: The course of true love never did run smooth.
Midsummer Night's Dream 1.1.134

3427 ANTONY: There's beggary in the love that can be reckon'd.
Antony and Cleopatra 1.1.15

3428 FALSTAFF [soliloquy]: O powerful love, that in some respects makes a beast a man; in some other, a man a beast.
Merry Wives of Windsor 5.5.4

3429 IAGO: Base men being in love have then a nobility in their natures more than is native to them.
Othello 2.1.215

3430 LAERTES: Nature is fine in love, and where 'tis fine,
It sends some precious instance of itself
After the thing it loves.
Hamlet 4.5.162

3431 BENEDICK [soliloquy]: I do much wonder that one man, seeing how much another man is a fool when he dedicates his behaviors to love, will, after he hath laugh'd at such shallow follies in others, become the argument of his own scorn by falling in love.
Much Ado About Nothing 2.3.7

3432 CELIA: The oath of a lover is no stronger than the word of a tapster; they are both the confirmer of false reckonings.
As You Like It 3.4.30

3433 ROSALIND: The sight of lovers feedeth those in love.
As You Like It 3.4.58

3434 JULIET [soliloquy]: Love's heralds should be thoughts,

Which ten times faster glides than the sun's beams,
Driving back shadows over low'ring hills.
Romeo and Juliet 2.5.4

3435 MRS. PAGE [reading a letter from Falstaff]: "Though Love use Reason for his precisian, he admits him not for his counsellor."
Merry Wives of Windsor 2.1.4
[*precisian:* puritanical spiritual adviser]

3436 OLIVIA: Love sought is good, but given unsought is better.
Twelfth Night 3.1.156

3437 PLAYER QUEEN: Where love is great, the littlest doubts are fear;
When little fears grow great, great love grows there.
Hamlet 3.2.171

3438 Love is a spirit all compact of fire.
Venus and Adonis 149

3439 Love's best habit is a soothing tongue.
The Passionate Pilgrim i.11

3440 CLOWN: Journeys end in lovers meeting,
Every wise man's son doth know.
Twelfth Night 2.3.43

3441 CRESSIDA: All lovers swear more performance than they are able, and yet reserve an ability that they never perform; vowing more than the perfection of ten, and discharging less than the tenth part of one.
Troilus and Cressida 3.2.84

3442 LUCETTA: They love least that let men know their love.
Two Gentlemen of Verona 1.2.32

3443 OLIVIA: A murd'rous guilt shows not itself more soon
Than love that would seem hid: love's night is noon.
Twelfth Night 3.1.147

3444 BEROWNE: A lover's eyes will gaze an eagle blind.
A lover's ears will hear the lowest sound.
Love's Labor's Lost 4.3.331

3445 SILVIUS: If thou rememb'rest not the slightest folly
That ever love did make thee run into,
Thou hast not lov'd.
As You Like It 2.4.34

3446 CELIA: It is as easy to count atomies as to resolve the propositions of a lover.
As You Like It 3.2.232
[*atomies:* atoms, minute specks]

3447 BEROWNE [soliloquy]: By heaven, I do love, and it hath taught me to rhyme and to be mallicholy.
Love's Labor's Lost 4.3.12
[*mallicholy:* melancholy]

3448 PHEBE: Good shepherd, tell this youth what 'tis to love.
SILVIUS [to Ganymede]: It is to be all made of sighs and tears . . .
It is to be all made of faith and service . . .
It is to be all made of fantasy,
All made of passion, and all made of wishes,
All adoration, duty, and observance,
All humbleness, all patience, and impatience,
All purity, all trial, all observance.
As You Like It 5.2.83

3449 ARVIRAGUS: Love's reason's without reason.
Cymbeline 4.2.22

3450 WOLSEY: Love thyself last, cherish those hearts that hate thee.
Henry VIII 3.2.443

3451 Fie, fie, fond love, thou art as full of fear
As one with treasure laden, hemm'd with thieves.
Venus and Adonis 1021

3452 There is no hate in loving.
Rape of Lucrece 240

3453 SOOTHSAYER: Be more beloving than beloved.
Antony and Cleopatra 1.2.23

3454 HELENA: Miserable most, to love unlov'd?
Midsummer Night's Dream 3.2.234

3455 DUKE: Believe not that the dribbling dart of love
Can pierce a complete bosom.
Measure for Measure 1.3.2

3456 Art thou a woman's son and canst not feel
What 'tis to love, how want of love tormenteth?
Venus and Adonis 201

3457 KING: Love that comes too late,
Like a remorseful pardon slowly carried,
To the great sender turns a sour offense.
All's Well That Ends Well 5.3.57

3458 THESEUS: Lovers and madmen have such seething brains,
Such shaping fantasies, that apprehend
More than cool reason ever comprehends.
Midsummer Night's Dream 5.1.4

3459 EGLAMOUR: Lovers break not hours,
Unless it be to come before their time.
Two Gentlemen of Verona 5.1.4

3460 HOLOFERNES: Who understandeth thee not, loves thee not.
Love's Labor's Lost 4.2.99

3461 PROTEUS: Love
Will creep in service where it cannot go.
Two Gentlemen of Verona 4.2.19

3462 MERCUTIO: This drivelling love is like a great natural that runs lolling up and down to hide his bable in a hole.
Romeo and Juliet 2.4.91
[*bable:* bauble, a stick carried by a court jester]

3463 O, learn to read what silent love hath writ:
To hear with eyes belongs to love's fine wit.
Sonnet 23

3464 My love is as a fever.
Sonnet 147

3465 Love can comment upon every woe.
Venus and Adonis 714

3466 How love makes young men thrall, and old men dote.
Venus and Adonis 837

3467 SCROOP: Sweet love, I see, changing his property,
Turns to the sourest and most deadly hate.
Richard II 3.2.135

3468 HELENA: What power is it which mounts my love so high,
That makes me see, and cannot feed mine eye?
All's Well That Ends Well 1.1.220

3469 COUNTESS: Our blood to us, this to our blood is born.
It is the show and seal of nature's truth,
Where love's strong passion is impress'd in youth.
By our remembrances of days foregone,
Such were our faults, or then we thought them none.
All's Well That Ends Well 1.3.131

3470 O most potential love! vow, bond, nor space
In thee hath neither sting, knot, nor confine,
For thou art all, and all things else are thine.
A Lover's Complaint 264

3471 Love's arms are peace, 'gainst rule, 'gainst sense, 'gainst shame,
And sweetens, in the suff'ring pangs it bears,

The aloes of all forces, shocks, and fears.
A Lover's Complaint 271
[*sweetens:* i.e. love sweetens; *aloes:* i.e. bitterness]

3472 VALENTINE: I have done penance for contemning Love,
Whose high imperious thoughts have punish'd me
With bitter fasts, with penitential groans,
With nightly tears, and daily heart-sore sighs,
For in revenge of my contempt of love,
Love hath chas'd sleep from my enthralled eyes,
And made them watchers of mine own heart's sorrow.
Two Gentlemen of Verona 2.4.129

3473 JULIA [to Lucetta]: Didst thou but know the inly touch of love,
Thou wouldst as soon go kindle fire with snow
As seek to quench the fire of love with words.
LUCETTA: I do not seek to quench your love's hot fire,
But qualify the fire's extreme rage,
Lest it should burn above the bounds of reason.
JULIA: The more thou dam'st it up, the more it burns.
Two Gentlemen of Verona 2.7.18

3474 OTHELLO [to Desdemona]: I do love thee! and when I love thee not,
Chaos is come again.
Othello 3.3.91

3475 CRESSIDA: The strong base and building of my love
Is as the very centre of the earth,
Drawing all things to it.
Troilus and Cressida 4.2.103

3476 Love is too young to know what conscience is.
Sonnet 151

3477 ROMEO: Alas that love, whose view is muffled still,

Should, without eyes, see pathways to
his will!
Romeo and Juliet 1.1.171

3478 HAMLET: Is this a prologue, or
the posy of a ring?
OPHELIA: 'Tis brief, my lord.
HAMLET: As woman's love.
Hamlet 3.2.152
[*posy of a ring:* short motto inscribed in a
ring]

3479 K. RICHARD [soliloquy]: I shall
despair; there is no creature loves
me,
And if I die no soul will pity me.
And wherefore should they, since that
I myself
Find in myself no pity to myself?
Richard III 5.3.200

3480 MACBETH: Th' expedition of my
violent love
Outrun the pauser, reason.
Macbeth 2.3.110

3481 SPEED: Love can feed on the air.
Two Gentlemen of Verona 2.1.173

3482 VALENTINE: Love hath twenty
pair of eyes.
Two Gentlemen of Verona 2.4.95

3483 JULIA: Fie, fie, how wayward is
this foolish love,
That (like a testy babe) will scratch the
nurse
And presently, all humbled, kiss the
rod!
Two Gentlemen of Verona 1.2.57

3484 DUMAINE [about Katherine]: I
would forget her, but a fever she
Reigns in my blood, and will
rememb'red be.
Love's Labor's Lost 4.3.93

3485 GAUNT: Love they to live that
love and honor have.
Richard II 2.1.138

3486 IMOGEN: [Grief] doth physic
love.
Cymbeline 3.2.34

3487 HELENA [soliloquy]: Things base
and vile, holding no quantity,
Love can transpose to form and
dignity.
Midsummer Night's Dream 1.1.232
[*holding no quantity:* lacking proportion,
unshapely]

3488 So true a fool is love that in your
will
(Though you do any thing) he thinks
no ill.
Sonnet 57

3489 VALENTINE: By love the young
and tender wit
Is turn'd to folly.
Two Gentlemen of Verona 1.1.47

3490 Ruin'd love when it is built anew
Grows fairer than at first, more strong,
far greater.
Sonnet 119

3491 O, learn to love, the lesson is but
plain,
And once made perfect, never lost
again.
Venus and Adonis 407

3492 CAESAR: The ostentation of our
love, which, left unshown,
Is often left unlov'd.
Antony and Cleopatra 3.6.52

3493 That love is merchandiz'd whose
rich esteeming
The owner's tongue doth publish every
where.
Sonnet 102

3494 Love thrives not in the heart that
shadows dreadeth.
Rape of Lucrece 270

3495 Against love's fire fear's frost
hath dissolution.
Rape of Lucrece 355

3496 All love's pleasure shall not
match his woe.
Venus and Adonis 1140

3497 POLONIUS [on Hamlet's strange behavior]: This is the very ecstasy of love,
Whose violent property fordoes itself,
And leads the will to desperate undertakings
As oft as any passion under heaven
That does afflict our natures.
Hamlet 2.1.99
[*fordoes:* destroys]

3498 BEROWNE: Love, first learned in a lady's eyes,
Lives not alone immured in the brain,
But with the motion of all elements,
Courses as swift as thought in every power,
And gives to every power a double power,
Above their functions and their offices.
Love's Labor's Lost 4.3.324

3499 BEROWNE: It adds a precious seeing to the eye.
Love's Labor's Lost 4.3.330

3500 BEROWNE: When Love speaks, the voice of all the gods
Make heaven drowsy with the harmony.
Love's Labor's Lost 4.3.341

3501 BOYET: Love doth approach disguis'd,
Armed in arguments.
Love's Labor's Lost 5.2.83

3502 DUKE: Love is like a child,
That longs for everything that he can come by.
Two Gentlemen of Verona 3.1.124

3503 ROMEO: Is love a tender thing? It is too rough,
Too rude, too boist'rous, and it pricks like thorn.
MERCUTIO: If love be rough with you, be rough with love;
Prick love for pricking, and you beat love down.
Romeo and Juliet 1.4.25

3504 CRANMER [to Gardiner]: Love and meekness . . .

Becomes a churchman better than ambition.
Henry VIII 5.2.97

3505 ANTIPHOLUS SYRACUSE [to Luciana]: It is thyself, mine own self's better part:
Mine eye's clear eye, my dear heart's dearer heart,
My food, my fortune, and my sweet hope's aim,
My sole earth's heaven, and my heaven's claim.
Comedy of Errors 3.2.61

3506 VALENTINE: Love delights in praises.
Two Gentlemen of Verona 2.4.148

3507 BEROWNE: Never durst poet touch a pen to write
Until his ink were temp'red with Love's sighs.
Love's Labor's Lost 4.3.343

3508 VALENTINE: Tell me, do you know Madam Silvia?
SPEED: She that your worship loves?
VALENTINE: Why, how know you that I am in love?
SPEED: Marry, by these special marks: first, you have learn'd, like Sir Proteus, to wreathe your arms, like a malecontent; to relish a love-song, like a robin-redbreast; to walk alone, like one that had the pestilence; to sigh, like a schoolboy that had lost his A B C; to weep, like a young wench that had buried her grandam; to fast, like one that takes diet; to watch, like one that fears robbing; to speak puling, like a beggar at Hallowmas. You were wont, when you laugh'd, to crow like a cock; when you walk'd, to walk like one of the lions; when you fasted, it was presently after dinner; when you look'd sadly, it was for want of money: and now you are metamorphis'd with a mistress, that when I look on you, I can hardly think you my master.
Two Gentlemen of Verona 2.1.15
[*malecontent:* malcontent; *puling:* whiningly]

3509 Were beauty under twenty locks
kept fast,
Yet love breaks through, and picks
them all at last.
Venus and Adonis 575

3510 VALENTINE [concerning Silvia]: I
have lov'd her ever since I saw her, and
still I see her beautiful.
SPEED: If you love her, you cannot see
her.
VALENTINE: Why?
SPEED: Because Love is blind.
Two Gentlemen of Verona 2.1.66

3511 TWO PAGES [singing]: Sweet
lovers love the spring.
As You Like It 5.3.21

3512 PROTEUS [soliloquy]: I to myself
am dearer than a friend.
Two Gentlemen of Verona 2.6.23

3513 PROTEUS: In love
Who respects friend?
Two Gentlemen of Verona 5.4.54

3514 For lovers say, the heart hath tre-
ble wrong
When it is barr'd the aidance of the
tongue.
An oven that is stopp'd, or river stay'd,
Burneth more hotly, swelleth with
more rage;
So of concealed sorrow may be said,
Free vent of words love's fire doth
assuage.
Venus and Adonis 329

3515 Love's gentle spring doth always
fresh remain,
Lust's winter comes ere summer half be
done;
Love surfeits not, Lust like a glutton
dies;
Love is all truth, Lust full of forged
lies.
Venus and Adonis 801

3516 Where Love reigns, disturbing
Jealousy
Doth call himself Affection's sentinel.
Venus and Adonis 649

3517 TOUCHSTONE: We that are true
lovers run into strange capers; but as
all is mortal in nature, so is all nature
in love mortal in folly.
As You Like It 2.4.54

3518 IMOGEN: Lovers
And men in dangerous bonds pray not
alike.
Cymbeline 3.2.36

3519 FRANCE: Love's not love
When it is mingled with regards that
stand
Aloof from th' entire point.
King Lear 1.1.238

3520 ROMEO: Stony limits cannot hold
love out,
And what love can do, that dares love
attempt.
Romeo and Juliet 2.2.67

3521 Love knows it is a greater grief
To bear love's wrong than hate's known
injury.
Sonnet 40

3522 VALENTINE [to Proteus]: Love is
your master, for he masters you;
And he that is so yoked by a fool,
Methinks should not be chronicled for
wise.
Two Gentlemen of Verona 1.1.39

3523 The strongest body shall it make
most weak,
Strike the wise dumb, and teach the
fool to speak.
Venus and Adonis 1145

3524 VALENTINE: To be in love—
where scorn is bought with groans;
Coy looks with heart-sore sighs; one
fading moment's mirth
With twenty watchful, weary, tedious
nights:
If happ'ly won, perhaps a hapless gain;
If lost, why then a grievous labor won.
Two Gentlemen of Verona 1.1.28

3525 ARMADO: Green indeed is the
color of lovers.
Love's Labor's Lost 1.2.86

3526 It shall be fickle, false, and full
of fraud,
Bud, and be blasted, in a breathing
while,
The bottom poison, and the top
o'erstraw'd
With sweets that shall the truest sight
beguile.
Venus and Adonis 1141

3527 OPHELIA [giving out flowers after
Polonius' death]: There's rosemary,
that's for remembrance; pray you, love,
remember. And there is pansies, that's
for thoughts.
Hamlet 4.5.175
[*rosemary:* used as a symbol of remembrance at weddings; *pansies:* emblems of
love and courtship]

3528 BERTRAM [about Diana]: She
knew her distance, and did angle for
me,
Maddening my eagerness with her restraint,
As all impediments in fancy's course
Are motives of more fancy, and in
fine,
Her inf'nite cunning, with her modern
grace,
Subdu'd me to her rate. She got the
ring.
All's Well That Ends Well 5.3.212
[*fancy's:* i.e. love's]

3529 SILVIUS [to Phebe]: Loose now
and then
A scatt'red smile, and that I'll live
upon.
As You Like It 3.5.103

3530 PARIS: Venus smiles not in a
house of tears.
Romeo and Juliet 4.1.8

3531 HELENA: We cannot fight for
love, as men do.
We should be woo'd, and were not
made to woo.
Midsummer Night's Dream 2.1.241

3532 ARMADO [soliloquy]: Love is a
familiar; Love is a devil; there is no
evil angel but Love.
Love's Labor's Lost 1.2.172
[*familiar:* attendant evil spirit, demon]

Lovers

3533 ROSALIND: The sight of lovers
feedeth those in love.
As You Like It 3.4.58

3534 CELIA: It is as easy to count
atomies as to resolve the propositions
of a lover.
As You Like It 3.2.232
[*atomies:* atoms, minute specks]

3535 CELIA: The oath of a lover is no
stronger than the word of a tapster;
they are both the confirmer of false
reckonings.
As You Like It 3.4.30

3536 JULIET: At lovers' perjuries
They say Jove laughs.
Romeo and Juliet 2.2.92

3537 BEROWNE: A lover's eyes will
gaze an eagle blind.
A lover's ear will hear the lowest
sound.
Love's Labor's Lost 4.3.331

3538 GRATIANO: Lovers ever run
before the clock.
Merchant of Venice 2.6.4

3539 EGLAMOUR: Lovers break not
hours,
Unless it be to come before their time.
Two Gentlemen of Verona 5.1.4

3540 Lovers' hours are long, though
seeming short.
Venus and Adonis 842

3541 CLOWN: Journeys end in lovers
meeting,
Every wise man's son doth know.
Twelfth Night 2.3.43

3542 ROMEO: How silver-sweet sound lovers' tongues by night,
Like softest music to attending ears!
Romeo and Juliet 2.2.166

3543 FRIAR LAWRENCE: A lover may bestride the gossamers
That idles in the wanton summer air,
And yet not fall; so light is vanity.
Romeo and Juliet 2.6.18
[*gossamers*: threads spun by spiders]

3544 CRESSIDA: They say all lovers swear more performance than they are able, and yet reserve an ability that they never perform.
Troilus and Cressida 3.2.84

3545 Lovers say, the heart hath treble wrong
When it is barr'd the aidance of the tongue.
Venus and Adonis 329

3546 JESSICA: Love is blind, and lovers cannot see
The pretty follies that themselves commit.
Merchant of Venice 2.6.36

3547 THESEUS: Lovers and madmen have such seething brains,
Such shaping fantasies, that apprehend
More than cool reason ever comprehends.
Midsummer Night's Dream 5.1.4

3548 IMOGEN: Lovers
And men in dangerous bonds pray not alike.
Cymbeline 3.2.36

3549 ROSALIND [about Oliver and Celia]: No sooner met but they look'd; no sooner look'd but they lov'd; no sooner lov'd but they sigh'd; no sooner sigh'd but they ask'd one another the reason; no sooner knew the reason but they sought the remedy: and in these degrees have they made a pair of stairs to marriage, which they will climb incontinent, or else be incontinent before marriage.
As You Like It 5.2.33

3550 DUKE: If ever thou shalt love,
In the sweet pangs of it remember me;
For such as I am, all true lovers are,
Unstaid and skittish in all motions else,
Save in the constant image of the creature
That is belov'd.
Twelfth Night 2.4.15

Lowliness

3551 BRUTUS [soliloquy]: Lowliness is young ambition's ladder.
Julius Caesar 2.1.22

3552 ANNE: I swear, 'tis better to be lowly born,
And range with humble livers in content,
Than to be perk'd up in a glist'ring grief
And wear a golden sorrow.
Henry VIII 2.3.19

Loyalty

3553 ENOBARBUS: The loyalty well held to fools does make
Our faith mere folly; yet he that can endure
To follow with allegiance a fall'n lord
Does conquer him that did his master conquer,
And earns a place i' th' story.
Antony and Cleopatra 3.13.42

3554 KING: O, where is faith? O, where is loyalty?
If it be banish'd from the frosty head,
Where shall it find a harbor in the earth?
2 Henry VI 5.1.166

3555 DESDEMONA: My noble father,
I do perceive here a divided duty:
To you I am bound for life and education;
My life and education both do learn me

How to respect you; you are the lord of
duty;
I am hitherto your daughter. But here's
my husband;
And so much duty as my mother
show'd
To you, preferring you before her
father,
So much I challenge that I may profess
Due to the Moor, my lord.
Othello 1.3.180

3556 ORLANDO [to Adam]: O good
old man, how well in thee appears
The constant service of the antique
world,
When service sweat for duty, not for
meed!
Thou art not for the fashion of these
times,
Where none will sweat but for promotion.
As You Like It 2.3.56
[*meed:* reward]

Luck

3557 POSTHUMUS: Many dream not to
find, neither deserve,
And yet are steep'd in favors.
Cymbeline 5.4.130

3558 MALVOLIO: All is fortune.
Twelfth Night 2.5.23

3559 STEPHANO: All is but fortune.
The Tempest 5.1.257

Lunacy

3560 THESEUS: Lovers and madmen
have such seething brains,
Such shaping fantasies, that apprehend
More than cool reason ever compre-
hends.
The lunatic, the lover, and the poet
Are of imagination all compact.
Midsummer Night's Dream 5.1.4

Lust

3561 Light and lust are deadly
enemies.
Rape of Lucrece 674

3562 While Lust is in his pride, no
exclamation
Can curb his heat, or rein his rash
desire.
Rape of Lucrece 705

3563 ROSALINE: The blood of youth
burns not with such excess
As gravity's revolt to wantonness.
Love's Labor's Lost 5.2.73

3564 The flesh being proud, Desire
doth fight with Grace,
For there it revels, and when that
decays,
The guilty rebel for remission prays.
Rape of Lucrece 712

3565 GHOST [to Hamlet]: Virtue, as it
never will be moved,
Though lewdness court it in a shape of
heaven,
So lust, though to a radiant angel
link'd,
Will sate itself in a celestial bed
And prey on garbage.
Hamlet 1.5.53

3566 Th' expense of spirit in a waste
of shame
Is lust in action, and till action, lust
Is perjur'd, murd'rous, bloody, full of
blame,
Savage, extreme, rude, cruel, not to
trust,
Enjoy'd no sooner but despised
straight,
Past reason hunted, and no sooner
had,
Past reason hated as a swallowed bait
On purpose laid to make the taker
mad:
Mad in pursuit and in possession so,
Had, having, and in quest to have,
extreme,
A bliss in proof, and prov'd, a very
woe,

Before, a joy propos'd, behind a
  dream.
All this world well knows, yet none
  knows well
To shun the heaven that leads men to
  this hell.
Sonnet 129

3567 IAGO: When the blood is made
dull with the act of sport, there should
be, again to inflame it and to give
satiety a fresh appetite, loveliness in
favor, sympathy in years, manners, and
beauties.
Othello 2.1.226

3568 SONG: Lust is but a bloody fire,
Kindled with unchaste desire,
Fed in heart, whose flames aspire,
As thoughts do blow them, higher and
  higher.
Merry Wives of Windsor 5.5.95

3569 Careless lust stirs up a desperate
  courage,
Planting oblivion, beating reason back,
Forgetting shame's pure blush and
  honor's wrack.
Venus and Adonis 556

3570 CLAUDIO: Time goes on crutches
till love have all his rites.
Much Ado About Nothing 2.1.357

3571 PROSPERO: Do not give dalliance
Too much the rein.
The Tempest 4.1.51

3572 Reason is the bawd to lust's
  abuse.
Venus and Adonis 792

3573 PERICLES: Murther's as near to
  lust as flame to smoke.
Pericles 1.1.138
[*murther:* murder]

3574 MACDUFF: Avarice
Sticks deeper, grows with more per-
  nicious root
Than summer-seeming lust.
Macbeth 4.3.84

3575 Pure Chastity is rifled of her
  store,
And Lust, the thief, far poorer than
  before.
Rape of Lucrece 692

3576 Tears harden lust, though marble
  wear with raining.
Rape of Lucrece 560

3577 Love comforteth like sunshine
  after rain,
But Lust's effect is tempest after sun;
Love's gentle spring doth always fresh
  remain,
Lust's winter comes ere summer half be
  done;
Love surfeits not, Lust like a glutton
  dies;
Love is all truth, Lust full of forged
  lies.
Venus and Adonis 799

Madness

3578 APEMANTUS: Like madness is the
  glory of this life.
Timon of Athens 1.2.134

3579 POLONIUS: To define true
  madness,
What is't but to be nothing else but
  mad?
Hamlet 2.2.93

3580 HAMLET: Madness would not err,
Nor sense to ecstasy was ne'er so
  thrall'd
But it reserv'd some quantity of choice.
Hamlet 3.4.73
[*thrall'd:* enslaved; *quantity of choice:* some
power to choose]

3581 QUEEN [to Hamlet, on his
  father's ghost]: This is the very
  coinage of your brain,
This bodiless creation ecstasy
Is very cunning in.
Hamlet 3.4.137

3582 FOOL: He's mad that trusts in the
tameness of a wolf, a horse's health, a
boy's love, or a whore's oath.
King Lear 3.6.18

3583 OTHELLO: It is the very error of the moon,
She comes more nearer earth than she was wont,
And makes men mad.
Othello 5.2.109

3584 DOCTOR: Infected minds
To their deaf pillows will discharge their secrets.
Macbeth 5.1.72

3585 KING: Madness in great ones must not unwatch'd go.
Hamlet 3.1.189

3586 CONSTANCE: I am not mad, I would to heaven I were!
For then 'tis like I should forget myself.
O, if I could, what grief should I forget!
King John 3.4.48

3587 HAMLET: I am but mad north-north-west. When the wind is southerly I know a hawk from a hand-saw.
Hamlet 2.2.378

3588 POLONIUS [about Hamlet's behavior]: Though this be madness, yet there is method in't.
Hamlet 2.2.205

3589 POLONIUS [about Hamlet]: How pregnant sometimes his replies are! a happiness that often madness hits on, which reason and sanity could not so prosperously be deliver'd of.
Hamlet 2.2.208

3590 K. LEAR: O, that way madness lies, let me shun that!
King Lear 3.4.21

3591 ROSALIND: Love is merely a madness, and I tell you, deserves as well a dark house and a whip as madmen do; and the reason why they are not so punish'd and cur'd is, that the lunacy is so ordinary that the whippers are in love too.
As You Like It 3.2.400

3592 THESEUS: Lovers and madmen have such seething brains,
Such shaping fantasies, that apprehend
More than cool reason ever comprehends.
Midsummer Night's Dream 5.1.4

3593 ABBESS: What's a fever but a fit of madness?
Comedy of Errors 5.1.76

Maids

3594 ROSALIND: Maids are May when they are maids, but the sky changes when they are wives.
As You Like It 4.1.148

3595 TRANIO [to Lucentio, about Bianca]: If you love the maid,
Bend thoughts and wits to achieve her.
Taming of the Shrew 1.1.178

3596 PORTIA: A maiden hath no tongue but thought.
Merchant of Venice 3.2.8

3597 MARIANA: The honor of a maid is her name.
All's Well That Ends Well 3.5.12

3598 LAERTES: The chariest maid is prodigal enough
If she unmask her beauty to the moon.
Hamlet 1.3.36

3599 EMILIA: Of all flow'rs
Methinks a rose is best . . .
It is the very emblem of a maid;
For when the west wind courts her gently,
How modestly she blows, and paints the sun
With her chaste blushes! When the north comes near her,
Rude and impatient, then, like chastity,
She locks her beauties in her bud again,
And leaves him to base briers.
Two Noble Kinsmen 2.2.135

Majesty

3600 PRINCE [soliloquy]: O majesty!
When thou dost pinch thy bearer,
   thou dost sit
Like a rich armor worn in heat of day,
That scald'st with safety.
                                    2 Henry IV 4.5.28
[*scald'st with safety:* i.e. both protects and
burns]

3601 ROSENCRANTZ: The cess of
   majesty
Dies not alone, but like a gulf doth
   draw
What's near it with it. Or it is a massy
   wheel
Fix'd on the summit of the highest
   mount,
To whose huge spokes ten thousand
   lesser things
Are mortis'd and adjoin'd, which when
   it falls,
Each small annexment, petty
   consequence,
Attends the boist'rous ruin. Never
   alone
Did the King sigh, but with a general
   groan.
                                    Hamlet 3.3.15
[*cess:* cessation]

3602 CLEOPATRA: Majesty, to keep
   decorum, must
No less beg than a kingdom.
                         Antony and Cleopatra 5.2.17

3603 BELARIUS: The gates of monarchs
Are arch'd so high that giants may jet
   through
And keep their impious turbands on.
                                    Cymbeline 3.3.4
[*jet:* strut]

3604 KENT: To plainness honor's
   bound,
When majesty falls to folly.
                                    King Lear 1.1.148

3605 KING: There's such divinity doth
   hedge a king
That treason can but peep to what it
   would.
                                    Hamlet 4.5.124

3606 KING: Majesty might never yet
   endure
The moody frontier of a servant brow.
                                    1 Henry IV 1.3.18

Malady

3607 BEROWNE: Abstinence engenders
   maladies.
                         Love's Labor's Lost 4.3.291

3608 LEAR: Where the greater malady
   is fix'd,
The lesser is scarce felt.
                                    King Lear 3.4.8

3609 SPEED: [to the love-sick Valen-
   tine]: Not an eye that sees you but is a
physician to comment on your malady.
                    Two Gentlemen of Verona 2.1.41

Malice

3610 ORLEANCE: Ill will never said
   well.
                                    Henry V 3.7.114

3611 HERO: One doth not know
How much an ill word may empoison
   liking.
                    Much Ado About Nothing 3.1.85

3612 CRANMER: Men that make
Envy and crooked malice nourishment
Dare bite the best.
                                    Henry VIII 5.2.78

3613 OTHELLO [to Lodovico and
   others]: Speak of me as I am;
   nothing extenuate,
Nor set down aught in malice.
                                    Othello 5.2.342

Malevolence

3614 DONALBAIN: There's daggers in
   men's smiles.
                                    Macbeth 2.3.140

Man

3615 MIRANDA: How beauteous
mankind is! O brave new world,
That has such creatures in't!
The Tempest 5.1.183

3616 HAMLET: What a piece of work is
a man, how noble in reason, how infinite in faculties, in form and moving,
how express and admirable in action,
how like an angel in apprehension,
how like a god! the beauty of the
world; the paragon of animals; and yet
to me what is this quintessence of
dust?
Hamlet 2.2.303
[*quintessence:* the fifth essence of ancient
philosophy, supposed to be the substance of
the heavenly bodies and to be latent in all
things]

3617 PANDARUS: Do you know what a
man is? Is not birth, beauty, good
shape, discourse, manhood, learning,
gentleness, virtue, youth, liberality,
and suchlike, the spice and salt that
season a man?
Troilus and Cressida 1.2.252

3618 BOTTOM: Man is but an ass . . .
Man is but a patch'd fool.
Midsummer Night's Dream 4.1.206

3619 All men are bad and in their
badness reign.
Sonnet 121

3620 BALTHAZAR: Men were deceivers
ever.
Much Ado About Nothing 2.3.63

3621 FALSTAFF: There is nothing but
roguery to be found in villainous man.
1 Henry IV 2.4.124

3622 NURSE [to Juliet]: There's no
trust,
No faith, no honesty in men, all perjur'd,
All forsworn, all naught, all dissemblers.
Romeo and Juliet 3.2.85

3623 CHANCELLOR: We all are men,
In our own natures frail, and capable
Of our flesh; few are angels.
Henry VIII 5.2.45

3624 DUKE [soliloquy]: O, what may
man within him hide,
Though angel on the outward side!
Measure for Measure 3.2.271

3625 In men, as in a rough-grown
grove, remain
Cave-keeping evils that obscurely sleep.
Rape of Lucrece 1249

3626 MARIANA: They say best men are
moulded out of faults,
And for the most, become much more
the better
For being a little bad.
Measure for Measure 5.1.439

3627 FALSTAFF: He is but the
counterfeit of a man who has not the
life of a man.
1 Henry IV 5.4.116

3628 GONERIL: O, the difference of
man and man!
King Lear 4.2.26

3629 ISABELLA: Man, proud man,
Dress'd in a little brief authority,
Most ignorant of what he's most assur'd
(His glassy essence), like an angry ape
Plays such fantastic tricks before high
heaven
As make the angels weep.
Measure for Measure 2.2.117
[*glassy:* fragile, highly susceptible of
damage]

3630 ALBANY: Humanity must per-
force prey on itself,
Like monsters of the deep.
King Lear 4.2.48

3631 TIMON [soliloquy]: Ingrateful
man, with liquorish draughts
And morsels unctuous, greases his pure
mind,
That from it all consideration slips.
Timon of Athens 4.3.194

3632 EDMUND: Know thou this, that men
Are as the time is.
King Lear 5.3.30

3633 PROTEUS: O heaven, were man
But constant, he were perfect.
Two Gentlemen of Verona 5.4.110

3634 HAMLET [soliloquy]: What is a man,
If his chief good and market of his time
Be but to sleep and feed? a beast, no more.
Sure He that made us with such large discourse,
Looking before and after, gave us not
That capability and godlike reason
To fust in us unus'd.
Hamlet 4.4.33

[*fust:* grow mouldy]

3635 APEMANTUS [to Timon, about his guests]: I wonder men dare trust themselves with men.
Methinks they should invite them without knives:
Good for their meat, and safer for their lives.
Timon of Athens 1.2.43

3636 AJAX: I do hate a proud man, as I hate the engend'ring of toads.
Troilus and Cressida 2.3.158

3637 FALSTAFF [soliloquy]: O powerful love, that in some respects makes a beast a man; in some other, a man a beast.
Merry Wives of Windsor 5.5.4

3738 DUKE: However we do praise ourselves,
Our fancies are more giddy and unfirm,
More longing, wavering, sooner lost and worn,
Than women's are.
Twelfth Night 2.4.32

3739 Though men can cover crimes with bold stern looks,

Poor women's faces are their own faults' books.
Rape of Lucrece 1252

3640 HAMLET [to Horatio]: Give me that man
That is not passion's slave, and I will wear him
In my heart's core, ay, in my heart of heart.
Hamlet 3.2.71

3641 WOLSEY [soliloquy]: This is the state of man: to-day he puts forth
The tender leaves of hopes, tomorrow blossoms,
And bears his blushing honors thick upon him;
The third day comes a frost, a killing frost,
And when he thinks, good easy man, full surely
His greatness is a-ripening, nips his root,
And then he falls as I do.
Henry VIII 3.2.352

3642 CERIMON: I hold it ever
Virtue and cunning were endowments greater
Than nobleness and riches. Careless heirs
May the two latter darken and expend;
But immortality attends the former,
Making a man a god.
Pericles 3.2.27

3643 JAQUES: All the world's a stage,
And all the men and women merely players;
They have their exits and their entrances,
And one man in his time plays many parts,
His acts being seven ages. At first the infant,
Mewling and puking in the nurse's arms.
Then the whining schoolboy, with his satchel
And shining morning face, creeping like snail

Unwillingly to school. And then the
    lover,
Sighing like furnace, with a woeful
    ballad
Made to his mistress' eyebrow. Then a
    soldier,
Full of strange oaths, and bearded like
    the pard,
Jealous in honor, sudden, and quick in
    quarrel,
Seeking the bubble reputation
Even in the cannon's mouth. And then
    the justice,
In fair round belly with good capon
    lin'd,
With eyes severe and beard of formal
    cut,
Full of wise saws and modern in-
    stances;
And so he plays his part. The sixt age
    shifts
Into the lean and slipper'd pantaloon,
With spectacles on nose, and pouch on
    side,
His youthful hose, well sav'd, a world
    too wide
For his shrunk shank, and his big
    manly voice,
Turning again toward childish treble,
    pipes
And whistles in his sound. Last scene
    of all,
That ends this strange eventful history,
Is second childishness, and mere
    oblivion,
Sans teeth, sans eyes, sans taste, sans
    every thing.
                        As You Like It 2.7.139
[*sixt:* sixth]

3644 DESDEMONA: Men's natures
wrangle with inferior things,
Though great ones are their object.
                        Othello 3.4.144

3645 ULYSSES: O heavens, what some
    men do,
While some men leave to do!
How some men creep in skittish For-
    tune's hall,
Whiles others play the idiots in her
    eyes!
                        Troilus and Cressida 3.3.132

3646 EMILIA: Men are mad things.
                        Two Noble Kinsmen 2.2.126

Manhood

3647 BEATRICE: He that hath a beard
is more than a youth, and he that hath
no beard is less than a man.
                        Much Ado About Nothing 2.1.36

3648 SIR TOBY: It comes to pass oft
that a terrible oath, with a swaggering
accent sharply twang'd off, gives
manhood more approbation than ever
proof itself would have earn'd him.
                        Twelfth Night 3.4.179

3649 COMINIUS: Manhood is call'd
    foolery when it stands
Against a falling fabric.
                        Coriolanus 3.1.245
[*stands against:* opposes]

Manners

3650 ANGELO [soliloquy]: O place, O
    form,
How often dost thou with thy case, thy
    habit,
Wrench awe from fools, and tie the
    wiser souls
To thy false seeming!
                        Measure for Measure 2.4.12

3651 CORIN: Those that are good
manners at the court are as ridiculous
in the country as the behavior of the
country is most mockable at the court.
                        As You Like It 3.2.45

3652 FALSTAFF [soliloquy]: It is certain
that either wise bearing or ignorant
carriage is caught, as men take
diseases, one of another; therefore let
men take heed of their company.
                        2 Henry IV 5.1.75

3653 GRIFFITH: Men's evil manners
    live in brass, their virtues
We write in water.
                        Henry VIII 4.2.45

3654 PALAMON: 'Tis in our power
(Unless we fear that apes can tutor 's) to
Be masters of our manners.
Two Noble Kinsmen 1.2.43
['s: us]

3655 WORCESTER: Defect of manners,
want of government,
Pride, haughtiness, opinion, and disdain,
The least of which haunting a noble-
man
Loseth men's hearts and leaves behind
a stain
Upon the beauty of all parts besides,
Beguiling them of commendation.
1 Henry IV 3.1.182
[*government:* self-control; *opinion:* conceit]

March

3656 PERDITA: Daffadils,
That come before the swallow dares
... take
The winds of March with beauty.
Winter's Tale 4.4.118
[*daffadils:* daffodils]

3657 SOOTHSAYER [to Caesar]: Beware
the ides of March.
Julius Caesar 1.2.18

3658 CAESAR: The ides of March are
come.
SOOTHSAYER: Ay, Caesar, but not
gone.
Julius Caesar 3.1.1

Market

3659 ROSALIND [to Phebe, on the
love-struck Silvius]: Sell when you
can, you are not for all markets.
As You Like It 3.5.60

Master

3660 IAGO: We cannot all be masters,
nor all masters
Cannot be truly follow'd.
Othello 1.1.43

3661 CASSIUS: Men at some time are
masters of their fates.
Julius Caesar 1.2.139

3662 K. RICHARD: Lions make leopards tame.
Richard II 1.1.174

Match

3663 FIRST SOLDIER: Half won is the
match well made.
All's Well That Ends Well 4.3.225

3664 K. EDWARD: The harder
match'd, the greater victory.
3 Henry VI 5.1.70

Maternity

3665 EGEON: The pleasing punishment that women bear.
Comedy of Errors 1.1.47

3666 MIRANDA: Good wombs have
borne bad sons.
The Tempest 1.2.120

Matrimony

3667 TOUCHSTONE [to Jaques]: As the
ox hath his bow, sir, the horse his
curb, and the falcon her bells, so man
hath his desires; and as pigeons bill, so
wedlock would be nibbling.
As You Like It 3.3.79

3668 ROSALIND: Men are April when
they woo, December when they wed;
maids are May when they are maids,
but the sky changes when they are
wives.
As You Like It 4.1.147

3669 GLOUCESTER: Hasty marriage
seldom proveth well.
3 Henry VI 4.1.18

3670 BERTRAM: War is no strife
To the dark house and the detested
wife.
All's Well That Ends Well 2.3.292

3671 PAROLLES: A young man married is a man that's marr'd.
All's Well That Ends Well 2.3.298

3672 FIRST CITIZEN [on Blanch and the Dolphin]: He is the half part of a blessed man,
Left to be finished by such as she,
And she a fair divided excellence,
Whose fullness of perfection lies in him.
O, two such silver currents when they join
Do glorify the banks that bound them in.
King John 2.1.437

3673 BENEDICK [soliloquy]: I do wonder that one man, seeing how much another man is a fool when he dedicates his behaviors to love, will, after he hath laugh'd at such shallow follies in others, become the argument of his own scorn by falling in love.
Much Ado About Nothing 2.3.7

3674 BEATRICE: Wooing, wedding, and repenting, is as a Scotch jig, a measure, and a cinquepace; the first suit is hot and hasty, like a Scotch jig, and full as fantastical; the wedding, mannerly-modest, as a measure, full of state and ancientry; and then comes repentance, and with his bad legs falls into the cinquepace faster and faster, till he sink into his grave.
Much Ado About Nothing 2.1.73
[*cinquepace:* lively dance]

3675 NERISSA: Hanging and wiving goes by destiny.
Merchant of Venice 2.9.83

3676 PORTIA: A light wife doth make a heavy husband.
Merchant of Venice 5.1.130

3677 BENEDICK [soliloquy]: When I said I would die a bachelor, I did not think I should live till I were married.
Much Ado About Nothing 2.3.242

3678 PLAYER QUEEN: The instances that second marriage move

Are base respects of thrift, but none of love.
Hamlet 3.2.182

3679 LEONTES: Should all despair
That have revolted wives, the tenth of mankind
Would hang themselves.
Winter's Tale 1.2.198
[*revolted:* unfaithful]

3680 SUFFOLK: What is wedlock forced, but a hell,
An age of discord and continual strife?
Whereas the contrary bringeth bliss,
And is a pattern of celestial peace.
1 Henry VI 5.5.62

3681 CLOWN: Many a good hanging prevents a bad marriage.
Twelfth Night 1.5.19

3682 CINNA: Wisely, I say, I am a bachelor.
CITIZEN: That's as much to say, they are fools that marry.
Julius Caesar 3.3.16

3683 KATHERINA: I am asham'd that women are so simple
To offer war where they should kneel for peace,
Or seek for rule, supremacy, and sway,
When they are bound to serve, love, and obey.
Taming of the Shrew 5.2.161

3684 DUKE: Let still the woman take
An elder than herself, so wears she to him;
So sways she level in her husband's heart.
Twelfth Night 2.4.29

3685 FRIAR LAWRENCE: She's not well married that lives married long,
But she's best married that dies married young.
Romeo and Juliet 4.5.77

3686 THESEUS: Earthlier happy is the rose distill'd,
Than that which withering on the virgin thorn

Grows, lives, and dies in single blessedness.
Midsummer Night's Dream 1.1.76

3687 CLOWN: I do marry that I may
repent.
All's Well That Ends Well 1.3.36

3688 ROSALIND [about Oliver and
Celia]: No sooner met but they look'd;
no sooner look'd but they lov'd; no
sooner lov'd but they sigh'd; no sooner
sigh'd but they ask'd one another the
reason; no sooner knew the reason but
they sought the remedy.
As You Like It 5.2.33

3689 PORTIA [commending herself to
Bassanio]: Happy in this, she is not
yet so old
But she may learn; happier than this,
She is not bred so dull but she can
learn;
Happiest of all, is that her gentle spirit
Commits itself to yours to be directed,
As from her lord, her governor, her
king.
Merchant of Venice 3.2.160

3690 KATHERINA: Thy husband is thy
lord, thy life, thy keeper,
Thy head, thy sovereign; one that cares
for thee,
And for thy maintenance; commits his
body
To painful labor, both by sea and
land;
To watch the night in storms, the day
in cold,
Whilst thou li'st warm at home, secure
and safe;
And craves no other tribute at thy
hands
But love, fair looks, and true
obedience—
Too little payment for so great a debt.
Taming of the Shrew 5.2.146

3691 KATHERINA: Such duty as the
subject owes the prince,
Even such a woman oweth to her husband;

And when she is froward, peevish,
sullen, sour,
And not obedient to his honest will,
What is she but a foul contending
rebel,
And graceless traitor to her loving
lord?
Taming of the Shrew 5.2.155

3692 CLOWN: If men could be contented to be what they are, there were
no fear in marriage.
All's Well That Ends Well 1.3.50

3693 JACHIMO: That hook of wiving,
Fairness which strikes the eye.
Cymbeline 5.5.167

3694 Q. ISABEL: Fell jealousy . . .
Troubles oft the bed of blessed
marriage.
Henry V 5.2.363

May

3695 Rough winds do shake the dar-
ling buds of May,
And summer's lease hath all too short
a date.
Sonnet 18

3696 ROSALIND: Maids are May when
they are maids, but the sky changes
when they are wives.
As You Like It 4.1.148

3697 DUMAINE: Love, whose month is
ever May . . .
Love's Labor's Lost 4.3.100

Meals

3698 ABBESS: Unquiet meals make ill
digestions.
Comedy of Errors 5.1.73

3699 ARCITE: Hunger needs no sauce.
Two Noble Kinsmen 3.3.24

Meaning

3700 K. EDWARD: 'Tis wisdom to conceal our meaning.
3 Henry VI 4.7.60

3701 HELENA [to widow]: Our plot, which if it speed,
Is wicked meaning in a lawful deed,
And lawful meaning in a lawful act,
Where both not sin, and yet a sinful fact.
All's Well That Ends Well 3.7.44

Means

3702 PAROLLES: There's place and means for every man alive.
All's Well That Ends Well 4.3.339

3703 CARLISLE: The means that heavens yield must be embrac'd,
And not neglected; else heaven would,
And we will not. Heaven's offer we refuse,
The proffered means of succors and redress.
Richard II 3.2.29

Meddler

3704 AARON: A long-tongu'd babbling gossip.
Titus Andronicus 4.2.150

Medicine

3705 CYMBELINE: By med'cine life may be prolong'd, yet death
Will seize the doctor too.
Cymbeline 5.5.29

3706 PANDULPH: Before the curing of a strong disease,
Even in the instant of repair and health,
The fit is strongest; evils that take leave,
On their departure most of all show evil.
King John 3.4.112

3707 NORTHUMBERLAND: In poison there is physic.
2 Henry IV 1.1.137

3708 TIMON: Trust not the physician,
His antidotes are poison, and he slays
Moe than you rob.
Timon of Athens 4.3.431
[*moe:* more]

3709 KING: Diseases desperate grown
By desperate appliances are reliev'd,
Or not at all.
Hamlet 4.3.9

3710 To see the salve doth make the wound ache more.
Rape of Lucrece 1116

3711 CLAUDIO: The miserable have no other medicine
But only hope.
Measure for Measure 3.1.2

3712 ISABELLA: 'Tis a physic
That's bitter to sweet end.
Measure for Measure 4.6.7

3713 MACBETH [to doctor, on Lady Macbeth]: Canst thou not minister to a mind diseas'd,
Pluck from the memory a rooted sorrow,
Raze out the written troubles of the brain,
And with some sweet oblivious antidote
Cleanse the stuff'd bosom of that perilous stuff
Which weighs upon the heart?
DOCTOR: Therein the patient
Must minister to himself.
MACBETH: Throw physic to the dogs,
I'll none of it.
Macbeth 5.3.40

Meditation

3714 OLIVER: Chewing the food of sweet and bitter fancy.
As You Like It 4.3.101

3715 OBERON: In maiden meditation, fancy-free.
Midsummer Night's Dream 2.1.164

Meekness

3716 ADRIANA: They can be meek that have no other cause.
Comedy of Errors 2.1.33

3717 CRANMER [to Gardiner]: Love and meekness . . .
Become a churchman better than ambition.
Henry VIII 5.2.97

Melancholy

3718 MESSENGER: Melancholy is the nurse of frenzy.
Taming of the Shrew, Intro. 2.133

3719 BELARIUS: O melancholy,
Who ever yet could sound thy bottom?
Cymbeline 4.2.203

3720 Distress likes dumps when time is kept with tears.
Rape of Lucrece 1127

3721 ABBESS: Sweet recreation barr'd, what doth ensue
But moody and dull melancholy.
Comedy of Errors 5.1.78

3722 JAQUES: I have neither the scholar's melancholy, which is emulation; nor the musician's, which is fantastical; nor the courtier's, which is proud; nor the soldier's, which is ambitious; nor the lawyer's, which is politic; nor the lady's, which is nice; nor the lover's, which is all these: but it is a melancholy of my own, compounded of many simples, extracted from many objects, and indeed the sundry contemplation of my travels, in which my often rumination wraps me in a most humorous sadness.
As You Like It 4.1.10

3723 BUSHY: Lay aside life-harming heaviness
And entertain a cheerful disposition.
Richard II 2.2.3

3724 ANTONIO [to Salerio and Solanio]: In sooth, I know not why I am so sad;
It wearies me, you say it wearies you;
But how I caught it, found it, or came by it,
What stuff 'tis made of, whereof it is born,
I am to learn.
Merchant of Venice 1.1.1

3725 HAMLET [soliloquy]: How weary, stale, flat, and unprofitable
Seem to me all the uses of this world!
Hamlet 1.2.133

3726 JAQUES: I can suck melancholy out of a song.
As You Like It 2.5.12

3727 PETER: When griping griefs the heart doth wound,
And doleful dumps the mind oppress,
Then music with her silver sound . . .
With speedy help doth lend redress.
Romeo and Juliet 4.5.126

3728 LEAR: We are not ourselves
When nature, being oppress'd, commands the mind
To suffer with the body.
King Lear 2.4.107

3729 HAMLET: I have of late—but wherefore I know not—lost all my mirth, forgone all custom of exercises; and indeed it goes so heavily with my disposition, that this goodly frame, the earth, seems to me a sterile promontory; this most excellent canopy, the air, look you, this brave o'erhanging firmament, this majestical roof fretted with golden fire, why, it appeareth nothing to me but a foul and pestilent congregation of vapors.
Hamlet 2.2.295

3730 ARCHBISHOP: Against ill chances
men are ever merry,
But heaviness foreruns the good event.
2 Henry IV 4.2.81

3731 BEROWNE [soliloquy]: By heaven,
I do love, and it hath taught me to
rhyme and to be mallicholy.
Love's Labor's Lost 4.3.12
[*mallicholy:* melancholy]

Memorabilia

3732 ROMEO [to Juliet]: All these woes
shall serve
For sweet discourses in our time to
come.
Romeo and Juliet 3.5.52

Memory

3733 PERCY: That is not forgot
Which ne'er I did remember.
Richard II 2.3.37

3734 PLAYER KING: Purpose is but the
slave to memory.
Hamlet 3.2.188

3835 BOYET: Contempt will kill the
speaker's heart,
And quite divorce his memory from his
part.
Love's Labor's Lost 5.2.149

3736 BULLINGBROOK: I count myself
in nothing else so happy
As in a soul remembering my good
friends.
Richard II 2.3.46

3737 MACDUFF [on the slaughter of
his family]: I cannot but remember
such things were,
That were most precious to me.
Macbeth 4.3.222

3738 ALONSO: How sharp the point of
this remembrance is!
The Tempest 5.1.138

3739 LADY MACBETH: Memory, the
warder of the brain,
Shall be a fume.
Macbeth 1.7.65
[*fume:* i.e. the fumes of wine would be suf-
ficient to deaden memory, after the murder
of Duncan]

3740 HAMLET [on his murdered
father]: O heavens, die two months
ago, and not forgotten yet? Then
there's hope a great man's memory
may outlive his life half a year.
Hamlet 3.2.130

3741 BENEDICK: If a man do not erect
in this age his own tomb ere he dies,
he shall live no longer in monument
than the bell rings and the widow
weeps . . . an hour in clamor and a
quarter in rheum.
Much Ado About Nothing 5.2.77

3742 PROSPERO: Let us not burthen
our remembrances with
A heaviness that's gone.
The Tempest 5.1.198
[*burthen:* burden]

Mending

3743 CLOWN: Any thing that's
mended is but patch'd.
Twelfth Night 1.5.47

3744 Were it not sinful then, striving
to mend,
To mar the object that before was
well?
Sonnet 103

3745 ALBANY: Striving to better, oft
we mar what's well.
King Lear 1.4.346

Mercantile

3746 ANTONY: To business that we
love we rise betime,
And go to't with delight.
Antony and Cleopatra 4.4.20

3747 Huge rocks, high winds, strong pirates, shelves and sand,
The merchant fears, ere rich at home he lands.
Rape of Lucrece 335

Mercy

3748 TAMORA: Sweet mercy is nobility's true badge.
Titus Andronicus 1.1.119

3749 FIRST SENATOR: Nothing emboldens sin so much as mercy.
Timon of Athens 3.5.3

3750 KING [soliloquy]: Whereto serves mercy
But to confront the visage of offense?
Hamlet 3.3.46

3751 PRINCE: Mercy but murders, pardoning those that kill.
Romeo and Juliet 3.1.197

3752 ESCALUS: Mercy is not itself, that oft looks so;
Pardon is still the nurse of second woe.
Measure for Measure 2.1.283

3753 PORTIA: The quality of mercy is not strain'd,
It droppeth as the gentle rain from heaven
Upon the place beneath. It is twice blest:
It blesseth him that gives and him that takes.
'Tis mightiest in the mightiest, it becomes
The throned monarch better than his crown.
Merchant of Venice 4.1.184

3754 ISABELLA: No ceremony that to great ones 'longs,
Not the king's crown, nor the deputed sword,
The marshal's truncheon, nor the judge's robe,

Become them with one half so good a grace
As mercy does.
Measure for Measure 2.2.59
[*'longs*: belongs]

3755 PORTIA: We do pray for mercy,
And that same prayer doth teach us all to render
The deeds of mercy.
Merchant of Venice 4.1.200

3756 PORTIA: Mercy is above this sceptred sway,
It is enthroned in the hearts of kings,
It is an attribute of God himself;
And earthly power doth then show likest God's
When mercy seasons justice.
Merchant of Venice 4.1.193

3757 ISABELLA [to Angelo]: All the souls that were were forfeit once,
And He that might the vantage best have took
Found out the remedy. How would you be,
If He, which is the top of judgment, should
But judge you as you are?
Measure for Measure 2.2.73

3758 ISABELLA: Merciful heaven,
Thou rather with thy sharp and sulphurous bolt
Splits the unwedgeable and gnarled oak
Than the soft myrtle; but man, proud man,
Dress'd in a little brief authority,
Most ignorant of what he's most assur'd
(His glassy essence), like an angry ape
Plays such fantastic tricks before high heaven
As make the angels weep.
Measure for Measure 2.2.114
[*glassy*: fragile, highly susceptible of damage]

3759 YORK [after being stabbed]: Open thy gate of mercy, gracious God!

My soul flies through these wounds to
seek out thee.
3 Henry VI 1.4.177

Merit

3760 FALSTAFF [about Gadshill]: If
men were to be sav'd by merit, what
hole in hell were hot enough for him.
1 Henry IV 1.2.107

3761 HAMLET: Use every man after his
desert, and who shall scape whipping?
Hamlet 2.2.529

3762 ARRAGON: Who shall go about
To cozen fortune, and be honorable
Without the stamp of merit? Let none
presume
To wear an undeserved dignity.
Merchant of Venice 2.9.37

3763 ARRAGON: O that estates,
degrees, and offices
Were not deriv'd corruptly, and that
clear honor
Were purchas'd by the merit of the
wearer!
Merchant of Venice 2.9.41

3764 ACHILLES: Not a man, for being
simply man,
Hath any honor, but honor for those
honors
That are without him, as place, riches,
and favor —
Prizes of accident as oft as merit.
Troilus and Cressida 3.3.80

3765 BELARIUS: Many times
Doth ill deserve by doing well.
Cymbeline 3.3.53

3766 TROILUS: Our head shall go bare
till merit crown it.
Troilus and Cressida 3.2.91

3767 NORFOLK [about Wolsey]: The
force of his own merit makes his
way —
A gift that heaven gives for him, which
buys
A place next to the King.
Henry VIII 1.1.64

Merriment

3768 AUTOLYCUS [singing]:
A merry heart goes all the day,
Your sad tires in a mile-a.
Winter's Tale 4.3.125

3769 SALERIO [quoting Antonio's advice to Bassanio]:
"Be merry, and employ your chiefest
thoughts
To courtship, and such fair ostents of
love."
Merchant of Venice 2.8.43

3770 MESSENGER: Frame your mind to
mirth and merriment,
Which bars a thousand harms and
lengthens life.
Taming of the Shrew, Intro. 2.135

3771 Sad souls are slain in merry
company.
Rape of Lucrece 1110

3772 DON PEDRO: In faith, lady, you
have a merry heart.
BEATRICE: Yea, my lord, I thank it —
poor fool, it keeps on the windy side
of care.
Much Ado About Nothing 2.1.312

3773 ROSALIND: I had rather have a
fool to make me merry than experience
to make me sad.
As You Like It 4.1.27

3774 DESDEMONA: I am not merry;
but I do beguile
The thing I am by seeming otherwise.
Othello 2.1.122

3775 K. HENRY: 'Tis ever common
That men are merriest when they are
from home.
Henry V 1.2.271

3776 K. RICHARD: Be merry, for our
time of stay is short.
Richard II 2.1.223

3777 HAMLET: What should a man do
but be merry.
Hamlet 3.2.125

3778 ROMEO [soliloquy]: How oft
when men are at the point of death
Have they been merry, which their
keepers call
A lightning before death!
Romeo and Juliet 5.3.88

Metamorphosis

3779 MENENIUS: There is differency
between a grub and a butterfly, yet
your butterfly was a grub.
Coriolanus 5.4.11

Method

3780 POLONIUS [on Hamlet's
behavior]: Though this be madness,
yet there is method in't.
Hamlet 2.2.205

Midnight

3781 HAMLET [soliloquy]: 'Tis now the
very witching time of night,
When churchyards yawn and hell itself
breathes out
Contagion to this world. Now could I
drink hot blood,
And do such bitter business as the day
Would quake to look on.
Hamlet 3.2.388

3782 THESEUS: The iron tongue of
midnight hath told twelve.
Lovers, to bed, 'tis almost fairy time.
Midsummer Night's Dream 5.1.363

3783 HORATIO: The dead waste and
middle of the night.
Hamlet 1.2.198
[Many editors prefer *vast* to *waste*.]

Might

3784 K. RICHARD: They well deserve
to have
That know the strong'st and surest way
to get.
Richard II 3.3.200

Mind

3785 MOROCCO: A golden mind
stoops not to shows of dross.
Merchant of Venice 2.7.20

3786 K. HENRY: All things are ready,
if our minds be so.
Henry V 4.3.71

3787 PETRUCHIO: 'Tis the mind that
makes the body rich.
Taming of the Shrew 4.3.172

3788 GLOUCESTER: 'Tis but a base ignoble mind
That mounts no higher than a bird can
soar.
2 Henry VI 2.1.13

3789 BEVIS: There's no better sign of a
brave mind than a hard hand.
2 Henry VI 4.2.19

3790 CASSIUS [soliloquy]: It is meet
That noble minds keep ever with their
likes;
For who so firm that cannot be se-
duc'd?
Julius Caesar 1.2.310

3791 GLOUCESTER: Fearless minds
climb soonest unto crowns.
3 Henry VI 4.7.62

3792 DUNCAN: There's no art
To find the mind's construction in the
face.
Macbeth 1.4.12

3793 CRESSIDA: The error of our eye
directs our mind.
What error leads must err.
Troilus and Cressida 5.2.110

3794 LEAR: We are not ourselves
When nature, being oppress'd, com-
mands the mind
To suffer with the body.
King Lear 2.4.107

3795 LONGAVILLE: The mind shall
banquet, though the body pine;

Fat paunches have lean pates; and
dainty bits
Make rich the ribs, but bankrout quite
the wits.
Love's Labor's Lost 1.1.25
[*bankrout:* bankrupt]

3796 ANTONIO: In nature there's no
blemish but the mind.
Twelfth Night 3.4.367

3797 QUEEN: Oft have I heard that
grief softens the mind,
And makes it fearful and degenerate.
2 Henry VI 4.4.1

3798 GLOUCESTER: Suspicion always
haunts the guilty mind.
3 Henry VI 5.6.11

3799 DOCTOR [on Lady Macbeth's ill-
ness]: Unnatural deeds
Do breed unnatural troubles; infected
minds
To their deaf pillows will discharge
their secrets.
Macbeth 5.1.71

3800 MACBETH [to doctor, on Lady
Macbeth]: Canst thou not minister
to a mind diseas'd,
Pluck from the memory a rooted
sorrow,
Raze out the written troubles of the
brain,
And with some sweet oblivious
antidote
Cleanse the stuff'd bosom of that
perilous stuff
Which weighs upon the heart?
Macbeth 5.3.40

3801 EDGAR [soliloquy]: Who alone
suffers, suffers most i' th' mind,
Leaving free things and happy shows
behind,
But then the mind much sufferance
doth o'erskip,
When grief hath mates, and bearing
fellowship.
King Lear 3.6.104

3802 COUNTESS: Where an unclean
mind carries virtuous qualities, there
commendations go with pity.
All's Well That Ends Well 1.1.41

3803 Men have marble, women waxen
minds.
Rape of Lucrece 1240

3804 HELENA [soliloquy]: Love looks
not with the eyes but with the mind.
Midsummer Night's Dream 1.1.234

3805 VALENTINE: Dumb jewels often
in their silent kind
More than quick words do move a
woman's mind.
Two Gentlemen of Verona 3.1.90

3806 HORATIO: If your mind dislike
any thing, obey it.
Hamlet 5.2.217

3807 K. LEAR: When the mind's free,
The body's delicate.
King Lear 3.4.11

3808 PANDULPH: Your mind is all as
youthful as your blood.
King John 3.4.125

3809 K. HENRY: When the mind is
quick'ned, out of doubt,
The organs, though defunct and dead
before,
Break up their drowsy grave, and newly
move
With casted slough and fresh legerity.
Henry V 4.1.20
[*legerity:* nimbleness]

3810 PERICLES [soliloquy]: The passions of the mind,
That have their first conception by
misdread,
Have after-nourishment and life by
care.
Pericles 1.2.11

3811 MACBETH: Better be with the
dead,
Whom we, to gain our peace, have
sent to peace,

Than on the torture of the mind to lie
In restless ecstasy.
Macbeth 3.2.19

Minute

3812 JULIET: In a minute there are
many days.
Romeo and Juliet 3.5.45

3813 Like as the waves make toward
the pibbled shore,
So do our minutes hasten to their end.
Sonnet 60
[*pibbled*: pebbled]

3814 Minutes fill up hours.
Rape of Lucrece 297

Miracles

3815 KENT: Nothing almost sees
miracles
But misery.
King Lear 2.2.165

3816 HELENA: Great floods have flown
From simple sources; and great seas
have dried
When miracles have by the great'st
been denied.
All's Well That Ends Well 2.1.139
[*great floods*: perhaps a reference to Moses
smiting the rock at Horeb; *great seas have
dried*: probably the parting of the Red Sea,
permitting the Israelites to escape Egypt]

3817 CANTERBURY: Miracles are
ceas'd;
And therefore we must needs admit
the means
How things are perfected.
Henry V 1.1.67

Mirror

3818 FOOL: There was never yet fair
woman but she made mouths in a
glass.
King Lear 3.2.35
[*made mouths*: practiced facial expressions;
glass: mirror]

3819 CLOTEN: It is not vainglory for a
man and his glass to confer in his own
chamber.
Cymbeline 4.1.7
[*glass*: mirror]

3820 GLOUCESTER [soliloquy]: Shine
out, fair sun, till I have bought a
glass,
That I may see my shadow as I pass.
Richard III 1.2.262
[*glass*: mirror]

Mirth

3821 BEROWNE: Mirth cannot move a
soul in agony.
Love's Labor's Lost 5.2.857

3822 Mirth doth search the bottom of
annoy,
Sad souls are slain in merry company.
Rape of Lucrece 1109

3823 SERVANT: Frame your mind to
mirth and merriment,
Which bars a thousand harms and
lengthens life.
Taming of the Shrew, Intro. 2.135

3824 GRATIANO: Let me play the fool,
With mirth and laughter let old
wrinkles come,
And let my liver rather heat with wine
Than my heart cool with mortifying
groans.
Merchant of Venice 1.1.79

3825 Who buys a minute's mirth to
wail a week?
Or sells eternity to get a toy?
For one sweet grape who will the vine
destroy?
Rape of Lucrece 213

3826 MACBETH: Be large in mirth.
Macbeth 3.4.11

3827 THESEUS [to Philostrate]: Awake
the pert and nimble spirit of mirth,
Turn melancholy forth to funerals.
Midsummer Night's Dream 1.1.13

Misanthropy

3828 HAMLET: Man delights not me—
nor women neither.

Hamlet 2.2.309

Misapplication

3829 CICERO: Men may construe
things after their fashion,
Clean from the purpose of the things
themselves.

Julius Caesar 1.3.34

3830 BEROWNE: Sow'd cockle reap'd
no corn.

Love's Labor's Lost 4.3.380

Mischance

3831 PRINCE: Let mischance be slave
to patience.

Romeo and Juliet 5.3.221

Mischief

3832 ROMEO [soliloquy]: O mischief,
thou art swift
To enter in the thoughts of desperate
men!

Romeo and Juliet 5.1.35

3833 OCTAVIUS: Some that smile have
in their hearts, I fear,
Millions of mischiefs.

Julius Caesar 4.1.50

3834 K. JOHN: How oft the sight of
means to do ill deeds
Makes deeds ill done!

King John 4.2.219

3835 ANTONY: Mischief, thou art
afoot,
Take thou what course thou wilt!

Julius Caesar 3.2.259

3836 DUKE: To mourn a mischief that
is past and gone

Is the next way to draw new mischief
on.

Othello 1.3.204

3837 LUCIANA: Ill deeds is doubled
with an evil word.

Comedy of Errors 3.2.20

3838 ELY: Playing the mouse in the
absence of the cat.

Henry V 1.2.172

Miser

3839 The aged man that coffers up his
gold
Is plagu'd with cramps and gout and
painful fits,
And scarce hath eyes his treasure to
behold,
But like still-pining Tantalus he sits,
And useless barns the harvest of his
wits;
Having no other pleasure of his gain
But torment that it cannot cure his
pain.

Rape of Lucrece 855

3840 Foul cank'ring rust the hidden
treasure frets,
But gold that's put to use more gold
begets.

Venus and Adonis 767

3841 FIRST FISHERMAN: I can compare
our rich misers to nothing so fitly as to
a whale; 'a plays and tumbles, driving
the poor fry before him, and at last
devours them all at a mouthful.

Pericles 2.1.29

['a: he]

Misery

3842 KENT: Nothing almost sees
miracles
But misery.

King Lear 2.2.165

3843 CLAUDIO: The miserable have no
other medicine
But only hope.

Measure for Measure 3.1.2

3844 KING: What's more miserable than discontent?
2 Henry VI 3.1.201

3845 GAUNT: Misery makes sport to mock itself.
Richard II 2.1.85

3846 TRINCULO: Misery acquaints a man with strange bedfellows.
The Tempest 2.2.39

3847 FIRST LORD: Misery doth part The flux of company.
As You Like It 2.1.51

3848 Misery is trodden on by many, And being low, never reliev'd by any.
Venus and Adonis 707

3849 KING: When sorrows come, they come not single spies, But in battalions.
Hamlet 4.5.78

3850 QUEEN: One woe doth tread upon another's heel, So fast they follow.
Hamlet 4.7.163

3851 HELENA: Miserable most, to love unlov'd?
Midsummer Night's Dream 3.2.234

3852 ABBESS: Sweet recreation barr'd, what doth ensue But moody and dull melancholy, Kinsman to grim and comfortless despair.
Comedy of Errors 5.1.78

3853 It easeth some, though none it ever cured, To think their dolor others have endured.
Rape of Lucrece 1581

3854 TALBOT: Kings and mightiest potentates must die, For that's the end of human misery.
1 Henry VI 3.2.136

3855 APEMANTUS: Willing misery Outlives incertain pomp.
Timon of Athens 4.3.242

3856 MORTIMER [dying]: Just Death, kind umpire of men's miseries, With sweet enlargement doth dismiss me hence.
1 Henry VI 2.5.29

Misfortune

3857 K. LEWIS [to Margaret]: Yield not thy neck To fortune's yoke, but let thy dauntless mind Still ride in triumph over all mischance.
3 Henry VI 3.3.16

3858 LUCIUS: Some falls are means the happier to arise.
Cymbeline 4.2.403

3859 EDGAR: The worst is not So long as we can say, "This is the worst."
King Lear 4.1.27

3860 DUKE: What cannot be preserv'd when Fortune takes, Patience her injury a mock'ry makes.
Othello 1.3.206

3861 MACBETH: My way of life Is fall'n into the sear, the yellow leaf, And that which should accompany old age, As honor, love, obedience, troops of friends, I must not look to have; but in their stead, Curses, not loud but deep, mouth-honor, breath, Which the poor heart would fain deny, and dare not.
Macbeth 5.3.22

3862 EDMUND [soliloquy]: This is the excellent foppery of the world, that when we are sick in fortune—often the surfeits of our own behavior—we make

guilty of our disasters the sun, the
moon, and stars.
                    King Lear 1.2.118

3863 BELARIUS [to Arviragus, on his
  fall from Cymbeline's favor]: Then
  was I as a tree
Whose boughs did bend with fruit:
  but in one night,
A storm or robbery (call it what you
  will)
Shook down my mellow hangings, nay,
  my leaves,
And left me bare to weather.
                    Cymbeline 3.3.60

3864 ROMEO [to the slain Paris]: O,
  give me thy hand,
One writ with me in sour misfortune's
  book!
                    Romeo and Juliet 5.3.82

3865 FLAVIUS: We have seen better
  days.
                    Timon of Athens 4.2.27

Misinterpretation

3866 WORCESTER: Look how we can,
  or sad or merrily,
Interpretation will misquote our looks.
                    1 Henry IV 5.2.12

Mismanagement

3867 MACBETH: Things bad begun
  make strong themselves by ill.
                    Macbeth 3.2.55

Mistrust

3868 PISTOL: Trust none;
For oaths are straws, men's faiths are
  wafer-cakes,
And Hold-fast is the only dog.
                    Henry V 2.3.50
[*wafer-cakes:* i.e. fragile; *Hold-fast:* an allusion to the proverb: Brag is a good dog, but
Holdfast is a better.]

3869 Q. ELIZABETH: Trust not him
  that hath once broken faith.
                    3 Henry VI 4.4.30

3870 WARWICK [to Somerset]: I hold
  it cowardice
To rest mistrustful where a noble heart
Hath pawn'd an open hand in sign of
  love.
                    3 Henry VI 4.2.8

3871 LEONTES: All's true that is
  mistrusted.
                    Winter's Tale 2.1.48

Misuse

3872 The hardest knife ill us'd doth
  lose his edge.
                    Sonnet 95

3873 The colt that's back'd and burthen'd being young,
Loseth his pride, and never waxeth
  strong.
                    Venus and Adonis 419
[*burthen'd:* burdened]

Mob

3874 CORIOLANUS: The beast
With many heads.
                    Coriolanus 4.1.1

3875 RUMOR: The blunt monster with
  uncounted heads,
The still-discordant wav'ring multitude.
                    2 Henry IV, Induction 18

3876 MARTIUS [to some dissentious
  citizens]: What would you have, you
  curs,
That like nor peace nor war? The one
  affrights you,
The other makes you proud. He that
  trusts to you,
Where he should find you lions, finds
  you hares;
Where foxes, geese. You are no surer,
  no,
Than is the coal of fire upon the ice,

Or hailstone in the sun. Your virtue is
To make him worthy whose offense
  subdues him,
And curse that justice did it. Who
  deserves greatness
Deserves your hate; and your affections
  are
A sick man's appetite, who desires
  most that
Which would increase his evil. He that
  depends
Upon your favors swims with fins of
  lead,
And hews down oaks with rushes.
  Hang ye!
                    Coriolanus 1.1.168

Mockery

3877 BOYET: The tongues of mocking
wenches are as keen
As is the razor's edge invisible.
            Love's Labor's Lost 5.2.256

3878 PORTIA: It is a sin to be a
mocker.
            Merchant of Venice 1.2.57

Moderation

3879 PANDARUS: Be moderate, be
moderate.
CRESSIDA: Why tell you me of moderation?
The grief is fine, full, perfect, that I
  taste,
And violenteth in a sense as strong
As that which causeth it. How can I
  moderate it?
            Troilus and Cressida 4.4.1
[*violenteth:* rages with violence]

3880 NERISSA: They are as sick that
surfeit with too much as they that
starve with nothing.
            Merchant of Venice 1.2.5

3881 FRIAR LAWRENCE: Love
moderately: long love doth so;
Too swift arrives as tardy as too slow.
            Romeo and Juliet 2.6.14

Modesty

3882 Soft slow tongue [is the] true
mark of modesty.
            Rape of Lucrece 1220

3883 HAMLET: O'erstep not the
modesty of nature.
            Hamlet 3.2.19

3884 STEWARD: We wound our
modesty, and make foul the clearness
of our deservings, when of ourselves we
publish them.
            All's Well That Ends Well 1.3.5

3885 DON PEDRO: It is the witness still
of excellency
To put a strange face on his own perfection.
            Much Ado About Nothing 2.3.46

3886 ANGELO [soliloquy]: Can it be
That modesty may more betray our
  sense
Than woman's lightness?
            Measure for Measure 2.2.167

3887 LAERTES [to Ophelia, on love's
  danger]: The chariest maid is prodigal enough
If she unmask her beauty to the moon.
Virtue itself scapes not calumnious
  strokes.
The canker galls the infants of the
  spring
Too oft before their buttons be
  disclos'd,
And in the morn and liquid dew of
  youth
Contagious blastments are most
  imminent.
Be wary then, best safety lies in fear.
            Hamlet 1.3.36

Monarch

3888 BELARIUS: The gates of monarchs
Are arch'd so high that giants may jet
  through
And keep their impious turbands on.
            Cymbeline 3.3.4
[*jet:* strut]

Money

3889 CHIEF JUSTICE: Your means are very slender, and your waste is great. FALSTAFF: I would it were otherwise, I would my means were greater and my waist slenderer.
2 Henry IV 1.2.140

3890 FALSTAFF: I can get no remedy against this consumption of the purse; borrowing only lingers and lingers it out, but the disease is incurable.
2 Henry IV 1.2.234

3891 SHALLOW: A friend i' th' court is better than a penny in purse.
2 Henry IV 5.1.30

3892 FORD: They say, if money goes before, all ways do lie open.
Merry Wives of Windsor 2.2.168

3893 FALSTAFF: Money is a good soldier, sir, and will on.
Merry Wives of Windsor 2.2.170

3894 GRUMIO: Nothing comes amiss, so money comes withal.
Taming of the Shrew 1.2.81

3895 FORD: Love like a shadow flies when substance love pursues.
Merry Wives of Windsor 2.2.207

3896 TIMON: The learned pate Ducks to the golden fool.
Timon of Athens 4.3.17
[*ducks:* bows]

3897 CORIN: He that wants money, means, and content is without three good friends.
As You Like It 3.2.24

3898 ARVIRAGUS: All gold and silver rather turn to dirt, As 'tis no better reckon'd, but of those Who worship dirty gods.
Cymbeline 3.6.53

3899 TIMON [soliloquy, on gold]: This yellow slave

Will knit and break religions, bless th' accurs'd, Make the hoar leprosy ador'd, place thieves, And give them title, knee, and approbation With senators on the bench.
Timon of Athens 4.3.34

3900 BAGOT [on the common people]: Their love Lies in their purses, and whoso empties them By so much fills their hearts with deadly hate.
Richard II 2.2.129

3901 ANNE [about Slender]: O, what a world of vild ill-favor'd faults Looks handsome in three hundred pounds a-year.
Merry Wives of Windsor 3.4.32
[*vild:* vile]

3902 IAGO: Put money in thy purse
... put but money in thy purse ... fill thy purse with money.
Othello 1.3.343

Monster

3903 CRESSIDA: They that have the voice of lions and the act of hares, are they not monsters?
Troilus and Cressida 3.2.88

Monument

3904 BENEDICK: If a man do not erect in this age his own tomb ere he dies, he shall live no longer in monument than the bells rings and the widow weeps.
Much Ado About Nothing 5.2.77

3905 Your monument shall be my gentle verse, Which eyes not yet created shall o'erread, And tongues to be your being shall rehearse,

When all the breathers of this world
are dead;
You still shall live (such virtue hath my
pen)
Where breath most breathes, even in
the mouths of men.
Sonnet 81

3906 DUKE: A forted residence 'gainst
the tooth of time
And razure of oblivion.
Measure for Measure 5.1.12

Moon

3907 TITANIA: The moon (the
governess of floods),
Pale in her anger, washes all the air,
That rheumatic diseases do abound.
And through this distemperature, we
see
The seasons alter.
Midsummer Night's Dream 2.1.103

3908 LAERTES: The chariest maid is
prodigal enough
If she unmask her beauty to the moon.
Hamlet 1.3.36

3909 OTHELLO: It is the very error of
the moon,
She comes more nearer earth than she
was wont,
And makes men mad.
Othello 5.2.109

3910 NERISSA: When the moon shone,
we did not see the candle.
PORTIA: So doth the greater glory dim
the less.
Merchant of Venice 5.1.92

Moonlight

3911 LORENZO [to Jessica]: How sweet
the moonlight sleeps upon this
bank!
Here we will sit, and let the sounds of
music
Creep in our ears. Soft stillness and the
night
Become the touches of sweet harmony.
Merchant of Venice 5.1.54

Moral

3912 FLUELLEN: Fortune is painted
blind, with a muffler afore her eyes, to
signify to you that Fortune is blind;
and she is painted also with a wheel,
to signify to you, which is the moral of
it, that she is turning, and inconstant,
and mutability, and variation; and her
foot, look you, is fixed upon a
spherical stone, which rolls, and rolls,
and rolls. In good truth, the poet
makes a most excellent description of
it. Fortune is an excellent moral.
Henry V 3.6.30

Morality

3913 AUFIDIUS: Our virtues
Lie in th' interpretation of the time.
Coriolanus 4.7.49

3914 IAGO: 'Tis in ourselves that we
are thus or thus.
Othello 1.3.319

3915 LUCIO: I had as lief have the foppery of freedom as the mortality of imprisonment.
Measure for Measure 1.2.133
[Most editors prefer *morality*, in antithesis
to *foppery*.]

Morning

3916 HORATIO: The cock, that is the
trumpet to the morn,
Doth with his lofty and shrill-sounding
throat
Awake the god of day.
Hamlet 1.1.150

3917 PUCK: Night's swift dragons cut
the clouds full fast,
And yonder shines Aurora's harbinger,
At whose approach, ghosts, wand'ring
here and there,
Troop home to churchyards.
Midsummer Night's Dream 3.2.379

3918 ROMEO: Night's candles are burnt out, and jocund day
Stands tiptoe on the misty mountain tops.

Romeo and Juliet 3.5.9

3919 HORATIO: But look, the morn in russet mantle clad
Walks o'er the dew of yon high eastward hill.

Hamlet 1.1.166

3920 TROILUS [to Cressida]: The busy day,
Wak'd by the lark, hath rous'd the ribald crows,
And dreaming night will hide our joys no longer.

Troilus and Cressida 4.2.8

3821 Lo here the gentle lark, weary of rest,
From his moist cabinet mounts up on high,
And wakes the morning, from whose silver breast
The sun ariseth in his majesty,
Who doth the world so gloriously behold
That cedar tops and hills seem burnish'd gold.

Venus and Adonis 853

3922 Full many a glorious morning have I seen
Flatter the mountain tops with sovereign eye,
Kissing with golden face the meadows green,
Gilding pale streams with heavenly alcumy;
Anon permit the basest clouds to ride
With ugly rack on his celestial face,
And from the forlorn world his visage hide,
Stealing unseen to west with this disgrace.

Sonnet 33

[*alcumy:* alchemy]

3923 RICHARD: See how the morning opes her golden gates,
And takes her farewell of the glorious sun!

How well resembles it the prime of youth,
Trimm'd like a younker prancing to his love!

3 Henry VI 2.1.21

[*younker:* stripling]

3924 FRIAR LAWRENCE: The grey-ey'd morn smiles on the frowning night,
Check'ring the eastern clouds with streaks of light,
And flecked darkness like a drunkard reels
From forth day's path and Titan's fiery wheels.

Romeo and Juliet 2.3.1

3925 DON PEDRO: Look, the gentle day,
Before the wheels of Phoebus, round about
Dapples the drowsy east with spots of grey.

Much Ado About Nothing 5.3.25

3926 PROSPERO: The morning steals upon the night,
Melting the darkness.

The Tempest 5.1.65

Mortality

3927 TOUCHSTONE: All is mortal in nature.

As You Like It 2.4.55

3928 PROSPERO: We are such stuff
As dreams are made on; and our little life
Is rounded with a sleep.

The Tempest 4.1.156

3929 JAQUES: 'Tis but an hour ago since it was nine,
And after one hour more 'twill be eleven,
And so, from hour to hour, we ripe and ripe,
And then from hour to hour, we rot and rot.

As You Like It 2.7.24

3930 GLOUCESTER: O, let me kiss that hand!
LEAR: Let me wipe it first, it smells of mortality.
King Lear 4.6.132

3931 WARWICK [soliloquy]: Why, what is pomp, rule, reign, but earth and dust?
And live we how we can, yet die we must.
3 Henry VI 5.2.27

3932 HAMLET: Imperious Caesar, dead and turn'd to clay,
Might stop a hole to keep the wind away.
O that that earth which kept the world in awe
Should patch a wall t' expel the winter's flaw!
Hamlet 5.1.213

3933 PUCK: Lord, what fools these mortals be!
Midsummer Night's Dream 3.2.115

3934 LORENZO: This muddy vesture of decay.
Merchant of Venice 5.1.64

Motherhood

3935 LADY MACBETH: I have given suck, and know
How tender 'tis to love the babe that milks me.
Macbeth 1.7.54

3936 EGEON: The pleasing punishment that women bear.
Comedy of Errors 1.1.46

3937 LADY MACDUFF: The poor wren,
The most diminutive of birds, will fight,
Her young ones in the nest, against the owl.
Macbeth 4.2.9

Motion

3938 ULYSSES: Things in motion sooner catch the eye
Than what not stirs.
Troilus and Cressida 3.3.183

3939 FALSTAFF: I were better to be eaten to death with a rust than to be scour'd to nothing with perpetual motion.
2 Henry IV 1.2.218

Mourning

3940 No longer mourn for me when I am dead
Than you shall hear the surly sullen bell
Give warning to the world that I am fled
From this vile world with vildest worms to dwell.
Sonnet 71

[*vildest:* vilest]

3941 O, if (I say) you look upon this verse,
When I (perhaps) compounded am with clay,
Do not so much as my poor name rehearse,
But let your love even with my life decay.
Sonnet 71

3942 LAFEW: Moderate lamentation is the right of the dead, excessive grief the enemy to the living.
All's Well That Ends Well 1.1.55

3943 Q. MARGARET: What cannot be avoided,
'Twere childish weakness to lament or fear.
3 Henry VI 5.4.37

3944 DUKE: To mourn a mischief that is past and gone
Is the next way to draw new mischief on.
Othello 1.3.204

3945 QUEEN [to Hamlet]: Do not for
ever with thy vailed lids
Seek for thy noble father in the dust.
Thou know'st 'tis common, all that
lives must die,
Passing through nature to eternity.
Hamlet 1.2.70

3946 Q. MARGARET: Wise men ne'er
sit and wail their loss,
But cheerly seek how to redress their
harms.
3 Henry VI 5.4.1

3947 GUIDERIUS: Notes of sorrow out
of tune are worse
Than priests and fanes that lie.
Cymbeline 4.2.241

Multitude

3948 ARCHBISHOP: An habitation
giddy and unsure
Hath he that buildeth on the vulgar
heart.
2 Henry IV 1.3.89
[*vulgar:* plebeian]

3949 THIRD CITIZEN: Ingratitude is
monstrous, and for the multitude to be
ingrateful were to make a monster of
the multitude.
Coriolanus 2.3.9

Murder (Murther)

3950 BRUTUS [soliloquy]: Between the
acting of a dreadful thing
And the first motion, all the interim is
Like a phantasma or a hideous dream.
The Genius and the mortal
instruments
Are then in council; and the state of
man,
Like to a little kingdom, suffers then
The nature of an insurrection.
Julius Caesar 2.1.63
[*The Genius:* the soul; *mortal instruments:*
man's reason and his will; *in council:* at
war]

3951 LADY MACBETH [soliloquy]:
Come, thick night,
And pall thee in the dunnest smoke of
hell,
That my keen knife see not the wound
it makes,
Nor heaven Tpeep through the blanket
of the dark
To cry, "Hold, hold!"
Macbeth 1.5.50

3952 MACBETH [to Lady Macbeth,
after Duncan's murder]:
Methought I heard a voice cry, "Sleep
no more!
Macbeth does murther sleep,"—the in-
nocent sleep,
Sleep that knits up the ravell'd sleave
of care,
The death of each day's life, sore
labor's bath,
Balm of hurt minds, great nature's sec-
ond course,
Chief nourisher in life's feast.
Macbeth 2.2.32

3953 MACBETH [soliloquy, after Dun-
can's murder]: Will all great Neptune's
ocean wash this blood
Clean from my hand? No; this my
hand will rather
The multitudinous seas incarnadine,
Making the green one red.
Macbeth 2.2.57

3954 LADY MACBETH: Out, damn'd
spot! out, I say!
Macbeth 5.1.35

3955 LADY MACBETH [haunted by
Duncan's murder]: Here's the smell of
the blood still. All the perfumes of
Arabia will not sweeten this little
hand. O, O, O!
Macbeth 5.1.50

3956 CLARENCE [to Gloucester's two
hired murderers]: The great King of
kings
Hath in the table of His law commanded
That thou shalt do no murther. Will
you then

Spurn at his edict, and fulfill a man's?
Take heed; for he holds vengeance in
his hand,
To hurl upon their heads that break
his law.
Richard III 1.4.195

3957 KING [soliloquy]: It hath the
primal eldest curse upon't,
A brother's murther.
Hamlet 3.3.37

3958 ALCIBIADES: To kill, I grant, is
sin's extremest gust,
But in defense, by mercy, 'tis most
just.
Timon of Athens 3.3.54

3959 HAMLET [soliloquy]: Murther,
though it have no tongue, will speak
With most miraculous organ.
Hamlet 2.2.593

3960 IAGO: Guiltiness will speak
Though tongues were out of use.
Othello 5.1.109

3961 PERICLES: Murther's as near to
lust as flame to smoke.
Pericles 1.1.138

3962 KING [to Laertes]: No place in-
deed should murther sanctuarize.
Revenge should have no bounds.
Hamlet 4.7.127

3963 K. HENRY: Treason and murther
ever kept together,
As two yoke-devils sworn to either's
purpose.
Henry V 2.2.105

3964 PRINCE: Mercy but murders, pardoning those that kill.
Romeo and Juliet 3.1.197

3965 K. RICHARD: Murthers, treasons,
and detested sins,
The cloak of night being pluck'd from
off their backs,
Stand bare and naked, trembling at
themselves.
Richard II 3.2.44

3966 BRUTUS: That we shall die, we
know, 'tis but the time,
And drawing days out, that men stand
upon.
CASCA: Why, he that cuts off twenty
years of life
Cuts off so many years of fearing
death.
BRUTUS: Grant that, and then is death
a benefit;
So are we Caesar's friends, that have
abridg'd
His time of fearing death.
Julius Caesar 3.1.99

Music

3967 LORENZO: The man that hath no
music in himself,
Nor is not moved with concord of
sweet sounds,
Is fit for treasons, stratagems, and
spoils;
The motions of his spirit are dull as
night,
And his affections dark as Erebus:
Let no such man be trusted.
Merchant of Venice 5.1.83
[*Erebus*: the hell of classical mythology]

3968 LUCENTIO [to Hortensio]:
Preposterous ass, that never read so
far
To know the cause why music was or-
dain'd!
Was it not to refresh the mind of man
After his studies or his usual pain?
Taming of the Shrew 3.1.9

3969 PETER: When griping griefs the
heart doth wound,
And doleful dumps the mind oppress,
Then music with her silver sound . . .
With speedy help doth lend redress.
Romeo and Juliet 4.5.126

3970 CLEOPATRA: Give me some
music; music, moody food
Of us that trade in love.
Antony and Cleopatra 2.5.1

3971 DUKE: If music be the food of
love, play on,

Give me excess of it; that surfeiting,
The appetite may sicken, and so die.
                        Twelfth Night 1.1.1

3972 DUKE: Music oft hath such a
   charm
To make bad good, and good provoke
   to harm.
              Measure for Measure 4.1.14

3973 DUKE: O, it came o'er my ear
   like the sweet sound
That breathes upon a bank of violets,
Stealing and giving odor.
                        Twelfth Night 1.1.5

3974 K. RICHARD [soliloquy]: How
   sour sweet music is
When time is broke, and no proportion kept!
So is it in the music of men's lives.
                        Richard II 5.5.42

3975 JESSICA: I am never merry when I
   hear sweet music.
                Merchant of Venice 5.1.69

3976 BENEDICK: Is it not strange that
sheep's guts should hale souls out of
men's bodies?
          Much Ado About Nothing 2.3.59
[*sheep's guts:* violin or lute strings]

3977 Music to hear, why hear'st thou
   music sadly?
Sweets with sweets war not, joy delights in joy.
Why lov'st thou that which thou receiv'st not gladly,
Or else receiv'st with pleasure thine
   annoy?
If the true concord of well-tuned
   sounds,
By unions married, do offend thine
   ear,
They do but sweetly chide thee, who
   confounds
In singleness the parts that thou
   shouldst bear.
Mark how one string, sweet husband to
   another,
Strikes each in each by mutual
   ordering;

Resembling sire, and child, and happy
   mother,
Who all in one, one pleasing note do
   sing:
Whose speechless song, being many,
   seeming one,
Sings this to thee, "Thou single wilt
   prove none."
                              Sonnet 8

3978 SONG: Orpheus with his lute
   made trees,
And the mountain tops that freeze,
Bow themselves when he did sing.
To his music plants and flowers
Ever sprung, as sun and showers
There had made a lasting spring.
Every thing that heard him play,
Even the billows of the sea,
Hung their heads, and then lay by.
In sweet music is such art,
Killing care and grief of heart
Fall asleep, or hearing, die.
                        Henry VIII 3.1.3

3979 PIRITHOUS: They say from iron
Came music's origin.
              Two Noble Kinsmen 5.4.60

Mutability

3980 Reckoning Time, whose million'd
   accidents
Creep in 'twixt vows, and change decrees of kings,
Tan sacred beauty, blunt the sharp'st
   intents,
Divert strong minds to th' course of
   alt'ring things.
                            Sonnet 115

3981 CAPULET [supposing Juliet to be
   dead]: All things that we ordained
   festival,
Turn from their office to black funeral:
Our instruments to melancholy bells,
Our wedding cheer to a sad burial
   feast;
Our solemn hymns to sullen dirges
   change;
Our bridal flowers serve for a buried
   corse;

And all things change them to the contrary.

Romeo and Juliet 4.5.84

Mystery

3982 HAMLET: There are more things in heaven and earth, Horatio, Than are dreamt of in your philosophy.

Hamlet 1.5.166

Name

3983 IAGO [to Othello]: Good name in man and woman, dear my lord, Is the immediate jewel of their souls. Who steals my purse steals trash; 'tis something, nothing; 'Twas mine, 'tis his, and has been slave to thousands; But he that filches from me my good name Robs me of that which not enriches him, And makes me poor indeed.

Othello 3.3.155

3984 FALSTAFF [to Prince Hal]: I would to God thou and I knew where a commodity of good names were to be bought.

1 Henry IV 1.2.82

3985 CAPTAIN: We go to gain a little patch of ground That hath in it no profit but the name.

Hamlet 4.4.18

3986 K. RICHARD: The King's name is a tower of strength.

Richard III 5.3.12

3987 MARIANA: The honor of a maid is her name.

All's Well That Ends Well 3.5.12

3988 JULIET: What's in a name? That which we call a rose By any other word would smell as sweet.

Romeo and Juliet 2.2.43

Nature

3989 ULYSSES: One touch of nature makes the whole world kin.

Troilus and Cressida 3.3.175

3990 KING: How quickly nature falls into revolt When gold becomes her object!

2 Henry IV 4.5.65

3991 HAMLET: Use almost can change the stamp of nature.

Hamlet 3.4.168

3992 ANTONIO: In nature there's no blemish but the mind.

Twelfth Night 3.4.367

3993 LEAR: We are not ourselves When nature, being oppress'd, commands the mind To suffer with the body.

King Lear 2.4.107

3994 HAMLET: O'erstep not the modesty of nature.

Hamlet 3.2.19

3995 MACDUFF: Boundless intemperance In nature is a tyranny; it hath been Th' untimely emptying of the happy throne, And fall of many kings.

Macbeth 4.3.67

3996 Every thing that grows Holds in perfection but a little moment.

Sonnet 15

3997 DUKE: Nature never lends The smallest scruple of her excellence, But like a thrifty goddess, she determines Herself the glory of a creditor, Both thanks and use.

Measure for Measure 1.1.36

3998 POLIXENES [to Perdita]: Nature is made better by no mean

But Nature makes that mean; so over
  that art
Which you say adds to Nature, is an art
That Nature makes. You see, sweet
  maid, we marry
A gentler scion to the wildest stock,
And make conceive a bark of baser
  kind
By bud of nobler race. This is an art
Which does mend Nature—change it
  rather; but
The art itself is Nature.
                    Winter's Tale 4.4.89

3999 LEAR: Nature's above art.
                    King Lear 4.6.86

4000 BELARIUS: How hard it is to hide
  the sparks of nature!
                    Cymbeline 3.3.79

4001 LEONTES: How sometimes nature
  will betray its folly!
It tenderness! and make itself a pastime
To harder bosoms!
                    Winter's Tale 1.2.151
[*pastime:* source of mirth]

4002 HELENA: The mightiest space in
  fortune nature brings
To join like likes, and kiss like native
  things.
            All's Well That Ends Well 1.1.222

4003 BELARIUS: O worthiness of
  nature! breed of greatness!
Cowards father cowards and base
  things sire base.
                    Cymbeline 4.2.25

4004 LAERTES: Nature her custom
  holds,
Let shame say what it will.
                    Hamlet 4.7.187

4005 K. LEAR: Allow not nature more
  than nature needs.
                    King Lear 2.4.266

4006 Nature's bequest gives nothing,
  but doth lend,

And being frank she lends to those are
  free.
                    Sonnet 4

4007 BRUTUS: Nature must obey
  necessity.
                    Julius Caesar 4.3.227

4008 HAMLET: 'Tis dangerous when
  the baser nature comes
Between the pass and fell incensed
  points
Of mighty opposites.
                    Hamlet 5.2.60
[*pass:* thrust; *fell incensed:* fiercely angered]

4009 DUKE SENIOR [to his companions
  in exile]: And this our life, exempt
  from public haunt,
Finds tongues in trees, books in running brooks,
Sermons in stones, and good in every
  thing.
                    As You Like It 2.1.15

4010 SOLANIO: Nature hath fram'd
  strange fellows in her time.
                Merchant of Venice 1.1.51

4011 SICINIUS: Nature teaches beasts
  to know their friends.
                    Coriolanus 2.1.6

4012 SOOTHSAYER: In nature's infinite
  book of secrecy
A little I can read.
                Antony and Cleopatra 1.2.10

4013 My nature is subdu'd
To what it works in, like the dyer's
  hand.
                    Sonnet 111

4014 HOTSPUR: Diseased nature often-
  times breaks forth
In strange eruptions; oft the teeming
  earth
Is with a kind of colic pinch'd and
  vex'd
By the imprisoning of unruly wind
Within her womb, which, for enlarge-
  ment striving,
Shakes the old beldame earth, and
  topples down
Steeples and moss-grown towers.
                    1 Henry IV 3.1.26

4015 VIOLA: Nature with a beauteous wall
Doth oft close in pollution.
Twelfth Night 1.2.48

4016 TOUCHSTONE: All is mortal in nature.
As You Like It 2.4.55

4017 QUEEN [to Hamlet]: Do not for ever with thy vailed lids
Seek for thy noble father in the dust.
Thou know'st 'tis common, all that lives must die,
Passing through nature to eternity.
Hamlet 1.2.70

4018 TIMON: Nature, as it grows again toward earth,
Is fashion'd for the journey, dull and heavy.
Timon of Athens 2.2.218

4019 LAERTES: Nature is fine in love, and where 'tis fine,
It sends some precious instance of itself
After the thing it loves.
Hamlet 4.5.162

4020 DOGBERRY: To be a well-favor'd man is the gift of fortune, but to write and read comes by nature.
Much Ado About Nothing 3.3.14
[*well-favor'd:* good-looking]

4021 COUNTESS: It is the show and seal of nature's truth,
Where love's strong passion is impress'd in youth.
By our remembrances of days foregone,
Such were our faults, or then we thought them none.
All's Well That Ends Well 1.3.132

4022 CLAUDIO: Our natures do pursue,
Like rats that ravin down their proper bane,
A thirsty evil, and when we drink we die.
Measure for Measure 1.2.128
[*ravin down:* devour greedily; *proper bane:* rat poison]

Neatness

4023 LEONTES [to Mamillius]: We must be neat; not neat, but cleanly.
Winter's Tale 1.2.123

Necessity

4024 GAUNT: There is no virtue like necessity.
Richard II 1.3.278

4025 LEAR: The art of our necessities is strange
And can make vild things precious.
King Lear 3.2.70
[*vild:* vile, worthless]

4026 K. RICHARD [to Queen]: I am sworn brother . . .
To grim Necessity, and he and I
Will keep a league till death.
Richard II 5.1.20

4027 K. EDWARD: What fates impose, that men must needs abide;
It boots not to resist both wind and tide.
3 Henry VI 4.3.58
[*boots:* helps]

4028 CLOWN: He must needs go that the devil drives.
All's Well That Ends Well 1.3.29

4029 ULYSSES: The elephant hath joints, but none for courtesy; his legs are legs for necessity, not for flexure.
Troilus and Cressida 2.3.105

4030 LEAR: Necessity's sharp pinch.
King Lear 2.4.211

Necromancy

4031 BANQUO: Oftentimes, to win us to our harm,
The instruments of darkness tell us truths,
Win us with honest trifles, to betray 's
In deepest consequence.
Macbeth 1.3.123

4032 GLENDOWER: I can call spirits from the vasty deep.
HOTSPUR: Why, so can I, or so can any man,
But will they come when you do call for them?
1 Henry IV 3.1.52

Need

4033 LEAR: O, reason not the need! our basest beggars
Are in the poorest things superfluous.
King Lear 2.4.264
[*superfluous:* i.e. they have some wretched things they could do without]

Negligence

4034 PATROCLUS: Omission to do what is necessary
Seals a commission to a blank of danger.
Troilus and Cressida 3.3.230

4035 CLEOPATRA: Celerity is never more admir'd
Than by the negligent.
Antony and Cleopatra 3.7.24

4036 The patient dies while the physician sleeps.
Rape of Lucrece 904

Neighbor

4037 K. HENRY: Our bad neighbor makes us early stirrers,
Which is both healthful and good husbandry.
Besides, they are our outward consciences
And preachers to us all, admonishing
That we should dress us fairly for our end.
Henry V 4.1.6

News

4038 TIME: Let Time's news
Be known when 'tis brought forth.
Winter's Tale 4.1.26

4039 MESSENGER: The nature of bad news infects the teller.
Antony and Cleopatra 1.2.95

4040 NORTHUMBERLAND: The first bringer of unwelcome news
Hath but a losing office, and his tongue
Sounds ever after as a sullen bell,
Rememb'red tolling a departed friend.
2 Henry IV 1.1.100

4041 CLEOPATRA: Though it be honest, it is never good
To bring bad news. Give to a gracious message
An host of tongues, but let ill tidings tell
Themselves when they be felt.
Antony and Cleopatra 2.5.85

4042 CELIA: Here comes Monsieur LeBeau.
ROSALIND: With his mouth full of news.
As You Like It 1.2.91

Night

4043 MALCOLM: The night is long that never finds the day.
Macbeth 4.3.240

4044 CORIN: A great cause of the night is lack of the sun.
As You Like It 3.2.28

4045 THIRD CITIZEN: When the sun sets, who doth not look for night?
Richard III 2.3.34

4046 Day's oppression is not eas'd by night.
Sonnet 28

4047 K. RICHARD: When the searching
 eye of heaven is hid
Behind the globe, that lights the lower
 world,
Then thieves and robbers range abroad
 unseen
In murthers and in outrage boldly
 here,
But when from under this terrestrial
 ball
He fires the proud tops of the eastern
 pines
And darts his light through every
 guilty hole,
Then murthers, treasons, and detested
 sins,
The cloak of night being pluck'd from
 off their backs,
Stand bare and naked, trembling at
 themselves.
                    Richard II 3.2.37
[*murthers:* murders]

4048 O comfort-killing Night, image
 of hell,
Dim register and notary of shame,
Black stage for tragedies and murthers
 fell,
Vast sin-concealing chaos, nurse of
 blame!
Blind muffled bawd, dark harbor for
 defame,
Grim cave of death, whisp'ring
 conspirator
With close-tongu'd treason and the
 ravisher!
                    Rape of Lucrece 764
[*murther:* murder]

4049 HERMIA: Dark night, that from
 the eye his function takes,
The ear more quick of apprehension
 makes;
Wherein it doth impair the seeing
 sense,
It pays the hearing double recompense.
        Midsummer Night's Dream 3.2.177

4050 BANQUO: There's husbandry in
 heaven,
Their candles are all out.
                    Macbeth 2.1.4

4051 MACBETH: Come, seeling night,
Scarf up the tender eye of pitiful day.
                    Macbeth 3.2.46

4052 JACHIMO: The crickets sing, and
 man's o'erlabor'd sense
Repairs itself by rest.
                    Cymbeline 2.2.11

4053 THESEUS: The iron tongue of
 midnight hath told twelve.
Lovers, to bed, 'tis almost fairy time.
        Midsummer Night's Dream 5.1.363

4054 LORENZO [to Jessica]: How sweet
 the moonlight sleeps upon this
 bank!
Here we will sit, and let the sounds of
 music
Creep in our ears. Soft stillness and the
 night
Become the touches of sweet harmony.
                Merchant of Venice 5.1.54

4055 Sable Night, mother of dread
 and fear,
Upon the world dim darkness doth
 display,
And in her vaulty prison stows the day.
                    Rape of Lucrece 117

4056 PUCK: Now the hungry lion
 roars,
And the wolf behowls the moon;
Whilst the heavy ploughman snores,
All with weary task foredone.
        Midsummer Night's Dream 5.1.371

4057 Give not a windy night a rainy
 morrow.
                    Sonnet 90

4058 KING: Black is the badge of hell,
The hue of dungeons, and the school
 of night.
                Love's Labor's Lost 4.3.250

4059 BOLINGBROOK: Deep night, dark
 night, the silent of the night ...
The time when screech-owls cry and
 ban-dogs howl,
And spirits walk, and ghosts break up
 their graves.
                    2 Henry VI 1.4.16
[*ban-dogs:* dogs on chains]

4060 PUCK: Night's swift dragons cut the clouds full fast,
And yonder shines Aurora's harbinger,
At whose approach, ghosts, wand'ring here and there,
Troop home to churchyards. Damned spirits all,
That in crossways and floods have burial,
Already to their wormy beds are gone.
For fear lest day should look their shames upon.
Midsummer Night's Dream 3.2.379

Nightingale

4061 PORTIA: The nightingale, if she should sing by day
When every goose is cackling, would be thought
No better a musician than the wren.
How many things by season season'd are
To their right praise and true perfection!
Merchant of Venice 5.1.104

4062 VALENTINE: This shadowy desert, unfrequented woods,
I better brook than flourishing peopled towns:
Here I can sit alone, unseen of any,
And to the nightingale's complaining notes
Tune my distresses and record my woes.
Two Gentlemen of Verona 5.4.2

Nimbleness

4063 Youth is nimble.
The Passionate Pilgrim xii.6

Nobility

4064 SUFFOLK: True nobility is exempt from fear.
2 Henry VI 4.1.129

4065 MOROCCO: A golden mind stoops not to shows of dross.
Merchant of Venice 2.7.20

4066 Unstain'd thoughts do seldom dream on evil.
Rape of Lucrece 87

4067 IAGO: Base men being in love have then a nobility in their natures more than is native to them.
Othello 2.1.215

4068 CASSIUS [soliloquy]: It is meet That noble minds keep ever with their likes;
For who so firm that cannot be seduc'd?
Julius Caesar 1.2.310

4069 CROMWELL: Men so noble,
However faulty, yet should find respect For what they have been.
Henry VIII 5.2.109

4070 TAMORA: Sweet mercy is nobility's true badge.
Titus Andronicus 1.1.119

4071 DUCHESS: That which in mean men we entitle patience
Is pale cold cowardice in noble breasts.
Richard II 1.2.33

4072 GLOUCESTER [criticizing the queen]: Great promotions
Are daily given to ennoble those
That scarce some two days since were worth a noble.
Richard III 1.3.79

4073 FLAVIUS: What vilder thing upon the earth than friends,
Who can bring noblest minds to basest ends!
Timon of Athens 4.3.463
[*vilder:* viler]

4074 BRUTUS: For mine own part,
I shall be glad to learn of noble men.
Julius Caesar 4.3.53

4075 WARWICK [to Somerset]: I hold
it cowardice
To rest mistrustful where a noble heart
Hath pawn'd an open hand in sign of
love.

3 Henry VI 4.2.6

Nonsense

4076 ROSALIND: I had rather have a
fool to make me merry than experience
to make me sad.

As You Like It 4.1.27

Nose

4077 FOOL: All that follow their noses
are led by their eyes but blind men,
and there's not a nose among twenty
but can smell him that's stinking.

King Lear 2.4.68

4078 CLOTEN: We will nothing pay
For wearing our own noses.

Cymbeline 3.1.13

Nothing

4079 LEAR: Nothing will come of
nothing.

King Lear 1.1.90

4080 MACBETH: Nothing is
But what is not.

Macbeth 1.3.141

4081 GLOUCESTER: The quality of
nothing hath not such need to hide
itself.

King Lear 1.2.33

4082 K. RICHARD [soliloquy]:
Whate'er I be,
Nor I, nor any man that but man is,
With nothing shall be pleas'd, till he
be eas'd
With being nothing.

Richard II 5.5.38

4083 THESEUS: The poet's eye, in a
fine frenzy rolling,

Doth glance from heaven to earth,
from earth to heaven;
And as imagination bodies forth
The forms of things unknown, the
poet's pen
Turns them to shapes, and gives an
aery nothing
A local habitation and a name.

Midsummer Night's Dream 5.1.12

4084 CLOWN [to Parolles]: To say
nothing, to do nothing, to know
nothing, and to have nothing, is to be
a great part of your title, which is
within a very little of nothing.

All's Well That Ends Well 2.4.24

4085 GRATIANO: I do know of these
That therefore only are reputed wise
For saying nothing.

Merchant of Venice 1.1.95

4086 WARWICK [on the defeated King
Henry]: Having nothing, nothing
can he lose.

3 Henry VI 3.3.152

Novelty

4087 SANDS: New customs,
Though they be never so ridiculous
(Nay, let 'em be unmanly), yet are fol-
low'd.

Henry VIII 1.3.3

4088 KING: Things done well
And with a care exempt themselves
from fear;
Things done without example, in their
issue
Are to be fear'd.

Henry VIII 1.2.88

4089 ULYSSES: All with one consent
praise new-born gawds,
Though they are made and moulded of
things past,
And give to dust, that is a little gilt,
More laud than gilt o'erdusted.

Troilus and Cressida 3.3.176

[*gawds:* trifles, toys; *gilt o'erdusted:* i.e.
true gold obscured with dust]

4090 If there be nothing new, but that which is
Hath been before, how are our brains beguil'd,
Which laboring for invention bear amiss
The second burthen of a former child!
Sonnet 59

4091 DUKE: Novelty is only in request, and, as it is, as dangerous to be ag'd in any kind of course, as it is virtuous to be constant in any undertaking.
Measure for Measure 3.2.224

Oak

4092 MESSENGER [telling of York's death]: Many strokes, though with a little axe,
Hews down and fells the hardest-timber'd oak.
3 Henry VI 2.1.54

4093 NESTOR: The splitting wind
Makes flexible the knees of knotted oaks.
Troilus and Cressida 1.3.49

Oath

4094 DIANA: 'Tis not the many oaths that makes the truth,
But the plain single vow, that is vow'd true.
All's Well That Ends Well 4.2.21

4095 CASSANDRA: It is the purpose that makes strong the vow,
But vows to every purpose must not hold.
Troilus and Cressida 5.3.23

4096 BEROWNE: Having sworn too hard-a-keeping oath,
Study to break it and not break my troth.
Love's Labor's Lost 1.1.65

4097 PROTEUS: Unheedful vows may heedfully be broken.
Two Gentlemen of Verona 2.6.11

4098 SALIBURY: It is a great sin to swear unto a sin,
But greater sin to keep a sinful oath.
Who can be bound by any solemn vow
To do a murd'rous deed, to rob a man,
To force a spotless virgin's chastity,
To reave the orphan of his patrimony,
To wring the widow from her custom'd right,
And have no other reason for this wrong
But that he was bound by a solemn oath?
2 Henry VI 5.1.182
[*reave:* bereave, rob; *custom'd right:* her part of her husband's estate]

4099 PROSPERO [to Ferdinand]: Do not give dalliance
Too much the rein. The strongest oaths are straw
To th' fire i' th' blood.
The Tempest 4.1.51

4100 PISTOL: Trust none;
For oaths are straws, men's faiths are wafer-cakes,
And Hold-fast is the only dog.
Henry V 2.3.50
[*wafer-cakes:* i.e. fragile; *Hold-fast:* an allusion to the proverb: Brag is a good dog, but Holdfast is a better.]

4101 CELIA: The oath of a lover is no stronger than the word of a tapster; they are both the confirmer of false reckonings.
As You Like It 3.4.30

4102 BEROWNE: What fool is not so wise
To lose an oath to win a paradise?
Love's Labor's Lost 4.3.70

4103 SIR TOBY: A terrible oath, with a swaggering accent sharply twang'd off, gives manhood more approbation than ever proof itself would have earn'd him.
Twelfth Night 3.4.179

4104 PERICLES [to Helicanus]: I'll take
thy word for faith, not ask thine
oath:
Who shuns not to break one will crack
them both.
Pericles 1.2.120

4105 AARON: An idiot holds his bauble for a god,
And keeps the oath which by that god
he swears.
Titus Andronicus 5.1.79
[*bauble:* fool's stick, trinket]

4106 JULIET: At lovers' perjuries
They say Jove laughs.
Romeo and Juliet 2.2.92

Obedience

4107 YORK: Let them obey that know
not how to rule.
2 Henry VI 5.1.6

4108 WOLSEY: The hearts of princes
kiss obedience,
So much they love it; but to stubborn
spirits
They swell and grow, as terrible as
storms.
Henry VIII 3.1.162

4109 LEAR: Thou hast seen a farmer's
dog bark at a beggar?
GLOUCESTER: Ay, sir.
LEAR: And the creature run from the
cur? There thou mightst behold the
great image of authority: a dog's
obey'd in office.
King Lear 4.6.154

4110 POSTHUMUS: Every good servant
does not all commands;
No bond, but to do just ones.
Cymbeline 5.1.6

4111 BATES: If his cause be wrong, our
obedience to the King wipes the crime
of it out of us.
Henry V 4.1.132

4112 THESEUS: To you your father
should be as a god.
Midsummer Night's Dream 1.1.47

4113 EDGAR: Obey thy parents, keep
thy word's justice, swear not.
King Lear 3.4.80

4114 CATHNESS: Give obedience where
'tis truly ow'd.
Macbeth 5.2.26

4115 CANTERBURY: Therefore doth
heaven divide
The state of man in divers functions,
Setting endeavor in continual motion;
To which is fixed, as an aim or butt,
Obedience.
Henry V 1.2.183

Obesity

4116 LONGAVILLE: Fat paunches have
lean pates; and dainty bits
Make rich the ribs, but bankrout quite
the wits.
Love's Labor's Lost 1.1.26
[*bankrout:* bankrupt]

4117 CAESAR: Let me have men about
me that are fat,
Sleek-headed men and such as sleep
a-nights.
Yond Cassius has a lean and hungry
look,
He thinks too much; such men are
dangerous.
Julius Caesar 1.2.192

4118 KING [to Falstaff]: Make less thy
body hence and more thy grace,
Leave gormandizing, know the grave
doth gape
For thee thrice wider than for other
men.
2 Henry IV 5.5.52

Oblivion

4119 KING [soliloquy]: O sleep! O
gentle sleep!

Nature's soft nurse, how have I
frighted thee,
That thou no more wilt weigh my
eyelids down,
And steep my senses in forgetfulness?
2 Henry IV 3.1.5

4120 AGAMEMNON: What's past and
what's to come is strew'd with husks
And formless ruin of oblivion.
Troilus and Cressida 4.5.166

Observation

4121 To see sad sights moves more
than hear them told.
Rape of Lucrece 1324

4122 ARMADO: How hast thou pur-
chased this experience?
MOTH: By my penny of observation.
Love's Labor's Lost 3.1.26

4123 BELARIUS: To apprehend . . .
Draws us a profit from all things we
see.
Cymbeline 3.3.17

4124 BASTARD [soliloquy]: He is but a
bastard to the time
That doth not smack of observation.
King John 1.1.207

Obstacle

4125 DESDEMONA: Men's natures
wrangle with inferior things,
Though great ones are their object.
Othello 3.4.144

4126 Though the rose have prickles,
yet 'tis pluck'd!
Venus and Adonis 574

Obstinacy

4127 CAMILLO: You may as well
Forbid the sea for to obey the moon
As or by oath remove or counsel shake

The fabric of his folly, whose
foundation
Is pil'd upon his faith.
Winter's Tale 1.2.425

4128 YORK: Direct not him whose way
himself will choose,
'Tis breath thou lack'st, and that
breath wilt thou lose.
Richard II 2.1.29

4129 KATHERINE [about Wolsey]: His
own opinion was his law.
Henry VIII 4.2.37

Occasion

4130 MENENIUS: A very little thief of
occasion will rob you of a great deal of
patience.
Coriolanus 2.1.28

4131 FLUELLEN: There is occasions and
causes why and wherefore in all things.
Henry V 5.1.3

4132 LAERTES: Occasion smiles upon a
second leave.
Hamlet 1.3.54

[*occasion:* opportunity]

Ocean

4133 EGEON: The always-wind-obeying
deep.
Comedy of Errors 1.1.64

Odor

4134 The rose looks fair, but fairer we
it deem
For that sweet odor which doth in it
live.
Sonnet 54

4135 Of their sweet deaths are sweetest
odors made.
Sonnet 54

4136 BOTTOM: Odors savors sweet.
Midsummer Night's Dream 3.1.84

4137 The summer's flow'r is to the
summer sweet,
Though to itself it only live and die,
But if that flow'r with base infection
meet,
The basest weed outbraves his dignity:
For sweetest things turn sourest by
their deeds;
Lilies that fester smell far worse than
weeds.
Sonnet 94
[*outbraves:* surpasses in splendor]

4138 FRIAR LAWRENCE: Within the infant rind of this weak flower
Poison hath residence and medicine
power;
For this, being smelt, with that part
cheers each part,
Being tasted, stays all senses with the
heart.
Romeo and Juliet 2.3.23
[*stays:* brings to a halt]

4139 JULIET: That which we call a rose
By any other word would smell as
sweet.
Romeo and Juliet 2.2.43

Offense

4140 KING: Where th' offense is, let
the great axe fall.
Hamlet 4.5.219

4141 GONERIL: All's not offense that
indiscretion finds.
King Lear 2.4.196

4142 CLAUDIO: Thus can the
demigod, Authority,
Make us pay down for our offense by
weight
The words of heaven.
Measure for Measure 1.2.120

4143 TROILUS: There is between my
will and all offenses
A guard of patience.
Troilus and Cressida 5.2.53

4144 KING: Th' offender's scourge is
weigh'd,
But never the offense.
Hamlet 4.3.6
[*scourge:* punishment; *weigh'd:* taken into
consideration]

4145 Th' offender's sorrow lends but
weak relief
To him that bears the strong offense's
cross.
Sonnet 34

4146 DUKE: Hence hath offense his
quick celerity,
When it is borne in high authority.
Measure for Measure 4.2.110

4147 KING [soliloquy, on his act of
murder]: May one be pardon'd and
retain th' offense?
In the corrupted currents of this world
Offense's gilded hand may shove by
justice,
And oft 'tis seen the wicked prize itself
Buys out the law, but 'tis not so above:
There is no shuffling, there the action
lies
In his true nature, and we ourselves
compell'd,
Even to the teeth and forehead of our
faults,
To give in evidence.
Hamlet 3.3.56
[*gilded hand:* offer of a bribe; *wicked prize:*
ill-gotten gains]

4148 WILLIAMS [to King]: All offenses,
my lord, come from the heart.
Henry V 4.8.46

4149 All my offenses that abroad you
see
Are errors of the blood, none of the
mind.
A Lover's Complaint 183

4150 CASCA [about Brutus]: O, he sits
high in all the people's hearts;
And that which would appear offense
in us,
His countenance, like richest alchymy,

Will change to virtue and to worthiness.

Julius Caesar 1.3.157

[*alchymy:* alchemy]

4151 PORTIA: To offend and judge are distinct offices,
And of opposed natures.

Merchant of Venice 2.9.61

Office

4152 IAGO: 'Tis the curse of service;
Preferment goes by letter and affection,
And not by the old gradation where each second
Stood heir to th' first.

Othello 1.1.35

[*old gradation:* seniority]

4153 LEAR [to Gloucester]: Thou hast seen a farmer's dog bark at a beggar
. . . And the creature run from the cur? There thou mightst behold the great image of authority: a dog's obey'd in office.

King Lear 4.6.154

4154 DUKE [soliloquy]: O place and greatness! millions of false eyes
Are stuck upon thee. Volumes of report
Run with these false, and most contrarious quests
Upon thy doings; thousand escapes of wit
Make thee the father of their idle dream,
And rack thee in their fancies.

Measure for Measure 4.1.59

Omens

4155 CALPHURNIA: When beggars die there are no comets seen;
The heavens themselves blaze forth the death of princes.

Julius Caesar 2.2.30

Omission

4156 PATROCLUS: Omission to do what is necessary
Seals a commission to a blank of danger.

Troilus and Cressida 3.3.230

Opinion

4157 SIMONIDES: Opinion's but a fool, that makes us scan,
The outward habit by the inward man.

Pericles 2.2.56

4158 THERSITES: A plague of opinion! a man may wear it on both sides, like a leather jerkin.

Troilus and Cressida 3.3.264

[*opinion:* self-conceit and self-respect]

4159 JAQUES: Weed your better judgments
Of all opinion that grows rank in them.

As You Like It 2.7.45

4160 NESTOR: As Ulysses says, opinion crowns
With an imperial voice.

Troilus and Cressida 1.3.186

4161 MACBETH: I have bought
Golden opinions from all sorts of people.

Macbeth 1.7.32

[*bought:* won]

4162 VERNON [to Somerset]: If I, my lord, for my opinion bleed,
Opinion shall be surgeon to my hurt.

1 Henry VI 2.4.53

4163 MARTIUS [to some citizens]:
What's the matter, you dissentious rogues,
That rubbing the poor itch of your opinion
Make yourselves scabs?

Coriolanus 1.1.164

4164 DUKE: Opinion [is] a sovereign mistress of effects.

Othello 1.3.224

4165 GRATIANO: There are a sort of men whose visages
Do cream and mantle like a standing pond,
And do a wilful stillness entertain,
With purpose to be dress'd in an opinion
Of wisdom, gravity, profound conceit,
As who should say, "I am Sir Oracle,
And when I ope my lips let no dog bark!"

Merchant of Venice 1.1.88

Opportunity

4166 BRUTUS [to Cassius, in the field]:
There is a tide in the affairs of men,
Which taken at the flood, leads on to fortune;
Omitted, all the voyage of their life
Is bound in shallows and in miseries.
On such a full sea are we now afloat,
And we must take the current when it serves,
Or lose our ventures.

Julius Caesar 4.3.218

4167 MENAS: Who seeks, and will not take when once 'tis offer'd,
Shall never find it more.

Antony and Cleopatra 2.7.83

4168 KING: That we would do,
We should do when we would; for this "would" changes.

Hamlet 4.7.118

4169 O Opportunity, thy guilt is great!
'Tis thou that execut'st the traitor's treason;
Thou sets the wolf where he the lamb may get;
Whoever plots the sin, thou 'point'st the season;
'Tis thou that spurn'st at right, at law, at reason.

Rape of Lucrece 876

4170 PAROLLES: There's place and means for every man alive.

All's Well That Ends Well 4.3.339

4171 LUCIUS: Some falls are means the happier to arise.

Cymbeline 4.2.403

4172 Every thing that grows
Holds in perfection but a little moment.

Sonnet 15

4173 CARLISLE: The means that heavens yield must be embrac'd,
And not neglected; else heaven would,
And we will not. Heaven's offer we refuse,
The proffered means of succors and redress.

Richard II 3.2.29

4174 ANTIPHOLUS SYRACUSE: There's a time for all things.

Comedy of Errors 2.2.65

4175 Make use of time, let not advantage slip,
Beauty within itself should not be wasted.
Fair flowers that are not gath'red in their prime
Rot, and consume themselves in little time.

Venus and Adonis 129

4176 ROSALIND [to Phebe, on the love-struck Silvius]:
Sell when you can, you are not for all markets.

As You Like It 3.5.60

4177 OLD LADY: Come pat betwixt too early and too late.

Henry VIII 2.3.84

4178 K. JOHN: How oft the sight of means to do ill deeds
Makes deeds ill done!

King John 5.2.219

4179 GLOUCESTER: A staff is quickly found to beat a dog.

2 Henry VI 3.1.171

4180 KING: Let's take the instant by the forward top;
For we are old, and on our quick'st decrees
Th' inaudible and noiseless foot of time
Steals ere we can effect them.
All's Well That Ends Well 5.3.39
[*forward top:* forelock]

4181 ELINOR [to John, on offering Blanch as bride to Lewis]: Urge them while their souls
Are capable of this ambition,
Lest zeal, now melted by the windy breath
Of soft petitions, pity, and remorse,
Cool and congeal again to what it was.
King John 2.1.475

Oppression

4182 Day's oppression is not eas'd by night.
Sonnet 28

4183 CHAMBERLAIN: Press not a falling man too far! 'tis virtue.
His faults lie open to the laws, let them,
Not you, correct him.
Henry VIII 3.2.333

4184 THIRD FISHERMAN: Master, I marvel how the fishes live in the sea.
FIRST FISHERMAN: Why, as men do a-land; the great ones eat up the little ones.
Pericles 2.1.26

4185 CLIFFORD: The smallest worm will turn, being trodden on.
3 Henry VI 2.2.17

4186 FALSTAFF: The camomile, the more it is trodden on, the faster it grows.
1 Henry IV 2.4.400

Oracle

4187 GRATIANO: I am Sir Oracle,
And when I ope my lips let no dog bark!
Merchant of Venice 1.1.93

Orator

4188 LUCIANA: Be not thy tongue thy own shame's orator.
Comedy of Errors 3.2.10

4189 Bid me discourse, I will enchant thine ear.
Venus and Adonis 145

4190 CANTERBURY [about Henry]:
When he speaks,
The air, a charter'd libertine, is still,
And the mute wonder lurketh in men's ears
To steal his sweet and honeyed sentences.
Henry V 1.1.50

Order

4191 MARIA [to Sir Toby]: You must confine yourself within the modest limits of order.
Twelfth Night 1.3.8

4192 CANTERBURY: So work the honey-bees,
Creatures that by a rule in nature teach
The act of order to a peopled kingdom.
Henry V 1.2.187

4193 ULYSSES: The heavens themselves, the planets, and this centre
Observe degree, priority, and place,
Insisture, course, proportion, season, form,
Office, and custom, in all line of order.
Troilus and Cressida 1.3.85
[*insisture:* steady continuance]

4194 NORFOLK: Order gave each thing view.
Henry VIII 1.1.44

Ornament

4195 BASSANIO: So may the outward
shows be least themselves —
The world is still deceiv'd with orna-
ment.
In law, what plea so tainted and cor-
rupt
But, being season'd with a gracious
voice,
Obscures the show of evil? In religion,
What damned error but some sober
brow
Will bless it, and approve it with a
text,
Hiding the grossness with fair orna-
ment?
There is no vice so simple but assumes
Some mark of virtue on his outward
parts.
How many cowards, whose hearts are
all as false
As stairs of sand, wear yet upon their
chins
The beards of Hercules and frowning
Mars,
Who inward search'd, have livers white
as milk,
And these assume but valor's excre-
ment
To render them redoubted! Look on
beauty,
And you shall see 'tis purchas'd by the
weight,
Which therein works a miracle in na-
ture,
Making them lightest that wear most
of it.
So are those crisped snaky golden locks,
Which make such wanton gambols
with the wind
Upon supposed fairness, often known
To be the dowry of a second head,
The skull that bred them in the sepul-
chre.
Thus ornament is but the guiled shore
To a most dangerous sea; the beau-
teous scarf
Veiling an Indian beauty; in a word,
The seeming truth which cunning
times put on
To entrap the wisest.
Merchant of Venice 3.2.73

[*valor's excrement:* beard of a brave man;
render them redoubted: make themselves
feared; *lightest:* most wanton]

4196 VALENTINE: Dumb jewels often
in their silent kind
More than quick words do move a
woman's mind.
Two Gentlemen of Verona 3.1.90

Ownership

4197 PETRUCHIO [concerning Kate]: I
will be master of what is mine own.
She is my goods, my chattels, she is
my house,
My household stuff, my field, my barn,
My horse, my ox, my ass, my any
thing;
And here she stands, touch her who-
ever dare.
Taming of the Shrew 3.2.229

Pain

4198 MACBETH: The labor we delight
in physics pain.
Macbeth 2.3.50

4199 LEAR: When the mind's free,
The body's delicate.
King Lear 3.4.11

4200 LEONATO: There was never yet
philosopher
That could endure the toothache patiently,
However they have writ the style of
gods,
And made a push at chance and sufferance.
Much Ado About Nothing 5.1.35

4201 FIRST JAILER: He that sleeps feels
not the toothache.
Cymbeline 5.4.172

4202 LEAR: Where the greater malady
is fix'd,
The lesser is scarce felt.
King Lear 3.4.8

4203 BENVOLIO: One fire burns out
another's burning,
One pain is less'ned by another's anguish.
Romeo and Juliet 1.2.45

4204 LEAR [to Cordelia]: Thou art a
soul in bliss, but I am bound
Upon a wheel of fire, that mine own
tears
Do scald like molten lead.
King Lear 4.7.45

4205 DESDEMONA: Let our finger ache,
and it endues
Our other healthful members even to a
sense
Of pain.
Othello 3.4.146

4206 K. HENRY: 'Tis good for men to
love their present pains
Upon example; so the spirit is eased.
Henry V 4.1.18

4207 BEROWNE: Why? all delights are
vain, but that most vain
Which, with pain purchas'd, doth inherit pain.
Love's Labor's Lost 1.1.72

4208 GAUNT: They breathe truth that
breathe their words in pain.
Richard II 2.1.8

4209 Pain pays the income of each
precious thing.
Rape of Lucrece 334

4210 ANTONY: The present pleasure,
By revolution low'ring, does become
The opposite of itself.
Antony and Cleopatra 1.2.124

4211 ADRIANA: A wretched soul,
bruis'd with adversity,
We bid be quiet when we hear it cry;
But were we burd'ned with like weight
of pain,
As much, or more, we should ourselves
complain.
Comedy of Errors 2.1.34

4212 ISABELLA: The poor beetle that
we tread upon
In corporal sufferance finds a pang as
great
As when a giant dies.
Measure for Measure 3.1.78

Painting

4213 Through the painter must you
see his skill.
Sonnet 24

4214 Perspective it is best painter's art.
Sonnet 24

4215 TIMON: The painting is almost
the natural man;
For since dishonor traffics with man's
nature,
He is but outside; pencill'd figures are
Even such as they give out.
Timon of Athens 1.1.157

Pardon

4216 PRINCE: Mercy but murders, pardoning those that kill.
Romeo and Juliet 3.1.197

4217 KING [soliloquy]: May one be
pardon'd and retain th' offense?
Hamlet 3.3.56

4218 DUCHESS [to Henry, begging pardon for her son]: If I were thy nurse,
thy tongue to teach,
"Pardon" should be the first word of
thy speech.
I never long'd to hear a word till now,
Say "pardon," King, let pity teach thee
how.
The word is short, but not so short as
sweet,
No word like "pardon" for kings'
mouths so meet.
Richard II 5.3.116

4219 ESCALUS: Mercy is not itself, that
oft looks so;
Pardon is still the nurse of second woe.
Measure for Measure 2.1.283

4220 K. JOHN [to King Philip, about the Pope]: You and all the kings of Christendom
Are led so grossly by this meddling priest,
Dreading the curse that money may buy out,
And by merit of vild gold, dross, dust,
Purchase corrupted pardon of a man
Who in that sale sells pardon from himself.
King John 3.1.162
[*vild:* vile]

4221 To you it doth belong
Your self to pardon of self-doing crime.
Sonnet 58

4222 PROSPERO: The rarer action is
In virtue than in vengeance.
The Tempest 5.1.27

4223 SILVIUS: The common executioner,
Whose heart th' accustom'd sight of death makes hard,
Falls not the axe upon the humbled neck
But first begs pardon.
As You Like It 3.5.3

Parents

4224 EDGAR: Obey thy parents, keep thy word's justice, swear not.
King Lear 3.4.80

4225 LAUNCELOT: It is a wise father that knows his own child.
Merchant of Venice 2.2.76

4226 THESEUS [to Hermia]: To you your father should be as a god;
One that compos'd your beauties; yea, and one
To whom you are but as a form in wax,
By him imprinted, and within his power,
To leave the figure, or disfigure it.
Midsummer Night's Dream 1.1.47

Parting

4227 JULIET [to Romeo]: Good night, good night! Parting is such sweet sorrow,
That I shall say good night till it be morrow.
Romeo and Juliet 2.2.184

4228 PROTEUS [soliloquy, on Julia]: What, gone without a word?
Ay, so true love should do: it cannot speak,
For truth hath better deeds than words to grace it.
Two Gentlemen of Verona 2.2.16

4229 JULIET [soliloquy, after her mother's departure]: Farewell! God knows when we shall meet again.
I have a faint cold fear thrills through my veins,
That almost freezes up the heat of life.
Romeo and Juliet 4.3.14

4230 Q. MARGARET [to Oxford and Somerset]: So part we sadly in this troublous world,
To meet with joy in sweet Jerusalem.
3 Henry VI 5.5.7

4231 LEBEAU [to Orlando]: Hereafter, in a better world than this,
I shall desire more love and knowledge of you.
As You Like It 1.2.284

4232 SUFFOLK [to Queen Margaret]: To die by thee were but to die in jest,
From thee to die were torture more than death.
2 Henry VI 3.2.400

Passion

4233 MACBETH: Th' expedition of my violent love
Outrun the pauser, reason.
Macbeth 2.3.110

4234 ANTONY [to servant, weeping at
    Caesar's death]:
Passion, I see, is catching, for mine
    eyes,
Seeing those beads of sorrow standing
    in thine,
Began to water.
                        Julius Caesar 3.1.283

4235 LEONATO: Men
Can counsel and speak comfort to that
    grief
Which they themselves not feel, but
    tasting it,
Their counsel turns to passion.
            Much Ado About Nothing 5.1.20

4236 PERICLES [soliloquy]: The pas-
    sions of the mind,
That have their first conception by
    misdread,
Have after-nourishment and life by
    care.
                        Pericles 1.2.11

4237 SHYLOCK: Affection,
Mistress of passion, sways it to the
    mood
Of what it likes or loathes.
            Merchant of Venice 4.1.50

4238 Affection is a coal that must be
    cool'd,
Else suffer'd it will set the heart on
    fire.
                Venus and Adonis 387

4239 PROSPERO [to Ferdinand]: Do not
    give dalliance
Too much the rein. The strongest oaths
    are straw
To th' fire i' th' blood. Be more abste-
    mious,
Or else good night your vow!
                    The Tempest 4.1.51

4240 Nothing can affection's course
    control,
Or stop the headlong fury of his speed.
                Rape of Lucrece 500

4241 OTHELLO: Passion, having my
    best judgment collied,
Assays to lead the way.
                    Othello 2.3.206
[*collied:* darkened]

4242 OLD ATHENIAN: Our own prece-
    dent passions do instruct us
What levity's in youth.
            Timon of Athens 1.1.133

4243 PUCELLE: Of all base passions,
    fear is most accurs'd.
                    1 Henry VI 5.2.18

4244 PLAYER KING: What to ourselves
    in passion we propose,
The passion ending, doth the purpose
    lose.
                    Hamlet 3.2.194

4245 HAMLET: O, it offends me to the
soul to hear a robustious periwig-pated
fellow tear a passion to totters, to very
rags, to spleet the ears of the groundlings, who for the most part are capable of nothing but inexplicable dumb
shows and noise. I would have such a
fellow whipt.
                        Hamlet 3.2.8
[*totters:* tatters; *spleet:* split; *groundlings:*
those who paid the lowest admission price
and stood on the ground to watch the play]

4246 HAMLET [to Horatio]: Give me
    that man
That is not passion's slave, and I will
    wear him
In my heart's core, ay, in my heart of
    heart.
                    Hamlet 3.2.71

4247 CLARENCE: A little fire is quickly
    trodden out,
Which being suffer'd, rivers cannot
    quench.
                    3 Henry VI 4.8.7

4248 Small lights are soon blown out,
    huge fires abide.
                Rape of Lucrece 647

4249 LUCETTA: Fire that's closest kept
burns most of all.
Two Gentlemen of Verona 1.2.30

4250 POET: The fire i' th' flint
Shows not till it be strook.
Timon of Athens 1.1.22
[*strook:* struck]

4251 PETRUCHIO: Where two raging
fires meet together,
They do consume the thing that feeds
their fury.
Taming of the Shrew 2.1.132

4252 BENVOLIO: One fire burns out
another's burning,
One pain is less'ned by another's anguish.
Romeo and Juliet 1.2.45

4253 COUNTESS: It is the show and
seal of nature's truth,
Where love's strong passion is im-
press'd in youth.
By our remembrances of days foregone,
Such were our faults, or then we
thought them none.
All's Well That Ends Well 1.3.132

4254 JULIA [to Lucetta]: The current
that with gentle murmur glides,
Thou know'st, being stopp'd, impa-
tiently doth rage;
But when his fair course is not hin-
dered,
He makes sweet music with th' ena-
mell'd stones,
Giving a gentle kiss to every sedge
He overtaketh in his pilgrimage.
Two Gentlemen of Verona 2.7.25

4255 CONSTANCE: O that my tongue
were in the thunder's mouth!
Then with a passion would I shake the
world.
King John 3.4.38

4256 IAGO: The blood is made dull
with the act of sport.
Othello 2.1.226

Past

4257 PAULINA: Every present time
doth boast itself
Above a better gone.
Winter's Tale 5.1.96

4258 ARCHBISHOP: O thoughts of men
accurs'd!
Past and to come seems best; things
present worst.
2 Henry IV 1.3.107

4259 PAULINA: What's gone and
what's past help
Should be past grief.
Winter's Tale 3.2.222

4260 ANTONIO: What's past is
prologue.
The Tempest 2.1.253

4261 ANTONY: Things that are past
are done with me.
Antony and Cleopatra 1.2.97

4262 LADY MACBETH: Things without
all remedy
Should be without regard: what's
done, is done.
Macbeth 3.2.11

4263 MACBETH: To-morrow, and to-
morrow, and to-morrow,
Creeps in this petty pace from day to
day,
To the last syllable of recorded time;
And all our yesterdays have lighted
fools
The way to dusty death.
Macbeth 5.5.19

4264 PROSPERO: Let us not burthen
our remembrances with
A heaviness that's gone.
The Tempest 5.1.198
[*burthen:* burden]

4265 Our dates are brief, and
therefore we admire
What thou dost foist upon us that is
old.
Sonnet 123
[*thou:* i.e. Time]

4266 AGAMEMNON: What's past and what's to come is strew'd with husks And formless ruin of oblivion.
Troilus and Cressida 4.5.166

4267 PROSPERO [to Miranda]: What seest thou else
In the dark backward and abysm of time?
The Tempest 1.2.49

Pasture

4268 CORIN: Good pasture makes fat sheep.
As You Like It 3.2.27

4269 KING: Most subject is the fattest soil to weeds.
2 Henry IV 4.4.54

Path

4270 The path is smooth that leadeth on to danger.
Venus and Adonis 788

4271 OPHELIA: Do not, as some ungracious pastors do,
Show me the steep and thorny way to heaven,
Whiles, like a puff'd and reckless libertine,
Himself the primrose path of dalliance treads,
And reaks not his own rede.
Hamlet 1.3.47
[*reaks:* recks, heeds; *rede:* advice]

Patience

4272 LEONATO: There was never yet philosopher
That could endure the toothache patiently.
Much Ado About Nothing 5.1.35

4273 NYM: Though patience be a tir'd mare, yet she will plod.
Henry V 2.1.23

4274 BRABANTIO: He bears the sentence well that nothing bears
But the free comfort which from thence he hears;
But he bears both the sentence and the sorrow
That, to pay grief, must of poor patience borrow.
Othello 1.3.212

4275 CLEOPATRA: Patience is sottish, and impatience does
Become a dog that's mad.
Antony and Cleopatra 4.15.79
[*sottish:* stupid, very foolish]

4276 MENENIUS: A very little thief of occasion will rob you of a great deal of patience.
Coriolanus 2.1.28

4277 IAGO: How poor are they who have not patience!
What wound did ever heal but by degrees?
Othello 2.3.370

4278 LEONATO: 'Tis all men's office to speak patience
To those that wring under the load of sorrow,
But no man's virtue nor sufficiency
To be so moral when he shall endure
The like himself.
Much Ado About Nothing 5.1.27

4279 DUCHESS: That which in mean men we entitle patience
Is pale cold cowardice in noble breasts.
Richard II 1.2.33

4280 PANDARUS: He that will have a cake out of the wheat must tarry the grinding.
Troilus and Cressida 1.1.14

4281 PRINCE: Let mischance be slave to patience.
Romeo and Juliet 5.3.221

4282 CLIFFORD: Patience is for poltroons.
3 Henry VI 1.1.62
[*poltroons:* arrant cowards]

4283 QUEEN [to Hamlet]: Upon the heat and flame of thy distemper Sprinkle cool patience.

Hamlet 3.4.123

4284 K. LEWIS [to Q. Margaret]: With patience calm the storm.

3 Henry VI 3.3.38

4285 ADRIANA: Patience unmov'd! no marvel though she pause—
They can be meek that have no other cause:
A wretched soul, bruis'd with adversity,
We bid be quiet when we hear it cry;
But were we burd'ned with like weight of pain,
As much, or more, we should ourselves complain.

Comedy of Errors 2.1.32

4286 MACBETH: Come what come may,
Time and the hour runs through the roughest day.

Macbeth 1.3.147

4287 DUKE: What cannot be preserv'd when Fortune takes,
Patience her injury a mock'ry makes.

Othello 1.3.206

4288 TYBALT: Patience perforce with willful choler meeting
Makes my flesh tremble in their different greeting.

Romeo and Juliet 1.5.89

[*different greeting:* i.e. the confrontation of these opposed states of mind]

4289 HELICANUS: Bear with patience Such griefs as you yourself do lay upon yourself.

Pericles 1.2.65

4290 TROILUS: There is between my will and all offenses
A guard of patience.

Troilus and Cressida 5.2.53

4291 FIRST SENATOR: To revenge is no valor, but to bear.

Timon of Athens 3.5.39

4292 OTHELLO: Had it pleas'd heaven
To try me with affliction, had they rain'd
All kinds of sores and shames on my bare head,
Steep'd me in poverty to the very lips,
Given to captivity me and my utmost hopes,
I should have found in some place of my soul
A drop of patience.

Othello 4.2.47

Patriotism

4293 COMINIUS: I do love
My country's good with a respect more tender,
More holy and profound, than mine own life.

Coriolanus 3.3.111

4294 BRUTUS: Who is here so vile that will not love his country?

Julius Caesar 3.2.32

4295 PUCELLE: One drop of blood drawn from thy country's bosom
Should grieve thee more than streams of foreign gore.

1 Henry VI 3.3.54

4296 VOLUMNIA: Had I a dozen sons, each in my love alike ... I had rather had eleven die nobly for their country than one voluptuously surfeit out of action.

Coriolanus 1.3.22

4297 BELARIUS: If in your country wars you chance to die,
That is my bed, too, lads, and there I'll lie.

Cymbeline 4.4.51

4298 SATURNINUS: To the love and favor of my country
Commit myself, my person, and the cause.

Titus Andronicus 1.1.58

4299 WOLSEY [to Cromwell]: Be just, and fear not:

Let all the ends thou aim'st at be thy
country's,
Thy God's, and truth's.
Henry VIII 3.2.446

Payment

4300 PORTIA: He is well paid that is
well satisfied.
Merchant of Venice 4.1.415

4301 PISTOL: Base is the slave that
pays.
Henry V 2.1.96

4302 DUKE: Haste still pays haste, and
leisure answers leisure;
Like doth quit like, and *Measure* still
for Measure.
Measure for Measure 5.1.410

4303 CAMILLO [to Archidamus]: You
pay a great deal too dear for what's
given freely.
Winter's Tale 1.1.17

Peace

4304 IMOGEN: Plenty and peace breeds
cowards; hardness ever
Or hardiness is mother.
Cymbeline 3.6.21

4305 BURGUNDY: Peace,
Dear nurse of arts, plenties, and joyful
births.
Henry V 5.2.34

4306 ARCHBISHOP OF YORK: A peace
is of the nature of a conquest,
For then both parties nobly are
subdued,
And neither party loser.
2 Henry IV 4.2.89

4307 GLOUCESTER [soliloquy]: Why, I,
in this weak piping time of peace,
Have no delight to pass away the time,
Unless to see my shadow in the sun.
Richard III 1.1.24

4308 K. HENRY: In peace there's
nothing so becomes a man
As modest stillness and humility.
Henry V 3.1.3

4309 DOLPHIN: It is most meet we
arm us 'gainst the foe;
For peace itself should not so dull a
kingdom
(Though war nor no known quarrel
were in question)
But that defenses, musters, prepara-
tions,
Should be maintain'd, assembled, and
collected,
As were a war in expectation.
Henry V 2.4.15

4310 GLOUCESTER [soliloquy, on King
Edward]: Now is the winter of our
discontent
Made glorious summer by this son of
York;
And all the clouds that low'r'd upon
our house
In the deep bosom of the ocean
buried.
Now are our brows bound with vic-
torious wreaths,
Our bruised arms hung up for monu-
ments,
Our stern alarums chang'd to merry
meetings,
Our dreadful marches to delightful
measures.
Grim-visag'd War hath smooth'd his
wrinkled front;
And now, in stead of mounting barbed
steeds
To fright the souls of fearful adver-
saries,
He capers nimbly in a lady's chamber
To the lascivious pleasing of a lute.
Richard III 1.1.1

4311 KING: Blessed are the
peacemakers on earth.
2 Henry VI 2.1.34

4312 WOLSEY: In thy right hand carry
gentle peace
To silence envious tongues.
Henry VIII 3.2.445

4313 TOUCHSTONE: I knew when seven justices could not take up a quarrel, but when the parties were met themselves, one of them thought but of an If, as, "If you said so, then I said so"; and they shook hands and swore brothers. Your If is the only peacemaker; much virtue in If.
As You Like It 5.4.98

4314 FIRST SERVANT: Let me have war, say I, it exceeds peace as far as day does night; it's spritely, waking, audible, and full of vent. Peace is a very apoplexy, lethargy, mull'd, deaf, sleepy, insensible, a getter of more bastard children than war's the destroyer of men.
SECOND SERVANT: 'Tis so . . . but peace is a great maker of cuckolds.
Coriolanus 4.5.221
[*cuckolds:* husbands of unfaithful wives]

4315 WOLSEY: I feel within me A peace above all earthly dignities, A still and quiet confidence.
Henry VIII 3.2.378

4316 CONSTANCE: Peace is to me a war.
King John 3.1.113

Perception

4317 MACBETH [soliloquy]: Mine eyes are made the fools o' th' other senses.
Macbeth 2.1.44

4318 TROILUS: My election Is led on in the conduct of my will, My will enkindled by mine eyes and ears, Two traded pilots 'twixt the dangerous shores Of will and judgment.
Troilus and Cressida 2.2.61
[*election:* choice; *traded pilots:* intermediaries constantly going back and forth]

4319 BELARIUS: To apprehend . . . Draws us a profit from all things we see.
Cymbeline 3.3.17

4320 Oft the eye mistakes, the brain being troubled.
Venus and Adonis 1068

4321 IMOGEN: Our very eyes Are sometimes like our judgments, blind.
Cymbeline 4.2.301

4322 HERMIA: Dark night, that from the eye his function takes, The ear more quick of apprehension makes; Wherein it doth impair the seeing sense, It pays the hearing double recompense.
Midsummer Night's Dream 3.2.177

Perfection

4323 ALBANY: Striving to better, oft we mar what's well.
King Lear 1.4.346

4324 SALISBURY: To gild refined gold, to paint the lily, To throw a perfume on the violet, To smooth the ice, or add another hue Unto the rainbow, or with taper-light To seek the beauteous eye of heaven to garnish, Is wasteful and ridiculous excess.
King John 4.2.11

4325 PORTIA: How many things by season season'd are To their right praise and true perfection!
Merchant of Venice 5.1.107

4326 Every thing that grows Holds in perfection but a little moment.
Sonnet 15

4327 No perfection is so absolute,
That some impurity doth not pollute.
                    Rape of Lucrece 853

4328 TROILUS: No perfection in reversion shall have a praise in the present.
                    Troilus and Cressida 3.2.92
[*perfection in reversion:* promise of future perfection]

4329 Truth needs no color with his color fix'd,
Beauty no pencil, beauty's truth to lay;
But best is best, if never intermix'd.
                    Sonnet 101

4330 PERICLES: He's no man on whom perfections wait
That, knowing sin within, will touch the gate.
                    Pericles 1.1.79

4331 PROTEUS: Were man
But constant, he were perfect.
                    Two Gentlemen of Verona 5.5.110

Perfidy

4332 GLOUCESTER [aside, kissing the young prince]:
To say the truth, so Judas kiss'd his master,
And cried "All hail!" when as he meant all harm.
                    3 Henry VI 5.7.33

Performance

4333 PAINTER: Promising is the very air o' th' time;
It opens the eyes of expectation.
Performance is ever the duller for his act.
                    Timon of Athens 5.1.22

4334 POINS: Is it not strange that desire should so many years outlive performance?
                    2 Henry IV 2.4.260

Perjury

4335 SHYLOCK: Shall I lay perjury upon my soul?
No, not for Venice.
                    Merchant of Venice 4.1.229

Perseverance

4336 MESSENGER [telling of York's death]: Many strokes, though with a little axe,
Hews down and fells the hardest-timber'd oak.
                    3 Henry VI 2.1.54

4337 ULYSSES [to Achilles]:
Perseverance, dear my lord,
Keeps honor bright; to have done is to hang
Quite out of fashion, like a rusty mail
In monumental mock'ry.
                    Troilus and Cressida 3.3.150
[*mail:* armor]

4338 ANTONIO [to Sebastian]: Do not, for one repulse forego the purpose
That you resolv'd t' effect.
                    The Tempest 3.3.12

4339 GLOUCESTER: Much rain wears the marble.
                    3 Henry VI 3.2.50

Perspective

4340 Perspective it is best painter's art.
                    Sonnet 24

4341 Through the painter must you see his skill.
                    Sonnet 24

Persuasion

4342 SECOND SENATOR: What thou wilt,
Thou rather shalt enforce it with thy smile
Than hew to't with thy sword.
                    Timon of Athens 5.4.44

4343 HERMIONE: You may ride 's
With one soft kiss a thousand furlongs
ere
With spur we heat an acre.
Winter's Tale 1.2.94
[*'s:* us; *heat:* gallop]

4344 PAULINA: The silence often of
pure innocence
Persuades when speaking fails.
Winter's Tale 2.2.39

4345 Beauty itself doth of itself
persuade
The eyes of men without an orator.
Rape of Lucrece 29

4346 VALENTINE [to Duke, on court-
ship]: Win her with gifts, if she
respect not words:
Dumb jewels often in their silent kind
More than quick words do move a
woman's mind.
Two Gentlemen of Verona 3.1.89

Philosophy

4347 LAFEW: They say miracles are
past, and we have our philosophical
persons, to make modern and familiar,
things supernatural and causeless.
Hence is it that we make trifles of terrors, ensconcing ourselves into seeming
knowledge, when we should submit
ourselves to an unknown fear.
All's Well That Ends Well 2.3.1
[*terrors:* i.e. occurrences that should inspire
awe]

4348 FIRST LORD: The web of our life
is of a mingled yarn, good and ill
together: our virtues would be proud,
if our faults whipt them not, and our
crimes would despair, if they were not
cherish'd by our virtues.
All's Well That Ends Well 4.3.71

4349 CASSIUS [to Brutus]: Of your
philosophy you make no use,
If you give place to accidental evils.
Julius Caesar 4.3.145

4350 LEONATO: There was never yet
philosopher
That could endure the toothache patiently,
However they have writ the style of
gods,
And made a push at chance and sufferance.
Much Ado About Nothing 5.1.35

4351 TOUCHSTONE: Hast any
philosophy in thee, shepherd?
CORIN: No more but that I know the
more one sickens the worse at ease he
is; and that he that wants money,
means, and content is without three
good friends; that the property of rain
is to wet and fire to burn; that good
pasture makes fat sheep; and that a
great cause of the night is lack of the
sun; that he that hath learn'd no wit
by nature, nor art, may complain of
good breeding, or comes of a very dull
kindred.
As You Like It 3.2.21

4352 CORIN: I am a true laborer: I
earn that I eat, get that I wear, owe no
man hate, envy no man's happiness,
glad of other men's good, content with
my harm, and the greatest of my pride
is to see my ewes graze and my lambs
suck.
As You Like It 3.2.73

4353 HAMLET: There are more things
in heaven and earth, Horatio,
Than are dreamt of in your philosophy.
Hamlet 1.5.166

4354 FRIAR LAWRENCE: Adversity's
sweet milk, philosophy.
Romeo and Juliet 3.3.55

Physic

4355 MACBETH: The labor we delight
in physics pain.
Macbeth 2.3.50

4356 IMOGEN: Some griefs are med'-cinable.
Cymbeline 3.2.33

4357 NORTHUMBERLAND: In poison there is physic.
2 Henry IV 1.1.137

4358 ISABELLA: 'Tis a physic
That's bitter to sweet end.
Measure for Measure 4.6.7

4359 MACBETH [to doctor, on Lady Macbeth]: Canst thou not minister to a mind diseas'd,
Pluck from the memory a rooted sorrow,
Raze out the written troubles of the brain,
And with some sweet oblivious antidote
Cleanse the stuff'd bosom of that perilous stuff
Which weighs upon the heart?
DOCTOR: Therein the patient
Must minister to himself.
MACBETH: Throw physic to the dogs, I'll none of it.
Macbeth 5.3.40

Physician

4360 TIMON: Trust not the physician,
His antidotes are poison, and he slays
Moe than you rob.
Timon of Athens 4.3.431
[*moe:* more]

4361 The patient dies while the physician sleeps.
Rape of Lucrece 904

Piety

4362 K. HENRY: Other devils that suggest by treasons
Do botch and bungle up damnation
With patches, colors, and with forms being fetch'd
From glist'ring semblances of piety.
Henry V 2.2.114

Pilgrim

4363 JULIA: A true-devoted pilgrim is not weary
To measure kingdoms with his feeble steps.
Two Gentlemen of Verona 2.7.9

Pitch

4364 DOGBERRY: They that touch pitch will be defil'd.
Much Ado About Nothing 3.3.57

Pity

4365 ALCIBIADES: Pity is the virtue of the law,
And none but tyrants use it cruelly.
Timon of Athens 3.5.8

4366 ANNE: No beast so fierce but knows some touch of pity.
Richard III 1.2.71

4367 Root pity in thy heart, that when it grows,
Thy pity may deserve to pitied be.
Sonnet 142

4368 Soft pity enters at an iron gate.
Rape of Lucrece 595

4369 BRUTUS: As fire drives out fire, so pity pity.
Julius Caesar 3.1.171

4370 VIOLA: I pity you.
OLIVIA: That's a degree to love.
Twelfth Night 3.1.123
[*degree:* step, grize]

4371 ORLANDO [to Duke Senior]: If ever you have look'd on better days,
If ever been where bells have knoll'd to church,
If ever sate at any good man's feast,
If ever from your eyelids wip'd a tear,
And know what 'tis to pity, and be pitied,

Let gentleness my strong enforcement
be.
As You Like It 2.7.113

[*sate:* sat]

4372 MARCUS: O heavens, can you
hear a good man groan
And not relent, or not compassion
him?
Titus Andronicus 4.1.123

4373 FIRST STRANGER: Men must learn
now with pity to dispense,
For policy sits above conscience.
Timon of Athens 3.2.86

Place

4374 DUKE [soliloquy]: O place and
greatness! millions of false eyes
Are stuck upon thee. Volumes of re-
port
Run with these false, and most con-
trarious quests
Upon thy doings; thousand escapes of
wit
Make thee the father of their idle
dream,
And rack thee in their fancies.
Measure for Measure 4.1.59

4375 ANGELO [soliloquy]: O place, O
form,
How often doth thou with thy case,
thy habit,
Wrench awe from fools, and tie the
wiser souls
To thy false seeming!
Measure for Measure 2.4.12

4376 PAROLLES: There's place and
means for every man alive.
All's Well That Ends Well 4.3.339

4377 WINCHESTER: Each hath his place
and function to attend.
1 Henry VI 1.1.173

Planets

4378 EDMUND [soliloquy]: When we
are sick in fortune—often the surfeits

of our own behavior—we make guilty
of our disasters the sun, the moon, and
stars, as if we were villains on necessity,
fools by heavenly compulsion, knaves,
thieves, and treachers by spherical predominance; drunkards, liars, and adulterers by an enforc'd obedience of
planetary influence; and all that we are
evil in, by a divine thrusting on.
King Lear 1.2.119

Planning

4379 LORD BARDOLPH: When we
mean to build,
We first survey the plot, then draw the
model,
And when we see the figure of the
house,
Then must we rate the cost of the
erection,
Which if we find outweighs ability,
What do we do then but draw anew
the model
In fewer offices, or at least desist
To build at all?
2 Henry IV 1.3.41

Play

4380 ROSALIND: If it be true that good
wine needs no bush, 'tis true that a
good play needs no epilogue. Yet to
good wine they do use good bushes;
and good plays prove the better by the
help of good epilogues.
As You Like It, Epilogue 3

4381 PRINCE: If all the year were playing holidays,
To sport would be as tedious as to
work.
1 Henry IV 1.2.204

4382 PROLOGUE: New plays and
maidenheads are near akin.
Two Noble Kinsmen, Prologue 1

4383 PRINCE: Thus we play the fools
with the time, and the spirits of the
wise sit in the clouds and mock us.
2 Henry IV 2.2.142

Pleasure

4384 LUCENTIO: No profit grows where is no pleasure ta'en.
Taming of the Shrew 1.1.39

4385 BEROWNE: All delights are vain, but that most vain
Which, with pain purchas'd, doth inherit pain.
Love's Labor's Lost 1.1.72

4386 IAGO: Pleasure and action make the hours seem short.
Othello 2.3.379

4387 All love's pleasure shall not match his woe.
Venus and Adonis 1140

4388 ANTONY: The present pleasure,
By revolution low'ring, does become
The opposite of itself.
Antony and Cleopatra 1.2.124

4389 FRIAR LAWRENCE: Violent delights have violent ends,
And in their triumph die, like fire and powder,
Which as they kiss consume.
Romeo and Juliet 2.6.9

4390 HECTOR: Pleasure and revenge
Have ears more deaf than adders to the voice
Of any true decision.
Troilus and Cressida 2.2.171

4391 Some glory in their birth, some in their skill,
Some in their wealth, some in their body's force,
Some in their garments, though newfangled ill,
Some in their hawks and hounds, some in their horse;
And every humor hath his adjunct pleasure,
Wherein it finds a joy above the rest.
Sonnet 91

4392 Why should the private pleasure of some one
Become the public plague of many moe?
Rape of Lucrece 1478
[*moe:* more]

4393 IMOGEN: Flow'rs are like the pleasures of the world.
Cymbeline 4.2.296

4394 BULLINGBROOK: I regreet
The daintiest last, to make the end most sweet.
Richard II 1.3.68
[*regreet:* greet, salute]

Plenty

4395 IMOGEN: Plenty and peace breeds cowards; hardness ever
Of hardiness is mother.
Cymbeline 3.6.21

4396 IMOGEN: To lapse in fullness
Is sorer than to lie for need.
Cymbeline 3.6.12

Poet

4397 THESEUS: The lunatic, the lover, and the poet
Are of imagination all compact.
Midsummer Night's Dream 5.1.7

4398 BEROWNE: Never durst poet touch a pen to write
Until his ink were temp'red with Love's sighs.
Love's Labor's Lost 4.3.343

4399 THESEUS: The poet's eye, in a fine frenzy rolling,
Doth glance from heaven to earth, from earth to heaven;
And as imagination bodies forth
The forms of things unknown, the poet's pen
Turns them to shapes, and gives to aery nothing
A local habitation and a name.
Midsummer Night's Dream 5.1.12

4400 HOTSPUR: I had rather be a kitten and cry mew
Than one of these same metre ballatmongers.
I had rather hear a brazen canstick turn'd,
Or a dry wheel grate on the axle-tree,
And that would set my teeth on edge,
Nothing so much as mincing poetry.
'Tis like the forc'd gait of a shuffling nag.
1 Henry IV 3.1.127
[*ballet:* ballad]

4401 TOUCHSTONE: When a man's verses cannot be understood, nor a man's good wit seconded with the forward child, understanding, it strikes a man more dead than a great reckoning in a little room.
As You Like It 3.3.12

4402 Who will believe my verse in time to come
If it were fill'd with your most high deserts?
Though yet heaven knows it is but as a tomb
Which hides your life, and shows not half your parts.
If I could write the beauty of your eyes,
And in fresh numbers number all your graces,
The age to come would say, "This poet lies,
Such heavenly touches ne'er touch'd earthly faces."
Sonnet 17

4403 CINNA: I am Cinna the poet, I am Cinna the poet.
PLEBEIAN: Tear him for his bad verses, tear him for his bad verses.
Julius Caesar 3.3.29
[Cinna the poet is mistaken by the mob for Cinna the conspirator and is killed.]

Poetry

4404 TOUCHSTONE: The truest poetry is the most feigning, and lovers are

given to poetry; and what they swear in poetry may be said as lovers they do feign.
As You Like It 3.3.19

4405 POET: Our poesy is as a gum, which oozes
From whence 'tis nourish'd. The fire i' th' flint
Shows not till it be strook; our gentle flame
Provokes itself and like the current flies
Each bound it chases.
Timon of Athens 1.1.21
[*strook:* struck]

4406 DUKE: Much is the force of heaven-bred poesy.
Two Gentlemen of Verona 3.2.71

4407 Not marble nor the gilded monuments
Of princes shall outlive this pow'rful rhyme,
But you shall shine more bright in these contents
Than unswept stone, besmear'd with sluttish time.
When wasteful war shall statues overturn
And broils root out the work of masonry,
Nor Mars his sword nor war's quick fire shall burn
The living record of your memory.
'Gainst death and all-oblivious enmity
Shall you pace forth; your praise shall still find room,
Even in the eyes of all posterity
That wear this world out to the ending doom.
Sonnet 55

4408 HOLOFERNES: The elegancy, facility, and golden cadence of poesy.
Love's Labor's Lost 4.2.121

Poison

4409 NORTHUMBERLAND: In poison there is physic.
2 Henry IV 1.1.137

4410 BULLINGBROOK: They love not poison that do poison need.
Richard II 5.6.38

Policy

4411 VOLUMNIA: Honor and policy, like unsever'd friends,
I' th' war do grow together.
Coriolanus 3.2.42

4412 FIRST STRANGER: Men must learn now with pity to dispense,
For policy sits above conscience.
Timon of Athens 3.2.86

4413 LADY MACBETH [to Macbeth]: To beguile the time,
Look like the time; bear welcome in your eye,
Your hand, your tongue; look like th' innocent flower,
But be the serpent under't.
Macbeth 1.5.63

Politician

4414 LEAR [to Gloucester]: Get thee glass eyes,
And like a scurvy politician, seem
To see the things thou dost not.
King Lear 4.6.170

4415 MORTIMER [to Plantagenet]: With silence, nephew, be thou politic.
1 Henry VI 2.5.101

4416 HAMLET: A politician ... one that would circumvent God.
Hamlet 5.1.78

Politics

4417 SERVANT: The devil knew not what he did when he made man politic; he cross'd himself by't.
Timon of Athens 3.3.29

4418 ARCHBISHOP: An habitation giddy and unsure

Hath he that buildest on the vulgar heart.
2 Henry IV 1.3.89
[*vulgar:* plebeian]

4419 ARRAGON: O that estates, degrees, and offices
Were not deriv'd corruptly, and that clear honor
Were purchas'd by the merit of the wearer!
Merchant of Venice 2.9.41

4420 YORK [soliloquy, on his plot to depose Henry]:
Watch thou, and wake when others be asleep,
To pry into the secrets of the state.
2 Henry VI 1.1.249

4421 MARCELLUS: Something is rotten in the state of Denmark.
Hamlet 1.4.90

4422 KING [soliloquy]: Oft 'tis seen the wicked prize itself
Buys out the law, but 'tis not so above.
Hamlet 3.3.59
[*wicked prize:* ill-gotten gains]

Pollution

4423 VIOLA: Nature with a beauteous wall
Doth oft close in pollution.
Twelfth Night 1.2.48

Pomp

4424 K. RICHARD: Within the hollow crown
That rounds the mortal temples of a king,
Keeps Death his court, and there the antic sits,
Scoffing his state and grinning at his pomp.
Richard II 3.2.160

4425 WARWICK [soliloquy]: What is pomp, rule, reign, but earth and dust?

And live we how we can, yet die we
must.

3 Henry VI 5.2.27

4426 DUKE SENIOR [to his companions
in exile]: Hath not old custom made
this life more sweet
Than that of painted pomp?

As You Like It 2.1.2

4427 CLOWN: I am for the house with
the narrow gate, which I take to be too
little for pomp to enter.

All's Well That Ends Well 4.5.50

4428 BELARIUS: The gates of monarchs
Are arch'd so high that giants may jet
through
And keep their impious turbands on.

Cymbeline 3.3.4

[*jet:* strut]

4429 LEAR: Take physic, pomp,
Expose thyself to feel what wretches
feel,
That thou mayst shake the superflux to
them,
And show the heavens more just.

King Lear 3.4.33

4430 HAMLET: Let the candied tongue
lick absurd pomp.

Hamlet 3.2.60

[*candied:* flattering]

4431 CLEOPATRA: O, behold,
How pomp is followed!

Antony and Cleopatra 5.2.150

4432 APEMANTUS: Willing misery
Outlives incertain pomp.

Timon of Athens 4.3.242

Pomposity

4433 AJAX: I do hate a proud man, as
I hate the engend'ring of toads.

Troilus and Cressida 2.3.158

Populace

4434 SECOND OFFICER: There have
been many great men that have flatter'd the people, who ne'er lov'd them;
and there may be many that they have
lov'd, they know not wherefore; so
that, if they love they know not why,
they hate upon no better ground.

Coriolanus 2.2.7

4435 THIRD CITIZEN: Ingratitude is
monstrous, and for the multitude to be
ingrateful were to make a monster of
the multitude.

Coriolanus 2.3.9

4436 CORIOLANUS: The mutable,
rank-scented meiny.

Coriolanus 3.1.66

[*meiny:* common herd, multitude]

Port

4437 GAUNT: All places that the eye
of heaven visits
Are to the wise man ports and happy
havens.

Richard II 1.3.275

Portent

4438 CLARENCE: Every cloud
engenders not a storm.

3 Henry VI 5.3.13

Possession

4439 FRIAR: That what we have we
prize not to the worth
Whiles we enjoy it, but being lack'd
and lost,
Why then we rack the value; then we
find
The virtue that possession would not
show us
Whiles it was ours.

Much Ado About Nothing 4.1.218

4440 BASTARD: Have is have, however men do catch.
King John 1.1.173

4441 The sweets we wish for turn to loathed sours
Even in the moment that we call them ours.
Rape of Lucrece 867

4442 CRESSIDA: Women are angels, wooing:
Things won are done, joy's soul lies in the doing.
Troilus and Cressida 1.2.286

Posterity

4443 From fairest creatures we desire increase,
That thereby beauty's rose might never die.
Sonnet 1

4444 By law of nature thou art bound to breed,
That thine may live, when thou thyself art dead;
And so in spite of death thou dost survive,
In that thy likeness still is left alive.
Venus and Adonis 171

4445 When forty winters shall besiege thy brow,
And dig deep trenches in thy beauty's field,
Thy youth's proud livery, so gaz'd on now,
Will be a totter'd weed of small worth held:
Then being ask'd, where all thy beauty lies,
Where all the treasure of thy lusty days,
To say within thine own deep-sunken eyes
Were an all-eating shame, and thriftless praise.
How much more praise deserv'd thy beauty's use,

If thou couldst answer, "This fair child of mine
Shall sum my count, and make my old excuse,"
Proving his beauty by succession thine.
Sonnet 2
[*totter'd weed:* tattered garment]

4446 BENVOLIO [about Juliet]: Then she hath sworn that she will still live chaste?
ROMEO: She hath, and in that sparing makes huge waste;
For beauty starv'd with her severity
Cuts beauty off from all posterity.
Romeo and Juliet 1.1.217

Poverty

4447 FOOL: Fortune, that arrant whore,
Ne'er turns the key to th' poor.
King Lear 2.4.52

4448 FALSTAFF: I can get no remedy against this consumption of the purse; borrowing only lingers and lingers it out, but the disease is incurable.
2 Henry IV 1.2.234

4449 CORIN: He that wants money, means, and content is without three good friends.
As You Like It 3.2.24

4450 CARDINAL: Clergy's bags
Are lank and lean.
2 Henry VI 1.3.128

4451 IAGO: Poor and content is rich, and rich enough,
But riches fineless is as poor as winter
To him that ever fears he shall be poor.
Othello 3.3.172
[*fineless:* boundless]

4452 POSTHUMUS [soliloquy]: Poor wretches that depend
On greatness' favor dream as I have done,
Wake, and find nothing.
Cymbeline 5.4.127

4453 DUKE [to the condemned Claudio]: If thou art rich, thou'rt poor,
For like an ass, whose back with ingots bows,
Thou bear'st thy heavy riches but a journey,
And death unloads thee.
Measure for Measure 3.1.25

4454 ANTONIO: It is still her [Fortune's] use
To let the wretched man outlive his weath,
To view with hollow eye and wrinkled brow
An age of poverty.
Merchant of Venice 4.1.268

4455 SECOND VARRO SERVANT: Who can speak broader than he that has no house to put his head in? Such may rail against great buildings.
Timon of Athens 3.4.63

4456 BASTARD [soliloquy]: Well, whiles I am a beggar, I will rail,
And say there is no sin but to be rich;
And being rich, my virtue then shall be
To say there is no vice but beggary.
King John 2.1.593

4457 K. HENRY: I may conquer fortune's spite
By living low, where fortune cannot hurt me.
3 Henry VI 4.6.19

4458 LEAR: Through tatter'd clothes small vices do appear;
Robes and furr'd gowns hide all.
King Lear 4.6.164

4459 CLOWN [to Countess]: 'Tis not so well that I am poor, though many of the rich are damn'd.
All's Well That Ends Well 1.3.17

4460 LEAR: Poor naked wretches, whereso'er you are,
That bide the pelting of this pitiless storm.

How shall your houseless heads and unfed sides,
Your loop'd and window'd raggedness, defend you
From seasons such as these? O, I have ta'en
Too little care of this! Take physic, pomp,
Expose thyself to feel what wretches feel,
That thou mayst shake the superflux to them,
And show the heavens more just.
King Lear 3.4.28

4461 QUEEN [about Eleanor]: She bears a duke's revenues on her back,
And in her heart she scorns our poverty.
2 Henry VI 1.3.80

4462 HAMLET: Why should the poor be flatter'd?
Hamlet 3.2.59

4463 OLIVIA: O world, how apt the poor are to be proud!
Twelfth Night 3.1.127

4464 FIRST CITIZEN: They say poor suitors have strong breaths.
Coriolanus 1.1.59

4465 APOTHECARY [selling poison to Romeo]: My poverty, but not my will, consents.
Romeo and Juliet 5.1.75

Power

4466 K. RICHARD: They well deserve to have
That know the strong'st and surest way to get.
Richard II 3.3.200

4467 AUFIDIUS: Power, unto itself most commendable,
Hath not a tomb so evident as a chair
T' extol what it hath done.
Coriolanus 4.7.51

4468 ISABELLA: O, it is excellent
To have a giant's strength; but it is
tyrannous
To use it like a giant.
Measure for Measure 2.2.107

4469 ANTONY: When Caesar says,
"Do this," it is perform'd.
Julius Caesar 1.2.10

4470 ANTONY: The hated, grown to
strength,
Are newly grown to love.
Antony and Cleopatra 1.3.48

4471 HAMLET: The power of beauty
will sooner transform honesty from
what it is to a bawd than the force of
honesty can translate beauty into his
likeness.
Hamlet 3.1.110

4472 TAMORA: The eagle suffers little
birds to sing.
Titus Andronicus 4.4.83

4473 CARLISLE [to Richard]: Fear not,
my lord, that Power that made you
king
Hath power to keep you king in spite
of all.
The means that heavens yield must be
embrac'd,
And not neglected; else heaven would,
And we will not. Heaven's offer we
refuse,
The proffered means of succor and
redress.
Richard II 3.2.27

Praise

4474 Who is it that says most, which
can say more
Than this rich praise, that you alone
are you...?
Sonnet 84

4475 HERMIONE: Our praises are our
wages.
Winter's Tale 1.2.94

4476 VALENTINE: Love delights in
praises.
Two Gentlemen of Verona 2.4.148

4477 ULYSSES: The present eye praises
the present object.
Troilus and Cressida 3.3.180

4478 PRINCESS: A giving hand, though
foul, shall have fair praise.
Love's Labor's Lost 4.1.23

4479 POET: When we for recompense
have prais'd the vild,
It stains the glory in that happy verse
Which aptly sings the good.
Timon of Athens 1.1.15
[*vild:* vile]

4480 KING: Praising what is lost
Makes the remembrance dear.
All's Well That Ends Well 5.3.19

4481 BEATRICE: There's not one wise
man among twenty that will praise
himself.
Much Ado About Nothing 5.2.73

4482 AENEAS: The worthiness of praise
distains his worth,
If that the prais'd himself bring the
praise forth.
Troilus and Cressida 1.3.241
[*distains:* taints]

4483 You to your beauteous blessings
add a curse,
Being fond on praise, which makes
your praises worse.
Sonnet 84

4484 ANTONY [in The Forum]:
Friends, Romans, countrymen, lend
me your ears!
I come to bury Caesar, not to praise
him.
The evil that men do lives after them,
The good is oft interred with their
bones;
So let it be with Caesar. The noble
Brutus
Hath told you Caesar was ambitious;
If it were so, it was a grievous fault,
And grievously hath Caesar answer'd it.

Here, under leave of Brutus and the
rest
(For Brutus is an honorable man,
So are they all, all honorable men),
Come I to speak in Caesar's funeral.
He was my friend, faithful and just to
me;
But Brutus says he was ambitious,
And Brutus is an honorable man.
He hath brought many captives home
to Rome,
Whose ransoms did the general coffers
fill;
Did this in Caesar seem ambitious?
When that the poor have cried, Caesar
hath wept;
Ambition should be made of sterner
stuff:
Yet Brutus says he was ambitious,
And Brutus is an honorable man.
You all did see that on the Lupercal
I thrice presented him a kingly crown,
Which he did thrice refuse. Was this
ambition?
Yet Brutus says he was ambitious,
And sure he is an honorable man.
I speak not to disprove what Brutus
spoke,
But here I am to speak what I do
know.
You all did love him once, not without
cause;
What cause withholds you then to
mourn for him?
O judgment! thou art fled to brutish
beasts,
And men have lost their reason. Bear
with me,
My heart is in the coffin there with
Caesar,
And I must pause till it come back to
me.
> *Julius Caesar* 3.2.73

4485 TROILUS: No perfection in reversion shall have a praise in present.
> *Troilus and Cressida* 3.2.92

[*perfection in reversion:* promise of future
perfection]

4486 LAUNCE: Good things should be
prais'd.
> *Two Gentlemen of Verona* 3.1.347

4487 HERMIONE: One good deed dying tongueless
Slaughters a thousand waiting upon
that.
> *Winter's Tale* 1.2.92

4488 DESDEMONA: O heavy ignorance!
thou praisest the worst best.
> *Othello* 2.1.143

4489 PORTIA: The nightingale, if she
should sing by day
When every goose is cackling, would
be thought
No better a musician than the wren.
How many things by season season'd
are
To their right praise and true perfection!
> *Merchant of Venice* 5.1.104

4490 BEROWNE: To things of sale a
seller's praise belongs.
> *Love's Labor's Lost* 4.3.236

4491 TIMON: No man
Can justly praise but what he does
affect.
> *Timon of Athens* 1.2.214

4492 What can mine own praise to my
own self bring?
> *Sonnet 39*

4493 LUCIUS: When no friends are by,
men praise themselves.
> *Titus Andronicus* 5.3.118

4494 HERMIONE: You may ride 's
With one soft kiss a thousand furlongs
ere
With spur we heat an acre.
> *Winter's Tale* 1.2.94

[*'s:* us; *heat:* gallop]

4495 ENOBARBUS: I will praise any
man that will praise me.
> *Antony and Cleopatra* 2.6.88

4496 LAFEW [concerning Helena]:
Your commendations, madam, get
from her tears.

COUNTESS: 'Tis the best brine a
maiden can season her praise in.
          All's Well That Ends Well 1.1.46

Prayer

4497 ANGELO: I am that way going to
temptation,
Where prayers cross.
          Measure for Measure 2.2.157

4498 IMOGEN: Lovers
And men in dangerous bonds pray not
alike.
          Cymbeline 3.2.36

4499 MENECRATES: We, ignorant of
ourselves,
Beg often our own harm, which the
wise pow'rs
Deny us for our good; so find we profit
By losing of our prayers.
          Antony and Cleopatra 2.1.5

4500 KING: Let never day nor night
unhallowed pass,
But still remember what the Lord hath
done.
          2 Henry VI 2.1.83

4501 DUCHESS: O happy vantage of a
kneeling knee!
          Richard II 5.3.132

4502 KING [rising from prayer]: My
words fly up, my thoughts remain
below:
Words without thoughts never to
heaven go.
          Hamlet 3.3.97

4503 ISABELLA: True prayers . . .
Shall be up at heaven, and enter there
Ere sun-rise, prayers from preserved
souls,
From fasting maids, whose minds are
dedicate
To nothing temporal.
          Measure for Measure 2.2.151

4504 HAMLET [to Ophelia]: Nymph,
in thy orisons
Be all my sins rememb'red.
          Hamlet 3.1.88

4505 JULIET [to her nurse]: I pray thee
leave me to myself to-night,
For I have need of many orisons
To move the heavens to smile upon my
state,
Which, well thou knowest, is cross and
full of sin.
          Romeo and Juliet 4.3.2

4506 SOLANIO: Let me say amen
betimes, lest the devil cross my prayer.
          Merchant of Venice 3.1.20

4507 KATHERINE: I am past all comforts here but prayers.
          Henry VIII 4.2.123

4508 SUFFOLK: Rather let my head
Stoop to the block than these knees
bow to any
Save to the God of heaven and to my
king.
          2 Henry VI 4.1.124

4509 RIVERS: A virtuous and Christian-
like conclusion—
To pray for them that have done scathe
to us.
          Richard III 1.3.315

Preacher

4510 PORTIA: It is a good divine that
follows his own instructions; I can
easier teach twenty what were good to
be done, than to be one of the twenty
to follow mine own teaching.
          Merchant of Venice 1.2.14

4511 OPHELIA: Do not, as some
ungracious pastors do,
Show me the steep and thorny way to
heaven,
Whiles, like a puff'd and reckless libertine,

Himself the primrose path of dalliance
treads,
And reaks not his own rede.
Hamlet 1.3.47
[*reaks:* recks, heeds; *rede:* advice]

4512 DUKE [soliloquy]: He who the
sword of heaven will bear
Should be as holy as severe.
Measure for Measure 3.2.261

4513 LANCASTER [to the Archbishop]:
Your flock, assembled by the bell,
Encircled you to hear with reverence
Your exposition on the holy text.
2 Henry IV 4.2.5

Precaution

4514 Danger deviseth shifts, wit waits
on fear.
Venus and Adonis 690

4515 LAERTES: Best safety lies in fear.
Hamlet 1.3.43

4516 THIRD CITIZEN: When clouds are
seen, wise men put on their cloaks.
Richard III 2.3.32

4517 CLARENCE: A little fire is quickly
trodden out,
Which being suffer'd, rivers cannot
quench.
3 Henry VI 4.8.7

4518 Who sees the lurking serpent
steps aside.
Rape of Lucrece 362

4519 DOLPHIN: In cases of defense 'tis
best to weigh
The enemy more mighty than he
seems.
Henry V 2.4.43

4520 ARIEL [singing]: If of life you
keep a care,
Shake off slumber, and beware.
Awake, awake!
The Tempest 2.1.303

Precocity

4521 GLOUCESTER [aside, about Prince
Edward]: So wise so young, they say
do never live long.
Richard III 3.1.79

4522 YORK: Small herbs have grace,
great weeds do grow apace.
Richard III 2.4.13

Predicament

4523 TITUS: Now I stand as one upon
a rock,
Environ'd with a wilderness of sea,
Who marks the waxing tide grow wave
by wave,
Expecting ever when some envious
surge
Will in his brinish bowels swallow him.
Titus Andronicus 3.1.93

Preeminence

4524 Gnats are unnoted wheresoe'er
they fly,
But eagles gaz'd upon with every eye.
Rape of Lucrece 1014

Preferment

4525 CLOTEN: Be but duteous, and
true preferment shall tender itself to
thee.
Cymbeline 3.5.153

4526 IAGO: 'Tis the curse of service;
Preferment goes by letter and affection,
And not by the old gradation, where
each second
Stood heir to th' first.
Othello 1.1.35
[*old gradation:* seniority]

Premonition

4527 QUEEN: Some unborn sorrow,
ripe in fortune's womb,

Is coming towards me, and my inward
soul
With nothing trembles; at something
it grieves,
More than with parting from my lord
the King.
BUSHY: Each substance of a grief hath
twenty shadows,
Which shows like grief itself, but are
not so.
Richard II 2.2.10

Preparation

4528 ANTONY: The spirit of a youth
That means to be of note, begins
betimes.
Antony and Cleopatra 4.4.26

4529 LORD BARDOLPH: When we
mean to build,
We first survey the plot, then draw the
model,
And when we see the figure of the
house,
Then must we rate the cost of the
erection,
Which if we find outweighs ability,
What do we then but draw anew the
model
In fewer offices, or at least desist
To build at all?
2 Henry IV 1.3.41

4530 DOLPHIN: It is most meet we
arm us 'gainst the foe;
For peace itself should not so dull a
kingdom,
(Though war nor no known quarrel
were in question)
But that defenses, musters, prepara-
tions,
Should be maintain'd, assembled, and
collected,
As were a war in expectation.
Henry V 2.4.15

Present

4531 ARCHBISHOP: Past and to come
seems best; things present worse.
2 Henry IV 1.3.108

4532 PAULINA: Every present time
doth boast itself
Above a better gone.
Winter's Tale 5.1.96

4533 ULYSSES: The present eye praises
the present object.
Troilus and Cressida 3.3.180

4534 Every present sorrow seemeth
chief.
Venus and Adonis 970

Presumption

4535 HELENA: It is not so with Him
that all things knows
As 'tis with us that square our guess by
shows;
But most it is presumption in us when
The help of heaven we count the act of
men.
All's Well That Ends Well 2.1.149

4536 HELICANUS: How dares the
plants look up to heaven, from
whence
They have their nourishment?
Pericles 1.2.55

4537 K. HENRY: The man that once
did sell the lion's skin
While the beast liv'd, was kill'd with
hunting him.
Henry V 4.3.93

Pretension

4538 TIMON: There is boundless theft
In limited professions.
Timon of Athens 4.3.427
[*limited:* officially regulated]

4539 CLEON: Who makes the fairest
show means most deceit.
Pericles 1.4.75

4540 K. LEAR [to Gloucester]: Get
thee glass eyes,
And like a scurvy politician, seem
To see the things thou dost not.
King Lear 4.6.170

4541 OLIVIA: 'Twas never merry world
Since lowly feigning was call'd compliment.
Twelfth Night 3.1.98
[*lowly feigning:* pretending humility]

4542 FOOL: That sir which serves and
seeks for gain,
And follows but for form,
Will pack when it begins to rain,
And leave thee in the storm.
King Lear 2.4.78

4543 VALENTINE: A woman sometimes
scorns what best contents her.
Two Gentlemen of Verona 3.1.93

4544 CAESAR: The ostentation of our
love, which, left unshown,
Is often left unlov'd.
Antony and Cleopatra 3.6.52

4545 FIRST GENTLEMAN: Not a courtier,
Although they wear their faces to the
bent
Of the King's looks, hath a heart that
is not
Glad at the thing they scowl at.
Cymbeline 1.1.12

Price

4546 Pain pays the income of each
precious thing.
Rape of Lucrece 334

Pride

4547 AGAMEMNON: He that is proud
eats up himself. Pride is his own glass,
his own trumpet, his own chronicle,
and whatever praises itself but in the
deed, devours the deed in the praise.
Troilus and Cressida 2.3.154

4548 AJAX: I do hate a proud man, as
I hate the engend'ring of toads.
Troilus and Cressida 2.3.158

4549 SALISBURY: Pride went before,
ambition follows him.
2 Henry VI 1.1.180

4550 SUFFOLK: Small things make
base men proud.
2 Henry VI 4.1.106

4551 OLIVIA: O world, how apt the
poor are to be proud!
Twelfth Night 3.1.127

4552 K. RICHARD: Pride must have a
fall, and break the neck
Of that proud man that did usurp his
back.
Richard II 5.5.88

4553 ULYSSES: Pride hath no other
glass
To show itself but pride; for supple
knees
Feed arrogance and are the proud
man's fees.
Troilus and Cressida 3.3.47

4554 JAQUES: Who cries out on pride
That can therein tax any private party?
Doth it not flow as hugely as the
sea...?
As You Like It 2.7.70

4555 SICINIUS [about Martius]: Such a
nature,
Tickled with good success, disdains the
shadow
Which he treads on at noon.
Coriolanus 1.1.259

4556 IAGO: 'Tis pride that pulls the
country down.
Othello 2.3.95

4557 YORK: 'Tis beauty that doth oft
make women proud.
3 Henry VI 1.4.128

4558 CONSTANCE: I will instruct my
sorrows to be proud,
For grief is proud and makes his owner
stoop.
King John 3.1.68

4559 EDGAR: Set not thy sweet heart on proud array.
                              King Lear 3.4.82

4560 WOLSEY [soliloquy]: I have ventur'd,
Like little wanton boys that swim on bladders,
This many summers in a sea of glory,
But far beyond my depth. My high-blown pride
At length broke under me, and now has left me,
Weary and old with service, to the mercy
Of a rude stream that must forever hide me.
Vain pomp and glory of this world, I hate ye!
                              Henry VIII 3.2.358

4561 ROSALIND: My pride fell with my fortunes.
                              As You Like It 1.2.252

4562 ISABELLA: Man, proud man,
Dress'd in a little brief authority,
Most ignorant of what he's most assur'd
(His glassy essence), like an angry ape
Plays such fantastic tricks before high heaven
As make the angels weep.
                              Measure for Measure 2.2.117
[*glassy:* fragile, highly susceptible of damage]

4563 The colt that's back'd and burthen'd being young,
Loseth his pride, and never waxeth strong.
                              Venus and Adonis 419
[*burthen'd:* burdened]

4564 KING: That title of respect
Which the proud soul ne'er pays but to the proud.
                              1 Henry IV 1.3.8

4565 BELARIUS: O, this life
Is nobler than attending for a check;
Richer than doing nothing for a bable;

Prouder than rustling in unpaid-for silk.
                              Cymbeline 3.3.21
[*bable:* bribe]

4566 PRINCESS: All pride is willing pride.
                              Love's Labor's Lost 2.1.36

4567 CLEOPATRA: O, behold,
How pomp is followed!
                              Antony and Cleopatra 5.2.151

Prince

4568 Princes are the glass, the school, the book,
Where subjects' eyes do learn, do read, do look.
                              Rape of Lucrece 615
[*glass:* mirror]

4569 WOLSEY: The hearts of princes kiss obedience,
So much they love it; but to stubborn spirits,
They swell and grow, as terrible as storms.
                              Henry VIII 3.1.162

4570 WOLSEY [soliloquy]: O how wretched
Is that poor man that hangs on princes' favors!
There is, betwixt that smile we would aspire to,
That sweet aspect of princes, and their ruin,
More pangs and fears than wars or women have.
                              Henry VIII 3.2.366

4571 BRAKENBURY: Princes have but their titles for their glories,
An outward honor for an inward toil,
And for unfelt imaginations
They often feel a world of restless cares;
So that betwixt their titles and low name
There's nothing differs but the outward fame.
                              Richard III 1.4.78

4572 CALPHURNIA: When beggars die
there are no comets seen;
The heavens themselves blaze forth the
death of princes.
Julius Caesar 2.2.30

4573 FALSTAFF [about Prince Hal]:
The true prince may (for recreation
sake) prove a false thief.
1 Henry IV 1.2.154

4574 SIMONIDES: Princes are
A model which heaven makes like to
itself.
As jewels lose their glory if neglected,
So princes their renowns if not re-
spected.
Pericles 2.2.10

Priority

4575 LEPIDUS: Small to greater matters
must give way.
Antony and Cleopatra 2.2.11

4576 HECTOR: Life every man holds
dear, but the dear man
Holds honor far more precious-dear
than life.
Troilus and Cressida 5.3.27

Prison

4577 CASSIUS: Stoney tower, nor walls
of beaten brass,
Nor airless dungeon, nor strong links
of iron,
Can be retentive to the strength of
spirit.
Julius Caesar 1.3.93

4578 ROMEO: Stoney limits cannot
hold love out.
Romeo and Juliet 2.2.67

4579 ARVIRAGUS: Our cage
We make a choir, as doth the prison'd
bird,
And sing our bondage freely.
Cymbeline 3.3.42

Prisoner

4580 ANGELO: The jury, passing on
the prisoner's life,
May in the sworn twelve have a thief or
two
Guiltier than him they try.
Measure for Measure 2.1.19

4581 GLOUCESTER: How hath your
lordship brook'd imprisonment?
HASTINGS: With patience, noble lord,
as prisoners must.
Richard III 1.1.125

4582 MACBETH: I am cabin'd, cribb'd,
confin'd, bound in
To saucy doubts and fears.
Macbeth 3.4.24

Privilege

4583 BASTARD: Some sins do bear
their privilege on earth.
King John 1.1.261

4584 PEMBROKE: Impatience hath his
privilege.
King John 4.3.32

Prize

4585 CRESSIDA: Women are angels,
wooing:
Things won are done, joy's soul lies in
the doing.
That she belov'd knows nought that
knows not this:
Men prize the thing ungain'd more
than it is.
Troilus and Cressida 1.2.286

4586 GRATIANO: All things that are,
Are with more spirit chased than
enjoy'd.
Merchant of Venice 2.6.12

4587 BAPTISTA: 'Tis deeds must win
the prize.
Taming of the Shrew 2.1.342

Procrastination

4588 REIGNIER: Defer no time, delays have dangerous ends.
1 Henry VI 3.2.33

4589 KING: That we would do,
We should do when we would; for this "would" changes,
And hath abatements and delays as many
As there are tongues, are hands, are accidents,
And then this "should" is like a spendthrift's sigh,
That hurts by easing.
Hamlet 4.7.118
[*spendthrift's sigh*: a sigh, which, it was supposed, drew blood from the heart]

4590 The patient dies while the physician sleeps,
The orphan pines while the oppressor feeds,
Justice is feasting while the widow weeps,
Advice is sporting while infection breeds.
Rape of Lucrece 904

4591 MACBETH: To-morrow, and to-morrow, and to-morrow,
Creeps in this petty pace from day to day,
To the last syllable of recorded time;
And all our yesterdays have lighted fools
The way to dusty death.
Macbeth 5.5.19

4592 CAPUCHIUS: The King's request that I would visit you,
Who grieves much for your weakness, and by me
Sends you his princely commendations,
And heartily entreats you take good comfort.
KATHERINE: O my good lord, that comfort comes too late,
'Tis like a pardon after execution.
That gentle physic given in time had cur'd me;
But now I am past all comforts here but prayers.
Henry VIII 4.2.116

Prodigality

4593 FOOL: He that keeps nor crust nor crumb,
Weary of all, shall want some.
King Lear 1.4.198

Profanity

4594 ISABELLA: That in the captain's but a choleric word,
Which in the soldier is flat blasphemy.
Measure for Measure 2.2.130

4595 LUCIANA: Ill deeds is doubled with an evil word.
Comedy of Errors 3.2.20

4596 SIR TOBY: It comes to pass oft that a terrible oath, with a swaggering accent sharply twang'd off, gives manhood more approbation than ever proof itself would have earn'd him.
Twelfth Night 3.4.179

4597 CLOTEN: When a gentleman is dispos'd to swear, it is not for any standers-by to curtal his oaths.
Cymbeline 2.1.10
[*curtal*: curtail]

4598 CALIBAN [to Miranda]: You taught me language, and my profit on't
Is, I know how to curse. The red plague rid you
For learning me your language!
The Tempest 1.2.363

Profession

4599 TIMON: There is boundless theft In limited professions.
Timon of Athens 4.3.427
[*limited*: officially regulated]

Profit

4600 POMPEY: 'Tis not my profit that does lead mine honor;
Mine honor, it.
Antony and Cleopatra 2.7.76

4601 BELARIUS: To apprehend . . .
Draws us a profit from all things we
see.
Cymbeline 3.3.17

4602 TRANIO: No profit grows where is
no pleasure ta'en.
Taming of the Shrew 1.1.39

4603 PISTOL: Profits will accrue.
Henry V 2.1.112

Prologue

4604 PROLOGUE: For us, and for our
tragedy,
Here stooping to your clemency,
We beg your hearing patiently.
Hamlet 3.2.149

4605 HAMLET: Is this a prologue, or
the posy of a ring?
OPHELIA: 'Tis brief, my lord.
HAMLET: As woman's love.
Hamlet 3.2.152
[*posy of a ring:* short motto inscribed in a
ring]

4606 ANTONIO: What's past is prologue.
The Tempest 2.1.253

Promise

4607 POLONIUS: I do know,
When the blood burns, how prodigal
the soul
Lends the tongue vows.
Hamlet 1.3.115

4608 MACBETH [on the witches'
predictions]: Be these juggling fiends
no more believ'd,
That palter with us in a double sense,
That keep the word of promise to our
ear,
And break it to our hope.
Macbeth 5.8.19

4609 PAINTER: Promising is the very
air o' th' time;
It opens the eyes of expectation.

Performance is ever the duller for his
act,
And but in the plainer and simpler
kind of people
The deed of saying is quite out of use.
To promise is most courtly and fashionable;
Performance is a kind of will or testa-
ment
Which argues a great sickness in his
judgment
That makes it.
Timon of Athens 5.1.22
[*deed of saying:* the fulfillment of a
promise]

Promotion

4610 VENTIDIUS: Who does i' th' wars
more than his captain can
Becomes his captain's captain.
Antony and Cleopatra 3.1.21

4611 ORLANDO [to Adam]: O good
old man, how well in thee appears
The constant service of the antique
world,
When service sweat for duty, not for
meed!
Thou art not for the fashion of these
times,
Where none will sweat but for promotion.
As You Like It 2.3.56
[*meed:* reward]

Promptness

4612 MACBETH: The flighty purpose
never is o'ertook
Unless the deed go with it.
Macbeth 4.1.145

4613 FORD: Better three hours too
soon than a minute too late.
Merry Wives of Windsor 2.2.312

Proof

4614 IAGO [soliloquy]: Trifles light as
air

Are to the jealous confirmations strong
As proofs of holy writ.
Othello 3.3.322

4615 LUCIUS: Let proof speak.
Cymbeline 3.1.77

Propagation

4616 From fairest creatures we desire increase,
That thereby beauty's rose might never die.
Sonnet 1

4617 When forty winters shall besiege thy brow,
And dig deep trenches in thy beauty's field,
Thy youth's proud livery, so gaz'd on now,
Will be a totter'd weed of small worth held:
Then being ask'd, where all thy beauty lies,
Where all the treasure of thy lusty days,
To say within thine own deep-sunken eyes
Were an all-eating shame, and thriftless praise.
How much more praise deserv'd thy beauty's use,
If thou couldst answer, "This fair child of mine
Shall sum my count, and make my old excuse,"
Proving his beauty by succession thine.
Sonnet 2
[*totter'd weed:* tattered garment]

Prophecy

4618 WARWICK: There is a history in all men's lives,
Figuring the natures of the times deceas'd,
The which observ'd, a man may prophesy,
With a near aim, of the main chance of things

As yet not come to life, who in their seeds
And weak beginnings lie intreasured.
2 Henry IV 3.1.80

4619 SOOTHSAYER: In nature's infinite book of secrecy
A little I can read.
Antony and Cleopatra 1.2.10

4620 REGAN: Jesters do oft prove prophets.
King Lear 5.3.71

Proportion

4621 K. RICHARD [soliloquy]: How sour sweet music is
When time is broke, and no proportion kept!
So is it in the music of men's lives.
Richard II 5.5.42

Prosperity

4622 CAMILLO: Prosperity's the very bond of love.
Winter's Tale 4.4.573

4623 COSTARD: Welcome the sour cup of prosperity! Affliction may one day smile again, and till then, sit thee down, sorrow!
Love's Labor's Lost 1.1.313

Proverbs

4624 LEONATO: Patch grief with proverbs, make misfortune drunk
With candle-wasters.
Much Ado About Nothing 5.1.17
[*candle-wasters:* those who study late into the night]

4625 SHYLOCK: Fast bind, fast find—
A proverb never stale in thrifty mind.
Merchant of Venice 2.5.54

4626 ROMEO: I am proverb'd with a grandsire phrase.
Romeo and Juliet 1.4.37
[*grandsire phrase:* old proverb]

Providence

4627 Q. KATHERINE: Heaven is above all yet; there sits a judge
That no king can corrupt.
Henry VIII 3.1.100

4628 HAMLET: There's a divinity that shapes our ends,
Rough-hew them how we will.
Hamlet 5.2.10

4629 HAMLET: There's a special providence in the fall of a sparrow.
Hamlet 5.2.219

4630 ADAM: He that doth the ravens feed,
Yea, providently caters for the sparrow,
Be comfort to my age!
As You Like It 2.3.43

Provocation

4631 HASTINGS: To fly the boar before the boar pursues
Were to incense the boar to follow us,
And make pursuit where he did mean no chase.
Richard III 3.2.28

Prudence

4632 CHIEF JUSTICE: Wake not a sleeping wolf.
2 Henry IV 1.2.153

4633 NORFOLK: Heat not a furnace for your foe so hot
That it do singe yourself. We may outrun
By violent swiftness that which we run at,
And lose by overrunning.
Henry VIII 1.1.140

4634 GARDENER: Superfluous branches We lop away, that bearing boughs may live.
Richard II 3.4.63

4635 FOOL: Have more than thou showest,
Speak less than thou knowest,
Lend less than thou owest,
Ride more than thou goest,
Learn more than thou trowest,
Set less than thou throwest.
King Lear 1.4.118

4636 COUNTESS [to Bertram]: Love all, trust a few,
Do wrong to none. Be able for thine enemy
Rather in power than use, and keep thy friend
Under thy own life's key. Be check'd for silence,
But never tax'd for speech.
All's Well That Ends Well 1.1.64

4637 FALSTAFF [soliloquy]: Well, 'tis no matter, honor pricks me on. Yea, but how if honor prick me off when I come on? how then? Can honor set to a leg? No. Or an arm? No. Or take away the grief of a wound? No. Honor hath no skill in surgery then? No. What is honor? A word. What is in that word honor? What is that honor? Air. A trim reckoning! Who hath it? He that died a' Wednesday. Doth he feel it? No. Doth he hear it? No. 'Tis insensible then? Yea, to the dead. But will't not live with the living? No. Why? Detraction will not suffer it. Therefore I'll none of it, honor is a mere scutcheon. And so ends my catechism.
1 Henry IV 5.1.129
[*scutcheon:* an emblem carried in funerals]

Pruning

4638 GARDENER: Superfluous branches We lop away, that bearing boughs may live.
Richard II 3.4.63

Punctuality

4639 FRIAR LAWRENCE: Too swift arrives as tardy as too slow.
Romeo and Juliet 2.6.15

4640 FORD: Better three hours too
soon than a minute too late.
Merry Wives of Windsor 2.2.312

Punishment

4641 ANTONY: Bid that welcome
Which comes to punish us, and we
punish it
Seeming to bear it lightly.
Antony and Cleopatra 4.14.136

4642 DUKE: Now, as fond fathers,
Having bound up the threat'ning twigs
of birch,
Only to stick it in their children's sight
For terror, not to use, in time the rod
Becomes more mock'd than fear'd; so
our decrees,
Dead to infliction, to themselves are
dead.
Measure for Measure 1.3.23

4643 K. HENRY: Some, peradventure,
have on them the guilt of
premeditated and contriv'd murther;
some, of beguiling virgins with the
broken seals of perjury; some, making
the wars their bulwark, that have
before gor'd the gentle bosom of peace
with pillage and robbery. Now, if these
men have defeated the law and outrun
native punishment, though they can
outstrip men, they have no wings to fly
from God.
Henry V 4.1.161
[*murther:* murder]

Purity

4644 Best is best, if never intermix'd.
Sonnet 101

4645 IAGO: Who has that breast so
pure
But some uncleanly apprehensions
Keep leets and law-days and in sessions
sit
With meditations lawful?
Othello 3.3.138
[*keep leets:* hold courts]

Purpose

4646 CASSANDRA: It is the purpose
that makes strong the vow.
Troilus and Cressida 5.3.23

4647 PLAYER KING: What to ourselves
in passion we propose,
The passion ending, doth the purpose
lose.
Hamlet 3.2.194

4648 PRINCE: In every thing the purpose must weigh with the folly.
2 Henry IV 2.2.175

4649 MACBETH: The flighty purpose
never is o'ertook
Unless the deed go with it.
Macbeth 4.1.145

4650 ANTONIO [to Sebastian]: Do not
for one repulse forgo the purpose
That you resolv'd t' effect.
The Tempest 3.3.12

4651 PLAYER KING: What we do
determine, oft we break.
Purpose is but the slave to memory.
Hamlet 3.2.187

Purse

4652 IAGO: Who steals my purse steals
trash; 'tis something, nothing;
'Twas mine, 'tis his, and has been slave
to thousands;
But he that filches from me my good
name
Robs me of that which not enriches
him,
And makes me poor indeed.
Othello 3.3.157

4653 SHALLOW: A friend i' th' court is
better than a penny in purse.
2 Henry IV 5.1.30

4654 FALSTAFF: I can get no remedy
against this consumption of the purse;

borrowing only lingers and lingers it out, but the disease is incurable.
2 Henry IV 1.2.236

4655 BAGOT [on the common people]: Their love
Lies in their purses, and whoso empties them
By so much fills their hearts with deadly hate.
Richard II 2.2.129

4656 IAGO: Put money in thy purse
... put but money in thy purse ...
fill thy purse with money.
Othello 1.3.343

4657 PETRUCHIO [to Kate]: Our purses shall be proud, our garments poor,
For 'tis the mind that makes the body rich.
Taming of the Shrew 4.3.171

Pursuit

4658 GRATIANO: All things that are, Are with more spirit chased than enjoy'd.
Merchant of Venice 2.6.12

4659 CRESSIDA: Men prize the thing ungain'd more than it is.
Troilus and Cressida 1.2.289

Qualification

4660 CLEOPATRA: I do not like "but yet," it does allay
The good precedence; fie upon "but yet"!
"But yet" is as a jailer to bring forth Some monstrous malefactor.
Antony and Cleopatra 2.5.50
[*good precedence:* i.e. the good news that preceded the *but yet*]

Quarrel

4661 POLONIUS: Beware
Of entrance to a quarrel, but being in,

Bear't that th' opposed may beware of thee.
Hamlet 1.3.65

4662 HAMLET [soliloquy]: Rightly to be great
Is not to stir without great argument,
But greatly to find quarrel in a straw When honor's at the stake.
Hamlet 4.4.53

4663 EDMUND: The best quarrels, in the heat, are curs'd
By those that feel their sharpness.
King Lear 5.3.56

4664 KING: Thrice is he arm'd that hath his quarrel just;
And he but naked, though lock'd up in steel,
Whose conscience with injustice is corrupted.
2 Henry VI 3.2.233

4665 BENEDICK: In a false quarrel there is no true valor.
Much Ado About Nothing 5.1.120

4666 NORTHUMBERLAND [on the rebellion]: Contention, like a horse Full of high feeding, madly hath broke loose,
And bears down all before him.
2 Henry IV 1.1.9

4667 MERCUTIO [to Benvolio]: Thou! why, thou wilt quarrel with a man that hath a hair more or a hair less in his beard than thou hast. Thou wilt quarrel with a man for cracking nuts, having no other reason but because thou hast hazel eyes.
Romeo and Juliet 3.1.16

4668 TITANIA: The spring, the summer,
The chiding autumn, angry winter, change
Their wonted liveries; and the mazed world,
By their increase, now knows not which is which.
And this same progeny of evils comes

From our debate, from our dissension;
We are their parents and original.
Midsummer Night's Dream 2.1.111

Quietness

4669 ANTONY: Quietness, grown sick
of rest, would purge
By any desperate change.
Antony and Cleopatra 1.3.53

4670 GLOUCESTER: Thy greatest help is
quiet.
2 Henry VI 2.4.67

Quotations

4671 ANTONIO: The devil can cite
Scripture for his purpose.
Merchant of Venice 1.3.98

Rage

4672 NESTOR: The thing of courage,
As rous'd with rage, with rage doth
sympathize.
Troilus and Cressida 1.3.51

4673 MENENIUS: Put not your worthy
rage into your tongue.
Coriolanus 3.1.240

4674 MENENIUS: This tiger-footed
rage, when it shall find
The harm of unscann'd swiftness, will
too late
Tie leaden pounds to 's heels.
Coriolanus 3.1.310
[*unscann'd:* thoughtless; *'s:* its]

4675 IAGO: Men in rage strike those
that wish them best.
Othello 2.3.243

Raiment

4676 SLY: Ne'er ask me what raiment
I'll wear; for I have no more doublets
than backs, no more stockings than

legs, nor no more shoes than feet; nay,
sometime more feet than shoes, or
such shoes as my toes look through the
over-leather.
Taming of the Shrew, Induction 2.10

Rain

4677 GLOUCESTER: Much rain wears
the marble.
3 Henry VI 3.2.50

4678 CORIN: The property of rain is to
wet and fire to burn.
As You Like It 3.2.26

Rainbow

4679 CERES: Hail, many-colored
messenger, that ne'er
Dost disobey the wife of Jupiter;
Who with thy saffron wings upon my
flow'rs
Diffusest honey-drops, refreshing
show'rs,
And with each end of thy blue bow
dost crown
My bosky acres and my unshrubb'd
down,
Rich scarf to my proud earth.
The Tempest 4.1.76

Rancor

4680 GLOUCESTER: Rancor will out.
2 Henry VI 1.1.142

Rapacity

4681 GAUNT: With eager feeding food
doth choke the feeder.
Richard II 2.1.37

Rapier

4682 ROSENCRANTZ: Many wearing
rapiers are afraid of goose-quills.
Hamlet 2.2.343
[*goose-quills:* the pens of satirical writers]

Rapprochement

4683 GLOUCESTER: 'Tis death to me to be at enmity;
I hate it, and desire all good men's love.
Richard III 2.1.61

Rashness

4684 MONTJOY: Advantage is a better soldier than rashness.
Henry V 3.6.120

4685 POLONIUS: I do know,
When the blood burns, how prodigal the soul
Lends the tongue vows.
Hamlet 1.3.115

4686 CHARLES: One sudden foil shall never breed distrust.
1 Henry VI 3.3.11
[*foil:* repulse]

4687 OTHELLO: My blood begins my safer guides to rule,
And passion, having my best judgment collied,
Assays to lead the way.
Othello 2.3.205
[*collied:* darkened]

4688 NORFOLK: We may outrun
By violent swiftness that which we run at,
And lose by over-running.
Henry VIII 1.1.141

4689 HAMLET: Our indiscretion sometimes serves us well.
Hamlet 5.2.8

Readiness

4690 K. HENRY: All things are ready, if our minds be so.
Henry V 4.3.71

4691 COUNTESS: Be able for thine enemy
Rather in power than use.
All's Well That Ends Well 1.1.65

4692 HAMLET: If it be now, 'tis not to come; if it be not to come, it will be now; if it be not now, yet it will come—the readiness is all.
Hamlet 5.2.220

Reading

4693 DOGBERRY: To be a well-favor'd man is the gift of fortune, but to read and write comes by nature.
Much Ado About Nothing 3.3.14
[*well-favor'd:* good-looking]

4694 LADY MACBETH [to Macbeth]:
Your face, my thane, is as a book, where men
May read strange matters.
Macbeth 1.5.62

4695 CYMBELINE: Who is't can read a woman?
Cymbeline 5.5.48

Reaping

4696 TOUCHSTONE: They that reap must sheaf and bind.
As You Like It 3.2.107

Reason

4697 CRESSIDA: Blind fear that seeing reason leads finds safer footing than blind reason stumbling without fear.
Troilus and Cressida 3.2.71

4698 ENOBARBUS [soliloquy]: When valor preys on reason,
It eats the sword it fights with.
Antony and Cleopatra 3.13.198

4699 SIR TOBY: [Judgment and reason] have been grand-jurymen since before Noah was a sailor.
Twelfth Night 3.2.16

4700 LYSANDER: The will of man is by his reason sway'd.
Midsummer Night's Dream 2.2.115

4701 LEWIS: Strong reasons make strange actions.
King John 3.4.182

4702 BOTTOM: To say the truth, reason and love keep little company together now-a-days.
Midsummer Night's Dream 3.1.143

4703 ISABELLA [to Duke]: Do not banish reason
For inequality, but let your reason serve
To make the truth appear, where it seems hid,
And hide the false seems true.
Measure for Measure 5.1.64

4704 IAGO: If the beam of our lives had not one scale of reason to poise another of sensuality, the blood and baseness of our natures would conduct us to most preposterous conclusions. But we have reason to cool our raging motions, our carnal stings, our unbitted lusts.
Othello 1.3.326
[*beam*: balance; *motions*: desires, appetites]

4705 HAMLET: Reason panders will.
Hamlet 3.4.88

4706 LADY MACBETH: Little is the wisdom, where the flight
So runs against all reason.
Macbeth 4.2.13

4707 POLONIUS [to Queen, on Hamlet]: Mad let us grant him then, and now remains
That we find out the cause of this effect,
Or rather say, the cause of this defect,
For this effect defective comes by cause.
Hamlet 2.2.100

4708 BRUTUS: Good reasons must of force give place to better.
Julius Caesar 4.3.203

4709 DROMIO SYRACUSE: Every why hath a wherefore.
Comedy of Errors 2.2.44

4710 FLUELLEN: There is occasions and causes why and wherefore in all things.
Henry V 5.1.3

4711 Let reason rule things worthy blame.
The Passionate Pilgrim xviii.3

4712 NORFOLK: With the sap of reason you would quench ... the fire of passion.
Henry VIII 1.1.148

4713 Reason is the bawd to lust's abuse.
Venus and Adonis 792

4714 MRS. PAGE [reading a letter from Falstaff]: "Though Love use Reason for his precisian, he admits him not for his counsellor."
Merry Wives of Windsor 2.1.4
[*precisian*: puritanical spiritual adviser]

4715 ARVIRAGUS: Love's reason's without reason.
Cymbeline 4.2.22

4716 LUCETTA [on Proteus as Julia's best prospect]: I have no other but a woman's reason:
I think him so, because I think him so.
Two Gentlemen of Verona 1.2.23

4717 MACBETH: Th' expedition of my violent love
Outrun the pauser, reason.
Macbeth 2.3.110

4718 TROILUS: Reason flies the object of all harm.
Troilus and Cressida 2.2.41

4719 HAMLET: So, oft it chances in particular men,
That for some vicious mole of nature in them,
As in their birth, wherein they are not guilty

(Since nature cannot choose his origin),
By their o'ergrowth of some com-
plexion
Oft breaking down the pales and forts
of reason,
Or by some habit, that too much o'er-
leavens
The form of plausive manners — that
these men,
Carrying, I say, the stamp of one de-
fect . . .
Shall in the general censure take cor-
ruption
From that particular fault.
Hamlet 1.4.23

4720 THESEUS: Lovers and madmen
have such seething brains,
Such shaping fantasies, that apprehend
More than cool reason ever compre-
hends.
Midsummer Night's Dream 5.1.4

4721 HAMLET [soliloquy]: He that
made us with such large discourse,
Looking before and after, gave us not
That capability and godlike reason
To fust in us unus'd.
Hamlet 4.4.36
[*fust:* grow mouldy]

4722 FALSTAFF [to Poins]: Give you a
reason on compulsion? if reasons were
as plentiful as blackberries, I would
give no man a reason upon compulsion.
1 Henry IV 2.4.238

4723 TROILUS: Reason and respect
Make livers pale and lustihood deject.
Troilus and Cressida 2.2.49

4724 BASSANIO: Gratiano speaks an infinite deal of nothing, more than any
man in all Venice. His reasons are as
two grains of wheat hid in two bushels
of chaff; you shall seek all day ere you
find them, and when you have them,
they are not worth the search.
Merchant of Venice 1.1.114

Rebellion

4725 NORTHUMBERLAND [on the
rebellion]: Contention, like a horse
Full of high feeding, madly hath broke
loose,
And bears down all before him.
2 Henry IV 1.1.9

4726 MENENIUS: There was a time
when all the body's members
Rebell'd against the belly; thus accus'd
it:
That only like a gulf it did remain
I' th' midst a' th' body, idle and
unactive,
Still cupboarding the viand, never
bearing
Like labor with the rest, where th'
other instruments
Did see and hear, devise, instruct,
walk, feel,
And, mutually participate, did min-
ister
Unto the appetite and affection com-
mon
Of the whole body . . .
Note me this, good friend:
Your most grave belly was deliberate,
Not rash like his accusers, and thus
answered:
"True is it, my incorporate friends,"
quoth he,
"That I receive the general food at first
Which you do live upon; and fit it is,
Because I am the store-house and the
shop
Of the whole body. But, if you do re-
member,
I send it through the rivers of your
blood,
Even to the court, the heart, to th' seat
o' th' brain,
And, through the cranks and offices of
man,
The strongest nerves and small inferior
veins
From me receive that natural compe-
tency
Whereby they live. And though all at
once . . . cannot
See what I do deliver out to each,
Yet I can make my audit up, that all

From me do back receive the flour of
all,
And leave me but the bran."
Coriolanus 1.1.96
[*a':* of]

Recklessness

4727 FRIAR LAWRENCE: Violent
delights have violent ends,
And in their triumph die, like fire and
powder,
Which as they kiss consume.
Romeo and Juliet 2.6.9

4728 SECOND MURDERER [accepting
Macbeth's hire to kill Banquo]: I am
one, my liege,
Whom the vile blows and buffets of
the world
Have so incens'd that I am reckless
what
I do to spite the world.
Macbeth 3.1.108

Reckoning

4729 BRUTUS [to Cassius, on the eve
of battle]: O, that a man might
know
The end of this day's business ere it
come!
But it sufficeth that the day will end,
And then the end is known.
Julius Caesar 5.1.122

Recompense

4730 TIMON: There's none
Can truly say he gives if he receives.
Timon of Athens 1.2.10

Reconciliation

4731 A smile recures the wounding of
a frown.
Venus and Adonis 465

4732 O benefit of ill, now I find true
That better is by evil still made better,

And ruin'd love when it is built anew
Grows fairer than at first, more strong,
far greater.
Sonnet 119

4733 K. RICHARD [to two quarreling
lords]: Deep malice makes too deep
incision.
Forget, forgive, conclude and be
agreed.
Richard II 1.1.155

4734 OTHELLO [to Desdemona, before
killing her]: If you bethink yourself
of any crime
Unreconcil'd as yet to heaven and
grace,
Solicit for it straight.
Othello 5.2.26

Recovery

4735 ROSSE: Things at the worst will
cease, or else climb upward
To what they were before.
Macbeth 4.2.24

Recreation

4736 ABBESS: Sweet recreation barr'd,
what doth ensue
But moody and dull melancholy,
Kinsman to grim and comfortless
despair,
And at her heels a huge infectious
troop
Of pale distemperatures and foes to
life?
Comedy of Errors 5.1.78

4737 IAGO: Pleasure and action make
the hours seem short.
Othello 2.3.379

4738 THESEUS: How shall we beguile
The lazy time, if not with some
delight?
Midsummer Night's Dream 5.1.40

Redemption

4739 ISABELLA: All the souls that were
were forfeit once,
And He that might the vantage best
have took
Found out the remedy.
Measure for Measure 2.2.73

4740 KING: Let never day nor night
unhallowed pass,
But still remember what the Lord has
done.
2 Henry VI 2.1.83

Redress

4741 YORK: Things past redress are
now with me past care.
Richard II 2.3.171

4742 BRUTUS [to his fellow con-
spirators]: What need we any spur
but our own cause,
To prick us to redress?
Julius Caesar 2.1.123

4743 Broken glass no cement can redress.
The Passionate Pilgrim xiii.10

Reflection

4744 OTHELLO [to Desdemona]: Think
on thy sins.
Othello 5.2.39

Reformation

4745 CLOWN: Virtue that transgresses
is but patch'd with sin, and sin that
amends is but patch'd with virtue.
Twelfth Night 1.5.48

4746 CANTERBURY: Never came reformation in a flood.
Henry V 1.1.33

4747 BENEDICK [soliloquy]: Happy are
they that hear their detractions, and
can put them to mending.
Much Ado About Nothing 2.3.229

4748 MARIANA: They say best men are
moulded out of faults,
And for the most, become much more
the better
For being a little bad.
Measure for Measure 5.1.439

4749 CLOWN: Bid the dishonest man
mend himself: if he mend, he is no
longer dishonest; if he cannot, let the
botcher mend him.
Twelfth Night 1.5.45
[*botcher:* one who mends shoes or clothes]

4750 PRINCE [soliloquy]: So when this
loose behavior I throw off
And pay the debt I never promised,
By how much better than my word I
am,
By so much shall I falsify men's hopes,
And like bright metal on a sullen
ground,
My reformation, glitt'ring o'er my
fault,
Shall show more goodly and attract
more eyes
Than that which hath no foil to set it
off.
I'll so offend, to make offense a skill,
Redeeming time when men think least
I will.
1 Henry IV 1.2.208

4751 CLEOPATRA: My desolation does
begin to make
A better life.
Antony and Cleopatra 5.2.1

Relief

4752 SILVIUS: Wherever sorrow is,
relief would be.
As You Like It 3.5.86

Religion

4753 HAMLET [to the Queen, on her
marriage]: Such a deed
As from the body of contraction plucks
The very soul, and sweet religion

Makes a rhapsody of words. Heaven's
   face does glow
O'er this solidity and compound mass
With heated visage, as against the
   doom;
Is thought-sick at the act.
                              Hamlet 3.4.45

4754 WARWICK: My soul intends to
   live
With that dread King that took our
   state upon him,
To free us from his Father's wrathful
   curse.
                           2 Henry VI 3.2.153

4755 PANDULPH: It is religion that
   doth make vows kept.
                           King John 3.1.279

4756 BASSANIO: In religion,
What damned error but some sober
   brow
Will bless it, and approve it with a
   text,
Hiding the grossness with fair ornament?
                   Merchant of Venice 3.2.77

4757 CRANMER [to Gardiner]: Love
   and meekness . . .
Become a churchman better than am-
   bition;
Win staying souls with modesty again,
Cast none away.
                           Henry VIII 5.2.97

4758 HECTOR: 'Tis mad idolatry
To make the service greater than the
   god.
                   Troilus and Cressida 2.2.56

4759 BEATRICE [about Benedick]: He
wears his faith but as the fashion of his
hat: it ever changes with the next
block.
             Much Ado About Nothing 1.1.75

Remedy

4760 HELENA: Our remedies oft in
   ourselves do lie,
Which we ascribe to heaven.
             All's Well That Ends Well 1.1.216

4761 IMOGEN: Certainties
Either are past remedies, or, timely
   knowing,
The remedy then born.
                           Cymbeline 1.6.96

4762 PUCELLE: Care is no cure, but
   rather corrosive,
For things that are not to be remedied.
                           1 Henry VI 3.3.3

4763 LADY MACBETH: Things without
   all remedy
Should be without regard: what's
   done, is done.
                           Macbeth 3.2.11

4764 DUKE: When remedies are past,
   the griefs are ended.
                           Othello 1.3.202

4765 KING: Diseases desperate grown
By desperate appliance are reliev'd,
Or not at all.
                           Hamlet 4.3.9

Remembrance

4766 KING: Let never day nor night
   unhallowed pass,
But still remember what the Lord has
   done.
                           2 Henry VI 2.1.83

4767 COUNTESS: It is the show and
   seal of nature's truth,
Where love's strong passion is impress'd in youth.
By our remembrances of days foregone,
Such were our faults, or then we
   thought them none.
             All's Well That Ends Well 1.3.132

4768 BULLINGBROOK: I count myself
   in nothing else so happy
As in a soul remembering my good
   friends.
                           Richard II 2.3.46

4769 KING: Praising what is lost
Makes the remembrance dear.
             All's Well That Ends Well 5.3.19

4770 MACDUFF [on the slaughter of his family]: I cannot but remember such things were,
That were most precious to me.
Macbeth 4.3.222

4771 Your monument shall be my gentle verse,
Which eyes not yet created shall o'er-read,
And tongues to be your being shall re-hearse,
When all the breathers of this world are dead;
You still shall live (such virtue hath my pen)
Where breath most breathes, even in the mouths of men.
Sonnet 81

4772 When to the sessions of sweet silent thought
I summon up remembrance of things past,
I sigh the lack of many a thing I sought,
And with old woes new wail my dear time's waste;
Then can I drown an eye (unus'd to flow)
For precious friends hid in death's dateless night,
And weep afresh love's long since cancell'd woe,
And moan th' expense of many a vanish'd sight.
Sonnet 30

4773 MARTIUS: I have some wounds upon me, and they smart
To hear themselves rememb'red.
Coriolanus 1.9.28

4774 ALONSO: How sharp the point of this remembrance is!
The Tempest 5.1.138

4775 PROSPERO: Let us not burthen our remembrances with
A heaviness that's gone.
The Tempest 5.1.198
[*burthen:* burden]

4776 OPHELIA [giving out flowers after Polonius' death]: There's rosemary, that's for remembrance; pray you, love, remember. And there is pansies, that's for thoughts.
Hamlet 4.5.175
[*rosemary:* used as a symbol of remembrance at both weddings and funerals]

Remorse

4777 KING: Oft our displeasures, to ourselves unjust,
Destroy our friends, and after weep their dust.
All's Well That Ends Well 5.3.63

4778 LADY MACBETH [soliloquy, on Duncan's assassination]: Come, you spirits
That tend on mortal thoughts, unsex me here,
And fill me from the crown to the toe topful
Of direst cruelty! Make thick my blood,
Stop up th' access and passage to remorse,
That no compunctious visitings of nature
Shake my fell purpose, nor keep peace between
Th' effect and it!
Macbeth 1.5.40

4779 K. RICHARD: What is done cannot be now amended:
Men shall deal unadvisedly sometimes,
Which after-hours give leisure to repent.
Richard III 4.4.291

4780 DOCTOR [on Lady Macbeth's sleepwalking confession]: Foul whisp'rings are abroad. Unnatural deeds
Do breed unnatural troubles; infected minds
To their deaf pillows will discharge their secrets.
Macbeth 5.1.71

4781 MACBETH: To know my deed,
'twere best not know myself.
Macbeth 2.2.70

4782 MACBETH [to Lady Macbeth, on
Duncan's murder]: I am afraid to
think what I have done;
Look on't again I dare not.
Macbeth 2.2.48

4783 SECOND MURDERER: The urging
of that word "judgment" hath bred a
kind of remorse in me.
Richard III 1.4.107

4784 GHOST [to Hamlet, on the
Queen]: Leave her to heaven,
And to those thorns that in her bosom
lodge
To prick and sting her.
Hamlet 1.5.86

4785 OTHELLO [to Iago]: Abandon all
remorse;
On horror's head horrors accumulate.
Othello 3.3.369

Repartee

4786 BEATRICE: I wonder that you will
still be talking, Signior Benedick,
nobody marks you.
BENEDICK: What, my dear Lady Disdain! are you yet living?
Much Ado About Nothing 1.1.116

Repentance

4787 MARIANA: They say best men are
moulded out of faults,
And for the most, become much more
the better
For being a little bad.
Measure for Measure 5.1.439

4788 ARIEL: [Repentance] is nothing
but heart's sorrow,
And a clear life ensuing.
The Tempest 3.3.81

4789 BENEDICK [soliloquy]: Happy are
they that hear their detractions, and
can put them to mending.
Much Ado About Nothing 2.3.229

4790 Th' offender's sorrow lends but
weak relief
To him that bears the strong offense's
cross.
Sonnet 34

4791 VALENTINE: Who by repentance
is not satisfied
Is nor of heaven nor earth.
Two Gentlemen of Verona 5.4.79

4792 PROVOST: I have seen
When, after execution judgment hath
Repented o'er his doom.
Measure for Measure 2.2.10

4793 PAULINA: All faults I make,
when I shall come to know them,
I do repent.
Winter's Tale 3.2.219

4794 FALSTAFF: Well, I'll repent, and
that suddenly, while I am in some liking. I shall be out of heart shortly, and
then I shall have no strength to repent.
1 Henry IV 3.3.4

4795 HENRY V [to Falstaff after his
coronation]: Presume not that I am
the thing I was,
For God doth know, so shall the world
perceive,
That I have turn'd away my former
self;
So will I those that kept me company.
2 Henry IV 5.5.56

4796 HAMLET [to the Queen]: Confess
yourself to heaven,
Repent what's past, avoid what is to
come,
And do not spread the compost on the
weeds
To make them ranker.
Hamlet 3.4.149

4797 OPHELIA [to Gertrude]: There's
rue for you, and here's some for me;

we may call it herb of grace a' Sundays. You may wear your rue with a difference.
Hamlet 5.4.181
[*rue:* an emblem for repentance, which, when mixed with holy water, was then called the *herb of grace*; *a':* on]

Repose

4798 JACHIMO: The crickets sing, and man's o'erlabor'd sense
Repairs itself by rest.
Cymbeline 2.2.11

4799 DOCTOR: Our foster-nurse of nature is repose . . .
Whose power
Will close the eye of anguish.
King Lear 4.4.12

4800 BELARIUS: Weariness
Can snore upon the flint, when resty sloth
Finds the down pillow hard.
Cymbeline 3.6.33

4801 GARDINER: These should be hours for necessities,
Not for delights; times to repair our nature
With comforting repose, and not for us
To waste these times.
Henry VIII 5.1.3

Repression

4802 CLARENCE: A little fire is quickly trodden out,
Which being suffer'd, rivers cannot quench.
3 Henry VI 4.8.7

Reproof

4803 MRS. PAGE: Better a little chiding than a great deal of heartbreak.
Merry Wives of Windsor 5.3.9

4804 ORLANDO: I will chide no breather in the world but myself, against whom I know most faults.
As You Like It 3.2.280

4805 KING [to Thomas, on dealing with Prince Henry]: Chide him for faults, and do it reverently,
When you perceive his blood inclin'd to mirth.
2 Henry IV 4.4.37

Repulsion

4806 JULIA: Love will not be spurr'd to what it loathes.
Two Gentlemen of Verona 5.2.7

Reputation

4807 IAGO: Good name in man and woman . . .
Is the immediate jewel of their souls.
Othello 3.3.155

4808 IAGO: He that filches from me my good name
Robs me of that which not enriches him,
And makes me poor indeed.
Othello 3.3.159

4809 CASSIO: Reputation, reputation, reputation! O, I have lost my reputation! I have lost the immortal part of myself, and what remains is bestial.
Othello 2.3.262

4810 IAGO: Reputation is an idle and most false imposition; oft got without merit, and lost without deserving.
Othello 2.3.268

4811 ANTONY: I have offended reputation,
A most unnoble swerving.
Antony and Cleopatra 3.11.49

4812 FALSTAFF [to Prince Hal]: I would to God thou and I knew where a commodity of good names were to be bought.

1 Henry IV 1.2.82

4813 MARIANA: The honor of a maid is her name.

All's Well That Ends Well 3.5.12

4814 GRIFFITH: Men's evil manners live in brass, their virtues
We write in water.

Henry VIII 4.2.45

4815 MOWBRAY: The purest treasure mortal times afford
Is spotless reputation; that away,
Men are but gilded loam or painted clay.

Richard II 1.1.177

4816 HAMLET [on his murdered father]: O heavens, die two months ago, and not forgotten yet? Then there's hope a great man's memory may outlive his life half a year.

Hamlet 3.2.130

Resignation

4817 K. HENRY: Let me embrace thee, sour adversities,
For wise men say it is the wisest course.

3 Henry VI 3.1.24

4818 ANTONY: Bid that welcome
Which comes to punish us, and we punish it
Seeming to bear it lightly.

Antony and Cleopatra 4.14.136

4819 GLOUCESTER: Henceforth I'll bear
Affliction till it do cry out itself
"Enough, enough," and die.

King Lear 4.6.75

4820 DUKE: When remedies are past, the griefs are ended
By seeing the worst, which late on hopes depended.
To mourn a mischief that is past and gone

Is the next way to draw new mischief on.

Othello 1.3.202

4821 LADY MACBETH: Things without all remedy
Should be without regard: what's done, is done.

Macbeth 3.2.11

4822 PAULINA: What's gone and what's past help
Should be past grief.

Winter's Tale 3.2.222

4823 PAGE: What cannot be eschew'd must be embrac'd.

Merry Wives of Windsor 5.5.237

4824 Q. MARGARET: What cannot be avoided,
'Twere childish weakness to lament or fear.

3 Henry VI 5.4.37

4825 K. EDWARD: What fates impose, that men must needs abide.

3 Henry VI 4.3.58

4826 PERICLES [to Antiochus]: Ready for the way of life or death,
I wait the sharpest blow.

Pericles 1.1.54

4827 HAMLET [to Horatio]: Thou hast been
As one in suff'ring all that suffers nothing,
A man that Fortune's buffets and rewards
Hast ta'en with equal thanks.

Hamlet 3.2.65

4828 K. LEAR [to his daughters]:
Know that we have divided
In three our kingdom; and 'tis our fast intent
To shake all cares and business from our age,
Conferring them on younger strengths, while we
Unburthen'd crawl toward death.

King Lear 1.1.37

[*unburthen'd:* unburdened]

Resolution

4829 ANTONIO: What I will, I will.
Two Gentlemen of Verona 1.3.65

4830 OTHELLO: To be once in doubt
Is once to be resolv'd.
Othello 3.3.179

4831 HAMLET [soliloquy]: The native
hue of resolution
Is sicklied o'er with the pale cast of
thought,
And enterprises of great pitch and
moment
With this regard their currents turn
awry,
And lose the name of action.
Hamlet 3.1.83

4832 BASTARD [to King John]: Be stir-
ring as the time, be fire with fire,
Threaten the threat'ner, and outface
the brow
Of bragging horror; so shall inferior
eyes,
That borrow their behaviors from the
great,
Grow great by your example and put
on
The dauntless spirit of resolution.
King John 5.1.48

4833 IAGO: It makes us, or it mars us.
Othello 5.1.4

4834 ANTONIO [to Sebastian]: Do not
for one repulse forego the purpose
That you resolv'd t' effect.
The Tempest 3.3.13

4835 MACBETH: The flighty purpose
never is o'ertook
Unless the deed go with it.
Macbeth 4.1.145

4836 MACBETH: From this moment
The very firstlings of my heart shall be
The firstlings of my hand. And even
now,
To crown my thoughts with acts, be it
thought and done.
Macbeth 4.1.146

4837 NYM: I have a sword, and it shall
bite upon my necessity.
Merry Wives of Windsor 2.1.131

4838 K. LEWIS [to Margaret]: Yield
not thy neck
To fortune's yoke, but let thy dauntless
mind
Still ride in triumph over all
mischance.
3 Henry VI 3.3.16

4839 YORK [soliloquy, on his plot to
depose Henry]:
Steel thy fearful thoughts,
And change misdoubt to resolution;
Be that thou hop'st to be, or what
thou art
Resign to death.
2 Henry VI 3.1.331

Respect

4840 True respect will prison false
desire.
Rape of Lucrece 642

4841 CROMWELL: Men so noble,
However faulty, yet should find respect
For what they have been.
Henry VIII 5.2.109

4842 PORTIA: Nothing is good, I see,
without respect.
Merchant of Venice 5.1.99

4843 OTHELLO [to Brabantio]: Good
signior, you shall more command
with years
Than with your weapons.
Othello 1.2.60

4844 Respect and reason wait on
wrinkled age!
Rape of Lucrece 275

Responsibility

4845 K. HENRY [soliloquy]: What infinite heart's ease
Must kings neglect, that private men
enjoy!

And what have kings, that privates
have not too,
Save ceremony, save general ceremony?
Henry V 4.1.236

4846 TOUCHSTONE: It is meat and
drink to me to see a clown. By my
troth, we that have good wits have
much to answer for.
As You Like It 5.1.10
[*clown:* country yokel]

4847 BATES: We know enough, if we
know we are the King's subjects. If his
cause be wrong, our obedience to the
King wipes the crime of it out of us.
Henry V 4.1.131

4848 K. HENRY: Every subject's duty
is the King's, but every subject's soul is
his own.
Henry V 4.1.176

4849 EDMUND [soliloquy]: When we
are sick in fortune . . . we make guilty
of our disasters the sun, the moon, and
stars, as if we were villains on necessity,
fools by heavenly compulsion, knaves,
thieves, and treachers by spherical predominance; drunkards, liars, and adulterers by an enforc'd obedience of
planetary influence; and all that we are
evil in, by a divine thrusting on.
King Lear 1.2.119

4850 CASSIUS: The fault, dear Brutus,
is not in our stars,
But in ourselves, that we are
underlings.
Julius Caesar 1.2.140

4851 CLEOPATRA: Be it known that
we, the greatest, are misthought
For things that others do; and when we
fall,
We answer others' merits in our name,
And therefore to be pitied.
Antony and Cleopatra 5.2.176

Rest

4852 WORCESTER: For mine own part,
I could be well content

To entertain the lag end of my life
With quiet hours.
1 Henry IV 5.1.23

4853 JACHIMO: The crickets sing, and
man's o'erlabor'd sense
Repairs itself by rest.
Cymbeline 2.2.11

Restlessness

4854 MACBETH: Better be with the
dead . . .
Than on the torture of the mind to lie
In restless ecstasy.
Macbeth 3.2.19

Restraint

4855 CLAUDIO: As surfeit is the father
of much fast,
So every scope by the immoderate use
Turns to restraint.
Measure for Measure 1.2.126
[*scope:* freedom]

4856 MENENIUS: Do not cry havoc,
where you should hunt
With modest warrant.
Coriolanus 3.1.273
[*havoc:* an order to pillage and initiate a
general slaughter]

4857 SHALLOW: Keep a gamester from
the dice, and a good student from his
book, and it is wonderful.
Merry Wives of Windsor 3.1.38
[*studient:* student]

Results

4858 MACBETH: Things bad begun
make strong themselves by ill.
Macbeth 3.2.55

4859 PRINCE: Let the end try the man.
2 Henry IV 2.2.47

4860 ALBANY: Striving to better, oft
we mar what's well.
King Lear 1.4.346

4861 HELENA: Great floods have flown
From simple sources; and great seas
have dried
When miracles have by the great'st
been denied.
All's Well That Ends Well 2.1.139
[*great floods:* perhaps a reference to Moses
smiting the rock at Horeb; *great seas have
dried:* probably the parting of the Red Sea,
permitting the Israelites to escape Egypt]

4862 FRIAR LAWRENCE: Violent
delights have violent ends,
And in their triumph die, like fire and
powder,
Which as they kiss consume.
Romeo and Juliet 2.6.9

Retirement

4863 WORCESTER: I could be well
content
To entertain the lag end of my life
With quiet hours.
1 Henry IV 5.1.23

4864 DUKE SENIOR [to his companions
in exile]: Our life, exempt from
public haunt,
Finds tongues in trees, books in the
running brooks,
Sermons in stones, and good in everything.
As You Like It 2.1.15

Retribution

4865 NORFOLK: Heat not a furnace for
your foe so hot
That it do singe yourself.
Henry VIII 1.1.140

4866 EDGAR: The gods are just, and of
our pleasant vices
Make instruments to plague us.
King Lear 5.3.171

4867 MACBETH [soliloquy]: We but
teach
Bloody instructions, which, being
taught, return

To plague th' inventor. This even-
handed justice
Commends th' ingredients of our
poison'd chalice
To our own lips.
Macbeth 1.7.8

4868 LADY MACBETH [soliloquy]:
Nought's had, all's spent,
Where our desire is got without
content;
'Tis safer to be that which we destroy
Than by destruction dwell in doubtful
joy.
Macbeth 3.2.5

4869 HAMLET: 'Tis the sport to have
the enginer
Hoist with his own petar.
Hamlet 3.4.206
[*enginer:* constructor of military engines and
possibly artillery weapons; *hoist with:* blown
up by; *petar:* a small engine of war used to
blow in a door or to make a breech]

4870 BEROWNE: Sow'd cockle reap'd
no corn.
Love's Labor's Lost 4.3.380

4871 EDMUND: The wheel is come full
circle.
King Lear 5.3.175
[*wheel:* i.e. of fortune]

4872 FIRST SENATOR: He forfeits his
own blood that spills another.
Timon of Athens 3.5.87

Revelry

4873 PLAYER KING: Where joy most
revels, grief doth most lament;
Grief joys, joy grieves, on slender
accident.
Hamlet 3.2.198

4874 SONG: Come, thou monarch of
the vine,
Plumpy Bacchus with pink eyne!
In thy fats our cares be drown'd,
With thy grapes our hairs be crown'd!

Cup us, till the world go round,
Cup us, till the world go round!
Antony and Cleopatra 2.7.113
[*pink eyne:* half-shut eyes]

Revenge

4875 CLOWN: The whirligig of time
brings in his revenges.
Twelfth Night 5.1.376

4876 FIRST SENATOR: To revenge is no
valor, but to bear.
Timon of Athens 3.5.39

4877 PROSPERO: The rarer action is
In virtue than in vengeance.
The Tempest 5.1.27

4878 HECTOR: Pleasure and revenge
Have ears more deaf than adders to the
voice
Of any true decision.
Troilus and Cressida 2.2.171

4879 NORFOLK: Heat not a furnace for
your foe so hot
That it do singe yourself.
Henry VIII 1.1.140

4880 'Tis a meritorious fair design
To chase injustice with revengeful
arms.
Rape of Lucrece 1692

4881 MACBETH: Blood will have
blood.
Macbeth 3.4.121

4882 KING: Revenge should have no
bounds.
Hamlet 4.7.128

4883 PARIS: Can vengeance be pursued
further than death?
Romeo and Juliet 5.3.55

4884 AARON: Vengeance is in my
heart, death in my hand,
Blood and revenge are hammering in
my head.
Titus Andronicus 2.3.38

4885 LAERTES: It warms the very
sickness in my heart.
Hamlet 4.7.55

4886 MALCOLM [to Rosse and Mac-
duff]: Let's make us med'cines of our
great revenge
To cure this deadly grief.
Macbeth 4.3.214

4887 ANTONY: Cry "Havoc!" and let
slip the dogs of war.
Julius Caesar 3.1.273
[*Havoc:* a war-cry, meaning "give no
quarter"]

4888 SHYLOCK: If a Jew wrong a
Christian, what is his humility?
Revenge. If a Christian wrong a Jew,
what should his sufferance be by Chris-
tian example? Why, revenge.
Merchant of Venice 3.1.68

4889 RICHARD [on York's death]: I
cannot weep; for all my body's
moisture
Scarce serves to quench my furnace-
burning heart;
Nor can my tongue unload my heart's
great burthen,
For self-same wind that I should speak
withal
Is kindling coals that fires all my
breast,
And burns me up with flames that
tears would quench.
3 Henry VI 2.1.79
[*burthen:* burden]

Reverence

4890 SUFFOLK: Rather let my head
Stoop to the block than these knees
bow to any
Save to the God of heaven and to my
king.
2 Henry VI 4.1.124

4891 ANTONY [in The Forum]: But
yesterday the word of Caesar might
Have stood against the world; now lies
he there,
And none so poor to do him reverence.
Julius Caesar 3.2.118

4892 BELARIUS: Though mean and mighty, rotting
Together, have one dust, yet reverence
(That angel of the world) doth make distinction
Of place 'tween high and low.
Cymbeline 4.2.246

Revolt

4893 KING: How quickly nature falls into revolt
When gold becomes her object!
2 Henry IV 4.5.65

Reward

4894 FIRST MURDERER: Remember our reward when the deed's done.
SECOND MURDERER: 'Zounds, he dies! I had forgot the reward.
FIRST MURDERER: Where's thy conscience now?
SECOND MURDERER: O, in the Duke of Gloucester's purse.
FIRST MURDERER: When he opens his purse to give us our reward, thy conscience flies out.
SECOND MURDERER: 'Tis no matter, let it go. There's few or none will entertain it.
Richard III 1.4.126

Rhetoric

4895 TOUCHSTONE: It is a figure in rhetoric that drink, being pour'd out of a cup into a glass, by filling the one doth empty the other.
As You Like It 5.1.41

4896 ARMADO: Sweet smoke of rhetoric!
Love's Labor's Lost 3.1.63

Rhymes

4897 BEROWNE: Rhymes are guards on wanton Cupid's hose.
Love's Labor's Lost 4.3.56

4898 BEROWNE [soliloquy]: By heaven, I do love, and it hath taught me to rhyme, and to be mallicholy.
Love's Labor's Lost 4.3.12
[*mallicholy:* melancholy]

4899 K. HENRY: These fellows of infinite tongue, that can rhyme themselves into ladies' favors, they do always reason themselves out again.
Henry V 5.2.155

4900 K. HENRY: A rhyme is but a ballad.
Henry V 5.2.158

Riches

4901 PETRUCHIO: 'Tis the mind that makes the body rich.
Taming of the Shrew 4.3.172

4902 Poorly rich, so wanteth in his store,
That cloy'd with much, he pineth still for more.
Rape of Lucrece 97

4903 BASTARD [soliloquy]: Well, whiles I am a beggar, I will rail,
And say there is no sin but to be rich;
And being rich, my virtue then shall be
To say there is no vice but beggary.
King John 2.1.593

4904 JULIET: They are but beggars that can count their worth.
Romeo and Juliet 2.6.32

4905 DUKE [to the condemned Claudio]: If thou art rich, thou'rt poor,
For like an ass, whose back with ingots bows,
Thou bear'st thy heavy riches but a journey,
And death unloads thee.
Measure for Measure 3.1.25

4906 IAGO: Poor and content is rich, and rich enough,

But riches fineless is as poor as winter
To him that ever fears he shall be
poor.
Othello 3.3.172
[*fineless:* boundless]

4907 NERISSA: Superfluity comes
sooner by white hairs, but competency
lives longer.
Merchant of Venice 1.2.8

4908 TIMON: Faults that are rich are
fair.
Timon of Athens 1.2.13

Ridicule

4909 BOYET: The tongues of mocking
wenches are as keen
As is the razor's edge invisible.
Love's Labor's Lost 5.2.256

Right

4910 BASSANIO [to Duke, about
Shylock]: To do a great right, do a
little wrong,
And curb this cruel devil of his will.
Merchant of Venice 4.1.216

Ripeness

4911 EDGAR: Men must endure
Their going hence even as their coming
hither,
Ripeness is all.
King Lear 5.2.9

4912 JAQUES: And so from hour to
hour, we ripe and ripe,
And then from hour to hour, we rot
and rot.
As You Like It 2.7.26

4913 K. RICHARD: The ripest fruit first
falls.
Richard II 2.1.153

Risk

4914 LUCIO: Our doubts are traitors,
And make us lose the good we oft
might win,
By fearing to attempt.
Measure for Measure 1.4.77

4915 CASSIUS: The storm is up, and all
is on the hazard.
Julius Caesar 5.1.68
[*on the hazard:* at stake]

Rivalry

4916 PRINCE: Two stars keep not their
motion in one sphere.
1 Henry IV 5.4.65

4917 Tell me thou lov'st elsewhere,
but in my sight,
Dear heart, forbear to glance thine eye
aside;
What need'st thou wound with cunning when thy might
Is more than my o'erpress'd defense
can bide?
Sonnet 139

River

4918 JULIA [to Lucetta]: The current
that with gentle murmur glides,
Thou know'st, being stopp'd, impa-
tiently doth rage;
But when his fair course is not hin-
dered,
He makes sweet music with th' enam-
ell'd stones,
Giving a gentle kiss to every sedge
He overtaketh in his pilgrimage.
Two Gentlemen of Verona 2.7.25

Robbery

4919 DUKE: The robb'd that smiles
steals something from the thief.
Othello 1.3.208

4920 OTHELLO: He that is robb'd, not
wanting what is stol'n,

Let him not know't, and he's not
robb'd at all.
Othello 3.3.342

4921 K. RICHARD: When the searching
eye of heaven is hid
Behind the globe, that lights the lower
world,
Then thieves and robbers range abroad
unseen
In murthers and in outrage boldly
here.
Richard II 3.2.37
[*murthers:* murders]

4922 CLIFFORD: What makes robbers
bold but too much lenity?
3 Henry VI 2.6.22

Rogue

4923 FALSTAFF: There is nothing but
roguery to be found in villainous man.
1 Henry IV 2.4.124

4924 KENT [about Oswald]: Such smiling rogues as these,
Like rats, oft bite the holy cords
a-twain
Which are t' intrinse t' unloose;
smooth every passion
That in the natures of their lords rebel,
Being oil to fire, snow to the colder
moods;
Renege, affirm, and turn their halcyon
beaks
With every gale and vary of their
masters,
Knowing nought (like dogs) but
following.
King Lear 2.2.73
[*smooth:* humor, flatter; *renege:* deny; *gale
and vary:* changing wind]

Rome

4925 TITINIUS [on Cassius' death]: The
sun of Rome is set.
Our day is gone,
Clouds, dews, and dangers come; our
deeds are done!
Julius Caesar 5.3.63

Rose

4926 Though the rose have prickles,
yet 'tis pluck'd!
Venus and Adonis 574

4927 O how much more doth beauty
beauteous seem
By that sweet ornament which truth
doth give!
The rose looks fair, but fairer we it
deem
For that sweet odor which doth in it
live.
Sonnet 54

4928 JULIET: What's in a name? That
which we call a rose
By any other word would smell as
sweet.
Romeo and Juliet 2.2.43

4929 EMILIA: Of all flow'rs
Methinks a rose is best.
WOMAN: Why, gentle madam?
EMILIA: It is the very emblem of a
maid;
For when the west wind courts her
gently,
How modestly she blows, and paints
the sun
With her chaste blushes! When the
north comes near her,
Rude and impatient, then, like
chastity,
She locks her beauties in her bud
again,
And leaves him to base briers.
Two Noble Kinsmen 2.2.135

Royalty

4930 K. RICHARD: The King's name is
a tower of strength,
Which they upon the adverse party
want.
Richard III 5.3.12

4931 KING: There's such divinity doth
hedge a king
That treason can but peep to what it
would.
Hamlet 4.5.124

4932 PORTIA: A substitute shines brightly as a king
Until a king be by, and then his state
Empties itself, as doth an inland brook
Into the main of waters.
Merchant of Venice 5.1.94

4933 PRINCE [soliloquy]: O majesty!
When thou dost pinch thy bearer, thou dost sit
Like a rich armor worn in heat of day,
That scald'st with safety.
2 Henry IV 4.5.28
[*scald'st with safety:* i.e. both protects and burns]

4934 K. RICHARD: Within the hollow crown
That rounds the mortal temples of a king
Keeps Death his court, and there the antic sits,
Scoffing his state and grinning at his pomp.
Richard II 3.2.160

4935 KING [soliloquy]: Uneasy lies the head that wears a crown.
2 Henry IV 3.1.31

4936 GLOUCESTER: Fearless minds climb soonest unto crowns.
3 Henry VI 4.7.63

4937 YORK [soliloquy]: Let pale-fac'd fear keep with the mean-born man,
And find no harbor in a royal heart.
2 Henry VI 3.1.335

4938 BELARIUS: The gates of monarchs
Are arch'd so high that giants may jet through
And keep their impious turbands on.
Cymbeline 3.3.4
[*jet:* strut]

4939 PERICLES: Heaven forbid
That kings should let their ears hear their faults hid!
Pericles 1.2.61
[*their faults hid:* i.e. listen to talk that hides their faults, as in flattery]

4940 BRAKENBURY: Princes have but their titles for their glories,
An outward honor for an inward toil,
And for unfelt imaginations
They often feel a world of restless cares;
So that between their titles and low name
There's nothing differs but the outward fame.
Richard III 1.4.78

4941 MALCOLM: The king-becoming graces,
As justice, verity, temp'rance, stableness,
Bounty, perseverance, mercy, lowliness,
Devotion, patience, courage, fortitude,
I have no relish of them.
Macbeth 4.3.91

4942 WOLSEY [soliloquy]: O how wretched
Is that poor man that hangs on princes' favors!
There is, betwixt that smile we would aspire to,
That sweet aspect of princes, and their ruin,
More pangs and fears than wars and women have;
And when he falls, he falls like Lucifer,
Never to hope again.
Henry VIII 3.2.366

4943 K. RICHARD: Let us sit upon the ground
And tell sad stories of the death of kings:
How some have been depos'd, some slain in war,
Some haunted by the ghosts they have deposed,
Some poisoned by their wives, some sleeping kill'd,
All murthered.
Richard II 3.2.155
[*murthered:* murdered]

4944 YORK [about Richard, on the castle wall]: Yet looks he like a king!
Behold, his eye,

As bright as is the eagle's, lightens
forth
Controlling majesty.
              Richard II 3.3.68

Ruin

4945 KING RICHARD: Cry woe,
destruction, ruin, and decay:
The worst is death, and death will have
his day.
             Richard II 3.2.102

4946 SHYLOCK [to Gratiano]: Repair
thy wit, good youth, or it will fall
To cureless ruin.
      Merchant of Venice 4.1.141

4947 WOLSEY [soliloquy]: I have
touch'd the highest point of all my
greatness,
And, from that full meridian of my
glory,
I haste now to my setting. I shall fall
Like a bright exhalation in the
evening,
And no man see me more.
           Henry VIII 3.2.223

4948 Ruin hath taught me thus to
ruminate,
That Time will come and take my love
away.
This thought is as a death, which cannot choose
But weep to have that which it fears to
lose.
                Sonnet 64

4949 SECOND LORD: Goodly buildings
left without a roof
Soon fall to ruin.
            Pericles 2.4.36

Rumor

4950 ROSSE: Cruel are the times when
we are traitors,
And do not know ourselves; when we
hold rumor

From what we fear, yet know not what
we fear.
             Macbeth 4.2.18

4951 WARWICK: Rumor doth double,
like the voice and echo,
The numbers of the feared.
           2 Henry IV 3.1.97

4952 DOCTOR: Foul whisp'rings are
abroad.
             Macbeth 5.1.71

4953 RUMOR: Open your ears; for
which of you will stop
The vent of hearing when loud Rumor
speaks?
I, from the orient to the drooping west
(Making the wind my post-horse), still
unfold
The acts commenced on this ball of
earth.
Upon my tongue continual slanders
ride,
The which in every language I pro-
nounce,
Stuffing the ears of men with false
reports.
I speak of peace, while covert enmity
Under the smile of safety wounds the
world;
And who but Rumor, who but only I,
Make fearful musters and prepar'd de-
fense,
Whiles the big year, swoll'n with some
other grief,
Is thought with child by the stern
tyrant war,
And no such matter? Rumor is a pipe
Blown by surmises, jealousies, conjec-
tures,
And of so easy and so plain a stop
That the blunt monster with un-
counted heads,
The still-discordant wav'ring multitude,
Can play upon it.
      2 Henry IV, Induction 1.1

4954 AARON: A long-tongu'd babbling gossip.
          Titus Andronicus 4.2.150

Running

4955 NORFOLK: We may outrun
By violent swiftness that which we run
    at,
And lose by overrunning.
                    Henry VIII 1.1.141

Rust

4956 Foul cank'ring rust the hidden
    treasure frets,
But gold that's put to use more gold
    begets.
                    Venus and Adonis 767

4957 FALSTAFF: I were better to be
eaten to death with a rust than to be
scour'd to nothing with perpetual
motion.
                    2 Henry IV 1.2.218

Ruthlessness

4958 MACBETH: The flighty purpose
    never is o'ertook
Unless the deed go with it. From this
    moment
The very firstlings of my heart shall be
The firstlings of my hand.
                    Macbeth 4.1.145

Sack

4959 FALSTAFF [soliloquy]: A good
sherris-sack hath a twofold operation in
it. It ascends me into the brain, dries
me there all the foolish and dull and
crudy vapors which environ it, makes it
apprehensive, quick, forgetive, full of
nimble, fiery, and delectable shapes,
which deliver'd o'er to the voice, the
tongue, which is the birth, becomes
excellent wit. The second property of
your excellent sherris is the warming of
the blood, which before (cold and
settled) left the liver white and pale,
which is the badge of pusillanimity
and cowardice; but the sherris warms
it, and makes it course from the inwards to the parts' extreme. It illumineth the face, which as a beacon
gives warning to all the rest of this little kingdom, man, to arm, and then
the vital commoners and inland petty
spirits muster me all to their captain,
the heart, who great and puff'd up
with this retinue, doth any deed of
courage; and this valor comes of sherris. So that skill in the weapon is
nothing without sack (for that sets it a-
work) and learning a mere hoard of
gold kept by a devil, till sack commences it and sets it in act and use.
                    2 Henry IV 4.3.96

4960 FALSTAFF: If sack and sugar be a
fault, God help the wicked!
                    1 Henry IV 2.4.470

4961 FALSTAFF: A coward is worse
than a cup of sack with lime in it.
                    1 Henry IV 2.4.126

Sadness

4962 Sad souls are slain in merry
company.
                    Rape of Lucrece 1110

4963 PRINCESS: A heavy heart bears
    not a humble tongue.
                    Love's Labor's Lost 5.2.737

4964 AUTOLYCUS [singing]:
A merry heart goes all the day,
Your sad tires in a mile-a.
                    Winter's Tale 4.3.125

4965 ORLANDO [declining Rosalind's
advice not to combat the King's feared
wrestler, Charles]: If I be foil'd, there
is but one sham'd that was never gracious; if kill'd, but one dead that is
willing to be so. I shall do my friends
no wrong, for I have none to lament
me; the world no injury, for in it I
have nothing. Only in the world I fill
up a place, which may be better supplied when I have made it empty.
                    As You Like It 1.2.187

4966 JAQUES: I have neither the scholar's melancholy, which is emulation; nor the musician's, which is fantastical; nor the courtier's, which is proud; nor the soldier's, which is ambitious; nor the lawyer's, which is politic; nor the lady's, which is nice; nor the lover's, which is all these: but it is a melancholy of my own, compounded of many simples, extracted from many objects, and indeed the sundry contemplation of my travels, in which my often rumination wraps me in a most humorous sadness.
As You Like It 4.1.10

4967 Distress likes dumps when time is kept with tears.
Rape of Lucrece 1127

4968 ANTONIO [to Salerio and Solanio]: In sooth, I know not why I am so sad;
It wearies me, you say it wearies you;
But how I caught it, found it, or came by it,
What stuff 'tis made of, whereof it is born,
I am to learn.
Merchant of Venice 1.1.1

4969 PETER: When griping griefs the heart doth wound,
And doleful dumps the mind oppress,
Then music with her silver sound . . .
With speedy help doth lend redress.
Romeo and Juliet 4.5.126

4970 BUSHY: Lay aside life-harming heaviness
And entertain a cheerful disposition.
Richard II 2.2.3

4971 PRINCE HAL [on the death of Henry IV]: Be sad, good brothers,
For by my faith it very well becomes you . . .
Be sad,
But entertain no more of it, good brothers,
Than a joint burden laid upon us all.
2 Henry IV 5.2.49

4972 PROSPERO: Let us not burthen our remembrances with
A heaviness that's gone.
The Tempest 5.1.198
[*burthen:* burden]

4973 FALSTAFF: A plague of sighing and grief, it blows a man up like a bladder.
1 Henry IV 2.4.331

4974 MESSENGER: Too much sadness hath congealed your blood.
Taming of the Shrew, Intro. 2.132

Safety

4975 LAERTES: Best safety lies in fear.
Hamlet 1.3.43

4976 HOTSPUR: Out of this nettle, danger, we pluck this flower, safety.
1 Henry IV 2.3.9

4977 BOY: I would give all my fame for a pot of ale and safety.
Henry V 3.2.12

Sage

4978 Sad pause and deep regard beseems the sage.
Rape of Lucrece 277

Salvation

4979 PORTIA: In the course of justice, none of us
Should see salvation. We do pray for mercy,
And that same prayer doth teach us all to render
The deeds of mercy.
Merchant of Venice 4.1.199

4980 KING: God's goodness hath been great to thee.
Let never day nor night unhallowed pass,
But still remember what the Lord hath done.
2 Henry VI 2.1.82

Salve

4981 To see the salve doth make the wound ache more.

Rape of Lucrece 1116

Satiety

4982 CLAUDIO: Surfeit is the father of much fast.

Measure for Measure 1.2.126

4983 LYSANDER: A surfeit of the sweetest things
The deepest loathing to the stomach brings.

Midsummer Night's Dream 2.2.137

4984 K. HENRY [on Richard II's reign]: They surfeited with honey and began
To loathe the taste of sweetness, whereof a little
More than a little is by much too much.

1 Henry IV 3.2.71

4985 KING: Goodness, growing to a plurisy,
Dies in his own too much.

Hamlet 4.7.117

[*plurisy:* excess, plethora]

4986 NERISSA: They are as sick that surfeit with too much as they that starve with nothing.

Merchant of Venice 1.2.5

4987 GRATIANO: Who riseth from a feast
With that keen appetite that he sits down?
Where is the horse that doth untread again
His tedious measures with the un-abated fire
That he did pace them first? All things that are,
Are with more spirit chased than en-joy'd.

Merchant of Venice 2.6.8

4988 BRUTUS: Enough, with over-measure.

Coriolanus 3.1.140

4989 FRIAR LAWRENCE: Violent delights have violent ends,
And in their triumph die, like fire and powder,
Which as they kiss consume. The sweetest honey
Is loathsome in his own deliciousness,
And in the taste confounds the appe-tite.
Therefore love moderately.

Romeo and Juliet 2.6.9

Satire

4990 THERSITES: Wit larded with malice.

Troilus and Cressida 5.1.57

4991 ROSENCRANTZ: Many wearing rapiers are afraid of goose-quills.

Hamlet 2.2.343

[*goose-quills:* the pens of satirical writers]

4992 PAINTER: It is a pretty mocking of the life.

Timon of Athens 1.1.35

4993 BOYET: The tongues of mocking wenches are as keen
As is the razor's edge invisible,
Cutting a smaller hair than may be seen;
Above the sense of sense, so sensible
Seemeth their conference, their con-ceits have wings
Fleeter than arrows, bullets, wind, thought, swifter things.

Love's Labor's Lost 5.2.256

Satisfaction

4994 PORTIA: He is well paid that is well satisfied.

Merchant of Venice 4.1.415

4995 Nor gives it satisfaction to our blood

That we must curb it upon others'
proof,
To be forbod the sweets that seem so
good
For fear of harms that preach in our
behoof.
O appetite, from judgment stand
aloof!

A Lover's Complaint 162

[*forbod:* forbidden]

Sauce

4996 ARCITE: Hunger needs no sauce.
Two Noble Kinsmen 3.3.24

Scandal

4997 ANGELO [soliloquy]: Authority
bears of a credent bulk,
That no particular scandal once can
touch
But it confounds the breather.
Measure for Measure 4.4.26

[*credent bulk:* massive credibility]

4998 What care I who calls me well or
ill,
So you o'er-green my bad, my good
allow?
Sonnet 112

4999 WORCESTER: We in the world's
wide mouth
Live scandaliz'd and foully spoken of.
1 Henry IV 1.3.153

5000 DUKE [soliloquy]: No might nor
greatness in mortality
Can censure scape; back-wounding
calumny
The whitest virtue strikes. What king
so strong
Can tie the gall up in the slanderous
tongue?
Measure for Measure 3.2.185

[*scape:* escape]

5001 The mightier man, the mightier
is the thing

That makes him honor'd, or begets
him hate;
For greatest scandal waits on greatest
state.
Rape of Lucrece 1004

5002 CAMILLO: The injury of tongues.
Winter's Tale 1.2.338

5003 GAUNT [on Richard's unwise
rule]: Ah, would the scandal vanish
with my life,
How happy then were my ensuing
death!
Richard II 2.1.67

Scars

5004 ROMEO: He jests at scars that
never felt a wound.
Romeo and Juliet 2.2.1

5005 YORK [to Somerset]: Show me
one scar character'd on thy skin:
Men's flesh preserv'd so whole do
seldom win.
2 Henry VI 3.1.300

5006 LAFEW: A scar nobly got, or a
noble scar, is a good liv'ry of honor.
All's Well That Ends Well 4.5.99

Sceptre

5007 PORTIA: Sceptre shows the force
of temporal power.
Merchant of Venice 4.1.190

5008 PANDULPH: A sceptre snatch'd
with an unruly hand
Must be as boisterously maintain'd as
gain'd.
King John 3.4.135

5009 EXETER: 'Tis much, when sceptres are in children's hands.
1 Henry VI 4.1.192

Scolding

5010 MISTRESS PAGE: Better a little chiding than a great deal of heart-break.
Merry Wives of Windsor 5.3.9

5011 BENEDICK [about Beatrice]: She speaks poniards, and every word stabs ... While she is here, a man may live as quiet in hell as in a sanctuary.
Much Ado About Nothing 2.1.247

5012 PETRUCHIO [to Gremio, about Kate]: Think you a little din can daunt mine ears?
Have I not in my time heard lions roar?
Have I not heard the sea, puff'd up with winds,
Rage like an angry boar chafed with sweat?
Have I not heard great ordnance in the field,
And heaven's artillery thunder in the skies?
Have I not in a pitched battle heard
Loud 'larums, neighing steeds, and trumpets' clang?
And do you tell me of a woman's tongue,
That gives not half so great a blow to hear
As will a chestnut in a farmer's fire?
Taming of the Shrew 1.2.199
['*larums:* alarums, calls to arms]

5013 ABBESS: Unquiet meals make ill digestions.
Comedy of Errors 5.1.74

Scorn

5014 VALENTINE: Scorn at first makes after-love the more.
Two Gentlemen of Verona 3.1.95

5015 Hot desire converts to cold disdain.
Rape of Lucrece 691

5016 VALENTINE: A woman sometimes scorns what best contents her.
Two Gentlemen of Verona 3.1.93

Scripture

5017 GLOUCESTER [soliloquy]: Thus I clothe my naked villainy
With odd old ends stol'n forth of holy writ,
And seem a saint, when most I play the devil.
Richard III 1.3.335

5018 ANTONIO: The devil can cite Scripture for his purpose.
Merchant of Venice 1.3.98

Sea

5019 TITUS: If the winds rage, doth not the sea wax mad,
Threat'ning the welkin with his big-swoll'n face?
Titus Andronicus 3.1.222

5020 EGEON: The always-wind-obeying deep.
Comedy of Errors 1.1.64

5021 MACBETH [soliloquy, on Duncan's murder]: What hands are here?
Hah! they pluck out mine eyes.
Will all great Neptune's ocean wash this blood
Clean from my hand? No; this my hand will rather
The multitudinous seas incarnadine,
Making the green one red.
Macbeth 2.2.56

5022 The sea, all water, yet receives rain still,
And in abundance addeth to his store.
Sonnet 135

Season

5023 TITANIA: The moon (the governess of floods),

Pale in her anger, washes all the air,
That rheumatic diseases do abound.
And through this distemperature, we
see
The seasons alter: hoary-headed frosts
Fall in the fresh lap of the crimson
rose,
And on old Hiems' thin and icy crown
An odorous chaplet of sweet summer
buds
Is, as in mockery, set; the spring, the
summer,
The chiding autumn, angry winter,
change
Their wonted liveries; and the mazed
world,
By their increase, now knows not which
is which.
Midsummer Night's Dream 2.1.103

5024 PORTIA: How many things by
season season'd are
To their right praise and true perfection!
Merchant of Venice 5.1.107

5025 GLOUCESTER: The seasons change
their manners.
2 Henry IV 4.4.123

Secrecy

5026 LUCIANA: Be not thy tongue thy
own shame's orator.
Comedy of Errors 3.2.10

5027 SOOTHSAYER: In nature's infinite
book of secrecy
A little I can read.
Antony and Cleopatra 1.2.10

5028 HOTSPUR: Constant you are,
But yet a woman, and for secrecy,
No lady closer, for I well believe
Thou wilt not utter what thou dost not
know,
And so far will I trust thee, gentle
Kate.
1 Henry IV 2.3.108

5029 PORTIA: How hard it is for
women to keep counsel!
Julius Caesar 2.4.8

5030 CRESSIDA: Who shall be true to
us,
When we are so unsecret to ourselves?
Troilus and Cressida 3.2.124

5031 NURSE: Two may keep counsel,
putting one away.
Romeo and Juliet 2.4.197

5032 AARON: Two may keep counsel
when the third's away.
Titus Andronicus 4.2.144

5033 LUCETTA: Fire that's closest kept
burns most of all.
Two Gentlemen of Verona 1.2.30

5034 MONTAGUE: But he, his own
affections' counsellor,
Is to himself (I will not say how true)
But to himself so secret and so close,
So far from sounding and discovery,
As is the bud bit with an envious
worm,
Ere he can spread his sweet leaves to
the air
Or dedicate his beauty to the sun.
Romeo and Juliet 1.1.147

Sect

5035 FIRST SENATOR: Quarrelling . . .
Is valor misbegot, and came into the
world
When sects and factions were newly
born.
Timon of Athens 3.5.27

Security

5036 HECAT: Security
Is mortals' chiefest enemy.
Macbeth 3.5.32

5037 DUKE: There is scarce truth
enough alive to make societies secure,
but security enough to make
fellowships accurs'd.
Measure for Measure 3.2.226

5038 ALCIBIADES: Reverend ages love
Security.
Timon of Athens 3.5.79

Seduction

5039 KING [reading from Diana's letter]: "A seducer flourishes, and a poor maid is undone."
All's Well That Ends Well 5.3.145

5040 K. HENRY: Some, peradventure, have on them the guilt . . . of beguiling virgins with the broken seals of perjury.
Henry V 4.1.163

5041 BANQUO: Oftentimes, to win us to our harm,
The instruments of darkness tell us truths,
Win us with honest trifles, to betray 's
In deepest consequence.
Macbeth 1.3.124

Self

5042 PROTEUS [soliloquy]: I to myself am dearer than a friend.
Two Gentlemen of Verona 2.6.23

5043 To give away yourself keeps yourself still.
Sonnet 16

5044 IAGO: 'Tis in ourselves that we are thus or thus.
Othello 1.3.319

5045 CASSIUS [alluding to Caesar]: I cannot tell what you and other men
Think of this life; but, for my single self,
I had as lief not be as live to be
In awe of such a thing as I myself.
Julius Caesar 1.2.93

5046 TROILUS: You cannot shun yourself.
Troilus and Cressida 3.2.146

5047 PAROLLES: Our remedies oft in ourselves do lie,
Which we ascribe to heaven.
All's Well That Ends Well 1.1.216

Self-control

5048 MACDUFF: Boundless intemperance
In nature is a tyranny.
Macbeth 4.3.67

5049 LUCIANA: Headstrong liberty is lash'd with woe.
Comedy of Errors 2.1.15

5050 ROSSE [to Lady Macduff]: I pray you school yourself.
Macbeth 4.2.15
[*school:* control]

5051 CHARMIAN: Keep yourself within yourself.
Antony and Cleopatra 2.5.75

5052 PANDULPH [to King Philip]: Better conquest never canst thou make
Than arm thy constant and thy nobler parts
Against these giddy loose suggestions.
King John 3.1.290

5053 HAMLET [to the Queen]: Refrain to-night,
And that shall lend a kind of easiness
To the next abstinence, the next more easy;
For use almost can change the stamp of nature.
Hamlet 3.4.165

Self-defense

5054 ALCIBIADES: To kill, I grant, is sin's extremest gust,
But in defense, by mercy, 'tis most just.
Timon of Athens 3.5.54

5055 LEAR: Thou'dst shun a bear,
But if thy flight lay toward the roaring sea,
Thou'dst meet the bear i' th' mouth.
King Lear 3.4.8

5056 CLIFFORD: The smallest worm will turn, being trodden on,

And doves will peck in safeguard of
their brood.
3 Henry VI 2.2.17

Self-denial

5057 PERICLES: He's no man on whom
perfections wait
That, knowing sin within, will touch
the gate.
Pericles 1.1.79

Self-examination

5058 ISABELLA [to Angelo]: Go to your
bosom,
Knock there, and ask your heart what
it doth know
That's like my brother's fault. If it
confess
A natural guiltiness such as is his,
Let it not sound a thought upon your
tongue
Against my brother's life.
Measure for Measure 2.2.136

5059 ORLANDO: I will chide no
breather in the world but myself,
against whom I know most faults.
As You Like It 3.2.280

Self-fulfillment

5060 KING: Honors thrive,
When rather from our acts we them
derive
Than our foregoers.
All's Well That Ends Well 2.3.135

Self-knowledge

5061 Men's faults do seldom to
themselves appear.
Rape of Lucrece 633

5062 CLOWN [to Duke, concerning a
fault he found in his friends]: Sir, they
praise me, and make an ass of me.
Now my foes tell me plainly I am an

ass; so that by my foes, sir, I profit in
the knowledge of myself, and by my
friends I am abus'd.
Twelfth Night 5.1.17

Selflessness

5063 TIMON: There's none
Can truly say he gives if he receives.
Timon of Athens 1.2.10

Self-love

5064 IAGO: I have look'd upon the
world for four times seven years, and
since I could distinguish betwixt a
benefit and an injury, I never found
man that knew how to love himself.
Othello 1.3.311

5065 WOLSEY: Love thyself last,
cherish those hearts that hate thee.
Henry VIII 3.2.443

5066 PAROLLES: Self-love . . . is the
most inhibited sin in the canon.
All's Well That Ends Well 1.1.144

5067 DOLPHIN [to French King]: Self-
love, my liege, is not so vile a sin
As self-neglecting.
Henry V 2.4.74

5068 PROTEUS [soliloquy]: I to myself
am dearer than a friend.
Two Gentlemen of Verona 2.6.23

5069 Sin of self-love possesseth all
mine eye,
And all my soul, and all my every
part;
And for this sin there is no remedy,
It is so grounded inward in my heart.
Sonnet 62

5070 YOUNG CLIFFORD [soliloquy]: He
that is truly dedicate to war
Hath no self-love.
2 Henry VI 5.2.37

5071 Q. KATHERINE [to King]: Love yourself, and in that love Not unconsidered leave your honor.
Henry VIII 1.2.14

Self-pity

5072 GLOUCESTER: None can help our harms by wailing them.
Richard III 2.2.103

Self-praise

5073 What can mine own praise to mine own self bring?
Sonnet 39

5074 AGAMEMNON: Whatever praises itself but in the deed, devours the deed in the praise.
Troilus and Cressida 2.3.156

5075 STEWARD: We wound our modesty, and make foul the clearness of our deservings, when of ourselves we publish them.
All's Well That Ends Well 1.3.5

5076 AENEAS: The worthiness of praise distains his worth, If that the prais'd himself bring the praise forth.
Troilus and Cressida 1.3.241
[*distains:* taints]

5077 BEATRICE: There's not one wise man in twenty that will praise himself.
Much Ado About Nothing 5.2.73

Self-reliance

5078 HELENA: Our remedies oft in ourselves do lie, Which we ascribe to heaven.
All's Well That Ends Well 1.1.216

5079 PISTOL: The world's mine oyster, Which I with sword will open.
Merry Wives of Windsor 2.2.3

5080 CORIN: I earn that I eat, get that I wear, owe no man hate, envy no man's happiness, glad of other men's good, content with my harm.
As You Like It 3.2.73

5081 CORIOLANUS: I'll never Be such a gosling to obey instinct, but stand As if a man were author of himself, And knew no other kin.
Coriolanus 5.3.34

5082 Where is truth, if there be no self-trust?
Rape of Lucrece 158

5083 POMPEY: I know not What counts harsh Fortune casts upon my face, But in my bosom shall she never come, To make my heart her vassal.
Antony and Cleopatra 2.6.53

5084 CONRADE [to Don John]: It is impossible you should take true root but by the fair weather that you make yourself. It is needful that you frame the season for your own harvest.
Much Ado About Nothing 1.3.24

5085 CLAUDIO [soliloquy]: Let every eye negotiate for itself, And trust no agent.
Much Ado About Nothing 2.1.178

5086 BANQUO [to the three witches]: If you can look into the seeds of time, And say which grain will grow, and which will not, Speak then to me, who neither beg nor fear Your favors nor your hate.
Macbeth 1.3.60

Self-reproach

5087 PATROCLUS: Those wounds heal ill that men do give themselves.
Troilus and Cressida 3.3.229

5088 To you it doth belong
Your self to pardon of self-doing
crime.
Sonnet 58

5089 When in disgrace with Fortune
and men's eyes
I all alone beweep my outcast state,
And trouble deaf heaven with my
bootless cries,
And look upon myself and curse my
fate,
Wishing me like to one more rich in
hope,
Featur'd like him, like him with
friends possess'd,
Desiring this man's art, and that man's
scope,
With what I most enjoy contented
least;
Yet in these thoughts myself almost
despising,
Haply I think on thee, and then my
state
(Like to the lark at break of day arising
From sullen earth) sings hymns at
heaven's gate,
For thy sweet love rememb'red such
wealth brings,
That then I scorn to change my state
with kings.
Sonnet 29

Self-slaughter

5090 IMOGEN: Against self-slaughter
There is a prohibition so divine
That cravens my weak hand.
Cymbeline 3.4.76
[*cravens:* renders cowardly]

5091 HAMLET [soliloquy]: O that this
too too sallied flesh would melt,
Thaw, and resolve itself into a dew!
Or that the Everlasting had not fix'd
His canon 'gainst self-slaughter!
Hamlet 1.2.129
[*sallied:* sullied; many editors prefer *solid*]

Self-will

5092 HAMLET: There's a divinity that
shapes our ends,
Rough-hew them how we will.
Hamlet 5.2.10

Selling

5093 COSTARD: To sell a bargain well
is as cunning as fast and loose.
Love's Labor's Lost 3.1.103

5094 BEROWNE: To things of sale a
seller's praise belongs.
Love's Labor's Lost 4.3.236

5095 ROSALIND [to Phebe, on the
love-struck Silvius]:
Sell when you can, you are not for all
markets.
As You Like It 3.5.60

5096 PARIS: Fair Diomed, you do as
chapmen do,
Dispraise the thing that they desire to
buy,
But we in silence hold this virtue well,
We'll not commend what we intend to
sell.
Troilus and Cressida 4.1.76

5097 AUTOLYCUS [singing]:
Gloves as sweet as damask roses,
Masks for faces and for noses;
Bugle-bracelet, necklace amber,
Perfume for a lady's chamber;
Golden quoifs and stomachers
For my lads to give their dears;
Pins and poking-sticks of steel;
What maids lack from head to heel:
Come buy of me, come; come buy,
come buy,
Buy, lads, or else your lasses cry:
Come buy.
Winter's Tale 4.4.220

Senility

5098 GONERIL: Old fools are babes
again, and must be us'd
With checks as flatteries.
                              King Lear 1.3.18

Senses

5099 MACBETH [soliloquy]: Mine eyes
are made the fools o' th' other
senses.
                              Macbeth 2.1.44

5100 KING: What impossibility would
slay
In common sense, sense saves another
way.
           All's Well That Ends Well 2.1.177
[*sense saves:* i.e. reason saves]

5101 HERMIA: Dark night, that from
the eye his function takes,
The ear more quick of apprehension
makes;
Wherein it doth impair the seeing
sense,
It pays the hearing double recompense.
           Midsummer Night's Dream 3.2.177

5102 TROILUS: My election
Is led on in the conduct of my will,
My will enkindled by mine eyes and
ears,
Two traded pilots 'twixt the dangerous
shores
Of will and judgment.
              Troilus and Cressida 2.2.63
[*election:* choice; *traded pilots:* intermediaries constantly going back and
forth]

5103 IMOGEN: Our very eyes
Are sometimes like our judgments,
blind.
                              Cymbeline 4.2.301

5104 BELARIUS: To apprehend . . .
Draws us a profit from all things we
see.
                              Cymbeline 3.3.17

5105 SEBASTIAN: Let fancy still my
sense in Lethe steep;
If this be thus to dream, still let me
sleep!
                              Twelfth Night 4.1.62

Sensibility

5106 Men have marble, women waxen
minds.
                         Rape of Lucrece 1240

Sensitivity

5107 EMILIA [to Othello]: Thou hast
not half that pow'r to do me harm
As I have to be hurt.
                              Othello 5.2.162
[*be hurt:* i.e. endure hurt]

Sensuality

5108 IAGO: If the beam of our lives
had not one scale of reason to poise
another of sensuality, the blood and
baseness of our natures would conduct
us to most prepost'rous conclusions.
                              Othello 1.3.326
[*beam:* balance]

5109 TIMON [soliloquy]: Ingrateful
man, with liquorish draughts
And morsels unctuous, greases his pure
mind,
That from it all consideration slips.
                         Timon of Athens 4.3.194

Sentence

5110 CLOWN: A sentence is but a
chev'ril glove to a good wit.
How quickly the wrong side may be
turn'd outward!
                              Twelfth Night 3.1.11
[*chev'ril:* kidskin]

5111 CANTERBURY [about Henry]:
When he speaks,
The air, a charter'd libertine, is still,

And the mute wonder lurketh in men's
ears
To steal his sweet and honeyed sentences.
Henry V 1.1.50

Separation

5112 All days are nights to see till I
see thee,
And nights bright days when dreams
do show thee me.
Sonnet 43

Serpent

5113 LADY MACBETH [to Macbeth]:
Look like th' innocent flower,
But be the serpent under't.
Macbeth 1.5.65

5114 Who sees the lurking serpent
steps aside.
Rape of Lucrece 362

5115 BRUTUS: [soliloquy]: It is the
bright day that brings forth the
adder,
And that craves wary walking.
Julius Caesar 2.1.14

Servant

5116 POSTHUMUS: Every good servant
does not all commands;
No bond, but to do just ones.
Cymbeline 5.1.6

Service

5117 PROTEUS: Love
Will creep in service where it cannot
go.
Two Gentlemen of Verona 4.2.19

5118 IAGO: 'Tis the curse of service;
Preferment goes by letter and affection,

And not by old gradation, where each
second
Stood heir to th' first.
Othello 1.1.35
[*old gradation:* seniority]

5119 HECTOR: 'Tis mad idolatry
To make the service greater than the
god.
Troilus and Cressida 2.2.56

5120 CLOWN: Things may serve long,
but not serve ever.
All's Well That Ends Well 2.2.58

5121 PETRUCHIO: The poorest service
is repaid with thanks.
Taming of the Shrew 4.3.45

5122 WOLSEY: Had I but serv'd my
God with half the zeal
I serv'd my king, He would not in
mine age
Have left me naked to mine enemies.
Henry VIII 3.2.455

5123 ORLANDO [to Adam]: O good
old man, how well in thee appears
The constant service of the antique
world,
When service sweat for duty, not for
meed!
Thou art not for the fashion of these
times,
Where none will sweat but for promotion.
As You Like It 2.3.56
[*meed:* reward]

5124 To give away yourself keeps
yourself still.
Sonnet 16

Servitude

5125 IAGO: We cannot all be masters,
nor all masters
Cannot be truly follow'd.
Othello 1.1.43

5126 POSTHUMUS: Every good servant
does not all commands;
No bond, but to do just ones.
Cymbeline 5.1.6

Shadows

5127 ARRAGON: Some there be that
shadows kiss,
Such have but a shadow's bliss.
Merchant of Venice 2.9.66

5128 At his own shadow let the thief
run mad.
Rape of Lucrece 997

5129 K. RICHARD [to Ratcliffe]:
Shadows to-night
Have strook more terror to the soul of
Richard
Than can the substance of ten thou-
sand soldiers
Armed in proof and led by shallow
Richmond.
Richard III 5.3.216
[*strook:* struck]

Shame

5130 LUCIANA: Be not thy tongue thy
own shame's orator.
Comedy of Errors 3.2.10

5131 LUCIANA: Shame hath a bastard
fame, well managed.
Comedy of Errors 3.2.19

5132 LEONTES: Past all shame . . .
So past all truth.
Winter's Tale 3.2.84

5133 HAMLET: O shame, where is thy
blush?
Hamlet 3.4.81

5134 GONERIL: Shame itself doth
speak
For instant remedy.
King Lear 1.4.246

5135 MARTIUS: I have wounds upon
me, and they smart
To hear themselves rememb'red.
Coriolanus 1.9.28

5136 Shame folded up in blind concealing night,
When most unseen, then most doth
tyrannize.
Rape of Lucrece 675

5137 FIRST SENATOR: Never shame to
hear
What you have nobly done.
Coriolanus 2.2.67

5138 SECOND MURDERER: [Conscience]
is a blushing shame-fac'd spirit.
Richard III 1.4.137

Sheep

5139 BENEDICK: Is it not strange that
sheep's guts should hale souls out of
men's bodies?
Much Ado About Nothing 2.3.59
[*sheep's guts:* violin or lute strings]

5140 CORIN: Good pasture makes fat
sheep.
As You Like It 3.2.27

Shepherd

5141 KING [soliloquy, near the bat-
tlefield]: The shepherd's homely
curds,
His cold thin drink out of his leather
bottle,
His wonted sleep under a fresh tree's
shade,
All which secure and sweetly he enjoys,
Is far beyond a prince's delicates—
His viands sparkling in a golden cup,
His body crouched in a curious bed,
When care, mistrust, and treason waits
on him.
3 Henry VI 2.5.47

Sherris (Sherry)

5142 FALSTAFF: Valor comes of sherris.
2 Henry IV 4.3.113

Should

5143 KING: "Should" is like a spendthrift's sigh,
That hurts by easing.
Hamlet 4.7.122
[*spendthrift's sigh:* a sigh which, it was supposed, drew blood from the heart]

Showers

5144 GAUNT: Small show'rs last long,
but sudden storms are short.
Richard II 2.1.35

Sickness

5145 LUCIO'S SERVANT: Many do keep
their chambers are not sick.
Timon of Athens 3.4.73

5146 CORIN: The more one sickens the
worse at ease he is.
As You Like It 3.2.23

5147 Testy sick men, when their
deaths be near,
No news but health from their physicians know.
Sonnet 140

5148 NERISSA: They are as sick that
surfeit with too much as they that
starve with nothing.
Merchant of Venice 1.2.5

5149 HELENA: Sickness is catching.
Midsummer Night's Dream 1.1.186

5150 LEAR: Infirmity doth still neglect
all office
Whereto our health is bound.
King Lear 2.4.106

Sighing

5151 ULYSSES: Welcome ever smiles,
And farewell goes out sighing.
Troilus and Cressida 3.3.168

5152 FALSTAFF: A plague of sighing
and grief, it blows a man up like a
bladder.
1 Henry IV 2.4.331

5153 LAUNCE: If the wind were down,
I could drive the boat with my sighs.
Two Gentlemen of Verona 2.3.52

5154 HAMLET: Windy suspiration of
forc'd breath.
Hamlet 1.2.79

Sight

5155 ROMEO: He that is strooken blind
cannot forget
The precious treasure of his eyesight
lost.
Romeo and Juliet 1.1.232
[*strooken:* stricken]

5156 To see sad sights moves more
than hear them told,
For then the eye interprets to the ear.
Rape of Lucrece 1324

5157 ROSALIND: To have seen much,
and to have nothing, is to have rich
eyes and poor hands.
As You Like It 4.1.23

5158 He sees his love, and nothing
else he sees,
For nothing else with his proud sight
agrees.
Venus and Adonis 287

Silence

5159 CLAUDIO: Silence is the
perfectest herald of joy.
Much Ado About Nothing 2.1.306
[*herald:* herald]

5160 EMILIA: Silence often of pure innocence
Persuades when speaking fails.
Winter's Tale 2.2.39

5161 GRATIANO: Silence is only commendable
In a neat's tongue dried and a maid not vendible.
Merchant of Venice 1.1.111
[*neat's:* ox's; *vendible:* salable, i.e. marriageable]

5162 COUNTESS: Be check'd for silence,
But never tax'd for speech.
All's Well That Ends Well 1.1.67

5163 GRATIANO: I do know of these
That therefore only are reputed wise
For saying nothing.
Merchant of Venice 1.1.95

5164 PROTEUS [soliloquy, on Julia]:
What, gone without a word?
Ay, so true love should do: it cannot speak,
For truth hath better deeds than words to grace it.
Two Gentlemen of Verona 2.2.16

5165 MORTIMER [to Plantagenet]:
With silence, nephew, be thou politic.
1 Henry VI 2.5.101

Silver

5166 BASSANIO: Thou pale and common drudge
'Tween man and man.
Merchant of Venice 3.2.103

5167 FIRST MUSICIAN: Silver hath a sweet sound.
Romeo and Juliet 4.5.131

Simplicity

5168 THESEUS: Never anything can be amiss,

When simpleness and duty tender it.
Midsummer Night's Dream 5.1.83

5169 Q. ELIZABETH: An honest tale speeds best being plainly told.
Richard III 4.4.358

Sin

5170 Who buys a minute's mirth to wail a week?
Or sells eternity to get a toy?
Rape of Lucrece 213

5171 ANGELO [soliloquy]: Most dangerous
Is that temptation that doth goad us on
To sin in loving virtue.
Measure for Measure 2.2.180

5172 CLOWN: Virtue that transgresses is but patch'd with sin, and sin that amends is but patch'd with virtue.
Twelfth Night 1.5.48

5173 K. RICHARD: Sin will pluck on sin.
Richard III 4.2.64

5174 BASTARD: Some sins do bear their privilege on earth.
King John 1.1.261

5175 KING: Forbear to judge, for we are sinners all.
2 Henry VI 3.3.31

5176 FIRST SENATOR: Nothing emboldens sin so much as mercy.
Timon of Athens 3.5.3

5177 PERICLES: Few love to hear the sins they love to act.
Pericles 1.1.92

5178 ESCALUS: Some rise by sin, and some by virtue fall;
Some run from brakes of ice and answer none,
And some condemned for a fault alone.
Measure for Measure 2.1.38

5179 LEAR: Through tatter'd clothes small vices do appear;
Robes and furr'd gowns hide all.
King Lear 4.6.164

5180 LEAR: Plate sin with gold,
And the strong lance of justice hurtless breaks;
Arm it in rags, a pigmy's straw does pierce it.
King Lear 4.6.165

5181 CLAUDIO: O, what authority and show of truth
Can cunning sin cover itself withal!
Much Ado About Nothing 4.1.35

5182 ISABELLA: O, 'tis the cunning livery of hell,
The damned'st body to invest and cover
In prenzie guards!
Measure for Measure 3.1.94

5183 PERICLES: How courtesy would seem to cover sin.
Pericles 1.1.121

5184 PERICLES: He's no man on whom perfections wait
That, knowing sin within, will touch the gate.
Pericles 1.1.79

5185 SALISBURY: It is a great sin to swear unto a sin,
But greater sin to keep a sinful oath.
2 Henry VI 5.1.182

5186 GLOWER: Best custom what they did begin
Was with long use account'd no sin.
Pericles, Prologue 29

5187 PERICLES [soliloquy]: One sin, I know, another doth provoke:
Murther's as near to lust as flame to smoke;
Poison and treason are the hands of sin,
Ay, and the targets to put off the shame.
Pericles 1.1.137

[*murther:* murder]

5188 O, in what sweets dost thou thy sins enclose!
Sonnet 95

5189 PERICLES: Kings are earth's gods; in vice their law's their will.
Pericles 1.1.103

5190 Sin ne'er gives a fee,
He gratis comes.
Rape of Lucrece 913

5191 PORTIA: It is a sin to be a mocker.
Merchant of Venice 1.2.57

5192 K. HENRY: 'Tis sin to flatter.
3 Henry VI 5.6.3

5193 HELICANUS: Flattery is the bellows blows up sin.
Pericles 1.2.39

5194 WOLSEY [to Cromwell]: I charge thee, fling away ambition!
By that sin fell the angels.
Henry VIII 3.2.440

5195 PAROLLES: Self-love … is the most inhibited sin in the canon.
All's Well That Ends Well 1.1.144

5196 HAMLET: Mother, for love of grace,
Lay not that flattering unction to your soul,
That not your trespass but my madness speaks;
It will but skin and film the ulcerous place,
Whiles rank corruption, mining all within,
Infects unseen. Confess yourself to heaven,
Repent what's past, avoid what is to come,
And do not spread the compost on the weeds
To make them ranker.
Hamlet 3.4.144

5197 Think but how vile a spectacle it were
To view thy present trespass in another.
Men's faults do seldom to themselves appear,

Their own transgressions partially they
smother.
                        Rape of Lucrece 631

5198 ALCIBIADES: To kill, I grant, is
sin's extremest gust.
                        Timon of Athens 3.5.54

5199 OTHELLO [to Desdemona]: Con-
fess thee freely of thy sin;
For to deny each article with oath
Cannot remove nor choke the strong
conception
That I do groan withal.
                        Othello 5.2.53

5200 OTHELLO [to Desdemona]: Think
on thy sins.
                        Othello 5.2.39

5201 HAMLET [soliloquy]: Foul deeds
will rise,
Though all the earth o'erwhelm them,
to men's eyes.
                        Hamlet 1.2.256

Sincerity

5202 FIRST BANDITTI: There is no time
so miserable but a man may be true.
                        Timon of Athens 4.3.456

5203 IAGO: Men should be what they
seem,
Or those that be not, would they
might seem none!
                        Othello 3.3.126

5204 HAMLET: Suit the action to the
word, the word to the action, with this
special observance, that you o'erstep
not the modesty of nature.
                        Hamlet 3.2.17

5205 OTHELLO: Speak of me as I am;
nothing extenuate.
                        Othello 5.2.342

Singing

5206 PORTIA: The crow doth sing as
sweetly as the lark
When neither is attended.
                        Merchant of Venice 5.1.102

Skepticism

5207 HECTOR: Modest doubt is call'd
The beacon of the wise, the tent that
searches
To th' bottom of the worst.
                        Troilus and Cressida 2.2.15
[*tent:* probe]

Sky

5208 HAMLET: This most excellent
canopy, the air, look you, this brave
o'erhanging firmament, this majestical
roof fretted with golden fire, why, it
appeareth nothing to me but a foul
and pestilent congregation of vapors.
                        Hamlet 2.2.299

5209 SCROOP: Men judge by the complexion of the sky
The state and inclination of the day.
                        Richard II 3.2.194

5210 BULLINGBROOK: The more fair
and crystal is the sky,
The uglier seem the clouds that in it
fly.
                        Richard II 1.1.41

5211 K. JOHN: So foul a sky clears not
without a storm.
                        King John 4.2.108

Slander

5212 HAMLET: Be thou as chaste as
ice, as pure as snow, thou shalt not
escape calumny.
                        Hamlet 3.1.135

5213 DUKE [soliloquy]: No might nor
greatness in mortality
Can censure scape; back-wounding
calumny
The whitest virtue strikes. What king
so strong
Can tie the gall up in the slanderous
tongue?
                        Measure for Measure 3.2.185

5214 LAERTES: Virtue itself scapes not calumnious strokes.
Hamlet 1.3.38

5215 OLIVIA: There is no slander in an allow'd fool, though he do nothing but rail.
Twelfth Night 1.5.94

5216 PISANIO: 'Tis slander,
Whose edge is sharper than the sword, whose tongue
Outvenoms all the worms of Nile, whose breath
Rides on the posting winds and doth belie
All corners of the world. Kings, queens, and states,
Maids, matrons, nay, the secrets of the grave
This viperous slander enters.
Cymbeline 3.4.33

5217 RUMOR: Upon my tongues continual slanders ride.
2 Henry IV, Induction 6

5218 BALTHAZAR: Slander lives upon succession,
For ever hous'd where it gets possession.
Comedy of Errors 3.1.105

5219 Slander's mark was ever yet the fair;
The ornament of beauty is suspect,
A crow that flies in heaven's sweetest air.
So thou be good, slander doth but approve
Thy worth the greater.
Sonnet 70

5220 WOLSEY: We must not stint
Our necessary actions in the fear
To cope malicious censurers.
Henry VIII 1.2.76

5221 JULIET [to Paris]: That is no slander, sir, which is a truth.
Romeo and Juliet 4.1.33

5222 OLIVIA: To be generous . . . is to take those things for bird-bolts that you deem cannon-bullets.
Twelfth Night 1.5.91
[*bird-bolts:* blunt-headed arrows for shooting birds]

5223 HERO: How much an ill word may empoison liking.
Much Ado About Nothing 3.1.86

5224 MENENIUS [to some factious citizens]: You slander
The helms o' th' state, who care for you like fathers,
When you curse them as enemies.
Coriolanus 1.1.76

5225 ANTONY: Read not my blemishes in the world's report.
Antony and Cleopatra 2.3.5

Slave

5226 PISTOL: Base is the slave that pays.
Henry V 2.1.96

5227 CASCA: Every bondsman in his own hand bears
The power to cancel his captivity.
Julius Caesar 1.3.101

5228 CLEOPATRA [to Seleucus]: O slave, of no more trust
Than love that's hir'd!
Antony and Cleopatra 5.2.154

Sleep

5229 BELARIUS: Weariness
Can snore upon the flint, when resty sloth
Finds the down pillow hard.
Cymbeline 3.6.33

5230 K. HENRY [soliloquy]: O sleep! O gentle sleep!
Nature's soft nurse, how have I frighted thee,
That thou no more wilt weigh my eyelids down,

And steep my senses in forgetfulness?
Why rather, sleep, liest thou in smoky
 cribs,
Upon uneasy pallets stretching thee,
And hush'd with buzzing night-flies to
 thy slumber,
Than in the perfum'd chambers of the
 great,
Under the canopies of costly state,
And lull'd with sound of sweetest
 melody?
O thou dull god, why li'st thou with
 the vile
In loathsome beds, and leavest the
 kingly couch
A watch-case or a common 'larum-bell?
Wilt thou upon the high and giddy
 mast
Seal up the ship-boy's eyes, and rock
 his brains
In cradle of the rude imperious surge,
And in the visitation of the winds,
Who take the ruffian billows by the
 top,
Curling their monstrous heads and
 hanging them
With deafening clamor in the slippery
 clouds,
That with the hurly death itself
 awakes?
Canst thou, O partial sleep, give then
 repose
To the wet sea-boy in an hour so rude,
And in the calmest and most stillest
 night,
With all appliances and means to boot,
Deny it to a king? Then happy low, lie
 down!
Uneasy lies the head that wears a
 crown.
                    2 Henry IV 3.1.5
[*hurly:* tumult; *low:* lowly ones]

5231 K. HENRY [soliloquy]: 'Tis not
 the balm, the sceptre, and the ball,
The sword, the mace, the crown
 imperial,
The intertissued robe of gold and
 pearl ...
The throne he sits on, nor the tide of
 pomp
That beats upon the high shore of this
 world ...

Not all these, laid in bed majestical,
Can sleep so soundly as the wretched
 slave;
Who, with a body fill'd and vacant
 mind,
Gets him to rest, cramm'd with
 distressful bread ...
Winding up days with toil and nights
 with sleep.
                    Henry V 4.1.260

5232 DOCTOR: Our foster-nurse of
 nature is repose.
                    King Lear 4.4.12

5233 Though woe be heavy, yet it
 seldom sleeps.
                    Rape of Lucrece 1574

5234 SEBASTIAN: It seldom visits sorrow; when it doth,
It is a comforter.
                    The Tempest 2.1.195

5235 HELENA: Sleep, that sometimes
 shuts up sorrow's eye,
Steal me a while from mine own
 company.
                    Midsummer Night's Dream 3.2.435

5236 FIRST JAILER: He that sleeps feels
 not the toothache.
                    Cymbeline 5.4.172

5237 GARDINER: These should be
 hours for necessities,
Not for delights; times to repair our
 nature
With comforting repose, and not for us
 To waste these times.
                    Henry VIII 5.1.2

5238 DUKE [to the condemned
 Claudio]: The best of rest is sleep,
And that thou oft provok'st, yet grossly
 fear'st
Thy death, which is no more.
                    Measure for Measure 3.1.17

5239 HAMLET [soliloquy]: To die, to
 sleep —
To sleep, perchance to dream — ay,
 there's the rub,

For in that sleep of death what dreams
may come,
When we have shuffled off this mortal
coil,
Must give us pause.

Hamlet 3.1.64

5240 FRIAR LAWRENCE: Care keeps his
watch in every old man's eye,
And where care lodges, sleep will never
lie;
But where unbruised youth with
unstuff'd brain
Doth couch his limbs, there golden
sleep doth reign.

Romeo and Juliet 2.3.35

5241 LADY MACBETH: The sleeping
and the dead
Are but as pictures.

Macbeth 2.2.50

5242 MACDUFF: Downy sleep, death's
counterfeit.

Macbeth 2.3.76

5243 AGAMEMNON: A stirring dwarf
we do allowance give
Before a sleeping giant.

Troilus and Cressida 2.3.137

5244 GLENDOWER [interpreting to
Lord Mortimer what his wife, who
speaks only Welsh, is saying to him]:
She bids you on the wanton rushes lay
you down,
And rest your gentle head upon her
lap,
And she will sing the song that
pleaseth you,
And on your eyelids crown the god of
sleep,
Charming your blood with pleasing
heaviness,
Making such difference 'twixt wake and
sleep
As is the difference betwixt day and
night
The hour before the heavenly-harness'd
team
Begins his golden progress in the east.

1 Henry IV 3.1.217

5245 MACBETH [soliloquy]: Now o'er
the one half world
Nature seems dead, and wicked dreams
abuse
The curtain'd sleep.

Macbeth 2.1.49

5246 MACBETH [to Lady Macbeth,
after Duncan's murder]:
Methought I heard a voice cry, "Sleep
no more!
Macbeth does murther sleep" — the innocent sleep,
Sleep that knits up the ravell'd sleave
of care,
The death of each day's life, sore
labor's bath,
Balm of hurt minds, great nature's second course,
Chief nourisher in life's feast.

Macbeth 2.2.32

[*murther:* murder]

5247 DOCTOR [on Lady Macbeth's
sleepwalking confession]:
Foul whisp'rings are abroad. Unnatural
deeds
Do breed unnatural troubles; infected
minds
To their deaf pillows will discharge
their secrets.

Macbeth 5.1.71

5248 BRUTUS: Boy! Lucius! Fast
asleep? It is no matter,
Enjoy the honey-heavy dew of slumber.
Thou hast no figures nor no fantasies,
Which busy care draws in the brains of
men;
Therefore thou sleep'st so sound.

Julius Caesar 2.1.229

5249 IAGO: There are a kind of men,
so loose of soul,
That in their sleeps will mutter their
affairs.

Othello 3.3.416

5250 ALONSO: I wish mine eyes
Would, with themselves, shut up my
thoughts.

The Tempest 2.1.191

Smell

5251 The rose looks fair, but fairer we
it deem
For that sweet odor which doth in it
live.
Sonnet 54

5252 JULIET: That which we call a rose
By any other word would smell as
sweet.
Romeo and Juliet 2.2.43

5253 The summer's flow'r is to the
summer sweet,
Though to itself it only live and die,
But if that flow'r with base infection
meet,
The basest weed outbraves his dignity:
For sweetest things turn sourest by
their deeds;
Lilies that fester smell far worse than
weeds.
Sonnet 94
[*outbraves:* surpasses in splendor]

5254 FRIAR LAWRENCE: Within the infant rind of this weak flower
Poison hath residence and medicine
power;
For this, being smelt, with that part
cheers each part,
Being tasted, stays all senses with the
heart.
Romeo and Juliet 2.3.23
[*stays:* brings to a halt]

Smiling

5255 A smile recures the wounding of
a frown.
Venus and Adonis 465

5256 DUKE: The robb'd that smiles
steals something from the thief.
Othello 1.3.208

5257 ULYSSES: Welcome ever smiles,
And farewell goes out sighing.
Troilus and Cressida 3.3.168

5258 OCTAVIUS: Some that smile have
in their hearts, I fear,
Millions of mischiefs.
Julius Caesar 4.1.50

5259 HAMLET: One may smile, and
smile, and be a villain!
Hamlet 1.5.108

5260 DONALBAIN: There's daggers in
men's smiles.
Macbeth 2.3.140

5261 GLOUCESTER [soliloquy]: I can
smile, and murther whiles I smile.
3 Henry VI 3.2.182
[*murther:* murder]

5262 SECOND SENATOR: What thou
wilt,
Thou rather shalt enforce it with thy
smile
Than hew to't with thy sword.
Timon of Athens 5.4.44

5263 SILVIUS [to Phebe]: Loose now
and then
A scatt'red smile, and that I'll live
upon.
As You Like It 3.5.103

5264 PARIS: Venus smiles not in a
house of tears.
Romeo and Juliet 4.1.8

Snake

5265 PETRUCHIO: Is the adder better
than the eel,
Because his painted skin contents the
eye?
Taming of the Shrew 4.3.177

5266 BRUTUS [soliloquy]: It is the
bright day that brings forth the
adder,
And that craves wary walking.
Julius Caesar 2.1.14

5267 LADY MACBETH [to Macbeth]:
Look like th' innocent flower,
But be the serpent under't.
Macbeth 1.5.65

Society

5268 IMOGEN: Society is no comfort
To one not sociable.
Cymbeline 4.2.12

5269 DUKE: There is scarce truth
enough alive to make societies secure,
but security enough to make
fellowships accurs'd.
Measure for Measure 3.2.226

5270 NATHANIEL: Society, saith the
text, is the happiness of life.
Love's Labor's Lost 4.2.161

Soil

5271 CORIN: Good pasture makes fat
sheep.
As You Like It 3.2.27

5272 KING: Most subject is the fattest
soil to weeds.
2 Henry IV 4.4.54

Soldier

5273 The painful warrior famoused for
fight,
After a thousand victories once foil'd,
Is from the book of honor rased quite,
And all the rest forgot for which he
toil'd.
Sonnet 25
[*rased:* erased, blotted out]

5274 TIMON [to Alcibiades]: Thou art
a soldier, therefore seldom rich,
It comes in charity to thee; for all thy
living
Is 'mongst the dead, and all the lands
thou hast
Lie in a pitch'd field.
Timon of Athens 1.2.222

5275 K. HENRY: Therefore should
every soldier in the wars do as every
sick man in his bed, wash every mote
out of his conscience; and dying so,
death is to him advantage; or not dying, the time was blessedly lost

wherein such preparation was gain'd;
and in him that escapes, it were not
sin to think that making God so free
an offer, He let him outlive that day to
see His greatness and to teach others
how they should prepare.
Henry V 4.1.178

5276 FIRST GENTLEMAN: There's not a
soldier of us all, that in the thanksgiv-
ing before meat, do relish the petition
well that prays for peace.
Measure for Measure 1.2.14

5277 OTHELLO: 'Tis the soldier's life
To have their balmy slumbers wak'd
with strife.
Othello 2.3.257

5278 YOUNG CLIFFORD [soliloquy]: He
that is truly dedicate to war
Hath no self-love.
2 Henry VI 5.2.37

5279 REIGNIER: I am a soldier, and
unapt to weep,
Or to exclaim on fortune's fickleness.
1 Henry VI 5.3.133

5280 VENTIDIUS: Ambition [is]
The soldier's virtue.
Antony and Cleopatra 3.1.22

5281 ISABELLA: That in the captain's
but a choleric word,
Which in the soldier is flat blasphemy.
Measure for Measure 2.2.130

5282 AGAMEMNON: May that soldier a
mere recreant prove,
That means not, hath not, or is not in
love!
Troilus and Cressida 1.3.287

5283 LADY MACBETH [sleepwalking]:
Fie, my lord, fie, a soldier, and afeard?
Macbeth 5.1.36

5284 CONSTABLE [about English
soldiers]: Give them great meals of
beef and iron and steel, they will eat
like wolves and fight like devils.
Henry V 3.7.149

5285 JAQUES: A soldier,
Full of strange oaths, and bearded like
the pard,
Jealous in honor, sudden, and quick in
quarrel,
Seeking the bubble reputation
Even in the cannon's mouth.
As You Like It 2.7.149

Solitude

5286 VALENTINE [soliloquy]: This
shadowy desert, unfrequented
woods,
I better brook than flourishing peopled
towns:
Here I can sit alone, unseen of any,
And to the nightingale's complaining
notes
Tune my distresses and record my
woes.
O thou that dost inhabit in my breast,
Leave not the mansion so long tenant-
less,
Lest growing ruinous, the building fall
And leave no memory of what it was!
Repair me with thy presence, Silvia.
Two Gentlemen of Verona 5.4.2

Sons

5287 MIRANDA: Good wombs have
borne bad sons.
The Tempest 1.2.119

5288 K. EDWARD: 'Tis a happy thing
To be father unto many sons.
3 Henry VI 3.2.104

5289 CONSTANCE: O Lord, my boy,
my Arthur, my fair son!
My life, my joy, my food, my all the
world!
My widow-comfort, and my sorrows'
cure!
King John 3.4.103

5290 K. HENRY: Happy always was it
for that son
Whose father for his hoarding went to
hell.
3 Henry VI 2.2.47

5291 POLIXENES: Methinks a father
Is at the nuptial of his son a guest
That best becomes the table.
Winter's Tale 4.4.394

5292 VOLUMNIA: Had I a dozen sons,
each in my love alike ... I had rather
had eleven die nobly for their country
than one voluptuously surfeit out of
action.
Coriolanus 1.3.22

Sorrow

5293 KING: When sorrows come, they
come not single spies,
But in battalions.
Hamlet 4.5.78

5294 CLEON: One sorrow never comes
but brings an heir
That may succeed as his inheritor.
Pericles 1.4.63

5295 QUEEN: One woe doth tread
upon another's heel,
So fast they follow.
Hamlet 4.7.163

5296 Sorrow, like a heavy hanging
bell,
Once set on ringing, with his own
weight goes;
Then little strength rings out the
doleful knell.
Rape of Lucrece 1493

5297 DUCHESS: Sorrow ends not when
it seemeth done.
Richard II 1.2.61

5298 BULLINGBROOK: Fell Sorrow's
tooth doth never rankle more
Than when he bites, but lanceth not
the sore.
Richard II 1.3.302

5299 How hard true sorrow hits.
Sonnet 120

5300 Sorrow ebbs, being blown with
wind of words.
Rape of Lucrece 1330

5301 An oven that is stopp'd, or river stay'd,
Burneth more hotly, swelleth with more rage;
So of concealed sorrow may be said,
Free vent of words love's fire doth assuage.
Venus and Adonis 331

5302 MARCUS: Sorrow concealed, like an oven stopp'd,
Doth burn the heart to cinders.
Titus Andronicus 2.4.36

5303 MARCUS: To weep with them that weep doth ease some deal,
But sorrow flouted at is double death.
Titus Andronicus 3.1.244

5304 MALCOLM [to Rosse]: Give sorrow words. The grief that does not speak
Whispers the o'er-fraught heart, and bids it break.
Macbeth 4.3.209

5305 GUIDERIUS: Notes of sorrow out of tune are worse
Than priests and fanes that lie.
Cymbeline 4.2.241

5306 MALCOLM: To show an unfelt sorrow is an office
Which the false man does easy.
Macbeth 2.3.136

5307 MACDUFF: Each new morn
New widows howl, new orphans cry, new sorrows
Strike heaven on the face.
Macbeth 4.3.4

5308 BRAKENBURY: Sorrow breaks seasons and reposing hours,
Makes the night morning and the noontide night.
Richard III 1.4.76

5309 Thus ebbs and flows the current of her sorrow,
And time doth weary time with her complaining;
She looks for night, and then she longs for morrow,

And both she thinks too long with her remaining.
Short time seems long in sorrow's sharp sustaining;
Though woe be heavy, yet it seldom sleeps,
And they who watch see time how slow it creeps.
Rape of Lucrece 1569

5310 It easeth some, though none it ever cured,
To think their dolor others have endured.
Rape of Lucrece 1581

5311 Every present sorrow seemeth chief.
Venus and Adonis 970

5312 BENEDICK: Everyone can master a grief but he that has it.
Much Ado About Nothing 3.2.28

5313 EDGAR: Bad is the trade that must play fool to sorrow.
King Lear 4.1.38

5314 SILVIUS: Where ever sorrow is, relief would be.
As You Like It 3.5.86

5315 DESDEMONA: I am not merry; but I do beguile
The thing I am by seeming otherwise.
Othello 2.1.122

5316 ANNE: 'Tis better to be lowly born,
And range with humble livers in content,
Than to be perk'd up in a glist'ring grief
And wear a golden sorrow.
Henry VIII 2.3.19

5317 GAUNT: Gnarling sorrow hath less power to bite
The man that mocks at it and sets it light.
Richard II 1.3.292

5318 CONSTANCE: I will instruct my sorrows to be proud,

For grief is proud and makes his owner
stoop.
                              King John 3.1.68

5319 QUEEN: Joy, being altogether
wanting,
It doth remember me the more of
sorrow.
                              Richard II 3.4.13

5320 DEMETRIUS: Sorrow's heaviness
doth heavier grow
For debt that bankrout sleep doth sorrow owe.
        Midsummer Night's Dream 3.2.84
[*bankrout:* bankrupt]

5321 ROSSE [to Siward, on his son's
death]: Your cause of sorrow
Must not be measur'd by his worth, for
then
It hath no end.
                              Macbeth 5.9.10

5322 SEBASTIAN: [Sleep] seldom visits
sorrow; when it doth,
It is a comforter.
                        The Tempest 2.1.195

5323 TITUS [to Lavinia]: Come and
take choice of all my library,
And so beguile thy sorrow.
                    Titus Andronicus 4.1.34

5324 GLOUCESTER: Henceforth I'll bear
Affliction till it do cry out itself
"Enough, enough," and die.
                        King Lear 4.6.75

5325 TROILUS: Sorrow that is couch'd
in seeming gladness
Is like that mirth fate turns to sudden
sadness.
              Troilus and Cressida 1.1.39

5326 PROTEUS: Cease to lament for
that thou canst not help,
And study help for that which thou
lament'st.
Time is the nurse and breeder of all
good.
          Two Gentlemen of Verona 3.1.243

5327 OPHELIA [to Gertrude]: There's
rue for you, and here's some for me;
we may call it herb of grace a' Sundays. You may wear your rue with a
difference.
                        Hamlet 4.5.181
[*rue:* symbolic of sorrow and repentance; *a':*
on]

5328 LEAR: Down, thou climbing
sorrow,
Thy element's below.
                      King Lear 2.4.57

Soul

5329 ISABELLA: All the souls that were
were forfeit once,
And He that might the vantage best
have took
Found out the remedy.
              Measure for Measure 2.2.73

5330 CASSIO: Well, God's above all;
and there be souls must be sav'd, and
there be souls must not be sav'd.
                        Othello 2.3.102

5331 LORENZO: Soft stillness and the
night
Become the touches of sweet har-
mony . . .
Such harmony is in immortal souls,
But whilst this muddy vesture of decay
Doth grossly close it in, we cannot hear
it.
              Merchant of Venice 5.1.56

5332 K. HENRY: Every subject's duty
is the King's, but every subject's soul is
his own.
                        Henry V 4.1.176

5333 ADRIANA: A wretched soul,
bruis'd with adversity,
We bid be quiet when we hear it cry;
But were we burden'd with like weight
of pain,
As much, or more, we should ourselves
complain.
              Comedy of Errors 2.1.34

5334 WARWICK: My soul intends to live
With that dread King that took our state upon him,
To free us from his Father's curse.
2 Henry VI 3.2.153

5335 IAGO: There are a kind of men, so loose of soul,
That in their sleep will mutter their affairs.
Othello 3.3.416

5336 YORK [after being stabbed]:
Open thy gate of mercy, gracious God!
My soul flies through these wounds to seek out thee.
3 Henry VI 1.4.177

5337 ANTONIO: An evil soul producing holy witness
Is like a villain with a smiling cheek,
A goodly apple rotten at the heart.
Merchant of Venice 1.3.99

5338 KING [to Simpcox]: Poor soul, God's goodness hath been great to thee.
Let never day nor night unhallowed pass,
But still remember what the Lord hath done.
2 Henry VI 2.1.82

5339 K. RICHARD [falling, wounded by Exton]: Mount, mount, my soul! thy seat is up on high,
Whilst my gross flesh sinks downward, here to die.
Richard II 5.5.112

5340 HAMLET [to Horatio, on the ghost before them]: I do not set my life at a pin's fee,
And for my soul, what can it do to that,
Being a thing immortal as itself.
Hamlet 1.4.65

5341 My body or my soul, which was the dearer,
When the one pure, the other made divine?

Whose love of either to myself was nearer,
When both were kept for heaven and Collatine?
Ay me, the bark pill'd from the lofty pine,
His leaves will wither and his sap decay;
So must my soul, her bark being pill'd away.
Rape of Lucrece 1163
[*pill'd:* peeled, stripped off]

5342 K. JOHN [to Hubert]: Within this wall of flesh
There is a soul counts thee her creditor.
King John 3.3.20

5343 LAFEW [about Parolles]: The soul of this man is his clothes.
All's Well That Ends Well 2.5.43

5344 CHARMIAN: The soul and body rive not more in parting
Than greatness going off.
Antony and Cleopatra 4.13.5
[*rive:* cleave]

Speech

5345 HAMLET: A knavish speech sleeps in a foolish ear.
Hamlet 4.2.22

5346 PRINCESS: A heavy heart bears not a humble tongue.
Love's Labor's Lost 5.2.737

5347 LEAR [to Cordelia]: Mend your speech a little,
Lest you may mar your fortunes.
King Lear 1.1.93

5348 COUNTESS: Be check'd for silence, But never tax'd for speech.
All's Well That Ends Well 1.1.67

5349 ISABELLA: It oft falls out,
To have what we would have, we speak not what we mean.
Measure for Measure 2.4.117

5350 SUFFOLK: Things are often spoke and seldom meant.
2 Henry VI 3.1.268

5351 CORDELIA: That glib and oily art, To speak and purpose not.
King Lear 1.1.224

5352 FOOL: Speak less than thou knowest.
King Lear 1.4.119

5353 HAMLET: We must speak by the card, or equivocation will undo us.
Hamlet 5.1.137

5354 BOYET: Contempt will kill the speaker's heart,
And quite divorce his memory from his part.
Love's Labor's Lost 5.2.149

5355 TRANIO: Balk logic with acquaintances that you have,
And practice rhetoric in your common talk.
Taming of the Shrew 1.1.34
[*balk logic:* chop logic, bandy words]

5356 BASSANIO: In law, what plea so tainted and corrupt
But, being season'd with a gracious voice,
Obscures the show of evil?
Merchant of Venice 3.2.75

5357 VIOLA [disguised as a page, to Olivia]: I would be loath to cast away my speech; for besides that it is excellently well penn'd, I have taken great pains to con it.
Twelfth Night 1.5.172
[*con:* memorize]

5358 K. JOHN [to Hubert]: I had a thing to say,
But I will fit it with some better time.
King John 3.3.25

5359 CANTERBURY [about Henry]: When he speaks,
The air, a charter'd libertine, is still,

And the mute wonder lurketh in men's ears
To steal his sweet and honeyed sentences.
Henry V 1.1.50

5360 VIOLA: They that dally nicely with words may quickly make them wanton.
King John 3.3.25

5361 FIRST GENTLEMAN [concerning Leontes' and Camillo's reaction when Perdita is revealed as the King's lost daughter]: There was speech in their dumbness, language in their very gesture.
Winter's Tale 5.2.13

5362 ULYSSES [about Cressida]: There's language in her eye, her cheek, her lip,
Nay, her foot speaks.
Troilus and Cressida 4.5.55

5363 DON PEDRO: Speak low if you speak love.
Much Ado About Nothing 2.1.99

5364 LADY GREY: 'Tis better said than done.
3 Henry VI 3.2.90

Speed

5365 CLEOPATRA: Celerity is never more admir'd
Than by the negligent.
Antony and Cleopatra 3.7.23

5366 HELENA: The dove pursues the griffin; the mild hind
Makes speed to catch the tiger—bootless speed,
When cowardice pursues and valor flies.
Midsummer Night's Dream 2.1.232
[*griffin:* fabulous monster with the body of a lion and the head of an eagle]

5367 FRIAR LAWRENCE: Wisely and slow, they stumble that run fast.
Romeo and Juliet 2.3.94

5368 FRIAR LAWRENCE: Too swift arrives as tardy as too slow.
Romeo and Juliet 2.6.15

Spendthrift

5369 FOOL: He that keeps nor crust nor crumb,
Weary of all, shall want some.
King Lear 1.4.198

Spirit

5370 CASSIUS: Stoney tower, nor walls of beaten brass,
Nor airless dungeon, nor strong links of iron,
Can be retentive to the strength of spirit.
Julius Caesar 1.3.93

5371 HOLOFERNES: This is a gift that I have, simple, simple; a foolish extravagant spirit, full of forms, figures, shapes, objects, ideas, apprehensions, motions, revolutions. These are begot in the ventricle of memory, nourish'd in the womb of pia mater, and delivered upon the mellowing of occasion.
Love's Labor's Lost 4.2.65

5372 CLEOPATRA: I shall show the cinders of my spirits
Through th' ashes of my chance.
Antony and Cleopatra 5.2.173
[*chance:* her misfortune]

Spirits

5373 GLENDOWER: I can call spirits from the vasty deep.
HOTSPUR: Why, so can I, or so can any man,
But will they come when you do call for them?
1 Henry IV 3.1.52

5374 DUKE: Spirits are not finely touch'd
But to fine issues.
Measure for Measure 1.1.35

Sport

5375 PRINCESS: There's no such sport as sport by sport o'erthrown.
Love's Labor's Lost 5.2.153

5376 PRINCE: If all the year were playing holidays,
To sport would be as tedious as to work.
1 Henry IV 1.2.204

5377 A summer's day will seem an hour but short,
Being wasted in such time-beguiling sport.
Venus and Adonis 23

5378 ABBESS: Sweet recreation barr'd, what doth ensue
But moody and dull melancholy,
Kinsman to grim and comfortless despair,
And at her heels a huge infectious troop
Of pale distemperatures and foes to life?
Comedy of Errors 5.1.78

5379 Youth is full of sport.
The Passionate Pilgrim xii.5

5380 HAMLET: 'Tis the sport to have the enginer
Hoist with his own petar.
Hamlet 3.4.206
[*enginer:* constructor of military engines and possibly artillery weapons; *hoist with:* blown up by; *petar:* a small engine of war used to blow in a door or to make a breech]

5381 GLOUCESTER: As flies to wanton boys are we to th' gods,
They kill us for their sport.
King Lear 4.1.36

5382 KING [soliloquy, on being a shepherd]: So many hours must I tend my flock,
So many hours must I take my rest,
So many hours must I contemplate,
So many hours must I sport myself.
3 Henry VI 2.5.31

Spring

5383 SONG [of spring]:
When daisies pied, and violets blue,
And lady-smocks all silver-white,
And cuckoo-buds of yellow hue
Do paint the meadows with delight.
Love's Labor's Lost 5.2.894

5384 TWO PAGES [singing]:
In spring time, the only pretty ring time,
When birds do sing, hey ding a ding, ding,
Sweet lovers love the spring.
As You Like It 5.3.16

5385 CAPULET: Well-apparell'd April on the heel
Of limping winter treads.
Romeo and Juliet 1.2.27

5386 When proud-pied April (dress'd in all his trim)
Hath put a spirit of youth in everything.
Sonnet 98

5387 SONG: Primrose, first-born child of Ver,
Merry spring-time's harbinger,
With her bells dim;
Oxlips in their cradles growing,
Marigolds on death-beds blowing.
Two Noble Kinsmen 1.1.7
[*Ver:* an old name for spring]

5388 AUTOLYCUS [singing]:
When daffadils begin to peer,
With heigh, the doxy over the dale!
Why, then comes in the sweet o' the year,
For the red blood reigns in the winter's pale.
Winter's Tale 4.3.1
[*daffadils:* daffodils]

5389 Love's gentle spring doth always fresh remain.
Venus and Adonis 801

Spying

5390 YORK [soliloquy, on his plot to depose Henry]:
Watch thou, and wake when others be asleep,
To pry into the secrets of the state.
2 Henry VI 1.1.249

Stage

5391 JAQUES: All the world's a stage,
And all the men and women merely players;
They have their exits and their entrances,
And one man in his time plays many parts.
As You Like It 2.7.139

5392 ANTONIO: I hold the world but as the world, Gratiano,
A stage, where every man must play a part,
And mine a sad one.
Merchant of Venice 1.1.77

5393 LEAR: When we are born, we cry that we are come
To this great stage of fools.
King Lear 4.6.182

Stars

5394 PRINCE: Two stars keep not their motion in one sphere.
1 Henry IV 5.4.65

5395 CASSIUS: Men at some time are masters of their fates;
The fault, dear Brutus, is not in our stars,
But in ourselves, that we are underlings.
Julius Caesar 1.2.139

5396 KENT: It is the stars,
The stars above us govern our conditions.
King Lear 4.3.33

5397 LORENZO [to Jessica]: Look how
the floor of heaven
Is thick inlaid with patens of bright
gold.
There's not the smallest orb which
thou behold'st
But in his motion like an angel sings,
Still quiring to the young-ey'd
cherubins;
Such harmony is in immortal souls,
But whilst this muddy vesture of decay
Doth grossly close it in, we cannot hear
it.
Merchant of Venice 5.1.58
[*quiring:* singing in harmony]

5398 CAESAR: The skies are painted
with unnumb'red sparks,
They are all fire, and every one doth
shine;
But there's but one in all doth hold his
place.
Julius Caesar 3.1.63

5399 HAMLET: This majestical roof
fretted with golden fire.
Hamlet 2.2.301

5400 Those gold candles fix'd in
heaven's air.
Sonnet 21

5401 BASSANIO: These blessed candles
of the night.
Merchant of Venice 5.1.220

States

5402 CRESSIDA: Mighty states
characterless are grated
To dusty nothing.
Troilus and Cressida 3.2.188

Station

5403 Q. MARGARET: They that stand
high have many blasts to shake
them.
Richard III 1.3.258

Stealing

5404 DEMETRIUS: Easy it is
Of a cut loaf to steal a shive.
Titus Andronicus 2.1.86
[*shive:* slice]

Stealth

5405 SUFFOLK: The fox barks not
when he would steal the lamb.
2 Henry VI 3.1.55

Stillness

5406 ULYSSES: Things in motion
sooner catch the eye
Than what stirs not.
Troilus and Cressida 3.3.183

Storm

5407 THIRD CITIZEN: Untimely storms
make men expect a dearth.
Richard III 2.3.35

5408 GAUNT: Small show'rs last long,
but sudden storms are short.
Richard II 2.1.35

5409 CLARENCE: Every cloud
engenders not a storm.
3 Henry VI 5.3.13

5410 FIRST PLAYER: We often see,
against some storm,
A silence in the heavens, the rack
stand still,
The bold winds speechless, and the orb
below
As hush as death.
Hamlet 2.2.483
[*rack:* cloud-mass]

5411 K. LEAR: Blow, winds, and crack
your cheeks! rage, blow!
You cataracts and hurricanoes, spout
Till you have drench'd our steeples,
drown'd the cocks!

You sulph'rous and thought-executing fires,
Vaunt-couriers of oak-cleaving thunder-bolts,
Singe my white head! And thou, all-shaking thunder,
Strike flat the thick rotundity o' th' world!
Crack nature's moulds, all germains spill at once
That makes ingrateful man!
King Lear 3.2.1

[*germains:* seeds of all living things]

5412 K. JOHN: So foul a sky clears not without a storm.
King John 4.2.108

Straightforwardness

5413 BRUTUS: There are no tricks in plain and simple faith.
Julius Caesar 4.2.22

Strength

5414 ISABELLA: O, it is excellent
To have a giant's strength; but it is tyrannous
To use it like a giant.
Measure for Measure 2.2.106

5415 CARLISLE: To fear the foe, since fear oppresseth strength,
Gives in your weakness strength unto your foe.
Richard II 3.2.180

5416 K. RICHARD: The King's name is a tower of strength,
Which they upon the adverse faction want.
Richard III 5.3.12

5417 MESSENGER [telling of York's death]: Hercules himself must yield to odds;
And many strokes, though with a little axe,
Hews down and fells the hardest-timber'd oak.
3 Henry VI 2.1.53

5418 JULIET: Love give me strength!
and strength shall help afford.
Romeo and Juliet 4.1.125

5419 ANGELO: We are made to be no stronger
Than faults may shake our frames.
Measure for Measure 2.4.132

Strictness

5420 SECOND SENATOR: What thou wilt,
Thou rather shalt enforce it with thy smile
Than hew to't with thy sword.
Timon of Athens 5.4.44

Stubbornness

5421 REGAN: To wilful men,
The injuries that they themselves procure
Must be their schoolmasters.
King Lear 2.4.302

Study

5422 BEROWNE: Study is like the heaven's glorious sun,
That will not be deep search'd with saucy looks;
Small have continual plodders ever won,
Save base authority from others' books.
Love's Labor's Lost 1.1.84

5423 TRANIO [to Lucentio]: No profit grows where is no pleasure ta'en.
In brief, sir, study what you most affect.
Taming of the Shrew 1.1.39

5424 BEROWNE: So study evermore is overshot:
While it doth study to have what it would,
It doth forget to do the thing it should;

And when it hath the thing it hunteth most,
'Tis won as towns with fire — so won, so lost.
Love's Labor's Lost 1.1.142

5425 BEROWNE: What is the end of study, let me know.
KING: Why, that to know which else we should not know.
BEROWNE: Things hid and barr'd (you mean) from common sense.
KING: Ay, that is study's godlike recompense.
Love's Labor's Lost 1.1.55

5426 LONGAVILLE: The mind shall banquet, though the body pine.
Love's Labor's Lost 1.1.25

Style

5427 Q. ELIZABETH: Plain and not honest is too harsh a style.
Richard III 4.4.359

5428 Q. ELIZABETH: An honest tale speeds best being plainly told.
Richard III 4.4.358

5429 Why write I still all one, ever the same,
And keep invention in a noted weed,
That every word doth almost tell my name,
Showing their birth, and where they did proceed?
Sonnet 76

5430 BEROWNE: O, never will I trust to speeches penn'd . . .
Taffata phrases, silken terms precise,
Three-pil'd hyperboles, spruce affection,
Figures pedantical.
Love's Labor's Lost 5.2.402

5431 AMIENS [to Duke Senior, in exile]: Happy is your Grace,
That can translate the stubbornness of fortune
Into so quiet and so sweet a style.
As You Like It 2.1.18

Subjugation

5432 TIMON [to Apemantus]: If thou wert the lion, the fox would beguile thee; if thou wert the lamb, the fox would eat thee; if thou wert the fox, the lion would suspect thee, when peradventure thou wert accus'd by the ass; if thou wert the ass, thy dullness would torment thee, and still thou liv'dst but as a breakfast to the wolf; if thou wert the wolf, thy greediness would afflict thee, and oft thou shouldst hazard thy life for thy dinner; wert thou the unicorn, pride and wrath would confound thee and make thine own self the conquest of thy fury; wert thou a bear, thou wouldst be kill'd by the horse; wert thou a horse, thou wouldst be seiz'd by the leopard; wert thou a leopard, thou wert germane to the lion, and the spots of thy kindred were jurors on thy life; all thy safety were remotion and thy defense absence. What beast couldst thou be, that were not subject to a beast? And what a beast art thou already, that seest not thy loss in transformation?
Timon of Athens 4.3.328

Submission

5433 ANTONY: Bid that welcome
Which comes to punish us, and we punish it
Seeming to bear it lightly.
Antony and Cleopatra 4.14.136

Substance

5434 GUILDENSTERN: The very substance of the ambitious is merely the shadow of a dream.
Hamlet 2.2.257

5435 BUSHY: Each substance of a grief hath twenty shadows,
Which shows like grief itself, but is not so.
Richard II 2.2.14

5436 What is your substance, whereof
are you made,
That millions of strange shadows on
you tend?
Since every one hath, every one, one
shade,
And you, but one, can every shadow
lend.
Sonnet 53

Substitute

5437 PORTIA: A substitute shines
brightly as a king
Until a king be by.
Merchant of Venice 5.1.94

Subtlety

5438 Time's glory is . . .
To mock the subtle in themselves be-
guil'd.
Rape of Lucrece 939

Success

5439 BRUTUS [soliloquy]: Lowliness is
young ambition's ladder,
Whereto the climber-upward turns his
face;
But when he once attains the upmost
round,
He then unto the ladder turns his
back,
Looks in the clouds, scorning the base
degrees
By which he did ascend.
Julius Caesar 2.1.22

5440 Q. MARGARET: They that stand
high have many blasts to shake
them,
And if they fall, they dash themselves
to pieces.
Richard III 1.3.258

5441 NESTOR: Success,
Although particular, shall give a
scantling
Of good or bad unto the general.
Troilus and Cressida 1.3.340
[*give a scantling:* provide a sample of what
is to come]

5442 NORFOLK: To climb steep hills
Requires slow pace at first.
Henry VIII 1.1.131

5443 CLOTEN: Winning will put any
man into courage.
Cymbeline 2.3.7

5444 KING [watching a tempest approach the Shrewsbury battlefield]:
With the losers let it sympathize,
For nothing can seem foul to those
that win.
1 Henry IV 5.1.7

5445 K. HENRY: Didst thou never
hear
That things ill got had ever bad
success?
3 Henry VI 2.2.45

5446 MALVOLIO: Thou art made if
thou desir'st to be so.
Twelfth Night 2.5.155

Succession

5447 EDMUND: The younger rises
when the old doth fall.
King Lear 3.3.25

Sufferance

5448 HOSTESS: Of sufferance comes
ease.
2 Henry IV 5.4.25

Suffering

5449 ANTONY: Bid that welcome
Which comes to punish us, and we
punish it
Seeming to bear it lightly.
Antony and Cleopatra 4.14.136

5450 BENVOLIO: One fire burns out
another's burning,
One pain is less'ned by another's
anguish.
Romeo and Juliet 1.2.45

5451 EDGAR [soliloquy]: Who alone
 suffers, suffers most i' th' mind,
Leaving free things and happy shows
 behind,
But then the mind much sufferance
 doth o'erskip,
When grief hath mates, and bearing
 fellowship.
King Lear 3.6.104

5452 BEROWNE: Mirth cannot move a
 soul in agony.
Love's Labor's Lost 5.2.857

5453 How want of love tormenteth.
Venus and Adonis 202

5454 HAMLET [to Horatio]: Thou hast
 been
As one, in suffering all, that suffers
 nothing,
A man that fortune's buffets and
 rewards
Hast taken with equal thanks.
Hamlet 3.2.65

Suicide

5455 HAMLET [soliloquy]: To be, or
 not to be, that is the question:
Whether 'tis nobler in the mind to
 suffer
The slings and arrows of outrageous
 fortune,
Or to take arms against a sea of
 troubles,
And by opposing, end them. To die,
 to sleep—
No more, and by a sleep to say we end
The heart-ache and the thousand natural shocks
That flesh is heir to; 'tis a consummation
Devoutly to be wish'd. To die, to
 sleep—
To sleep, perchance to dream—ay,
 there's the rub,
For in that sleep of death what dreams
 may come,
When we have shuffled off this mortal
 coil,

Must give us pause; there's the respect
That makes calamity of so long life.
Hamlet 3.1.55

5456 HAMLET [soliloquy]: For who
 would bear the whips and scorns of
 time,
Th' oppressor's wrong, the proud man's
 contumely,
The pangs of despis'd love, the law's
 delay,
The insolence of office, and the spurns
That patient merit of th' unworthy
 takes,
When he himself might his quietus
 make
With a bare bodkin...?
Hamlet 3.1.69
[*bare bodkin:* dagger]

5457 HAMLET [soliloquy]: O that this
 too too sallied flesh would melt,
Thaw, and resolve itself into a dew!
Or that the Everlasting had not fix'd
His canon 'gainst self-slaughter! O
 God, God,
How weary, stale, flat, and unprofit-
 able
Seem to me all the uses of this world!
Hamlet 1.2.129
[*sallied:* sullied; many editors prefer *solid*]

5458 CASCA: Every bondsman in his
 own hand bears
The power to cancel his captivity.
Julius Caesar 1.3.101

5459 MENENIUS: He that hath a will
to die by himself fears it not from another.
Coriolanus 5.2.104

5460 CLEOPATRA: Is it sin
To rush into the secret house of death
Ere death dare come to us?
Antony and Cleopatra 4.15.80

5461 BRUTUS: I do find it cowardly
 and vile,
For fear of what might fall, so to
 prevent
The time of life.
Julius Caesar 5.1.103

5462 IMOGEN: Against self-slaughter
There is a prohibition so divine
That cravens my weak hand.
Cymbeline 3.4.76

[*cravens:* renders cowardly]

Summer

5463 Rough winds do shake the dar-
ling buds of May,
And summer's lease hath all too short
a date;
Sometime too hot the eye of heaven
shines,
And often is his gold complexion
dimm'd,
And every fair from fair sometime
declines,
By chance or nature's changing course
untrimm'd:
But thy eternal summer shall not fade,
Nor lose possession of that fair thou
ow'st.
Sonnet 18

[*ow'st:* ownest]

5464 GLOUCESTER: Short summers
lightly have a forward spring.
Richard III 3.1.94

Sun

5465 BEROWNE: 'Tis the sun that
maketh all things shine!
Love's Labor's Lost 4.3.242

5466 PERDITA [about Polixenes]: The
self-same sun that shines upon his
court
Hides not his visage from our cottage,
but
Looks on alike.
Winter's Tale 4.4.444

5467 FRIAR LAWRENCE: Now ere the
sun advance his burning eye,
The day to cheer and night's dank dew
to dry.
Romeo and Juliet 2.3.5

5468 The sun itself sees not till heaven
clears.
Sonnet 148

5469 APEMANTUS: Men shut their
doors against a setting sun.
Timon of Athens 1.2.145

5470 VIOLA: That orbed continent the
fire
That severs day from night.
Twelfth Night 5.1.271

5471 GLENDOWER: The heavenly-
harness'd team
Begins his golden progress in the east.
1 Henry IV 3.1.221

5472 K. RICHARD: He fires the proud
tops of the eastern pines
And darts his light through every
guilty hole.
Richard II 3.2.43

Sunrise

5473 AARON: The golden sun salutes
the morn,
And, having gilt the ocean with his
beams,
Gallops the zodiac in his glistering
coach,
And overlooks the highest-peering
hills.
Titus Andronicus 2.1.5

Sunset

5474 RICHMOND: The weary sun hath
made a golden set,
And by the bright track of his fiery car
Gives token of a goodly day to-
morrow.
Richard III 5.3.19

5475 THIRD CITIZEN: When the sun
sets, who doth not look for night?
Richard III 2.3.34

5476 CAPTAIN: The gaudy, blabbing,
and remorseful day
Is crept into the bosom of the sea.
2 Henry VI 4.1.1

Superfluity

5477 NERISSA: Superfluity comes sooner by white hairs, but competency lives longer.
Merchant of Venice 1.2.8

Supernatural

5478 LAFEW: They say miracles are past, and we have our philosophical persons, to make modern and familiar, things supernatural and causeless. Hence is it that we make trifles of terrors, ensconcing ourselves into seeming knowledge, when we should submit ourselves to an unknown fear.
All's Well That Ends Well 2.3.1
[*terrors:* i.e. occurrences that should inspire awe]

5479 HAMLET: There are more things in heaven and earth, Horatio,
Than are dreamt of in your philosophy.
Hamlet 1.5.166

Superstition

5480 Look how the world's poor people are amazed
At apparitions, signs, and prodigies.
Venus and Adonis 925

5481 EDMUND [soliloquy]: This is the excellent foppery of the world, that when we are sick in fortune—often the surfeits of our own behavior—we make guilty of our disasters the sun, the moon, and stars, as if we were villains on necessity, fools by heavenly compulsion, knaves, thieves, and treachers by spherical predominance; drunkards, liars, and adulterers by an enforc'd obedience of planetary influence; and all that we are evil in, by a divine thrusting on.
King Lear 1.2.118

Support

5482 PANDULPH: He that stands upon a slipp'ry place
Makes nice of no vild hold to stay him up.
King John 3.4.137
[*vild:* vile]

Supposition

5483 HERMIONE [to Leontes]: If I shall be condemn'd
Upon surmises (all proofs sleeping else
But what your jealousies awake), I tell you
'Tis rigor and not law.
Winter's Tale 3.2.111

Suppression

5484 JULIA [to Lucetta]: The current that with gentle murmur glides,
Thou know'st, being stopp'd, impatiently doth rage;
But when his fair course is not hindered,
He makes sweet music with th' enamell'd stones,
Giving a gentle kiss to every sedge
He overtaketh in his pilgrimage.
Two Gentlemen of Verona 2.7.25

Supremacy

5485 K. RICHARD: Lions make leopards tame.
Richard II 1.1.174

Surety

5486 HECTOR: The wound of peace is surety,
Surety secure.
Troilus and Cressida 2.2.14
[*wound of peace:* a sense of false security]

Surfeit

5487 KING [about Richard II's reign]: They surfeited with honey and began
To loathe the taste of sweetness, whereof a little
More than a little is by much too much.

1 Henry IV 3.2.71

5488 NERISSA: They are as sick that surfeit with too much as they that starve with nothing.

Merchant of Venice 1.2.5

5489 The profit of excess
Is but to surfeit.

Rape of Lucrece 138

5490 ARCHBISHOP: We are all diseas'd,
And with our surfeiting and wanton hours
Have brought ourselves into a burning fever,
And we must bleed for it.

2 Henry IV 4.1.54
[*bleed:* to be bled, as a medical treatment]

5491 LYSANDER: A surfeit of the sweetest things
The deepest loathing to the stomach brings.

Midsummer Night's Dream 2.2.137

5492 CLAUDIO: As surfeit is the father of much fast,
So every scope by the immoderate use
Turns to restraint.

Measure for Measure 1.2.126
[*scope:* freedom]

5493 IAGO: When the blood is made dull with the act of sport, there should be, again to inflame it and to give satiety fresh appetite, loveliness in favor, sympathy in years, manners, and beauties.

Othello 2.1.226

Suspicion

5494 K. HENRY [to Gloucester]: The bird that hath been limed in a bush,
With trembling wings misdoubteth every bush.

3 Henry VI 5.6.13
[Birdlime, a sticky substance, was used to catch birds.]

5495 WARWICK: Who finds the heifer dead and bleeding fresh,
And sees fast by a butcher with an axe,
But will suspect 'twas he that made the slaughter?

2 Henry VI 3.2.188

5496 GLOUCESTER: Suspicion always haunts the guilty mind;
The thief doth fear each bush an officer.

3 Henry VI 5.6.11

5497 OTHELLO: To be once in doubt is once to be resolved.

Othello 3.3.179

5498 IAGO [soliloquy]: Trifles light as air
Are to the jealous confirmations strong
As proofs of holy writ.

Othello 3.3.322

5499 IAGO: Oft my jealousy
Shapes faults that are not.

Othello 3.3.147

5500 IAGO: O, what damned minutes tells he o'er
Who dotes, yet doubts, suspects, yet strongly loves!

Othello 3.3.169

5501 NORTHUMBERLAND [on the death of his son]: See what a ready tongue suspicion hath!
He that but fears the thing he would not know
Hath by instinct knowledge from others' eyes
That what he fear'd is chanced.

2 Henry IV 1.1.84

Swearing

5502 TOUCHSTONE [to Rosalind and Celia, concerning a knight he once knew]: If you swear by that that is not, you are not forsworn. No more was this knight, swearing by his honor, for he never had any.
As You Like It 1.2.76

Sweat

5503 BELARIUS: The sweat of industry would dry and die,
But for the end it works to.
Cymbeline 3.6.31

5504 FIRST QUEEN: Bootless toil must recompense itself
With its own sweat.
Two Noble Kinsmen 1.1.153

Sweets

5505 Sweets grown common lose their dear delight.
Sonnet 102

5506 The sweets we wish for turn to loathed sours
Even in the moment that we call them ours.
Rape of Lucrece 867

5507 Sweets with sweets war not.
Sonnet 8

5508 GAUNT: Things sweet to taste prove in digestion sour.
Richard II 1.3.236

5509 O, in what sweets dost thou thy sins enclose!
Sonnet 95

5510 TOUCHSTONE: Sweetest nut hath sourest rind.
As You Like It 3.2.109

Swiftness

5511 FRIAR LAWRENCE: Too swift arrives as tardy as too slow.
Romeo and Juliet 2.6.15

5512 LYSANDER [to Hermia, on the rough course of love]: Swift as a shadow, short as any dream,
Brief as the lightning in the collied night,
That, in a spleen, unfolds both heaven and earth;
And ere a man hath power to say "Behold!"
The jaws of darkness do devour it up.
Midsummer Night's Dream 1.1.144

5513 JULIET: The lightning ... doth cease to be
Ere one can say it lightens.
Romeo and Juliet 2.2.119

5514 CLEOPATRA: Celerity is never more admir'd
Than by the negligent.
Antony and Cleopatra 3.7.24

Sword

5515 PISTOL [singing]:
Sword and shield
In bloody field
Doth win immortal fame.
Henry V 3.2.9

5516 DUKE [soliloquy]: He who the sword of heaven will bear
Should be as holy as severe.
Measure for Measure 3.2.261

5517 EDMUND: To be tender-minded
Does not become a sword.
King Lear 5.3.31

5518 ROSENCRANTZ: Many wearing rapiers are afraid of goose-quills.
Hamlet 2.2.343
[*goose-quills:* the pens of satirical writers]

5519 SECOND SENATOR: What thou wilt,

Thou rather shalt enforce it with thy smile
Than hew to't with thy sword.
Timon of Athens 5.4.44

5520 K. HENRY [to archbishop of Canterbury]: Take heed how you impawn our person,
How you awake our sleeping sword of war.
Henry V 1.2.21
[*impawn:* pledge, commit]

5521 OTHELLO: Keep up your bright swords, for the dew will rust them.
Othello 1.2.59

5522 PISANIO [on Imogen's plea to kill her]: Hence, vile instrument!
Thou shalt not damn my hand.
Cymbeline 3.4.74

5523 OXFORD: Every man's conscience is a thousand men.
Richard III 5.2.17
[Most other editions have: Every man's conscience is a thousand swords.]

5524 MACDUFF [to Malcolm]: Avarice Sticks deeper, grows with more pernicious root
Than summer-seeming lust; and it hath been
The sword of our slain kings.
Macbeth 4.3.84

5525 NYM: I have a sword, and it shall bite upon my necessity.
Merry Wives of Windsor 2.1.131

Sympathy

5526 Grief best is pleas'd with grief's society.
Rape of Lucrece 1111

5527 DESDEMONA: Let our finger ache, and it endues
Our other healthful members even to a sense
Of pain.
Othello 3.4.146

5528 GROOM [to Richard, in prison]: What my tongue dares not, that my heart shall say.
Richard II 5.5.97

Taciturnity

5529 BOY: Men of few words are the best men.
Henry V 3.2.36

5530 POLONIUS: Give thy thoughts no tongue,
Nor any unproportion'd thought his act.
Hamlet 1.3.59

Tact

5531 HAMLET: Suit the action to the word, the word to the action, with this special observance, that you o'erstep not the modesty of nature.
Hamlet 3.2.17

Tale

5532 Q. ELIZABETH: An honest tale speeds best being plainly told.
Richard III 4.4.358

5533 LADY CAPULET: That book in many's eyes doth share the glory,
That in gold clasps locks in the golden story.
Romeo and Juliet 1.3.91

5534 MAMILLIUS: A sad tale's best for winter.
Winter's Tale 2.1.25

5535 JAQUES: 'Tis but an hour ago since it was nine,
And after one hour more 'twill be eleven,
And so from hour to hour, we ripe and ripe,
And then from hour to hour, we rot and rot;
And thereby hangs a tale.
As You Like It 2.7.24

5536 AGRIPPA: Truths would be tales,
Where now half tales be truths.
Antony and Cleopatra 2.2.133

Talking

5537 FIRST MURDERER: Talkers are no
good doers.
Richard III 1.3.350

5538 BOY: Men of few words are the
best men.
Henry V 3.2.36

5539 All orators are dumb when
beauty pleadeth.
Rape of Lucrece 268

5540 CLOWN: Many a man's tongue
shakes out his master's undoing.
All's Well That Ends Well 2.4.23

5541 HERO: One doth not know
How much an ill word may empoison
liking.
Much Ado About Nothing 3.1.85

5542 SUFFOLK: Things are often spoke
and seldom meant.
2 Henry VI 3.1.268

5543 HOTSPUR [about Glendower]: He
is as tedious
As a tired horse, a railing wife,
Worse than a smokey house. I had
rather live
With cheese and garlic in a windmill,
far,
Than feed on cates and have him talk
to me
In any summer house in Christendom.
1 Henry IV 3.1.157
[*cates:* delicacies]

5544 BASSANIO: Gratiano speaks an infinite deal of nothing, more than any
man in all Venice. His reasons are as
two grains of wheat hid in two bushesls
of chaff; you shall seek all day ere you
find them, and when you have them,
they are not worth the search.
Merchant of Venice 1.1.114

5545 Lovers say, the heart hath treble
wrong
When it is barr'd the aidance of the
tongue.
Venus and Adonis 329

5546 PETRUCHIO [to Gremio, about
Kate]: Think you a little din can
daunt mine ears?
Have I not in my time heard lions
roar?
Have I not heard the sea, puff'd up
with winds,
Rage like an angry boar chafed with
sweat?
Have I not heard great ordnance in the
field,
And heaven's artillery thunder in the
skies?
Have I not in a pitched battle heard
Loud 'larums, neighing steeds, and
trumpets' clang?
And do you tell me of a woman's
tongue,
That gives not half so great a blow to
hear
As will a chestnut in a farmer's fire?
Taming of the Shrew 1.2.199
['*larums:* alarums, calls to arms]

5547 LORENZO [about Launcelot]: The
fool hath planted in his memory
An army of good words, and I do
know
A many fools, that stand in better
place,
Garnish'd like him, that for a tricksy
word
Defy the matter.
Merchant of Venice 3.5.66
[*tricksy:* ingenious, clever]

5548 LORENZO: How every fool can
play upon the word! I think the best
grace of wit will shortly turn into
silence, and discourse grow commendable in none only but parrots.
Merchant of Venice 3.5.43

5549 BEATRICE: I wonder that you will
still be talking, Signior Benedick,
nobody marks you.

BENEDICK: What, my dear Lady Disdain! are you yet living?
Much Ado About Nothing 1.1.116

5550 ROSALIND: Do you not know I am a woman? when I think, I must speak.
As You Like It 3.2.249

Tameness

5551 Youth is wild, and age is tame.
The Passionate Pilgrim xii.8

5552 The colt that's back'd and burthen'd being young,
Loseth his pride, and never waxeth strong.
Venus and Adonis 419
[*burthen'd:* burdened]

5553 GARDINER: Those that tame wild horses
Pace 'em not in their hands to make 'em gentle,
But stop their mouths with stubborn bits and spur 'em
Till they obey the manage.
Henry VIII 5.2.56

5554 DON PEDRO: In time the savage bull doth bear the yoke.
Much Ado About Nothing 1.1.261

Tardiness

5555 FRIAR LAWRENCE: Too swift arrives as tardy as too slow.
Romeo and Juliet 2.6.15

5556 FORD: Better three hours too soon than a minute too late.
Merry Wives of Windsor 2.2.312

Task

5557 ANTONY [to Eros, on his suicide]: The long day's task is done,
And we must sleep.
Antony and Cleopatra 4.14.35

Taste

5558 BENEDICK [soliloquy]: A man loves the meat in his youth that he cannot endure in his age.
Much Ado About Nothing 2.3.238

5559 GAUNT: Things sweet to taste prove in digestion sour.
Richard II 1.3.236

5560 VIOLA: I have heard of some kind of men that put quarrels purposely on others, to taste their valor.
Twelfth Night 3.4.242

Taxes

5561 Q. KATHERINE [to Wolsey, protesting a tax levied by his commission]: These exactions
(Whereof my sovereign would have note), they are
Most pestilent to th' hearing, and, to bear 'em,
The back is sacrifice to th' load.
Henry VIII 1.2.47

5562 KING [on a tax levied by Wolsey's commission]: We must not rend our subjects from our laws,
And stick them in our will. Sixt part of each?
A trembling contribution! Why, we take
From every tree, lop, bark, and part o' th' timber;
And, though we leave it with a root, thus hack'd,
The air will drink the sap.
Henry VIII 1.2.93
[*sixt:* sixth]

5563 BRUTUS: By heaven, I had rather coin my heart
And drop my blood for drachmaes than to wring
From the hard hands of peasants their vile trash
By any indirection.
Julius Caesar 4.3.72

Teaching

5564 REGAN: To wilful men,
The injuries that they themselves
   procure
Must be their schoolmasters.
   King Lear 2.4.302

5565 FOOL: We'll set thee to school to
an ant, to teach thee there's no laboring i' th' winter.
   King Lear 2.4.67

5566 PORTIA: It is a good divine that
follows his own instructions; I can
easier teach twenty what were good to
be done, than to be one of the twenty
to follow mine own teaching.
   Merchant of Venice 1.2.14

Tears

5567 RICHARD: To weep is to make
   less the depth of grief.
   3 Henry VI 2.1.85

5568 LEAR: When we are born, we cry
   that we are come
To this great stage of fools.
   King Lear 4.6.182

5569 K. RICHARD: Two together weeping make one woe.
   Richard II 5.1.86

5570 Distress likes dumps when time
   is kept with tears.
   Rape of Lucrece 1127

5571 COUNTESS: 'Tis the best brine a
maiden can season her praise in.
   All's Well That Ends Well 1.1.48

5572 LEONATO [about Claudio's un-
cle]: Did he break into tears?
MESSENGER: In great measure.
LEONATO: A kind overflow of kindness.
There are no faces truer than those that
are so wash'd.
   Much Ado About Nothing 1.1.24

5573 LEONTES: How sometimes nature
will betray its folly!
Its tenderness! and make itself a
   pastime
To harder bosoms!
   Winter's Tale 1.2.151
[*pastime:* source of mirth]

5574 Tears harden lust, though marble
   wear with raining.
   Rape of Lucrece 560

5575 What a hell of witchcraft lies
In the small orb of one particular tear!
   A Lover's Complaint 288

5576 PARIS: Venus smiles not in a
   house of tears.
   Romeo and Juliet 4.1.8

5577 OTHELLO: If that the earth could
   teem with woman's tears,
Each drop she falls would prove a
   crocodile.
   Othello 4.1.245
[The reference is to an old belief that a
crocodile sheds tears over the body of the
man as it eats him.]

5578 LEAR: Let not women's weapons,
   water-drops,
Stain my man's cheeks . . .
No, I'll not weep.
I have full cause of weeping, but this
   heart
Shall break into a hundred thousand
   flaws
Or ere I'll weep.
   King Lear 2.4.277

5579 ENOBARBUS [to Antony, on the
death of Fulvia]: The tears live in an
onion that should water this sorrow.
   Antony and Cleopatra 1.2.169

5580 SALISBURY [on Hubert's weeping
for Arthur]: Trust not those cunning
waters of his eyes,
For villainy is not without such rheum.
   King John 4.3.107

5581 DUNCAN: My plenteous joys,
Wanton in fullness, seek to hide
   themselves
In drops of sorrow.
   Macbeth 1.4.33

5582 EXETER [to Henry, on Suffolk's and York's deaths]: I had not so much of man in me,
And all my mother came into mine eyes
And gave me up to tears.
Henry V 4.6.30

5583 RICHARD [on York's death]: I cannot weep; for all my body's moisture
Scarce serves to quench my furnace-burning heart.
3 Henry VI 2.1.79

5584 ANTONY [to servant weeping at Caesar's death]: Thy heart is big; get thee apart and weep.
Passion, I see, is catching, for mine eyes,
Seeing those beads of sorrow stand in thine,
Begin to water.
Julius Caesar 3.1.282

5585 FATHER [who has just killed his son in battle]: Ah, boy, if any life be left in thee,
Throw up thine eye! See, see what show'rs arise,
Blown with the windy tempest of my heart
Upon thy wounds, that kills mine eye and heart!
3 Henry VI 2.5.85

5586 VALENTINE: Eye-offending brine.
Twelfth Night 1.1.29

Tediousness

5587 HOTSPUR [about Glendower]: O, he is as tedious
As a tired horse, a railing wife,
Worse than a smokey house. I had rather live
With cheese and garlic in a windmill, far,
Than feed on cates and have him talk to me
In any summer house in Christendom.
1 Henry IV 3.1.157
[*cates:* delicacies]

5588 LEWIS: Life is as tedious as a twice-told tale
Vexing the dull ear of a drowsy man.
King John 3.4.108

5589 POLONIUS [to King]: Since brevity is the soul of wit,
And tediousness the limbs and outward flourishes,
I will be brief.
Hamlet 2.2.90

5590 FIRST MURDERER: I would speak with Clarence, and I came hither on my legs.
BRAKENBURY: What, so brief?
SECOND MURDERER: 'Tis better, sir, than to be tedious.
Richard III 1.4.86

Temper

5591 PORTIA: The brain may devise laws for the blood, but a hot temper leaps o'er a cold decree.
Merchant of Venice 1.2.18

5592 IAGO: Men in rage strike those that wish them best.
Othello 2.3.243

5593 KATHERINA: A woman mov'd is like a fountain troubled,
Muddy, ill-seeming, thick, bereft of beauty.
Taming of the Shrew 5.2.142

Temperament

5594 Every humor hath his adjunct pleasure,
Wherein it finds a joy above the rest.
Sonnet 91

Temperance

5595 APEMANTUS: Great men should drink with harness on their throats.
Timon of Athens 1.2.52

5596 CASSIO: Every inordinate cup is unbless'd, and the ingredient is a devil.

Othello 2.3.307

5597 IAGO: Come, come; good wine is a good familiar creature, if it be well us'd.

Othello 2.3.309

5598 ADAM: I look old, yet I am strong and lusty;
For in my youth I never did apply
Hot and rebellious liquors in my blood.

As You Like It 2.3.47

5599 CLAUDIO: As surfeit is the father of much fast,
So every scope by the immoderate use
Turns to restraint.

Measure for Measure 1.2.126

[*scope:* freedom]

5600 LEAR: Allow not nature more than nature needs.

King Lear 2.4.266

5601 KING [to Falstaff]: Make less thy body hence, and more thy grace,
Leave gormandizing.

2 Henry IV 5.5.52

5602 KING [to his three ascetic lords]:
Brave conquerors—for so you are,
That war against your own affections
And the huge army of the world's desires.

Love's Labor's Lost 1.1.8

5603 NORFOLK [to Buckingham]: Ask God for temp'rance, that's th' appliance only
Which your disease requires.

Henry VIII 1.1.124

Tempest

5604 OTHELLO [on being welcomed home by Desdemona]:
If after every tempest comes such calms,

May the winds blow till they have waken'd death!
And let the laboring bark climb hills of seas
Olympus-high, and duck again as low
As hell's from heaven!

Othello 2.1.185

5605 LEAR: Blow, winds, and crack your cheeks! rage, blow!
You cataracts and hurricanoes, spout
Till you have drench'd our steeples, drown'd the cocks!
You sulph'rous and thought-executing fires,
Vaunt-couriers of oak-cleaving thunderbolts,
Singe my white head! And thou, all-shaking thunder,
Strike flat the thick rotundity o' th' world!
Crack nature's moulds, all germains spill at once
That make ungrateful man!

King Lear 3.2.1

[*germains:* seeds of all living things]

5606 PRINCE: The southern wind
Doth play the trumpet to his purposes,
And by his hollow whistling in the leaves
Foretells a tempest and a blust'ring day.

1 Henry IV 5.1.3

Temptation

5607 ANGELO [soliloquy]: The tempter, or the tempted, who sins most?

Measure for Measure 2.2.163

5608 ANGELO: I am that way going to temptation,
Where prayers cross.

Measure for Measure 2.2.158

5609 ANGELO [soliloquy]: Most dangerous
Is that temptation that doth goad us on
To sin in loving virtue.

Measure for Measure 2.2.180

5610 ROMEO: Tempt not a desp'rate man.

Romeo and Juliet 5.3.59

5611 BEROWNE: Devils soonest tempt, resembling spirits of light.

Love's Labor's Lost 4.3.253

5612 IAGO [soliloquy]: When devils will the blackest sins put on, They do suggest at first with heavenly shows.

Othello 2.3.351

5613 BANQUO: Oftentimes, to win us to our harm, The instruments of darkness tell us truths, Win us with honest trifles, to betray 's In deepest consequence.

Macbeth 1.3.123

5614 BRUTUS [soliloquy]: Between the acting of a dreadful thing And the first motion, all the interim is Like a phantasma or a hideous dream. The Genius and the mortal instruments Are then in council; and the state of man, Like to a little kingdom, suffers then The nature of an insurrection.

Julius Caesar 2.1.63

[*the Genius:* the soul; *mortal instruments:* man's reason and his will; *in council:* at war]

5615 TROILUS: Sometimes we are devils to ourselves, When we will tempt the frailty of our powers, Presuming on their changeful potency.

Troilus and Cressida 4.4.95

5616 Rich preys make true men thieves.

Venus and Adonis 724

5617 K. JOHN: How oft the sight of means to do ill deeds Makes deeds ill done!

King John 4.2.219

5618 PROSPERO [to Ferdinand]: Do not give dalliance Too much the rein. The strongest oaths are straw To th' fire i' th' blood.

The Tempest 4.1.51

5619 ROMAN: The fittest time to corrupt a man's wife is when she's fall'n out with her husband.

Coriolanus 4.3.32

5620 PERICLES: He's no man on whom perfections wait That, knowing sin within, will touch the gate.

Pericles 1.1.79

5621 ANGELO: 'Tis one thing to be tempted, Escalus, Another thing to fall.

Measure for Measure 2.1.17

5622 IAGO: 'Tis the strumpet's plague To beguile many and be beguil'd by one.

Othello 4.1.96

5623 BRUTUS [soliloquy]: It is the bright day that brings forth the adder, And that craves wary walking.

Julius Caesar 2.1.14

5624 PANDULPH [to King Philip]: Better conquest never canst thou make Than arm thy constant and nobler parts Against these giddy loose suggestions.

King John 3.1.290

5625 Two loves I have, of comfort and despair, That like two spirits do suggest me still: My better angel is a man (right fair), My worser spirit a woman (color'd ill). To win me soon to hell, my female evil Tempteth my better angel from my side; And would corrupt my saint to be a devil.

The Passionate Pilgrim ii.5

5626 CLAUDIO [aside, about Benedick]: Bait the hook well, this fish will bite.
Much Ado About Nothing 2.3.108

Tenderness

5627 EDMUND: To be tender-minded Does not become a sword.
King Lear 5.3.31

Terror

5628 LAFEW: We make trifles of terrors, ensconcing ourselves into seeming knowledge, when we should submit ourselves to an unknown fear.
All's Well That Ends Well 2.3.3
[*terrors:* i.e. occurrences that should inspire awe]

5629 Cold terror doth men's minds confound.
Venus and Adonis 1048

Testing

5630 PRINCE: Let the end try the man.
2 Henry IV 2.2.47

Thankfulness

5631 PETRUCHIO: The poorest service is repaid with thanks.
Taming of the Shrew 4.3.45

5632 BASSIANUS: Thanks to men Of noble minds is honorable meed.
Titus Andronicus 1.1.215
[*meed:* recompense, reward]

5633 KING: Proffers not took reap thanks for their reward.
All's Well That Ends Well 2.1.147

5634 BULLINGBROOK: Evermore thanks [is] the exchequer of the poor.
Richard II 2.3.65
[Gratitude being the only payment the poor can make for favors.]

5635 HAMLET: Beggar that I am, I am even poor in thanks.
Hamlet 2.2.272

5636 KING: God's goodness hath been great to thee.
Let never day nor night unhallowed pass,
But still remember what the Lord hath done.
2 Henry VI 2.1.83

Thievery

5637 ABHORSON: Every true man's apparel fits your thief. If it be too little for your thief, your true man thinks it big enough; if it be too big for your thief, your thief thinks it little enough; so every true man's apparel fits your thief.
Measure for Measure 4.2.43

5638 ANGELO: Thieves for their robbery have authority
When judges steal themselves.
Measure for Measure 2.2.175

5639 LEAR [to Gloucester]: A man may see how this world goes with no eyes. Look with thine ears; see how yond justice rails upon yond simple thief. Hark in thine ear: change places, and handy-dandy, which is the justice, which is the thief?
King Lear 4.6.150

5640 CLIFFORD: What makes robbers bold but too much lenity?
3 Henry VI 2.6.23

5641 Rich preys make true men thieves.
Venus and Adonis 724

5642 TIMON: There is boundless theft In limited professions.
Timon of Athens 4.3.427
[*limited:* officially regulated]

5643 GLOUCESTER: Suspicion always haunts the guilty mind;

The thief doth fear each bush an
officer.

3 Henry VI 5.6.11

5644 TIMON: I'll example you with
thievery:
The sun's a thief, and with his great
attraction
Robs the vast sea; the moon's an arrant
thief,
And her pale fire she snatches from the
sun;
The sea's a thief, whose liquid surge
resolves
The moon into salt tears; the earth's a
thief,
That feeds and breeds by a composture
stol'n
From gen'ral excrement; each thing's a
thief.
The laws, your curb and whip, in their
rough power
Have uncheck'd theft.

Timon of Athens 4.3.435

5645 DUKE: The robb'd that smiles
steals something from the thief;
He robs himself that spends a bootless
grief.

Othello 1.3.208

5646 ROSALIND: Beauty provoketh
thieves sooner than gold.

As You Like It 1.3.110

5647 OTHELLO: He that is robb'd, not
wanting what is stol'n,
Let him not know't, and he's not
robb'd at all.

Othello 3.3.342

5648 IAGO: Who steals my purse steals
trash; 'tis something, nothing;
'Twas mine, 'tis his, and has been slave
to thousands;
But he that filches from me my good
name
Robs me of that which not enriches
him,
And makes me poor indeed.

Othello 3.3.157

5649 SHYLOCK [before Portia, dis-
guised as a judge]: Nay, take my life
and all, pardon not that:
You take my house when you do take
the prop
That doth sustain my house; you take
my life
When you do take the means whereby
I live.

Merchant of Venice 4.1.374

5650 TROILUS [to Hector concerning
Helen, the stolen wife of the Greek
Menelaus]: O theft most base,
That we have stol'n what we do fear to
keep!

Troilus and Cressida 2.2.92

5651 FALSTAFF: A plague upon it
when thieves cannot be true one to
another!

1 Henry IV 2.2.27

5652 SUFFOLK: The fox barks not
when he would steal the lamb.

2 Henry VI 3.1.55

Things

5653 CICERO: Men may construe
things after their fashion,
Clean from the purpose of the things
themselves.

Julius Caesar 1.3.34

Thorn

5654 Though the rose have prickles,
yet 'tis pluck'd.

Venus and Adonis 574

Thought

5655 PARIS: Hot blood begets hot
thoughts, and hot thoughts beget hot
deeds.

Troilus and Cressida 3.1.129

5656 Nimble thought can jump both sea and land.
Sonnet 44

5657 CHORUS: So swift a pace hath thought.
Henry V, Prologue 5.15

5658 FLAVIUS: Thought is bounty's foe;
Being free itself, it thinks all others so.
Timon of Athens 2.2.232

5659 HOTSPUR [dying]: Thoughts, the slaves of live, and life, time's fool,
And time, that takes survey of all the world,
Must have a stop.
1 Henry IV 5.4.81

5660 STEPHANO: Thought is free.
The Tempest 3.2.123

5661 Thoughts are but dreams till their effects be tried.
Rape of Lucrece 353

5662 ISABELLA: Thoughts are no subjects,
Intents but merely thoughts.
Measure for Measure 5.1.453

5663 K. RICHARD: No thought is contended.
Richard II 5.5.11

5664 K. RICHARD [soliloquy]:
Thoughts tending to ambition, they do plot
Unlikely wonders.
Richard II 5.5.18

5665 K. RICHARD [soliloquy]:
Thoughts tending to content flatter themselves
That they are not the first of fortune's slaves,
Nor shall they be the last.
Richard II 5.5.23

5666 HAMLET [soliloquy]: A thought ... quarter'd hath but one part wisdom
And ever three parts coward.
Hamlet 4.4.42

5667 CAESAR: Make not your thoughts your prison.
Antony and Cleopatra 5.2.185

5668 The fault unknown is as a thought unacted.
Rape of Lucrece 527

5669 PLAYER KING: Our thoughts are ours, their ends none of our own.
Hamlet 3.2.213

5670 POLONIUS: Give thy thoughts no tongue,
Nor any unproportion'd thought his act.
Hamlet 1.3.59

5671 Unstain'd thoughts do seldom dream on evil.
Rape of Lucrece 87

5672 BULLINGBROOK: O, who can hold a fire in his hand
By thinking on the frosty Caucasus?
Or cloy the hungry edge of appetite
By bare imagination of a feast?
Or wallow naked in December snow
By thinking on fantastic summer's heat?
Richard II 1.3.294

5673 SALERIO [quoting Antonio's advice to Bassanio]: "Be merry, and employ your chiefest thoughts
To courtship, and such fair ostents of love
As shall conveniently become you there."
Merchant of Venice 2.8.43

5674 PORTIA: A maiden hath no tongue but thought.
Merchant of Venice 3.2.8

5675 PROTEUS: Hope is a lover's staff; walk hence with that
And manage it against despairing thoughts.
Two Gentlemen of Verona 3.1.248

5676 JULIET [soliloquy]: Love's heralds should be thoughts,
Which ten times faster glides than the sun's beams,
Driving back shadows over low'ring hills.
Romeo and Juliet 2.5.4

5677 ROSALIND: A woman's thought runs before her actions.
As You Like It 4.1.140

5678 ORLANDO: Thoughts . . . are wing'd.
As You Like It 4.1.142

5679 What's in that brain that ink may character
Which hath not figur'd to thee my true spirit?
What's new to speak, what now to register,
That may express my love, or thy dear merit?
Sonnet 108

5680 GLOUCESTER: Banish the canker of ambitious thoughts!
2 Henry VI 1.2.18

5681 ROMEO [soliloquy]: O mischief, thou art swift
To enter in the thoughts of desperate men!
Romeo and Juliet 5.1.35

5682 When to sessions of sweet silent thought
I summon up remembrance of things past,
I sigh the lack of many a thing I sought,
And with old woes new wail my dear time's waste.
Sonnet 30

5683 YORK [soliloquy, on his plot to depose King Henry]: Steel thy fearful thoughts,
And change misdoubt to resolution;
Be that thou hop'st to be, or what thou art
Resign to death.
2 Henry VI 3.1.331

5684 PRINCE: I never thought to hear you speak again.
KING: Thy wish was father, Harry, to that thought.
2 Henry IV 4.5.91

5685 HAMLET [soliloquy]: The native hue of resolution
Is sicklied o'er with the pale cast of thought.
Hamlet 3.1.83

5686 KING [rising from prayer]: My words fly up, my thoughts remain below:
Words without thoughts never to heaven go.
Hamlet 3.3.97

5687 KING: I am wrapp'd in dismal thinkings.
All's Well That Ends Well 5.3.128

5688 OPHELIA [giving out flowers after Polonius' death]: There's rosemary, that's for remembrance; pray you, love, remember. And there is pansies, that's for thoughts.
Hamlet 4.5.175
[*rosemary:* used at both weddings and funerals as a symbol of remembrance; *pansies:* emblems of love and courtship]

5689 BASTARD [to King John]: Be great in act, as you have been in thought.
King John 5.1.45

5690 FERDINAND: Sweet thoughts do even refresh my labors.
The Tempest 3.1.14

Thrift

5691 SHYLOCK: Thrift is blessing, if men steal it not.
Merchant of Venice 1.3.90

Thunder

5692 LEAR: You sulph'rous and thought-executing fires,

Vaunt-couriers of oak-cleaving thunder-
bolts,
Singe my white head! And thou, all-
shaking thunder,
Strike flat the thick rotundity o' th'
world!
Crack nature's moulds, all germains
spill at once
That make ingrateful man!
King Lear 3.2.4

[*germains:* seeds of all living things]

Tide

5693 BRUTUS: There is a tide in the
affairs of men,
Which taken at the flood, leads on to
fortune;
Omitted, all the voyage of their life
Is bound in shallows and in miser-
ies . . .
We must take the current when it
serves,
Or lose our ventures.
Julius Caesar 4.3.218

Time

5694 Misshapen Time, copesmate of
ugly Night,
Swift subtle post, carrier of grisly care,
Eater of youth, false slave to false
delight,
Base watch of woes, sin's pack-horse,
virtue's snare!
Thou nursest all, and murth'rest all
that are.
Rape of Lucrece 925

[*copesmate:* companion; *murth'rest:*
murderest]

5695 HECTOR: The end crowns all,
And that old common arbitrator,
Time,
Will one day end it.
Troilus and Cressida 4.5.224

5696 PERICLES: Time's the king of
men,
He's both their parent, and he is their
grave,

And gives them what he will, not what
they crave.
Pericles 2.3.45

5697 ULYSSES: Beauty, wit,
High birth, vigor of bone, desert in
service,
Love, friendship, charity, are subjects
all
To envious and calumniating Time.
Troilus and Cressida 3.3.171

5698 Time doth transfix the flourish
set on youth,
And delves the parallels in beauty's
brow.
Sonnet 60

5699 IAGO: Pleasure and action make
the hours seem short.
Othello 2.3.379

5700 K. RICHARD [soliloquy]: I wasted
time, and now doth time waste me.
Richard II 5.5.49

5701 DROMIO SYRACUSE: There's no
time for a man to recover his hair that
grows bald by nature.
Comedy of Errors 2.2.72

5702 DROMIO SYRACUSE: Time himself
is bald, and therefore, to the world's
end, will have bald followers.
Comedy of Errors 2.2.106

5703 IAGO: There are many events in
the womb of time which will be deliver'd.
Othello 1.3.369

5704 CAESAR [to Octavia]: Cheer your
heart,
Be you not troubled with the time.
Antony and Cleopatra 3.6.81

5705 PROTEUS: Time is the nurse and
breeder of all good.
Two Gentlemen of Verona 3.1.243

5706 K. RICHARD [soliloquy]: How
sour sweet music is

When time is broke, and no propor-
tion kept!
So is it in the music of men's lives.
Richard II 5.5.42

5707 ARCHBISHOP: Past and to come
seems best; things present worst.
2 Henry IV 1.3.108

5708 SALISBURY: O, call back yesterday, bid time return.
Richard II 3.2.69

5709 TROILUS: Injurious time now
with a robber's haste
Crams his rich thiev'ry up, he knows
not how.
As many farewells as be stars in
heaven,
With distinct breath and consign'd
kisses to them,
He fumbles up into a loose adieu;
And scants us with a single famish'd
kiss.
Troilus and Cressida 4.4.42

5710 ROSALIND: Time travels in divers
places with divers persons. I'll tell you
who Time ambles withal, who Time
trots withal, who Time gallops withal,
and who he stands still withal.
ORLANDO: I prithee, who doth he trot
withal?
ROSALIND: Marry, he trots hard with a
young maid between the contract of
her marriage and the day it is sol-
emniz'd. If the interim be but a se'n-
night, Time's pace is so hard that it
seems the length of seven year.
ORLANDO: Who ambles Time withal?
ROSALIND: With a priest that lacks
Latin, and a rich man that hath not
the gout; for the one sleeps easily
because he cannot study, and the other
lives merrily because he feels no pain;
the one lacking the burthen of lean
and wasteful learning, the other knowing no burthen of heavy tedious
penury. These Time ambles withal.
ORLANDO: Who does he gallop withal?
ROSALIND: With a thief to the gallows;
for though he go as softly as foot can
fall, he thinks himself too soon there.

ORLANDO: Who stays it still withal?
ROSALIND: With lawyers in the vaca-
tion; for they sleep between term and
term, and then they perceive not how
Time moves.
As You Like It 3.2.308
[*se'nnight:* week; *burthen:* burden]

5711 MACBETH: Come what come may,
Time and the hour runs through the
roughest day.
Macbeth 1.3.147

5712 CORDELIA: Time shall unfold
what plighted cunning hides,
Who covers faults, at last with shame
derides.
King Lear 1.1.279
[*plighted:* pleated]

5713 ROSALIND [to Orlando, on his
promise to keep their date]: Well,
Time is the old justice that examines
all such offenders, and let Time try.
As You Like It 4.1.199

5714 HOTSPUR [dying]: Thoughts, the
slaves of life, and life, time's fool,
And time, that takes survey of all the
world,
Must have a stop.
1 Henry IV 5.4.82

5715 AGAMEMNON: What's past and
what's to come is strew'd with husks
And formless ruin of oblivion.
Troilus and Cressida 4.5.166

5716 O how shall summer's honey
breath hold out
Against the wrackful siege of batt'ring
days,
When rocks impregnable are not so
stout,
Nor gates of steel so strong, but Time
decays?
Sonnet 65

5717 Lovers' hours are long, though
seeming short.
Venus and Adonis 842

5718 CLAUDIO: Time goes on crutches till love have all his rites.
Much Ado About Nothing 2.1.357

5719 OLIVIA: The clock upbraids me with the waste of time.
Twelfth Night 3.1.130

5720 TIME: Let Time's news
Be known when 'tis brought forth.
Winter's Tale 4.1.26

5721 Like as the waves make towards the pibbled shore,
So do our minutes hasten to their end,
Each changing place with that which goes before,
In sequent toil all forwards do contend.
Sonnet 60
[*pibbled:* pebbled; *sequent:* one after another]

5722 Make use of time, let not advantage slip.
Beauty within itself should not be wasted.
Fair flowers that are not gath'red in their prime
Rot, and consume themselves in little time.
Venus and Adonis 129

5723 ULYSSES: Time is like a fashionable host
That slightly shakes his parting guest by th' hand,
And with his arms outstretch'd as he would fly,
Grasps in the comer. The welcome ever smiles,
And farewell goes out sighing.
Troilus and Cressida 3.3.165

5724 KING: Let's take the instant by the forward top;
For we are old, and on our quick'st decrees
Th' inaudible and noiseless foot of time
Steals ere we can effect them.
All's Well That Ends Well 5.3.39
[*forward top:* forelock]

5725 KING [soliloquy, near the battlefield]: O God! methinks it were a happy life
To be no better than a homely swain,
To sit upon a hill, as I do now,
To carve out dials quaintly, point by point,
Thereby to see the minutes how they run:
How many make the hour full complete,
How many hours bring about the day,
How many days will finish up the year,
How many years a mortal man may live.
When this is known, then to divide the times:
So many hours must I tend my flock,
So many hours must I take my rest,
So many hours must I contemplate,
So many hours must I sport myself,
So many days my ewes have been with young,
So many weeks ere the poor fools will ean,
So many years ere I shall shear the fleece:
So minutes, hours, days, months, and years,
Pass'd over to the end they were created,
Would bring white hairs unto a quiet grave.
Ah! what a life were this! how sweet! how lovely!
3 Henry VI 2.5.21
[*homely swain:* simple shepherd; *ean:* yean, bring forth]

5726 PRINCE: We play the fools with the time, and the spirits of the wise sit in the clouds and mock us.
2 Henry IV 2.2.142

5727 HASTINGS: We are time's subjects, and time bids be gone.
2 Henry IV 1.3.110

5728 CLOWN: Youth's a stuff will not endure.
Twelfth Night 2.3.52

5729 ULYSSES [to Achilles]: Time
hath, my lord, a wallet at his back,
Wherein he puts alms for oblivion,
A great-siz'd monster of ingratitudes.
Those scraps are good deeds past,
  which are devour'd
As fast as they are made, forgot as
  soon
As done.
Troilus and Cressida 3.3.145

5730 Time's glory is to calm contending kings,
To unmask falsehood, and bring truth
to light,
To stamp the seal of time in aged
things,
To wake the morn, and sentinel the
night,
To wrong the wronger till he render
right,
To ruinate proud buildings with thy
hours,
And smear with dust their glitt'ring
golden tow'rs.
Rape of Lucrece 939

5731 Ruin hath taught me thus to
ruminate,
That Time will come and take my love
away.
This thought is as a death, which cannot choose
But weep to have that which it fears to
lose.
Sonnet 64

5732 Thou art thy mother's glass, and
she in thee
Calls back the lovely April of her
prime,
So thou through windows of thine age
shall see,
Despite of wrinkles, this thy golden
time.
Sonnet 3

5733 TIME: The same I am, ere ancient'st order was,
Or what is now receiv'd. I witness to
The times that brought them in; so
  shall I do

To th' freshest things now reigning,
and make stale
The glistering of this present.
Winter's Tale 4.1.10

5734 Time doth weary time with her
complaining.
Rape of Lucrece 1570

5735 Distress likes dumps when time
is kept with tears.
Rape of Lucrece 1127

5736 BULLINGBROOK: Grief makes one
hour ten.
Richard II 1.3.261

5737 Short time seems long in sorrow's
sharp sustaining.
Rape of Lucrece 1573

5738 They that watch see time how
slow it creeps.
Rape of Lucrece 1575

5739 DROMIO SYRACUSE: Time is a
very bankrout and owes more than
he's worth to season.
Nay, he's a thief too: have you not
heard men say,
That Time comes stealing on by night
and day?
Comedy of Errors 4.2.57
[*bankrout:* bankrupt]

5740 Devouring Time, blunt thou the
lion's paws,
And make the earth devour her own
sweet brood;
Pluck the keen teeth from the fierce
tiger's jaws,
And burn the long-liv'd phoenix in her
blood;
Make glad and sorry seasons as thou
fleet'st,
And do what e'er thou wilt, swift-
footed Time,
To the wide world and all her fading
sweets:
But I forbid thee one most heinous
crime,
O, carve not with thy hours my love's
fair brow,

Nor draw no lines there with thine antique pen;
Him in thy course untainted do allow,
For beauty's pattern to succeeding men.
Yet do thy worst, old Time: despite thy wrong,
My love shall in my verse ever live young.

Sonnet 19

5741 Q. MARGARET: Time suppresseth wrongs.

3 Henry VI 3.3.77

5742 CLOWN: The whirligig of time brings in his revenges.

Twelfth Night 5.1.376

5743 AUFIDIUS: Our virtues
Lie in th' interpretation of the time.

Coriolanus 4.7.49

5744 EDMUND: Know thou this, that men
Are as the time is.

King Lear 5.3.30

5745 ENOBARBUS: Every time
Serves for the matter that is then born in't.

Antony and Cleopatra 2.2.9

5746 ANTIPHOLUS SYRACUSE: There's a time for all things.

Comedy of Errors 2.2.65

Tomorrow

5747 MACBETH: To-morrow, and to-morrow, and to-morrow,
Creeps in this petty pace from day to day,
To the last syllable of recorded time;
And all our yesterdays have lighted fools
The way to dusty death.

Macbeth 5.5.19

Tongue

5748 K. HENRY: The tongues of men are full of deceits.

Henry V 5.2.117

5749 CLOWN: Many a man's tongue shakes out his master's undoing.

All's Well That Ends Well 2.4.23

5750 PRINCESS: A heavy heart bears not a humble tongue.

Love's Labor's Lost 5.2.737

5751 HAMLET [soliloquy]: Murther, though it have no tongue, will speak
With most miraculous organ.

Hamlet 2.2.593

[*murther:* murder]

5752 IAGO: Guiltiness will speak,
Though tongues were out of use.

Othello 5.1.109

5753 CLEOPATRA: Give to a gracious message
An host of tongues, but let ill tidings tell
Themselves when they be felt.

Antony and Cleopatra 2.5.86

5754 NORTHUMBERLAND: The first bringer of unwelcome news
Hath but a losing office, and his tongue
Sounds ever after as a sullen bell,
Remanb'red tolling a departed friend.

2 Henry IV 1.1.100

5755 STEPHANO: While thou liv'st, keep a good tongue in thy head.

The Tempest 3.2.112

5756 LUCIANA: Be not thy tongue thy own shame's orator.

Comedy of Errors 3.2.10

5757 PORTIA: A maiden hath no tongue but thought.

Merchant of Venice 3.2.8

5758 VALENTINE: That man hath a tongue, I say is no man,

If with his tongue he cannot win a
woman.
Two Gentlemen of Verona 3.1.104

5759 Lovers say, the heart hath treble
wrong
When it is barr'd the aidance of the
tongue.
Venus and Adonis 329

5760 Love's best habit is a soothing
tongue.
The Passionate Pilgrim i.11

5761 ROMEO: How silver-sweet sound
lovers' tongues by night,
Like softest music to attending ears!
Romeo and Juliet 2.2.165

5762 K. HENRY: These fellows of infinite tongue, that can rhyme
themselves into ladies' favors, they do
always reason themselves out again.
Henry V 5.2.155

5763 BOYET: The tongues of mocking
wenches are as keen
As is the razor's edge invisible,
Cutting a smaller hair than may be
seen;
Above the sense of sense, so sensible
Seemeth their conference, their con-
ceits have wings
Fleeter than arrows, bullets, wind,
thought, swifter things.
Love's Labor's Lost 5.2.256

5764 ROSALINE: A jest's prosperity lies
in the ear
Of him that hears it, never in the
tongue
Of him that makes it.
Love's Labor's Lost 5.2.861

5765 HAMLET: Let the candied tongue
lick absurd pomp.
Hamlet 3.2.60
[*candied:* flattering]

5766 MENENIUS: Put not your worthy
rage into your tongue.
Coriolanus 3.1.240

5767 Soft slow tongue [is the] true
mark of modesty.
Rape of Lucrece 1220

5768 CONSTANCE: O that my tongue
were in the thunder's mouth!
Then with a passion would I shake the
world.
King John 3.4.38

5769 PETRUCHIO [to Gremio, about
Kate]: Think you a little din can
daunt mine ears?
Have I not in my time heard lions
roar?
Have I not heard the sea, puff'd up
with winds,
Rage like an angry boar chafed with
sweat?
Have I not heard great ordnance in the
field,
And heaven's artillery thunder in the
skies?
Have I not in a pitched battle heard
Loud 'larums, neighing steeds, and
trumpets' clang?
And do you tell me of a woman's
tongue,
That gives not half so great a blow to
hear
As will a chestnut in a farmer's fire?
Taming of the Shrew 1.2.199
[*'larums:* alarums, calls to arms]

5770 MOWBRAY: My tongue's use is to
me no more
Than an unstringed viol or a harp.
Richard II 1.3.161

5771 GAUNT: They say the tongues of
dying men
Enforce attention like deep harmony.
Where words are scarce, they are
seldom spent in vain,
For they breathe truth that breathe
their words in pain.
Richard II 2.1.5

5772 The heart's attorney.
Venus and Adonis 335

Toothache

5773 LEONATO: There was never yet philosopher
That could endure the toothache patiently,
However they have writ the style of the gods,
And made a push at chance and sufferance.
Much Ado About Nothing 5.1.35

5774 FIRST JAILER: He that sleeps feels not the toothache.
Cymbeline 5.4.172

Torture

5775 That deep torture may be call'd a hell,
When more is felt than one hath power to tell.
Rape of Lucrece 1287

Touch

5776 ULYSSES: One touch of nature makes the whole world kin.
Troilus and Cressida 3.3.175

Toys

5777 MACBETH: All is but toys.
Macbeth 2.3.94

5778 What win I if I gain the thing I seek?
A dream, a breath, a froth of fleeting joy.
Who buys a minute's mirth to wail a week?
Or sells eternity to get a toy?
Rape of Lucrece 211

Trade

5779 EDGAR: Bad is the trade that must play fool to sorrow.
King Lear 4.1.37

5780 PANDER: If there be not a conscience to be us'd in every trade, we shall never prosper.
Pericles 4.2.12

5781 What win I if I gain the thing I seek?
A dream, a breath, a froth of fleeting joy.
Who buys a minute's mirth to wail a week?
Or sells eternity to get a toy?
Rape of Lucrece 211

Tradesman

5782 BEROWNE: To things of sale a seller's praise belongs.
Love's Labor's Lost 4.3.236

5783 AUTOLYCUS: Let me have no lying. It becomes none but tradesmen.
Winter's Tale 4.4.722

5784 PARIS: Fair Diomed, you do as chapmen do,
Dispraise the thing that they desire to buy.
Troilus and Cressida 4.1.76

5785 Huge rocks, high winds, strong pirates, shelves and sands
The merchant fears, ere rich at home he lands.
Rape of Lucrece 335

Tranquility

5786 SUFFOLK: Smooth runs the water where the brook is deep.
2 Henry VI 3.1.53

5787 KING: To the brightest beams Distracted clouds give way.
All's Well That Ends Well 5.3.34

Transformation

5788 HELENA [soliloquy]: Things base and vile, holding no quantity,

Love can transpose to form and dignity.
Midsummer Night's Dream 1.1.232
[*holding no quantity:* lacking proportion, unshapely]

5789 MARIANA: They say best men are moulded out of faults,
And for the most, become much more the better
For being a little bad.
Measure for Measure 5.1.439

Transience

5790 CLOWN: I see things may serve long, but not serve ever.
All's Well That Ends Well 2.2.58

Travellers

5791 JULIA: A true-devoted pilgrim is not weary
To measure kingdoms with his feeble steps.
Two Gentlemen of Verona 2.7.9

5792 ROSALIND: To have seen much, and to have nothing, is to have rich eyes and poor hands.
As You Like It 4.1.23

5793 LAFEW: A good traveller is something at the latter end of a dinner, but one that lies three thirds, and uses a known truth to pass a thousand nothings with, should be once heard and thrice beaten.
All's Well That Ends Well 2.5.28

5794 ANTONIO: Travellers ne'er did lie,
Though fools at home condemn 'em.
The Tempest 3.3.26

5795 VALENTINE [to Proteus]: Home-keeping youth have ever homely wits . . .
I rather would entreat thy company,
To see the wonders of the world abroad,

Than (living dully sluggardiz'd at home)
Wear out thy youth with shapeless idleness.
Two Gentlemen of Verona 1.1.2

5796 TOUCHSTONE: When I was at home, I was in a better place, but travellers must be content.
As You Like It 2.4.17

5797 K. HENRY: 'Tis ever common That men are merriest when they are from home.
Henry V 1.2.271

5798 GAUNT: All places that the eye of heaven visits
Are to the wise man ports and happy havens.
Richard II 1.3.275

5799 CLOWN [singing]:
Journeys end in lovers meeting,
Every wise man's son doth know.
Twelfth Night 2.3.43

5800 Weary with toil, I haste me to my bed,
The dear repose for limbs with travel tired,
But then begins a journey in my head
To work my mind, when body's work's expired;
For then my thoughts (from far where I abide)
Intend a zealous pilgrimage to thee,
And keep my drooping eyelids open wide,
Looking on darkness which the blind do see;
Save that my soul's imaginary sight
Presents thy shadow to my sightless view,
Which like a jewel hung in ghastly night,
Makes black night beauteous, and her old face new.
Sonnet 27

Treachery

5801 PERICLES: 'Tis time to fear when tyrants seem to kiss.

Pericles 1.2.79

5802 LANCASTER: That man that sits within a monarch's heart,
And ripens in the sunshine of his favor,
Would he abuse the countenance of the King,
Alack, what mischiefs might he set abroach
In shadow of such greatness?

2 Henry IV 4.2.11

5803 LADY MACBETH [to Macbeth]:
Look like th' innocent flower,
But be the serpent under't.

Macbeth 1.5.65

5804 CAESAR: Et tu Brute!

Julius Caesar 3.1.77

[And thou, Brutus!]

5805 SUFFOLK [about Gloucester]:
Smooth runs the water where the brook is deep,
And in his simple show he harbors treason.
The fox barks not when he would steal the lamb.

2 Henry VI 3.1.53

Treason

5806 LORENZO: The man that hath no music in himself,
Nor is not moved with concord of sweet sounds,
Is fit for treasons, stratagems, and spoils;
The motions of his spirit are dull as night,
And his affections dark as Erebus:
Let no such man be trusted.

Merchant of Venice 5.1.83

[*Erebus:* the hell of classical mythology]

5807 K. HENRY: Treason and murther ever kept together,

As two yolk-devils sworn to either's purpose.

Henry V 2.2.105

[*murther:* murder]

5808 K. RICHARD: When the searching eye of heaven is hid,
Behind the globe, that lights the lower world,
Then thieves and robbers range abroad unseen
In murthers and in outrage boldly here,
But when from under this terrestrial ball
He fires the proud tops of the eastern pines
And darts his light through every guilty hole,
Then murthers, treasons, and detested sins,
The cloak of night being pluck'd from off their backs,
Stand bare and naked, trembling at themselves.

Richard II 3.2.37

[*murthers:* murders]

5809 KING: There's such divinity doth hedge a king
That treason can but peep to what it would.

Hamlet 4.5.124

5810 IMOGEN: Though those that are betray'd
Do feel the treason sharply, yet the traitor
Stands in worse case of woe.

Cymbeline 3.4.85

5811 K. RICHARD: We must be brief when traitors brave the field.

Richard III 4.3.57

5812 WORCESTER: Treason is but trusted like the fox,
Who never so tame, so cherish'd and lock'd up,
Will have a wild trick of his ancestors.

1 Henry IV 5.2.9

5813 LANCASTER [about Hastings, Mowbray and Scroop]: Some guard these traitors to the block of death,
Treason's true bed and yielder-up of breath.

2 Henry IV 4.2.122

5814 GLOUCESTER [aside, kissing the young prince]: To say the truth, so Judas kiss'd his master,
And cried "All hail!" when as he meant all harm.

3 Henry VI 5.7.33

5815 VOLUMNIA [predicting what historians would say about Coriolanus should he conquer Rome]: "The man was noble,
But with his last attempt he wip'd it out,
Destroy'd his country, and his name remains
To th' ensuing age abhorr'd."

Coriolanus 5.3.145

5816 KING [soliloquy]: The shepherd's homely curds,
His cold thin drink out of his leather bottle,
His wonted sleep under a fresh tree's shade,
All which secure and sweetly he enjoys,
Is far beyond a prince's delicates—
His viands sparkling in a golden cup,
His body couched in a curious bed,
When care, mistrust, and treason waits on him.

3 Henry VI 2.5.47

Treatment

5817 To see the salve doth make the wound ache more.

Rape of Lucrece 1116

Tree

5818 FALSTAFF: The tree may be known by the fruit, as the fruit by the tree.

1 Henry IV 2.4.428

5819 ADRIANA [to Antipholus Syracuse]: Come, I will fasten on this sleeve of thine:
Thou art an elm, my husband, I a vine,
Whose weakness, married to thy stronger state,
Makes me with thy strength to communicate.

Comedy of Errors 2.2.173

Trial

5820 HERMIA: Let us teach our trial patience,
Because it is a customary cross.

Midsummer Night's Dream 1.1.152

5821 CRANMER [to King Henry, on his arrest for trial before the Council]: I humbly thank your Highness,
And am right glad to catch this good occasion
Most thoroughly to be winnowed, where my chaff
And corn shall fly asunder.

Henry VIII 5.1.109

Trifles

5822 IAGO [soliloquy]: Trifles light as air
Are to the jealous confirmations strong
As proof of holy writ.

Othello 3.3.322

5823 BANQUO: Oftentimes, to win us to our harm,
The instruments of darkness tell us truths,
Win us with honest trifles, to betray 's
In deepest consequence.

Macbeth 1.3.123

5824 SUFFOLK: Small things make base men proud.

2 Henry VI 4.1.106

5825 MESSENGER [telling of York's death]: Many strokes, though with a little axe,

Hews down and fells the hardest-
timber'd oak.

3 Henry VI 2.1.54

5826 HELENA: He that of greatest
works is finisher
Oft does them by the weakest minister.

All's Well That Ends Well 2.1.136

Triviality

5827 DESDEMONA: Men's natures
wrangle with inferior things,
Though great ones are their object.

Othello 3.4.144

Trouble

5828 LUCIANA: No evil lost is wail'd
when it is gone.

Comedy of Errors 4.2.24

5829 DOCTOR: Unnatural deeds
Do breed unnatural troubles.

Macbeth 5.1.71

5830 YORK: Comfort's in heaven, and
we are on the earth,
Where nothing lives but crosses, cares,
and grief.

Richard II 2.2.78

5831 CAESAR [to Octavia]: Cheer your
heart,
Be you not troubled.

Antony and Cleopatra 3.6.81

5832 KING: To the brightest beams
Distracted clouds give way.

All's Well That Ends Well 5.3.34

Trueness

5833 POLONIUS: This above all: to
thine own self be true,
And it must follow, as the night the
day,
Thou canst not then be false to any
man.

Hamlet 1.3.78

5834 FIRST BANDITTI: There is no time
so miserable but a man may be true.

Timon of Athens 4.3.456

Trumpet

5835 MACDUFF [attacking Macbeth]:
Make all our trumpets speak, give
them all breath,
Those clamorous harbingers of blood
and death.

Macbeth 5.6.9

Trust

5836 HOTSPUR [to Kate]: Constant
you are,
But yet a woman, and for secrecy,
No lady closer, for I well believe
Thou wilt not utter what thou dost not
know,
And so far will I trust thee.

1 Henry IV 2.3.114

5837 BENEDICK: All women shall pardon me. Because I will not do them
the wrong to mistrust any, I will do
myself the right to trust none ... I
will live a bachelor.

Much Ado About Nothing 1.1.242

5838 PISTOL: Trust none;
For oaths are straws, men's faiths are
wafer-cakes,
And Hold-fast is the only dog.

Henry V 2.3.50

[*wafer-cakes:* i.e. fragile; *Hold-fast:* an allusion to the proverb: Brag is a good dog, but
Holdfast is a better.]

5839 CLAUDIO [soliloquy]: Let every
eye negotiate for itself,
And trust no agent.

Much Ado About Nothing 2.1.178

5840 Q. ELIZABETH: Trust not him
that hath once broken faith.

3 Henry VI 4.4.30

5841 FOOL: He's mad that trusts in the
tameness of a wolf, a horse's health, a
boy's love, or a whore's oath.

King Lear 3.6.18

5842 APEMANTUS: Grant I may never prove so fond,
To trust a man on his oath or bond;
Or a harlot for her weeping,
Or a dog that seems a-sleeping,
Or a keeper with my freedom,
Or my friends, if I should need 'em.
Timon of Athens 1.2.65

5843 VALENTINE: Who should be trusted, when one's right hand
Is perjured to the bosom? Proteus,
I am sorry I must never trust thee more,
But count the world a stranger for thy sake.
Two Gentlemen of Verona 5.4.67

Truth

5844 PROTEUS [soliloquy]: Truth hath better deeds than words to grace it.
Two Gentlemen of Verona 2.2.17

5845 AGRIPPA: Truth would be tales,
Where now half tales be truths.
Antony and Cleopatra 2.2.133

5846 PERICLES: Truth can never be confirm'd enough,
Though doubts did ever sleep.
Pericles 5.1.201

5847 FOOL: Truth's a dog must to kennel, he must be whipt out.
King Lear 1.4.111

5848 DUKE: There is scarce truth enough alive to make societies secure, but security enough to make fellowships accurs'd. Much upon this riddle runs the wisdom of the world.
Measure for Measure 3.2.226

5849 Q. KATHERINE: Truth loves open dealing.
Henry VIII 3.1.39

5850 MOWBRAY: Truth hath a quiet breast.
Richard II 1.3.96

5851 LAUNCELOT: Truth will come to light ... In the end truth will out.
Merchant of Venice 2.2.79

5852 O how much more doth beauty beauteous seem
By that sweet ornament which truth doth give!
The rose looks fair, but fairer we it deem
For that sweet odor which doth in it live.
Sonnet 54

5853 Truth needs no color with his color fix'd,
Beauty no pencil, beauty's truth to lay;
But best is best, if never intermix'd.
Sonnet 101

5854 Both truth and beauty on my love depends.
Sonnet 101

5855 ENOBARBUS: That truth should be silent I had almost forgot.
Antony and Cleopatra 2.2.108

5856 HOTSPUR: O, while you live, tell the truth and shame the devil!
1 Henry IV 3.1.62

5857 DIANA: 'Tis not the many oaths that make the truth,
But the plain single vow that is vow'd true.
All's Well That Ends Well 4.2.21

5858 Love is all truth, Lust full of forged lies.
Venus and Adonis 804

5859 When my love swears that she is made of truth,
I do believe her, though I know she lies.
Sonnet 138

5860 GAUNT: They say the tongues of dying men
Enforce attention like deep harmony.
Where words are scarce, they are seldom spent in vain,

For they breathe truth that breathe
their words in pain.
Richard II 2.1.8

5861 FALSTAFF: Is not the truth the
truth?
1 Henry IV 2.4.230

5862 ISABELLA: Truth is truth
To th' end of reck'ning.
Measure for Measure 5.1.45

5863 ISABELLA [to Duke]: Do not
banish reason
For inequality, but let your reason
serve
To make the truth appear, where it
seems hid,
And hide the false seems true.
Measure for Measure 5.1.64

5864 JULIET [to Paris]: That is no
slander, sir, which is a truth.
Romeo and Juliet 4.1.33

5865 Time's glory is . . .
To unmask falsehood, and bring truth
to light.
Rape of Lucrece 939

5866 CLAUDIO: O, what authority and
show of truth
Can cunning sin cover itself withal!
Much Ado About Nothing 4.1.35

5867 POLONIUS: If circumstances leads
me, I will find
Where truth is hid, though it were hid
indeed
Within the centre.
Hamlet 2.2.157
[*centre:* i.e. of the earth]

5868 BANQUO: Oftentimes, to win us
to our harm,
The instruments of darkness tell us
truths,
Win us with honest trifles, to betray 's
In deepest consequence.
Macbeth 1.3.123

5869 Where is truth, if there be no
self-trust?
Rape of Lucrece 158

5870 LEONTES: All's true that is
mistrusted.
Winter's Tale 2.1.48

5871 PROLOGUE: Wonder on till truth
make all things plain.
Midsummer Night's Dream 5.1.128

5872 POLONIUS: This above all: to
thine own self be true,
And it must follow, as the night the
day,
Thou canst not then be false to any
man.
Hamlet 1.3.78

5873 GONZALO [to Sebastian]: The
truth you speak doth lack some
gentleness,
And time to speak it in. You rub the
sore,
When you should bring the plaster.
The Tempest 2.1.137

5874 TROILUS: Whiles others fish with
craft for great opinion,
I with great truth catch mere simp-
plicity;
Whilst some with cunning gild their
copper crowns,
With truth and plainness I do wear
mine bare.
Fear not my truth: the moral of my wit
Is "plain and true"; there's all the
reach of it.
Troilus and Cressida 4.4.103

Twilight

5875 DON PEDRO: Look, the gentle
day,
Before the wheels of Phoebus, round
about
Dapples the drowsy east with spots of
grey.
Much Ado About Nothing 5.3.25

5876 CAPTAIN: The gaudy, blabbing,
and remorseful day
Is crept into the bosom of the sea.
2 Henry VI 4.1.1

Tyranny

5877 BRUTUS [soliloquy]: Th' abuse of greatness is when it disjoins Remorse from power.
Julius Caesar 2.1.18

5878 ISABELLA: O, it is excellent To have a giant's strength; but it is tyrannous To use it like a giant.
Measure for Measure 2.2.107

5879 MACDUFF: Boundless intemperance In nature is a tyranny.
Macbeth 4.3.67

5880 Q. MARGARET: How can tyrants safely govern home, Unless abroad they purchase great alliance?
3 Henry VI 3.3.69

5881 PERICLES: 'Tis time to fear when tyrants seem to kiss.
Pericles 1.2.79

5882 GLOUCESTER: Tyranny ... sways, not as it hath power, but as it is suffer'd.
King Lear 1.2.50

5883 PERICLES: Tyrants' fears Decrease not, but grow faster than the years.
Pericles 1.2.84

5884 HERMIONE: Innocence shall make False accusation blush, and tyranny Tremble at patience.
Winter's Tale 3.2.30

Uncertainty

5885 IMOGEN: Doubting things go ill often hurts more Than to be sure they do.
Cymbeline 1.6.95

5886 LUCIO: Our doubts are traitors, And make us lose the good we oft might win, By fearing to attempt.
Measure for Measure 1.4.77

5887 MACBETH: Nothing is But what is not.
Macbeth 1.3.141

5888 OPHELIA: We know what we are, but know not what we may be.
Hamlet 4.5.43

5889 CASSIUS: The affairs of men rest still uncertain.
Julius Caesar 5.1.95

5890 LEONTES: I am a feather for each wind that blows.
Winter's Tale 2.3.154

Undependableness

5891 MARTIUS [to some factious citizens]: You are no surer, no, Than is the coal of fire upon the ice, Or hailstone in the sun.
Coriolanus 1.1.172

Understanding

5892 TOUCHSTONE: When a man's verses cannot be understood, nor a man's good wit seconded with the forward child, understanding, it strikes a man more dead than a great reckoning in a little room.
As You Like It 3.3.12

5893 CICERO: Men may construe things after their fashion, Clean from the purpose of the things themselves.
Julius Caesar 1.3.34

5894 HOLOFERNES: Who understandeth thee not, loves thee not.
Love's Labor's Lost 4.2.99

Undertaking

5895 DUKE: It is virtuous to be constant in any undertaking.
Measure for Measure 3.2.225

5896 POLONIUS [on Hamlet's strange behavior]: This is the very ecstasy of love,
Whose violent property fordoes itself,
And leads the will to desperate undertakings
As oft as any passion under heaven
That does afflict our natures.
Hamlet 2.1.99

[*fordoes:* destroys]

Unfaithfulness

5897 NURSE [to Juliet]: There's no trust,
No faith, no honesty in men, all perjur'd,
All forsworn, all naught, all dissemblers.
Romeo and Juliet 3.2.85

5898 VIOLA [soliloquy]: How easy it is for the proper-false
In women's waxen hearts to set their forms!
Twelfth Night 2.2.29

5899 DEMETRIUS: Easy it is
Of a cut loaf to steal a shive.
Titus Andronicus 2.1.86

[*shive:* slice]

5900 VALENTINE: Who should be trusted, when one's right hand
Is perjured to the bosom? Proteus,
I am sorry I must never trust thee more,
But count the world a stranger for thy sake.
The private wound is deepest: O time most accurst!
'Mongst all foes that a friend should be the worst!
Two Gentlemen of Verona 5.4.67

5901 ABBESS [to Adriana concerning Antipholus Ephesus]: Hath not else his eye

Stray'd his affection in unlawful love—
A sin prevailing much in youthful men,
Who give their eyes the liberty of gazing?
Comedy of Errors 5.1.50

Unhappiness

5902 ORLANDO [on the marriage of Oliver to Celia]: O, how bitter a thing it is to look into happiness through another man's eyes!
As You Like It 5.2.43

5903 DUKE SENIOR: We are not all alone unhappy.
As You Like It 2.7.136

Unintelligibility

5904 CASCA: It was Greek to me.
Julius Caesar 1.2.284

Uniqueness

5905 Which can say more
Than this rich praise, that you alone are you...?
Sonnet 84

5906 GLOUCESTER: I am myself alone.
3 Henry VI 5.6.83

Unkindness

5907 ANTONIO: In nature there's no blemish but the mind;
None can be call'd deform'd but the unkind.
Twelfth Night 3.4.367

5908 OPHELIA: Rich gifts wax poor when givers prove unkind.
Hamlet 3.1.100

5909 ADRIANA: If voluble and sharp discourse be marr'd,
Unkindness blunts it more than marble hard.
Comedy of Errors 2.1.92

4910 BRUTUS: Give me a bowl of wine.
In this I bury all unkindness.
Julius Caesar 4.3.158

5911 LEAR: Sharp-tooth'd unkindness.
King Lear 2.4.135

Unruliness

5912 GARDENER: Unruly children make their sire stoop.
Richard II 3.4.30

Unselfishness

5913 FRIAR LAWRENCE [soliloquy]:
Nought so vile that on the earth doth live
But to the earth some special good doth give;
Nor aught so good but, strain'd from that fair use,
Revolts from true birth, stumbling on abuse.
Virtue itself turns vice, being misapplied,
And vice sometime by action dignified.
Romeo and Juliet 2.3.17

5914 Foul cank'ring rust the hidden treasure frets,
But gold that's put to use more gold begets.
Venus and Adonis 767

Unsociableness

5915 IMOGEN: Society is no comfort
To one not sociable.
Cymbeline 4.2.12

Unwariness

5916 Birds never limed no secret bushes fear.
Rape of Lucrece 88
[Birdlime, a sticky substance, was used to catch birds.]

5917 Unstain'd thoughts do seldom dream on evil.
Rape of Lucrece 87

Urgency

5918 GARDINER: Affairs that walk
(As they say spirits do) at midnight, have
In them a wilder nature than the business
That seeks dispatch by day.
Henry VIII 5.1.13

Use

5919 VALENTINE: How use doth breed a habit in a man!
Two Gentlemen of Verona 5.4.1

5920 LUCIO: Use and liberty . . .
Have for long run by the hideous law,
As mice by lions.
Measure for Measure 1.4.62

5921 Torches are made to light, jewels to wear,
Dainties to taste, fresh beauty for use,
Herbs for their smell, and sappy plants to bear:
Things growing to themselves are growth's abuse.
Venus and Adonis 163

5922 HAMLET [soliloquy]: How weary, stale, flat, and unprofitable
Seem to me all the uses of this world!
Hamlet 1.2.133

5923 ALBANY: She that herself will sliver and disbranch
From her material sap, perforce must wither,
And come to deadly use.
King Lear 4.2.34
[*sliver and disbranch*: cut off]

5924 HAMLET: To what base uses we may return, Horatio!
Why may not imagination trace the noble dust of

Alexander, till 'a find it stopping a bunghole?

Hamlet 5.1.202

['a: he]

5925 Make use of time, let not advantage slip.

Venus and Adonis 129

5926 HAMLET: Use almost can change the stamp of nature.

Hamlet 3.4.168

Usurpation

5927 PANDULPH: A sceptre snatch'd with an unruly hand
Must be as boisterously maintain'd as gain'd.

King John 3.4.135

Usury

5928 That use is not forbidden usury,
Which happies those that pay the willing loan.

Sonnet 6

5929 LEAR: The usurer hangs the cozener.

King Lear 4.6.163

[That is, the judge—himself guilty of usury—condemns the petty cheat.]

Vainglory

5930 AJAX: I do hate a proud man, as I hate the engend'ring of toads.

Troilus and Cressida 2.3.158

5931 CLOTEN: It is not vainglory for a man and his glass to confer in his own chamber.

Cymbeline 4.1.7

[*glass:* mirror]

Valor

5932 CAESAR: Cowards die many times before their deaths,

The valiant never taste of death but once.

Julius Caesar 2.2.32

5933 FIRST SENATOR: He's truly valiant that can wisely suffer
The worst that man can breathe, and make his wrongs
His outsides, to wear them like his raiment, carelessly,
And ne'er prefer his injuries to his heart,
To bring it into danger.

Timon of Athens 3.5.31

5934 FALSTAFF: The better part of valor is discretion.

1 Henry IV 5.4.119

5935 NORTHUMBERLAND: What valor were it, when a cur doth grin,
For one to thrust his hand between his teeth,
When he might spurn him with his foot away?

3 Henry VI 1.4.56

5936 COMINIUS: It is held
That valor is the chiefest virtue, and
Most dignifies the haver.

Coriolanus 2.2.83

5937 BENEDICK: In a false quarrel there is no true valor.

Much Ado About Nothing 5.1.120

5938 True valor still a true respect should have.

Rape of Lucrece 201

5939 ENOBARBUS [soliloquy]: When valor preys on reason,
It eats the sword it fights with.

Antony and Cleopatra 3.13.198

5940 NESTOR: Valor's show and valor's worth divide
In storms of fortune.

Troilus and Cressida 1.3.46

5941 VIOLA: I have heard of some kind of men that put quarrels purposely on others, to taste their valor.

Twelfth Night 3.4.242

5942 GREGORY: To be valiant is to stand.
Romeo and Juliet 1.1.9

5943 BASTARD [to Lady Faulconbridge]: He that perforce robs lions of their hearts
May easily win a woman's.
King John 1.1.268

5944 FABIAN: There is no love-broker in the world can more prevail in man's commendation with woman than report of valor.
Twelfth Night 3.2.36

5945 MARTIUS [to his soldiers, preparing for battle]: Put your shields before your hearts, and fight
With hearts more proof than shields.
Coriolanus 1.4.24

5946 MACBETH [soliloquy, on Banquo]: 'Tis much he dares,
And to that dauntless temper of his mind,
He hath a wisdom that doth guide his valor
To act in safety.
Macbeth 3.1.51

5947 FALSTAFF: Valor comes of sherris.
2 Henry IV 4.3.113

Value

5948 FRIAR: That what we have we prize not to the worth
Whiles we enjoy it, but being lack'd and lost,
Why then we rack the value; then we find
The virtue that possession would not show us
Whiles it was ours.
Much Ado About Nothing 4.1.218

5949 LEAR: The art of our necessities is strange
And can make vild things precious.
King Lear 3.2.70
[*vild:* vile, worthless]

5950 LADY MACBETH [soliloquy]:
Nought's had, all's spent,
Where our desire is got without content.
Macbeth 3.2.5

5951 OLD LADY: Our content
Is our best having.
Henry VIII 2.3.23

5952 CRESSIDA: Men prize the thing ungain'd more than it is.
Troilus and Cressida 1.2.289

5953 JEWELLER: Things of like value differing in the owners
Are prized by their masters.
Timon of Athens 1.1.170

5954 TROILUS: What's aught, but as 'tis valued?
HECTOR: But value dwells not in particular will,
It holds his estimate and dignity
As well wherein 'tis precious of itself
As in the prizer.
Troilus and Cressida 2.2.52

Vanity

5955 MOROCCO: A golden mind stoops not to shows of dross.
Merchant of Venice 2.7.20

5956 GAUNT: Light vanity, insatiate cormorant,
Consuming means, soon preys upon itself.
Richard II 2.1.38
[*cormorant:* voracious bird of prey]

5957 FOOL: There was never yet fair woman but she made mouths in a glass.
King Lear 3.2.35
[*made mouths:* practiced facial expressions; *glass:* mirror]

5958 CLOTEN: It is not vainglory for a man and his glass to confer in his own chamber.
Cymbeline 4.1.7
[*glass:* mirror]

5959 FRIAR LAWRENCE: A lover may
bestride the gossamers
That idles in the wanton summer air,
And yet not fall; so light is vanity.
Romeo and Juliet 2.6.18
[*gossamers:* threads spun by spiders]

5960 Some glory in their birth, some
in their skill,
Some in their wealth, some in their
body's force,
Some in their garments, though new-
fangled ill,
Some in their hawks and hounds, some
in their horse;
And every humor hath his adjunct
pleasure,
Wherein it finds a joy above the rest.
Sonnet 91

5961 GLOUCESTER [soliloquy]: Shine
out, fair sun, till I have bought a
glass,
That I may see my shadow as I pass.
Richard III 1.2.262
[*glass:* mirror]

5962 You to your beauteous blessing
add a curse,
Being fond on praise, which makes
your praises worse.
Sonnet 84

5963 CONRADE: The fashion wears out
more apparel than the man.
Much Ado About Nothing 3.3.139

5964 What win I if I gain the thing I
seek?
A dream, a breath, a froth of fleeting
joy.
Rape of Lucrece 211

Variety

5965 CANTERBURY: Therefore doth
heaven divide
The state of man in divers functions,
Setting endeavor in continual motion.
Henry V 1.2.183

5966 ULYSSES: All with one consent
praise new-born gawds.
Troilus and Cressida 3.3.176
[*gawds:* trifles, toys]

5967 MACBETH: All is but toys.
Macbeth 2.3.94

Vehemence

5968 NORFOLK: Heat not a furnace for
your foe so hot
That it do singe yourself.
Henry VIII 1.1.140

Venture

5969 BRUTUS [to Cassius, in the field]:
There is a tide in the affairs of men,
Which taken at the flood, leads on to
fortune;
Omitted, all the voyage of their life
Is bound in shallows and in miseries.
On such a full sea are we now afloat,
And we must take the current when it
serves,
Or lose our ventures.
Julius Caesar 4.3.218

5970 CASCA [to Cassius, on the con-
spiracy]: I will set this foot of mine
as far
As who goes farthest.
Julius Caesar 1.3.119

5971 JACHIMO: Diseas'd ventures . . .
Play with all infirmities for gold
Which rottenness can lend nature; such
boil'd stuff
As well might poison poison.
Cymbeline 1.6.123
[*diseas'd ventures:* risks taken for commer-
cial profits]

5972 Things out of hope are compass'd
oft with vent'ring.
Venus and Adonis 567
[*vent'ring:* venturing]

Verse

5973 POET: When we for recompense
have prais'd the vild,
It stains our glory in that happy verse
Which aptly sings the good.
Timon of Athens 1.1.15
[*vild:* vile]

5974 TOUCHSTONE: When a man's
verses cannot be understood, nor a
man's good wit seconded with the forward child, understanding, it strikes a
man more dead than a great reckoning
in a little room.
As You Like It 3.3.12

5975 Was it the proud full sail of his
great verse,
Bound for the prize of all-too-precious
you,
That did my ripe thoughts in my brain
inhearse,
Making their tomb the womb wherein
they grew?
Sonnet 86
[*inhearse:* bury]

5976 Who will believe my verse in
time to come
If it were fill'd with your most high
deserts?
Though yet heaven knows it is but as a
tomb
Which hides your life, and shows not
half your parts.
Sonnet 17

5977 Do thy worst, old Time: despite
thy wrong,
My love shall in my verse ever live
young.
Sonnet 19

5978 CINNA: I am Cinna the poet, I
am Cinna the poet.
PLEBEIAN: Tear him for his bad verses,
tear him for his bad verses.
Julius Caesar 3.3.29
[Cinna the poet is mistaken by the mob for
Cinna the conspirator and is killed.]

Vessel

5979 BOY: The saying is true, "The
empty vessel makes the greatest
sound."
Henry V 4.4.68

Vice

5980 BASSANIO: There is no vice so
simple but assumes
Some mark of virtue on his outward
parts.
Merchant of Venice 3.2.81

5981 PERICLES: Vice repeated is like
the wand'ring wind,
Blows dust in others' eyes, to spread
itself.
Pericles 1.1.96

5982 ISABELLA: Authority, though it
err like others,
Hath yet a kind of medicine in itself,
That skins the vice o' th' top.
Measure for Measure 2.2.134
[*skins the vice:* i.e. grows new skin over the
sore]

5983 LEAR: Through tatter'd clothes
small vices do appear;
Robes and furr'd gowns hide all.
King Lear 4.6.163

5984 LUCIANA [to Antipholus
Syracuse]: Apparel vice like virtue's
harbinger;
Bear a fair presence, though your heart
be tainted.
Comedy of Errors 3.2.12

5985 CLOWN: Virtue that transgresses
is but patch'd with sin, and sin that
amends is but patch'd with virtue.
Twelfth Night 1.5.48

5986 FRIAR LAWRENCE [soliloquy]: Virtue itself turns vice, being
misapplied,
And vice sometime by action dignified.
Romeo and Juliet 2.3.21

5987 O, what a mansion have those
vices got

Which for their habitation chose out
thee,
Where beauty's veil doth cover every
blot,
And all things turn to fair that eyes
can see!
Sonnet 95

5988 Canker vice the sweetest buds
doth love.
Sonnet 70

5989 EDGAR: The gods are just, and of
our pleasant vices
Make instruments to plague us.
King Lear 5.3.171

5990 HAMLET: In the fatness of these
pursy times
Virtue itself of vice must pardon beg.
Hamlet 3.4.153

5991 PERICLES: Few love to hear the
sins they love to act.
Pericles 1.1.92

5992 PERICLES [soliloquy]: One sin, I
know, another doth provoke:
Murther's as near to lust as flame to
smoke;
Poison and treason are the hands of
sin,
Ay, and the targets to put off the
shame.
Pericles 1.1.137
[*murther:* murder]

5993 LEONTES: I ne'er heard yet
That any of these bolder vices wanted
Less impudence to gainsay what they
did
Than to perform it first.
Winter's Tale 3.2.54

Vicissitudes

5994 GLOUCESTER: Sometimes hath
the brightest day a cloud,
And after summer evermore succeeds
Barren winter, with his wrathful nip-
ping cold;

So cares and joys abound, as seasons
fleet.
2 Henry VI 2.4.1

5995 LEAR [to Cordelia]: Thou art a
soul in bliss, but I am bound
Upon a wheel of fire, that mine own
tears
Do scald like molten lead.
King Lear 4.7.45

Victim

5996 DUKE: The robb'd that smiles
steals something from the thief.
Othello 1.3.208

5997 Th' offender's sorrow lends but
weak relief
To him that bears the strong offense's
cross.
Sonnet 34

Victory

5998 KING: To whom God will, there
be the victory!
3 Henry VI 2.5.15

5999 CLIFFORD: God on our side,
doubt not victory
2 Henry VI 4.8.52

6000 LEONATO: A victory is twice itself
when the achiever brings home full
numbers.
Much Ado About Nothing 1.1.8

6001 K. EDWARD: The harder
match'd, the greater victory.
3 Henry VI 5.1.70

6002 OTHELLO: They laugh that win.
Othello 4.1.122

6003 KING [watching a tempest approach the Shrewsbury battlefield]:
With the losers let it sympathize,
For nothing can seem foul to those
that win.
1 Henry IV 5.1.7

Vigor

6004 IMOGEN: Plenty and peace breed
cowards; hardness ever
Of hardiness is mother.
Cymbeline 3.6.21

Vileness (Vildness)

6005 LEAR: The art of our necessities is
strange
And can make vild things precious.
King Lear 3.2.70

6006 ALBANY: Wisdom and goodness
to the vild seem vild,
Filths savor but themselves.
King Lear 4.2.38

6007 DOGBERRY: They that touch
pitch will be defil'd.
Much Ado About Nothing 3.3.57

6008 HELENA [soliloquy]: Things base
and vile, holding no quantity,
Love can transform to form and
dignity.
Midsummer Night's Dream 1.1.232
[*holding no quantity:* lacking proportion,
unshapely]

6009 'Tis better to be vile than vile
esteemed.
Sonnet 121

6010 POET: When we for recompense
have prais'd the vild,
It stains the glory in that happy verse
Which aptly sings the good.
Timon of Athens 1.1.15

Villainy

6011 TIMON [soliloquy]: All's obliquy;
There's nothing level in our cursed
natures
But direct villainy.
Timon of Athens 4.3.18

6012 GOWER: No visor does become
black villainy
So well as soft and tender flattery.
Pericles 4.4.44

6013 FALSTAFF: There is nothing but
roguery to be found in villainous man.
1 Henry IV 2.4.124

6014 BASSANIO: I like not fair terms
and a villain's mind.
Merchant of Venice 1.3.179

6015 HAMLET: One may smile, and
smile, and be a villain!
Hamlet 1.5.108

6016 FALSTAFF: Company, villainous
company, hath been the spoil of me.
1 Henry IV 3.3.11

6017 IAGO [soliloquy]: When devils
will their blackest sins put on,
They do suggest at first with heavenly
shows.
Othello 2.3.351

6018 K. RICHARD [soliloquy]: My conscience hath a thousand several
tongues,
And every tongue brings in a several
tale,
And every tale condemns me for a
villain.
Richard III 5.3.193

6019 EDMUND [soliloquy]: This is the
excellent foppery of the world, that
when we are sick in fortune—often the
surfeits of our own behavior—we make
guilty of our disasters the sun, the
moon, and stars, as if we were villains
on necessity, fools by heavenly compulsion, knaves, thieves, and treachers by
spherical predominance; drunkards,
liars, and adulterers by an enforc'd
obedience of planetary influence; and
all that we are evil in, by a divine
thrusting on.
King Lear 1.2.118

6020 BORACHIO: When rich villains
have need of poor ones, poor ones may
make what price they will.
Much Ado About Nothing 3.3.113

6021 SALISBURY [on Hubert's weeping for Arthur]: Trust not those cunning waters of his eyes,
For villainy is not without such rheum.
King John 4.3.108

6022 IAGO [soliloquy]: Knavery's plain face is never seen till us'd.
Othello 2.1.312

6023 HUME: A crafty knave does need no broker.
2 Henry VI 1.2.100

Vindication

6024 HAMLET: Let Hercules himself do what he may,
The cat will mew, and dog will have his day.
Hamlet 5.1.291
[That is, nothing under the sun can prevent justice being done for his father's murder.]

Vine

6025 ADRIANA [to Antipholus Syracuse]: Come, I will fasten on this sleeve of thine:
Thou art an elm, my husband, I a vine,
Whose weakness, married to thy stronger state,
Makes me with thy strength to communicate.
Comedy of Errors 2.2.173

Virgin

6026 ISABELLA: Fasting maids, whose minds are dedicate
To nothing temporal.
Measure for Measure 2.2.154

6027 THESEUS: But earthlier happy is the rose distill'd,
Than that which withering on the virgin thorn
Grows, lives, and dies in single blessedness.
Midsummer Night's Dream 1.1.76

6028 DUKE: Women are as roses, whose fair flow'r
Being once display'd, doth fall that very hour.
Twelfth Night 2.4.38

Virginity

6029 PROSPERO [to Ferdinand about Miranda]: If thou dost break her virgin-knot before
All sanctimonious ceremonies may
With full and holy rite be minist'red,
No sweet aspersion shall the heavens let fall
To make this contract grow; but barren hate,
Sour-ey'd disdain, and discord shall bestrew
The union of your bed with weeds so loathly
That you shall hate it both. Therefore take heed.
The Tempest 4.1.15

Virtue

6030 ANTONIO: Virtue is beauty.
Twelfth Night 3.4.369

6031 DUKE: Virtue is bold, and goodness never fearful.
Measure for Measure 3.1.208

6032 GHOST [to Hamlet]: Virtue ... never will be moved,
Though lewdness court it in a shape of heaven.
Hamlet 1.5.53

6033 ARTEMIDORUS: My heart laments that virtue cannot live
Out of the teeth of emulation.
Julius Caesar 2.3.13

6034 PRINCESS: Virtue's office never breaks men's troth.
Love's Labor's Lost 5.2.350

6035 BASSANIO: There is no vice so simple but assumes

Some mark of virtue on his outward parts.
Merchant of Venice 3.2.81

6036 ANGELO [soliloquy]: Most dangerous
Is that temptation that doth goad us on
To sin in loving virtue.
Measure for Measure 2.2.180

6037 ULYSSES: Let not virtue seek
Remuneration for the thing it was;
For beauty, wit,
High birth, vigor of bone, desert in service,
Love, friendship, charity, are subjects all
To envious and calumniating Time.
Troilus and Cressida 3.3.169

6038 AGRIPPA: Virtue and ... general graces speak
That which none else can utter.
Antony and Cleopatra 2.2.129

6039 Q. KATHERINE: Virtue finds no friends.
Henry VIII 3.1.126

6040 CERIMON: I hold it ever
Virtue and cunning were endowments greater
Than nobleness and riches. Careless heirs
May the two latter darken and expend;
But immortality attends the former,
Making a man a god.
Pericles 3.2.27

6041 DUKE: If our virtues
Did not go forth of us, 'twere all alike
As if we had them not.
Measure for Measure 1.1.33

6042 URSULA [to Antonio]: Can virtue hide itself? Go to, mum, you are he.
Graces will appear, and there's an end.
Much Ado About Nothing 2.1.122
[*mum:* be silent]

6043 KING: What stronger breastplate than a heart untainted!

Thrice is he armed that hath his quarrel just,
And he but naked, though locked up in steel,
Whose conscience with injustice is corrupted.
2 Henry VI 3.2.232

6044 GLOUCESTER: A heart unspotted is not easily daunted.
2 Henry VI 3.1.100

6045 Unstain'd thoughts do seldom dream on evil.
Rape of Lucrece 87

6046 KING: From lowest place when virtuous things proceed,
The place is dignified by th' doer's deed.
Where great additions swell 's, and virtue none,
It is a dropsied honor. Good alone
Is good, without a name.
All's Well That Ends Well 2.3.125
[*additions:* honorific titles and other marks of distinction; *'s:* us]

6047 Unruly blasts wait on the tender spring,
Unwholesome weeds take root with precious flow'rs,
The adder hisses where the sweet birds sing,
What virtue breeds iniquity devours.
Rape of Lucrece 869

6048 ALL: He lives in fame, that died in virtue's cause.
Titus Andronicus 1.1.390

6049 HAMLET: Virtue cannot so inoculate our old stock but we shall relish of it.
Hamlet 3.1.116
[That is, virtue cannot so change our nature that we do not retain some trace or taste of the original.]

6050 DUKE: It is virtuous to be constant in any undertaking.
Measure for Measure 3.2.225

6051 COMINIUS: It is held
That valor is the chiefest virtue, and
Most dignifies the haver.
Coriolanus 2.2.83

6052 YORK: 'Tis beauty that doth oft
make women proud . . .
'Tis virtue that doth make them most
admir'd . . .
'Tis government that makes them seem
divine.
3 Henry VI 1.4.128
[*government:* discipline, self-control]

6053 POSTHUMUS: The vows of women
Of no more bondage be to where they
are made
Than they are to their virtues, which is
nothing.
Cymbeline 2.4.110

6054 LAUNCE: To be slow in words is a
woman's only virtue.
Two Gentlemen of Verona 3.1.334

6055 FERDINAND: For several virtues
Have I lik'd several women, never any
With so full soul but some defect in
her
Did quarrel with the noblest grace she
ow'd,
And put it to the foil.
The Tempest 3.1.42

6056 KING [about Margaret]: Her virtues, graced with external gifts,
Do breed love's settled passions in my
heart.
1 Henry VI 5.5.3

6057 FIRST LORD: The web of our life
is of a mingled yarn, good and ill
together: our virtues would be proud,
if our faults whipt them not, and our
crimes would despair, if they were not
cherish'd by our virtues.
All's Well That Ends Well 4.3.71

6058 CLOWN: Virtue that transgresses
is but patch'd with sin, and sin that
amends is but patch'd with virtue.
Twelfth Night 1.5.48

6059 ESCALUS: Some rise by sin, and
some by virtue fall.
Measure for Measure 2.1.38

6060 FRIAR LAWRENCE [soliloquy]: Virtue itself turns vice, being misapplied,
And vice sometime by action dignified.
Romeo and Juliet 2.3.21

6061 GLOUCESTER: Virtue is chok'd
with foul ambition.
2 Henry VI 3.1.143

6062 LAERTES: Virtue itself scapes not
calumnious strokes.
Hamlet 1.3.38

6063 LEONTES: Calumny will sear
Virtue itself.
Winter's Tale 2.1.73

6064 HAMLET: Be thou chaste as ice,
as pure as snow, thou shalt not escape
calumny.
Hamlet 3.1.135

6065 GRIFFITH: Men's evil manners
live in brass, their virtues
We write in water.
Henry VIII 4.2.45

6066 PROSPERO: The rarer action is
In virtue than in vengeance.
The Tempest 5.1.27

6067 GAUNT: There is no virtue like
necessity.
Richard II 1.3.278

6068 AUFIDIUS: Our virtues
Lie in th' interpretation of the time.
Coriolanus 4.7.49

6069 MARIANA: The honor of a maid
is her name.
All's Well That Ends Well 3.5.12

6070 HAMLET: In the fatness of these
pursy times
Virtue itself of vice must pardon beg.
Hamlet 3.4.153

6071 HAMLET [to the Queen]: Assume a virtue, if you have it not.
Hamlet 3.4.160

Vituperation

6072 BASTARD [soliloquy]: Well, whiles I am a beggar, I will rail, And say there is no sin but to be rich; And being rich, my virtue then shall be
To say there is no vice but beggary.
King John 2.1.593

6073 MOWBRAY: The bitter clamor of two eager tongues.
Richard II 1.1.49

Voice

6074 BOY: The saying is true, "The empty vessel makes the greatest sound."
Henry V 4.4.68

6075 BASSANIO: In law, what plea so tainted and corrupt
But, being season'd with a gracious voice,
Obscures the show of evil? In religion, What damned error but some sober brow
Will bless it, and approve it with a text,
Hiding the grossness with fair ornament?
Merchant of Venice 3.2.75

6076 ROMEO: How silver-sweet sound lovers' tongues by night,
Like softest music to attending ears!
Romeo and Juliet 2.2.165

6077 K. LEAR [about Cordelia]: Her voice was ever soft,
Gentle, and low, an excellent thing in a woman.
King Lear 5.3.273

Vows

6078 LONGAVILLE: Vows are but breath, and breath a vapor is.
Love's Labor's Lost 4.3.66

6079 PROTEUS: Unheedful vows may be heedfully broken.
Two Gentlemen of Verona 2.6.11

6080 POLONIUS: When the blood burns, how prodigal the soul
Lends the tongue vows.
Hamlet 1.3.116

6081 PANDULPH: It is religion that doth make vows kept.
King John 3.1.279

6082 IMOGEN: Men's vows are women's traitors.
Cymbeline 3.4.54

6083 DIANA: 'Tis not the many oaths that make the truth,
But the plain single vow that is vow'd true.
All's Well That Ends Well 4.2.21

6084 POSTHUMUS: The vows of women Of no more bondage be to where they are made
Than they are to their virtues, which is nothing.
Cymbeline 2.4.110

6085 Vows were ever brokers to defiling.
A Lover's Complaint 173

6086 CLEOPATRA: Those mouth-made vows,
Which break themselves in swearing!
Antony and Cleopatra 1.3.30

Wages

6087 PORTIA: He is well paid that is well satisfied.
Merchant of Venice 4.1.415

6088 HERMIONE: Our praises are our wages.
Winter's Tale 1.2.94

Want

6089 BEROWNE: Where nothing wants that want itself doth seek.
Love's Labor's Lost 4.3.233

6090 CAESAR: Want will perjure
The ne'er-touch'd vestal.
Antony and Cleopatra 3.12.30

6091 FOOL: He that keeps nor crust nor crumb,
Weary of all, shall want some.
King Lear 1.4.198

6092 CORIN: He that wants money, means, and content is without three good friends.
As You Like It 3.2.24

Wantonness

6093 IAGO [to Othello, about Desdemona]: O, 'tis the spite of hell, the fiend's arch-mock,
To lip a wanton in a secure couch,
And to suppose her chaste!
Othello 4.1.70

6094 ARCHBISHOP: We are all diseas'd,
And with our surfeiting and wanton hours
Have brought ourselves into a burning fever,
And we must bleed for it.
2 Henry IV 4.1.54
[*bleed:* to be bled, as a medical treatment]

War

6095 WILLIAMS: There are few die well that die in a battle.
Henry V 4.1.141

6096 BERTRAM: War is no strife
To the dark house and the detested wife.
All's Well That Ends Well 2.3.291

6097 CONSTANCE: Peace is to me a war.
King John 3.1.113

6098 HOTSPUR: The arms are fair
When the intent of bearing them is just.
1 Henry IV 5.2.87

6099 LEWIS [to Pandulph]: Your breath first kindled the dead coals of war . . .
And brought in matter that should feed this fire;
And now 'tis far too huge to be blown out
With that same weak wind which enkindled it.
King John 5.2.83

6100 EXETER: Hungry war
Opens his vasty jaws.
Henry V 2.4.104

6101 CHORUS: Now all the youth of England are on fire,
And silken dalliance in the wardrobe lies;
Now thrive the armorers, and honor's thought
Reigns solely in the breast of every man.
Henry V, Prologue 2.1

6102 PAROLLES: To th' wars, my boy, to th' wars!
He wears his honor in a box unseen,
That hugs his kicky-wicky here at home,
Spending his manly marrow in her arms,
Which should sustain the bound and high curvet
Of Mars's fiery steed.
All's Well That Ends Well 2.3.278

6103 MACDUFF [attacking Macbeth]:
Make all our trumpets speak, give them all breath,
Those clamorous harbingers of blood and death.
Macbeth 5.6.9

6104 NORTHUMBERLAND: It is war's prize to take all vantages.
3 Henry VI 1.4.59

6105 YOUNG CLIFFORD [soliloquy]: O war, thou son of hell,
Whom angry heavens do make their minister,
Throw in the frozen bosoms of our part
Hot coals of vengeance! Let no soldier fly.
He that is truly dedicate to war
Hath no self-love.
2 Henry VI 5.2.33

6106 ANTONY: Cry "Havoc!" and let slip the dogs of war.
Julius Caesar 3.1.273
[*Havoc:* a war-cry, meaning "give no quarter"]

6107 TIMON [to Alcibiades]: Follow thy drum,
With man's blood paint the ground, gules, gules.
Religious canons, civil laws are cruel;
Then what should war be?
Timon of Athens 4.3.59
[*gules:* red]

6108 KING JOHN [warning Angiers of the French]: The cannons have their bowels full of wrath,
And ready mounted are they to spit forth
Their iron indignation 'gainst your walls.
King John 2.1.210

6109 BASTARD [at Angiers]: O now doth Death line his dead chaps with steel,
The swords of soldiers are his teeth, his fangs,
And now he feasts, mousing the flesh of men,
In undetermin'd differences of kings.
King John 2.1.352

6110 K. HENRY [at the battle of Harfleur]: Once more into the breach, dear friends, once more;

Or close the wall up with our English dead.
Henry V 3.1.1

6111 EDWARD: Sound trumpets! Let our bloody colors wave!
And either victory, or else a grave.
3 Henry VI 2.2.173

6112 CAPTAIN: The bay-trees in our country all are wither'd,
And meteors fright the fixed stars of heaven,
The pale-fac'd moon looks bloody on the earth,
And lean-look'd prophets whisper fearful change,
Rich men look sad, and ruffians dance and leap,
The one in fear to lose what they enjoy,
The other to enjoy by rage and war.
Richard II 2.4.8

6113 K. HENRY: In peace there's nothing so becomes a man
As modest stillness and humility;
But when the blast of war blows in our ears,
Then imitate the action of the tiger;
Stiffen the sinews, conjure up the blood,
Disguise fair nature with hard-favor'd rage.
Henry V 3.1.3

6114 MARTIUS [to some dissentious citizens]: What would you have, you curs,
That like nor peace nor war? The one affrights you,
The other makes you proud.
Coriolanus 1.1.168

6115 FIRST SERVANT: Let me have war, say I, it exceeds peace as far as day does night; it's spritely, waking, audible, and full of vent. Peace is a very apoplexy, lethargy, mull'd, deaf, sleepy, insensible, a getter of more bastard children than war's a destroyer of men.

SECOND SERVANT: 'Tis so . . . but peace is a great maker of cuckolds.

Coriolanus 4.5.221

[*cuckolds:* husbands of unfaithful wives]

6116 BELARIUS: The toil o' the' war,
A pain that only seems to seek out danger
I' th' name of fame and honor which dies i' th' search.

Cymbeline 3.3.49

6117 MOWBRAY: A woman's war,
The bitter clamor of two eager tongues.

Richard II 1.1.48

6118 HOTSPUR [on hearing Henry's army was advancing to attack]: Let them come!
They come like sacrifices in their trim,
And to the fire-ey'd maid of smoky war
All hot and bleeding will we offer them.
The mailed Mars shall on his altar sit
Up to the ears in blood.

1 Henry IV 4.1.112

Warrior

6119 The painful warrior famoused for fight,
After a thousand victories once foil'd,
Is from the book of honor rased quite,
And all the rest forgot for which he toil'd.

Sonnet 25

[*rased:* erased, blotted out]

Waste

6120 DEMETRIUS: More water glideth by the mill
Than wots the miller of.

Titus Andronicus 2.1.85

[*wots:* knows]

6121 Who lets so fair a house fall to decay,
Which husbandry in honor might uphold

Against the stormy gusts of winter's day
And barren rage of death's eternal cold?
O, none but unthrifts!

Sonnet 13

6122 PEMBROKE: To gild refined gold, to paint the lily,
To throw a perfume on the violet,
To smooth the ice, or add another hue
Unto the rainbow, or with taper-light
To seek the beauteous eye of heaven to garnish,
Is wasteful and ridiculous excess.

King John 4.2.11

6123 CHIEF JUSTICE: Your means are very slender, and your waste is great.
FALSTAFF: I would it were otherwise, I would my means were greater and my waist slenderer.

2 Henry IV 1.2.140

Watching

6124 HAMLET: Some must watch while some must sleep.

Hamlet 3.2.273

Water

6125 SUFFOLK: Smooth runs the water where the brook is deep.

2 Henry VI 3.1.53

6126 Deep sounds make lesser noise than shallow fords.

Rape of Lucrece 1329

6127 APEMANTUS: Here's that which is too weak to be a sinner,
Honest water, which ne'er left man i' th' mire.

Timon of Athens 1.2.58

6128 THIRD CITIZEN: By divine instinct men's minds mistrust
Ensuing danger; as by proof we see
The water swell before a boist'rous storm.

Richard III 2.3.44

6129 JULIA [to Lucetta]: The current
that with gentle murmur glides,
Thou know'st, being stopp'd, impa-
tiently doth rage;
But when his fair course is not
hindered,
He makes sweet music with th' enam-
ell'd stones,
Giving a gentle kiss to every sedge
He overtaketh in his pilgrimage.
Two Gentlemen of Verona 2.7.25

Weakness

6130 LEONTES: How sometimes nature
will betray its folly!
Its tenderness! and make itself a
pastime
To harder bosoms!
Winter's Tale 1.2.151
[*pastime:* source of mirth]

6131 HELENA: He that of greatest
works is finisher
Oft does them by the weakest minister:
So holy writ in babes hath judgment
shown,
When judges have been babes.
All's Well That Ends Well 2.1.136

6132 K. LEAR: We are not ourselves
When nature, being oppress'd, com-
mands the mind
To suffer with the body.
King Lear 2.4.107

Wealth

6133 PLAYER KING: Hitherto doth
love on fortune tend,
For who not needs shall never lack a
friend.
Hamlet 3.2.206

6134 FORD: They say, if money goes
before, all ways do lie open.
FALSTAFF: Money is a good soldier, sir,
and will on.
Merry Wives of Windsor 2.2.168

6135 TIMON: Faults that are rich are
fair.
Timon of Athens 1.2.13

6136 ANNE [about Slender]: O, what
a world of vild ill-favor'd faults
Looks handsome in three hundred
pounds a-year!
Merry Wives of Windsor 3.4.32
[*vild:* vile]

6137 DUKE [to the condemned
Claudio]: If thou art rich, thou'rt
poor,
For like an ass, whose back with ingots
bows,
Thou bear'st thy heavy riches but a
journey,
And death unloads thee.
Measure for Measure 3.1.25

6138 ARVIRAGUS: All gold and silver
rather turn to dirt,
As 'tis no better reckon'd, but of those
Who worship dirty gods.
Cymbeline 3.6.53

6139 GRUMIO: Nothing comes amiss,
so money comes withal.
Taming of the Shrew 1.2.81

6140 TIMON: I am wealthy in my
friends.
Timon of Athens 2.2.184

Weariness

6141 BELARIUS: Weariness
Can snore upon the flint, when resty
sloth
Finds the down pillow hard.
Cymbeline 3.6.33

6142 HAMLET [soliloquy]: How weary,
stale, flat, and unprofitable
Seem to me all the uses of this world!
Hamlet 1.2.133

Weather

6143 NATHANIEL: Many can brook the
weather that love not the wind.
Love's Labor's Lost 4.2.33

6144 SCROOP: Men judge by the complexion of the sky
The state and inclination of the day.
Richard II 3.2.194

6145 CONRADE [to Don John]: It is impossible you should take true root but by the fair weather that you make yourself.
Much Ado About Nothing 1.3.24

Wedlock

6146 PRINCESS: A world-without-end bargain.
Love's Labor's Lost 5.2.789

6147 BEATRICE: Wooing, wedding, and repenting, is as a Scotch jig, a measure, and a cinquepace; the first suit is hot and hasty, like a Scotch jig, and full as fantastical; the wedding, mannerly-modest, as a measure, full of state and ancientry; and then comes repentance, and with his bad legs falls into the cinquepace faster and faster, till he sink into his grave.
Much Ado About Nothing 2.1.73
[*cinquepace:* lively dance]

6148 SUFFOLK: What is wedlock forced, but a hell,
An age of discord and continual strife?
Whereas the contrary bringeth bliss,
And is a pattern of celestial peace.
1 Henry VI 5.5.62

6149 EMILIA: If she be not honest, chaste, and true,
There's no man happy.
Othello 4.2.17

6150 JACHIMO: To think that man, who knows
By history, report, or his own proof,
What woman is, yea, what she cannot choose
But must be, will 's free hours languish for
Assured bondage.
Cymbeline 1.6.69
[*'s:* his]

6151 BERTRAM: War is no strife
To the dark house and the detested wife.
All's Well That Ends Well 2.3.291

Weeds

6152 ANTONY: We bring forth weeds
When our quick winds lie still.
Antony and Cleopatra 1.2.109
[*quick winds:* fresh breezes thought to be good for the soil]

6153 KING: Most subject is the fattest soil to weeds.
2 Henry IV 4.4.54

6154 GARDENER: Noisome weeds . . . without profit suck
The soil's fertility from wholesome flowers.
Richard II 3.4.38

6155 QUEEN: Now 'tis spring, and weeds are shallow-rooted;
Suffer them now, and they'll o'ergrow the garden,
And choke the herbs for want of husbandry.
2 Henry VI 3.1.31

6156 YORK: Small herbs have grace, great weeds do grow apace.
Richard III 2.4.13

6157 The summer's flow'r is to the summer sweet,
Though to itself it only live and die,
But if that flow'r with base infection meet,
The basest weed outbraves his dignity:
For sweetest things turn sourest by their deeds;
Lilies that fester smell far worse than weeds.
Sonnet 94
[*outbraves:* surpasses in splendor]

6158 HAMLET [to the Queen]: Do not spread the compost on the weeds
To make them ranker.
Hamlet 3.4.151

6159 YORK: Sweet flow'rs are slow and weeds make haste.
Richard III 2.4.15

6160 YORK: Idle weeds are fast in growth.
Richard III 3.1.103

6161 Unwholesome weeds take root with precious flow'rs.
Rape of Lucrece 870

Weeping

6162 LEONATO: How much better is it to weep at joy than to joy at weeping!
Much Ado About Nothing 1.1.27

6163 RICHARD: To weep is to make less the depth of grief.
3 Henry VI 2.1.85

6164 LEAR: I have full cause of weeping, but this heart
Shall break into a hundred thousand flaws
Or ere I'll weep.
King Lear 2.4.284

6165 RICHARD [on York's death]: I cannot weep; for all my body's moisture
Scarce serves to quench my furnace-burning heart;
Nor can my tongue unload my heart's great burthen,
For self-same wind that I should speak withal
Is kindling coals that fires all my breast,
And burns me up with flames that tears would quench.
3 Henry VI 2.1.79
[*burthen:* burden]

6166 LEONTES: How sometimes nature will betray its folly!
Its tenderness! and make itself a pastime
To harder bosoms!
Winter's Tale 1.2.151
[*pastime:* source of mirth]

6167 K. RICHARD: Two together weeping make one woe.
Richard II 5.1.86

6168 Distress likes dumps when time is kept with tears.
Rape of Lucrece 1127

Welcome

6169 ULYSSES: Welcome ever smiles, And farewell goes out sighing.
Troilus and Cressida 3.3.168

6170 BALTHAZAR: Small cheer and great welcome makes a merry feast.
Comedy of Errors 3.1.26
[*cheer:* used here as a metaphor for food]

6171 ANTIPHOLUS EPHESUS: A table full of welcome makes scarce one dainty dish.
Comedy of Errors 3.1.23

6172 LAUNCE: I reckon this always, that a man is never undone till he be hang'd, nor never welcome to a place till some certain shot be paid and the hostess say "Welcome!"
Two Gentlemen of Verona 2.5.3

6173 BEDFORD: Unbidden guests Are often welcomest when they are gone.
1 Henry VI 2.2.54

6174 HAMLET: Th' appurtenance of welcome is fashion and ceremony.
Hamlet 2.2.371

6175 LADY MACBETH [to Macbeth]: Bear welcome in your eye,
Your hand, your tongue.
Macbeth 1.5.64

6176 ANTONY: Bid that welcome Which comes to punish us, and we punish it
Seeming to bear it lightly.
Antony and Cleopatra 4.14.136

6177 SILVIA [about Proteus]: His worth is warrant for his welcome.
Two Gentlemen of Verona 2.4.102

Wench

6178 BEROWNE: Light wenches may prove plagues to men forsworn.
Love's Labor's Lost 4.3.382

Wheel

6179 FOOL: Let go thy hold when a great wheel runs down a hill, lest it break thy neck with following; but the great one that goes upward, let him draw thee after.
King Lear 2.4.71

6180 LEAR [to Cordelia]: Thou art a soul in bliss, but I am bound
Upon a wheel of fire, that mine own tears
Do scald like molten lead.
King Lear 4.7.45

Whoredom

6181 IAGO [soliloquy]: 'Tis the strumpet's plague
To beguile many and be beguil'd by one.
Othello 4.1.96

Whipping

6182 HAMLET: Use every man after his desert, and who should scape whipping?
Hamlet 2.2.529

Wickedness

6183 K. HENRY: What rein can hold licentious wickedness
When down the hill he holds his fierce career?
Henry V 3.3.22

6184 K. HENRY: Some, peradventure, have on them the guilt of premeditated and contriv'd murther; some, of beguiling virgins with the broken seals of perjury; some, making the wars their bulwark, that have before gor'd the gentle bosom of peace with pillage and robbery. Now, if these men have defeated the law and outrun native punishment, though they can outstrip men, they have no wings to fly from God.
Henry V 4.1.161
[*murther:* murder]

6185 QUICKLY: 'Tis not good that children should know any wickedness.
Merry Wives of Windsor 2.2.128

6186 VIOLA [soliloquy]: Disguise, I see thou art a wickedness
Wherein the pregnant enemy does much.
Twelfth Night 2.2.27
[*pregnant enemy:* devil]

Wife

6187 ROSALIND: Maids are May when they are maids, but the sky changes when they are wives.
As You Like It 4.1.148

6188 NERISSA: Hanging and wiving goes by destiny.
Merchant of Venice 2.9.83

6189 LEONTES: Should all despair
That have revolted wives, the tenth of mankind
Would hang themselves.
Winter's Tale 1.2.198
[*revolted:* unfaithful]

6190 BERTRAM: War is no strife
To a dark house and the detested wife.
All's Well That Ends Well 2.3.291

6191 PORTIA: A light wife doth make a heavy husband.
Merchant of Venice 5.1.130

6192 KATHERINA: Thy husband is thy
lord, thy life, thy keeper,
Thy head, thy sovereign; one that cares
for thee,
And for thy maintenance; commits his
body
To painful labor, both by sea and
land;
To watch the night in storms, the day
in cold,
Whilst thou li'st warm at home, secure
and safe;
And craves no other tribute at thy
hands
But love, fair looks, and true obedi-
ence —
Too little payment for so great a debt.
Such duty as the subject owes the
prince,
Even such a woman oweth to her
husband;
And when she is froward, peevish,
sullen, sour,
And not obedient to his honest will,
What is she but a foul contending
rebel,
And graceless traitor to her loving
lord?
I am asham'd that women are so
simple
To offer war where they should kneel
for peace,
Or seek for rule, supremacy, and sway,
When they are bound to serve, love,
and obey.
Taming of the Shrew 5.2.146

6193 PETRUCHIO [concerning Kate]: I
will be master of what is mine own.
She is my goods, my chattels, she is
my house,
My household stuff, my field, my barn,
My horse, my ox, my ass, my any
thing;
And here she stands, touch her who-
ever dare.
Taming of the Shrew 3.2.229

6194 PORTIA [commending herself to
Bassanio]: Happy in this, she is not
yet so old
But she may learn; happier than this,
She is not bred so dull but she can
learn;
Happiest of all, is that her gentle spirit
Commits itself to yours to be directed,
As from her lord, her governor, her
king.
Merchant of Venice 3.2.160

6195 ADRIANA [to Antipholus
Syracuse]: Thou art an elm, my hus-
band, I a vine,
Whose weakness, married to thy
stronger state,
Makes me with thy strength to com-
municate.
Comedy of Errors 2.2.174

6196 ADRIANA: I will attend my hus-
band, be his nurse,
Diet his sickness, for it is my office.
Comedy of Errors 5.1.98

6197 LEONATO: Well, niece, I hope to
see you one day fitted with a husband.
BEATRICE: Not till God make men of
some other mettle than earth. Would
it not grieve a woman to be over-
master'd with a piece of valiant dust?
to make an account of her life to a
clod of wayward marl?
Much Ado About Nothing 2.1.60
[*mettle:* substance; *marl:* clay]

6198 PORTIA [to Brutus]: Am I
yourself
But, as it were, in sort or limitation.
To keep with you at meals, comfort
your bed,
And talk to you sometimes?
Julius Caesar 2.1.282

6199 OTHELLO [soliloquy]: O curse of
marriage!
That we can call these delicate crea-
tures ours,
And not their appetites!
Othello 3.3.268

6200 EMILIA: If she be not honest,
chaste, and true,
There's no man happy.
Othello 4.2.17

6201 EMILIA: Let husbands know
Their wives have sense like them; they
see, and smell,
And have their palates both for sweet
and sour,
As husbands have.
Othello 4.3.93

6202 BEROWNE [soliloquy]: What! I
love, I sue, I seek a wife —
A woman, that is like a German clock,
Still a-repairing, ever out of frame,
And never going aright, being a watch,
But being watch'd that it may still go
right!
Love's Labor's Lost 3.1.189

6203 VALENTINE [concerning Silvia]:
Why, man, she is mine own,
And I as rich in having such a jewel
As twenty seas, if all their sand were
pearl,
The water nectar, and the rocks pure
gold.
Two Gentlemen of Verona 2.4.168

6204 HECTOR: What nearer debt in all
humanity
Than wife is to the husband?
Troilus and Cressida 2.2.175

6205 ROMAN: The fittest time to corrupt a man's wife is when she's fall'n
out with her husband.
Coriolanus 4.3.32

6206 MISTRESS PAGE: Wives may be
merry, and yet honest too.
Merry Wives of Windsor 4.2.105

6207 BENEDICK [soliloquy]: One woman is fair, yet I am well; another is
wise, yet I am well; another virtuous,
yet I am well; but till all graces be in
one woman, one woman shall not
come in my grace. Rich she shall be,
that's certain; wise, or I'll none; virtuous, or I'll never cheapen her; fair,
or I'll never look on her; mild, or come
not near me; noble, or not I for an
angel; of good discourse, an excellent
musician, and her hair shall be of what
color it please God.
Much Ado About Nothing 2.3.26

6208 FORD: Money buys land, and
wives are sold by fate.
Merry Wives of Windsor 5.5.233

6209 DROMIO SYRACUSE: As from a
bear a man would run for life,
So fly I from her that would be my
wife.
Comedy of Errors 3.2.159

Wildness

6210 Youth is wild, and age is tame.
The Passionate Pilgrim xii.8

6211 DON PEDRO: In time the savage
bull doth bear the yoke.
Much Ado About Nothing 1.1.261

Wilfulness

6212 REGAN: To willful men,
The injuries that they themselves pro-
cure
Must be their schoolmasters.
King Lear 2.4.303

6213 TYBALT: Patience perforce with
willful choler meeting
Makes my flesh tremble in their
different greeting.
Romeo and Juliet 1.5.89
[*different greeting:* i.e. the confrontation of
these opposed states of mind]

Will

6214 PROTEUS: He wants wit that
wants resolved will.
Two Gentlemen of Verona 2.6.12

6215 LYSANDER: The will of man is by
his reason sway'd.
Midsummer Night's Dream 2.2.115

6216 ISABELLA: I am
At war 'twixt will and will not.
Measure for Measure 2.2.32

6217 Will is deaf and hears no heedful friends.

Rape of Lucrece 495

6218 YORK: All too late comes counsel to be heard,
Where will doth mutiny with wit's regard.

Richard II 2.1.27

6219 IAGO: Our bodies are our gardens, to the which our wills are gardeners; so that if we will plant nettles or sow lettuce, set hyssop and weed up tine, supply it with one gender of herbs or distract it with many, either to have it sterile with idleness or manur'd with industry—why, the power and corrigible authority of this lies in our wills.

Othello 1.3.320

[*tine:* tares, wild grasses]

6220 CAESAR: The cause is in my will.

Julius Caesar 2.2.71

6221 TROILUS: There is between my will and all offenses
A guard of patience.

Troilus and Cressida 5.2.53

6222 TROILUS: The will is infinite.

Troilus and Cressida 3.2.82

6223 PLAYER KING: Our wills and fates do so contrary run
That our devices still are overthrown,
Our thoughts are ours, their ends none of our own.

Hamlet 3.2.211

6224 HAMLET: Reason panders will.

Hamlet 3.4.88

6225 ORLEANCE: Ill will never said well.

Henry V 3.7.113

6226 ANTONIO: What I will, I will, and there's an end.

Two Gentlemen of Verona 1.3.65

6227 TROILUS: My election
Is led on in the conduct of my will,

My will enkindled by mine eyes and ears,
Two traded pilots 'twixt the dangerous shores
Of will and judgment.

Troilus and Cressida 2.2.62

[*election:* choice; *traded pilots:* intermediaries constantly going back and forth]

Willingness

6228 K. EDWARD: Willingness rids way.

3 Henry VI 5.3.21

Wind

6229 NATHANIEL: Many can brook the weather that love not the wind.

Love's Labor's Lost 4.2.33

6230 SON: Ill blows the wind that profits nobody.

3 Henry VI 2.5.55

6231 NESTOR: The splitting wind
Makes flexible the knees of knotted oaks.

Troilus and Cressida 1.3.49

6232 ANTONY: We bring forth weeds
When our quick winds lie still.

Antony and Cleopatra 1.2.109

Wine

6233 ROSALIND: Good wine needs no bush.

As You Like It, Epilogue 4

6234 SONG: Come, thou monarch of the vine,
Plumpy Bacchus with pink eyne!
In thy fats our cares be drown'd,
With thy grapes our hairs be crown'd!
Cup us, till the world go round,
Cup us, till the world go round!

Antony and Cleopatra 2.7.113

[*pink eyne:* half-shut eyes]

6235 ANTONY [at a feast]: Come, let's all take hands,
Till that the conquering wine hath steep'd our sense
In soft and delicate Lethe.
Antony and Cleopatra 2.7.106
[*Lethe:* forgetfulness]

6236 BRUTUS: Give me a bowl of wine.
In this I bury all unkindness.
Julius Caesar 4.3.158

6237 GRATIANO: Let my liver rather heat with wine
Than my heart cool with mortifying groans.
Merchant of Venice 1.1.81

6238 CASSIO: O thou invisible spirit of wine, if thou hast no name to be known by, let us call thee devil!
Othello 2.3.281

6239 CAESAR [drinking wine]: It's monstrous labor when I wash my brain
And it grows fouler.
Antony and Cleopatra 2.7.98

6240 CASSIO: O God, that men should put an enemy in their mouths to steal away their brains! that we should, with joy, pleasance, revel, and applause, transform ourselves into beasts!
Othello 2.3.289

6241 IAGO: Come, come; good wine is a good familiar creature, if it be well us'd.
Othello 2.3.309

6242 FALSTAFF [soliloquy]: A good sherris-sack hath a twofold operation in it. It ascends me into the brain, dries me there all the foolish and dull and crudy vapors which environ it, makes it apprehensive, quick, forgetive, full of nimble, fiery, and delectable shapes, which deliver'd o'er to the voice, the tongue, which is the birth, becomes excellent wit. The second property of your excellent sherris is the warming of the blood, which before (cold and settled) left the liver white and pale, which is the badge of pusillanimity and cowardice; but the sherris warms it, and makes it course from the inwards to the parts' extreme. It illumineth the face, which as a beacon gives warning to all the rest of this little kingdom, man, to arm, and then the vital commoners and inland petty spirits muster me all to their captain, the heart, who great and puff'd up with this retinue, doth any deed of courage; and this valor comes of sherris. So that skill in the weapon is nothing without sack (for that sets it a-work) and learning a mere hoard of gold kept by a devil, till sack commences it and sets it in act and use . . . If I had a thousand sons, the first humane principle I would teach them should be, to forswear thin potations and to addict themselves to sack.
2 Henry IV 4.3.96

6243 K. RICHARD: Give me a bowl of wine.
I have not that alacrity of spirit
Nor cheer of mind that I was wont to have.
Richard III 5.3.72

6244 TIMON: Go, suck the subtle blood o' th' grape,
Till the high fever seethe your blood to froth.
Timon of Athens 4.3.429

6245 MACBETH: The wine of life is drawn, and the mere lees
Is left this vault to brag of.
Macbeth 2.3.95

Winning

6246 OTHELLO: They laugh that win.
Othello 4.1.122

6247 KING: Nothing can seem foul to those that win.
1 Henry IV 5.1.8

6248 CLOTEN: Winning will put any man into courage.

Cymbeline 2.3.7

6249 K. HENRY: The gentler gamester is the soonest sinner.

Henry V 3.6.112

Winter

6250 SONG: When icicles hang by the wall,
And Dick the shepherd blows his nail,
And Tom bears logs into the hall,
And milk comes frozen home in pail.

Love's Labor's Lost 5.2.912

[*blows his nail:* i.e. blows on his finger-nails for warmth]

6251 For never-resting time leads summer on
To hideous winter and confounds him there,
Sap check'd with frost and lusty leaves quite gone,
Beauty o'ersnow'd and bareness every where.

Sonnet 5

6252 GRUMIO: Winter tames man, woman, and beast.

Taming of the Shrew 4.1.23

6253 THIRD CITIZEN: When great leaves fall, then winter is at hand.

Richard III 2.3.33

6254 MAMILLIUS: A sad tale's best for winter.

Winter's Tale 2.1.25

6255 Winter, which being full of care,
Makes summer's welcome thrice more wish'd.

Sonnet 56

6256 FOOL: We'll set thee to school to an ant, to teach thee there's no laboring i' th' winter.

King Lear 2.4.67

6257 CAPULET: Well-apparell'd April on the heel
Of limping winter treads.

Romeo and Juliet 1.2.27

Wisdom

6258 HELENA: Full oft we see
Cold wisdom waiting on superfluous folly.

All's Well That Ends Well 1.1.104

6259 TOUCHSTONE: The fool doth think he is wise, but the wise man knows himself to be a fool.

As You Like It 5.1.31

6260 FIRST LORD: To wisdom he's a fool that will not yield.

Pericles 2.4.54

6261 THIDIAS: Wisdom and fortune combating together,
If that the former dare but what it can,
No chance may shake it.

Antony and Cleopatra 3.13.79

6262 PRINCE: Wisdom cries out in the streets, and no man regards it.

1 Henry IV 1.2.88

6263 ALBANY: Wisdom and goodness to the vild seem vild,
Filths savor but themselves.

King Lear 4.2.38

[*vild:* vile]

6264 CLOWN: Well, God give them wisdom that have it; and those that are fools, let them use their talents.

Twelfth Night 1.5.14

6265 BEROWNE: Light, seeking light, doth light of light beguile.

Love's Labor's Lost 1.1.77

6266 ANGELO: Wisdom wishes to appear most bright
When it doth tax itself.

Measure for Measure 2.4.78

6267 ULYSSES: The amity that wisdom knits not, folly may easily untie.
Troilus and Cressida 2.3.101

6268 GRATIANO: There are a sort of men whose visages
Do cream and mantle like a standing pond,
And do a wilful stillness entertain,
With purpose to be dress'd in an opinion
Of wisdom, gravity, profound conceit,
As who should say, "I am Sir Oracle,
And when I ope my lips let no dog bark!"
Merchant of Venice 1.1.88

6269 Sad pause and deep regard beseems the sage.
Rape of Lucrece 277

6270 GONERIL [to Lear]: As you are old and reverend, [you] should be wise.
King Lear 1.4.240

6271 FOOL [to Lear]: Thou shouldst not have been old till thou hadst been wise.
King Lear 1.5.44

6272 Q. MARGARET: Wise men ne'er sit and wail their loss,
But cheerly seek how to redress their harms.
3 Henry VI 5.4.1

6273 LADY MACDUFF: Little is the wisdom, where the flight
So runs against all reason.
Macbeth 4.2.13

6274 THIRD CITIZEN: When clouds are seen, wise men put on their cloaks.
Richard III 2.3.32

6275 CRESSIDA: To be wise and love Exceeds man's might.
Troilus and Cressida 3.2.156

6276 CALPHURNIA [to Caesar]: Alas, my lord,
Your wisdom is consum'd in confidence.
Julius Caesar 2.2.49

6277 POLONIUS: Thus do we of wisdom and of reach,
With windlasses and with assays of bias,
By indirections find directions out.
Hamlet 2.1.61

6278 TOUCHSTONE: Learn of the wise, and perpend.
As You Like It 3.2.66
[*perpend:* consider]

6279 K. EDWARD: 'Tis wisdom to conceal our meaning.
3 Henry VI 4.7.60

6280 GLOUCESTER [aside, about Prince Edward]: So wise so young, they say do never live long.
Richard III 3.1.79

Wish

6281 CLEOPATRA: Wishers were ever fools.
Antony and Cleopatra 4.15.37

6282 BEROWNE: Where nothing wants that want itself doth seek.
Love's Labor's Lost 4.3.233

6283 PRINCE: I never thought to hear you speak again.
KING: Thy wish was father, Harry, to that thought.
2 Henry IV 4.5.91

Wit

6284 PROTEUS: He wants wit that wants resolved will.
Two Gentlemen of Verona 2.6.12

6285 LADY CAPULET: Some grief shows much of love,
But much grief shows still some want of wit.
Romeo and Juliet 3.5.72

6286 FALSTAFF: A good wit will make use of anything.
2 Henry IV 1.2.247

6287 YORK: All too late comes counsel to be heard,
Where will doth mutiny with wit's regard.
Richard II 2.1.27

6288 CELIA: Since the little wit that fools have was silenc'd, the little foolery that wise men have makes a great show.
As You Like It 1.2.88

6289 ISABELLA: Great men may jest with saints; 'tis wit in them,
But in the less foul profanation.
Measure for Measure 2.2.127

6290 ROSALINE: A jest's prosperity lies in the ear
Of him that hears it, never in the tongue
Of him that makes it.
Love's Labor's Lost 5.2.861

6291 DOGBERRY: When the age is in, the wit is out.
Much Ado About Nothing 3.5.34

6292 MARIA: Folly in fools bears not so strong a note
As fool'ry in the wise, when wit doth dote.
Love's Labor's Lost 5.2.75

6293 LONGAVILLE: Fat paunches have lean pates; and dainty bits
Make rich the ribs, but bankrout quite the wits.
Love's Labor's Lost 1.1.26
[*bankrout:* bankrupt]

6294 ANTIPHOLUS SYRACUSE: There's many a man hath more hair than wit.
Comedy of Errors 2.2.83

6295 DROMIO SYRACUSE: What he [Time] hath scanted men in hair he hath given them in wit.
Comedy of Errors 2.2.81

6296 VALENTINE: By love the young and tender wit
Is turn'd to folly.
Two Gentlemen of Verona 1.1.47

6297 VALENTINE: Home-keeping youth have ever homely wits.
Two Gentlemen of Verona 1.1.2

6298 Danger deviseth shifts, wit waits on fear.
Venus and Adonis 690

6299 DON PEDRO: What a pretty thing man is when he goes in his doublet and hose and leaves off his wit!
Much Ado About Nothing 5.1.199

6300 ROSALIND: Make the doors upon a woman's wit, and it will out at the casement; shut that, and 'twill out at the key-hole; stop that, 'twill fly with the smoke out at the chimney.
As You Like It 4.1.161

6301 CLOWN: Those wits that think they have thee do very oft prove fools; and I that am sure that I lack thee, may pass for a wise man. For what says Quinapalus? "Better a witty fool than a foolish wit."
Twelfth Night 1.5.33

6302 BEROWNE [to Katherine]: Your wit's too hot, it speeds too fast, 'twill tire.
Love's Labor's Lost 2.1.119

6303 TOUCHSTONE: I shall ne'er be ware of my own wit till I break my shins against it.
As You Like It 2.4.5

6304 THERSITES: I will keep where there is wit stirring, and leave the fashion of fools.
Troilus and Cressida 2.1.118

6305 CELIA: Always the dullness of the fool is the whetstone of the wits.
As You Like It 1.2.54

6306 SIR ANDREW: I am a great eater of beef, and I believe that does harm to my wit.
Twelfth Night 1.3.85

Woe

6307 KING: When sorrows come, they come not single spies,
But in battalions.
Hamlet 5.4.78

6308 QUEEN: One woe doth tread upon another's heel,
So fast they follow.
Hamlet 4.7.163

6309 CARLISLE: Wise men ne'er sit and wail their woes,
But presently prevent the ways to wail.
Richard II 3.2.178

6310 GAUNT: Gnarling sorrow hath less power to bite
The man that mocks at it and sets it light.
Richard II 1.3.292

6311 GAUNT: Woe doth the heavier sit
Where it perceives it is but faintly borne.
Richard II 1.3.280

6312 Fellowship in woe doth woe assuage,
As palmers' chat makes short their pilgrimage.
Rape of Lucrece 790

6313 JULIET: Sour woe delights in fellowship.
Romeo and Juliet 3.2.116

6314 K. RICHARD: Two together weeping make one woe.
Richard II 5.1.86

6315 GLOUCESTER: Woes by wrong imaginations lose
The knowledge of themselves.
King Lear 4.6.283

6316 ESCALUS: Mercy is not itself, that oft looks so;
Pardon is still the nurse of second woe.
Measure for Measure 2.1.283

6317 LUCIANA: Headstrong liberty is lash'd with woe.
Comedy of Errors 2.1.15

6318 Though woe be heavy, yet it seldom sleeps.
Rape of Lucrece 1574

6319 Love can comment upon every woe.
Venus and Adonis 714

6320 EDGAR [soliloquy]: When we our betters see bearing our woes,
We scarcely think our miseries our foes.
King Lear 3.6.102

6321 All love's pleasure shall not match his woe.
Venus and Adonis 1140

6322 Q. MARGARET [to Q. Elizabeth]: If sorrow can admit society,
Tell over your woes again by viewing mine.
Richard III 4.4.38

6323 FOOL: The man that makes his toe
What he his heart should make,
Shall of a corn cry woe,
And turn his sleep to wake.
King Lear 3.2.31

Woman

6324 ENOBARBUS [about Cleopatra]: Age cannot wither her, nor custom stale
Her infinite variety.
Antony and Cleopatra 2.2.234

6325 DUKE: However we do praise ourselves,
Our fancies are more giddy and unfirm,
More longing, wavering, sooner lost and worn,
Than women's are.
Twelfth Night 2.4.32

6326 ROSALIND: A woman's thought runs before her actions.
As You Like It 4.1.140

6327 ROSALIND: Make the doors upon a woman's wit, and it will out at the casement; shut that, and 'twill out at the key-hold; stop that, 'twill fly with the smoke out at the chimney.
As You Like It 4.1.163

6328 ORLANDO [soliloquy, about Rosalind]: Run, run, Orlando, carve on every tree
The fair, the chaste, and unexpressive she.
As You Like It 3.2.9
[*unexpressive:* inexpressible]

6329 BENEDICK [soliloquy]: One woman is fair, yet I am well; another is wise, yet I am well; another virtuous, yet I am well; but till all graces be in one woman, one woman shall not come in my grace.
Much Ado About Nothing 2.3.26

6330 HORTENSIO: Kindness in women, not their beauteous looks,
Shall win my love.
Taming of the Shrew 4.2.41

6331 CLOWN: A woman is a dish for the gods, if the devil dress her not.
Antony and Cleopatra 5.2.274

6332 DUKE: Women are as roses, whose fair flow'r
Being once display'd, doth fall that very hour.
Twelfth Night 2.4.38

6333 JAQUES: If ladies be but young and fair,
They have the gift to know it.
As You Like It 2.7.37

6334 FOOL: There was never yet fair woman but she made mouths in a glass.
King Lear 3.2.35
[*made mouths:* practiced facial expressions; *glass:* mirror]

6335 YORK: 'Tis beauty that doth oft make women proud . . .

'Tis virtue that doth make them most admir'd . . .
'Tis government that makes them seem divine.
3 Henry VI 1.4.128
[*government:* discipline, self-control]

6336 LAUNCE: To be slow in words is a woman's only virtue.
Two Gentlemen of Verona 3.1.334

6337 IAGO [to Emilia, on wives]: You are pictures out 'a doors,
Bells in your parlors, wild-cats in your kitchens,
Saints in your injuries, devils being offended,
Players in your huswifery, and huswives in your beds.
Othello 2.1.109
[*'a:* of]

6338 CASSIO [about Othello and Desdemona]: He hath achiev'd a maid
That paragons description and wild fame;
One that excels the quirks of blazoning pens,
And in th' essential vesture of creation
Does tire the ingener.
Othello 2.1.61
[*tire the ingener:* i.e. her beauty defies all attempts of the inventive poet to adequately praise her]

6339 BEROWNE: From women's eyes this doctrine I derive:
They sparkle still the right Promethean fire;
They are the books, the arts, the academes,
That show, contain, and nourish all the world.
Love's Labor's Lost 4.3.347

6340 YORK: Women are soft, mild, pitiful, and flexible.
3 Henry VI 1.4.141

6341 KATHERINA: Why are our bodies soft, and weak, and smooth,
Unapt to toil and trouble in the world,

But that our soft conditions, and our hearts,
Should well agree with our external parts?
Taming of the Shrew 5.2.165

6342 PORTIA: Ah me! How weak a thing
The heart of woman is!
Julius Caesar 2.4.39

6343 BOYET: Fair ladies mask'd are roses in their bud;
Dismask'd, their damask sweet commixture shown,
Are angels vailing clouds, or roses blown.
Love's Labor's Lost 5.2.295
[*damask:* red and white; *vailing:* letting fall, shedding]

6344 ROSALIND: That woman that cannot make her fault her husband's occasion, let her never nurse her child herself, for she will breed it like a fool!
As You Like It 4.1.173

6345 ABBESS: The venom clamors of a jealous woman
Poisons more deadly than a mad dog's tooth.
Comedy of Errors 5.1.69

6346 BENEDICK [concerning Beatrice]: She speaks poniards, and every word stabs. If her breath were as terrible as her terminations, there were no living near her, she would infect the north star.
Much Ado About Nothing 2.1.247

6347 CLOTEN: A woman's fitness comes by fits.
Cymbeline 4.1.5

6348 KATHERINA: A woman mov'd is like a fountain troubled,
Muddy, ill-seeming, thick, bereft of beauty.
Taming of the Shrew 5.2.142

6349 POSTHUMUS [soliloquy]: There's no motion

That tends to vice in man, but I affirm
It is the woman's part: be it lying, note it,
The woman's; flattering, hers; deceiving, hers;
Lust and rank thoughts, hers, hers; revenges, hers;
Ambitions, covetings, change of prides, disdain,
Nice longing, slanders, mutability,
All faults that may be named, nay, that hell knows,
Why, hers.
Cymbeline 2.5.20
[*change of prides:* varying vanities and extravagances; *nice longing:* wanton appetites]

6350 Though men can cover crimes with bold stern looks,
Poor women's faces are their own faults' books.
Rape of Lucrece 1252

6351 NURSE: Women grow by men.
Romeo and Juliet 1.3.95

6352 ENOBARBUS [about Cleopatra]: Her passions are made of nothing but the finest part of pure love. We cannot call her winds and waters, sighs and tears; they are greater storms and tempests than almanacs can report. This cannot be cunning in her; if it be, she makes a show'r of rain as well as Jove.
Antony and Cleopatra 1.2.146

6353 DEMETRIUS [concerning Lavinia]: She is a woman, therefore may be woo'd,
She is a woman, therefore may be won.
Titus Andronicus 2.1.82

6354 HELENA: We cannot fight for love, as men may do.
We should be woo'd, and were not made to woo.
Midsummer Night's Dream 2.1.241

6355 VALENTINE [to Duke, on courtship]: Never give her o'er,
For scorn at first makes after-love the more.

If she do frown, 'tis not in hate of you,
But rather to beget more love in you.
If she do chide, 'tis not to have you
gone,
For why, the fools are mad, if left
alone.
Take no repulse, what ever she doth
say;
For "get you gone," she doth not mean
"away!"
            Two Gentlemen of Verona 3.1.94

6356 VALENTINE: A woman sometimes
scorns what best contents her.
            Two Gentlemen of Verona 3.1.93

6357 Have you not heard it said full
oft,
A woman's nay doth stand for nought?
            The Passionate Pilgrim xviii.41

6358 ROSALIND: Do you not know I
am a woman? when I think, I must
speak.
                    As You Like It 3.2.249

6359 POSTHUMUS: The vows of women
Of no more bondage be to where they
are made
Than they are to their virtues, which is
nothing.
                    Cymbeline 2.4.110

6360 PORTIA: How hard it is for
women to keep counsel!
                    Julius Caesar 2.4.8

6361 HAMLET [to Ophelia]: You jig
and amble, and you lisp, and nickname God's creatures and make your
wantonness your ignorance.
                    Hamlet 3.1.144

6362 PATROCLUS: A woman impudent
and mannish grown
Is not more loath'd than an effeminate
man.
                    Troilus and Cressida 3.3.217

6363 HOTSPUR [to Kate]: Constant
you are,
But yet a woman, and for secrecy,
No lady closer, for I well believe

Thou wilt not utter what thou dost not
know,
And so far will I trust thee.
                    1 Henry IV 2.3.108

6364 CYMBELINE: O most delicate
fiend!
Who is't can read a woman?
                    Cymbeline 5.5.47

6365 CHAMBERLAIN: Two women
plac'd together makes cold weather.
                    Henry VIII 1.4.22

6366 KING: A child of our grand-
mother Eve, a female; or for thy more
sweet understanding, a woman.
                    Love's Labor's Lost 1.1.263

6367 HAMLET: Frailty, thy name is
woman!
                    Hamlet 1.2.146

6368 PISTOL: Fear and niceness
(The handmaids of all women, or more
truly
Woman its pretty self).
                    Cymbeline 3.4.155

Womb

6369 Where is she so fair whose
unear'd womb
Disdains the tillage of thy husbandry?
                    Sonnet 3

6370 MIRANDA: Good wombs have
borne bad sons.
                    The Tempest 1.2.119

Wonders

6371 CELIA: O wonderful, wonderful,
and most wonderful wonderful! and
yet again wonderful, and after that,
out of all hooping!
                    As You Like It 3.2.191
[*hooping:* whooping]

Woodman

6372 He is no woodman that doth
bend his bow
To strike a poor unseasonable doe.
Rape of Lucrece 580

Wooing

6373 VALENTINE: That man that hath
a tongue, I say is no man,
If with his tongue he cannot win a
woman.
Two Gentlemen of Verona 3.1.104

6374 DEMETRIUS [concerning Lavinia]:
She is a woman, therefore may be
woo'd,
She is a woman, therefore may be
won.
Titus Andronicus 2.1.82

6375 VALENTINE [to Duke, on court-
ship]: Win her with gifts, if she
respects not words:
Dumb jewels often in their silent kind
More than quick words do move a
woman's mind.
Two Gentlemen of Verona 3.1.89

6376 VALENTINE [to Duke, on the fine
art of courtship]: A woman
sometimes scorns what best contents
her.
Send her another; never give her o'er,
For scorn at first makes after-love the
more.
If she do frown, 'tis not in hate of you,
But rather to beget more love in you.
If she do chide, 'tis not to have you
gone,
For why, the fools are mad, if left
alone.
Take no repulse, what ever she doth
say;
For "get you gone," she doth not mean
"away!"
Two Gentlemen of Verona 3.1.93

6377 PETRUCHIO [soliloquy, about
Kate]: Say that she rail, why then I'll
tell her plain

She sings as sweetly as a nightingale;
Say that she frown, I'll say she looks as
clear
As morning roses newly wash'd with
dew;
Say she be mute, and will not speak a
word,
Then I'll commend her volubility,
And say she uttereth piercing elo-
quence;
If she do bid me pack, I'll give her
thanks,
As though she bid me stay by her a
week;
If she deny to wed, I'll crave the day
When I shall ask the banes, and when
be married.
Taming of the Shrew 2.1.170
[*banes:* banns, a public notice of a proposed
marriage]

6378 GREMIO [to any suitor, concerning Kate]: Woo her, wed her, and bed
her, and rid the house of her!
Taming of the Shrew 1.1.144

6379 When a woman woos, what
woman's son
Will sourly leave her till she have
prevailed?
Sonnet 41

6380 Affection faints not like a pale-
fac'd coward,
But then woos best when most his
choice is froward.
Venus and Adonis 569

6381 CRESSIDA: Women are angels,
wooing:
Things won are done, joy's soul lies in
the doing.
That she belov'd knows nought that
knows not this:
Men prize the thing ungain'd more
than it is.
Troilus and Cressida 1.2.286

6382 BERTRAM [to Diana]: A heaven
on earth I have won by wooing thee.
All's Well That Ends Well 4.2.66

6383 FENTON [to Anne Page]: Wooing
thee, I found thee of more value
Than stamps in gold, or sums in sealed
bags;
And 'tis the very riches of thyself
That I now aim at.
Merry Wives of Windsor 3.4.15

6384 HELENA: We cannot fight for
love, as men may do.
We should be woo'd, and were not
made to woo.
Midsummer Night's Dream 2.1.241

6385 SALERIO [quoting Antonio's advice to Bassanio]: "Be merry, and
employ your chiefest thoughts
To courtship, and such fair ostents of
love
As shall conveniently become you
there."
Merchant of Venice 2.8.43

6386 FIRST CITIZEN: They say poor
suitors have strong breaths.
Coriolanus 1.1.59

6387 ROSALIND: Men are April when
they woo, December when they wed;
maids are May when they are maids,
but the sky changes when they are
wives.
As You Like It 4.1.147

Words

6388 K. HENRY: 'Tis a kind of good
deed to say well,
And yet words are no deeds.
Henry VIII 3.2.153

6389 PANDARUS: Words pay no debts.
Troilus and Cressida 3.2.55

6390 BOY: Men of few words are the
best men.
Henry V 3.2.36

6391 ROSENCRANTZ: Many wearing
rapiers are afraid of goose-quills.
Hamlet 2.2.343
[*goose-quills:* the pens of satirical writers]

6392 BRABANTIO: Words are words; I
never yet did hear
That the bruis'd heart was pierced
through the ear.
Othello 1.3.218

6393 BRUTUS: Good words are better
than bad strokes.
Julius Caesar 5.1.29

6394 DROMIO EPHESUS: Words are but
wind.
Comedy of Errors 3.1.75

6395 BEATRICE: Foul words is but foul
wind, and foul wind is but foul
breath, and foul breath is noisome.
Much Ado About Nothing 5.2.52

6396 BEROWNE: Honest plain words
best pierce the ear of grief.
Love's Labor's Lost 5.2.753

6397 MALCOLM [to Rosse, after the
slaughter of Macduff's family]: Give
sorrow words. The grief that does
not speak
Whispers the o'er-fraught heart, and
bids it break.
Macbeth 4.3.209

6398 Sorrow ebbs, being blown with
wind of words.
Rape of Lucrece 1330

6399 LUCIANA: Ill deeds is doubled
with an evil word.
Comedy of Errors 3.2.20

6400 HERO: One doth not know
How much an ill word may empoison
liking.
Much Ado About Nothing 3.1.85

6401 BULLINGBROOK [on his years in
exile]: How long a time lies in one
little word!
Four lagging winters and four wanton
springs
End in a word: such is the breath of
kings.
Richard II 1.3.213

6402 ANTONY [at The Forum]: But yesterday the word of Caesar might Have stood against the world; now lies he there,
And none so poor to do him reverence.
Julius Caesar 3.2.118

6403 Q. ELIZABETH: Windy attorneys to their client woes,
Aery succeeders of interstate joys,
Poor breathing orators of miseries,
Let them have scope! though what they will impart
Help nothing else, yet do they ease the heart.
Richard III 4.4.127

6404 VIOLA: They that dally nicely with words may quickly make them wanton.
Twelfth Night 3.1.14

6405 TROILUS: Words, words, mere words, no matter from the heart.
Troilus and Cressida 5.3.108

6406 JULIA [to Lucetta]: Didst thou but know the inly touch of love,
Thou wouldst as soon go kindle fire with snow
As seek to quench the fire of love with words.
Two Gentlemen of Verona 2.7.18

6407 Free vent of words love's fire doth assuage.
Venus and Adonis 334

6408 LAUNCE: To be slow in words is a woman's only virtue.
Two Gentlemen of Verona 3.1.338

6409 KING [rising from prayer]: My words fly up, my thoughts remain below:
Words without thoughts never to heaven go.
Hamlet 3.3.97

6410 GAUNT: They say the tongues of dying men
Enforce attention like deep harmony.

Where words are scarce, they are seldom spent in vain,
For they breathe truth that breathe their words in pain.
Richard II 2.1.5

6411 CLOWN: Words are grown so false, I am loathe to prove reason with them.
Twelfth Night 3.1.24

6412 BEROWNE: O, never will I trust to speeches penn'd,
Nor to the motion of a schoolboy's tongue,
Nor never come in vizard to my friend,
Nor woo in rhyme, like a blind harper's song!
Taffata phrases, silken terms precise,
Three-pil'd hyperboles, spruce affection,
Figures pedantical.
Love's Labor's Lost 5.2.402

6413 MACBETH [soliloquy]: Words to the heat of deeds too cold breath gives.
Macbeth 2.1.61

6414 CLOWN: A sentence is but a chev'ril glove to a good wit.
Twelfth Night 3.1.11
[*chev'ril*: kidskin]

6415 LADY GREY: 'Tis better said than done.
3 Henry VI 3.2.90

6416 LORENZO: How every fool can play upon the word! I think the best grace of wit will shortly turn into silence, and discourse grow commendable in none only but parrots.
Merchant of Venice 3.5.43

6417 HAMLET: Suit the action to the word, the word to the action.
Hamlet 3.2.17

6418 CANTERBURY [about Henry]: When he speaks,
The air, a charter'd libertine, is still,

And the mute wonder lurketh in men's
ears
To steal his sweet and honeyed
sentences.

Henry V 1.1.50

Work

6419 MACBETH: The labor we delight
in physics pain.

Macbeth 2.3.50

6420 ANTONY: To business that we
love we rise betime,
And go to't with delight.

Antony and Cleopatra 4.4.20

6421 My nature is subdu'd
To what it works in, like the dyer's
hand.

Sonnet 111

6422 PEMBROKE: When workmen
strive to do better than well,
They do confound their skill in covetousness.

King John 4.2.28

6423 HAMLET: What a piece of work is
a man...!

Hamlet 2.2.303

World

6424 WIDOW: He that is giddy thinks
the world turns round.

Taming of the Shrew 5.2.20

6425 EDGAR: World, world, O world!
But that thy strange mutations make
us hate thee,
Life would not yield to age.

King Lear 4.1.10

6426 GRATIANO [to Antonio]: You
have too much respect upon the
world.
They lose it that do buy it with much
care.

Merchant of Venice 1.1.74

6427 JAQUES: All the world's a stage,
And all the men and women merely
players.

As You Like It 2.7.139

6428 ANTONIO: I hold the world but
as the world, Gratiano,
A stage, where every man must play a
part.

Merchant of Venice 1.1.77

6429 HAMLET [soliloquy]: How weary,
stale, flat, and unprofitable,
Seem to me all the uses of this world!
Fie on't, ah, fie! 'tis an unweeded
garden
That grows to seed, things rank and
gross in nature
Possess it merely.

Hamlet 1.2.133

6430 ROSALIND: O how full of briars is
this working-day world.

As You Like It 1.3.11

6431 ADAM [to Orlando]: O, what a
world is this, when what is comely
Envenoms him that bears it!

As You Like It 2.3.15

6432 BASTARD [soliloquy]: Mad world,
mad kings, mad composition!

King John 2.1.561

6433 SECOND MURDERER [to
Macbeth]: I am one, my liege,
Whom the vile blows and buffets of
the world
Have so incens'd that I am reckless
what
I do to spite the world.

Macbeth 3.1.108

6434 GLOUCESTER: The world is grown
so bad
That wrens make prey where eagles
dare not perch.

Richard III 1.3.69

6435 POET: How goes the world?
PAINTER: It wears, sir, as it grows.

Timon of Athens 1.1.2

6436 PISTOL: The world's my oyster
Which I with sword will open.
Merry Wives of Windsor 2.2.3

6437 TIMON: What wouldst thou do
with the world, Apemantus, if it lay in
thy power?
APEMANTUS: Give it the beasts, to be
rid of the men.
Timon of Athens 4.3.321

6438 MIRANDA: How beauteous
  mankind is! O brave new world
That has such people in't!
The Tempest 5.1.183

6439 HAMLET: Why, let the strooken
  deer go weep,
The hart ungalled play,
For some must watch while some must
  sleep,
Thus runs the world away.
Hamlet 3.2.271
[*strooken:* wounded; *ungalled:* unwounded]

6440 This huge stage presenteth
  nought but shows.
Sonnet 15

6441 GLOUCESTER: O ruin'd piece of
  nature! This great world
Shall so wear out to nought.
King Lear 4.6.134

6442 LADY MACDUFF: I am in this
  earthly world—where to do harm
Is often laudable, to do good sometime
Accounted dangerous folly.
Macbeth 4.2.75

6443 THIRD QUEEN: This world's a city
  full of straying streets,
And death's the market-place, where
  each one meets.
Two Noble Kinsmen 1.5.14

Worm

6444 HAMLET [to King]: Your worm is
your only emperor for diet: we fat all
creatures else to fat us, and we fat ourselves for maggots; your fat king and

your lean beggar is but variable service,
two dishes, but to one table—that's
the end.
Hamlet 4.3.21

6445 CLIFFORD: The smallest worm
will turn, being trodden on.
3 Henry VI 2.2.17

Worry

6446 SIR TOBY: I am sure care's an
  enemy to life.
Twelfth Night 1.3.2

Worship

6447 DOGBERRY: God is to be worshipp'd.
Much Ado About Nothing 3.5.39

6448 TIMON: What a god's gold
That he is worshipp'd in a baser
  temple
Than where swine feed!
Timon of Athens 5.1.47

Worst

6449 HECTOR: Modest doubt is call'd
The beacon of the wise, the tent that
  searches
To th' bottom of the worst.
Troilus and Cressida 2.2.15
[*tent:* probe]

6450 CRESSIDA: To fear the worst oft
cures the worst.
Troilus and Cressida 3.2.73

6451 ROSSE: Things at the worst will
  cease, or else climb upward
To what they were before.
Macbeth 4.2.24

6452 BULLINGBROOK: Apprehension
  of the good
Gives but the greater feeling to the
  worst.
Richard II 1.3.300

6453 ARCHBISHOP: Past and to come
seems best; things present worse.
2 Henry IV 1.3.108

6454 EDGAR: The worst is not
So long as we can say, "This is the
worst."
King Lear 4.1.27

6455 K. RICHARD: Cry woe, destruction, ruin, and decay:
The worst is death, and death will have
his day.
Richard II 3.2.102

6456 DUKE: When remedies are past,
the griefs are ended
By seeing the worst, which late on
hopes depended.
To mourn a mischief that is past and
gone
Is the next way to draw new mischief
on.
Othello 1.3.202

Worth

6457 FRIAR: It so falls out
That what we have we prize not to the
worth
Whiles we enjoy it, but being lack'd
and lost,
Why then we rack the value; then we
find
The virtue that possession would not
show us
Whiles it was ours.
Much Ado About Nothing 4.1.217

6458 TROILUS: What's aught but as 'tis
valued?
Troilus and Cressida 2.2.52

6459 JULIET: They are but beggars that
can count their worth.
Romeo and Juliet 2.6.32

6460 AARON: Let my deeds be witness
of my worth.
Titus Andronicus 5.1.103

6461 O, how thy worth with manners
may I sing,
When thou art all the better part of
me?
What can mine own praise to my own
self bring?
And what is't but mine own when I
praise thee?
Sonnet 39
[*manners:* proper modesty]

Worthiness

6462 LAUNCE: Good things should be
prais'd.
Two Gentlemen of Verona 3.1.347

Worthlessness

6463 GARDENER: Superfluous branches
We lop away, that bearing boughs may
live.
Richard II 3.4.63

Would

6464 KING: That we would do,
We should do when we would; for this
"would" changes,
And hath abatements and delays as
many
As there are tongues, are hands, are
accidents.
Hamlet 4.7.118

6465 LADY MACBETH [to Macbeth]:
Wouldst thou have that
Which thou esteem'st the ornament of
life,
And live a coward in thine own
esteem,
Letting "I dare not" wait upon "I
would,"
Like the poor cat i' th' adage?
Macbeth 1.7.41
[*th' adage:* i.e. "The cat would eat fish, and
would not wet her feet."]

Wounds

6466 ROMEO: He jests at scars that never felt a wound.
Romeo and Juliet 2.2.1

6467 IAGO: What wound did ever heal but by degrees?
Othello 2.3.371

6468 To see the salve doth make the wound ache more.
Rape of Lucrece 1116

6469 PATROCLUS: Those wounds heal ill that men do give themselves.
Troilus and Cressida 3.3.229

6470 HECTOR: The wound of peace is surety,
Surety secure.
Troilus and Cressida 2.2.14
[*wound of peace:* a false sense of security]

6471 VALENTINE: Proteus,
I am sorry I must never trust thee more,
But count the world a stranger for thy sake.
The private wound is deepest: O time most accurst!
'Mongst all foes that a friend should be the worst!
Two Gentlemen of Verona 5.4.71

Wren

6472 LADY MACDUFF: The poor wren,
The most diminutive of birds, will fight,
Her young ones in her nest, against the owl.
Macbeth 4.2.9

6473 GLOUCESTER: The world is grown so bad
That wrens make prey where eagles dare not perch.
Richard III 1.3.69

Writing

6474 DOGBERRY: To be a well-favor'd man is the gift of fortune, but to read and write comes by nature.
Much Ado About Nothing 3.3.14
[*well-favor'd:* good-looking]

6475 ARMADO: Devise, wit, write pen, for I am for whole volumes in folio.
Love's Labor's Lost 1.2.184

Wrongs

6476 FIRST SENATOR: He's truly valiant that can wisely suffer
The worst that man can breathe, and make his wrongs
His outsides, to wear them like his raiment, carelessly.
Timon of Athens 3.5.31

6477 ADRIANA [to Antipholus Syracuse]: Be it my wrong you are from me exempt,
But wrong not that wrong with a more contempt.
Comedy of Errors 2.2.171

6478 HECTOR: To persist
In doing wrong extenuates not wrong,
But makes it much more heavy.
Troilus and Cressida 2.2.186

6479 Q. MARGARET: Though usurpers sway the rule a while,
Yet heav'ns are just, and time suppresseth wrongs.
3 Henry VI 3.3.76

6480 BUCKINGHAM: Wrong hath but wrong, and blame the due of blame.
Richard III 5.1.29

6481 Wrong the wronger till he render right.
Rape of Lucrece 943

Yearnings

6482 When in disgrace with Fortune and men's eyes

I all alone beweep my outcast state,
And trouble deaf heaven with my
    bootless cries,
And look upon myself and curse my
    fate,
Wishing me like to one more rich in
    hope,
Featur'd like him, like him with
    friends possess'd,
Desiring this man's art, and that man's
    scope,
With what I most enjoy contented
    least;
Yet in these thoughts myself almost
    despising,
Haply I think on thee, and then my
    state
(Like to the lark at break of day arising
From sullen earth) sings hymns at
    heaven's gate,
For thy sweet love rememb'red such
    wealth brings,
That then I scorn to change my state
    with kings.
                                    Sonnet 29

Yesterdays

6483 MACBETH: To-morrow, and to-
morrow, and to-morrow,
Creeps in this petty pace from day to
    day,
To the last syllable of recorded time;
And all our yesterdays have lighted
    fools
The way to dusty death.
                                    Macbeth 5.5.19

6484 SALISBURY: O, call back yesterday, bid time return.
                                    Richard II 3.2.69

Youth

6485 CELIA: All's brave that youth
mounts and folly guides.
                                    As You Like It 3.4.45

6486 TIMON: Lust, and liberty,
Creep in the minds and marrows of
    our youth,

That 'gainst the stream of virtue they
    may strive,
And drown themselves in riot!
                                    Timon of Athens 4.1.25
[*riot:* licentious living]

6487 LAERTES [to Ophelia on love's
danger]: The canker galls the infants
    of the spring
Too oft before their buttons be
    disclos'd,
And in the morn and liquid dew of
    youth
Contagious blastments are most
    imminent.
                                    Hamlet 1.3.39

6488 PORTIA: The brain may devise
laws for the blood, but a hot temper
leaps o'er a cold decree—such a hare is
madness the youth, to skip o'er the
meshes of good counsel the cripple.
                                    Merchant of Venice 1.2.18

6489 OLIVIA: Youth is bought more
oft than begg'd or borrow'd.
                                    Twelfth Night 3.4.3

6490 KING: O God, that one might
    read the book of fate,
And see the revolution of the times
Make mountains level, and the conti-
    nent,
Weary of solid firmness, melt itself
Into the sea, and other times to see
The beachy girdle of the ocean
Too wide for Neptune's hips; how
    chance's mocks
And changes fill the cup of alteration
With divers liquors! O, if this were
    seen,
The happiest youth, viewing his prog-
    ress through,
What perils past, what crosses to
    ensue,
Would shut the book, and sit him
    down and die.
                                    2 Henry IV 3.1.45

6491 BEROWNE: Young blood doth
    not obey an old decree.
                                    Love's Labor's Lost 4.3.213

6492 GLOUCESTER [aside, about young Prince Edward]: So wise so young, they say do never live long.
Richard III 3.1.79

6493 PANDULPH: Your mind is all as youthful as your blood.
King John 3.4.125

6494 VALENTINE: Home-keeping youth have ever homely wits.
Two Gentlemen of Verona 1.1.2

6495 KING: Youth no less becomes
The light and careless livery that it wears
Than settled age his sables and his weeds,
Importing health and graveness.
Hamlet 4.7.77

6496 Crabbed age and youth cannot live together:
Youth is full of pleasance, age is full of care,
Youth is like summer morn, age like winter weather,
Youth like summer brave, age like winter bare.
Youth is full of sport, age's breath is short,
Youth is nimble, age is lame.
Youth is hot and bold, age is weak and cold,
Youth is wild, and age is tame.
Age, I do abhor thee, youth, I do adore thee.
The Passionate Pilgrim xii.1

6497 SHEPHERD: I would there were no age between ten and three-and-twenty, or that youth would sleep out the rest; for there is nothing in the between but getting wenches with child, wronging the ancientry, stealing, fighting.
Winter's Tale 3.3.59

6498 FALSTAFF: A man can no more separate age and covetousness than 'a can part young limbs and lechery.
2 Henry IV 1.2.228

['a: he]

6499 POLONIUS: It is common for the younger sort
To lack discretion.
Hamlet 2.1.113

6500 CLOWN: Youth's a stuff will not endure.
Twelfth Night 2.3.52

6501 ANTONY: The spirit of a youth
That means to be of note, begins betimes.
Antony and Cleopatra 4.4.26

6502 OLD ATHENIAN: Our own precedent passions do instruct us
What levity's in youth.
Timon of Athens 1.1.133

6503 FALSTAFF [to Chief Justice]: You that are old consider not the capacities of us that are young, you do measure the heat of our livers with the bitterness of your galls.
2 Henry IV 1.2.173

6504 FRIAR LAWRENCE: Care keeps his watch in every old man's eye,
But where care lodges, sleep will never lie;
But where unbruised youth with unstuff'd brain
Doth couch his limbs, there golden sleep doth reign.
Romeo and Juliet 2.3.35

6505 Time doth transfix the flourish set on youth,
And delves the parallels in beauty's brow.
Sonnet 60

6506 COUNTESS: It is the show and seal of nature's truth,
Where love's strong passion is impress'd in youth.
By our remembrances of days foregone,
Such were our faults, or then we thought them none.
All's Well That Ends Well 1.3.132

6507 EDMUND: The younger rises when the old doth fall.
King Lear 3.3.25

6508 Thou art thy mother's glass, and
  she in thee
Calls back the lovely April of her
  prime,
So thou through windows of thine age
  shall see,
Despite of wrinkles, this thy golden
  time.
Sonnet 3

6509 Misshapen Time, copesmate of
  ugly Night,
Swift subtle post, carrier of grisly care,
Eater of youth, false slave to false
  delight,
Base watch of woes, sin's pack-horse,
  virtue's snare!
Thou nursest all, and murth'rest all
  that are.
Rape of Lucrece 925
[*copesmate:* companion; *murth'rest:* mur-
derest]

6510 The conceit of this inconstant
  stay
Sets you most rich in youth before my
  sight,
Where wasteful Time debateth with
  Decay
To change your day of youth to sullied
  night,
And all in war with Time for love of
  you,
As he takes from you, I ingraft you
  new.
Sonnet 15

6511 FALSTAFF: For though the
camomile, the more it is trodden on,
the faster it grows, yet youth, the more
it is wasted, the sooner it wears.
1 Henry IV 2.4.399

6512 Proud-pied April (dress'd in all
  his trim)
Hath put a spirit of youth in every
  thing.
Sonnet 98

6513 CLEOPATRA: My salad days,
When I was green in judgment.
Antony and Cleopatra 1.5.73

6514 POLIXENES: To be boy eternal.
Winter's Tale 1.2.64

Zanies

6515 MALVOLIO: I take these wise men
that crow so at these set kind of
fools no better than fools' zanies.
Twelfth Night 1.5.89
[*fools' zanies:* fools' fools]

Zeal

6516 PRINCESS: Zeal strives to content,
  and the contents
Die in the zeal of that which it
  presents.
Love's Labor's Lost 5.2.517

Title Index

References are to the boldface serial numbers preceding each quote, rather than to page numbers.

Character Index

References are to the boldface serial numbers preceding each quote, rather than to page numbers. These abbreviations have been used:

AWTEW	All's Well That Ends Well
Ant. & Cleo.	Antony and Cleopatra
AYLI	As You Like It
Errors	The Comedy of Errors
Coriolanus	Coriolanus
Cymbeline	Cymbeline
Hamlet	Hamlet
1 H.IV	1 Henry IV
2 H.IV	2 Henry IV
H.V	Henry V
1 H.VI	1 Henry VI
2 H.VI	2 Henry VI
3 H.VI	3 Henry VI
H.VIII	Henry VIII
Caesar	Julius Caesar
John	King John
Lear	King Lear
LLL	Love's Labor's Lost
Macbeth	Macbeth
MM	Measure for Measure
MV	The Merchant of Venice
MWW	The Merry Wives of Windsor
MND	A Midsummer Night's Dream
Ado	Much Ado About Nothing
Othello	Othello
Pericles	Pericles
R.II	Richard II
R.III	Richard III
Rom. & Jul.	Romeo and Juliet
Shrew	The Taming of the Shrew
Tempest	The Tempest
Timon	Timon of Athens
Tit. Andr.	Titus Andronicus
Troil. & Cr.	Troilus and Cressida
TN	Twelfth Night
TGV	The Two Gentlemen of Verona
TNK	The Two Noble Kinsmen
WT	The Winter's Tale

Aaron *(Tit. Andr.)* on achievement 27; on betrayal by blushing 437, 481; comparing black to other hues 450; on counsel 964; on deeds as a measure of worth 1290; on gossip 2466; on meddlers 3704; on idiots' oaths 4105; on revenge 4884; on rumormongers 4954; on secrecy 5032; on sunrise 5473; on worth 6460

The Abbess *(Errors)* on anger's effect on appetite 240; on digestion 1418; on eating 1600; on straying eyes 1826; on fevers 2059; on poison in jealousy 3035; on madness 3593; on unquiet meals 3698; on melancholy 3721; on misery 3852; on recreation 4736; on scolding 5013; on sports 5378; on Antipholus' unfaithfulness 5901; on jealous women 6345

Abhorson *(MM)* on outfitting the thief 5637

Achilles *(Troil. & Cr.)* on fortune 2270; on greatness fallen out with fortune 2508; on honors 2751; on merit 3764

Adam *(AYLI)* on age 130; on age and fortune 152; on God's comfort 786; on seeking fortune 2277; on the providence of God 2408, 4630; on temperance 5598; on the world 6431

Adriana *(Errors)* on adversity 85; on blushing 486, on conceit 839; on sharp conversation 937; on discourse 1451; comparing her husabnd to an elm 2825, 5819; on the sickness of her husband 2828; on meekness 3716; on enduring pain 4211; on patience 4285; on wretched souls 5333; on unkindness 5909; on vines 6025; on being a wife 6195; on wrongs 6477

Aeneas *(Troil. & Cr.)* on blushing 483; on the worthiness of praise 4482; on self-praise 5076

Agamemnon *(Troil. & Cr.)* on action 48; on boats 498; on deeds and self-praise 1267, 5074; on distinction 1494; on dwarfs 1580; on forgetfulness 2220; on the future 2343; on sleeping giants 2379, 5243; on oblivion 4120; on what's past 4266; on the harm of pride 4547; on soldiers and love 5282; on the ruins of time 5715

Agrippa *(Ant. & Cleo.)* on lamenting deeds 1277; on excellence 1750; on Antony's faults 2003; on tales 5536; on truth 5845; on virtue 6038

Aguecheek, Andrew, Sir *(TN)* on Sir Toby's grace 2484; on what life consists of 3314; on harm to the wit 6306

Ajax *(Troil. & Cr.)* on conceit 835; on proud men 3636, 4548; on pomposity 4433; on vainglory 5930

Albany, Duke of *(Lear)* on deformity in woman 1304; on making errors 1705; on fiends 2074; on filth 2079; on striving for goals 2404; on goodness 2449; on humanity 2805; on improvements 2917; on mankind 3630; on mending 3745; on perfectionism 4323; on results 4860; on deadly use 5923; on vile men 6006; on wisdom 6263

Alcibiades *(Timon)* on age 125; on anger 211; on compassion in law 815; on defense 1299; on impiety 2909; on killing 3110; on law 3199, 3201; on lawlessness 3224; on pity 4365; on security in age 5038; on self-defense 5054; on killing as sin 5198

Alonso *(Tempest)* on loquacity 3374; on memory 3738; on the sharpness of remembrance 4774; on sleep 5250

Amiens *(AYLI)* on benefits 432; on Duke Senior's character 695; on amending fortune 2275; on friendship 2324; on man's ingratitude 2963; on changing style 5431

Andrew, Sir *see* Aguecheek

Andronicus, Marcus *(Tit. Andr.)* on sorrow 828, 5302, 5303; on pity 4372

Andronicus, Titus on books 522, 3268, on losers 3391; on his predicament 4523; on the sea 5019; on beguiling sorrow 5323

Angelo *(MM)* on appearances 221; on authority 299; on condemnations 842; on custom and the law 1104; on etiquette 1712; on corrupt judges 1740, 2835, 3063; on falling 1877; on faults 1992, 1998; on form 2236; on graces 2477; on injustice 2969; on jewels 3044; on judging others 3071, 3084; on juries 3087, 3092; on

Berowne *(LLL)* on abstinence 14; on beauty in the aged 143, 380; on agony 164; on astronomers 293; on bargaining 343; on beauty 381, 397; on Rosaline's beauty 403; on the influence of company on behavior 436, 807, 808; on young bloods 468; on books 520; on charity 698; on sowing cockle 778, 945; on Cupid 1086, 1090; on delights 1316; on desire 1334; on temptation by devils 1401; on disease 1473; on drunkards 1556; on grief's ear 1588; on lovers' ears 1593; on education 1619; on eloquence 1635; on first learning of love 1810, 3235; on beauty in a woman's eye 1811, 6339; on lovers' eyes 1812, 3444, 3537; his doctrine on women's eyes 1820; on falsehood 1882; on fame 1892; on futility 2338; on easing grief 2541; on inconstancy 2923; on intellect 3004; on intemperance 3010; on justice 3098; on knowledge 3166, 3167, 3170; on laughter 3196; on the law 3200; on learning 3231, 3232; on light seeking light 3340; on love 3409, 3447, 3498, 3499, 3500; on a poet's love 3507; on maladies 3607; on his melancholy 3731; on mirth 3821; on misapplication 3830; on oaths 4096, 4102; on pain inherited from pleasure 4207, 4385; on poets 4398; on a seller's praise 4490, 5782; on retribution 4870; on being taught to rhyme 4897, 4898; on selling 5094; on study 5422, 5424, 5425; on style 5430; on suffering 5452; on the sun 5465; on temptation 5611; on want 6089; on light wenches 6178; on seeking a wife 6202; on wisdom 6265; on wishing 6282; on Katherine's wit 6302; on honest words 6396; on trusting words 6412; on obedience in youth 6491

Bertram *(AWTEW)* on Helena's coquetry 943; on desire 1337; on fancy's course 1908; on flirtation and love 2138, 3528; on impediments to love 2905; on matrimony 3670; on war 6096; on wedlock 6151; on detested wives 6190; on wooing Diana 6382

Bevis, George *(2 H.VI)* on bravery 541; on dressing the commonwealth 1546; on fashion 1928; on a hard hand 2608; on a brave mind 3789

Bianca *(Othello)* on absence 9

Bianca *(Shrew)* on old fashions 1931

Bolingbrook, Roger *(2 H.VI)* on the night 4059

Borachio *(Ado)* on fashion 1927, 1932; on rich villains 6020

Bottom, Nick *(MND)* on fools 2187; on lions 3350; on love 3393; his opinion of man 3618; on odors 4136; on reason and love 4702

Boy *(H.V)* on blustering 488; on Pistol's blustering 490; on brevity 563; on his cowardice 1038; on fame 1905; on safety 4977; on taciturnity 5529; on talking 5538; on vessels 5979; on voice 6074; on words 6390

Boy *(TNK)* on flowers 2162

Boyet *(LLL)* on fair ladies as angels 201; on conceits 832; on contempt for speakers 912; on fairness 3178; on love 3501; on memory 3735; on mocking 3877; on ridicule 4909; on satire 4993; on speech 5354; on wenches' tongues 5763; on women 6343

Brabantio *(Othello)* on foppery 2215; on his great grief 2581; on a bruised heart 2684; on borrowing from patience 4274; on words 6392

Brakenbury *(R.III)* on the cares of princes 4571; on royalty 4940; on sorrow 5308

Brutus, Marcus *(Caesar)* on acting a dreadful thing 31; on ambition's ladder 186; on associating with noble men 287; on slaying Caesar 594; on causes 645; on ceremony 664; on his conspiracy against Caesar 897; on conspiracy 898; on cowardice 1025, 1027; on crime 1051; on the drawing out of days 1144; on death 1160; on making decisions 1260; on knowing the day's end 1652; on the eye 1834; on faith 1861; on fate 1951; on Cassius' faults 1988; on fear 2031; on fires 2093; on flattery 2124; on fortune 2257; on knowing the future 2347; on abuse of greatness 2512; on his honesty 2738; on honor 2749; on

petual night 1205; on fires 2084; on
the commandment against murder
3956; on quenching passion 4247;
on portents 4438; on precaution
4517; on repression 4802; on storms
5409

Claudio *(MM)* on the persuasion of
Isabella 260; on the demigod
Authority 304; on death 1162; 1170;
on a thirsty evil 1726; on excess
1758; on fasting 1937; on too much
liberty 2290, 2916, 3265; on hope
2776; on life 3300; on medicine
3711; on misery 3842; on men's
natures 4022; on payment for offenses 4142; on restraint 4855; on
satiety 4982; on surfeiting 5492; on
temperance 5599

Claudio *(Ado)* on authority as a cover
for sin 302; on beauty as a witch
385; on blushing 480; on Hero's
chastity 715; on deceit 1227, 1259; on
deeds 1284; on desire 1351; on eyes
1836; on fishing for suckers 2102; on
friendship in love 2321, 3421; on
gullibility 2601; on happiness 2625;
on hypocrisy 2844; on man's insensitivity 2990; on silent joy 3050; on
love 3395; on lust 3570; on self-
reliance 5085; on silence 5159; on
cunning sin 5181; on tempting
Benedick 5626; on lovers' time 5718;
on trust 5839; on truth 5866

Claudius, King *(Hamlet)* on affliction
117; on threats 367; on difficult
choices 584; on procrastination 680,
4589; on earthly corruption 948; on
promptness 1275; on diseases desper-
ately grown 1472, 2671; on the
divinity hedging a king 1504, 3122;
on dress 1550; on forgiveness 2233;
on the futility of charging Hamlet
2340; on goodness 2456; on madness
in great ones 2528, 2982; on the
justice of heaven 2692; on his indecision 2933; on retributive justice
3099; on killing his brother 3107,
3957; on the law 3215; on love
3424; on Hamlet's madness 3585; on
majesty 3605; on medicine 3709; on
mercy 3750; on miseries 3849; on
Hamlet's murder 3962; on offenses
4140, 4144, 4147; on opportunity

4168; on pardons 4217; on politics
4422; on his prayers 4502; on
desperate remedies 4765; on revenge
4882; on royalty 4931; on surfeiting
4985; on "should" 5143; on sorrow
5293; on words and thoughts in
prayer 5686, 6409; on treason 5809;
on his army of woes 6307; on the in-
tentions of "would" 6464; on the
livery of youth 6495

Cleomines *(WT)* on forgiveness of self
2231

Cleon *(Pericles)* on deceit 1230; on vacant houses 2803; on pretension
4539; on sorrows 5294

Cleopatra *(Ant. & Cleo.)* on acting 33;
on action 49; on adolescence 70; on
age and childishness 148; on immortality 280, 2901; on celerity 657; on
overcoming chance 676; on good
deeds 1287; on desolation 1353; on
doubt as a jailer 1531; on exceptions
1753; on folly 2173; on fools 2192;
on slandering greatness 2526; on
haste 2651; on immaturity 2889; on
impatience 2903; on majesty 3602;
on music and love 3970; on the
negligent 4035; on bad news 4041;
on patience 4275; on pomp 4431; on
pride 4567; on 'but yet' 4660; on
reformation 4751; on responsibility
4851; on a slave's hired love 5228;
on speed 5365; on her spirit 5372;
on suicide 5460; on swiftness 5514;
on tongues bearing ill tidings 5753;
on vows 6086; on wishing 6281; on
her youth 6513

Clifford, Lord Thomas *(2 H.VI)* on
courage and patience 985; on worms
and doves 993, 1532, 1534, 6445; on
cowardice 1033, 1035; on defense
1300; on courage in desperation
1371; on the evening 1714; on
lawlessness 3222; on lenity 3250; on
lions 3345; on oppression 4185; on
patience 4282; on robbers 4922; on
self-defense 5056; on thievery 5640;
on victory 5999

Clifford, Young *(2 H.VI)* on age 157;
on self-love 5070; on soldiers 5278;
on war 6105

Cloten *(Cymbeline)* on bribery 567; on
Britain 570; on Caesar 591; on

bull 5554; on the twilight 5875; on wildness 6211; on man's wit 6299

Donalbain *(Macbeth)* on daggers in smiles 1110, 5260; on malevolence 3614

Dromio Ephesus *(Errors)* on words 6394

Dromio Syracuse *(Errors)* on age and the wit 155; on argument 253; on his bachelorhood 320; on baldness 329, 330, 331, 5701, 5702; on causes 643; on eating with the devil 1398; on escaping marriage 1707; on fire 2098; on hair 2604; on light 3338; on reason 4709; on time as a thief 5739; on not wanting a wife 6209; on wit 6295

Duchess of York *(R.II)* on cowardice 1034, 1492, 4279; on nobility 4071; her plea for her son's pardon 4218; on prayer 4501; on sorrow 5297

Duchess of York *(R.III)* on Gloucester's deceit 1236, 2845; on wailing losses 3387

Duke *(MM)* on the danger of age 132; on anarchy 192; on angels 198; on outward appearances 226; on authority 300; on boldness 506; on life's breath 551; on breeding 560; on calumny 604; on celerity 658; on constancy 902; on correction for Pompey 947; on bravely facing death 1177, 1178, 1197, 1198; on decrees 1265; on difficulties 1416; on discipline 1434; on discontent 1446; on duplicity 1569; on falling 1879; on fame 1903; on faults 1982, 1999; on fear 2009; on fellowship 2055; on frailty 2285; on goodness 2454, 2457; on awe of greatness 2507; on greed 2532; on happiness 2623; on haste 2649; on heavenly lights 2697; on holiness in judging 2723; on hypocritic judges 2841; on hypocrisy in man 2843; on indulgence 2943; on Pompey's need of instruction 2998; on good judges 3064; on flaunted law 3205, 3209; on leisure 3243; on lenity 3254; on liberty 3263; on not loving life 3310; on the fears of life 3322; on love 3455; on the evil in men 3624; on monuments 3906; on the power of music 3972;

on nature 3997; on novelty 4091; on offenses by high authority 4146; on high offices 4154; on payments 4302; on awe of place 4374; on poverty of the rich 4453; on preachers 4512; on punishment 4642; on riches 4905; on scandals 5000; on security 5037; on slander 5213; on death as a sleep 5238; on security in society 5269; on the spirits 5374; on the sword of heaven 5516; on truth 5848; on undertakings 5895; on virtue 6031, 6041, 6050; on the burden of wealth 6137

Duke *(Othello)* on charity 704; on fortune 2245; on griefs 2548, 2553, 2556; on mischief 3836; on misfortune 3860; on mourning mischiefs 3944; on opinion 4164; on patience 4287; on things without remedy 4764, 4820; on robbery 4919; on smiling 5256; on thievery 5645; on victims 5996; on experiencing the worst 6456

Duke *(TN)* on aloneness 167; on the constancy of love 905; on desires in love 1344; on excess 1764; on men's giddy fancies 1912, 3638; on the food of love 3407; on the pangs of love 3550; on matrimony 3684; on music 3971, 3973; on virgins 6028; on women 6325, 6332

Duke *(TGV)* on love 3502; on poetry 4406

Duke Senior *(AYLI)* on adversity 80; on contentment 935; on custom 1103; on the force of gentleness 2375; on nature 4009; on painted pomp 4426; on retirement 4864; on unhappiness 5903

Dumaine *(LLL)* on wonder in an eye 1819; on love's fever 2061, 2227, 3484; on May as the month of lovers 3697

Duncan, King of Scotland *(Macbeth)* on character 690, 1844; on his joys 3060; on the mind's construction 3792; on his tears 5581

Edgar *(Lear)* on adversity 83; on aloneness 169; on bondage 512; on borrowing 528; on commiseration 795, 796; on conceit 836; on good conduct 849; on death 1175, 1188; on the devil as a gentleman 1393; on fellowship 2056; on fortune 2265; on retribution of the gods 2423, 3103; on grief 2574; on harlotry 2633; on indebtedness 2932; on life 3290, 3311; on suffering in the mind 3801; on misfortune 3859; on obedience 4113; on obedience to parents 4224; on pride 4559; on retribution 4866, 5989; on ripeness 4911; on borrowing sorrow 5313; on suffering alone 5451; on bad trades 5779; on bearing woes 6320; on the world's mutations 6425; on the worst 6454

Edmund *(Lear)* on astrology 288; on bastards 353; on the tender-minded 979, 5627; on excusing our behavior 1770; on man's folly 2176; on foppery 2213; on men 3632; on misfortune 3862; on the planets 4378; on quarrels 4663; on assigning responsibility 4849; on retribution 4871; on succession 5447; on superstition 5481; on the sword 5517; on time's effect upon men 5744; on the villainy of man 6019; on the succession of youth 6507

Edward, Earl of March, afterwards King Edward IV *(3 H.VI)* on war 6111

Edward IV *(3 H.VI)* on executions 503; on being a stepfather 733, 1957; on competition 820; on concealment 829; on accepting things of destiny 1378; on fate 1945; on fortune's malice 2268; on friends 2294; on matches 3664; on concealing meaning 3700, 6279; on necessity 4027; on resignation 4825; on sons 5288; on victory 6001; on willingness 6228

Edward, Prince *(R.III)* on Caesar's fame 598, 1902

Egeon *(Errors)* on age 137; on motherhood 3665, 3936; on the ocean 4133, 5020

Eglamour, Sir *(TGV)* on dating 1130; on lovers' hours 3459, 3539

Elinor, Queen *(John)* on seizing opportunity 4181

Elizabeth, Queen *(3 H.VI; R.III)* on her babes 317, 729; on betrayals 434, 653; on loss of confidence 853; on broken faith 1862; on an honest tale 2737; on mistrust 3869; on simplicity 5169; on style 5427, 5428; on telling tales 5532; on trust 5840; on words as attorneys 6403

Ely, Bishop of *(H.V)* on mischief 3838

Emilia *(Othello)* on chastity 705; on happiness in marriage 2628; on enduring harm 2637; on jealousy 3026, 3029; on sensitivity to hurt 5107; on wedlock 6149; on unchaste wives 6200; on equality of wives 6201

Emilia *(TNK)* on chastity 720, 3599, 4929; on flowers 2160; on men 3646

Emilia *(WT)* on the persuasion of silence 5160

Enobarbus *(Ant. & Cleo.)* on adaptation 62; on admiration 65; on age 160; on conquest 859; on consolation 896; on courage 980; on doves fighting 1533; on doing evil 1734; on facial cosmetics 1847; on Cleopatra's fascination 1922; on fear 2012; on fortune 2253; on fury 2336; on consolation in grief 2573; on influence 2953; on men's judgments 3073; on playing with lions 3346; on loyalty 3553; on praises 4495; on reason 4698; on tears for Fulvia 5579; on time 5745; on truth 5855; on valor 5939; on cunning women 6352

Escalus *(MM)* on falling 1873; on lenity 3252; on pardons 4219; on rising by sin 5178; on virtue 6059; on pardon as a cause of woe 6316

Escalus *(Rom. & Jul.)* on mercy 3752; on mischance 3831; on murder 3964; on pardons 4216; on patience 4281

Exeter, Duke of *(H.V)* on government 2467; explaining his tears 5582; on war 6100

Exeter, Duke of *(1 H.VI)* on envy as the cause of confusion 1685; on hate as a cause of ruin 2656; on rule by children 5009

Fabian *(TN)* on detractions 1387; on valor 5944

850; on contentment 936; on counsel 966; on eating 1604; on fathers as providers 1961; on following form 2238; on fortune 2259; on seeking for gain 2356; on following great ones 2525; on houses 2799; on winter laboring 3175; on madness 3582; on mirrors 3818; on noses 4077; on poverty 4447; on pretension 4542; on prudence 4635; on prodigality 4593; on speech 5352; on spendthrifts 5369; on the ant's teaching 5565; on trust 5841; on truth 5847; on vanity 5957; on want 6091; on great wheels 6179; on winter 6256; on wisdom 6271; on woes 6323; on women 6334

Ford, Frank *(MWW)* on access 19; on Alice's chastity 718; on experience 1792; on folly 2178; on lateness 3192; on love 3413; on money 3892; on the love of money 3895; on punctuality 4613, 4640; on tardiness 5556; on the influence of wealth 6134; on selling wives 6208

France, King of *(AWTEW)* on age 154; on distinction 264, 471, 557, 1414; on brightness 569; on clouds 771; on dearness of things lost 1148; on good deeds 1270; on his despair 1358; on displeasure 1485; on dismal thinking 1678, 5687; on experience 1796; on rash faults 1978, 2492; on gifts 2384; on goodness 2446; on gratitude 2486; on honor 2757, 2758; on impossibilities 2912; on losses 3383; on late love 3457; on opportunity 4180; on praising what is lost 4480, 4769; on remorse 4777; on self-fulfillment 5060; on using sense 5100; on offering thanks 5633; on the noiseless foot of time 5724; on tranquility 5787, 5832; on virtue 6046

France, King of *(Lear)* on bashfulness 352; on diffidence 1417; on faith 1869; on love 3519

France, Princes of *(LLL)* on amusement 191; on beauty 387; on charity 701; on confession 851; on contentment 932; on the eye's judgment 1802; on a giving hand 2364; 2611; on glory 2397; on a heavy heart 2678, 5750;

on humility 2806; on liberality 3260; on praising a foul hand 4478; on pride 4566; on sadness 4963; on speech 5346; on sport 5375; on virtue 6034; on wedlock 6146; on zeal 6516

Friar Francis *(Ado)* on enjoyment of possessions 1677; on prizing lost things 3382, 6457; on the virtue of possession 4439; on value 5948

Friar Lawrence *(Rom. & Jul.)* on adversity 88; on affliction 121; on age 123; on honey's effect on the appetite 239; on Romeo's fated calamity 601; on old men's cares 626; on the dawn 1133; on violent delights 1317; on some good found in evil 1718; on excess 1765; on eyes as the source of love 1809; on old men's eyes 1821; on flowers 2155; on Juliet's light foot 2210; on goodness 2448; on haste 2647, 2648; on honey 2740; on loving moderately 3420, 3881; on the vanity in lovers 3543, 5959; on matrimony 3685; on the morning 3924; on odors in flowers 4138, 5254; on philosophy 4354; on pleasures 4389; on punctuality 4639; on recklessness in love 4727; on results 4862; on care as a robber of sleep 5240; on speed 5367, 5368; on the sun 5467; on surfeiting 4989; on swiftness 5511; on tardiness 5555; on unselfishness 5913; on virtue and vice 5986, 6060; on unbruised youth 6504

Gardener *(R.II)* on unruly children 737, 5912; on discipline 1433; on disobedience 1483; on efficiency 1627; on fathers 1958; on fruitfulness 2334; on horticulture 2794; on lenity 3253; on prudence 4634; on pruning 4638; on noisome weeds 6154; on worthlessness 6463

Gardiner, Bishop of Winchester *(H.VIII)* on affairs 100; on the bed as a place for repair 410, 2797; on business at night 583; on discipline 1435; on taming wild horses 2792, 5553; on repose 4801, 5237; on urgent business 5918

Gaunt, John of, Duke of Lancaster *(R.II)* on adaptation 64; on Christ 457, 754; on Richard's flatterers 1067; on death 1190; on deathbed words 1209; on digestion of sweet things 1419; on disappointments 1430; on eating 1606; on men's ends 1649; on England 1670, 1671, 1676; on Richard's rashness 1680; on fires 2087; on food 2182; on fortitude 2240; on haste 2650; on havens 2663; on honor 2773; on journeymen 3049; on the love of life 3324; on love 3485; on misery 3845; on necessity 4024; on death's pain 4208; on ports 4437; on rapacity 4681; on the scandal of Richard's rule 5003; on showers 5144; on gnarling sorrow 5317; on storms 5408; on sweets 5508; on taste 5559; on the words of dying men 5771, 5860, 6410; on wise travellers 5798; on vanity 5956; on virtue 6067; on making light of woes 6310, 6311

Gentleman, First *(Cymbeline)* on courtiers 996, 1006; on dissimulation 1490; on hypocrisy 2854; on pretension 4545

Gentleman, First *(MM)* on soldiers 5276

Gentleman, First *(WT)* on absence 4; on eloquence 1638; on language 3184; on speech 5361

Gertrude, Queen of Denmark *(Hamlet)* on death 1207; on patience as a remedy for distress 1497; on Hamlet's ecstasy 1617; on eternal life 1709; on guilt 2595; on hallucinations 2607, 2885; on jealousy 3033; on mortality in nature 3323, 4017; on Hamlet's madness 3581; on miseries 3850; on Hamlet's mourning 3945; on patience 4283; on multiplying sorrows 5295, 6308

Ghost *(Hamlet)* on conceit 830; on conscience 894; on the queen's guilt 2597; on lewdness 3256; on lust 3565; on Gertrude's remorse 4784; on virtue 6032

Glendower, Owen *(R.II; 1 H.IV)* on contentment in love and song 934; on invocation of spirits 3020, 5373; on necromancy 4032; on sleep 5244;

on the sun 5471

Gloucester, Prince Humphrey, later Duke of *(2 H.IV; H.V; 1 & 2 H.VI)* on ambition 177, 181; on aspiration 279; on a base mind 347; on cankerous thoughts 614; on joys and cares 638; on courage 976; on an unspotted heart 2681; on innocence 2979; on reverence for the king 3127; on base minds 3788; on opportunity 4179; on the help of quietness 4670; on rancor 4680; on ambitious thoughts 5680; on vicissitudes 5994; on virtue 6044, 6061

Gloucester, Earl of *(Lear)* on accommodation with afflictions 118; on age 147; on bondage 512; on defects in man 1296; on excess 1763; on fortune 2265; on the gods 2424; on kissing Lear's hand 2612; on the quality of nothing 4081; on resignation 4819; on sorrow 5324; on sport of the gods 5381; on tyranny 5882; on woes 6315; on the ruined world 6441

Gloucester, Richard, Duke of *see* Richard and King Richard III

Gobbo *see* Launcelot

Goneril *(Lear)* on age 124; on flattery 2115; on old fools 2197; on indiscretion 2938; on the variety of men 3628; on offenses 4141; on senility 5098; on shame 5134; on age and wisdom 6270

Gonzalo *(Tempest)* on ungentle truth 5873

Gower *(H.V)* on beards 366

Gower, the Poet *(Pericles)* on sin in customs 1105, 5186; on flattery 2119, 6012

Gratiano *(MV)* on anticipation 214; on anxiety as a detriment to life 217; on appetite 238; on care of the world 629; on cheerfulness 726; on disappointments 1428; on dogmatism 1518; on feasting 2051; on the fire in horses 2791; on joy of the chase 3054; on laughter 3198; on livers 3359; on lovers' promptness 3538; on mirth 3824; on saying nothing 4085; on vain opinions 4165; on oracles 4187; on winning the prize

4586; on the pursuit of things 4658; on satiety 4987; on silence 5161, 5163; on wine 6237; on pretentious wisdom 6268; on losing the world 6426

Green *(R.II)* on futility 2339; on retribution of hell 2705

Gregory *(Rom. & Jul.)* on valor 5942

Gremio *(Shrew)* on learning 3230; on wooing Kate 6378

Grey, Lady *(3 H.VI; R.III)* inappropriateness 2921; on speech 5364, 6415

Griffith *(H.VIII)* on adversity 86; on the blessedness of being little 799; on Wolsey's death 1211; on remembrance of evil 1717; on fame 1897; on fearing God 2421; on Wolsey's grave 2501; on evil manners 3653; on men's reputations 4814; on men's virtues 6065

Groom *(R.II)* his sympathy for King Richard 5528

Grumio *(Shrew)* on money 3894; on wealth 6139; on winter 6252

Guiderius *(Cymbeline)* on blustering 489; on Cloten's brains 539; on equality of Thersites and Ajax 1693; on equality 1694; on fears 2046; on fools 2207; on mourning 3947; on sorrow 5305

Guildenstern *(Hamlet)* on ambition 187; on argument 259; on dreams 1537; on fortune 2264; on the substance of ambition 5434

Hamlet on God-given ability 1; on abstinence 16; on self-accusation 23; on acting 34, 36, 37, 38, 39; on action 51; on adultery 72, 73; on age and passion 150; on dreams 187; on deceptive appearances 227; on badness 326; on purposeful work 371; on preeminence in beasts 372; on beauty 393; on blushing 484; on bounty 530; on the briefness of a woman's love 565; on business 582; on Caesar 597; on calumny 603; on cats 642; on ceremony 666; on change 678; on Horatio's character 696; on charity 697; on choice in

madness 746; on clowns 776; on conception 840; on confession 852; on conscience 861, 869; on corruption 952; on cosmetics 956; on the devil's ability to counterfeit 971; on cowardice 1022, 1044; on crime 1049; on the kind use of cruelty 1074; on cunning 1084; on custom 1098, 1102; on the end of Caesar 1161; on death by suicide 1163, 1182; on death 1179; on deceit 1232, 1248; on foul deeds 1279; on defect in man 1294; on delay 1313; on employment 1314, 1640; on deserving 1324; on desire 1341; on his despair 1355; on his belief in destiny 1377, 1381; on the devil's pleasing shape 1390; on discretion 1460; on divinity 1503; on cats and dogs 1515; on doomsday 1520, 2736; on dreams 1537; on a foolish ear 1585; on the good earth 1597; on ecstasy 1616; on the end of heartache 1654; on equality of king and beggar 1689; on Horatio's equanimity 1698; on equivocation 1701; on evil 1735, 1737; on a kingly eye 1839; on women's faces 1845; on falsity 1890; on fame 1896; on fashion 1935; on fate 1942, 1943; on fattening creatures 1962; on the effects of one particular fault 1983; on fear of ghosts 2042; on frailty in women 2063, 6367; on fishing 2104; on flattery 2111; on the flesh 2131; his plea to Laertes for forgiveness 2230; on fortitude 2241; on fortune 2262, 2276; on frailty 2287; on the government of God 2414; on goodness 2447; on gossip 2460; on Alexander's grave dust 2493, 2494; on Caesar's dust 2495; on mighty opposites 2513; on greatness coveting honor 2524; on grief 2582; on guilt 2594, 2598, 2600; on habit 2603; on hands of little employment 2609; on honesty 2728, 2734; on his honesty 2731; on defending honor 2755; on hypocritic smiles 2838; on hypocrisy in women 2852; on idleness 2857, 2860; on imagination 2878; on immortality 2893, 2900; on inconstancy in women 2927; on his indecision to live 2936, 2937; on indiscretion

2939; on innocence 2978; on his supposed insanity 2983, 2985; on the insolence of office 2992; on good judgment 3074; on heaven's judgment 3076; on justice 3091; on his kinship to Claudius 3113; on kings as food for worms 3145; on knavery in men 3160; on a knavish speech 3162, 5345; on the ease of lying 3286; on weariness of life 3298; on life 3327; his love letter to Ophelia 3418; on woman's love 3478; on madness 3580; on his madness 3587; on the nobility of man 3616, 3634; on the dispassionate man 3640; on his melancholy 3725, 3729; on his father's memory 3740; on merit and punishment 3761; on merriment 3777; on the witching time 3781; on misanthropy 3828; on modesty 3883; on Caesar's mortality 3932; on murder speaking 3959; on mysteries 3982; on changing nature 3991; on the modesty of nature 3994; on base natures 4008; on play passions 4245; on conquerors of passion 4246; on philosophy 4353; on politicians 4416; on pomp 4430; on the poor 4462; on the power of beauty 4471; on intercessory prayer 4504; on prologues 4605; on providence 4628, 4629; on quarreling 4662; on rashness 4689; on readiness 4692; on reason 4705; on the breaking down of reason 4719; on man's godlike reasoning 4721; on religion 4753; on repentance 4796; on his father's reputation 4816; on Horatio's resignation 4827; on resolution 4831; on retribution 4869; on self-control 5053; on self-slaughter 5091; on self-will 5092; on shame 5133; on sighing 5154; on his mother's sin 5196; on sins 5201; on sincerity 5204; on the majesty of the sky 5208; on slander 5212; on death as a sleep 5239; on villains' smiles 5259; on the soul's immortality 5340; on speech 5353; on good sport 5380; on the stars 5399; on Horatio's suffering 5454; on suicide 5455, 5456, 5457; on the supernatural 5479; on using tact 5531; on giving thanks 5635; on

quartering a thought 5666; on the pale cast of thought 5685; on murder's miraculous tongue 5751; on flattering tongues 5765; on uses of this world 5922; on Alexander's final use 5924; on use 5926; on vice 5990; on villainy 6015; on vindications 6024; on virtue 6049, 6064, 6070, 6071; on watchmen 6124; on his weariness of the world 6142, 6429; on weeds 6158; on welcome 6174; on whippings 6182; on the will 6224; on the wantonness of women 6361; on words 6417; on the workmanship in man 6423; on the world 6439; on worms 6444

Hastings, Lord *(2 H.IV)* on hope 2777; on time's subjects 5727

Hastings, Lord *(3 H.VI; R.III)* on England 1668; on unwise flight 2134; on grace 2478; on imprisonment 4581; on provocations 4631

Hecat *(Macbeth)* on overconfidence as an enemy 855; on security 5036

Hector *(Troil. & Cr.)* on caution as a beacon of the wise 651; on the dearness of life 1146, 3294; on making decisions 1261; on modest doubt 1524; on importance of the end 1647; on the dearness of honor 2769; on idolatry 2864; on pleasure 4390; on priorities 4576; on religion 4758; on revenge 4878; on service 5119; on skepticism 5207; on surety 5486; on Time as an arbitrator 5695; on wives 6204; on searching for the worst 6449; on the wound of peace 6470; on wrongs 6478

Helena *(AWTEW)* on achievement 25; on endings 1645, 1646; on the failure of expectation 1780; on faith 1864; on great floods 2139; on superfluous folly 2164; on the works of God 2413, 2422; on the help of heaven 2695; on aged honor 2764; on industry 2947; on kissing 3155; on lions 3351; on the power of love 3468; on meaning 3701; on miracles 3816; on nature 4002; on presumptions 4535; on remedies 4760; on results 4861; on self-reliance 5078; on the use of trifles 5826; on using weak ministers 6131; on wisdom

limited choice 744; on kindness in women 3117, 6330

Hotspur *(R.II; 1 H.IV; also see* Percy, Henry) on action 50, 52; on the just use of arms 268; on ballads 334; on bargaining 344; on Glendower as a bore 525; on Kate's constancy 901; on courage 984, 994; on danger 1120, 1125; on his death 1214; on shaming the devil 1397; on doomsday 1522; on earthquakes 1599; on foppery 2216; on greatness 2504; on life 3293; on the end of life 3307; on hunting lions 3347; on diseased nature 4014; on necromancy 4032; on mincing poetry 4400; on safety 4976; on a woman's secrecy 5028; on calling up spirits 5373; on Glendower's talking 5543, 5587; his final thoughts 5659; on the end of time 5714; on trusting a woman with a secret 5836, 6363; on telling the truth 5856; on war 6098, 6118

Hubert *(John)* on war with France 464, 476; on lying 3278

Hume, John *(2 H.VI)* on brokers 571; on crafty knaves 1046, 3161; on cunning 1081; on villainy 6023

Iago *(Othello)* on favoritism in promotion 111, 745, 4152; on anger 208; on uncleanly apprehensions 248, 548; on balance between reason and passion 328; on beauty 396; on passion 470; his comparison of bodies to gardens 500; on candor in men 608, 610; on character 691; on concealment of intent 827; on conceit 831; on conscience 867, 875; on contentment and riches 921; on being critical 1059; on delay 1312, 1388, 2065; on devil's heavenly shows 1396; on disguise 1479; on dreams 1542; on drunkenness 1559; on the use of duplicity 1568; on knavery's plain face 1843, 3159; on faults 1984; on favoritism 2004; on men's frailty 2222; on ripening fruit 2331; on guilt 2592; on healing 2670; on honesty 2732; on honor 2762; on hypocrisy 2837; on idleness 2859; on

industry 2946; on Desdemona's provocative eye 3019; on jealousy 3024, 3025, 3028, 3031; on lords 3378; on the power of love to change 3429; on lust 3567; on masters 3660; on saving money 3902; on morality 3914; on guilt 3960; on a good name 3983; on nobility in base men 4067; on passion 4256; on patience 4277; on pleasure 4386; on poverty of the rich 4451; on preferment 4526; on pride 4556; on proofs of infidelity 4614; on purity 4645; on purses 4652, 4656; on rage 4675; on controlling sensuality 4704, 5108; on recreation 4737; on reputation 4807, 4808, 4810; on resolution 4833; on riches fineless 4906; on the self 5044; on self-love 5064; on the curse of service 5118; on servitude 5125; on sincerity 5203; on sleep-talk 5249; on loose souls 5335; on surfeiting 5493; on suspicions 5498, 5499, 5500; on temper 5592; on temperance 5597; on temptation 5612, 5622; on stealing one's reputation 5648; on pleasurable time 5699; on the womb of time 5703; on guilt's tongue 5752; on trifles 5822; on his villainy 6017, 6022; on Desdemona's wantonness 6093; on whoredom 6181; on men's will 6219; on wine 6241; on women 6337; on the healing of wounds 6467

Imogen *(Cymbeline)* on betrayals 435; on breeding 561; on certainties 669; on courtesy 1000; on cowardice 1023; on breach of custom 1099; on desires 1339; on differences in men 1415; on differences in dignity 1423; on doubting 1527; on excuse 1772; on misjudgment of the eyes 1830; on falsehood 1883; on flowers 2140; on fools 2185; on curing grief 2560; on blind judgment 3079; on lying 3275; on life 3289; on grief as a physic for love 3486; on the prayers of lovers 3518, 3548; on peace 4304; on perceptions 4321; on physic 4356; on pleasure in flowers 4393; on plenty 4395, 4396; on praying 4498; on remedies 4761; on self-slaughter 5090, 5462; on senses 5103; on

society 5268; on treason 5810; on
uncertainties 5885; on unsociableness
5915; on vigor 6004; on men's vows
6082

Iras *(Ant. & Cleo.)* on darkness 1129;
on the end of life 1142; on Cleopatra's death 1220; on the conse-
quences of Cleopatra's defeat 1293

Isabel, Queen of France *(H.V)* on
jealousy in marriage 3034, 3694

Isabella *(MM)* on affliction 116; on apprehension of death 247; on authority 298, 301; on pain in beetles 413;
on blasphemy 453, 621; her appeal
to Angelo's conscience 890; on
criticism 1054; on apprehension of
death 1218, 2037; on deceit 1247; on
the privilege in degrees 1306; on
faults 1985; on the death of giants
2380; on the strength of giants 2381;
on prerogatives of greatness 2521,
2522; on hell 2710; on hypocrisy
2839; on man's ignorance 2869; on
immortality of souls 2902; on impossibilities 2910; on indecision
2934; on intent 3012; on jesting
with saints 3039; on mercy in judgment 3075; on bending the law
3207; on the fragility of man 3629;
on medicine 3712; on mercy 3754;
on God's mercy 3757; on heaven's
mercy 3758; a comparison of pains
4212; on bitter physics 4358; on
power 4468; on prayers 4503; on
proud man 4562; on profanity 4594;
on reasoning truth 4703; on Christ's
redemption 4739; on self-
examination 5058; on cunning sin
5182; on profanity in soldiers 5281;
on redemption of the soul 5329; on
speech 5349; on strength 5414; on
thought 5662; on truth 5862, 5863;
on tyranny 5878; on vice in authority 5982; on virgins 6026; on *will* and
will not 6216; on great men's wit
6289

Jachimo *(Cymbeline)* on attractiveness
294; on bondage in marriage 516; on
eyes 1840; on matrimony 3693,
6150; on the night 4052; on repose

4798, 4853; on diseased ventures
5971

Jailer, First *(Cymbeline)* on pain 4201;
on sleep 5236; on toothaches 5774

Jaques *(AYLI)* on acting 35; on age
139, 3333; on the ages of man 156;
on compliments 825; on drama in
life 1535; on judges 3067; on
weeding judgments 3080, 4159; on
fair ladies 3179, 6333; on liberty
3267; on men as players 3643; on
melancholy 3722, 3726; on mortality
3929; on the universality of pride
4554; on ripening 4912; on his
sadness 4966; on soldiers seeking
reputation 5285; on the world as a
stage 5391, 6427; on tales 5535

Jessica *(MV)* on the blindness of love
458, 3412, 3546; on love's follies
2171; on music 3975

Jeweller *(Timon)* on things of like
value 5953

John, King on assassination 283; on
the midnight bell 429; on spilling
blood 461, 3108; his warning to
Angiers 616; on corruption in
religion 955; on crime 1048; on ill
deeds 1276; on haste 2209, 2652; on
sure foundations 2282; on humors of
kings 2816; on the majesty of kings
3142; on laughter 3197; on mischief
3834; on opportunity 4178; on buying church pardons 4220; on stormy
skies 5211, 5412; on speech 5358; on
temptation 5617; on war 6108

Julia *(TGV)* on aloofness 171; on aversion 314; on the caprice of foolish
love 619; on kindling fire with snow
2096; on looks as love's food 2181;
on hate 2657; on interference in love
matters 3015; on loathing 3364; on
Proteus' looks 3370; on love 3400,
3403, 3473, 3483, 4254; on pilgrims
4363; on repulsion 4806; on
stopped-up rivers 4918, 6129; on
suppression of love 5484; on
travellers 5791; on quenching love
with words 6406

Juliet *(Rom. & Jul.)* on beggars 415;
on boasting 494; on bondage 513;
on the bounty of her love 529; on
anticipation 741; on commiseration
793; on conceit 833; on courtship

1010, 1011; on Romeo's supposed deceit 1237; on her betrothal to Paris 1364; on expectation 1783; her farewell to Romeo 1920; on her fear 2041; on fellowship 2057; on the odor of a rose 2159, 4139, 4928, 5252; on fortune 2258; on the infiniteness of love 3408; on lovers' perjuries 3536; on minutes 3812; on what's in a name 3988; on lovers' oaths 4106; on lovers' partings 4227; on final partings 4229; on prayer 4505; on riches 4904; on truth and slander 5221; on strength 5418; on the swiftness of lightning 5513; on love's thoughts 5676; on truth 5864; on fellowship in woe 6313; on counting worth 6459

Katherina *(Shrew)* on anger in women 209, 5593, 6348; on anger 210; on a wife's duty 1575, 6192; on husbands 2820; on matrimony 3683, 3690, 3691; on women's soft conditions 6341

Katherine *(LLL)* on cheerfulness 723; on a light heart 2677; on long life 3316

Katherine, Queen, afterwards Dowager *(H.VIII)* on taxes 324, 576, 3361, 5561; on prayer 788, 4507; on deceptive faces 1846; on the justice of God 2411; on deceiving hearts 2683; on the rule of heaven 2691; on leaving honor 2772; on the incorruptible Judge 3065; on Wolsey's obstinacy 4129; on the king's procrastination 4592; on providence 4627; on self-love 5071; on truth 5849; on virtue 6039

Kent, Earl of *(Lear)* on anger 207; on appearances 229; on astrology 292; on his diligence 1425; on doctors 1510; on duty 1577; on good effects 1625; on flattery 2114; on fortune 2260; on honor 2760; on risking his life 3308; on folly in majesty 3604; on miracles 3815; on misery 3842; on roguery 4924; on the influences of stars 5396

Knight, First *(Pericles)* on equality 1695; on the marks of a gentleman 2374

Lady, Old *(H.VIII)* on contentment 919; on honor 2759; on opportunity 4177; on the value of content 5951

Laertes *(Hamlet)* on affection 107; on blessings 455; on calumny 602; on galling canker 615; on chastity 707; on desire 1328; on fear 2014; on immodesty 2892; on kings as subjects to birth 3126; on love 3430; on the prodigality of maids 3598; on modesty 3887; on the moon 3908; on nature 4004; on the nature of love 4019; on occasion 4132; on precaution 4515; on revenge 4885; on safety 4975; on slander 5214; on virtue 6062; on the blastments against youth 6487

Lafew *(AWTEW)* on Parolles' clothing 770, 1549, 2214; on fashion 1936; on fear 2020; on excessive grief 2562; on honor 2756; on moderate lamentation 3182, 3942; on philosophy 4347; on scars nobly got 5006; on Parolles' soul 5343; on things supernatural 5478; on unknown terrors 5628; on travellers 5793

Lancaster *(1 & 2 H.IV)* on preachers 4513; on treachery 5802; on treason's true bed 5813

Launce *(TGV)* on goodness 2442; on hanging 2618; on impossibilities 2911; on praise 4486; on sighing 5153; on woman's only virtue 6054, 6336; on welcomes 6172; on words 6408; on worthiness 6462

Launcelot Gobbo *(MV)* on children 734; on dilemmas 1424; on fathers 1956; on parentage 4225; on truth 5851

Lawrence, Friar *see* Friar Lawrence

Lear, King on affliction 120; on agony 165; on rich and poor apparel 218; on art and nature 276; on authority 297; on fighting a bear 362; on birth 444; on suffering in the body 502; on dividing his kingdom 637; on ungrateful children 738; on fight or flight 749; on greater and lesser

witches' promises 4608; on promptness 4612; on the flighty purpose
4649; on reason as a pauser 4717; on
remorse for Duncan's murder 4781,
4782; on resolution 4835, 4836; on
restlessness 4854; on ill results 4858;
on retribution 4867; on revenge
4881; on ruthlessness 4958; on the
sea washing his hands clean 5021; on
the senses 5099; on dream-abused
sleep 5245, 5246; on time 5711; on
tomorrows 5747; on toys 5777, 5967;
on Banquo's valor 5946; on the wine
of life 6245; on words and deeds
6413; on work 6419; on yesterdays
6483
Macbeth, Lady *(Macbeth)* on affection
112; on Duncan's murder 474, 3955;
on ceremony 665; on fears of
childhood 739, 1831, 2027; on conscience 892, 893; on contentment
920; on Macbeth's countenance 970,
1852, 4694; on courage and winning
991; on cowardice 1028; on her
cruelty 1075; on death 1217; on
deeds without remedy 1280; on
desire 1327; on doubtful joy in
destruction 1383; on determination
1385; on fear of the devil 1405; on
discontent 1443; on disguise 1478;
on eating at home 1603; on fear
2016; on finalities 2080, 2081; on
unwise flight 2135; on bloody hands
2614; on counterfeiting welcome
2855; on irrevocableness 3021; on
memory 3739; on motherhood 3935;
on plotting Duncan's assassination
3951; on things past 4262; on deceptive policy 4413; on reason 4706; on
things without remedy 4763, 4821;
her prayer to be rid of remorse 4778;
on retribution 4868; on serpents
5113, 5267; on death's resemblance
to sleep 5241; on Macbeth as a
soldier 5283; on values 5950; on
welcome 6175; on "would" 6465
Macduff *(Macbeth)* on avarice 310; his
orders for battle 357; his bereavement 433; on covetousness 1015; on
the loss of hope 2782; on the horror
of murder 2788; on intemperance in
nature 3009, 3995; on intemperance
in liberty 3262; on lust 3574; on

memories of precious things 3737,
4770; on self-control 5048; on
death's resemblance to sleep 5242;
on widows' sorrows 5307; on avarice
as a sword 5524; on sounding war
trumpets 5835, 6103; on tyranny in
nature 5879
Macduff, Lady *(Macbeth)* on affection
115; on commending evil 1721; on
folly 2175; on doing good 2455; on
lauding harms 2639; on motherhood
3937; on wisdom that's against
reason 6273; on the world's morality
6442; on the courage of the mother
wren 6472
Maecenas *(Ant. & Cleo.)* on anger 203
Malcolm *(Macbeth)* on angels 195; on
avarice 312; on children 730; on confusion 856; on Cawdor's brave death
1173; on falsity 1887; on flight 2136;
on grace 2476; on his greed 2534;
on unspoken grief 2543; on revenge
as a cure for grief 2544, 4886; on
griefs 2578; on haste 2653, 2655; on
hypocrisy 2853; on the graces of
kings 3137; on the night 4043; on
royalty 4941; on sorrows 5304, 5306;
on putting grief into words 6397
Malvolio *(TN)* on determination 1384;
on fate 1955; on fools' zanies 2200,
6515; on fortune 2272; on greatness
2509; on Viola's immaturity 2890;
on infirmities 2950; on luck 3558;
on success 5446
Mamillius *(WT)* on winter 5534, 6254
Marcellus *(Hamlet)* on the corruption
in Denmark 949, 4421
Margaret, Queen *(1, 2 & 3 H.VI;
R.III)* on adaptation 63; on ambition and its pitfall 178; on banishment 341; on lamenting things certain 668; on complacency 823; on
conscience 881; on courage of wise
men 982; on danger to great ones
1117, 2511; on death 1195; on destiny
1374; on endurance 1656; on suffering evil 1728; on fear 2030; on
gardening 2362; on the effect of
grief 2575; on redressing harms
2635, 6272; on an unspotted heart
2689; on the justice of heaven 2696;
on husbandry 2831; on Eleanor's insensitivity 2991; on lions 3344; on

Murderer, First *(Macbeth)* on his disastrous life 1359, 3297

Murderer, First *(R.III)* on action 54; on conscience 870; on rewards 4894; on talking 5537

Murderer, Second *(Macbeth)* on his despair 1359; on the vile blows of life 3297; on his recklessness 4728; on the buffets of the world 6433

Murderer, Second *(R.III)* on brevity 564; on conscience 865, 870; on judgment 3086; on his remorse 4783; on rewards 4894; on shame 5138; on tediousness 5590

Murellus *(Caesar)* on echoes 1613

Musician, First *(Rom. & Jul.)* on the sound of silver 5167

Nathaniel, Sir *(LLL)* on conversation 938; on endurance 1660; on happiness 2627; on society 5270; on weather 6143; on the wind 6229

Nerissa *(MV)* on age 128; on competency 818; on destiny 1375; on eating 1602; on excess 1757, 1762; on hanging 2619; on surfeiting as a cause of sickness 2819, 4986, 5148, 5488; on matrimony 3675; on moderation 3880; on the moon 3910; on riches 4907; on superfluity 5477; on wiving 6188

Nestor *(Troil. & Cr.)* on chance 674; on courage's sympathy with rage 977, 4672; on fortune 2255; on oaks 4093; on opinion 4160; on success 5441; on valor 5940; on the splitting wind 6231

Norfolk, Thomas Howard, Duke of *(H.VIII)* on ability 2; on anger 202, 204; on fire 2095; on Wolsey's merit 3767; on order 4194; on prudence 4633; on rashness 4688; on the use of reason 4712; on revenge 4865, 4879; on overrunning 4955; on gaining success 5442; on temperance 5603; on vehemence 5968

Northumberland, Earl of *(R.II; 1 & 2 H.IV)* on anticipation 216; on contention 917; on Morton's countenance 969; on life after death 1204, 3331; on fearing his son's death

2044; on joy in hope 2775, 3051; on immortality 2896; on medicine 3707; on unwelcome news 4040, 5754; on poison in physic 4357, 4409; on national quarreling 4666; on rebellion 4725; on suspicion's ready tongue 5501

Northumberland, Earl of *(3 H.VI)* on bravery 544, 5935

Nurse *(Rom. & Jul.)* on counsel 963; on men 3622; on secrecy 5031; on unfaithfulness 5897; on women 6351

Nym, Corporal *(H.V; MWW)* on patience 4273; on his resolution 4837; on his sword 5525

Oberon *(MND)* on the dawn 1135; on flowers 2142; on meditation 3715

Octavius *(also see* Caesar, Octavius) on smiles that conceal mischief 3833, 5258

Officer, Second *(Coriolanus)* on the populace 4434

Oliver *(AYLI)* on kindness 3118; on lions 3349; on meditation 3714

Olivia *(TN)* on candor 609; on compliments 824; on ignoring criticism 1060; on equanimity 1697; on falsity 1888; on her headstrong fault 1981; on fools 2193; on generosity 2366; on love 3436; on secret love 3443; on pity 4370; on the pride of the poor 4463, 4551; on pretension 4541; on slander 5215, 5222; on the waste of time 5719; on buying youth 6489

Ophelia *(Hamlet)* on charity 702; on ungracious clergymen 765; on dalliance 1112; on Hamlet as a fashion-setter 1934; on flowers 2161; on the future 2346; on gifts 2383; on hell as a primrose path 2709, 4271; on hypocrisy in clergymen 2850, 4511; on knowledge of self 3169; on uncertainty 5888; on unkindness 5908

Orlando *(AYLI)* on hope and belief 427; on judging others 700, 3068; on Rosalind's chastity 714; on cheerfulness 724; on civility 762; on striving for contentment 928; on courtesy

1003; on criticism 1055; on distress
1496; on envying other men's happiness 1682; on eternity 1711; on his
faults 1986; on the force of
gentleness 2378; on graces as
enemies 2479; on happiness in marriage 2629; on his humility 2809; on
labor 3176; on ways to enjoy life
3319; on Adam's loyalty 3556; on
pity 4371; on promotions 4611; on
self-reproof 4804; on his sad estate
4965; his self-examination 5059; on
service 5123; on the swiftness of
thought 5678; on unhappiness 5902;
on woman 6328
Orleance, Duke of *(H.V)* on the brave
flea 546, 2130, 3352; on fools 2188;
on malice 3610; on ill will 6225
Othello on patience in affliction 119;
on honoring age 149; on vain
boasting 495; on competition 819;
on the conscience of unfaithful wives
884; on Desdemona's cunning 1083;
on custom as a tyrant 1107; on happiness in death 1194; on his death
1203; on his despair 1360; on discretion 1459; on resolving doubts 1525;
on excess 1761; his farewell to arms
1917; on fate 1948; on seeking
forgiveness 2234; on a duty of
friendship 2309; on the plague of
great ones 2516; on happiness 2630;
on horror 2787; on love and jealousy
3027, 3030; on joy in winning 3058;
on laughter 3195; on losses by robbery 3380; on his love for
Desdemona 3474; on the moon as a
cause of madness 3583, 3909; on
malice 3613; on passion 4241; on his
patience 4292; on his rashness 4687;
on Desdemona's last prayer 4734,
4744; on remorse 4785; on resolution 4830; on respect for age 4843;
on robbery 4920; on Desdemona's
"sin" 5199, 5200; his plea for a
sincere report on his acts 5205; on a
soldier's life 5277; on suspicion
5497; on care of the sword 5521; on
woman's tears 5577; on tempests
5604; on thievery 5647; on victories
6002; on the appetites of wives 6199;
on winning 6246
Outlaw, First *(TGV)* on lawlessness

1768, 3223; on faults 1987
Oxford, Earl of *(3 H.VI; R.III)* on conscience 868, 5523

Page *(R.III)* on gold 2425
Page, Anne *(MWW)* on faults covered
by gold 1974, 2436, 3901
Page, Master George *(MWW)* on endurance 1655; on things without
remedy 4823
Page, Mistress *(MWW)* on chastity in
men 706; on chiding 728; on correction 946; on criticism 1056; on
avoiding grief 2572; on heartbreak
2690; on reproofs 4803; on the
benefits of a scolding 5010; on merry
wives 6206
Pages, Two *(AYLI)* on lovers in the
spring 3511, 5384
Painter *(Timon)* on promising and expectation 1781, 4609; on performance 4333; on satire 4992; on the
world 6435
Palamon *(TNK)* on manners 3654
Pandarus *(Troil. & Cr.)* on bees 412; on
patience 599, 4280; on debts 1221; on
futility 2341; on joy in doing 3053;
on the seasoning of a man 3617; on
moderation 3879; on words 6389
Pander *(Pericles)* on honest trades 5780
Pandulph, Cardinal *(John)* on a
youthful mind 467, 3808; on caution 654; on danger 1122; on desperation 1369; on discontent 1438; on
strong disease 1470; on departing
evils 1733; on falsehoods 1881; on
fortune 2243; on healing 2669; on
help 2713; on lying 3279; on
medicine 3706; on religion 4755; on
snatched scepters 5008; on self-
control 5052; on support 5482; on
temptation 5624; on usurpations
5927; on vows 6081; on youth 6493
Paris *(Rom. & Jul.)* on love 3530; on
revenge 4883; on smiles 5264; on
tears 5576
Paris *(Troil. & Cr.)* on bargaining 345;
on hot blood 469; on buying 586;
on disapprobation 1432; on selling
5096; on thoughts 5655; on
tradesmen 5784
Parolles *(AWTEW)* on authority 295;

on boasting 497; on braggarts 534; on the need for ceremony 667; on Dumaine's lying 3283; on matrimony 3671; on means 3702; on opportunity 4170; on place 4376; on self-reliance 5047; on self-love 5066, 5195; on going to war 6102

Patroclus *(Troil. & Cr.)* on the danger of omissions 1116, 4156; on effeminacy 1626; on error 1704; on negligence 4034; on self-reproach 5087; on manly women 6362; on self-inflicted wounds 6469

Paulina *(WT)* on condolence 848; on faults 1979; on fires made by the heretic 2097, 2717; on grief 2547; on help 2712; on the persuasion of innocence 2973, 4344; on times past 4257; on things past 4259; on the present 4532; on things without remedy 4822; on repentance of faults 4793

Pembroke, Earl of *(John)* on covetousness 1019; on excusing faults 1769, 1975; on hiding faults 1994; on impatience 2904, 4584; on waste 6122; on work 6422

Percy, Henry *(R.II; 1 H.IV; also see* Hotspur) on forgetfulness 2221; on memory 3733

Percy, Lady *(1 & 2 H.IV)* on Percy's influence 1744, 2954

Percy, Thomas *see* Worcester

Perdita *(WT)* on daffodils 1109; on flowers 2151, 2154; on the beauty of March 3656; on the sun 5466

Pericles on life as a breath 554; on life by care 632; on Helicanus' counsel 968; on courtesy and sin 1001; on death 1187; on doubts 1526; on his ecstasy 1618; on faith 1866; on fear of tyrants 2018; on Antiochus' greatness 2510; his riddle on a husband 2826; on kings 3120, 3143; on kissing tyrants 3154; on life 3312; on lust 3573; on the passions of the mind 3810; on murder 3961; on oaths 4104; on passion 4236; on perfection 4330; on his resignation 4826; on royalty 4939; on self-denial 5057; on sin 5177; on courtesy as a cover for sin 5183; on resisting sin 5184; on sin provoking sin 5187; on

decreed sin 5189; on overcoming temptation 5620; on Time as king of men 5696; on treachery 5801; on truth 5846; on tyrants 5881, 5883; on vice 5981, 5991, 5992

Peter *(Rom. & Jul.)* on music 1363, 2583, 3969; on melancholy 3727, 4969

Petruchio *(Shrew)* on the value of birds 443; on blushing 485; on mind and body 499; on braving a woman's tongue 545; on frivolous circumstance 757, 2327; on clothing as no indicator of honor 769; his comparison of birds 811; on contentment 924; on courtship 1009; on dress 1552; on the dress of birds 1553; the eel and adder compared 1623; on fires 2086, 2090; on fury 2337; on honor in the poor 2743; on jays 3023; on larks 3191; on lateness 3193; on the mind 3787; on ownership 4197; on passions 4251; on proud purses 4657; on riches 4901; on Kate's scolding 5012, 5546; on poor service 5121; on snakes 5265; on giving thanks 5631; on his wife Kate 5769, 6193; on wooing a shrew 6377

Phebe *(AYLI)* on diplomacy 1427; on Ganymede's eyes 1838; on love at first sight 3419

Philostrate *(MND)* on acting 41; on delights 1315

Pirithous *(TNK)* on music 3979

Pisanio *(Cymbeline)* on fortune 2248; on slander 5216; on the sword 5522

Pistol *(2 H.IV; H.V; MWW)* on baseness 350; on bondage 514; on trusting men 655; on discretion 1463; on men's faiths 1859; on hope 2779; on mistrust 3868; on men's oaths 4100; on payments 4301; on profits 4603; on self-reliance 5079; on slaves 5226; on the sword 5515; on trust 5838; on pretty women 6368; on the world 6436

Player, First *(Hamlet)* on fortune 2273; on storms 5410

Player King *(Hamlet)* on change in fortune 685; on paying debts 1222; on hollow friends 1665, 2298; on forgetfulness 2223; on grief 2566, 2567; on joy 3056; on memory

3301

Roman *(Coriolanus)* on cuckolds 2822; on seducing wives 5619, 6205

Romeo on banishment 335, 336, 337; on Juliet's beauty 376; on blindness 459, 1816, 3381; on boasting 491; on Juliet's vow of chastity 713; on dancing 1113; on the breaking of day 1137; on merriment in death 1156, 3778; on engrossing death 1202; on desperation 1368, 1370, 5681; on evil 1738; on exile 1776, 1777, 1778; on experiencing wounds 1789; on the peril in Juliet's eyes 1837; his farewell 1918; on gold 2438; on sad hours 2798; on jesting at scars 3041; on the lark 3189; on love 3397, 3406, 3416, 3477, 3520; on the tenderness of love 3503; on lovers' tongues 3542, 5761, 6076; on remembrances 3732; on mischief 3832; on misfortune 3864; on the morning 3918; on Juliet's posterity 4446; on prisons 4578; on proverbs 4626; on scars 5004; on the preciousness of sight 5155; on temptation 5610; on wounds 6466

Rosalind *(AYLI)* single men compared to April 250; on beauty 382; on Cupid 1085; marrying men compared to December 1252; on desire 1348; on epilogues 1688; on excess 1766; on experience 1795; on rich eyes 1823, 5157; on women's faults 1991; on fortune 2271; on beauty and gold 2439; on love as insanity 2988, 3411; on love 3433; on the reason of love 3414; on lovers 3533, 3549; on madness 3591; on maids 3594; on the marketability of Phebe 3659; on matrimony 3668, 3688; maids compared to May 3696; on merriment 3773; on LeBeau's news 4042; on nonsense 4076; on opportunity for marriage 4176; on good plays 4380; on the fall of pride 4561; on selling 5095; on a woman's talking 5550, 6358; on a woman's thoughts 5677; on the company Time keeps 5710; on Time as an examiner 5713; on travellers 5792; on wives 6187; on wine 6233; on wit 6300; on woman 6326, 6327; on blaming husbands 6344; on wooing

6387; on the briars of the world 6430

Rosaline *(LLL)* on past care 631, 1095; on the prosperity of a jest 1589, 3038; on humor 2814; on lust 3563; on jesting tongues 5764; on wit 6290

Rosencrantz *(Hamlet)* on age 129; on cowardice 1029; on friends 2310; on revealing griefs 2555; on honesty 2736; on the fall of kings 3144; on protection of life 3313; on the cess of majesty 3601; on those wearing rapiers 4682, 5518; on satire 4991; on fear of words 6391

Rosse, Thane of *(Macbeth)* on crisis 1053; on fear 2021; on griefs 2578; on hope 2783; on recovery 4735; on rumor 4950; on self-control 5050; on death's sorrow 5321; on improvement from the worst 6451

Rossillion, Countess of *see under* Countess

Rumor *(2 H.IV)* on mobs 3875; on rumor 4953; on slander 5217

Salisbury, Earl of *(2 & 3 H.VI)* on ambition 174; on sinful oaths 4098, 5185; on pride 4549

Salisbury, Earl of *(John)* on conscience 878; on excess 1755; on extravagance 1798; on flowers 2153; on perfection 4324; on counterfeit tears 5580; on Hubert's villainy 6021

Salisbury, Earl of *(R.II)* on his despair 1357; on discomfort 1437; on bidding time return 5708; on yesterdays 6484

Sands, Lord *(H.VIII)* on new customs 1100; on fashions 1925; on novelty 4087

Saturninus *(Tit. Andr.)* on patriotism 4298

Say, Lord *(2 H.VI)* on ambition in great men 2517; on flying to heaven 2699; on the curse of ignorance 2867; on knowledge 3168

Scroop, Archbishop of York *(1 & 2 H.IV)* on challenges 673; on building a constituency 908; on forecasting weather 1138, 5209, 6144; on discontent 1440; on disease 1475; on doubts 1528; on foreboding 2217; on hopes for the future 2342; on hate 2660; on changing love 3467; on melancholy 3730; on the fickleness of the multitude 3948; on remembering times past 4258; on peace as a conquest 4306; on politics 4418; on present things 4531; on surfeiting 5490; on the best times 5707; on wantonness 6094; on the worst times 6453

Sebastian *(Tempest)* on sleep as a comforter to sorrow 5234, 5322

Sebastian *(TN)* on dreams 1543; on fancy 1909; on senses 5105

Sempronius *(Timon)* on bating honor 2761

Senator, First *(Coriolanus)* on shame 5137

Senator, First *(Timon)* on spilling blood 465; on true bravery 543, 5933; on character 693; on courage 987; on factions 1857; on folly 2174; on hazarding life 2665; on judgment for blood 3085; on killing 3111; on law enforcement 3221; on mercy 3749; on patience 4291; on retribution 4872; on revenge 4876; on sects 5035; on mercy as a breeder of sin 5176; on suffering wrongs 6476

Senator, Second *(Timon)* on the use of arms 269; on gentleness versus the sword 2376, 3116, 5519; on persuasive smiles 4342, 5262, 5420

Sergeant *(Macbeth)* on discomfort 1436

Servant *(Shrew)* on mirth 3823

Servant *(Timon)* on politics 1389, 4417

Servant *(WT)* on Perdita's beauty 402

Servant, First *(Coriolanus)* on war 1078, 6115; on peace 4314

Servant, Second *(Coriolanus)* on peace 1078, 6115; on cuckolds 4314

Shallow, Robert *(2 H.IV; MWW)* on having influence at court 999, 2952; on death 1215; on friends 2293; on money 3891; on purses 4653; on restraint 4857

Shepherd *(WT)* on being a gentleman 2373; on the wildness of youth 6497

Shylock *(MV)* on affection 108; on aversion 315; his discrimination against Gentiles 1468; on foppery 2212; on Jews 3046, 3047, 3048; on killing 3109; on loathing 3365; on

passion 4237; on perjury 4335; on proverbs 4625; on revenge 4888; on cureless ruin 4946; on thievery 5649; on thrift 5691

Sicinius Velutus *(Coriolanus)* on friendship 369, 2308; on cities 760; on nature 4011; on Martius' pride 4555

Silvia *(TGV)* on duty 1571; on plural faith 1863; on Proteus' welcome 6177

Silvius *(AYLI)* on executions 1773; on the power of fancy 1910; on the follies of love 2169, 3445; on what it is to love 3448; living on love 3529; on the executioner's pardon 4223; on relief 4752; on love's smiles 5263; on sorrow 5314

Simonides *(Pericles)* on dress 1547; on fashions 1926; on opinions 4157; on princes 4574

Sly, Christopher *(Shrew)* on his raiment 768, 4676; on his firmness 2100

Solanio *(MV)* on the devil 1407; on nature's strange fellows 2053, 4010; on men without humor 2817; on his prayer 4506

Soldier, First *(AWTEW)* on winning the match 3663

Son *(3 H.VI)* on blessings 456; on ill winds 6230

Soothsayer *(Ant. & Cleo.)* on loving 3453; on reading nature 4012, 5027; on prophecy 4619

Soothsayer *(Caesar)* on the ides of March 3657, 3658

Speed *(TGV)* on love 3481; on the marks of love 3508; on the blindness of love 3510; on Valentine's malady 3609

Stephano *(Tempest)* on civility 761; on courtesy in conversation 1004; on death 1154; on debts 1224; on luck 3559; on thought 5660; on a wise tongue 5755

Steward *(AWTEW)* on conceit 834; on publishing our deeds 1325; on modesty 2891, 3884; on self-praise 5075

Stranger, First *(Timon)* on conscience 879; on expediency 1787; on foregoing pity 4373; on policy above conscience 4412

Suffolk, Earl of *(1 & 2 H.VI)* on base men 348; on the majesty of beauty 392; on deceit, deception 1238, 1240, 1255; on eloquence 1637; on fear 2034; on the fox 2279; on serving God 2416; on great men's deaths 2505; on hell in marriage 2707; on law 3219; on forced marriages 3680; on nobility 4064; on parting 4232; on prayer 4508; on pride in base men 4550; his reverence 4890; on speech 5350; on stealth 5405; on insincere talk 5542; on thievery 5652; on tranquility 5786; on Gloucester's treachery 5805; on the trifles of base men 5824; on brook waters 6125; on forced wedlock 6148

Talbot, Lord John *(1 H.VI)* his death on the battlefield 1169; death as the end of misery 1201, 3854; on God 2242, 2406

Tamora *(Tit. Andr.)* on eagles 1581; on mercy 3748; on nobility's true badge 4070; on the use of power 4472

Thersites *(Troil. & Cr.)* on bastards 355; on folly 2177; on fools 2204; on Achilles' ignorance 2874; on opinions 4158; on satire 4990; on stirring wits 6304

Theseus *(MND)* on amusement 190; on bears 361; on her betrothal 439; on fantasies of the brain 536; on fear of bushes 580; on desires 1340; on duty 1570; on fathers 1960; on fear 2028; on fiction 2069; on imagination 2879, 2880; on insanity 2987; on leisure 3244; on love 3458; on lovers' fantasies 3547; on lunacy 3560; on madness 3592; on matrimony 3686; on midnight 3782; on mirth 3827; on night 4053; on the poets' aery nothings 4083; on obedience owed a father 4112; on parentage 4226; on poets 4397, 4399; on cool reason 4720; on recreation 4738; on simplicity 5168; on virgins 6027

Thidias *(Ant. & Cleo.)* on fortune 2246; on wisdom 6261

Thurio *(TGV)* on fools in love 2202; on hazarding for love 2667

Time *(WT)* on reporting the news 4038, 5720; on time 5733

Timon on ingratitude in the aged 140; on art 277; on supposing Apemantus a beast 373; on ceremony 661; on charity 703; on consideration 895; on deceit caused by gold 1243; on distinction in faults 1493; on doctors 1508; on rich faults 1973, 4908; on faults 1980; on flattery 2121, 2122, 2125; on fortune 2252; on friends 2296, 2304; on true friendship 2323; on generosity 2365; on giving 2385; on gold 2428; on the power and influence of gold 2433, 2434, 2437; on scorn in greatness 2530; on helping the feeble 2714; on man's ingratitude 2959, 3631; on lawyers 3225; on learning 3237; on medicine 3708; on the influence of money 3896; on the power of money 3899; on age in nature 4018; on painting 4215; on physicians 4360; on praise 4491; on pretension 4538; on professions 4599; on recompense 4730; on selflessness 5063; on sensuality 5109; on the life of a soldier 5274; on Apemantus' subjugation 5432; on thievery 5642; his examples of thievery 5644; on men's villainy 6011; on war's cruelty 6107; on wealth 6135, 6140; on drinking wine 6244; on the worship of gold 6448; on the riot of youth 6486

Titania *(MND)* on autumn 307; on the change of seasons 688, 5023; on the moon as a washer of the air 3907; on quarreling 4668

Titinius *(Caesar)* on the decline of Rome 4925

Toby, Sir *see* Belch

Touchstone *(AYLI)* on the degrees in a quarrel 256, 1307; on bachelors 318; on beauty 389; on chastity 708; on clowns 775; on conciliation 841; on folly 2172; on fools 2190; on harvesting 2645; on longing for home 2724; on honesty 2729, 2735; on *If* 2866; on lying 3272; on the degrees in lying 3273; on folly in love 3517; on matrimony 3667; on mortality in nature 3927, 4016; on making peace 4313; on poets 4401; on feigning in poetry 4404; on reaping 4696; on responsibility 4846; on rhetoric 4895; on swearing 5502; on sweets 5510; on traveling 5796; on understanding verse 5892, 5974; on wisdom 6259; on following wisdom 6278; on his wit 6303

Tranio *(Shrew)* on adversaries 78; on competition in law 821; on eating 1609; on gains 2352; on friendship of lawyers 3227; on logic 3367; on winning a maid 3595; on pleasure in profit 4602; on practicing speech 5355; on study 5423

Trinculo *(Tempest)* on adversity 82; on misery 3846

Troilus on anticipation 215; on choosing 748; on daybreak 1140; on being one's own enemy 1403; on use of the ear 1596; on envy 1684; on expectation 1782; on use of the eyes 1835; on the frailty of mankind 2286; on imagination 2822; on will and judgment 3082; on merit 3766; on the morning 3920; on patience in offenses 4143, 4290; on perceptions 4318; on perfection 4328; on praise 4485; on reason 4718; on cowards' use of reason 4723; on the self 5046; the senses' effect on the will 5102; on sorrow 5325; on temptation 5615; on the theft of Helen 5650; on injurious time 5709; on plain, simple truth 5874; on value 5954; on the patience of will 6221; on the will 6222, 6227; on words 6405; on worth 6458

Tybalt *(Rom. & Jul.)* on choler 750; on patience 4288; on wilfulness 6213

Ulysses *(Troil. & Cr.)* on achievement 28; on acting 43; on action 56; on affection 114; on amity 188; on anarchy 193; on appetite as a universal prey 242; on aristocracy 265; on arrogance 270; on Cressida's beauty 404; on courtesy in elephants 1002, 1631; on good deeds past 1278; degrees a necessity for order 1305; on

emulation 1641, 1643; on envy 1687; on Cressida's coquetry 1797; on the eye 1801, 1805; on farewells 1915; on folly 2165; on fortune 2263; on friendship 2320; on deadly gall 2358; on historians 2718; on honor 2742; on protecting honor 2771; on ingratitude 2965; on integrity 3003; on kinship in nature 3112; on supple knees 3163; on hard knots 3165; on body language 3185; on lords 3377; on the doings of men 3645; on motion 3938; on nature 3989; on novelties 4089; on order in the universe 4193; on perseverance 4337; on praise 4477; on the present eye 4533; on pride 4553; on sighing 5151; on smiling 5257; on speech 5362; on stillness 5406; on the subjects of Time 5697; on Time as a host 5723; on forgetful time 5729; on nature's touch 5776; on variety 5966; on virtue as a subject to Time 6037; on welcomes 6169; on wisdom in amity 6267

Valentine *(TN)* on tears 5586

Valentine *(TGV)* on absence 10, 11; on adversity 87; on banishment 338; on coquetry 941; on courtship 1008; on custom 1097; on friends as the worst enemies 1666; on flattery 2120; on folly 2170; on friends 2317; on courting with gifts 2386; on habit 2602; on hate in love 2662; on home-keeping youth 2726, 6494; on idleness in youth 2863; on jewels 3045; on love 3404, 3482, 3489, 3506; on his love for Silvia 3422, 3510; on penance for love 3472; on the mastery of love 3522; on the griefs of love 3524; on a woman's mind 3805; on the nightingale 4062; on ornaments 4196; on persuasion with gifts 4346; on praises 4476; on a woman's pretension 4543; on repentance 4791; on scorn 5014; on a woman's scorn 5016; on solitude 5286; on a courting man's tongue 5758; on traveling 5795; on trusting Proteus 5843; on unfaithful friends 5900; on use 5919;

on the value of his wife 6203; on wit turned to folly 6296; on homely wit 6297; on wooing a woman 6355, 6373, 6375, 6376; on the scorn of a woman 6356; on wounds inflicted by friends 6471

Varro Servant, Second *(Timon)* on those without houses 2801; on poverty 4455

Ventidius *(Ant. & Cleo.)* on becoming captain 620; on deeds 1283; on fame 1900; on earning promotion 4610; on soldiers 5280

Vernon *(1 H.VI)* on paying for opinions 4162

Viola *(TN)* on appearance in nature 224; on challenge 672; on disguise 1477; on echoes 1612; on fools 2195; on woman's frailty 2288; on Olivia's childlessness 2502; on ingratitude 2960; on pollution in nature 4015, 4423; on her speech 5357; on speech 5360; on the sun 5470; on tasting valor 5560; on women's unfaithfulness 5898; on valor 5941; on the wickedness of disguise 6186; on wanton words 6404

Volumnia *(Coriolanus)* on action 44; on anger 205; on buildings of fancy 574, 1911; on courage in her sons 992; on eloquence 1632; on honor in war 2765; on patriotism 4296; on policy in war 4411; on honorable sons 5292; on treason 5815

Warwick, Earl of *(2 H.IV)* on using history to prophesy 2719, 4618; on rumor 4951

Warwick, Earl of *(1, 2, & 3 H.VI)* on his death 504, 1213; on Christ 753; on trusting noble men 1041, 3870, 4075; on the certainty of death 1174; his defiance of Gloucester 1301; on distrust 1501; on evidence 1715; on eternal loyalty to God 2420; on his judgment 3077; on deposing a king 3146; on law 3217; on mortality 3931; on having nothing to lose 4086; on transitory pomp 4425; on his religion 4754; on his soul 5334; on suspicions 5495

Westmerland, Earl of *(2 H.IV)* on rotten causes 646

Widow *(Shrew)* on the world 6424

Williams, Michael *(H.V)* on dying in battle 356, 1181; on offenses 4148; on war 6095

Witch, Second *(Macbeth)* on Macbeth's battle against Scottish rebels 359

Wolsey, Cardinal *(H.VIII)* on action 53; on ambition 173, 183; on censurers 659; on the state of man 681, 3641; on a quiet conscience 887; on corruption 951; on fear of criticism 1061; on his dependency on royal favor 1319; on the destiny of man 1379; on duty 1572; on ends to aim at 1653; on falling 1878; his farewell to greatness 1916, 2527; on his fall from glory 2395, 2523; on serving God 2417, 5122; on cherishing hostile hearts 2679; on honesty 2733; on too much honor 2770; on being just 3102; on princes kissing obedience 3153, 4108; on Christian love 3450; on patriotism 4299; on peace 4312; on self-peace 4315; on his high-blown pride 4560; on princes 4569, 4570; on the fall of royalty 4942; on his ruin 4947; on self-love 5065; on ambition as sin 5194; on fear of slander 5220

Worcester, Thomas Percy, Earl of *(1 II.IV)* on appearances 228; on contentment in retirement 927, 4852, 4863; on facial expressions 1851; on trusting the fox 2281; on being the subject of gossip 2462; on interpretation 3017; on defect in manners 3655; on misinterpretations 3866; on scandals of great ones 4999; on treason 5812

York, Archbishop of *(2 H.IV) see* Scroop

York, Duke of *(1, 2 & 3 H.VI)* on beauty 394; on beggars mounted 416; on his death 1206; on dishonor 1481; on steeling doubts 1530; on fear 2032; on flying to God 2415; on government 2468; on the self-control

Topical Index

References are to the boldface serial numbers preceding each quote, rather than to page numbers.

following of 1931; and the interpretation of virtue 3016; as a hin-
drance to law 3212; *see also*
Ceremony, Etiquette, Fashion, Manners, Use

Daffodils 1109 *see also* Flowers, Rose,
Spring
Dagger 1110 *see also* Conscience,
Knife, Mind, Rapier, Sword
Dalliance 1111–1112; by unfaithful wives
6199; *see also* Amusement, Delay
Dancing 1113–1114 *see also* Mirth,
Music, Singing
Danger 1115–1125; of conceits 830, 831;
in mighty opposites 2513; in the
night 4047, 4048, 4059; *see also*
Fear, Hazard, Risk, Venture, War
Daring 1126; beards as an indication of
365; a challenge for 939; hard times
a breeder of 1023; as a reaction to
danger 1123; borrowed from the
great 2520; of love 3520; effect of
lust on 3569, of rage on 4672, of
reason on 4723, of lenity on 5176, of
wine on 6242; as a prerequisite to
fortune 5969; *see also* Boldness,
Bravery, Self-reliance
Darkness 1127–1129; lust's affinity for
3339; danger in 4047, 4048, 4059;
see also Evening, Night
Dating 1130; promptness in 3538; *see
also* Bachelor, Courtship, Maids,
Wooing
Dawn 1131–1136 *see also* Day, Lark,
Morning, Sunrise
Day 1137–1144 *see also* Darkness,
Dawn, Dew, Evening, Hours, Mid-
night, Minute, Moonlight, Morning,
Night, Sunrise, Sunset, Twilight
Daydream 1145; of place and greatness
2507; *see also* Ambition, Dreams,
Illusion
Dearness 1146–1150; in love 3505;
remembrance of 4770; *see also*
Affection, Devotion, Love, Passion
Death 1151–1220; banishment equated
with 336, 337, 338, 340, 341; of
Caesar 593, 594, 595, 596; as an end
to bondage 622; fame as a result of
1899; fear as a cause of 2035; as the
end of all fears 2046; of great ones

2519; by hanging 2616, 2617; hope
an obstacle to 2785; negligence as a
cause of 4036; as the end of thought
5659; *see also* Bereavement, Cure,
Despair, Doctor, Execution, Farewell,
Fear, Gallows, Grave, Grief, Hanging, Heaven, Hell, Mourning, Murder, Nature, Posterity, Sleep, Soldier,
Suicide, Sword, Time, War, Worm
Debts 1221–1224; as a result of unwise
spending 325; death as an end of
3309; *see also* Borrowing, Lending,
Liability, Purse, Usury
Decay 1225–1226; of buildings 573,
6121; of spring's flowers 615; *see also*
Canker, Corruption, Ruin
Deceit 1227–1250; in men 2853, 3624;
in evil souls 3274; in scurvy politicians 4414; in courtship 5762; in
women's vows 6053; *see also* Cunning, Deception, Dissimulation,
Duplicity, Flowers
December 1251–1252 *see also* April,
March, May, Season; Matrimony,
Wooing
Deception 1253–1259; in cowards 365;
of the fool 2190; in heresies 2716; of
devils 2837, 2846, 2847; of villains
2838, 2849; in men 2840, 2843; in
sin 2844; in beauty 2851; in women
2852; of Love's eyes 2877; knavery
and 6022; *see also* Counterfeit, Cunning, Deceit, Devil, Disguise,
Duplicity, Falsehood, Falsity, Flattery, Hypocrisy, Knavery, Lies, Lying, Pretension, Tears, Treachery,
Villainy
Decision 1260–1262; on flight or fight
362; dependent upon the eyes and
ears 1596; thought's effect upon
5685; *see also* Choice, Decree,
Determination, Judgment
Decline 1263; of great ones 2270,
2508, 2511, 2523, 2525, 2526, 2527;
see also Ambition, Decay, Destruction, Falling, Ruin
Decree 1264–1265; countenancing of
3209; *see also* Command, Order
Deeds 1266–1291; beauty measured by
406; ceremony devised to set a gloss
on 2323; blamed on great ones
2526; sweetest things affected by
4137; of vice and virtue 5980; that

make sweetest things sour 6157; *see
also* Achievement, Act, Murder, Opportunity, Talking

Deer 1292; as a mate for the lion 3351;
see also Beast

Defeat 1293; fear as a cause of 2015;
effect of indecision on 2937; as a
means for new opportunities 3858;
see also Conquest, Destruction,
Disappointment, Loss, Ruin, Subjugation, Suppression

Defect 1294–1297; the mending of
683, 1994; in judgment a cause of
fear 2026; in perfection 2918; the
mind and 3796; as a molder of the
best men 4748; in authority 5982;
concealed by beauty 2987; *see also*
Blemish, Corruption, Effect, Error,
Faults, Imperfection, Weakness

Defense 1298–1300; readiness in 4691;
effect of peace on 5486; *see also* Caution, Courage, Preparation, Prudence, Safety, Security, Sword, War

Defiance 1301; of fond fathers 192; as a
result of lost degree 193; *see also*
Challenge, Contempt, Disdain,
Disobedience, Rebellion, Revolt

Defilement 1302; caused by broken
vows 6085; *see also* Blemish, Corruption, Dishonor, Pitch

Deformity 1303–1304 *see also* Blemish,
Defect, Imperfection

Degrees 1305–1308; in profane
language 453; in crimes 1050; in joy
2390; in honor, hate 2515; in a
quarrel 3272; observed by heaven
and earth 4193; *see also* Lies, Lying,
Proportion

Delay 1309–1313; "would" and
"should" as a cause of 6464; *see also*
Dalliance, Haste, Impatience, Lateness, Law, Procrastination, Tardiness,
Time

Delicacy 1314; in women 6340, 6341,
6342, 6367; *see also* Frailty, Indulgence, Tenderness, Weakness,
Woman

Delight 1315–1318; youth full of 727;
in joy 3057; in life and death 3306;
in praises 4476; Time as a slave to
5694; in work 6419, 6420; *see also*
Amusement, Cheerfulness, Enjoyment, Entertainment, Fascination,

Happiness, Joy, Pleasure

Dependency 1319–1321; upon the
vulgar heart 908; upon the favor of
greatness 2005, of princes 4570;
upon the grace of men 2478; of
pride on fortune 4561; in traitors
5840; in friends 5842, 5843; *see also*
Beggar, Help, Relief, Support

Depravity 1322 *see also* Corruption,
Evil, Morality, Vice

Deserts 1323–1326 *see also* Penalty,
Punishment

Desire 1327–1352; effect of age on 150;
the restraint of reason upon 328;
beauty's charms a cause of 385;
effect on vows 460; for bondage by
man 516; commonality and 801; for
life or death 3306; as a hook for
matrimony 3667, 3693; in youth for
love 4253; for yesterdays 4257, 4258;
for place and greatness 4374; as an
instigator of thought 5684; as the
downfall of a virgin 6090; *see also*
Ambition, Appetite, Aspiration,
Covetousness, Greed, Hope, Lust,
Passion, Wish, Yearnings

Desolation 1353; caused by war 4945;
caused by rumor 4953; as a glory of
Time 5730; of buildings 6121; *see
also* Distress, Melancholy, Misery,
Resignation, Ruin, Sadness, Sorrow,
Woe

Despair 1354–1367; Death the arbitrator
of 1168; effect of words on 1588,
5300, 5301, 5304, 6403, of recreation
on 4736; in affairs of love 3497; the
overcoming of 5972; *see also* Death,
Disgrace, Futility, Grief, Melancholy,
Resignation, Sorrow, Suicide

Desperation 1368–1371; its effect upon
boldness 1532, 1534; and hope 2776;
see also Boldness, Difficulty, Distress,
Rashness, Recklessness, Wildness

Destiny 1372–1382; as a result of chance
20; dependent upon the stars, planets
288, 289, 290, 291, 292; unavoidableness of 1954; *see also* Chance,
Doomsday, Fate, Fortune, Future,
Luck, Misfortune, Opportunity

Destruction 1383; appetite and 242;
pride and 4556; *see also* Desolation,
Loss, Murder, Ruin, War

Determination 1384–1385; a conqueror

of mischance 508; as a prerequisite to fortune 5446, 5969; of value 5949, 5953, 5954; to see justice done 6024; *see also* Boldness, Decision, Fortitude, Obstinacy, Perseverance, Resolution, Stubbornness, Will

Detraction 1386–1387; virtue not immune to 5212, 5214; might and greatness the target of 4999, 5001, 5213; *see also* Calumny, Scandal, Slander

Device 1388 *see also* Delay

Devil 1389–1408; love as a 3532; and the fall of the angels 5194; and woman 6331; *see also* Adversary, Evil, Fiend, Spirits, Villainy, Wine

Devotion 1409–1410; division in 1576; to God and king 2416, 2417, 4299; love made of 2448; engendered by a king 3127; to country 4293, 4294, 4296, 4297, 4298, 4299; based on personal gain 4542; *see also* Adulation, Affection, Constancy, Dearness, Faithfulness, Fidelity, Love, Loyalty, Patriotism, Piety, Religion, Reverence, Worship, Zeal

Dew 1411–1413 *see also* Dawn, Morning

Differences 1414–1415; in men 315; death as a result of 1152; in age 1484; in value of like things 5953; of kings 6109; *see also* Discord, Disparity, Dissension, Distinction, Inequality, Variety

Difficulty 1416; patience in 119; *see also* Adversity, Affliction, Challenge, Crisis, Dilemma, Misfortune, Obstinacy, Predicament, Trouble, Worry

Diffidence 1417; slow tongue a sign of 3882; *see also* Bashfulness, Blushing, Fear, Modesty

Digestion 1418–1420 *see also* Dining, Eating, Feasting, Food, Meals, Wine

Dignity 1421–1423; as a prize of accident 2751; resulting from valor 5936; *see also* Honor, Majesty, Merit, Nobility, Preeminence

Dilemma 1424; in choice of duty 1506; in desires 5228; *see also* Choice, Difficulty, Predicament, Trouble

Diligence 1425; virtue in 902; *see also* Caution, Constancy, Industry

Dining 1426; ceremony in 1603; *see also* Digestion, Eating, Feasting,

Food, Meals

Diplomacy 1427; in the use of words 5531; *see also* Discretion, Prudence, Tact

Disappointment 1428–1431; in friends 2297, 2298, 2299, 2317; in love 3441; *see also* Adversity, Defeat, Discontent, Displeasure, Failure

Disapprobation 1432; its effect on action 53; as a cause of ill digestion 240; and repentance 683; *see also* Blame, Censure, Condemnation, Criticism, Dislike

Discipline 1433–1435; of the dull ass 281; of the rude beast 947; of stubborn spirits 4108; women made divine by 6052; *see also* Conduct, Correction, Order, Preparation, Punishment, Restraint, Self-examination, Study

Discomfort 1436–1437; sleep as a remedy for 4201; suffered by majesty 4933; in wearing crowns 4935; *see also* Distress, Pain, Suffering, Trouble

Discontent 1438–1448; zeal a cause of 932; envy a breeder of 1685; in man compared to sour music 4621; *see also* Disappointment, Discord, Dissension, Grief

Discord 1449–1450; envy a breeder of 1685 *see also* Confusion, Contention, Discontent, Dissension, Faction

Discourse 1451–1453; and godlike reason 1; effect of on fortune 5347; prudence in 5348, 5352; contempt in 5354; wantonness in 5360; *see also* Conversation, Orator, Speech, Talking

Discretion 1454–1466; in the fox 5652; in thought 5670; in women 5677; valor and 5935; *see also* Caution, Diplomacy, Prudence, Tact, Valor, Wisdom

Discrimination 1467–1468; of noble minds 286; *see also* Judgment, Preferment

Disdain 1469; resulting from a loss of degree 193; effect on after-love 2662; *see also* Arrogance, Contempt, Defiance, Mockery, Pride, Ridicule, Scorn

Disease 1470–1476; patience in 119; borrowing compared to 526; as a cause of despair 1437; love as 1921,

on valor 5947; *see also* Beast, Brain, Company, Custom, Devil, Sack, Sherris, Valor, Wine

Duplicity 1565–1569; in evil souls 3274; in courtship 5762; *see also* Deceit, Deception, Dissimulation, Hypocrisy, Pretention

Duty 1570–1579; and fear of censure 1061; of a true friend 2316; to God and king 2416, 2417; of wife to husband 2828, 3690, 3691; of subject to king 3127; love made of 3448; based on personal gain 4542; *see also* Burden, God, King, Office, Responsibility, Task, Trust

Dwarf 1580 *see also* Giant, Strength

Eagles 1581–1582; king's eye compared to 4944; *see also* Birds, Cock, Crow, Dove, Lark, Jay, Nightingale, Wren

Ear 1583–1596; choice influenced by eye and 6227; *see also* Body, Perception

Earth 1597–1598; as a place for crosses, cares, grief 785; as home for all devils 1400; *see also* Humanity, Nature, World

Earthquake 1599 *see also* Nature

Eating 1600–1611; effect of on the temperament 1940, on the wit 6293, 6306; *see also* Digestion, Dining, Feasting, Food, Meals, Welcome

Echo 1612–1613 *see also* Ear, Gossip

Economy 1614–1615; in nature 3997, 4005, 4006, 4007; *see also* Providence

Ecstasy 1616–1618; expectation as a cause of 1782; *see also* Delight, Joy, Love, Madness

Education 1619–1622; of the dull ass 281; of the rude beast 947; of wild horses 2792; the goal of 3167; as food for the mind 3795; *see also* Books, Instruction, Knowledge, Language, Learning, Library, Reading, Study, Tongue, Writing

Eel 1623 *see also* Serpent, Worm

Effect 1624–1625; of passion on vows 15; of love on things base and vile 316; of words on love 1625; of a good deed 1748; of counsel on a felt grief 1793; of judgment on fortune 2253; of speech on fortune 2274; of gold on faults 2436; of grace on

lasting beauty 2457; of mirth and merriment on life 2634; of the company one keeps 2888, 2923; of innocence in persuasion 2973, 2974; of drinking on man 3005, 3007, 3008; of jewels on women 3045; of kingdoms overthrown 3144; of music's charm 3972; of a jest 6290; of a pardon 6316; of ill words 6400; of enjoyable work 6419, 6420; *see also* Cause, Influence, Results

Effeminacy 1626; foppery and 1640, 2216; and the sword 5517; *see also* Delicacy, Weakness, Woman

Efficiency 1627; and promotion 4610; *see also* Ability, Competency

Effort 1628; effect of borrowing on 2830, of praise on 4475, of thought on 5690; sweat as the only recompense for 5504; *see also* Labor, Venture, Work

Egotist 1629–1630; self-love in 5066; self-praise in 5074, 5075, 5076; *see also* Boasting, Conceit, Pride, Self-love, Vanity

Elephant 1631 *see also* Beast

Eloquence 1632–1638; its influence on justice and religious beliefs 6075; *see also* Glibness, Poetry, Speech

Empathy 1639; in the hangman 360; sharing tears in 794, 1639; effectiveness of plain words in 1588; *see also* Commiseration, Compassion, Pity, Sympathy

Employment 1640; effect of borrowing on 2830; joy in 3053; *see also* Business, Industry, Labor, Task, Work

Emulation 1641–1643; of great ones 2507; as a cause of melancholy in scholars 3722; as the cause of primeval evil 5194; *see also* Ambition, Promotion, Rivalry

End 1644–1654; of learning 5425; of life 5714; of love 6378; *see also* Death, Doomsday, Epilogue, Goals, Purpose

Endurance 1655–1660; of youth 68, 5740; of affliction 119; of true love 2326; of a merry heart 2622; of things 2908; of desire 4334; of tyranny 5882; in verse 5977; *see also* Affliction, Fortitude, Patience, Perseverance, Strength

Enemy 1661–1667; security seen as 855;

between Desire and Grace 1347; *see also* Fatness, Humanity

Flight 2134–2136; from native law and punishment 2410; from martial love 6190, 6207, 6209; of cowards 1027, 1033, 1040; *see also* Battle, Coward, Escape, Haste, Love, Wife

Flirtation 2137–2138; use of restraint in 2138; and fidelity 4099; *see also* Coquetry, Courtship, Enticement, Invitation, Seduction, Wooing

Flood 2139; as a time for opportunity 5693; *see also* Storm, Tempest

Flowers 2140–2162; distillation of 4135; and canker vice 5988; *see also* Daffodils, Rose, Smell, Spring, Weeds

Folly 2163–2178; and age 151; in youth 2066, 2163, 4253; blamed on planetary influence 4378; *see also* Fools, Frivolity, Indiscretion, Nonsense

Food 2179–2183; its effect on temperament 1940, on the wit 6293, 6306; music as 3970, 3971; *see also* Appetite, Digestion, Dining, Eating, Feasting, Gluttony, Meals, Welcome

Fools 2184–2207; love a maker of 3445; *see also* Clown, Zanies

Foot 2208–2210 *see also* Body

Foppery 2211–2216; vanity of 5960; *see also* Affection, Egotist, Folly, Vainglory, Vanity

Foreboding 2217; of a new grief 4527; of tragedy 2041; *see also* Omens, Portent, Premonition, Prophecy

Foresight 2218–2219; in building 572; in defense preparations 1298; lacked by youth 6499; *see also* Preparation, Prudence, Wisdom

Forgetfulness 2220–2227; in friends 432; of good deeds done 1716, 1717, 5729; of the once-defeated warrior 2774; in ungrateful man 3631; sleep as a means to 5230; of men's virtues 6065; drinking wine and 6234, 6235, 6236; *see also* Fame, Ingratitude, Negligence, Oblivion, Omission, Unkindness, Wine

Forgiveness 2228–2235; of sin 752, 753, 5176; and enforcement of law 3209; effect of fasting on 1425; for little faults 3089; as nurse to second woe 3252; *see also* Compassion,

God, Kindness, Lenity, Mercy, Pardon, Repentance, Sin, Sympathy

Form 2236–2238; world deceived by 222; *see also* Ceremony

Fortitude 2239–2241; and achievement 27, 28; extremity as a test of 1800; hard hand a sign of 2608; as a prerequisite to fortune 5969; hard times as a producer of 6004; *see also* Courage, Obstinacy, Perseverance, Resolution, Stubbornness, Will

Fortress 2242 *see also* Strength

Fortune 2243–2278; of life compared to wind 20; dependent upon the stars, planets 288, 289, 290, 291, 292, 3310; unavoidableness of 1954; smoothed by flattery 2121; effect of behavior upon 2213; pride dependent upon 4561; thoughts as slaves of 5665; and valor 5940; *see also* Astrology, Chance, Destiny, Fate, Luck, Misfortune, Money, Providence, Riches, Stars, Venture, Wealth, Wheel, Woman, Worth

Fox 2279–2281 *see also* Beast, Cunning

Foundation 2282 *see also* Death

Fountain 2283 *see also* Ingratitude

Frailty 2284–2288; in men 3629; in women 6340, 6341, 6342, 6367; *see also* Delicacy, Defect, Effeminacy, Infirmity, Weakness, Woman

Freedom 2289–2291 *see also* Captivity, Liberty, Restraint

Frenzy 2292 *see also* Fury, Madness

Friend 2293–2318; forgetfulness in 432; ingratitude in 2963; *see also* Friendship, Love, Neighbor

Friendship 2319–2326; riches of 2296; effect of lending on 2301, of gossip on 2459; a subject to Time 6037; signs of 2316; dependent upon fortune 6133; as a source of wealth 6140; *see also* Amity, Association, Company, Fellowship, Friend, Rapprochement, Remembrance

Frivolity 2327; in youth 2163, 4253, 6502; blamed on planetary influence 4378; *see also* Folly, Indiscretion, Nonsense

Frown 2328; use of in courtship 6376; *see also* Displeasure, Smiling, Wound

Frugality 2329 *see also* Miser, Moderation, Prudence, Thrift

Fruit 2330–2333 *see also* Horticulture, Pruning, Ripeness

Fruitfulness 2334 *see also* Profit, Reward

Function 2335 *see also* Purpose, Use

Fury 2336–2337; of a jealous woman 3035; in woman compared to a troubled fountain 6348; *see also* Anger, Frenzy, Hate, Passion, Rage

Futility 2338–2341; in resisting fate 1374, 1378; in wailing a lost sorrow 3387; sweat the only recompense for 5504; hope a staff against 5675; *see also* Impossibility, Trifles

Future 2342–2349; dependent upon the stars, planets 288, 289, 290, 291, 292; and its promise of perfection 4485; *see also* Anticipation, Expectation, Foreboding, Heaven, Omens, Portent, Premonition, Prophecy, Time

Gain 2350–2357; use of flattery for 2123, 2125; *see also* Achievement, Acquisition, Benefits, Conquest, Fruitfulness, Profit, Reward

Gall 2358–2359 *see also* Courage, Liver, Rancor

Gallows 2360; as an aid to sleep 2616; as an end to all fear 2617; as a preventer of bad marriages 2620; courtesy on 2621; *see also* Death, Execution, Hanging

Gamble 2361; of life for gain 2350, 2353; of possessions for more possessions 2351; *see also* Chance, Risk, Uncertainty, Venture

Gardening 2362; man's will and body compared to 6219; *see also* Husbandry, Weeds

Gate 2363 *see also* Pomp

Generosity 2364–2368; merit in 530; effect of fasting on 1425; *see also* Abundance, Charity, Extravagance, Liberality, Plenty, Selflessness, Unselfishness

Gentlemen 2369–2374 *see also* Aristocracy, Nobility

Gentleness 2375–2378; not suitable to the sword 5627; *see also* Kindness, Meekness, Modesty, Tameness, Temperance, Tenderness

Giant 2379–2382 *see also* Dwarf, Strength

Gift 2383–2387; ability as a 1, 2; of imagination 2884; of God 4980; *see also* Courtesy, Favor, Legacy, Present

Glibness 2388; gift of 1636; its influence on justice and religious beliefs 6075; *see also* Eloquence

Glory 2389–2397; of kings compared to swan, eagles 2531, to his deputy 3119; *see also* Fame, Greatness, Honor, Majesty, Praise, Preeminence, Reputation

Gluttony 2398–2401; sickness caused by 1602; lust likened to 3577; its effect upon the wit 6293; *see also* Appetite, Excess, Surfeit, Sweets

Goals 2402–2404; got without content 4868; *see also* Ambition, Aspiration

God 2405–2422; gifts of 1, 2; the king as deputy to 3124; devotion to 4299; as the source of a king's earthly power 4473; and certain victory 5998; *see also* Christ, Christianity, Divinity, Grace, Heaven, Justice, Religion

Gods (The) 2423–2424; worshipped by idiots 4105; *see also* Devil, Evil, Invocation, Spirits

Gold 2425–2441; investment of for gain 2351; *see also* Avarice, Bribery, God, Greed, Money, Riches, Silver, Wealth

Goodness 2442–2458; in evil 223; evil in 224; the apprehension of 246; in Caesar 595; and evil in a flower 4138; as worthy of praise 4486; the counterfeiting of 5017; not immune to calumny 5212, 5214; Time the breeder of 5705; emanating from lowest places 6046; *see also* Excellence, Honesty, Merit, Morality, Piety, Virtue

Gossip 2459–2466; chastity and virtue not immune to 6062, 6064; *see also* Calumny, Lies, Lying, News, Rumor, Scandal, Slander

Government 2467–2475; personal ability in 2; gold's influence on 2430, 2431, 2437; dependent upon obe-

God 2409; love made of 3448; as an instigator of thought 5684; *see also* Ambition, Aspiration, Belief, Chance, Desire, Despair, Expectation, Faith, Heaven, Opportunity, Trust, Wish

Horror 2787–2788; in war 6100, 6103, 6107, 6109, 6112, 6118; *see also* Apprehension, Aversion, Fear, Repulsion, Terror

Horse 2789–2792; anger compared to 204; relationship of vanity to 5960; *see also* Beast, Speed

Horticulture 2793–2794 *see also* Fruit, Gardening, Husbandry, Pruning

Hostess 2795; cordiality of 6170, 6171, 6172; cold shoulder from 6173; *see also* Guest, Welcome

Hours 2796–2798; effect of sport on 3245, of pleasure and action on 4737; *see also* Day, Minute, Time

House 2799–2804 *see also* Home, Ruin

Humanity 2805; devil as an enemy of 1406; evil inherent in 1726; ingratitude in 2960, 2962, 2963, 2965, 2966; pomp as an impediment to 4429; Time as king of 5696, 5727; variety in 5965; *see also* Earth, Kindness, Man, Nature, World

Humility 2806–2813; self-praise as a wound to 493; love made of 3448; soft slow tongue a mark of 5767; *see also* Baseness, Lowliness, Meekness, Modesty

Humor 2814–2816; in men of vinegar aspect 2817; *see also* Jesting, Merriment, Mirth, Temperament, Wit

Humorless 2817 *see also* Humor

Hunger 2818–2819; lying while in 3275; *see also* Appetite, Desire, Lust

Husband 2820–2828; more honorable than a bachelor 318; effect of wife's unchastity on 2628; and light wenches 6178; *see also* Children, Cuckold, Lord, Love, Master, Matrimony, Wife

Husbandry 2829–2834; around the house 2802; *see also* Weeds, Work

Hypocrisy 2835–2856; of some in condemning sins in others 18, 1980, 5197; in law 2969, 2972; of the usurer 5929; *see also* Deception, Devil, Dissimulation, Falsity, Pretention

Idleness 2857–2863; advantage of action over 2379; preferred to motion 3229; as a cause of melancholy 3721; as an intensifier of aches, pains 3807; *see also* Inactivity, Laziness, Waste, Weeds

Idolatry 2864–2865; of planets, stars 288; *see also* Adulation, Gods (The)

If 2866 *see also* Hypocrisy, Quarrel, Should, Supposition, Would

Ignorance 2867–2874; in astronomy 293; in philosophy 4353; of verse and good wit 5974; *see also* Beast, Brain, Curse, Gullibility, Innocence, Intellect, Learning, Wit

Ill 2875–2876; as a begetter of ill 1729; *see also* Evil

Illusion 2877 *see also* Deception, Dreams, Fancy, Hallucination, Imagination, Love

Imagination 2878–2887; effect of night on 361; enchantment of 1782; of the poet 2993; in jealousy 3024; in lovers and madmen 3458; of men and women compared 3638; effect of on melancholy 4966; limits upon 5672; *see also* Dreams, Fancy, Hallucination, Illusion, Inspiration, Love, Madness

Imitation 2888; of humanity by players 37; of the great 1746; of heroes and princes 2954, 2955; of dishonest judges by thieves 5638; of virtue 6033; *see also* Counterfeit, Emulation

Immaturity 2889–2890 *see also* Youth

Immodesty 2891–2892; and the golden mind 5955; *see also* Wantonness

Immortality 2893–2902; in fame 1902; in verse 3337, 4402, 4407, 4771, 5977; in one's reputation 4809; *see also* Divinity, Eternity, Fame, God, Heaven, Life, Posterity, Reputation, Soul, Virtue

Impatience 2903–2904; anticipation as a cause of 741; love made of 3448; poverty of 4277; its effect on time

5562; *see also* Evil, Injury, Offense, Vice, Wickedness, Wrongs

Innocence 2973–2980; of love 3476; by reason of obedience to authority 4847; in children 6185; *see also* Blush, Candor, Chastity, Conscience, Integrity, Purity, Virginity

Insanity 2981–2989; in love 3397; melancholy as the nurse of 3718; grief the cause of 3797; unnatural deeds a breeder of 3799; moon as a cause of 3909; sleep a balm for 3952; *see also* Folly, Frenzy, Lunacy, Madness

Insensitivity 2990–2991 *see also* Arrogance

Insolence 2992; of the great 2530; *see also* Arrogance, Disdain, Egotist

Inspiration 2993; of love in poetry 3507; *see also* Imagination, Influence, Poet

Instinct 2994–2997; use of as a guide 3806; *see also* Cowardice

Instruction 2998–3001; of the dull ass 281; of wild horses 2792; *see also* Education, Learning, Teaching

Integrity 3002–3003 *see also* Honesty, Honor, Sincerity, Trust

Intellect 3004; as a servant to the will 4705; *see also* Brain, Experience, Knowledge, Learning, Library, Mind, Wisdom

Intemperance 3005–3010; as a cause of aging 130; effect of on the wit 1605; restraint resulting from 3261, 3265, 4855; *see also* Excess, Extravagance, Indulgence, Superfluity

Intensity 3011 *see also* Fury, Passion, Power, Strength

Intent 3012; slaughtered by lack of praise 4487; as a slave to memory 4651; words and 6388; *see also* Firmness, Purpose

Interest 3013–3014; lending with 2322; in the great 2461, 2462; in a wife 6202; *see also* Usury

Interference 3015; of age with opportunity 4180; *see also* Meddler

Interpretation 3016–3017; of a woman's mind 6375, 6376; *see also* Meaning, Purpose, Understanding

Investigation 3018 *see also* Study

Invitation 3019 *see also* Coquetry, Enticement, Flirtation

Invocation 3020 *see also* Apparition, Spirits, Supernatural

Irrevocableness 3021 *see also* Finality

Itch 3022 *see also* Desire

Jay 3023 *see also* Beauty, Birds, Cock, Crow, Dove, Eagles, Lark, Nightingale, Wren

Jealousy 3024–3037; a cause of division 1685; a breeder of rumors 4953; *see also* Canker, Covetousness, Doubt, Envy, Love, Madness, Preferment, Wife

Jesting 3038–3043; with men of vinegar aspect 2817; *see also* Clown, Humor, Wit

Jewel 3044–3045; chastity likened to 709; experience regarded as 1792; good reputation compared to 4807; a good wife seen as 6203; *see also* Ornament

Jews 3046–3048 *see also* Sufferance

Journeyman 3049 *see also* Work

Joy 3050–3061; as a medicine 723, 726, 4970; in death 1156, 1193, 1194; in the chase 1343, 2791; challenge as a cause of 2217; in a horse 2789; in new friends found 2303; as a prescription for long life 3316, 3320; abounding with cares 5994; in war 6112; *see also* Achievement, Cheerfulness, Delight, Ecstasy, Happiness, Laughter, Love, Matrimony, Merriment, Mirth, Pleasure, Satisfaction

Judge 3062–3067; influence of gold upon 2431; *see also* Authority, God, Judgment, Justice, King, Law, Mercy, Repentance, Retribution, Revenge, Sentence

Judgment 3068–3086; pity a virtue in 815; of the eye 1623; beauty bought by 1802; for those who escape native punishment 2410; gold's influence on 2431; of thieves by thieves 3211; effect of passion on 4687; of pleasant vices 5989; lacked by youth 6499; *see also* Judge, Jury, Remorse

Jury 3087; influence of a gracious voice on 3208; *see also* Judge, Judgment

Justice 3088–3106; of a good deceit 1240; and the gallows 2360; of

3310; obedience of the sea to 1868; *see also* Astrology, Astronomy, Comet, Lunacy, Madness, Planets, Stars, Sun

Moonlight 3911 *see also* Day, Night

Moral 3912 *see also* Truth

Morality 3913–3915; company's influence on 803, 804, 805, 806, 807, 808; *see also* Behavior, Chastity, Crime, Depravity, Law, Purity, Virtue

Morning 3916–3926 *see also* Dawn, Day, Sunrise

Mortality 3927–3934; inherent in youth 68; in kings 1201, 2493, 2494, 2495, 2496, 3132, 3133; in doctors 1507; of things 1659; *see also* Death, Grave, Life

Motherhood 3935–3537; joy of 735; *see also* Children, Father

Motion 3938–3939 *see also* Action, Activity

Mourning 3940–3947; for Caesar 594, 595; revenge as a cure for 4886; *see also* Bereavement, Fame, Grave, Grief, Heartbreak, Lamentation, Sadness, Sorrow, Tears, Weeping, Woe

Multitude 3948–3949 *see also* Mob, Populace

Murder 3950–3966; of kings 4943; *see also* Assassination, Blood, Conscience, Dagger, Death, Deed, Grave, Hand, Killing, King, Poison, Revenge, Sleep, Soul, Sword

Music 3967–3979; and eloquence compared 1633; government likened to 2467; of a lover's tongue 6076; of the gentle current 6129; *see also* Ballad, Dancing, Singing

Mutability 3980–3981 *see also* Change

Mystery 3982 *see also* Secrecy, Wonders

Name 3983–3988; as a treasure 2748; as a strength of the king 3147; *see also* Fame, Honor, Reputation, Rose

Nature 3989–4022; and the evil in man 1726; of man 2805; power of love to change 3428, 3429; iniquity and virtue in 6047; limitations of

virtue on 6049; *see also* Blemish, Character, Earth, Humanity, Kin, Man, Mind, Temperament, World, Youth

Neatness 4023; and trust 231; *see also* Order

Necessity 4024–4030; patience in 119; and pride 769; superfluity in 4033; as ambition's ladder 5439; *see also* Gift, Need, Poverty, Virtue

Necromancy 4031–4032 *see also* Invocation, Spirits

Need 4033; for a horse 2790; lying for 3275; for order 4193; *see also* Necessity, Poverty, Want

Negligence 4034–4036; of unthrifts 2802; *see also* Failure, Omission

Neighbor 4037 *see also* Friend

News 4038–4042; about great ones 2461, 2462; that eats up love 3036; *see also* Gossip, Rumor, Tongue

Night 4043–4060; lust's affinity for 3339; as a time for love's penance 3472; *see also* Day, Hell

Nightingale 4061–4062 *see also* Birds, Cock, Crow, Dove, Eagles, Jay, Lark, Wren

Nimbleness 4063 *see also* Youth

Nobility 4064–4075; things base and vile transformed to 346; in baseness 349; its vulnerability 2511; comparison of lowliness to 3552; a subject to Time 6037; *see also* Aristocracy, Blood, Breeding, Dignity, King, Majesty, Monarch

Nonsense 4076; in youth 2066; in speech 2536; *see also* Folly, Fools, Frivolity

Nose 4077–4078 *see also* Body, Caesar, Smell

Nothing 4079–4086 *see also* Imagination, Oblivion, Purse, Trifles, Triviality

Novelty 4087–4091; attraction of 2791; *see also* Change, Praise, Toys

Oak 4092–4093 *see also* Cedar, Tree, Wind

Oath 4094–4106; effect of religion on 6081; *see also* Cursing, Promise, Profanity, Swearing, Vows

to tapsters' 4101; of cooperation 5970; *see also* Chastity, Courtship, Inconstancy, Oath, Matrimony, Promise

Wages 6087–6088; of drunkenness 1555, 1560, 1563; of jealousy 3026, 3031, 3036; for contemning love 3472; for murder 3952; of pride 4547, 4552, 4556, 4560, 4563; of sin 5170, 5196; *see also* Business, Employment, Recompense, Smiling

Want 6089–6092; superfluity in 4033; *see also* Covetousness, Desire, Nature, Need, Poverty, Purse, Yearnings

Wantonness 6093–6094; in words 6404; *see also* Carnality, Immodesty, Lechery, Lewdness, Licentiousness

War 6095–6118; and ambition 1917; uncertainty in 2347; and kindness 5627; valor and 5932, 5945; twice a victory in 6000; *see also* Battle, Blood, Cannon, Captain, Danger, Death, Fame, Fear, Fighting, Honor, Immortality, King, Peace, Preparation, Quarrel, Reputation, Soldier, Strength, Sword, Valor, Warrior, Wound

Warrior 6119 *see also* War

Waste 6120–6123; of beauty 383; indecision as a cause of 2937; of youth 6511; *see also* Destruction, Extravagance, War

Watching 6124 *see also* Defense, Peace, Precaution, Preparation, War

Water 6125–6129; man's glory compared to a circle in 1893; *see also* Ocean, Sea, Tide

Weakness 6130–6132; conscience a cause of 872; peace and plenty a cause of 1023; effect of fury on 2336; in men 3623; in women 6340, 6341, 6342; *see also* Defect, Delicacy, Effeminacy, Faults, Frailty, Woman

Wealth 6133–6140; the mind as a source of 769; friendship dependent upon 2297, 2299, 2301; investment of for gain 2351; in a spotless reputation 2748; as a bond of love 3402; fearing the loss of 4451; con-

tentment as 4906; and content 5950, 5951; and value 5953, 5954; and vanity 5960; and small vices 5983; as a breeder of cowards 6004; in a good wife 6203, 6383; *see also* Abundance, Gold, Money, Plenty, Riches, Worth

Weariness 6141–6142; sadness as a cause of 3724; sleep a remedy for 3952; *see also* Bores, Ennui, Tediousness

Weather 6143–6145; forecast of 4057, 4438, 5144, 5211, 5407, 5410, 5464, 5474, 5606, 6257; *see also* Clouds, Rain, Showers, Sky, Storm, Tempest, Wind

Wedlock 6146–6151; hanging and 2620; unhappiness in 2628; virginity in 6029; *see also* Husband, Love, Matrimony, Wife

Weeds 6152–6161 *see also* Flowers, Husbandry

Weeping 6162–6168; its effect on sorrow 5303; *see also* Eye, Grief, Heartbreak, Lamentation, Mourning, Sadness, Sorrow, Tears

Welcome 6169–6177; ceremony devised for 2323; of summer 6255; *see also* Food, Guest, Hostess

Wench 6178 *see also* Bawd, Harlotry, Whoredom

Wheel 6179–6180 *see also* Fortune

Whoredom 6181 *see also* Bawd, Harlotry, Wench

Whipping 6182 *see also* Love, Madness, Punishment

Wickedness 6183–6186; universality of 1322; influence of inconstancy on 2924; in men 3622; emulation as a cause of 5194; in wine 6238, 6240; *see also* Corruption, Evil, Injustice, Malevolence, Sin, Wrongs

Wife 6187–6209; as a cause of husband's ill digestion 240; graces looked for in 2481; use of tongue to win a 5758; compared to heaven 6382; *see also* Children, Husband, Love, Mother, War

Wildness 6210–6211; in man 3625, 3630; effect of lenity on 5176; and youth 6497, 6498; *see also* Daring, Desperation, Rashness, Recklessness

Wilfulness 6212–6213; of foolish love